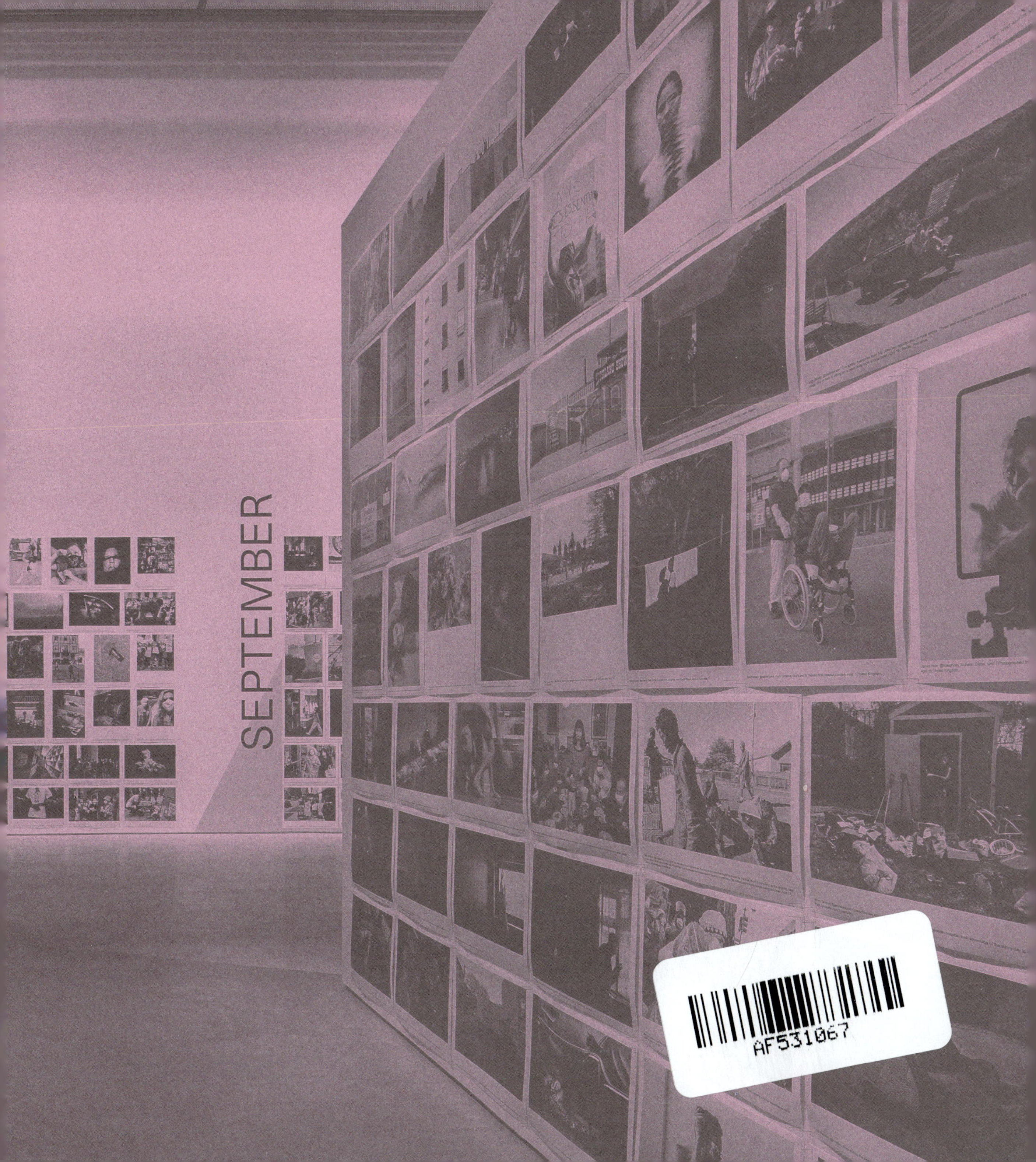
SEPTEMBER

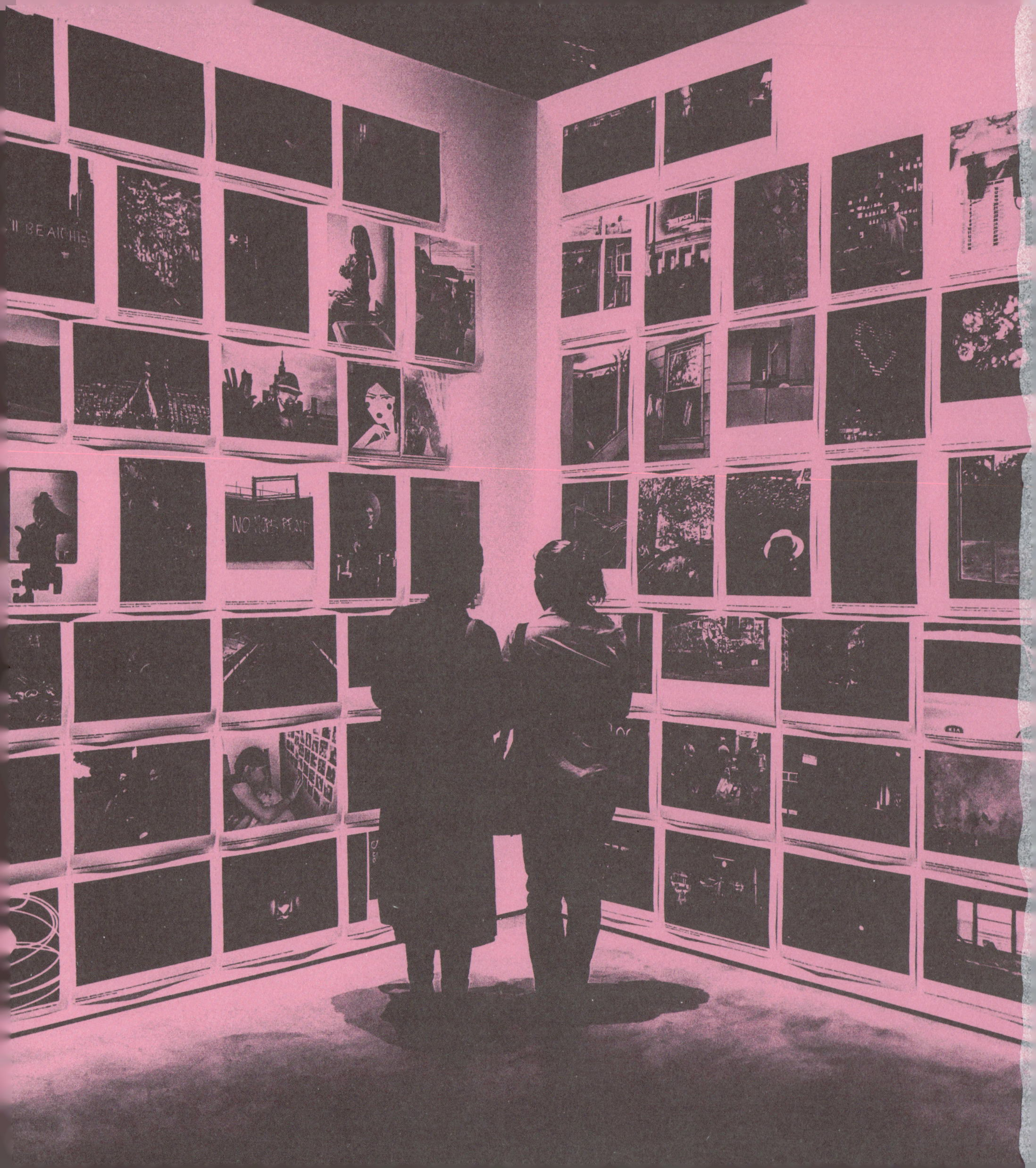

#ICPConcerned: Global Images for Global Crisis

FOREWORD | MARK LUBELL

INTRODUCTION | DAVID CAMPANY

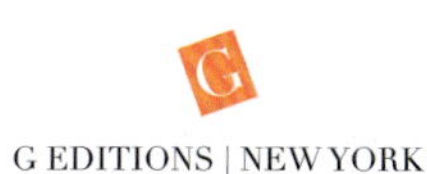

G EDITIONS | NEW YORK

CON

ALGERIA • ARGENTINA • AUSTRALIA • AUSTRIA • BANGLADESH • BELARUS • BELGIUM • BRAZIL • CANADA • CHILE • CHINA • COLOMBIA • CROATIA • CZECH REPUBLIC • DENMARK • ECUADOR • EGYPT • ETHIOPIA • FRANCE • GEORGIA • GERMANY • GHANA • GREECE • HUNGARY • INDIA • INDONESIA • IRAN • IRELAND • ISRAEL • ITALY • JAPAN • JORDAN • KENYA • LATVIA • LEBANON • LITHUANIA • LUXEMBOURG • MALTA • MEXICO • MOROCCO • NETHERLANDS • NICARAGUA • NIGERIA • NORWAY • PAKISTAN • PANAMA • PERU • PHILIPPINES • POLAND • PORTUGAL • QATAR • ROMANIA • RUSSIA • SINGAPORE • SAUDI ARABIA • SOUTH AFRICA • SOUTH KOREA • SPAIN • SWEDEN • SWITZERLAND • THAILAND • TUNISIA • TURKEY • UKRAINE • UNITED KINGDOM • UNITED ARAB EMIRATES • UNITED STATES OF AMERICA • URUGUAY • VENEZUELA • VIETNAM

TENTS

FOR EXACTLY 221 DAYS IN 70 COUNTRIES

FOREWORD

MARK LUBELL

EXECUTIVE DIRECTOR
INTERNATIONAL CENTER OF PHOTOGRAPHY, 2013-2021

CONCERNED PHOTOGRAPHY

On January 25, 2020, the International Center of Photography (ICP) opened its doors at its new home on Manhattan's Lower East Side, fulfilling a 20-year goal of re-uniting our museum and school under one roof. Seven weeks later, the COVID-19 pandemic forced us to close our doors and adapt as much of our programming as possible to an online environment. The situation challenged our most basic assumption as an institution—how could we continue to serve our community when our space was inaccessible and much of the world was locked down?

Harking back to ICP founder Cornell Capa's principle of "concerned photography"—the concept that socially and politically minded images can educate and change the world—we took action. On March 20, ICP announced a global open call for imagemakers to post images of their experiences as the pandemic unfolded. We hoped to witness and uplift how others were experiencing, creating, and adapting during this unprecedented time.

As of this writing, over 60,000 images have been tagged #ICPConcerned on Instagram, and I am proud that we were able to exhibit over 800 of them in ICP's galleries when we reopened our museum doors on October 1, 2020. Though our space was closed, our team worked tirelessly to produce online and on-site versions of the exhibition even when we weren't sure when we would be able to reopen.

The images in the *#ICPConcerned: Global Images for Global Crisis* have been shared as teaching tools in our classes and public programs, and will be preserved in ICP's collection. Individually and collectively, they illustrate not only our feelings of fear and isolation but our moments of joy, humor, and hopefulness. Their presentation in this published form plays an integral role in their preservation and continued life beyond ICP's walls and our individual screens, capturing this most challenging and significant moment in our collective history.

INTRODUCTION

DAVID CAMPANY

MANAGING DIRECTOR OF PROGRAMS
INTERNATIONAL CENTER OF PHOTOGRAPHY

A NECESSARY EXPERIMENT

This is the story and a celebration of a wild idea, dreamed up in deep uncertainty, at the onset of what turned out to be a tumultuous year. As the COVID-19 pandemic took hold in early 2020, the International Center of Photography (ICP) in New York City initiated a project that began online, led to the making of more than 60,000 images, and eventually developed into an exhibition with contributions from imagemakers in seventy countries around the world.

BY LATE FEBRUARY 2020, IT WAS CLEAR THE PANDEMIC WAS GLOBAL. Along with many other cultural institutions, we at ICP were facing the prospect of having to close our doors to the public. It was a harsh blow on many levels. Our brand-new building on Manhattan's Lower East Side had been open for just a few weeks. The new facilities of our renowned school were already buzzing, there were energetic public talks and discussions underway, and visitors were taking in our opening exhibitions. ICP was playing the thoughtful and reflective role in visual culture that is its aim. But on March 13, it all came to a halt.

Although our doors closed, an open mind was needed. We quickly pivoted, adapting many of our activities to online platforms, engaging with our international community. But our state-of-the-art museum could welcome no one, and what is an exhibition without an audience? Many museums and galleries were beginning to present "virtual tours" of the exhibitions they had been forced to close. As an institution dedicated to photography and visual culture, we at ICP wanted to do more. The world was in turmoil. If not now, when?

SO, ON MARCH 20, JUST A WEEK AFTER CLOSING, WE ANNOUNCED #ICPCONCERNED WITH AN INVITATION TO OUR COMMUNITY TO MAKE, UPLOAD, AND TAG IMAGES ON INSTAGRAM OF WHATEVER WAS GOING ON IN THEIR LIVES, WHEREVER THEY WERE. It was an open call, with no particular expectation, although the use of the word "concerned" derived from ICP's founding principle to be a home for socially and politically minded imagemaking that can educate and change the world.

For most, the month of March 2020 brought the first experience of lockdowns and social distancing. There was deep worry as to how long the pandemic would take to bring under control, and how many lives would be lost in the process. The virus itself was invisible, so how could it be represented? What could be pictured? While a handful of photographers had some access to medical facilities, most images were being made either in uncannily emptied streets or within the confines of domestic settings. There were striking documentary and photojournalistic images, but just as many photographers were staging situations in the home, using metaphor and even dark (or, occasionally optimistic) humor to make sense of the new realities.

BY APRIL 12, TEN THOUSAND #ICPCONCERNED IMAGES HAD BEEN UPLOADED TO INSTAGRAM. At the same time, New York City reached 10,000 confirmed cases of COVID-19 (a number that would soon look quaintly low). #ICPConcerned was becoming truly global: that month there were images from photographers in France, Norway, the United States, Japan, Singapore, Australia, Argentina, Belarus, Brazil, Ireland, Vietnam, China, Uruguay, South Korea, Indonesia, the UK, Bangladesh, Germany, Portugal, Belgium, Poland, Denmark, Panama, Greece, Romania, Peru, Italy, Nigeria, South Africa, Austria, Lithuania, Venezuela, Spain, Canada, Mexico, Ecuador, Turkey, Tunisia, Georgia, and Iran.

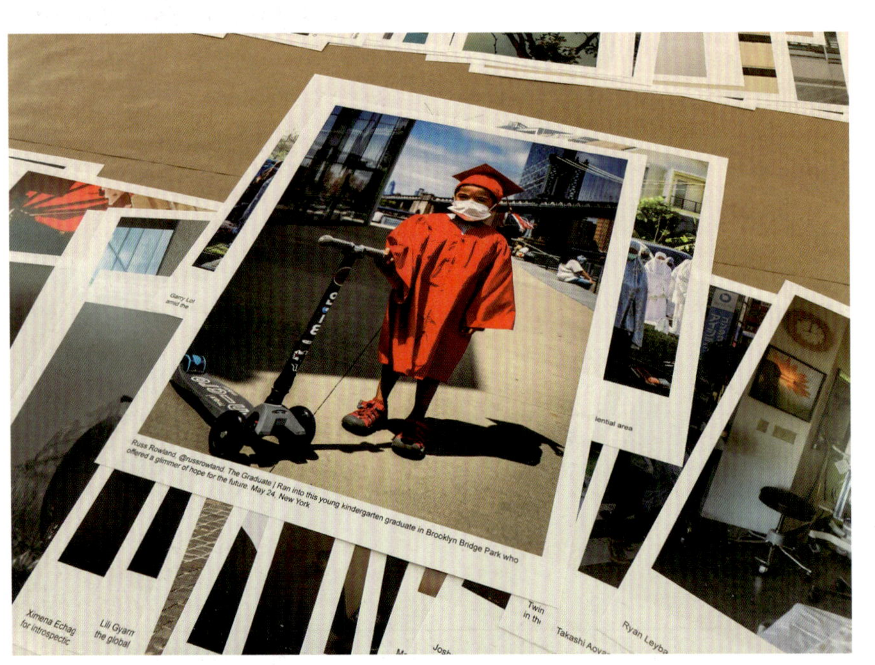

We at ICP followed the hashtag closely. Discussing the previous 24 hours in images became part of our daily ritual. With so many limitations on travel, the online experience was intensifying, becoming even more essential, and even more alienating. The internet makes connection possible but it also underscores the deep feelings of separation. Moreover, as April and early May passed, it was becoming scandalously clear that the pandemic was not affecting all communities and all countries equally. On the contrary, it was exposing the underlying inequalities that were already present. Lower income communities were being affected disproportionately. Given widespread and systemic racism, COVID-19 was taking a greater toll on Black and Brown families and bodies. We were "all in the same storm... but not in the same boat."

The character and tone of the imagery was shifting into anguish, anger, and outrage. At the same time, the invisibility of the virus made it easier for many governments to downplay or even ignore its effects.

AND THEN, ON MAY 25, GEORGE FLOYD WAS KILLED IN MINNEAPOLIS BY A WHITE POLICE OFFICER, DEREK CHAUVIN, DURING AN ARREST FOR ALLEGEDLY USING A COUNTERFEIT BILL. The incident was filmed by 17-year-old Darnella Frazier. Her video footage helped galvanize protests in support of Black lives and against police brutality. Within days, the streets went from empty to full. Isolation gave way to mass gatherings. Floyd's portrait appeared on banners and murals worldwide. In the United States alone, it is estimated that twenty million people took part in Black Lives Matter protests. Thousands of images of the demonstrations were uploaded and shared. Since most protestors were wearing PPE masks, individual identities were largely obscured. Emblazoned on many of those masks were George Floyd's haunting words, "I can't breathe." They took on a double resonance—a crying out against both racial injustice and the effects of the virus.

As the images on #ICPConcerned accumulated, ICP's galleries remained empty. Was a hashtag enough? Could ICP be doing more? How might a vast assemblage of online images be turned into a meaningful presentation? The galleries of ICP's museum are grand and sweeping. They needed to be filled with photographs. Could we make a physical exhibition, even with no immediate prospect of reopening? Could a real-life, large-scale show be installed, if only to be documented and shown online? What would an exhibition mean if the public might never see it in person? It seemed an unusual notion. But that's what we decided to do. We would make an exhibition about what was going on in the world, even if nobody could visit. We would document it, and show it on our website and through social media.

"Discussing the previous 24 hours in images became part of our daily ritual."

We quickly realized we would not be able to show all the uploaded images, which were nearing 35,000 at that point. So, a group of ICP staff, thirteen in all, volunteered to make selections from #ICPConcerned in a show titled *#ICPConcerned: Global Images for Global Crisis*. We came from many departments: Education, Public Programs, Marketing and Communications, and Exhibitions. There was only a loose discussion of the criteria for choosing the images. No iron-clad checklist of what to look for. This allowed each selector to use their own judgment, just as all the different photographers had used theirs. In this way, the exhibition would have no overriding agenda, no watertight argument or position, and no single mastermind to tame the multitude of views. If the selection embraced all perspectives, messily and without unity, then the exhibition would be an open invitation to each and every viewer to make their own interpretation.

Once an image had been selected, we reached out to the photographer. We outlined our project and asked for several things: permission to exhibit, caption information (including where and when the image was taken), permission to use the image for publicity and in book form, permission to archive a print in our collection, and a high-resolution file. The response was overwhelmingly positive. Over 800 photographers would have their work exhibited at ICP and become part of the initiative. Amateurs, professionals, students, artists, documentarists, and other visual storytellers.

Mass participation photo shows have a long and complicated history. They date back to the 1920s, when the spread of the modern mass media began to produce the illusion of democratic participation in a transnational culture open to all. Large-scale exhibitions appealed to the idea of a democracy of photography and a universal consciousness. In doing so, they often glossed over the deep inequities and uneven participation. The myth of the global village is that everyone can meet on equal terms. And, all too often in such exhibitions, photography has been held up as the innocent means of bringing people together, ignoring that fact that it is also a means of entrenching the power structures of the status quo. Having many selectors and no agreed criteria for *#ICPConcerned* was risky, but it brought the possibility of a more reflective and layered take on what the "democracy of photography" really means. Looking at the pages of this book, you can decide for yourself.

Much of today's exhibition culture is in the grip of easy consumerism. Many times, viewers' responses to what they are looking at are often neatly packaged into experiences with simple take-aways. At ICP, we attempt to recognize and draw attention to the contradictions of the modern world and the ambiguities of all images. We believe it is not our role to simplify, nor to make things palatable. This rewards for an active, rather than passive, engagement with images that is much greater. We trust our audiences with the challenges of response.

INSTALLATION OF *#ICPCONCERNED* BEGAN ON JUNE 19. A digital print station and viewing tables were set up in the gallery, making it feel more like a lab, or a project space. The images were printed along with their captions on Canon Luster paper, 17 x 22 inches. They were then hung with small steel pins as a chronological grid. The months would unfold around the largest of ICP's galleries, so that the walls would become a timeline. To move through the space would be to retrace the events of the recent past, while criss-crossing the globe. We continued to select images right through to the beginning of November, around the time of the election in the United States. At that point, the gallery space would be—we hoped—full.

Once the prints from March, April, May, and June were on the walls, we were up to speed and living in the moment. From here on, we added new images as the weeks and months passed. Staring at the blank walls allocated to the future was unsettling. July, August, September, October, November. What would happen in the world? And what images would be made of it? It was like gazing into the unknown. But this was a live project and we were going to see it through. With the pandemic still surging, there was no prospect of reopening anytime soon. Online, we announced our "unvisitable" show. How would it be received?

Even in a year of very few norms, a brand-new exhibition in a huge but closed gallery was a little odd, even to us. Even so, it had an important symbolic status. All these photographs, made first as immaterial images, were being printed and presented in a real space. ICP was honoring and celebrating the visions of these photographers and their experiences. In online forums, the exhibition began to gather a reputation: had ICP really installed a giant new show while most museums seemed to be inactive? Would the exhibition really come and go with no visitors at all? *#ICPConcerned* soon took on the status of a promise: one day it would have to open to the public.

As the exhibition grew through the summer, we committed to the idea that it would remain in place until we could welcome visitors once again. Looking to the future, we commissioned a separate website for the project, and invited many of the photographers to make audio recordings[i] about their selected image. By early September, there were positive signs that New York's cultural institutions might be able to welcome visitors. We readied ourselves: hand sanitizers around the building, timed ticketing, signs for social distancing.

ON OCTOBER 1, 2020, THE INTERNATIONAL CENTER OF PHOTOGRAPHY REOPENED. Stepping into the museum, visitors discovered the epic extent of *#ICPConcerned* as it snaked around corners and folded back on itself, so that the earliest images and the most recent were almost adjacent. Along walls, any number of stories, threads, motifs, and narratives could be traced. Did they add up? No. But then neither did the world. Did the exhibition speak in one voice? No. Neither did the world. But there was something salutary, cathartic, even redemptive in seeing so much of the previous year mirrored back. There it was, in its pain and difficulty, punctuated by moments of wit, hope, and possibility. For the first month we were open, our audience was stepping into an exhibition that was still evolving. Our print station remained there in the space, ready to take the chronology through to early November.

"Along walls, any number of stories, threads, motifs, and narratives could be traced. Did they add up? No. But then neither did the world."

As the US election loomed, the mood grew ever more fraught and divisive. The only things that seemed clear were the tough truths. The election result, either way, was not going

"No single approach dominates. Every genre and mode of photography is here."

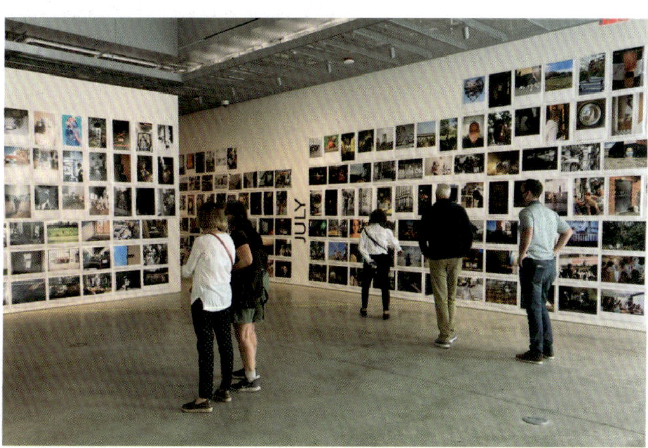

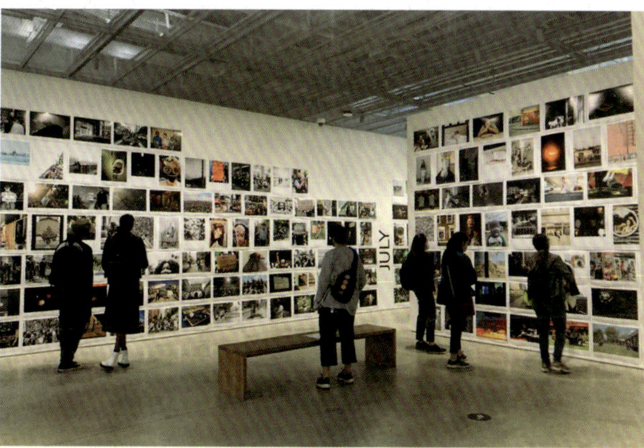

to bring stability overnight. An end to the pandemic was still a long way off. The world's economies would have to be rethought, not just restarted. And, a full reckoning with racial injustice, put off for so long, was more urgent than it had ever been. While the time period covered by the exhibition was coming to an end, we knew there were few conclusions. Neither were there any easy lessons to be drawn about the show, about the status of photography, or about the world in 2020.

Very little about the making *#ICPConcerned* had been predictable. It was an in-the-moment exhibition that evolved through some of the most turbulent months in recent history. And, there was one final twist in store for us.

ON OCTOBER 29, INSTAGRAM SUSPENDED THE "RECENT" SEARCH OPTION FOR HASHTAGS. It was a precautionary measure, aimed at preventing the spread of misinformation in the run up to the election. Too little and too late, of course, but it really put a wrench in our image selection process. Our show would have to wait for that final few days of images. We put a little sign in the gallery to explain. Our exhibition stayed open until January 3, 2021. Three days later, there was a violent assault on the US Capitol. With the hashtag search restored, we made our final image selections to close out the project. While those photographs never made it to the walls, we include them on these pages (and online).

Back in 1936, the anti-fascist playwright and cultural critic Bertolt Brecht laid out the profound and urgent task of representing an unpredictable world: "With the people struggling and changing reality before our eyes, we must not [...] derive realism as such from particular existing works, but we shall use every means, old and new, tried and untried, derived from art and derived from other sources, to render reality to men in a form they can master. [...] Our concept of realism must be wide and political, sovereign over all conventions."[ii]

Those were wise if difficult words, and worth bearing in mind as you move through the range of images that make up *#ICPConcerned.* No single approach dominates. Every genre and mode of photography is here. Portraits, landscapes, still life, reportage, and documentary, theatrical staging and raw witnessing, activism, and distant contemplation. These are strange times, with no guarantees as to what kind of image is effective, or for whom. There are few rules for describing a world with few rules, but it must be attempted. *#ICPConcerned* was a necessary experiment. While an exhibition may come and go, a book is permanent. It is there for generations to come. What will they make of *#ICPConcerned*, or of 2020? Time will tell.

[i] **WWW.ICPCONCERNED.ICP.ORG ; ICP.ORG/AUDIO**

[ii] **BERTOLT BRECHT,** *'Popularity and Realism' (1936),* in Walter Benjamin, Theodor W. Adorno, Ernst Bloch, Bertolt Brecht, and Georg Lukacs, Aesthetic and Politics, New Left Books, London, 1977, p.88.

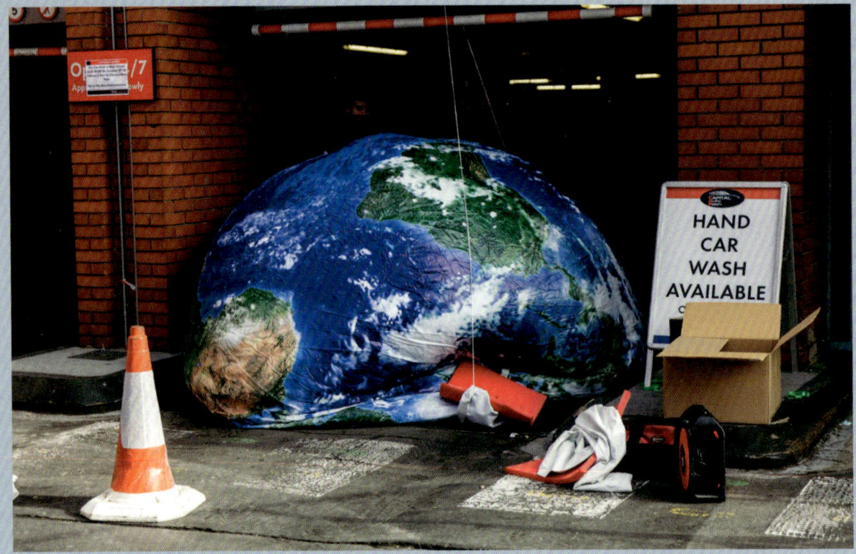

PAT MEAGHER, Flattening the Curve. SOHO, LONDON, UNITED KINGDOM

02·20

FEBRUARY

4_EU Vaccines War Explodes *(Reuters)*

9_Irish citizens flocked to the polls to vote for a new Prime Minister *(CNN)*

24_ Growing violence and protests in Haiti caused the area to cancel yearly Carnival *(CNN)*

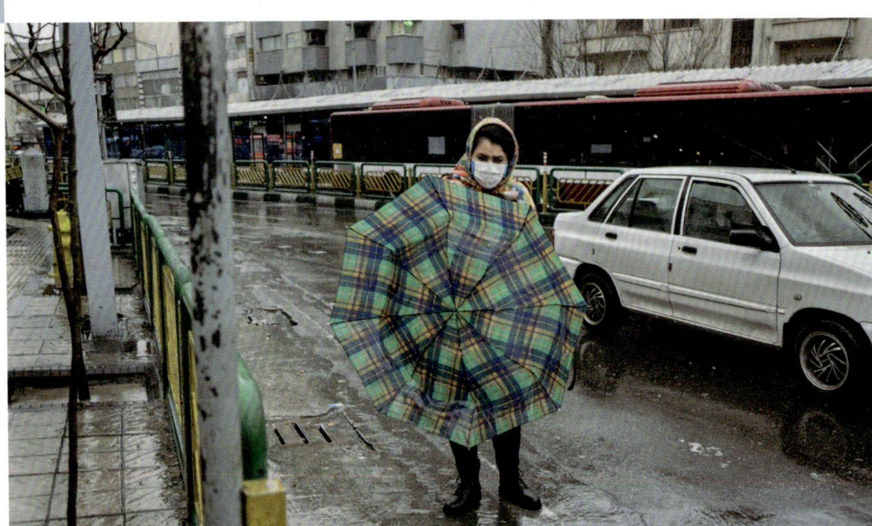

BITA HOUSHMAND, Nobody takes it very seriously from the first days but we are all scared of the coronavirus. Tehran was not locked down, but many people decided to stay at their homes.
TEHRAN, IRAN

JAN STRADTMANN, *Spend My Days Locked In A Haze I* From the Series "The Factor." LEIPZIG, GERMANY

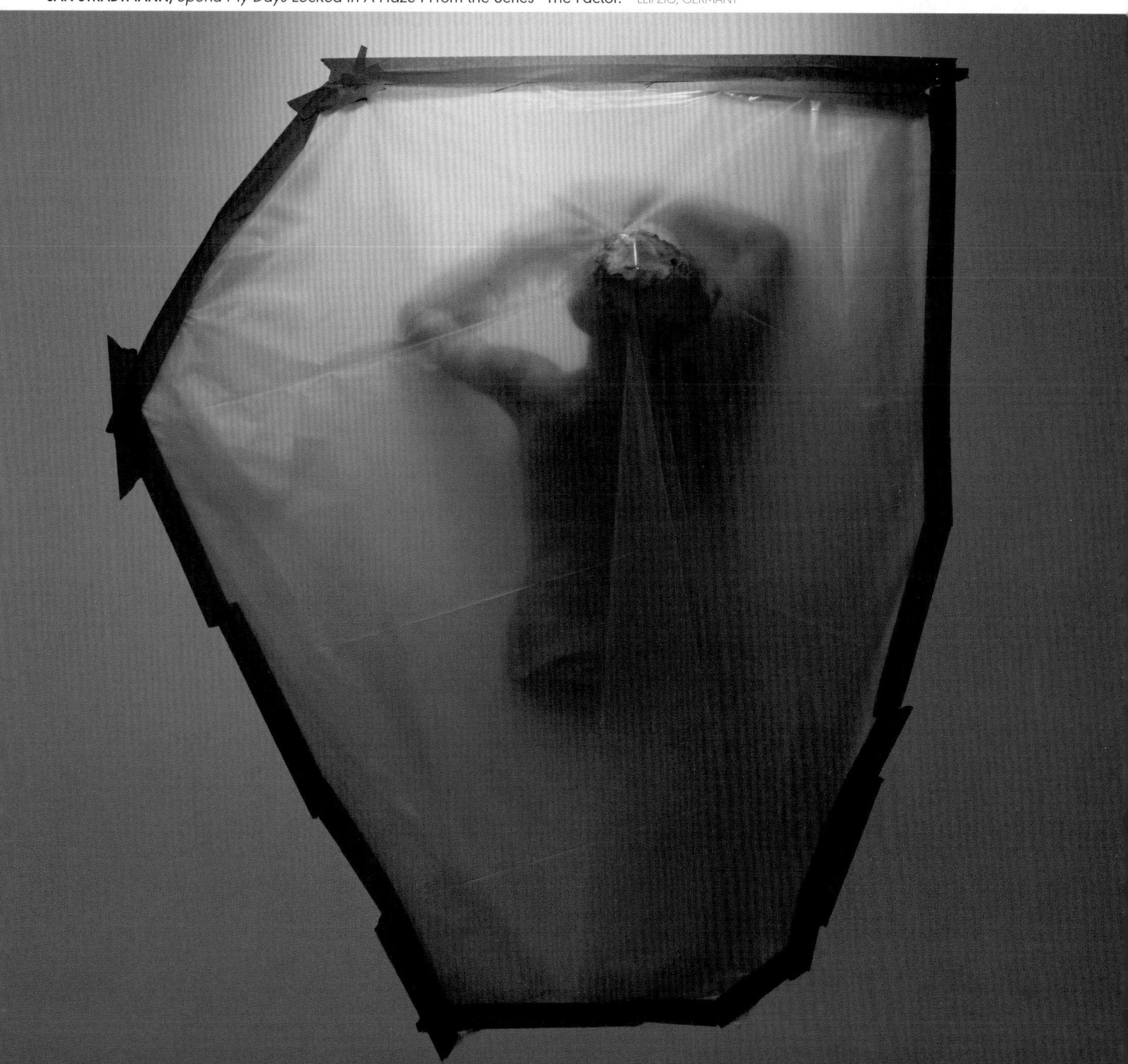

JAMIE RIVA, *Follow the Rainbow* |

Though the streets are not able to be flooded with big parades and parties this year, Pride and the grand celebration of equality and inclusion that it represents still need to be honored, in June and all year long. USA

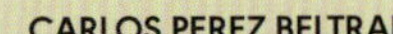

CARLOS PEREZ BELTRAN,

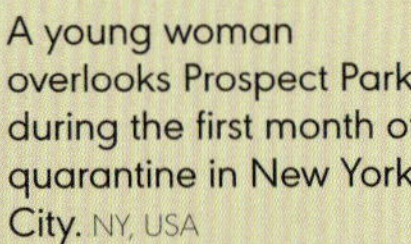

A young woman overlooks Prospect Park during the first month of quarantine in New York City. NY, USA

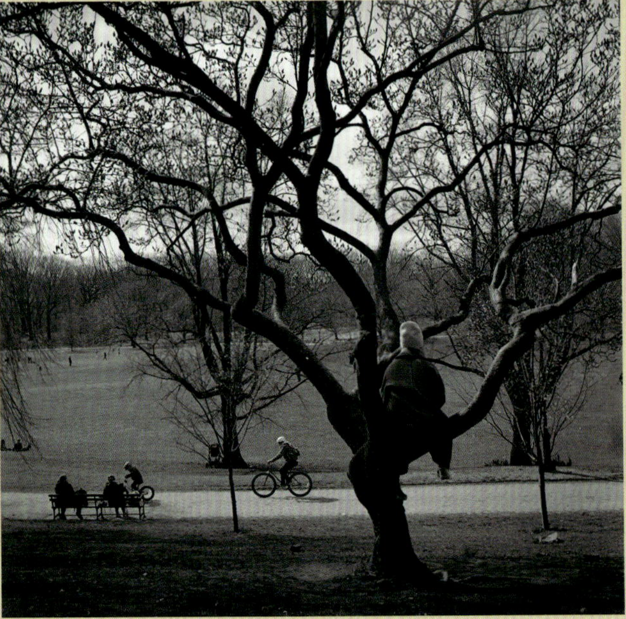

03·20

MARCH

4_Covid-19: l'executif reflechit a la mise en place d'un "passe sanitaire" pour se redonner un "cap

(Le Monde)

8_ First 20 cases in the US

(worldometers.info)

30_NEW DELHI - Migrant workers thronged in tens of thousands losing their jobs after the nationwide lockdown was announced *(IPS)*

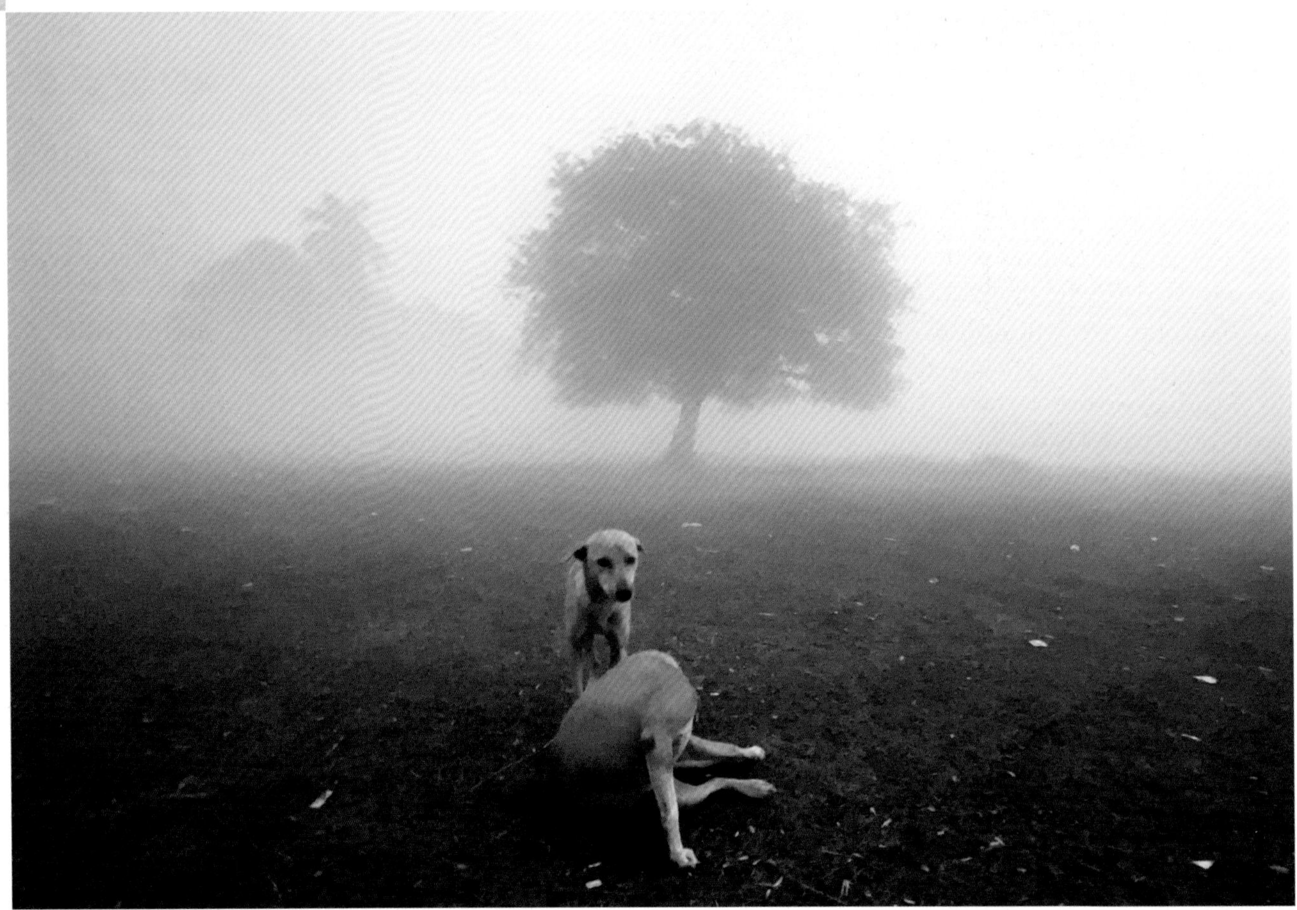

DIMPY BHALOTIA, Humans where are you? INDIA

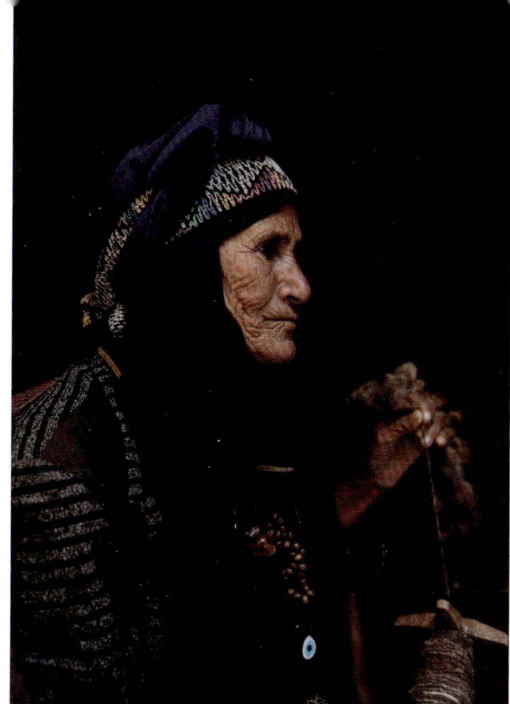

TINA BOYADJIEVA, Some things are worth traveling for during a pandemic. LITTLE PETRA, MA'AN, JORDAN

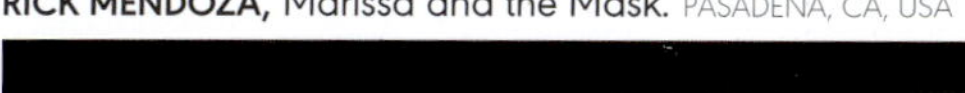

RICK MENDOZA, Marissa and the Mask. PASADENA, CA, USA

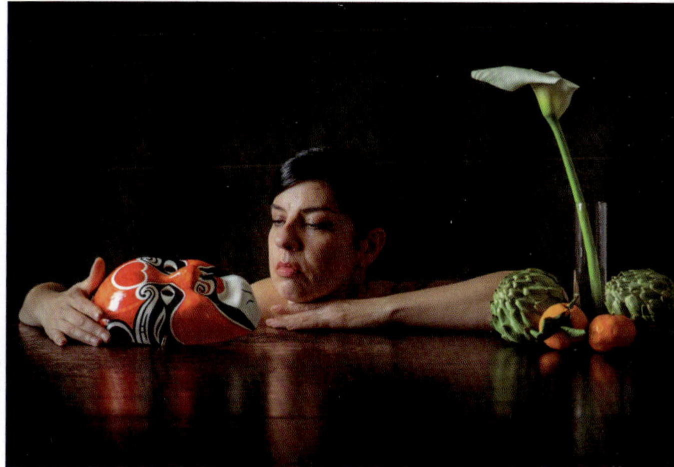

JANIQUE HELSON, *The Rediscovery* | Being home always, my dog and I are rediscovering each other. He never leaves my side. USA

LEILA SOLTANI, *The Unbearable Lightness of Being* | My home, Isfahan. IRAN

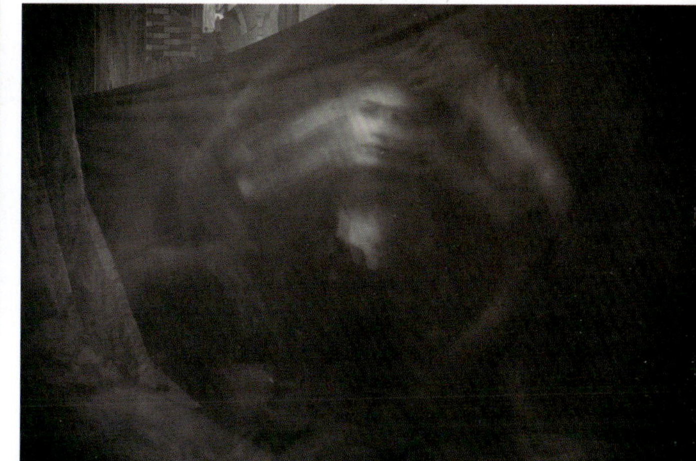

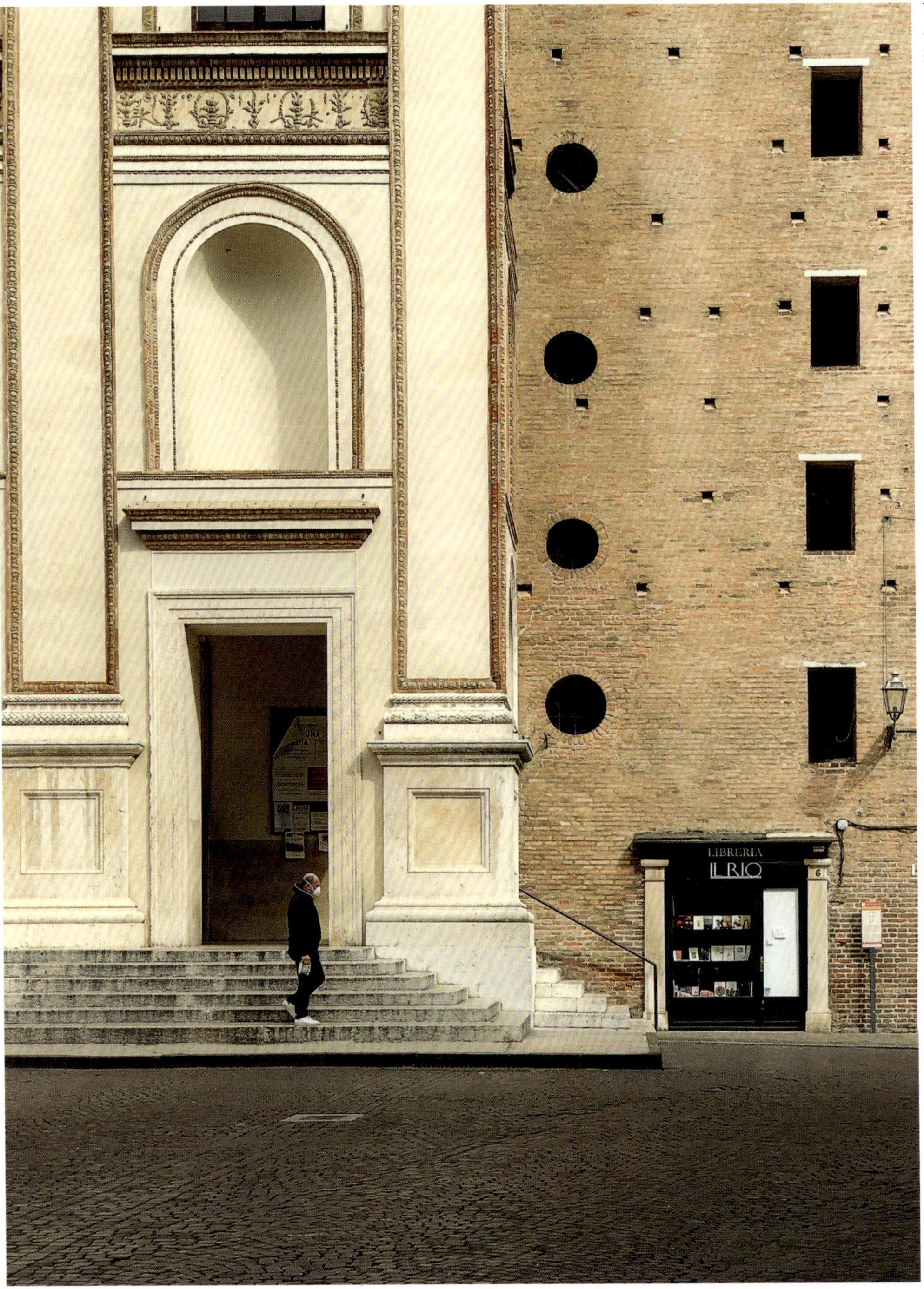

MINA HANNA,

This day will die,
and tomorrow is
a new beginning.
MANTUA, ITALY

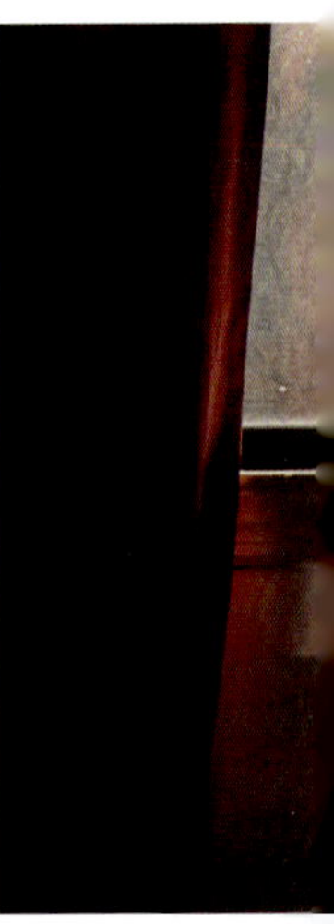

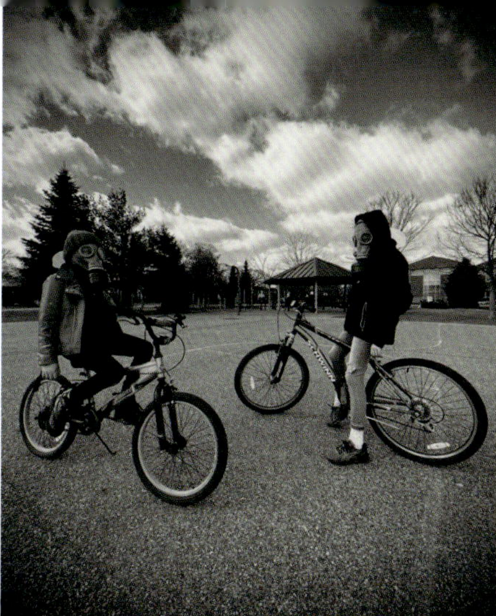

DOUGLAS TITUS, Girls Gas Masks Corona Day 1. GRAND RAPIDS, MI, USA

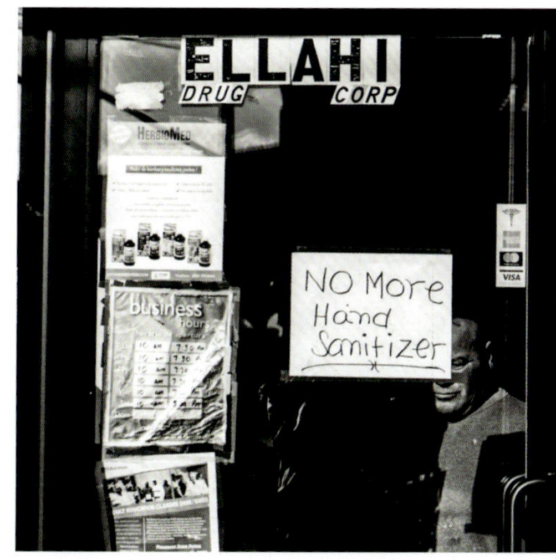

FARRAS ABDELNOUR, This photo was taken in Bushwick, in mid-March, when hand sanitizer demand peaked. BROOKLYN, NY, USA

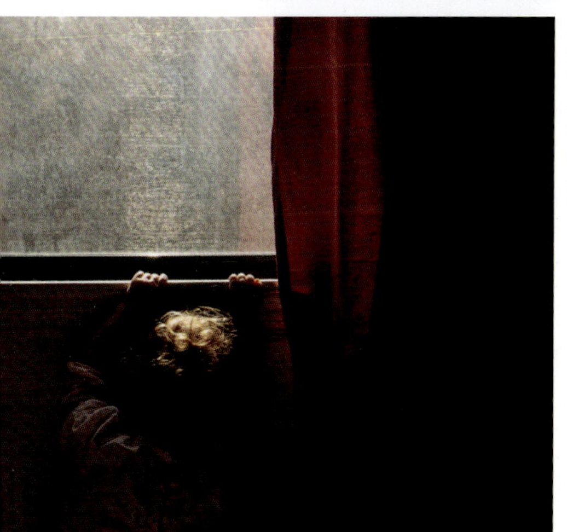

JENNIFER MCCLURE, She likes to stand in the window and wave at the few people who pass by. She yells at the birds, she asks to go to school. NEW YORK, NY, USA

CLAUDINE WILLIAMS, Orange You Glad You Have These Things. NEW YORK, NY, USA

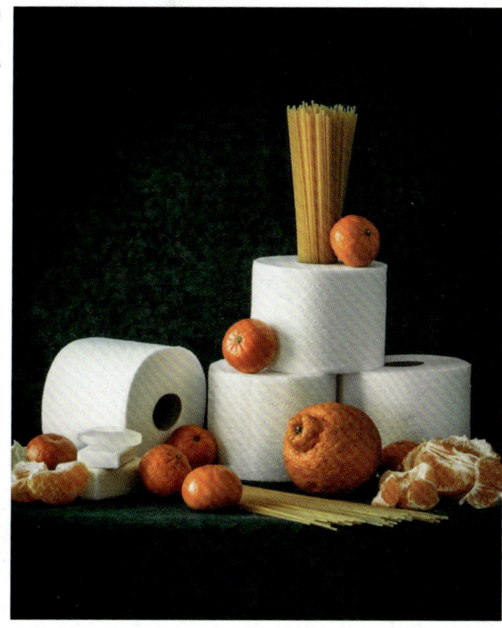

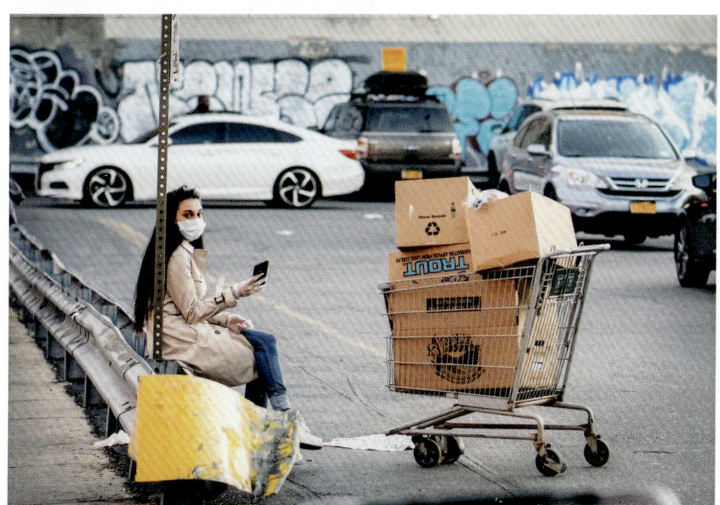

KATIE DEUTSCH, A woman waits in a supermarket parking lot in Brooklyn. The previous day a state of emergency had been declared in New York City. NEW YORK, NY, USA

JOHN FRANCIS PETERS, Empty grocery store shelves in the days leading up to California's statewide lockdown. SAN DIEGO, CA, USA

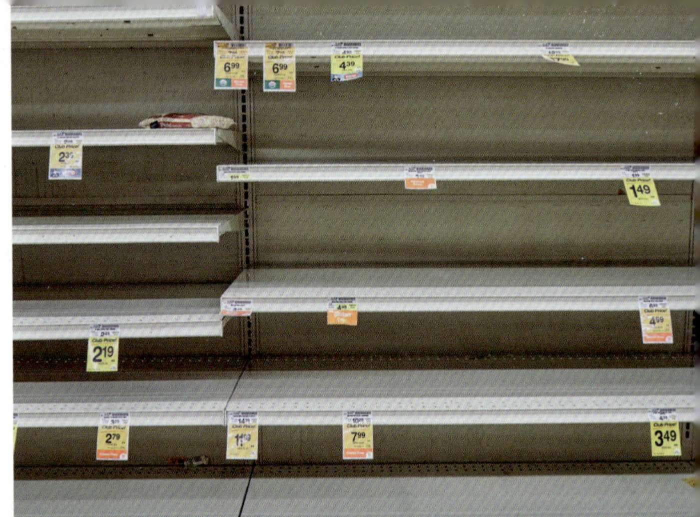

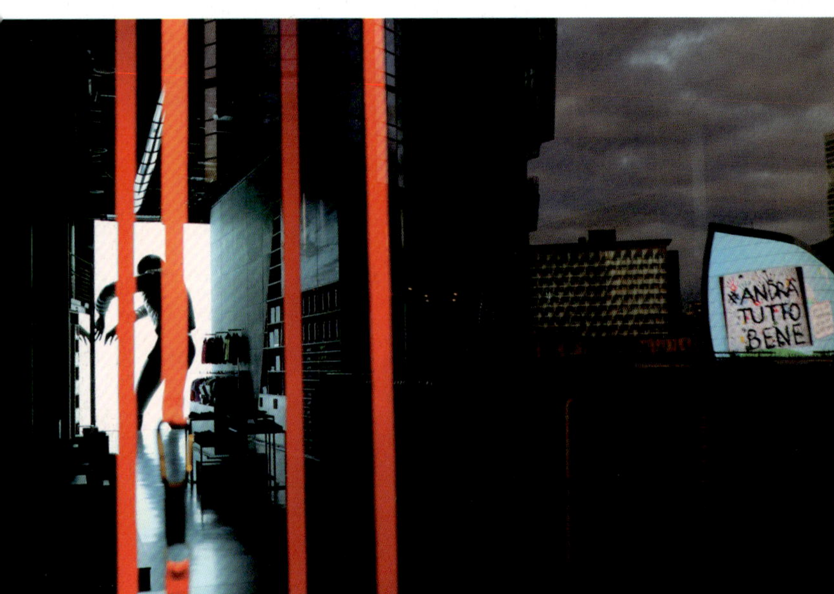

STUART PATON, *Everything Will Be Fine* | The Italian mantra. All that is missing is the question mark. MILAN, ITALY

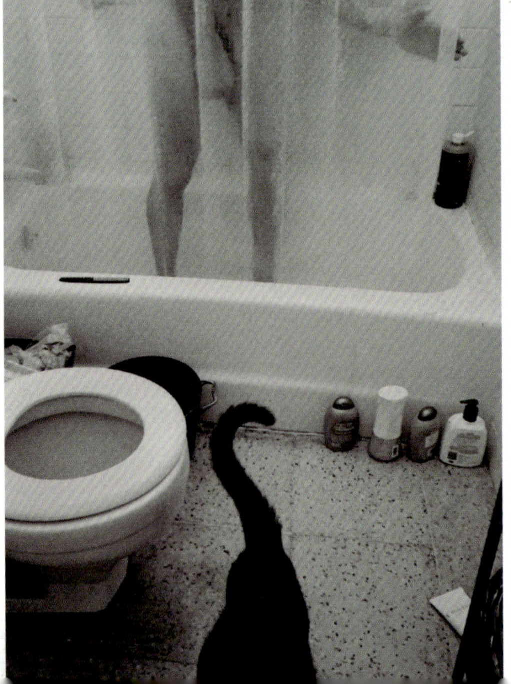

GABRIELLA N. BÁEZ, *Quarantine, curfew, and cats* | My cats Matcha and Chai have no idea there's a pandemic going on, they just know that recently they've been getting more pets. SAN JUAN, PUERTO RICO

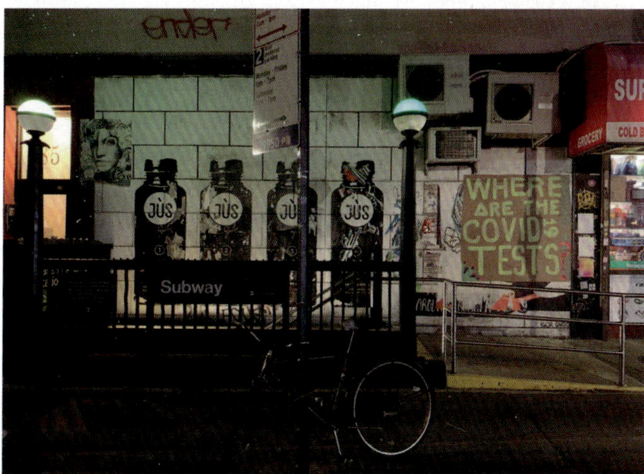

MEG ALLEN, The anxiety of quarantine and the lack of information from the government had already pushed most New Yorkers indoors. This was my last subway ride. BROOKLYN, NY, USA

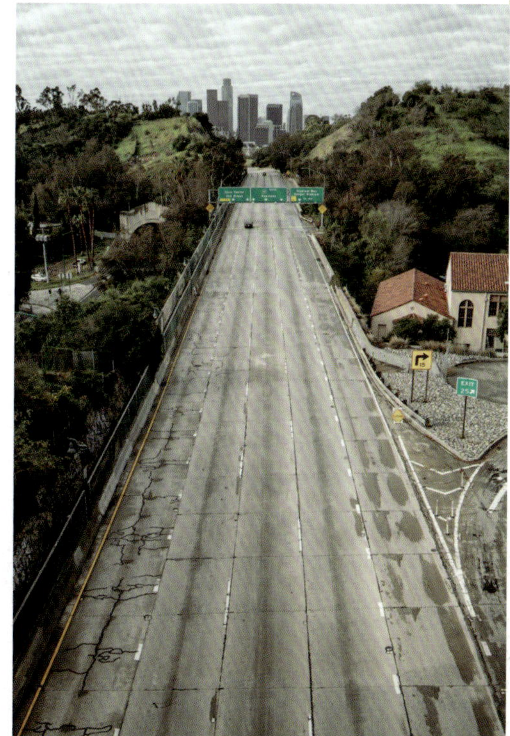

PATRICK WALSH, COVID-19, Interstate 5. LOS ANGELES, CA, USA

VINCENT KARCHER, A boy wearing mask and gloves around the Hoan Kiem lake, a popular gathering place for people in Hanoi. VIETNAM

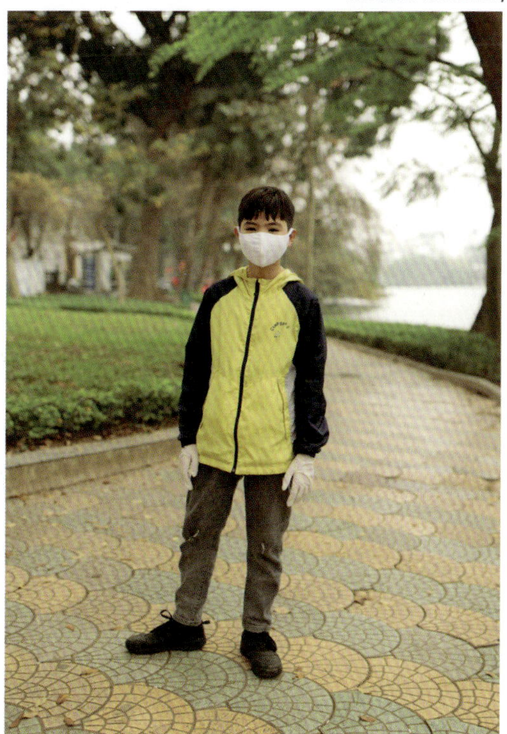

MAÍRA BARILLO, *Untitled* | Copacabana, Rio de Janeiro. The same week the first cases were confirmed in Brazil, nationalists got together for demonstrations provoked by the president to support his conservative actions in several cities. BRAZIL

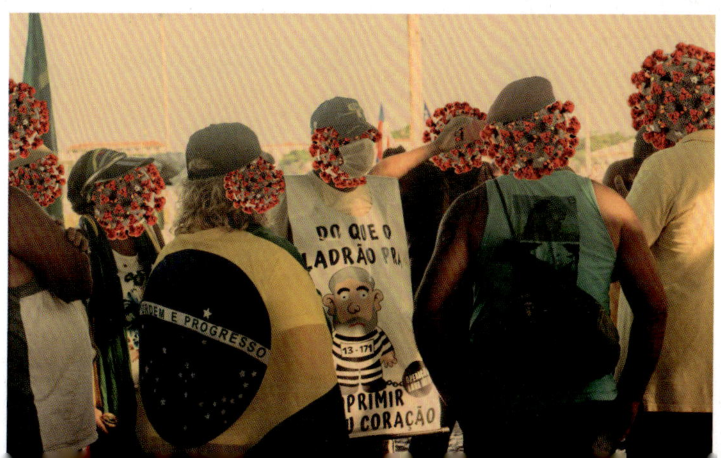

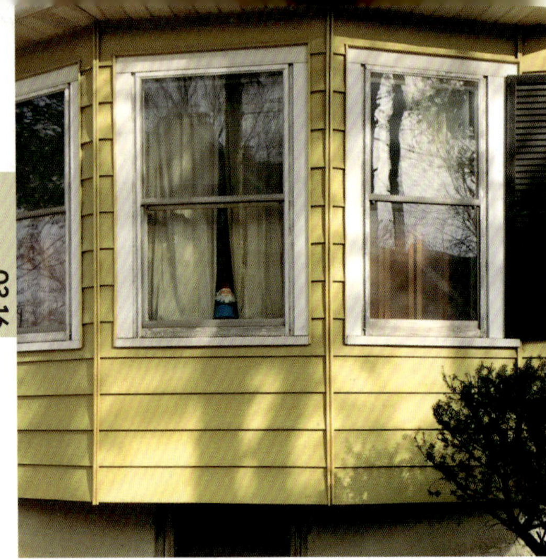

JOY BUSH,
Self-quarantine, even gnomes are doing it! HAMDEN, CT, USA

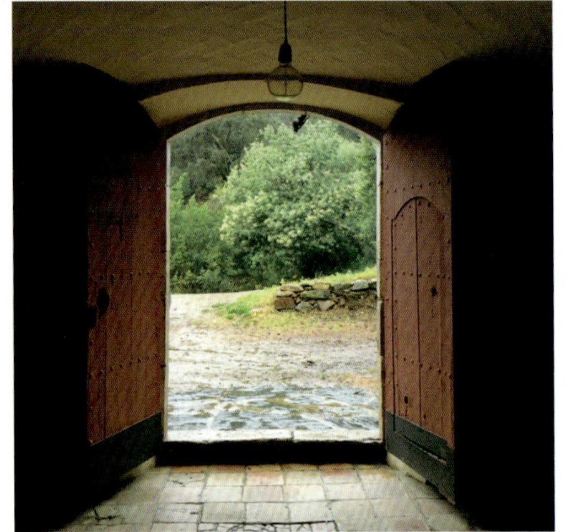

MICHELE CUREL, *Quarantine Day 7* | Mas Cabre, Gavarres Forest, Province of Girona, Catalonia. SPAIN

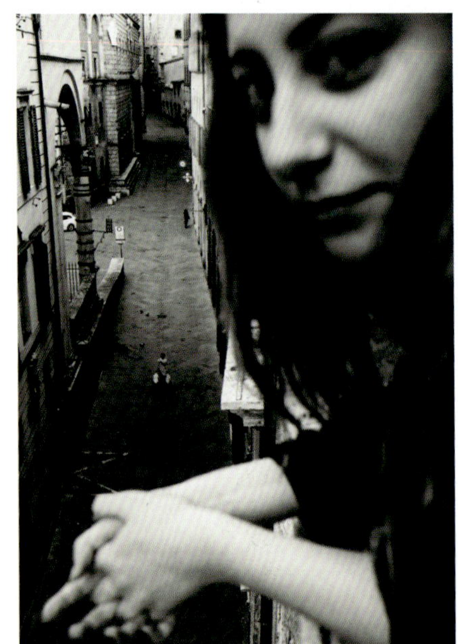

SALVATORE TERRASI,
Lockdown with roommate in Siena. TUSCANY, ITALY

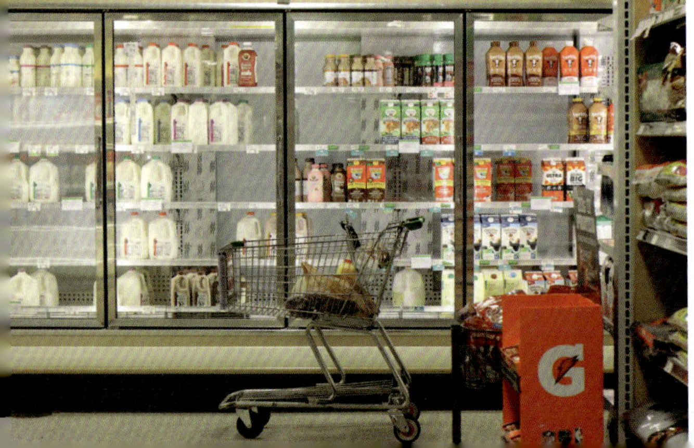

MABE FERNÁNDEZ-CONCHESO, *We still #gotmilk.* | On the first days of quarantine, milk was scarce in Miami and this was one of the few supermarkets that had any left. FL, USA

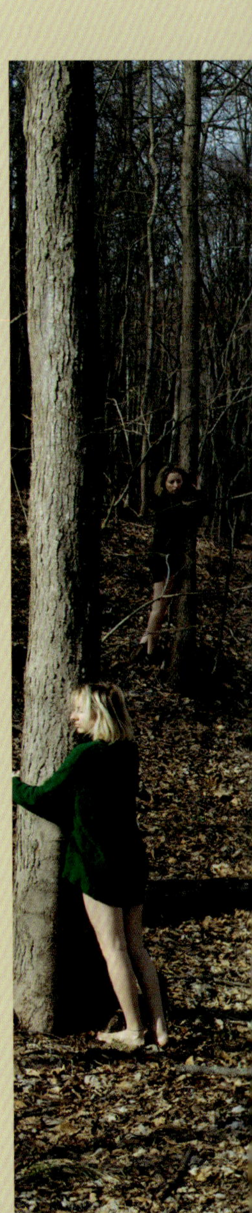

WANDA VON BREMEN, *Corona-free friends* |

When Coronavirus came to New York I decided to go upstate to get away from the city and to get away from all the things happening there. I put myself in isolation, which meant no human beings close to me and I was only surrounded by forest and nature. In search of emotional support and physical contact, I went into the forest and decided to hug trees. It was surprisingly calming to hug trees and to feel that nature is supporting us and is always there and always protecting us. NY, USA

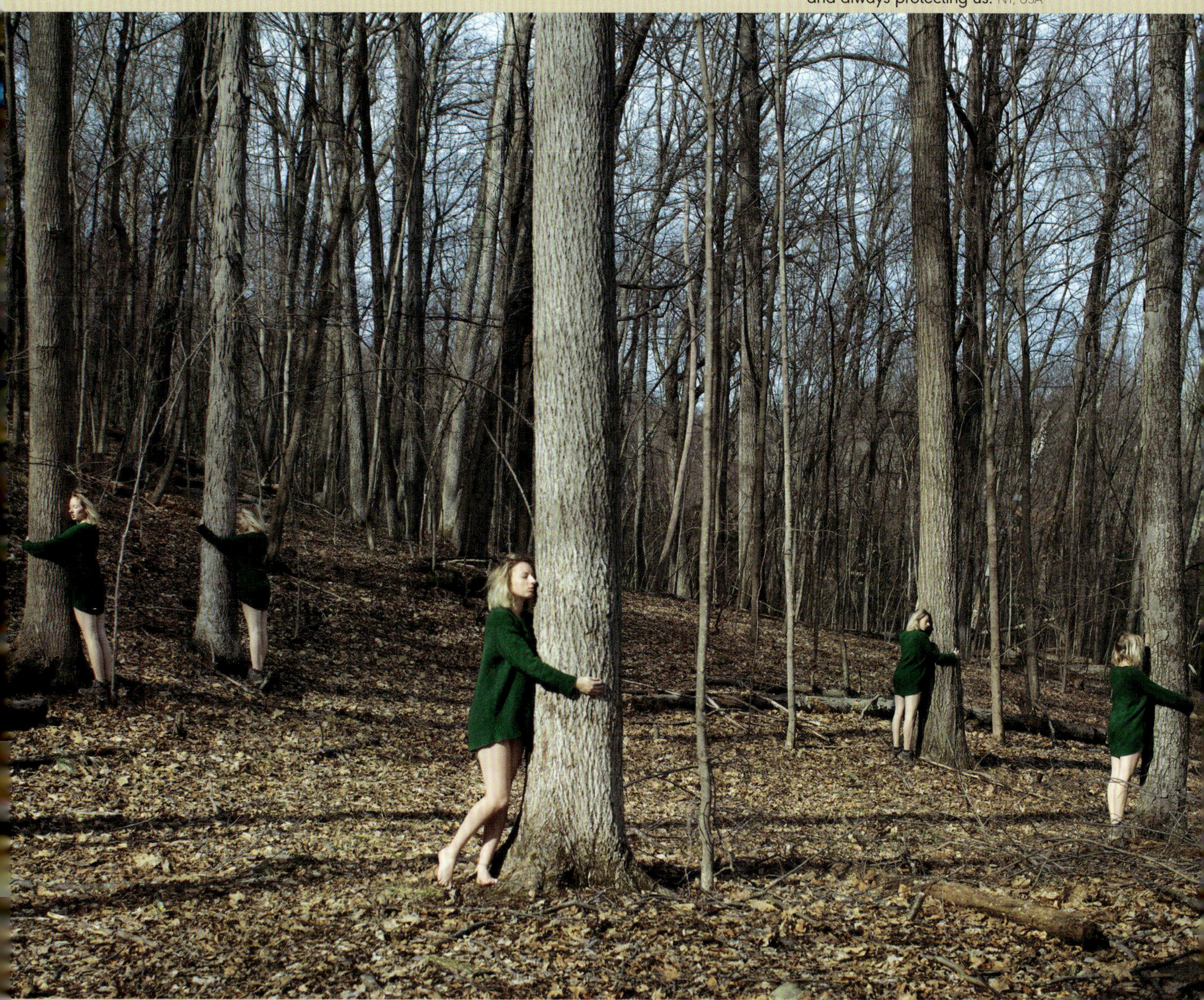

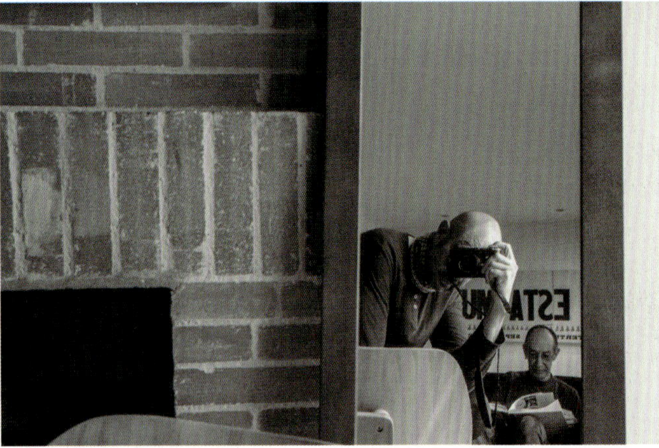

JUAN CRISTOBAL COBO,
My father and me on the very first day of lockdown in Bogotá. COLOMBIA

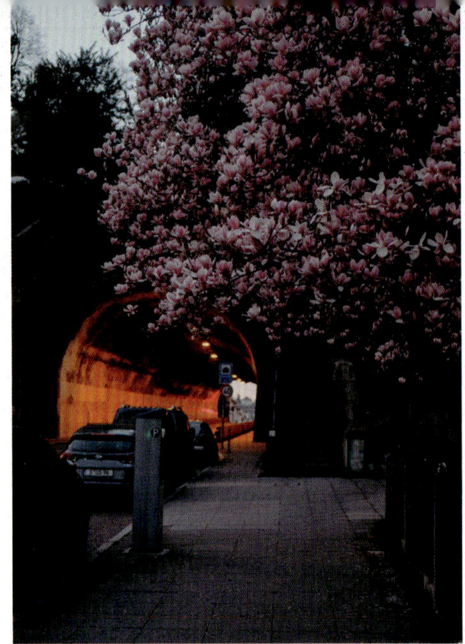

ILKAY KARAKURT, *Magnolia* | Through quarantine I pay attention to minor details around me. Also how nature transforms. Spring is coming. STUTTGART, BADEN-WÜRTTEMBERG, GERMANY

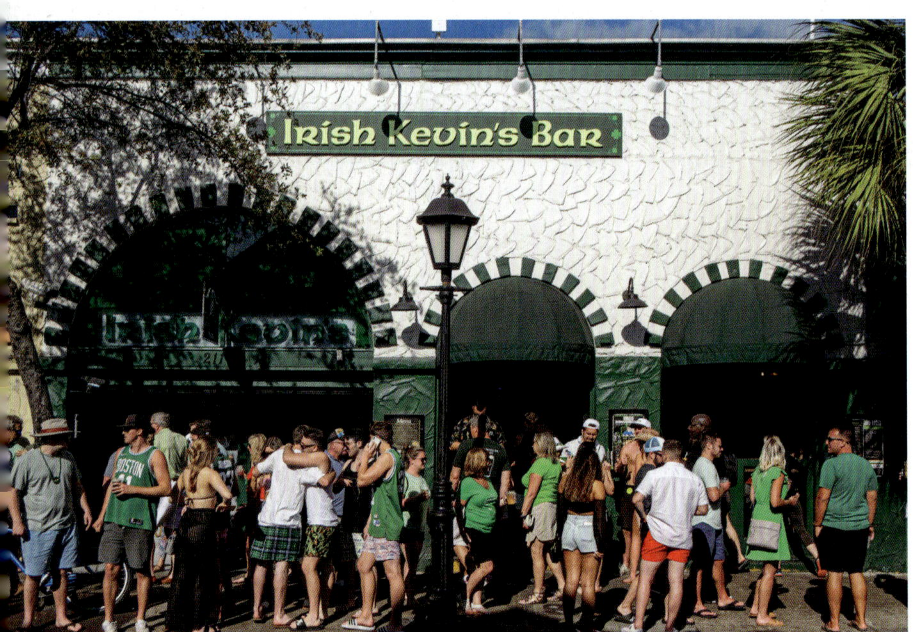

MARK HEDDEN, Key West, Spring Break and St. Patrick's Day, less than an hour before the bars were scheduled to close for lockdown. FL, USA

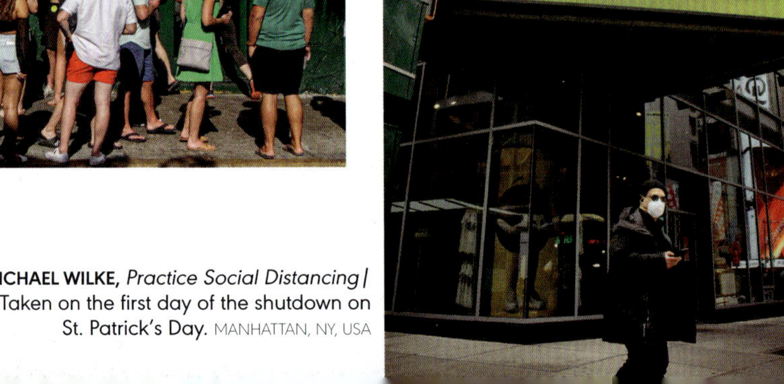

MICHAEL WILKE, *Practice Social Distancing* | Taken on the first day of the shutdown on St. Patrick's Day. MANHATTAN, NY, USA

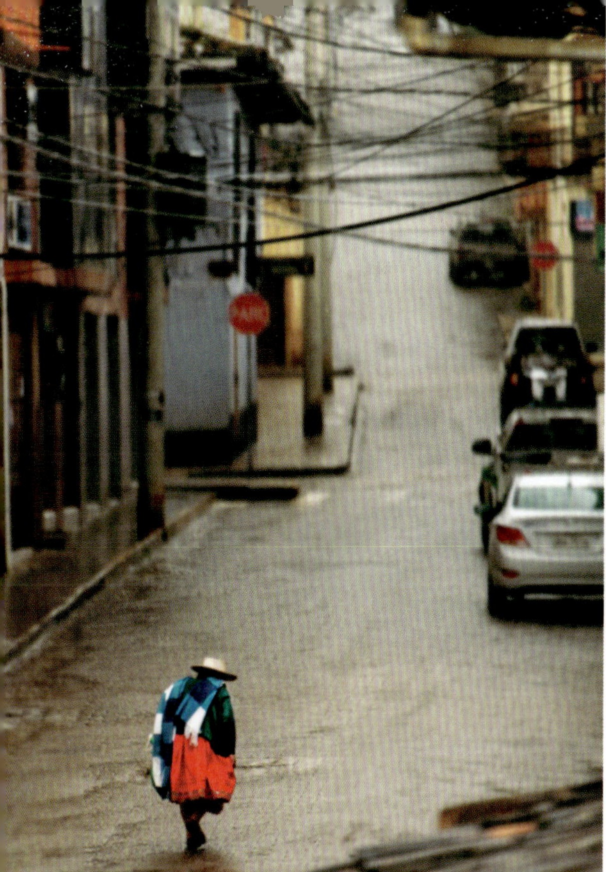

ILA CORONEL, *Cholita Sigseña, Sigsig* | Cholita buscando comida después del toque de queda. AZUAY, ECUADOR

RIF SPAHNI, *Dia 02* | Provisions. SACRED VALLEY, URUBAMBA, PERU

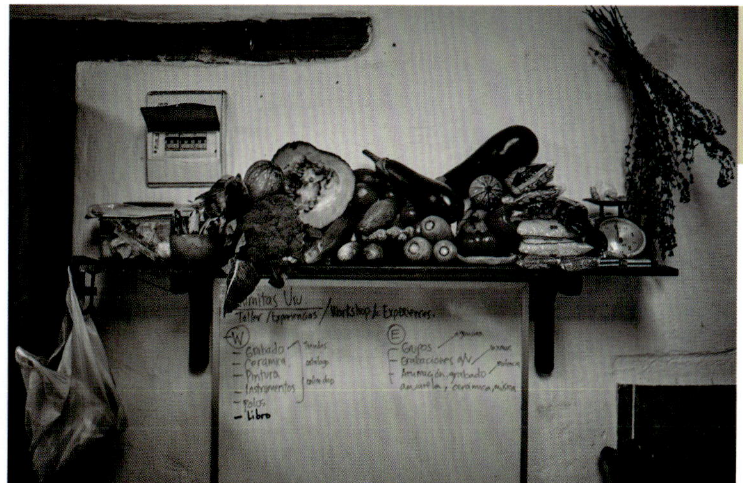

LUCÍA VÁZQUEZ, *Do we have a life during coronavirus time?* | Second Avenue, Upper East Side. NEW YORK, NY, USA

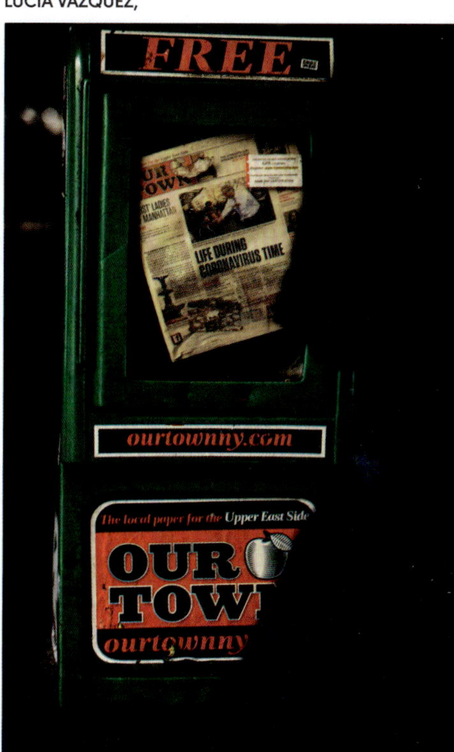

SHARON PULWER, A flight attendant on the El Al flight from Newark Liberty International Airport to Ben Gurion Airport in Tel Aviv. NJ, USA

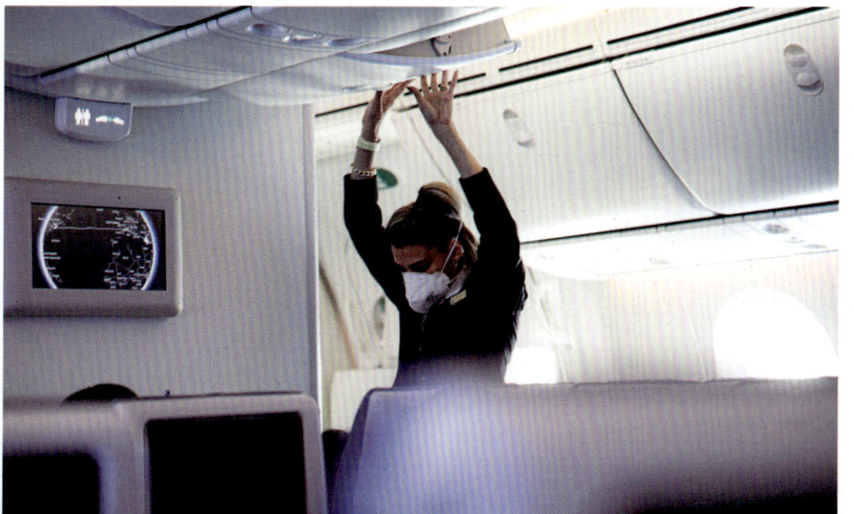

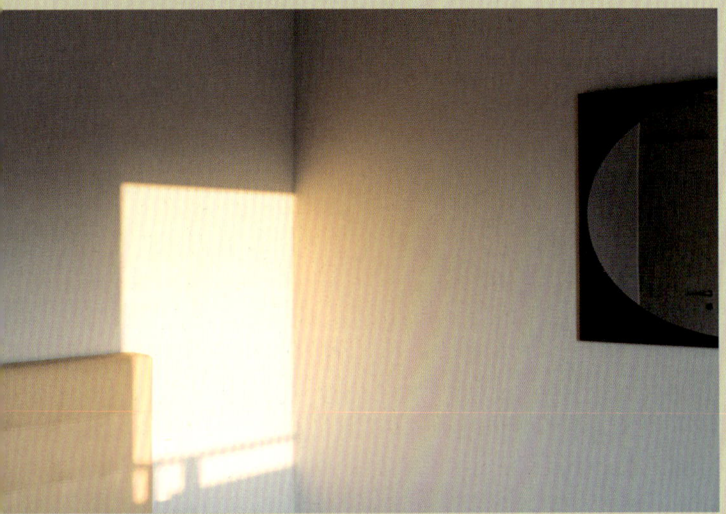

ALBA DEANGELIS, *On the Nature of Daylight* | Inspired by the song by Max Richter. A meditation about time, life, and death at this moment in history. This image was taken after about ten days alone, and I had just realized, looking at the sun on the wall of my bedroom, that this was the only physical element coming from the outside into my apartment, and the only external element connecting me to it. So as I was looking at the sun moving on the bedroom wall, I was also listening to the song by composer Max Richter called "On the Nature of Daylight," and I decided to record the entire movement of the sun on the following day. This photo is part of the bigger series in which you can see the sun slowly appearing on the initially dark wall, moving on it until it finally disappears again. At that point, thinking about the cycle of life itself was unavoidable, especially with the discomforting news of those days. MILAN, ITALY

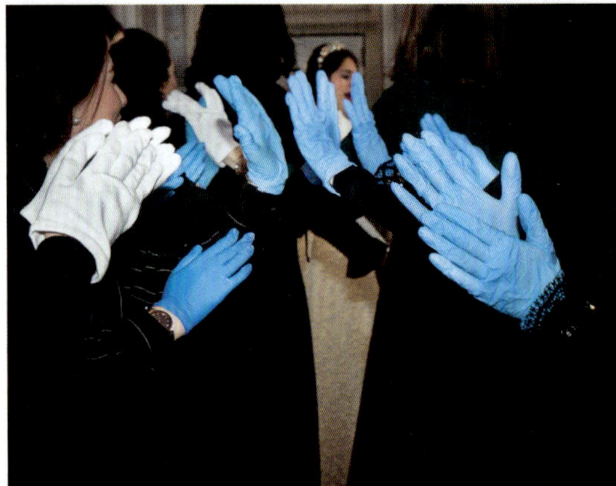

GHILA KRAJZMAN, This is a Hassidic wedding in Williamsburg. It was the last day it was possible to have a wedding before the city lockdown. NY, USA

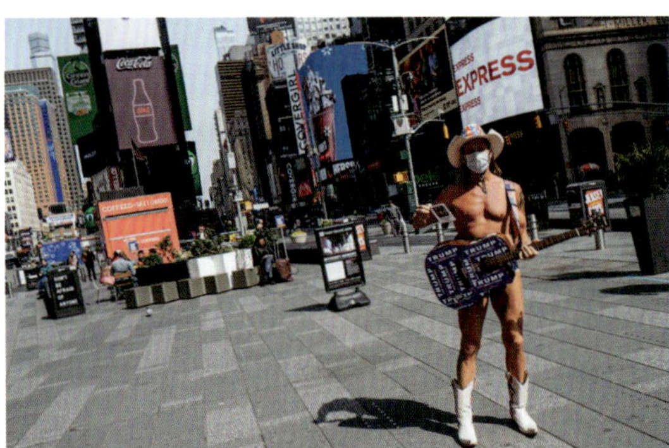

HWANHEE RYU, Vacancy. TIMES SQUARE, NEW YORK, NY, USA

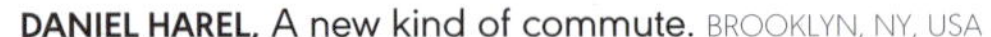

DANIEL HAREL, A new kind of commute. BROOKLYN, NY, USA

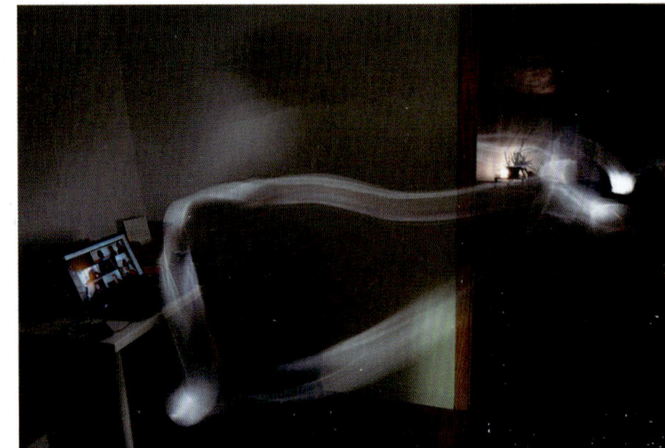

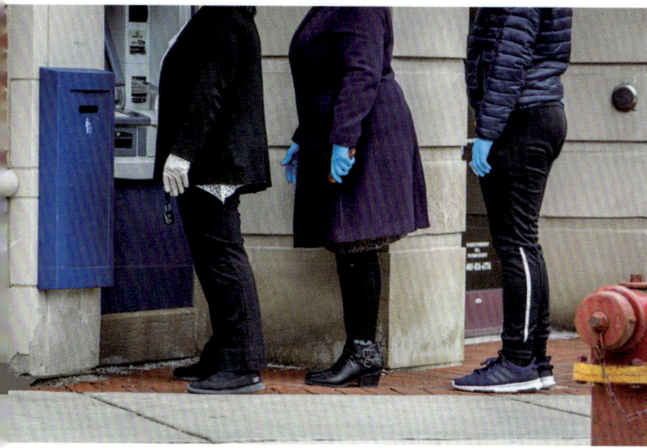

ADAM FRINT, COVID ATM Line. UKRAINIAN VILLAGE, CHICAGO, IL, USA

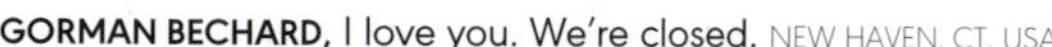

GORMAN BECHARD, I love you. We're closed. NEW HAVEN, CT, USA

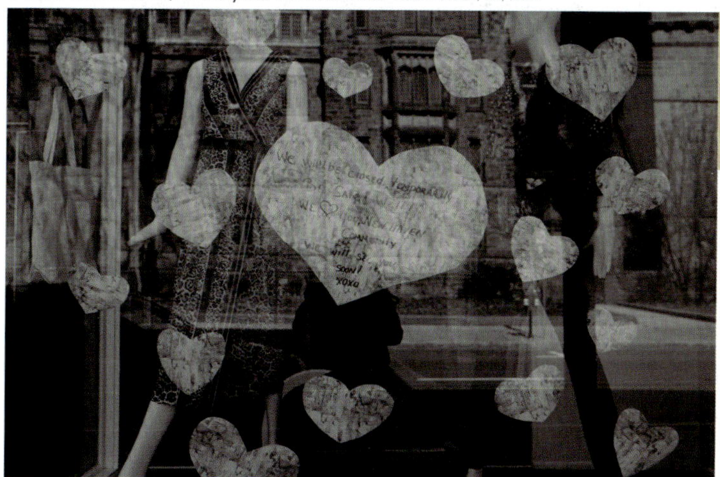

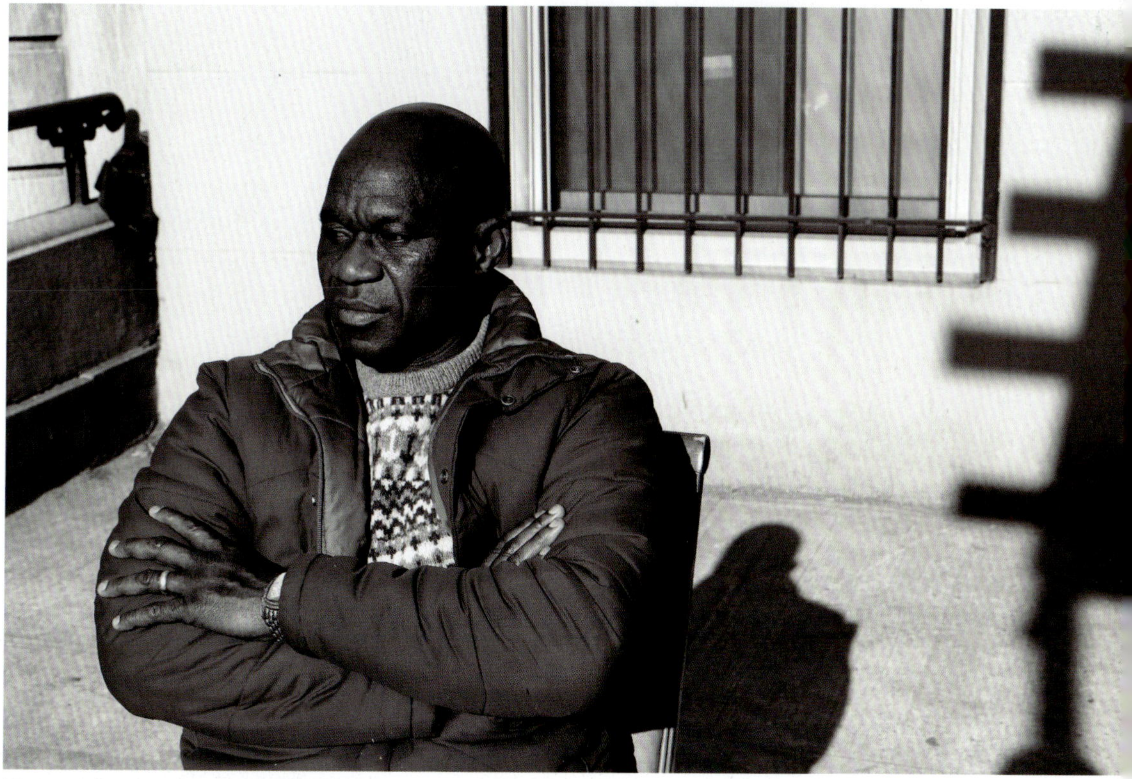

LORI AZIM, *Uncertainty* | Moussa sells newspapers on a sidewalk near my apartment. He requested this portrait two days before shutdown. As of August, he had yet to return. BROOKLYN, NY, USA

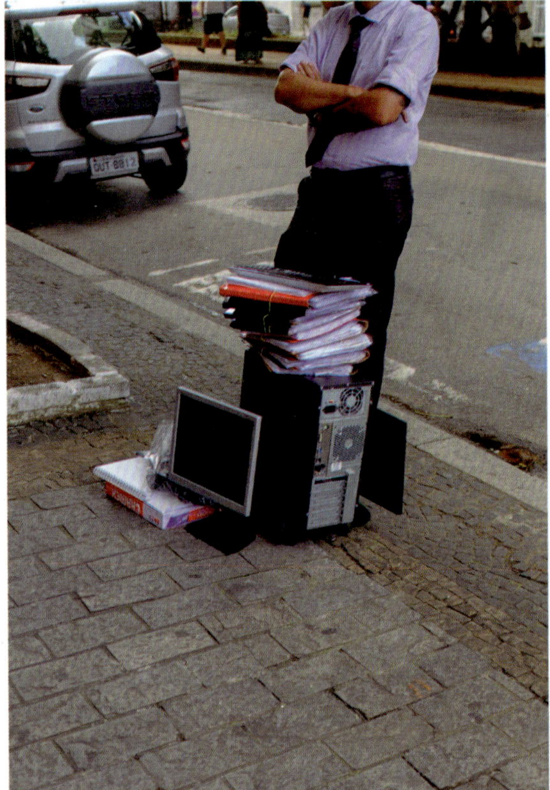

MATHEUS BONAFÉ, Companies adopt the home-office regime. Avenida Ipiranga, Central Zone of São Paulo. BRAZIL

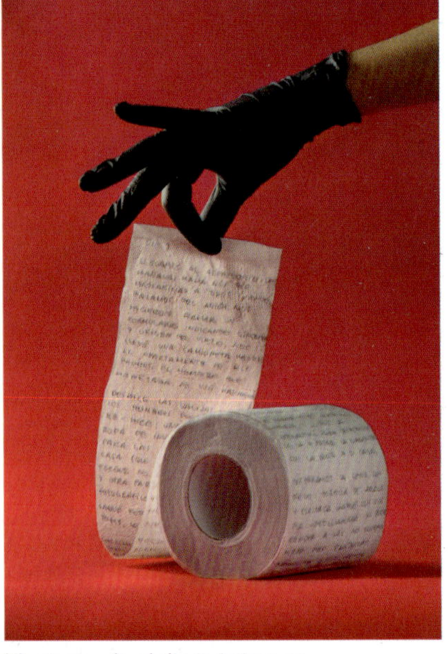

SABRINA SRUR, *Día 5* | Manteniendo el diario intimo actualizado. *si, sacrifique un papel higiénico por amor al arte. Lo que no quita que después que pase todo esto, sea nuevamente utilizable. POCITOS, MONTEVIDEO, URUGUAY

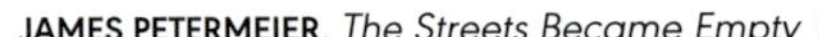

JAMES PETERMEIER, *The Streets Became Empty* | A City Tram in Den Haag during coronavirus restrictions. NETHERLANDS

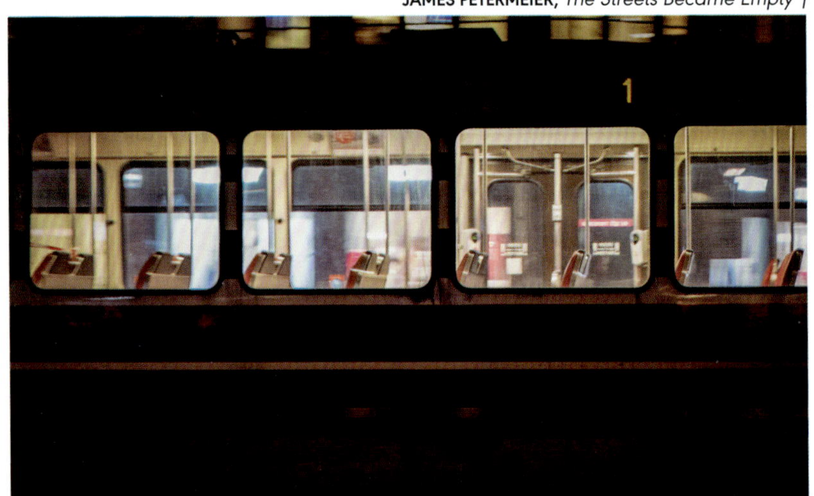

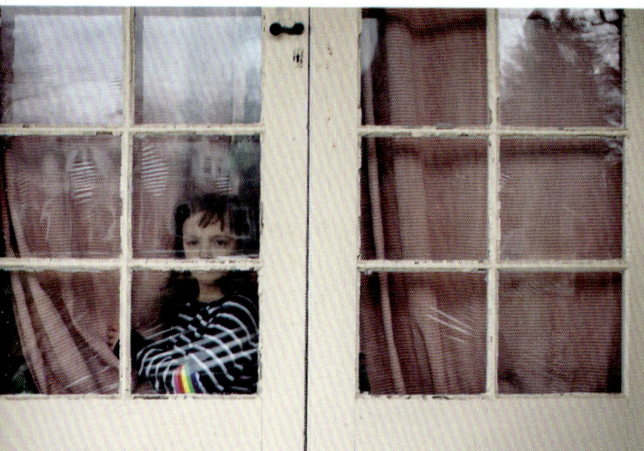

LUCY BOHNSACK, *Marian, Through the Window* | Many residents of New York City fled upstate early in the pandemic. Locals feared them but Marian enjoyed watching the strangers walk their dogs. CATSKILL, NY, USA

MARITA UPENIECE, Empty night city, London. UNITED KINGDOM

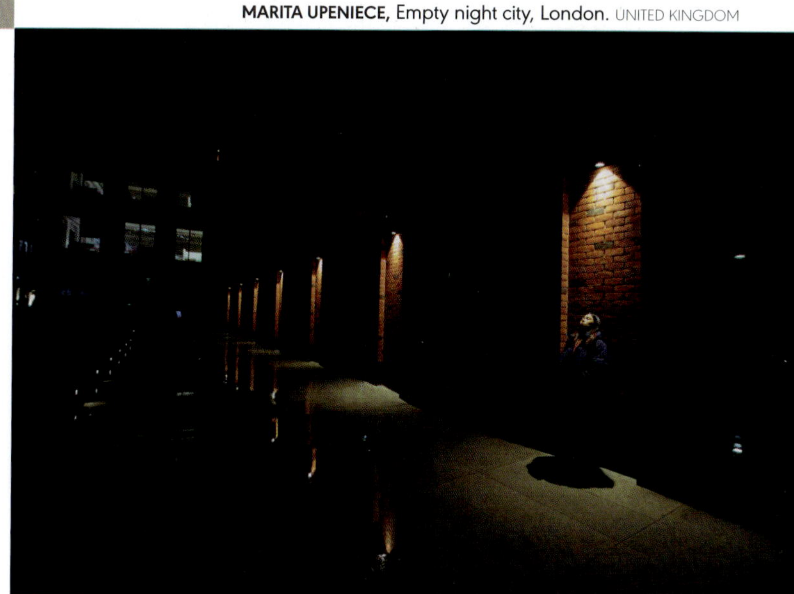

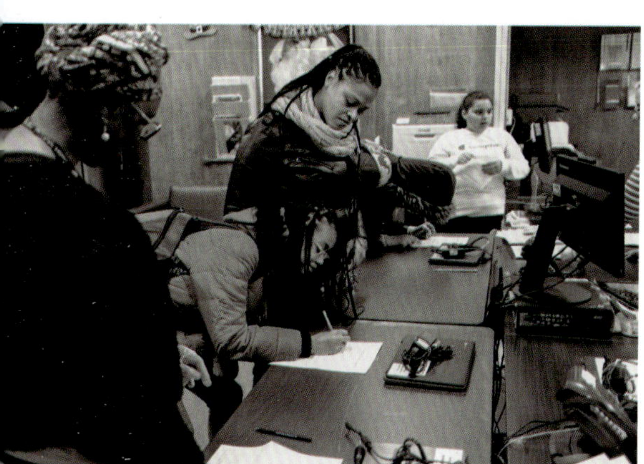

BEN RUSSELL, The High School of Fashion Industries staff distributes digital devices to students in preparation for online learning as New York City public school buildings close. NY, USA

VICTORIA WALCOTT, *Social distancing—not quite six feet* | Two boys playing outdoors demonstrate the strange experience of being young in the time of COVID-19. RALEIGH, NC, USA

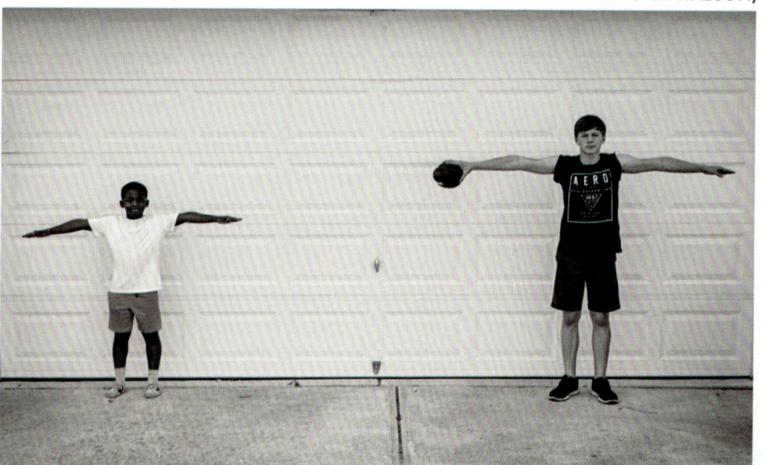

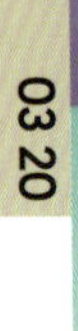

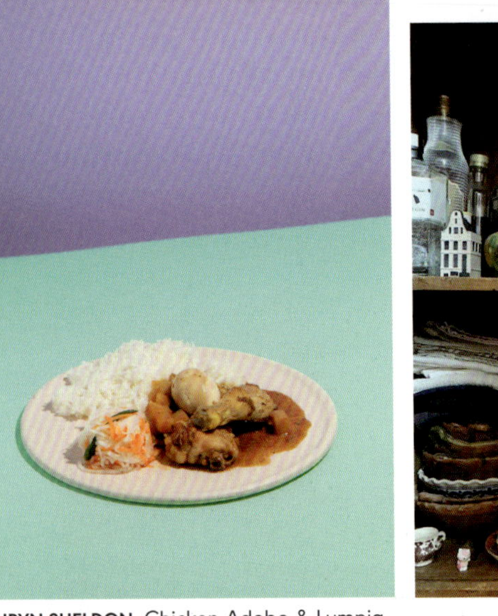

KATHRYN SHELDON, Chicken Adobo & Lumpia, from Chef Josh Sta Ana. BROOKLYN, NY, USA

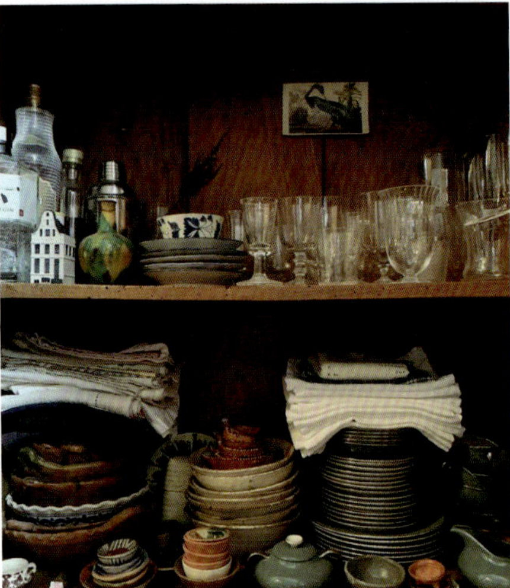

LISA SILVESTRI, *China Cabinet* | Preparing for the first virtual dinner party. NEW YORK, NY, USA

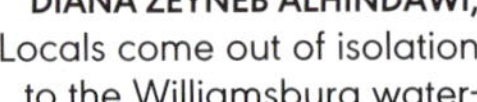

DIANA ZEYNEB ALHINDAWI, Locals come out of isolation to the Williamsburg waterfront in Brooklyn, on the first warm day of springtime, which under normal circumstances would have packed the streets of New York City. NY, USA

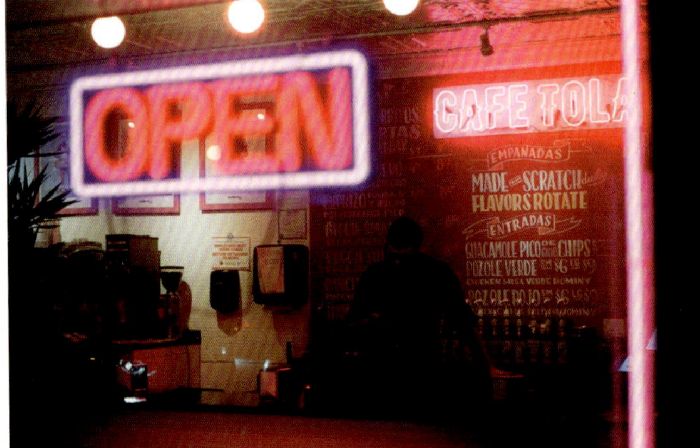

ZACHARY BRANIGAN, The Cafe Tola, Chicago. Shot during a lonely evening walk as Chicago began to fall quiet. IL, USA

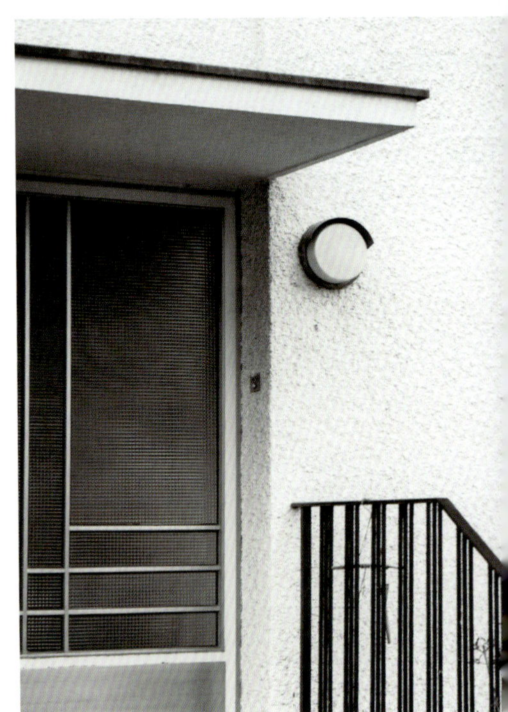

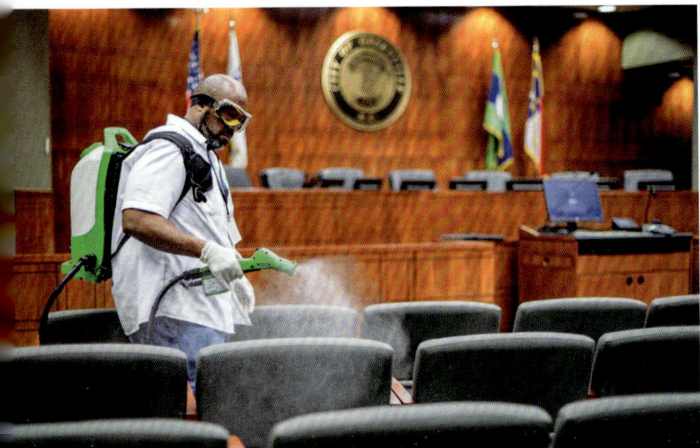

AARON HINES, City staff spray electrostatic disinfectant throughout the city council chambers after each use to prevent the spread of COVID-19. GREENVILLE, NC, USA

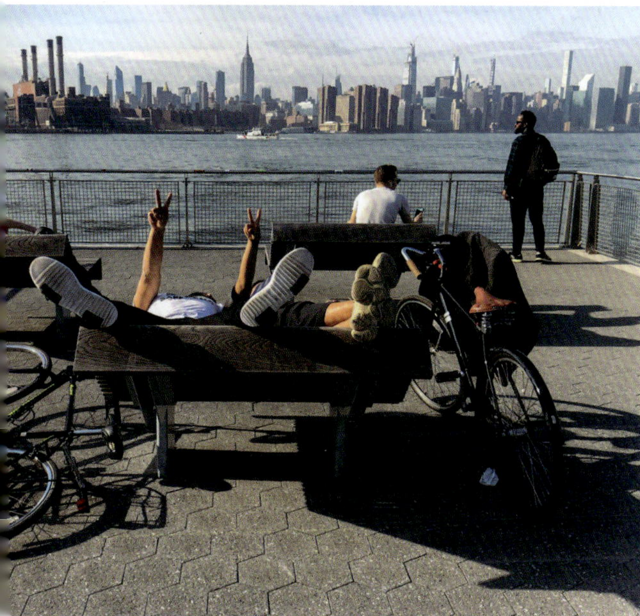

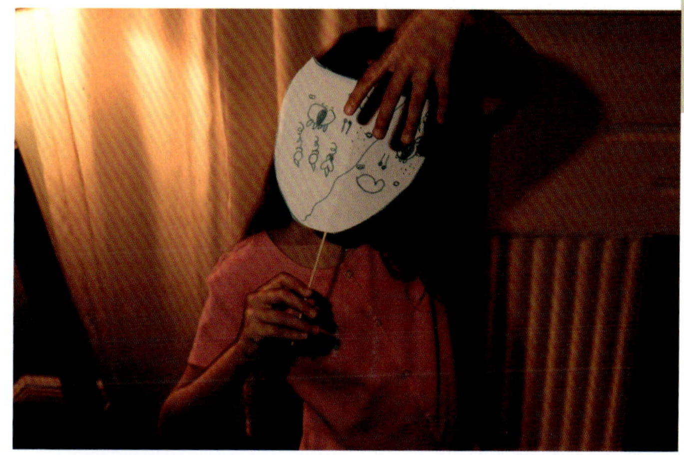

CARLO PIRRONGELLI, Part of my ongoing series "Not Far from Home." MIAMI, FL, USA

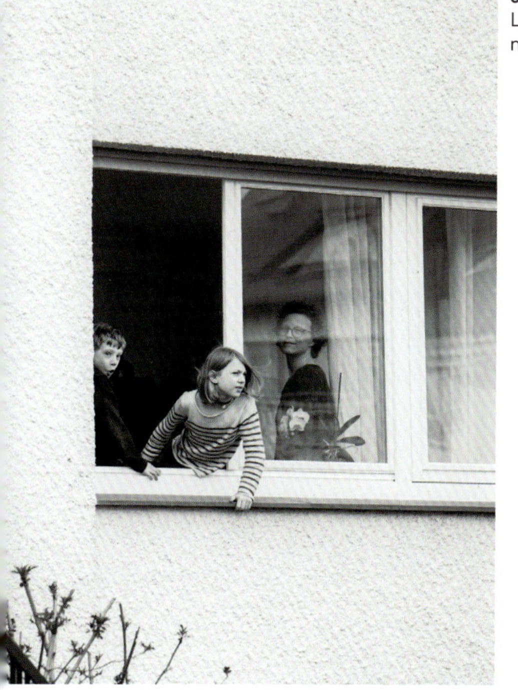

SVEN BECKER, *Confinement Portraits Project |* Luxembourg residents' confinement life, as coronavirus shuts down the country. BRIDEL, LUXEMBOURG

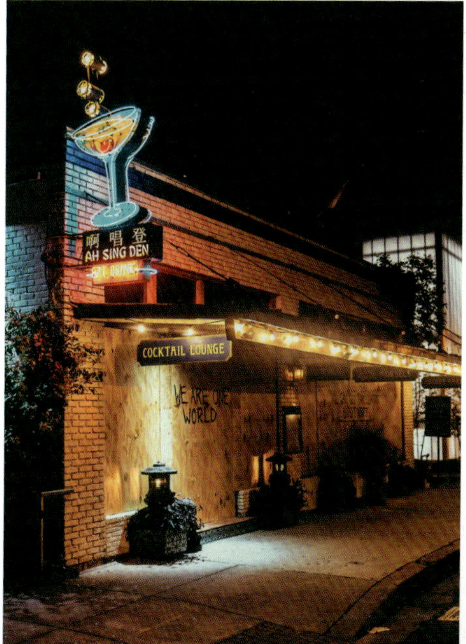

DANIEL CAVAZOS, We Are One World, SXSW. AUSTIN, TX, USA

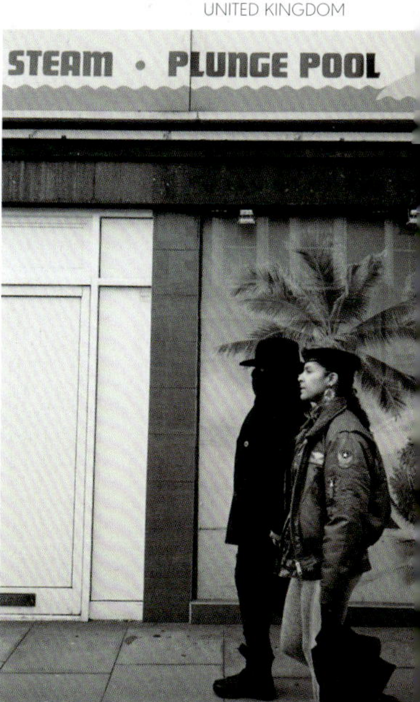

CHARLES CAVE, London, 2020. UNITED KINGDOM

MERIMA RAMDEDOVIĆ, *Growth During a Pandemic* |

This photo was taken the last time I took the train before quarantine, I wanted to create beauty within that cold and empty setting of the train. NEW YORK, NY, USA

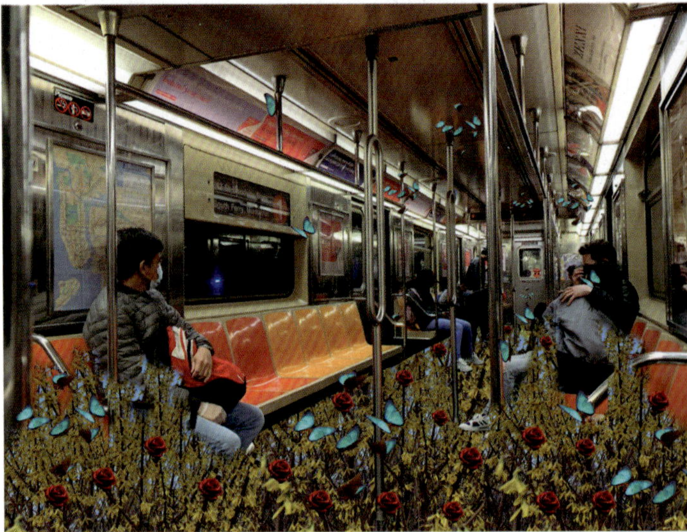

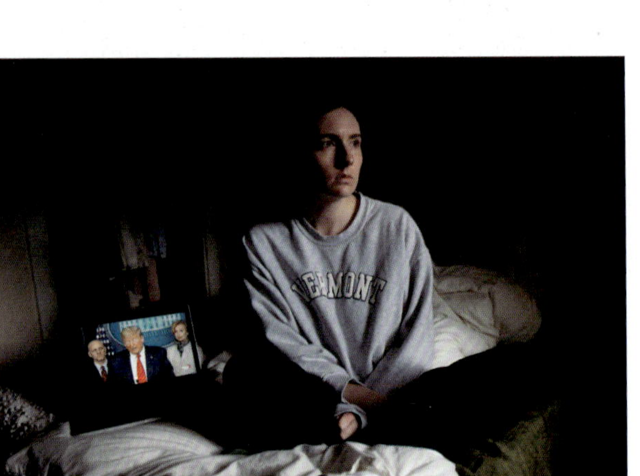

MEG JEUNKER, I—alongside millions of other Americans—was partially laid off from my full-time job, and lost my second job entirely. On the first day of local shutdowns, with a profound sense of personal significance and global history unfolding, I made this self-portrait. BOZEMAN, MT, USA

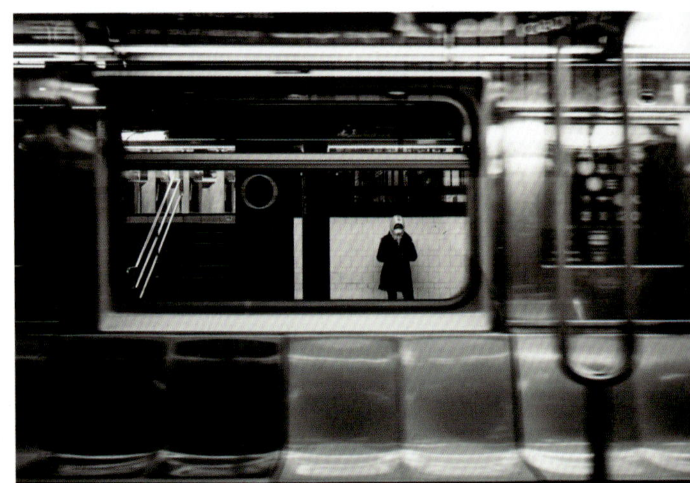

DERECK LARSEN, *Isolation* |

Shot through an empty, moving 6 train. UPPER EAST SIDE, NEW YORK, NY, USA

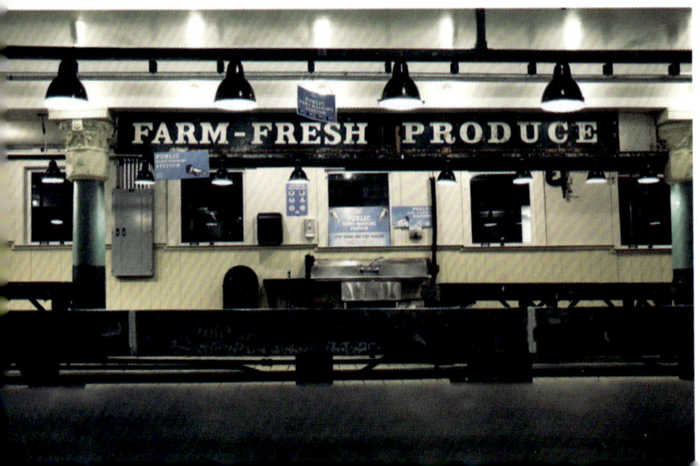

SONY THOMAS, *Leaving The Lights On* |
This was shot in an otherwise bustling, historic Pike Place Market in the heart of Seattle after the city was shutdown. WA, USA

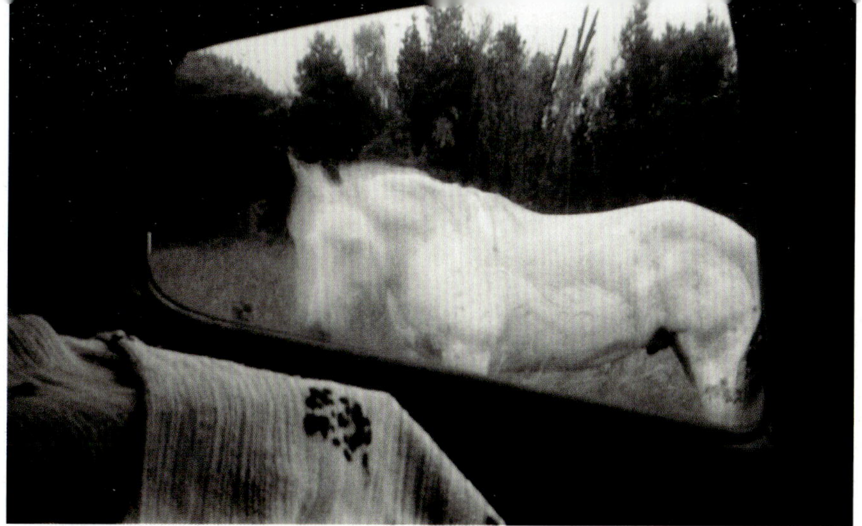

PAULINE ALIOUA, All things pass into the night. PROVENCE, FRANCE

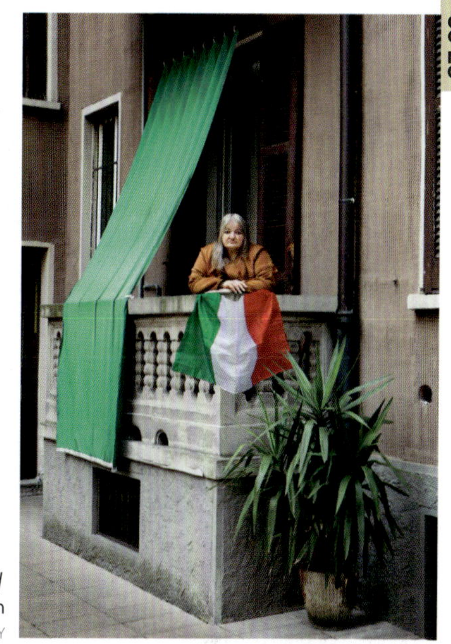

FABRIZIO SPUCCHES, *Comfort Zone |* A photo reportage, about isolation from COVID-19, inside a condo in Milano. ITALY

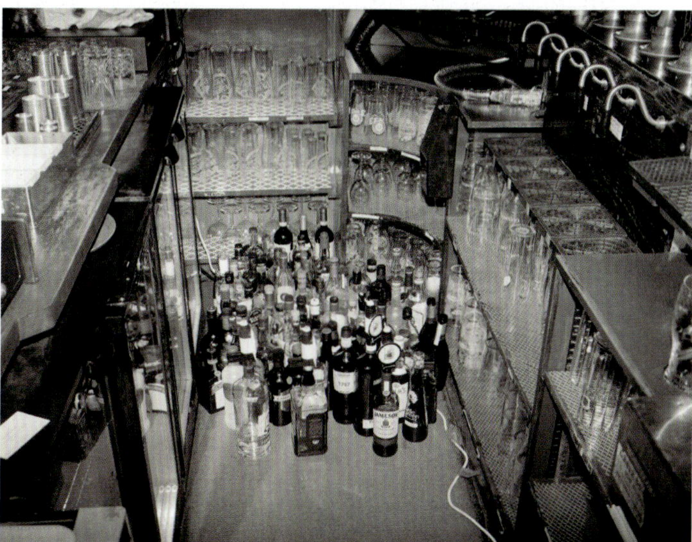

TOMMY SUSSEX, Bottles of alcoholic spirits are removed at the Queens Head Pub in Piccadilly Circus, as the bar is shutdown following government COVID-19 guidelines. LONDON, UNITED KINGDOM

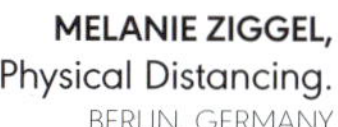

MELANIE ZIGGEL, Physical Distancing. BERLIN, GERMANY

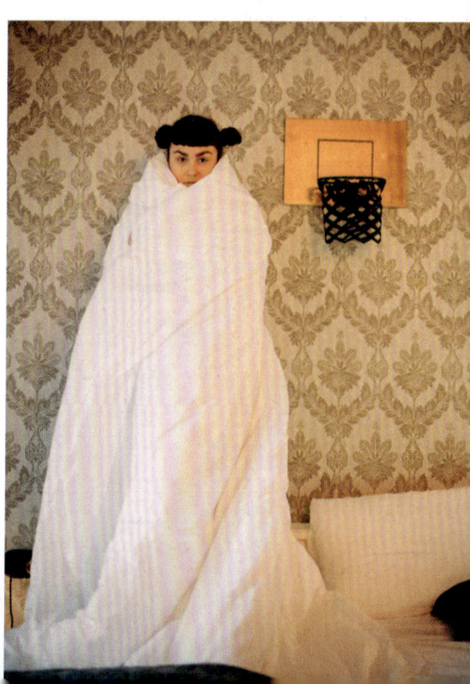

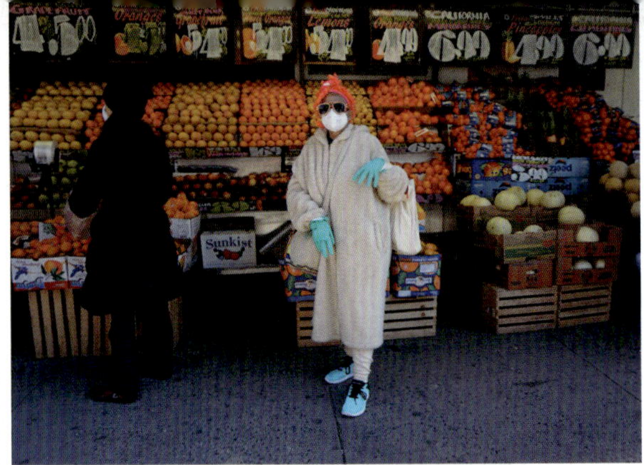

SARAH GELBARD, Sonia Lerebours waits in line for groceries one day before lockdown began in New York City. "You have to keep your sense of humor," she says, pointing to her turquoise shoes that match her turquoise gloves. NY, USA

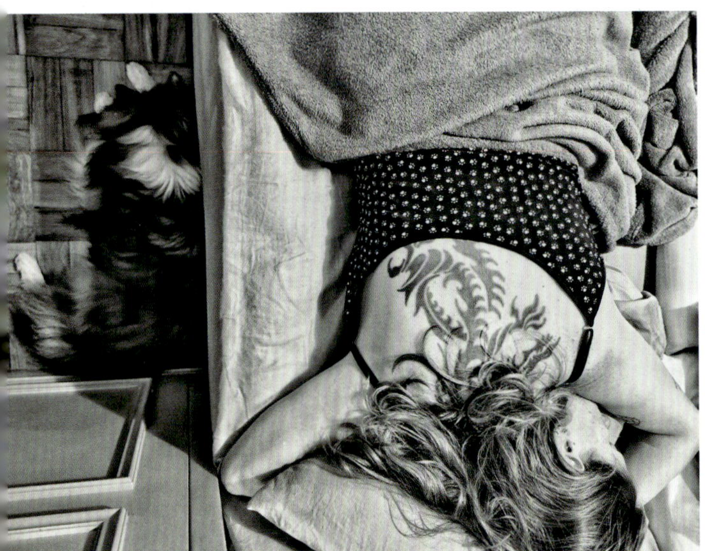

RENAM BRANDÃO, Dia 2 - e o tempo vazio? TIJUCA, RIO DE JANEIRO, BRAZIL

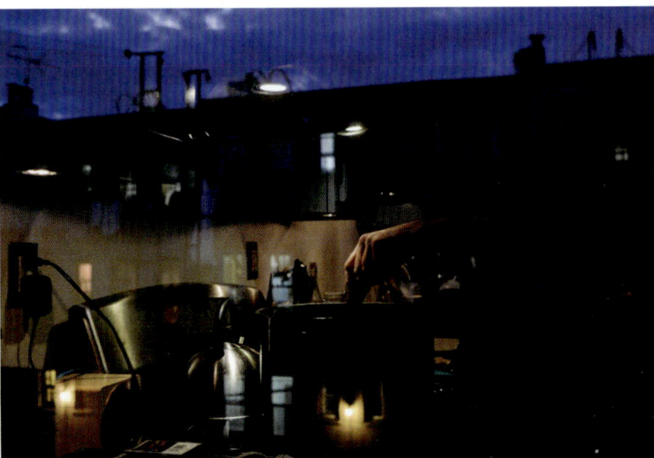

LAUREN CROTHERS, My partner making stock at dusk. He had been collecting vegetable peels and meat bones for weeks, and the end result took several hours of simmering on the stove. QUEENS, NY, USA

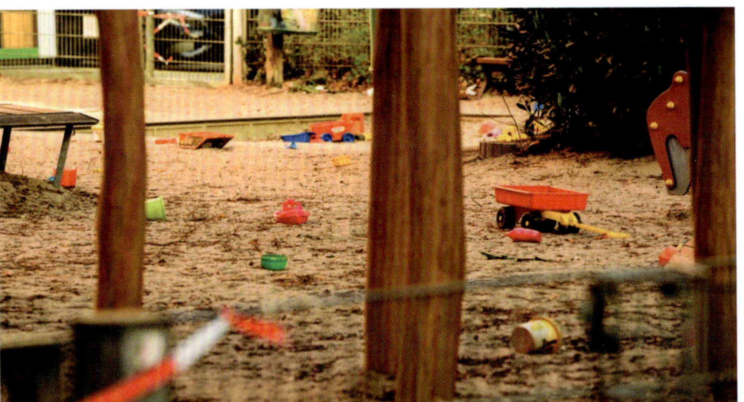

JAN SCHEUNERT, Barrier tape can be seen in front of a closed playground full of toys due to social distancing rules. BERLIN, GERMANY

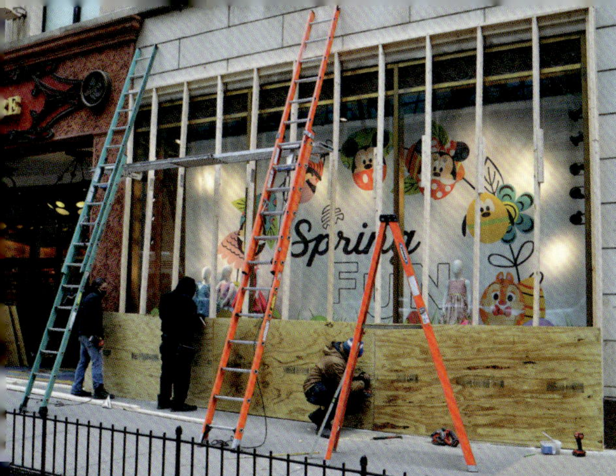

VICTOR HILITSKI, The Disney Store on Michigan Avenue was boarded with plywood to prevent looting during the pandemic, as Gov. J.B. Pritzker has issued a "stay-at-home" order and shut down "non-essential" businesses for the entire state. CHICAGO, IL, USA

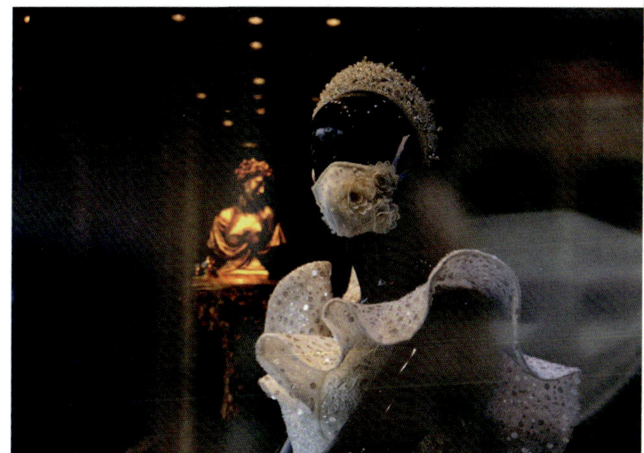

VIDA MOUSAVIAN, In Iran, donning a mask before going outside is now as routine as putting on a pair of shoes, widely considered a civic duty to protect others. A wedding dress store in Tehran designed and produced this luxury mask for ceremonies. IRAN

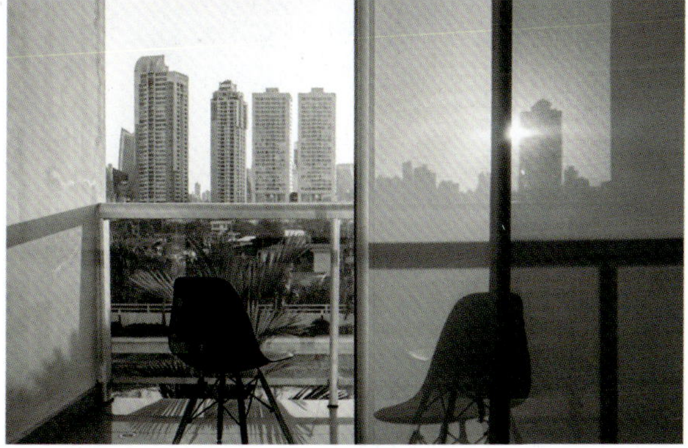

ALFREDO MARTIZ, Obligatory national quarantine. I never dreamed that a total lockdown would come and going outside would be linked to my ID number. PANAMA CITY, PANAMA

GIOVANNI DEL BRENNA, First Saturday night of lockdown, Place du Tertre, Montmartre, Paris, around 20h45. FRANCE

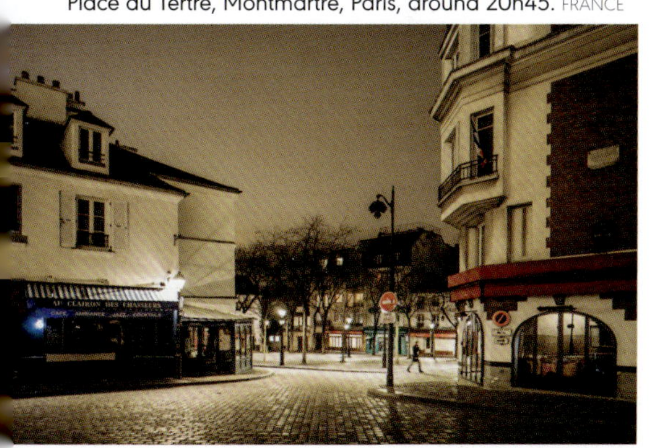

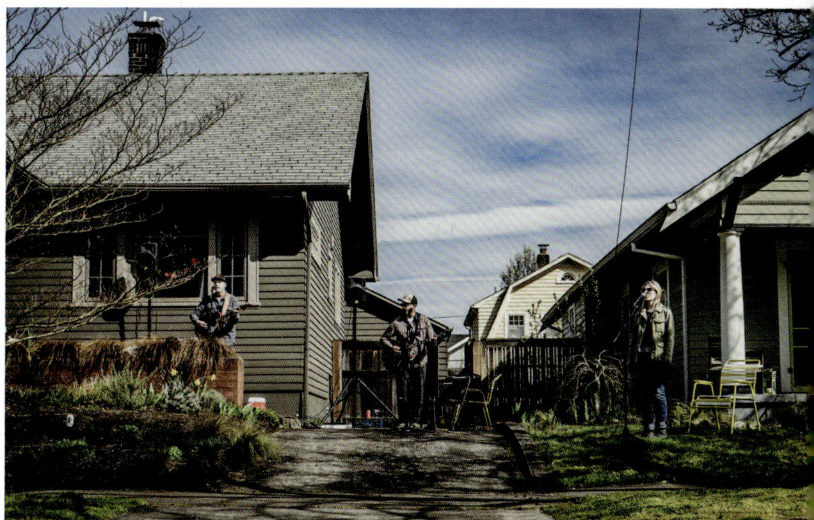

MICHELLE RADFORD, *Street Concert* | Local Musicians share their time and talents during the early stages of Isolation. PORTLAND, OR, USA

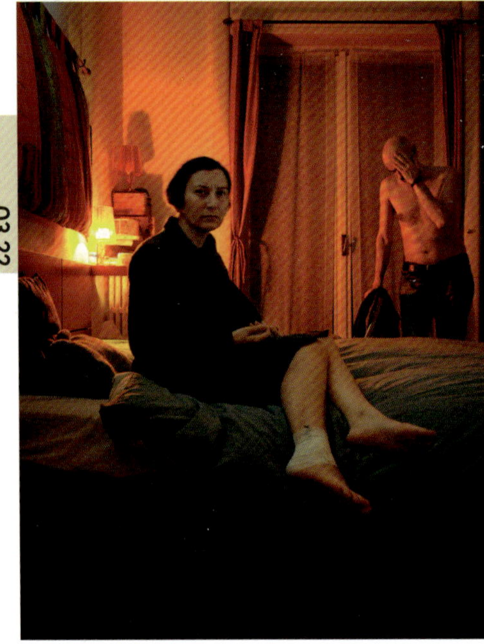

GIULIA BIANCHI, Self-portrait with my boyfriend the night that I sprained my ankle while I was trying to cheer up my dog. MILAN, ITALY

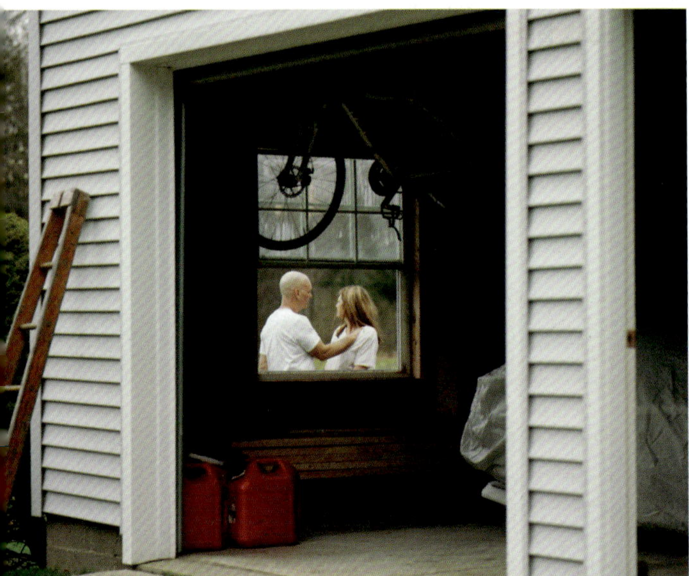

ASHLEY MARKLE, *I caught a glimpse* | My mother's relationships have always fascinated me. Coming home allowed me to view her relationship with my stepfather in its most natural state. STOW, OH, USA

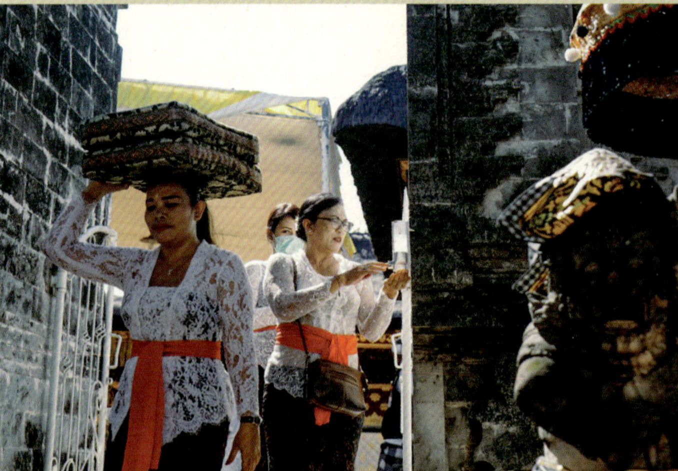

ADE ANGGA BHARGAWA, In this photograph a woman puts hand sanitizer on her hand. At the time we had a ceremony going on in our village temple. COVID-19 had just arrived in Indonesia, and some places had already begun to take precautions. The government already provided warnings, with health standards and instruction to avoid any new cases of COVID-19. Citizens and the government worked together to do their best. We know this is something new for us, but we believe we can pass this situation together. We are in the same storm, and to pass the storm we have to work together. BALI, INDONESIA

TIJANA PAKIĆ, During the pandemic I was confined with my husband and my daughter at our home. Starting on March 17, I began taking photos almost every day inside my home without any preconceived plan, allowing the process to develop over time. When the lockdown started I didn't think that it would influence me artistically in any big way because I usually work within my immediate surroundings. What I noticed instead is that the big change was happening outside of me. The rhythm of the whole country and the whole world synchronized with my own more relaxed artistic tempo. And while the world was quieting down, I, who doesn't usually work under the pressure of schedules, for the first time started creating a timetable for myself in order to gain control. I believe I was trying unconsciously to dissolve the bars of my 54-square meter jail, my apartment that I share with my husband and my daughter. As many others did, we tried to stay sane by exercising. One day, my daughter put on her running pants and took her father's boxing gloves, insisting that she pose for me. I like this image because it shows the contrast between her face, which radiates a childlike candor, and the strength that she will need in order to fight to become a woman in this complex society. PARIS, FRANCE

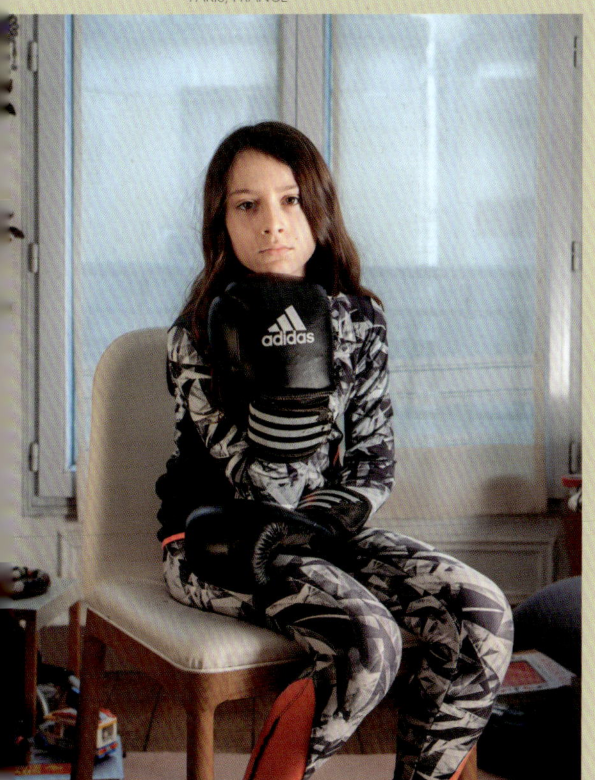

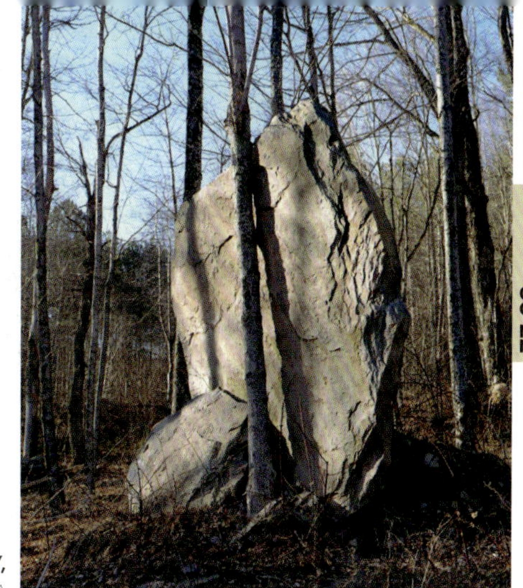

BRYAN WHITNEY, Resilience. USA

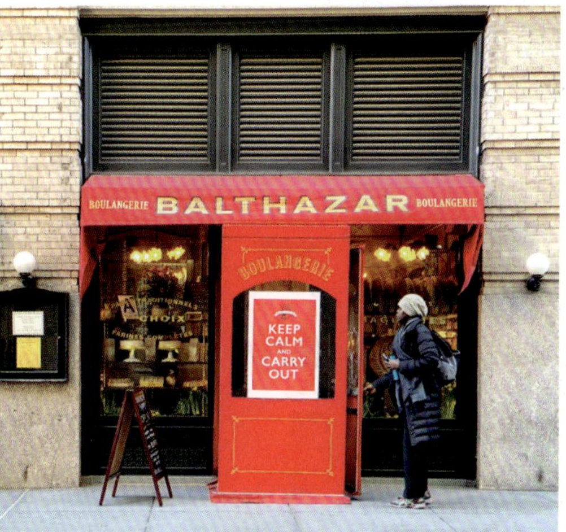

JANET SAMUELS, *What's for dinner?* | Soho, NYC. We had no idea about what was going to unfold... NY, USA

OSMAN SHARIF, *Abandoned Jackson Square* | This Jackson Square corner is an iconic bustling spot in New Orleans. The pandemic lockdown had transformed the French Quarter into an eerie ghost town. LA, USA

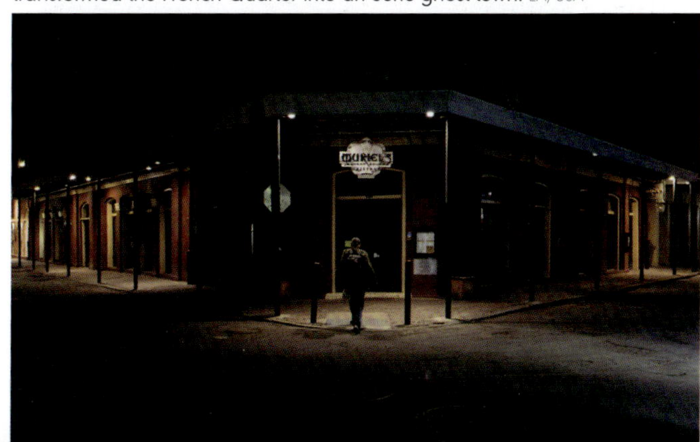

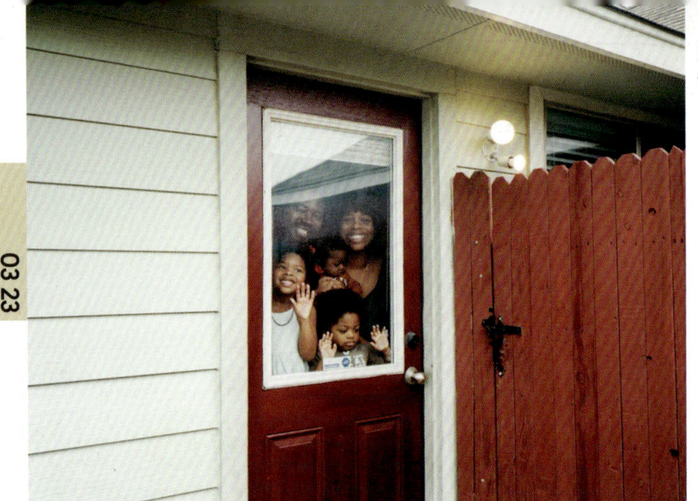

SUZANNE KOETT, Day 11: The Chieza family during the stay-at-home order in Austin. TX, USA

DANIEL ROLIDER, Avili and Ruti Levanon lie in the fields of Kiryat Tivon, during the national lockdown. ISRAEL

מעל נשארה פיסת שמיים
בדיוק לפי מידתנו

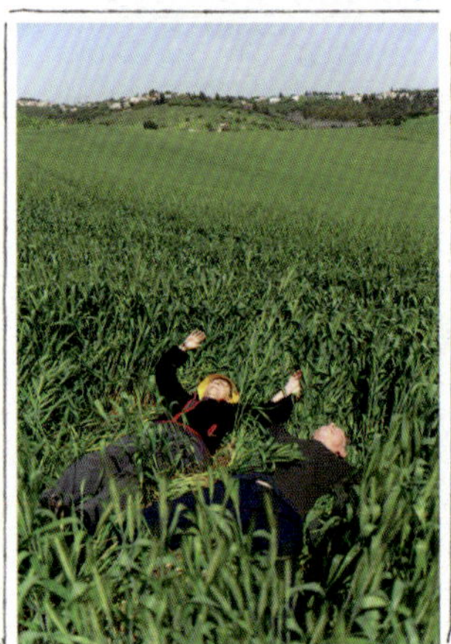

בהירה ומסנוורת והסנוניות
צללו מטה ומעלה ומסביב
רק שיבולים והעולם
שקפא

NIKLAS VIOLA, *Small Habits* | "Don't imitate me; it's as boring as the two halves of a melon" - Matsuo Basho. OKINAWA, JAPAN

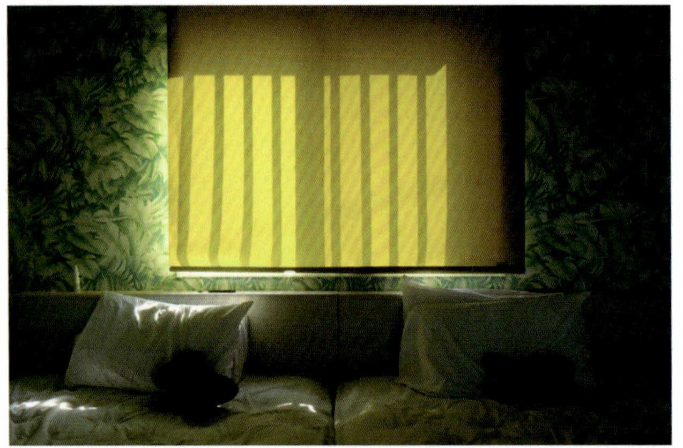

MOHAMMAD MOAZZEN, *Dawn of quarantine* | Zahedan, Sistan and Baluchestan. IRAN

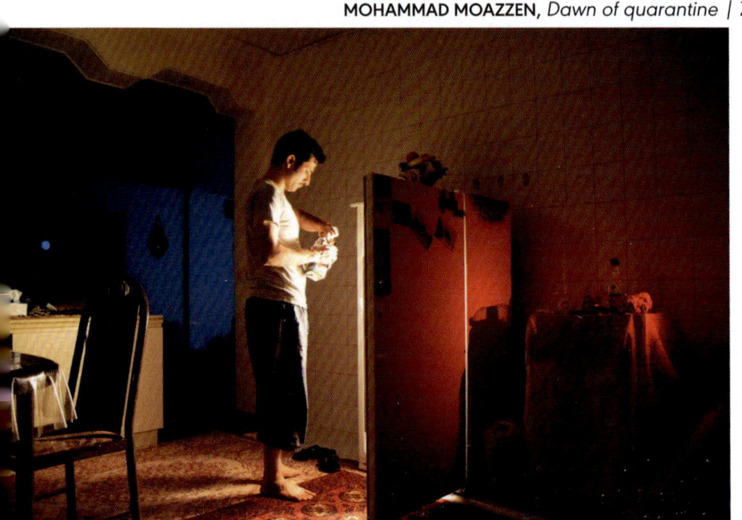

LINETTE KIELINSKI, *Last Banana Standing* | Part of my "Sill Series" of various produce items photographed on my kitchen window sill during the stay-at-home orders. PHILADELPHIA, PA, USA

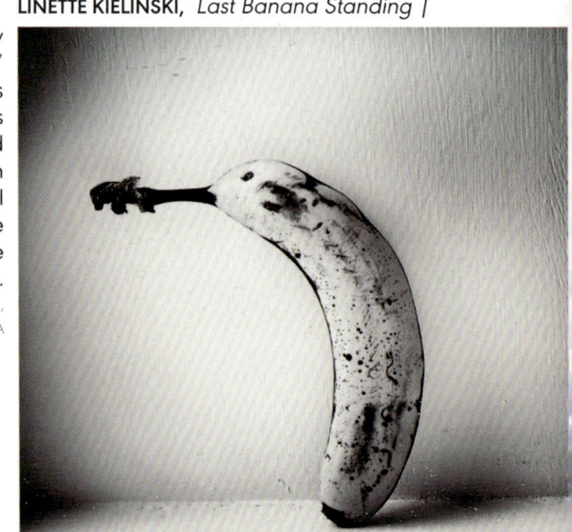

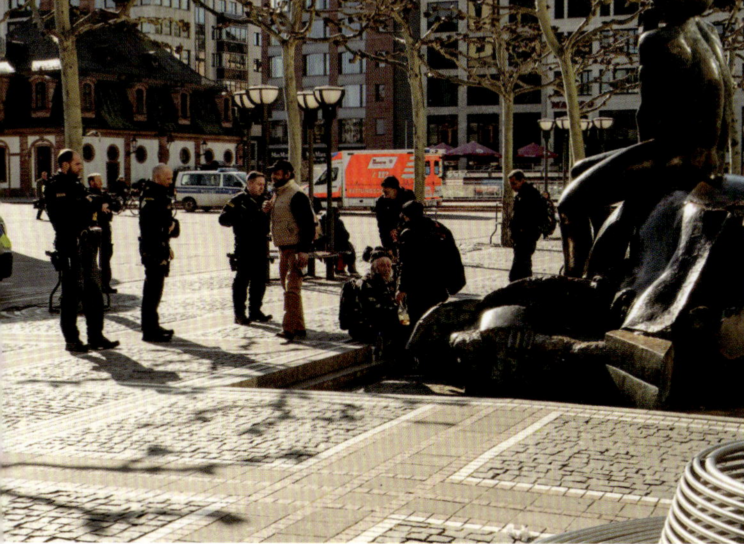

ABAYOMI AKANDE, *Police officers disperse a group of homeless men sitting in a group |* As an early measure, Germany barred groups of more than two people from gathering, except for families. FRANKFURT, GERMANY

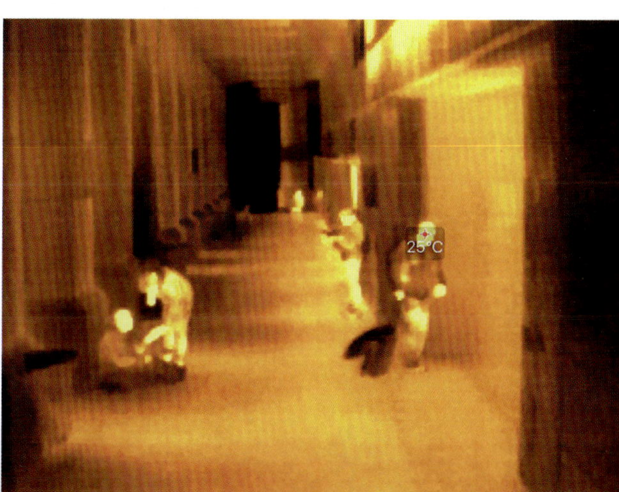

GILES PRICE, *The COVID-19 Dilemma* | What will the long-term civil liberties trade-off be in a world of growing state/corporate bio-surveillance? Westminster Underground Station. LONDON, UNITED KINGDOM

FLYNN LARSEN, *I Don't Know What to Do* |This moment conveys the disorientation and frequent aimlessness we are feeling. He's always saying, "but I don't know what to do!" HUDSON VALLEY, NY, USA

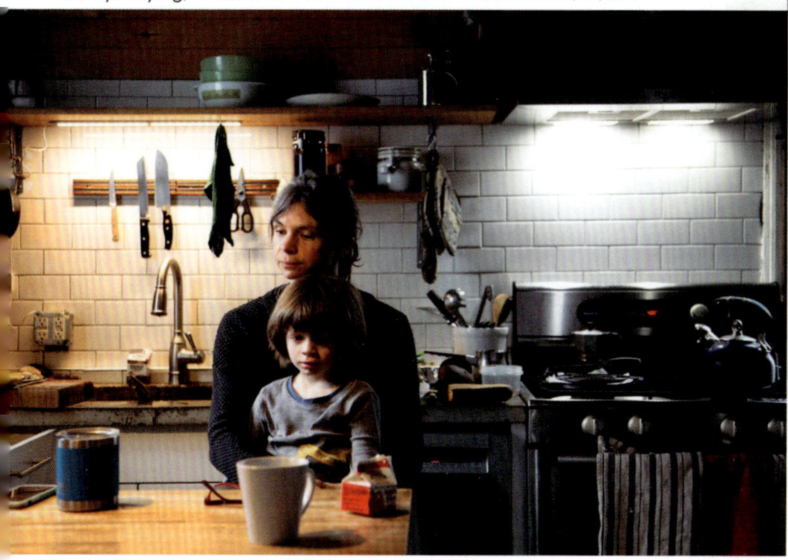

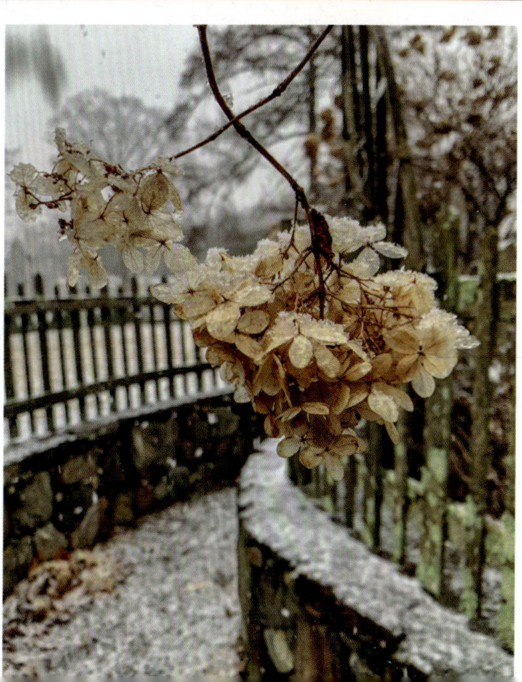

MELINA CRONIN, *Finding Beauty* | Just what I needed during this most crazy time, a reminder to find beauty everywhere. MOHEGAN LAKE, NY, USA

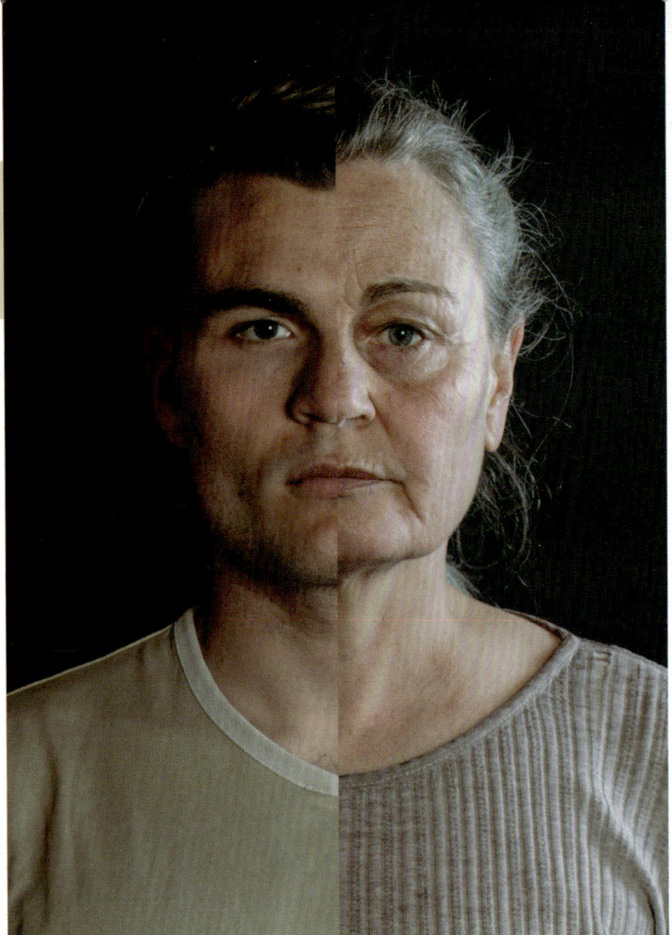

CLÉMENT DOUILLET, This dual being, made of my brother and mother, questions identity, genetic heritage, gender standards. It also reflects the lockdown experience: people reunified by force.
FRANCE

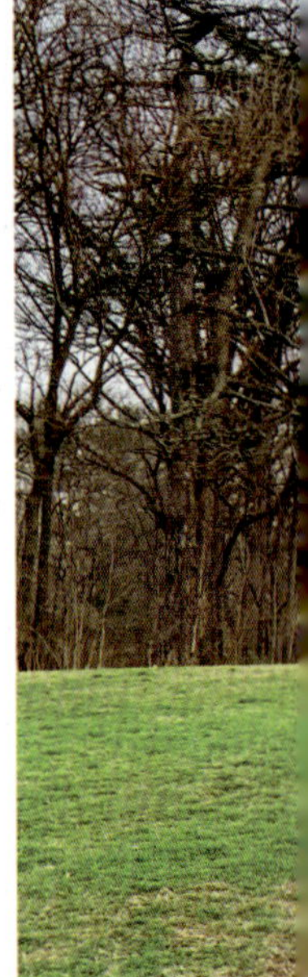

ALEX FONTECHA, *Friendship In the Time of Corona* | Taken at the start of COVID-19 on a daily walk in Prospect Park.
BROOKLYN, NY, USA

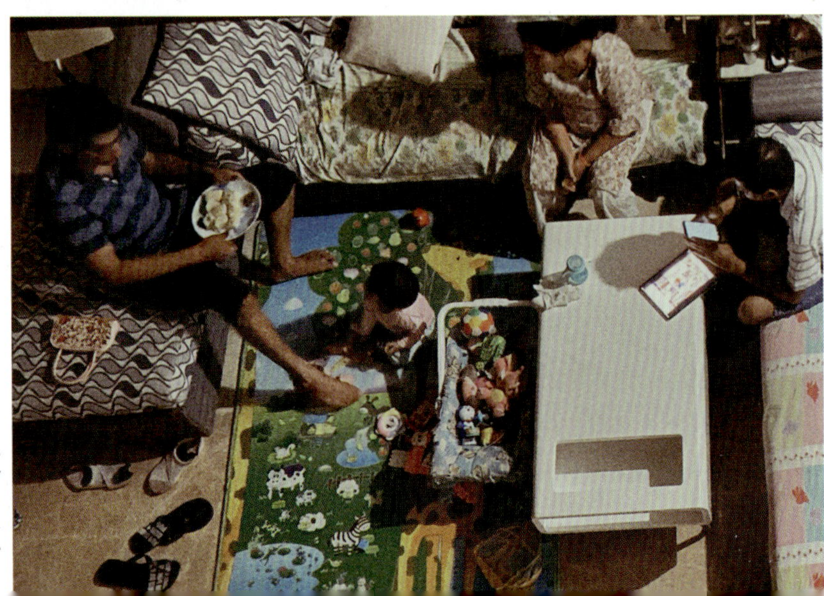

PRACHI SEKSARIA, A family stays indoors on the fifth day of curfew in the textile city of Bhilwara, the first COVID hotspot in India.
RAJASTHAN, INDIA

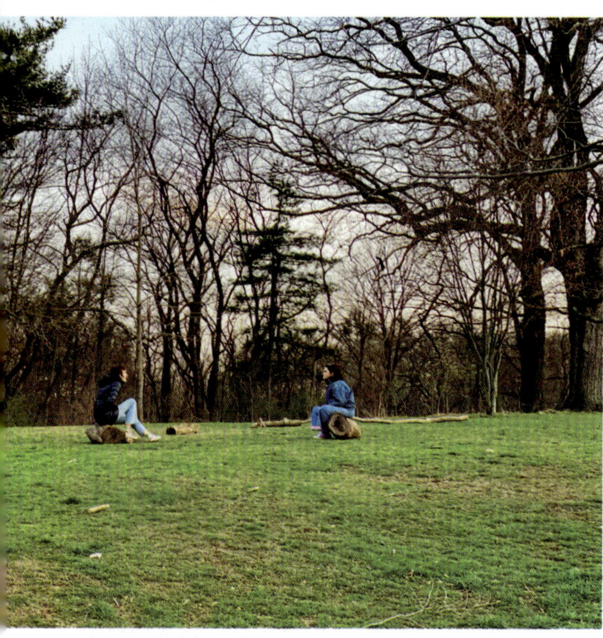

GHADAH ALRAWI, *Untitled* | Our dwindling supply of hand sanitizer on day 2 of self-imposed quarantine after moving back to the United States from Indonesia under Authorized Departure from the State Department. ARLINGTON, VA, USA

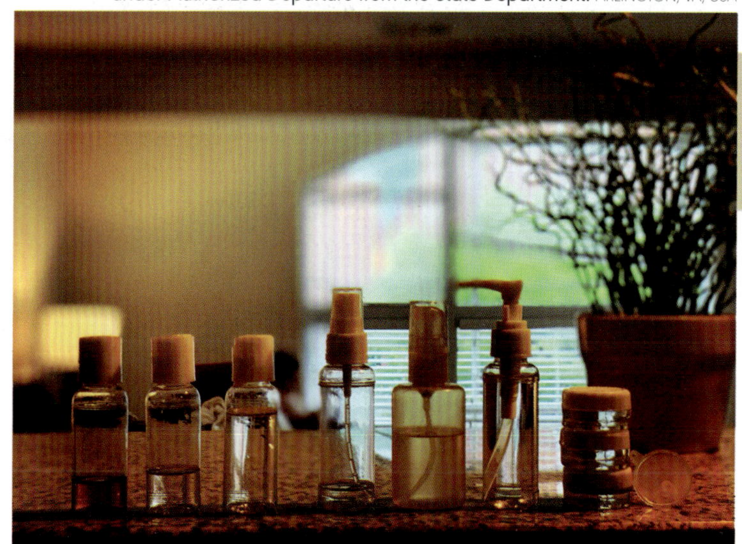

LORI ORDOVER, Decomposed...in quarantine...gracefully.
SANTA MONICA, CA, USA

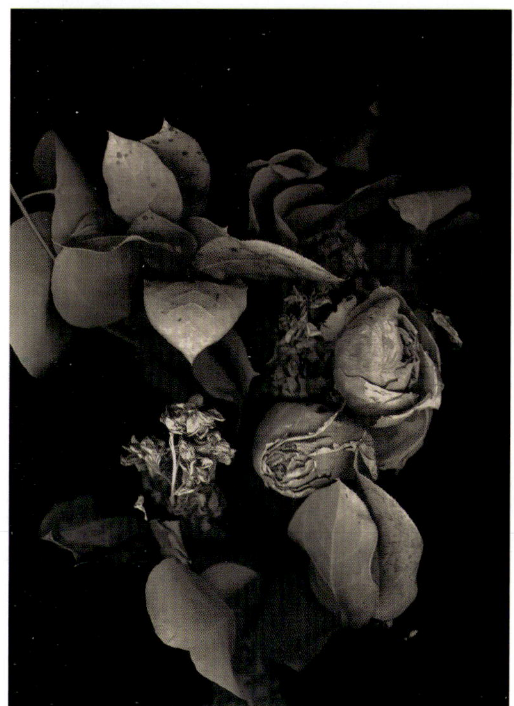

SERENA SALVADORI, *I need to touch this empty moment* | From the series: "You don't need to touch to feel," an autobiographical documentary about COVID-19 in quarantine.
MADRID, SPAIN

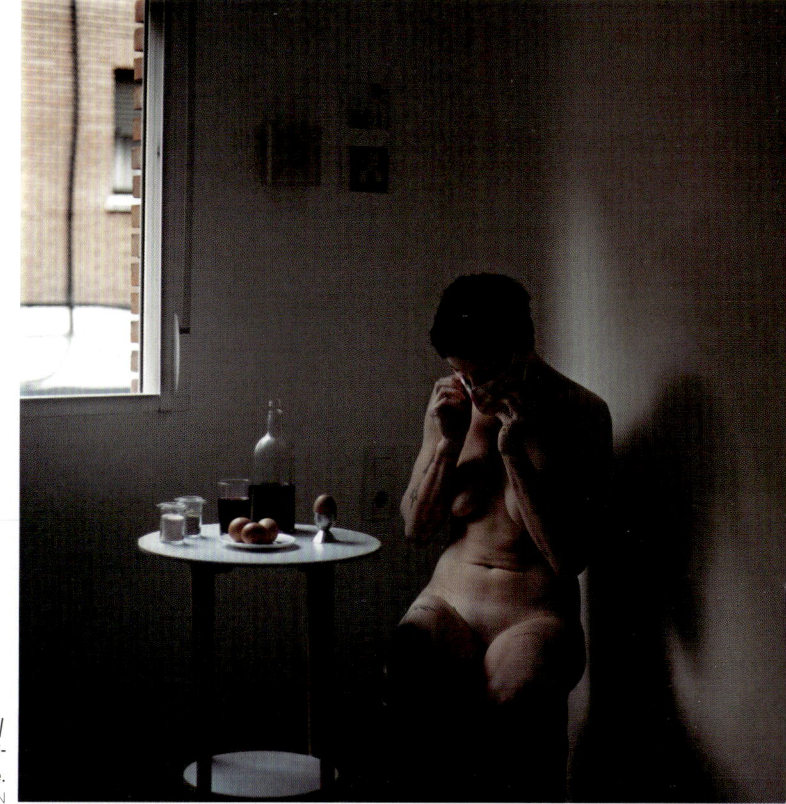

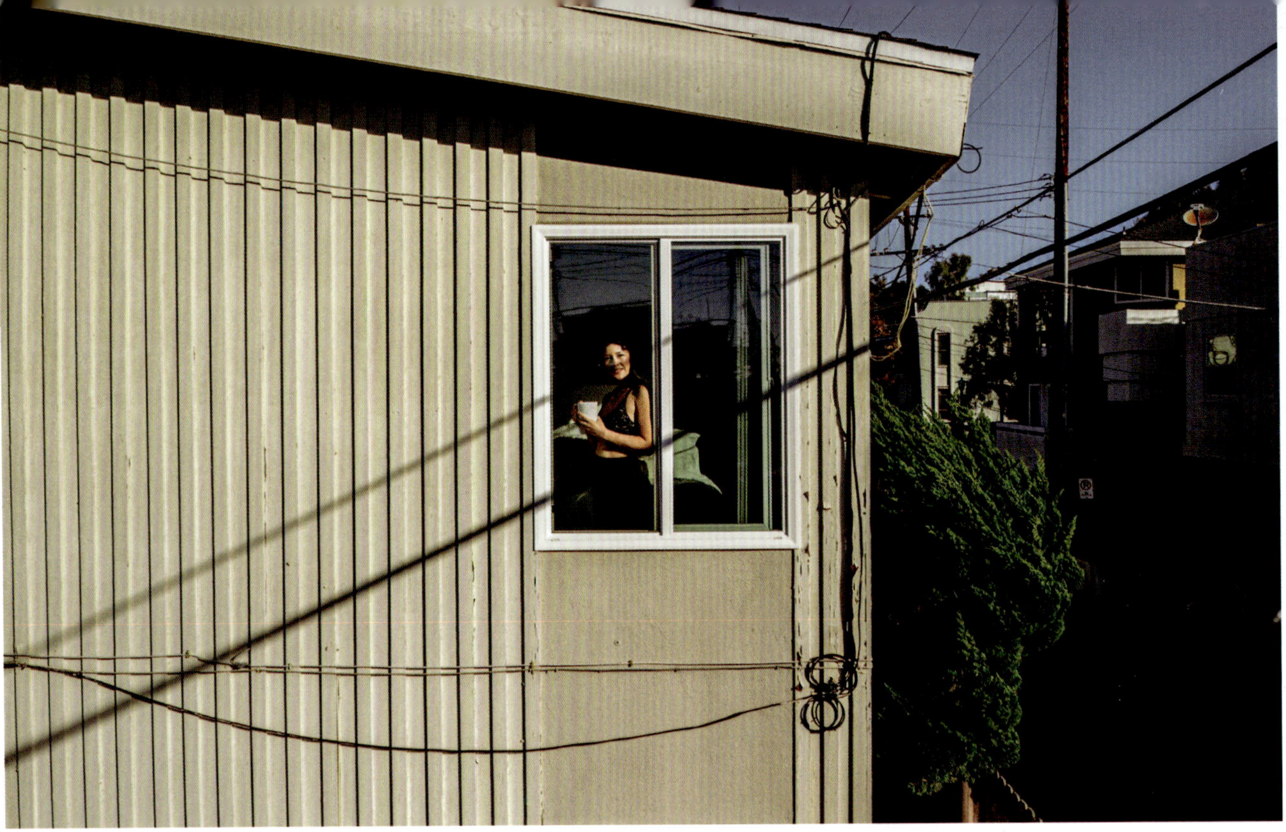

SAAM GABBAY, *8:30AM, Paula* | Canceled my birthday gathering due to quarantine, visited 29 guests at theirs instead, making portraits of them from the outside, looking in. VENICE BEACH, CA, USA

DAVID PEASE, Two days into lockdown and I was missing my three-year-old daughter. It would be another 108 days before we'd be able to see each other again. BILTON, WARSICKSHIRE, UNITED KINGDOM

AARON WESSLING, Legacy Emanuel Medical Center. PORTLAND, OR, USA

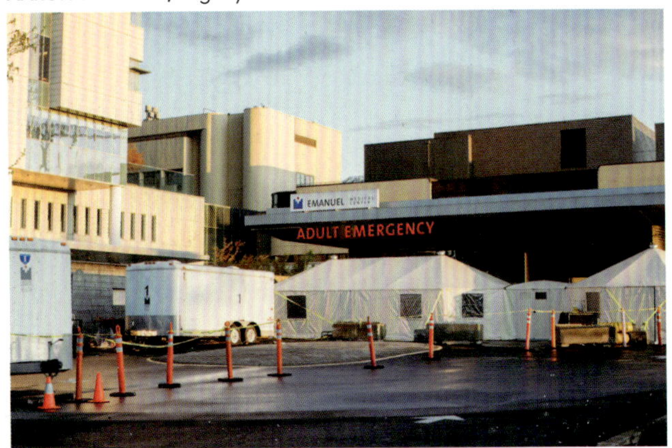

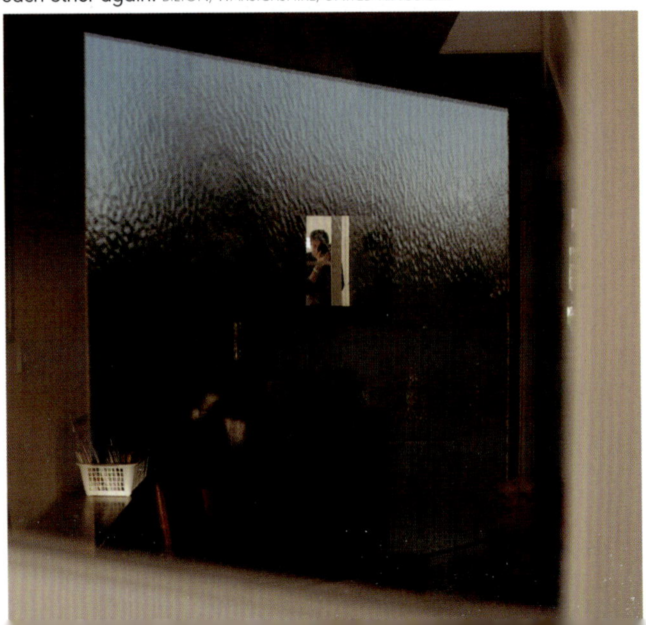

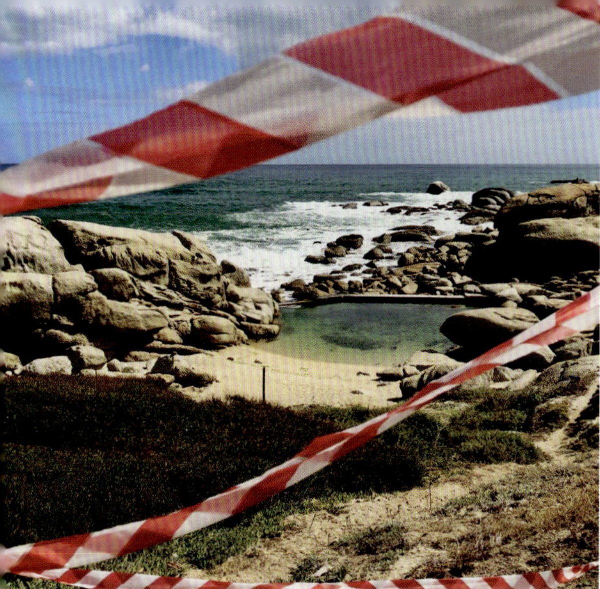

TESSA GORDON, Maiden's Cove Tidal Pool shuttered on the first day of the COVID-19 lockdown. CLIFTON, CAPE TOWN, SOUTH AFRICA

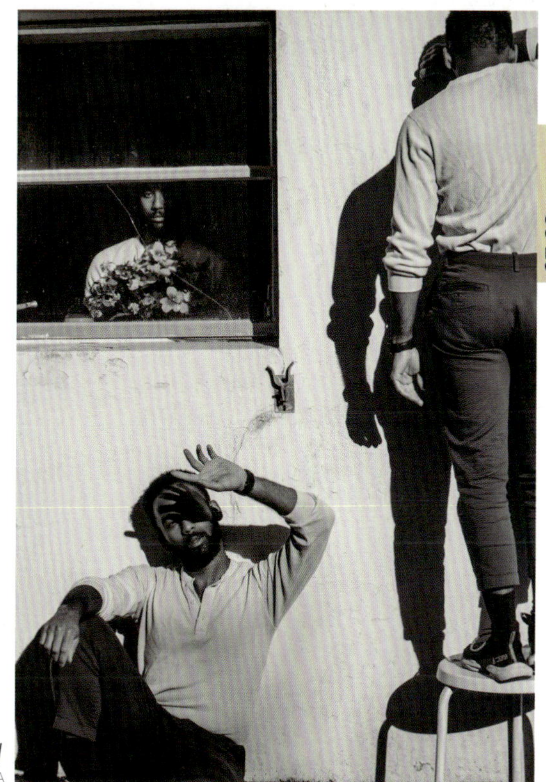

JADE GREENE, *Multiples (Self)* | Taken at my father's house outside of New York City. NY, USA

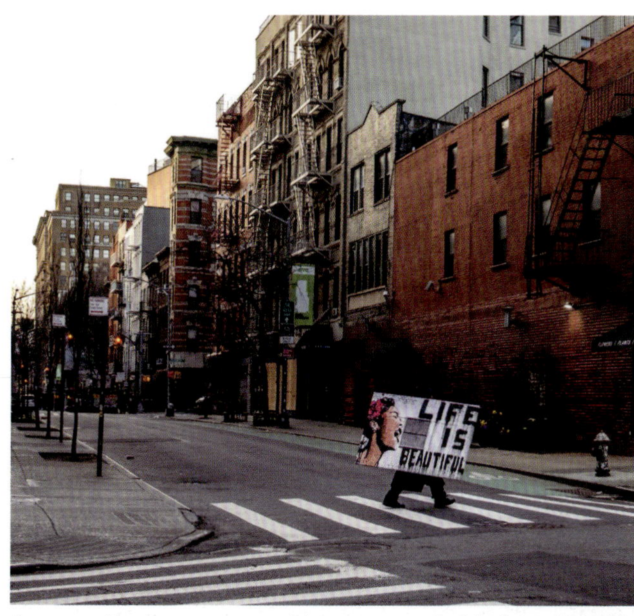

MARCO PETRINI, A man carries a message around the empty streets of the Lower East Side. NEW YORK, NY, USA

JOSHUA VAN PRAAG, Lockdown Kid. OXFORD, UNITED KINGDOM

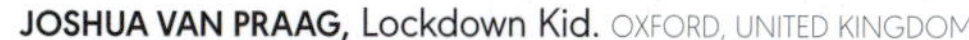

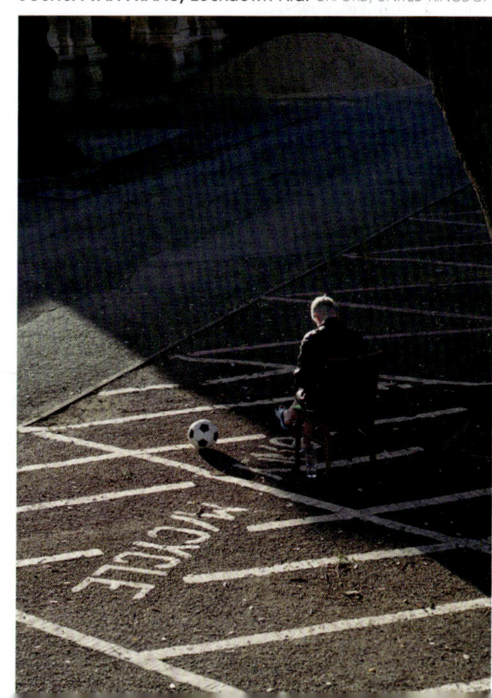

SANCHEZ MURRAY, A Tune of the Storm. PROSPECT PARK, BROOKLYN, NY, USA

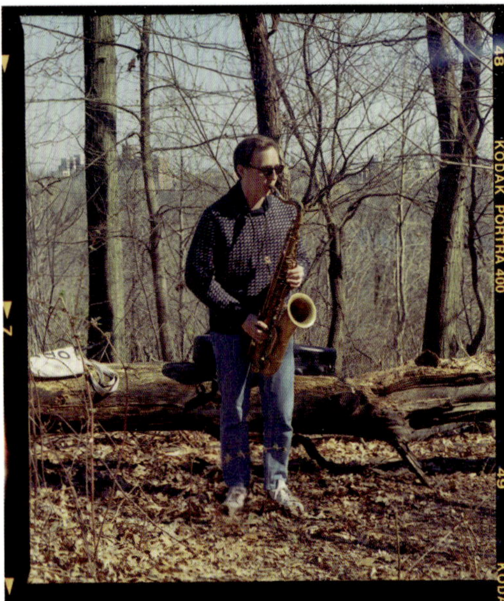

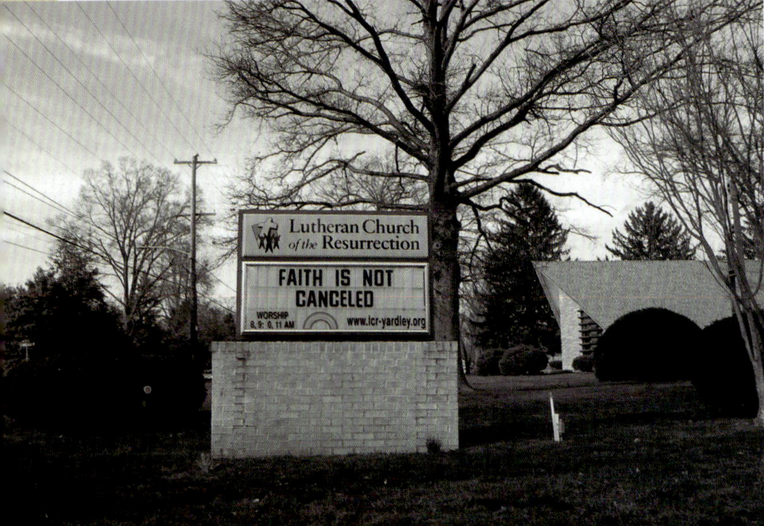

MADISON MCSHERRY, In a world filled with chaos,confusion and no sense of normality to be found, a local church offers some light in times that seem so dark. YARDLEY, PA, USA

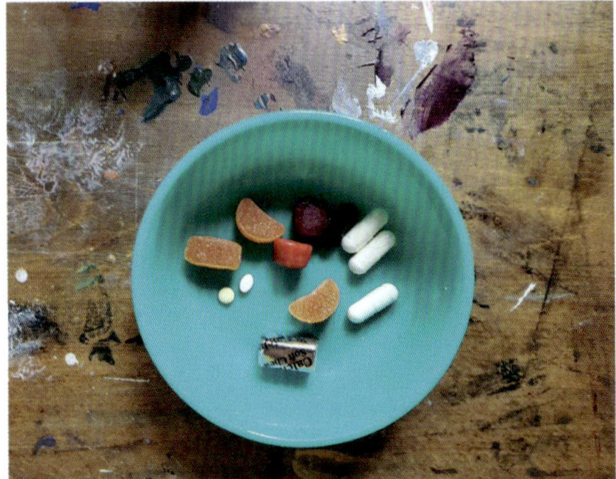

JENNY DITONA, *Fear* | I don't know if I'm becoming my dad or if I'm fearful that my compromised immune system wouldn't be able to handle this virus. VIRGINIA BEACH, VA, USA

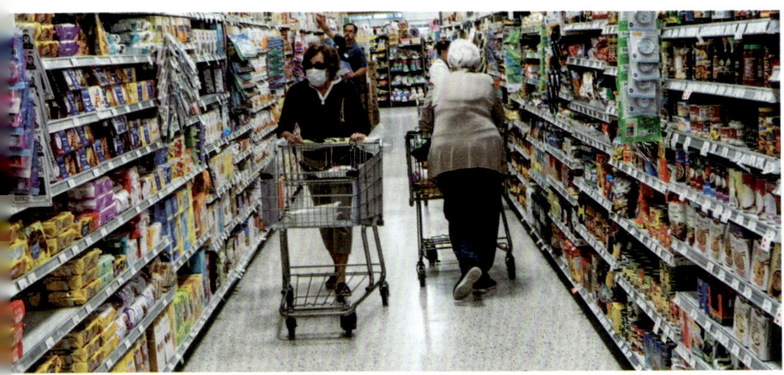

JOE GATO, At the local supermarket the elderly residents quickly adjusted to the new norms as items began to return to the shelves after an initial run. SOUTH BEACH, MIAMI, FL, USA

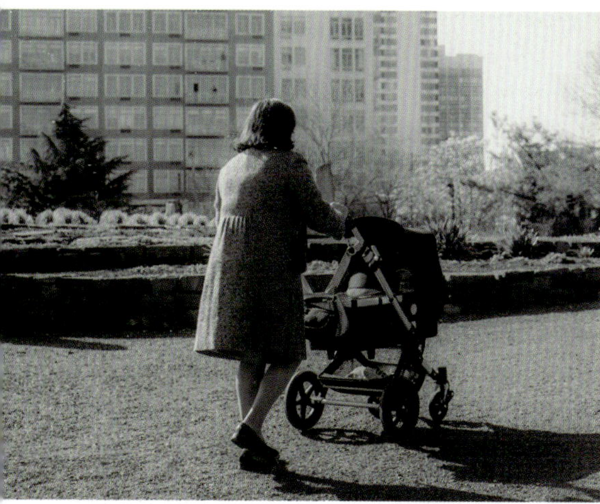

MARCUS MADDOX, Mother walking her child during the pandemic. PHILADELPHIA, PA, USA

MELISSA ANN PINNEY, *Threads That Bind* | These spools of silk thread came to me through my grandmother and mother, mementos signifying generations of women's work, character, and beauty. EVANSTON, IL, USA

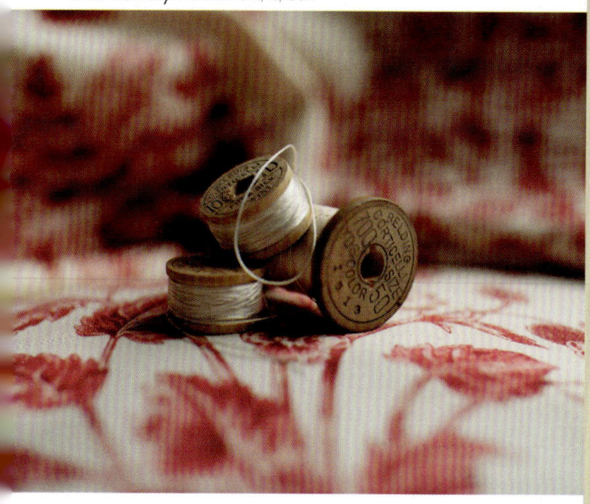

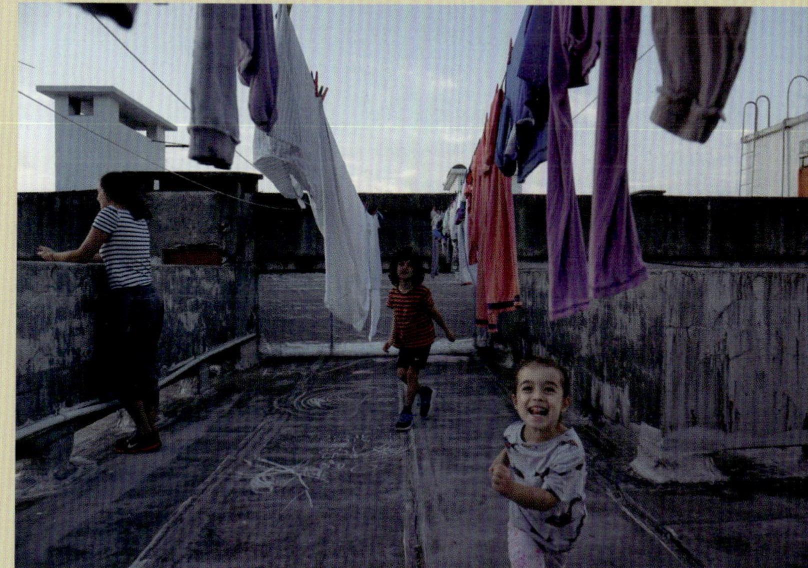

EITAN ABRAMOVICH,

I took this photo of my children and my wife on the rooftop of our apartment building, when we were following the government request to stay at home after the first cases of COVID-19 were reported in the country. The weather was still warm, and as the sun was setting my wife and I decided to get our children to the rooftop to get some daylight.

I posted this photo because I wanted to share the joy children can find at an unusual place to play, despite the uncertainty our society was living in at that stage of the pandemic. We passed through a lot of upset feelings during our quarantine. But to capture this cheer-up moment and make it last through photography is very comforting.

MONTEVIDEO, URUGUAY

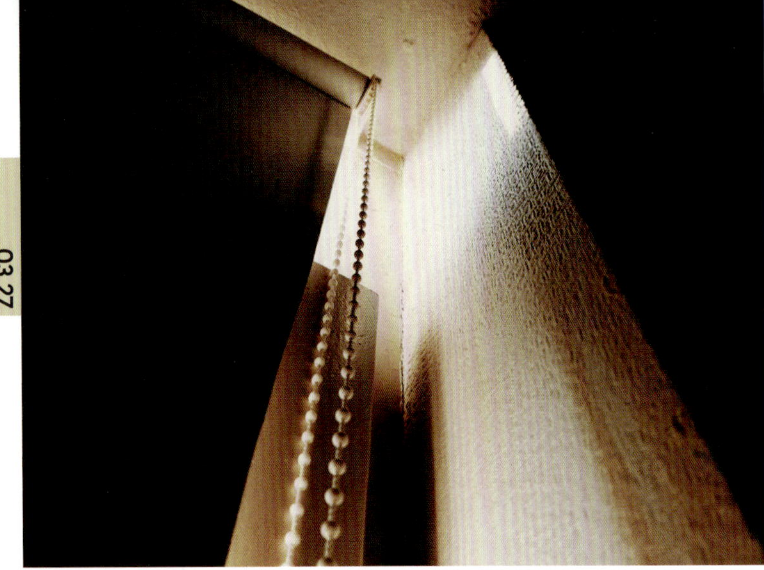

ROBERT KRUYSKAMP,
Corona Diaries—Waking up in the bedroom during the "intelligent" lockdown.
THE HAGUE, NETHERLANDS

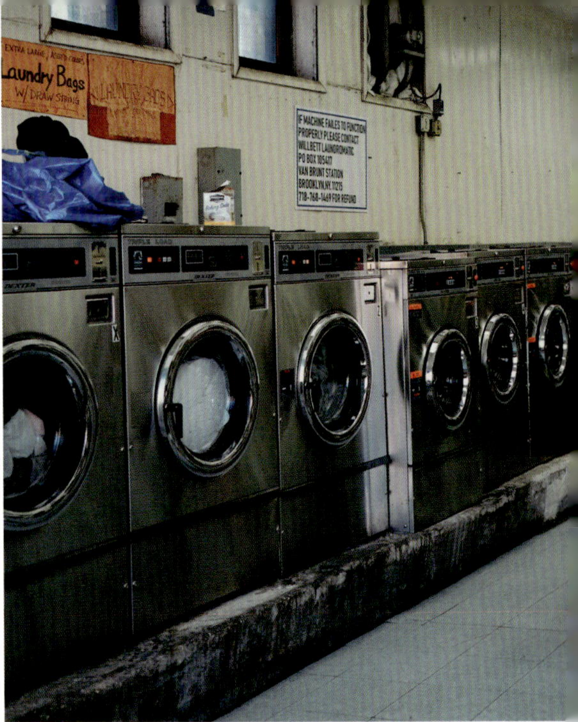

NAOMI HELLMANN, *Social distancing* | PIER 34, HUDSON RIVER PARK, NEW YORK, NY, USA

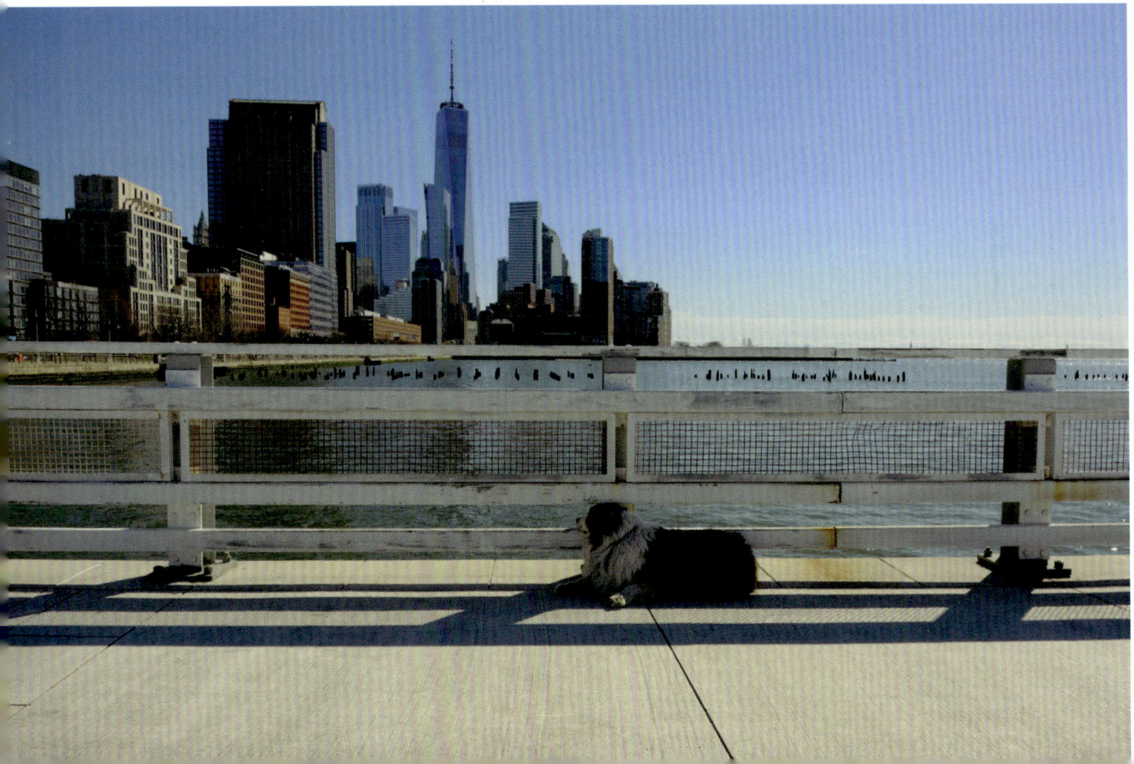

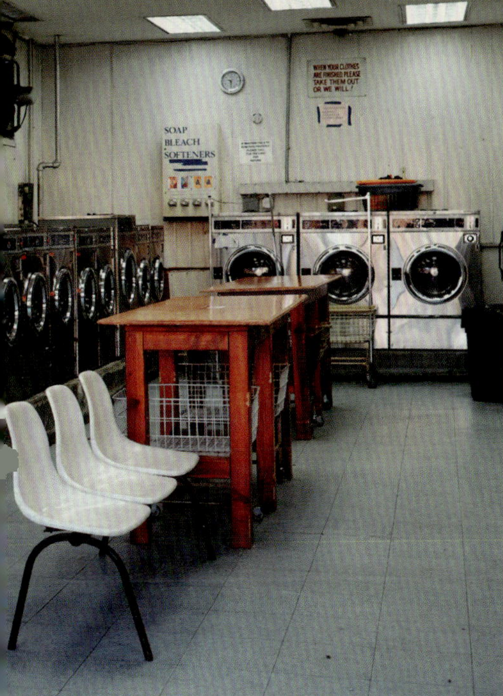

MARK SHERRY, Who will wash, dry, and fold now?
WINDSOR TERRACE, BROOKLYN, NY, USA

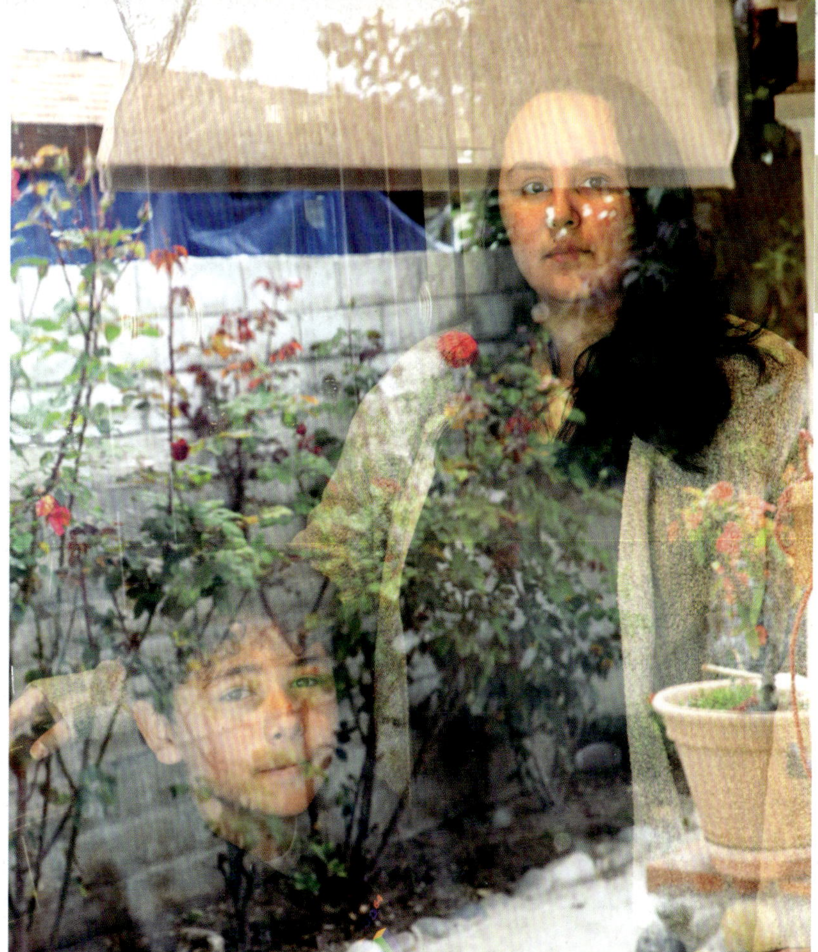

ARLENE MEJORADO, This image is part of a window into my familia during the "shelter in place" order for Los Angeles. Valerie is a pediatric nurse. Nicolas, her brother, is twelve years old. CA, USA

JUAN DIEGO REYES, *Self-portrait with Abby* | Day 13 of self-quarantine. MACON COUNTY, NC, USA

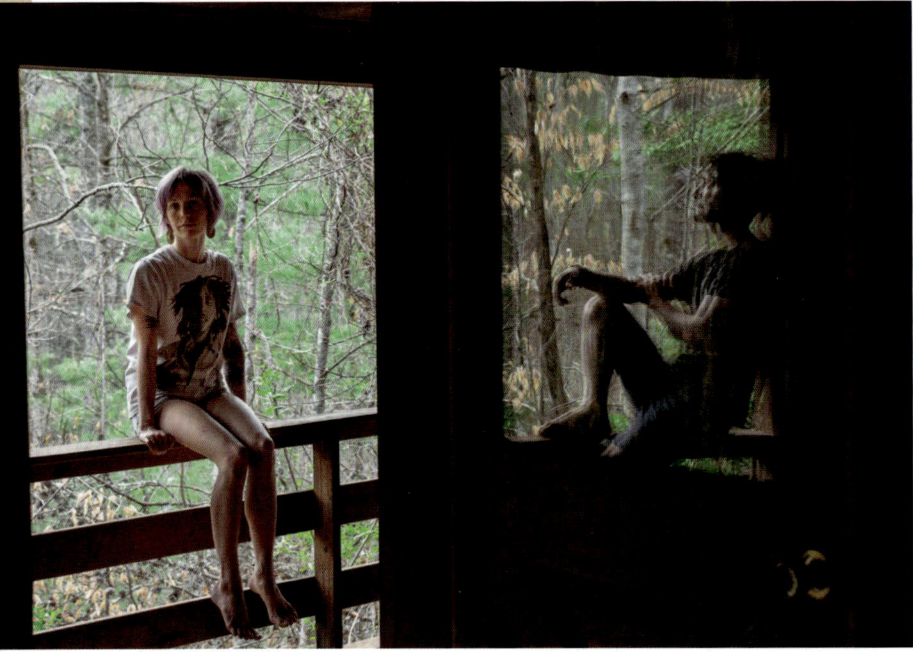

CÉLINE PANNETIER,

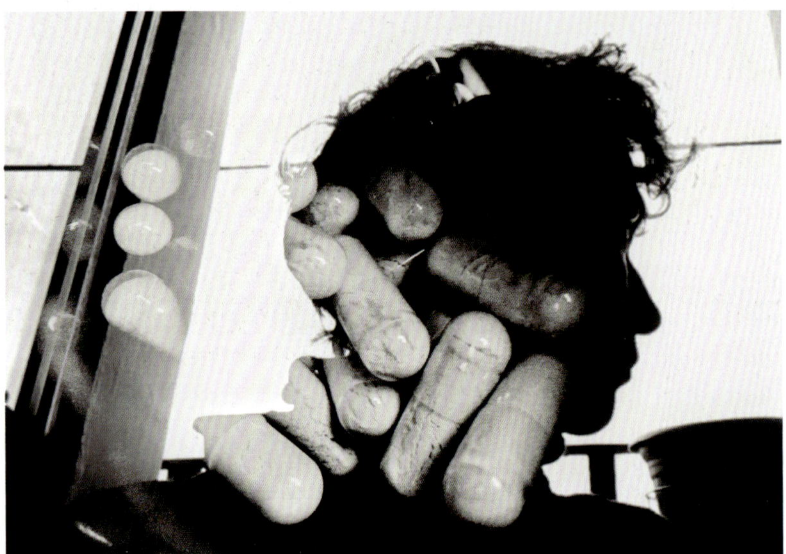

Day 26 of lockdown. From "Diary Of Boredom," a project realized exclusively with a mobile phone by a confined street photographer.
BARCELONA, SPAIN

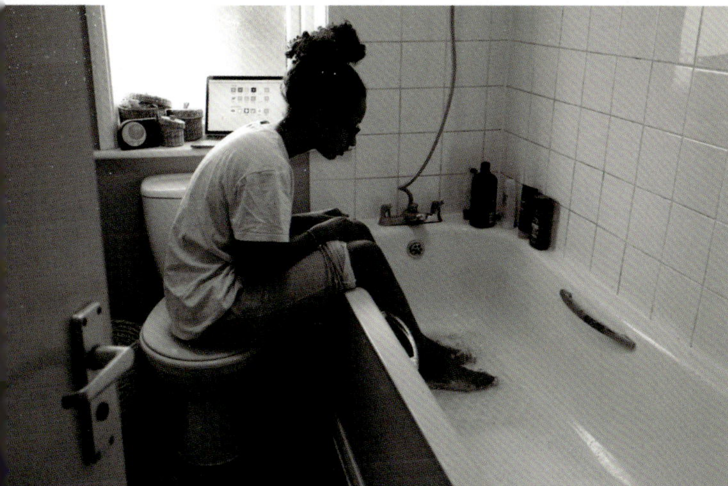

LYNNE PINNOCK, When You Can't Get to the Nail Salon.
LONDON, UNITED KINGDOM

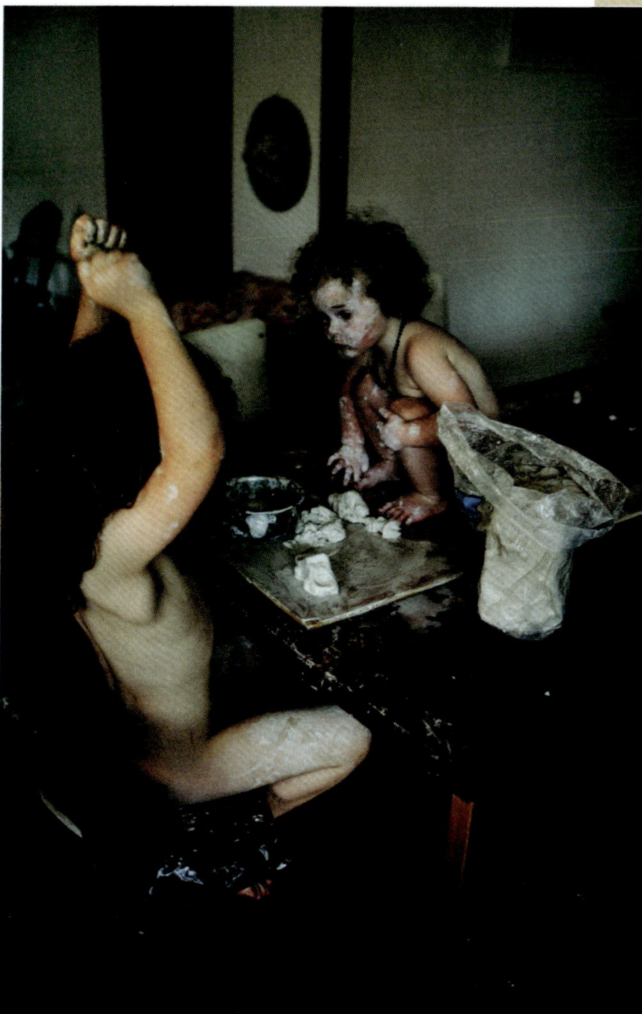

TAJETTE O'HALLORAN, Portrait of Isolation. MELBOURNE, AUSTRALIA

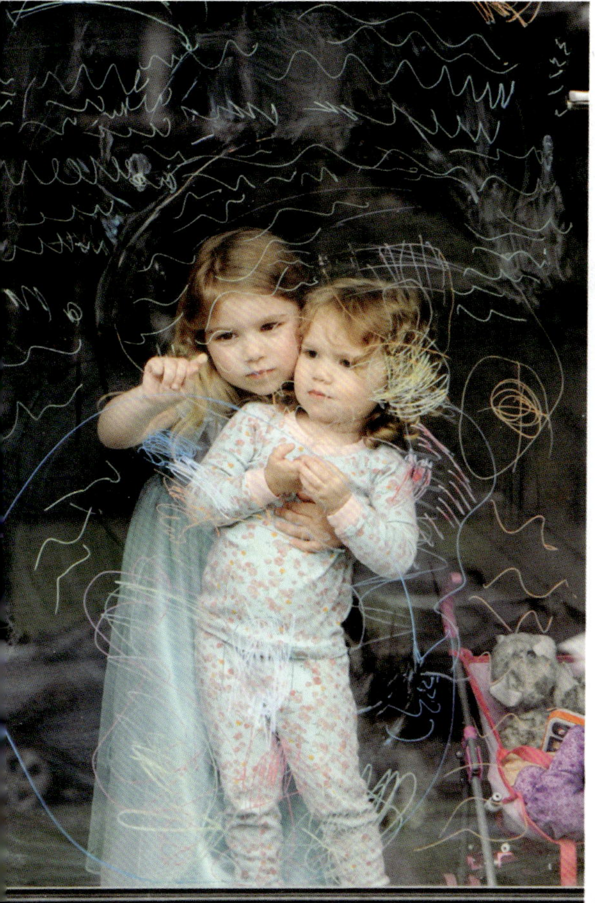

KATE ALBRIGHT, *Sisters* | Two weeks into lockdown and remote learning, sisters stand at their front door, scrawled with the drawings of the younger sister.
MONTCLAIR, NJ, USA

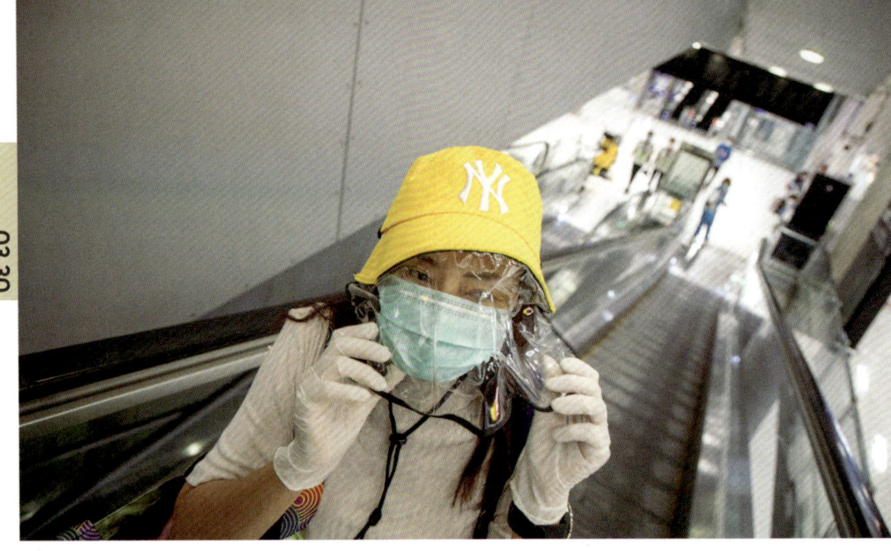

NAPAT WESSHASARTAR, My mom puts on her protective hat while picking me up at the Suvarnabhumi International Airport, Bangkok. THAILAND

WOONG-JAE SHIN,

The US Naval Hospital Ship Comfort arrived at Pier 90 in New York City with high expectations to help city hospitals. NEW YORK, NY, USA

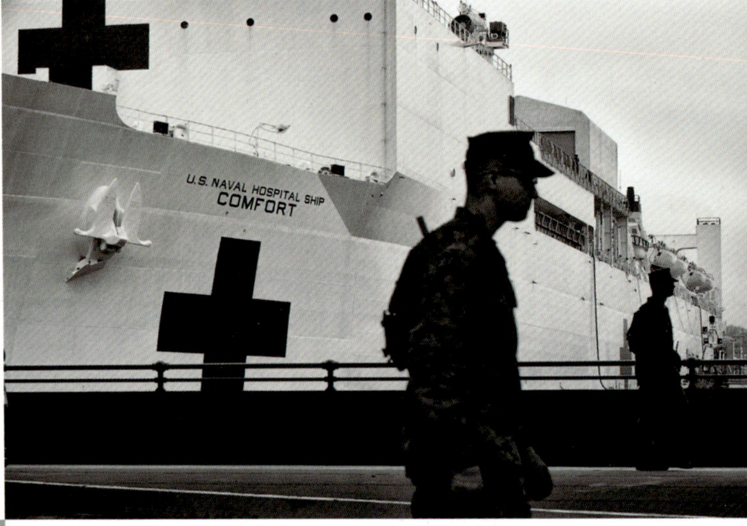

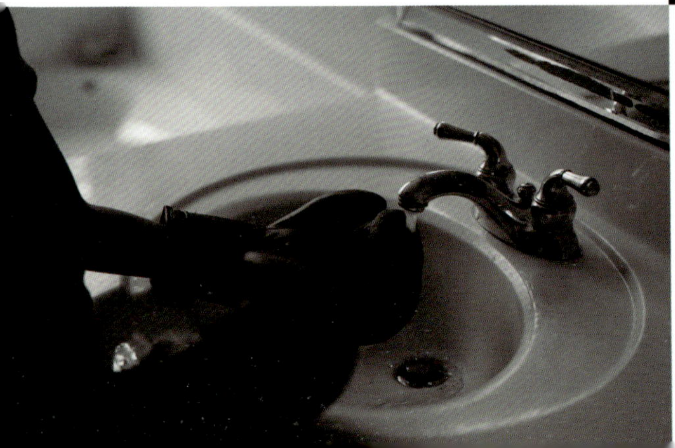

CATARINA LAY, WASH YOUR HANDS was the most popular phrase after the World Health Organization officially declared the outbreak of COVID-19 a pandemic on March 11. HOUSTON, TX

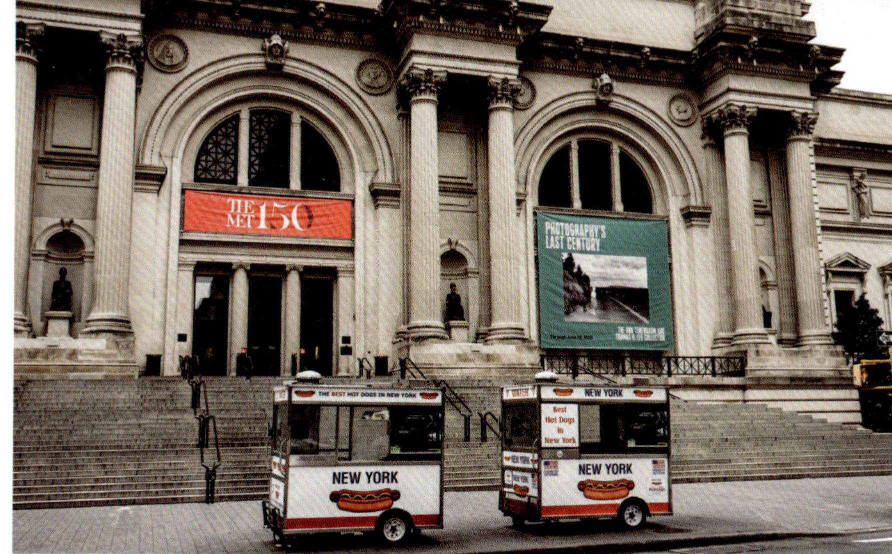

PATRICK STRAUB, Along a barren museum mile in Manhattan, two empty hot dog stands in front of an empty Metropolitan Museum stood out. NEW YORK, NY, USA

MIROSLAV MATEJČIĆ, Lonely Flowers. CRIKVENICA, CROATIA

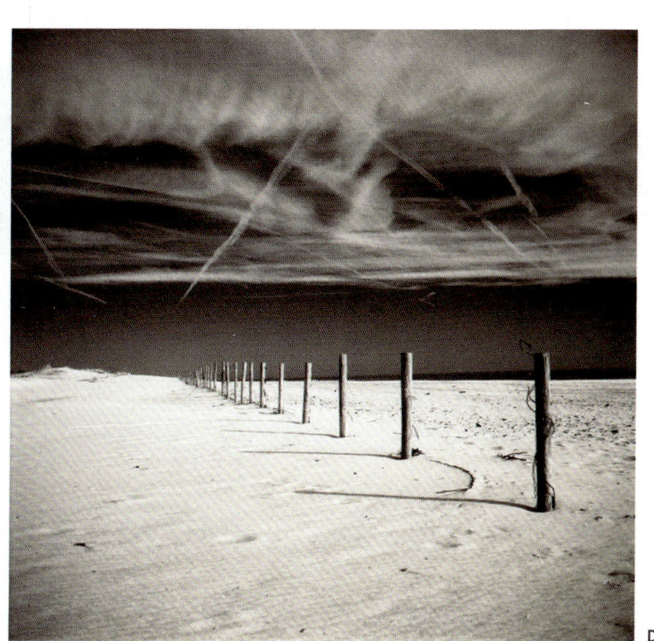

DALE RIO, Assateague Island. MD, USA

03 30

PARISA AMINOLAHI, *Our Quarantine* | At my studio, my daughter's happiness after finishing her schoolwork. NETHERLANDS

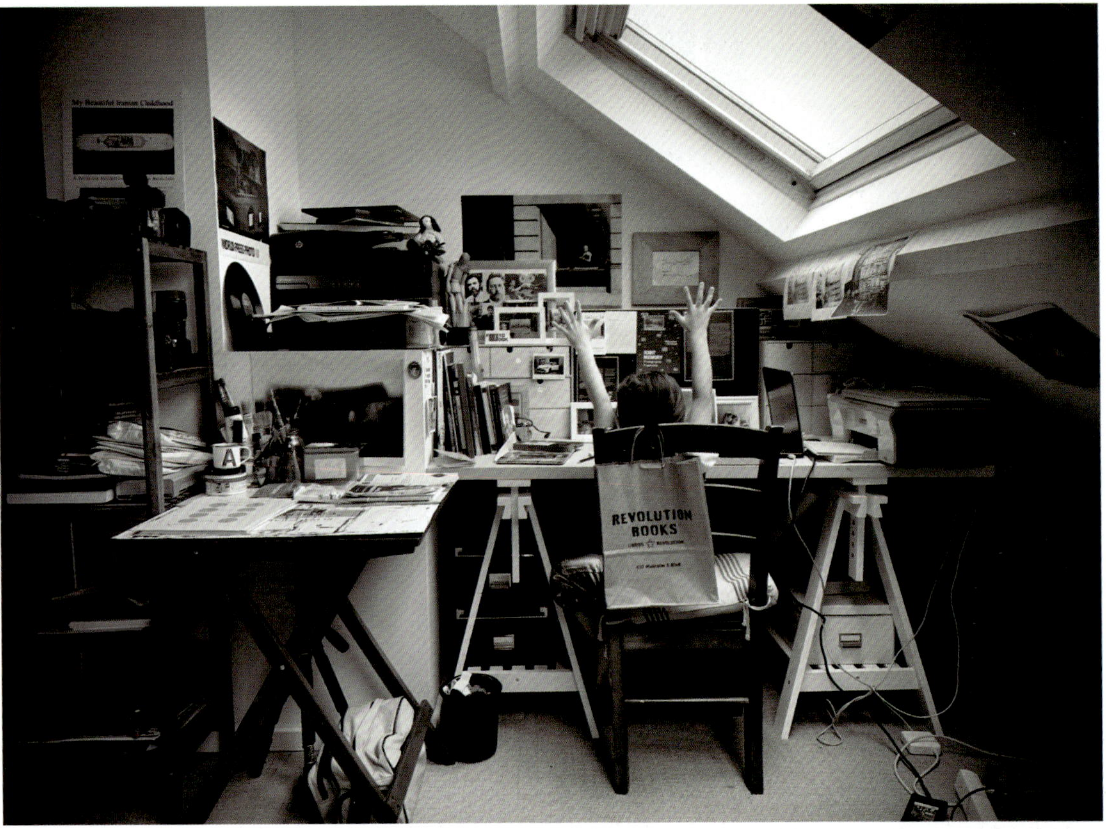

GIOVANNA MARIA DELL'ACQUA, *The price of value, Bologna* | A lady prepares "tortellini" during the lockdown. ITALY

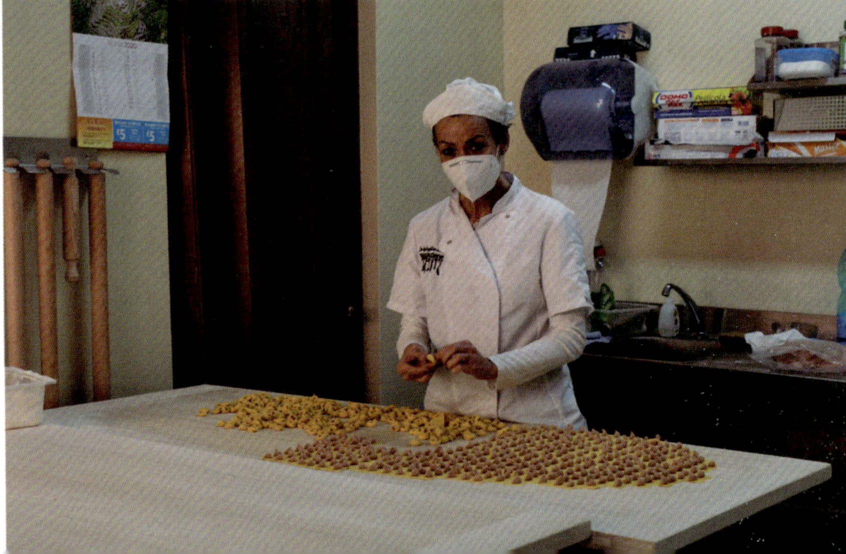

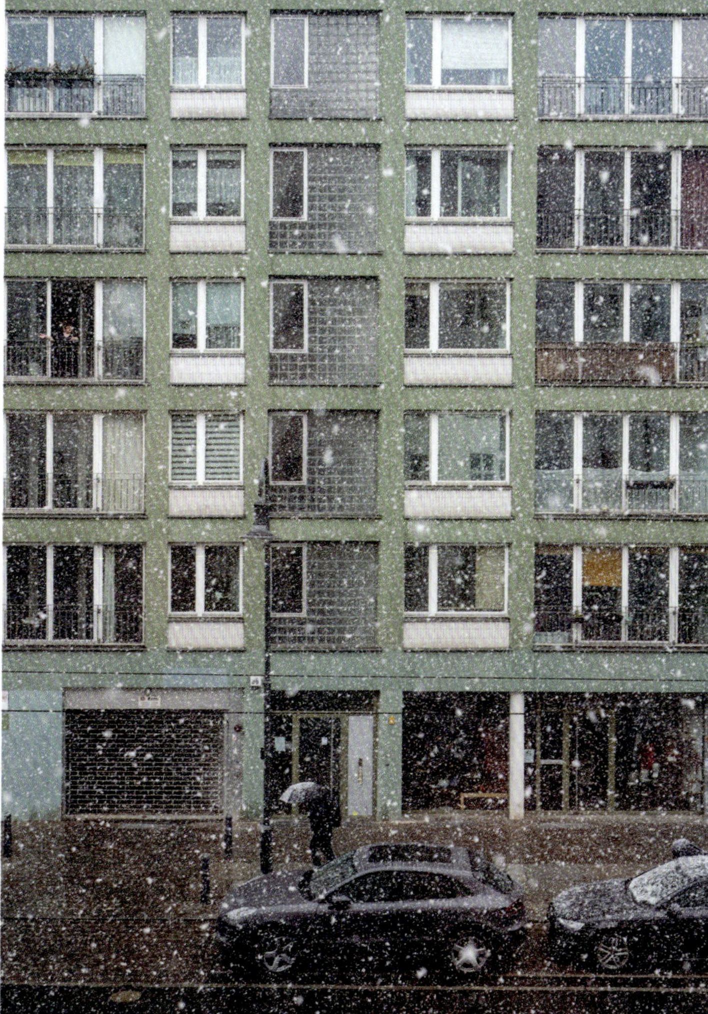

PEER KUGLER, A man walking through a street during the coronavirus lockdown in Berlin, while a woman in a window watches the snow. GERMANY

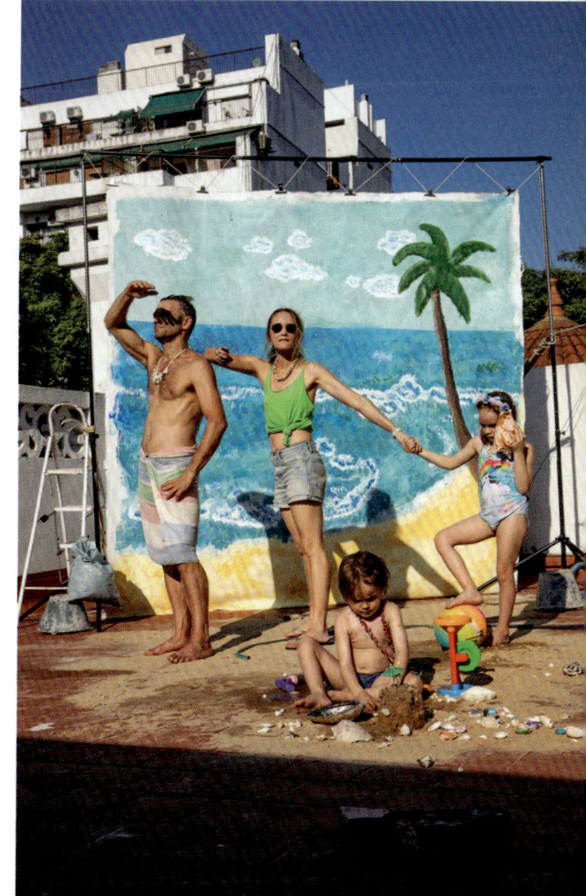

IRINA WERNING, On the seventh day... it was still boiling hot down in South America, so we had to get away somehow and the beach seemed like such a splendid idea. BUENOS AIRES, ARGENTINA

OLIVIA KOZIEL, A COVID-19 Family Portrait. NJ, USA

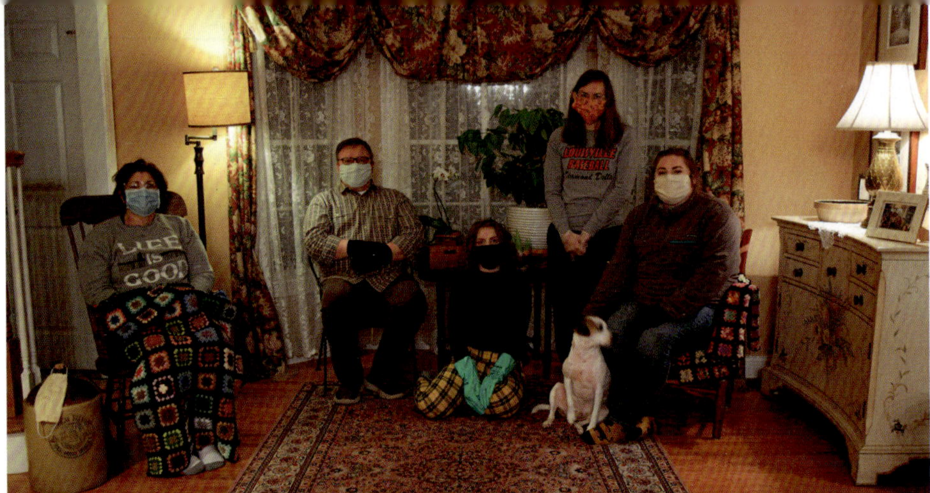

NICHOLAS HENDERSON, Abigail Henderson sewing homemade masks for at-risk persons and first responders in our home during lockdown. POST FALLS, ID, USA

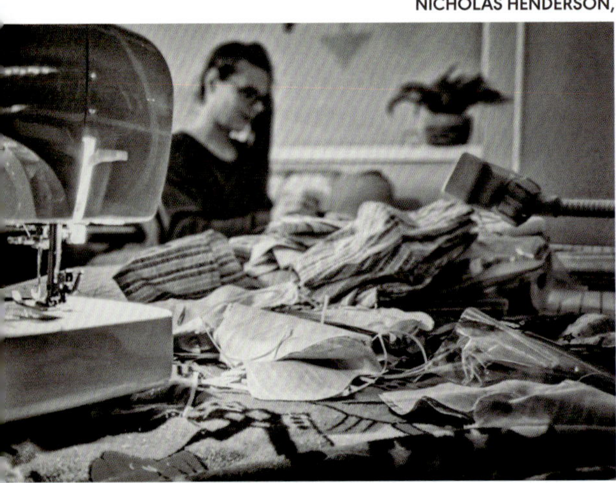

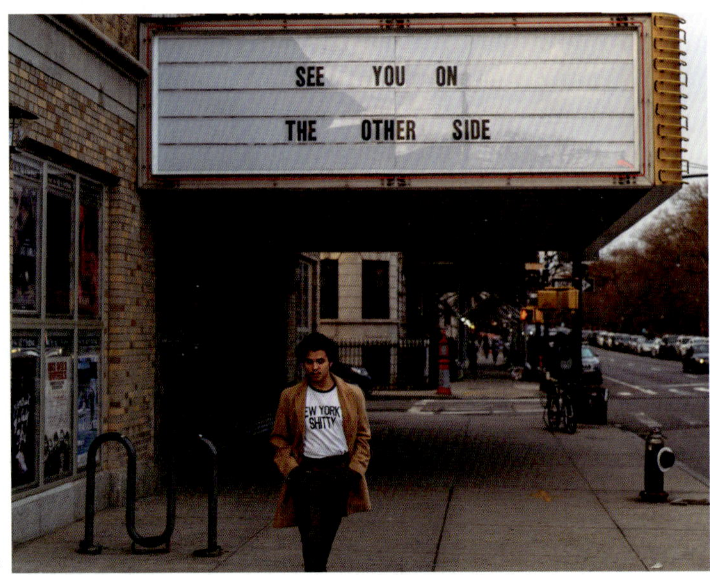

JULIE DODGE, See You on the Other Side. BROOKLYN, NY

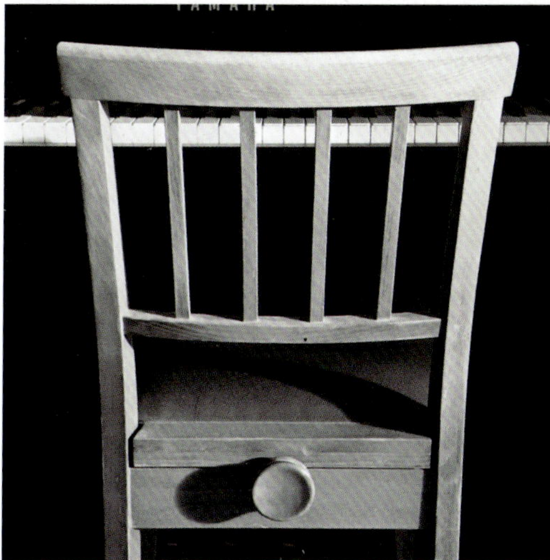

K LINNEA BACKE, Coming home to a postponed solo show here in Oslo, not being able to go back to NYC, I sat in the morning light quietly looking, contemplating. NORWAY

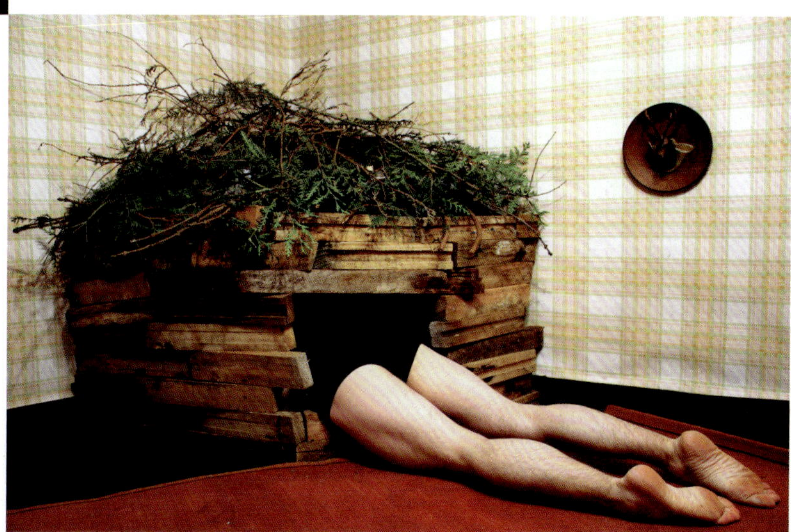

MEHRYL LEVISSE, *L'homme qui fut oiseau* | The man was a bird. CHARLEVILLE-MÉZIÈRES, FRANCE

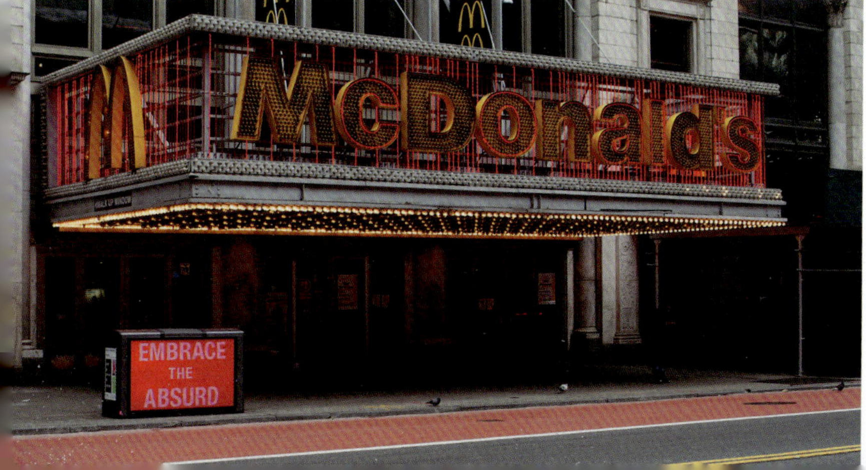

JELLE WAGENAAR, Embrace the Absurd. 42ND ST, NEW YORK, NY, USA

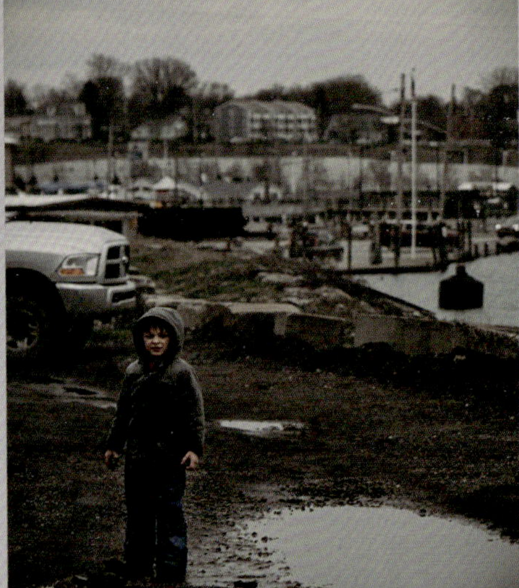

LENA AGNELLO, The first thing that came to mind when I saw this child while shooting some street photography is how lonely it must be being an only child during these times. ERIE, PA, USA

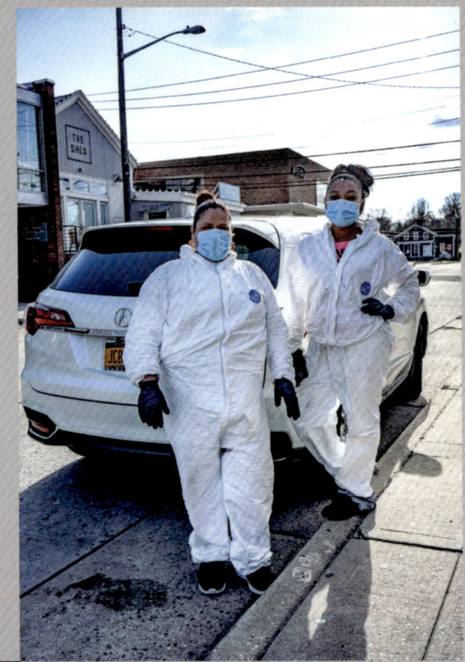

MICHAEL JOHNSON, Two young women prepare to clean a building in Huntington Village covered from head to toe to protect themselves and their clients. NEW YORK, NY, USA

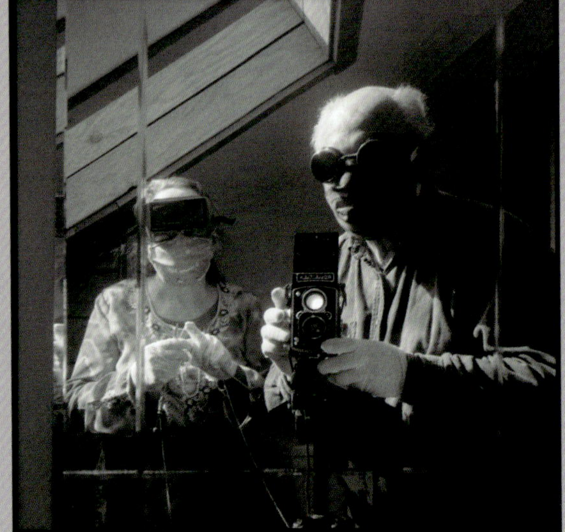

JIM HAIR, Portrait of the photographer and his wife at home in the time of pandemic. PORTLAND, OR, USA

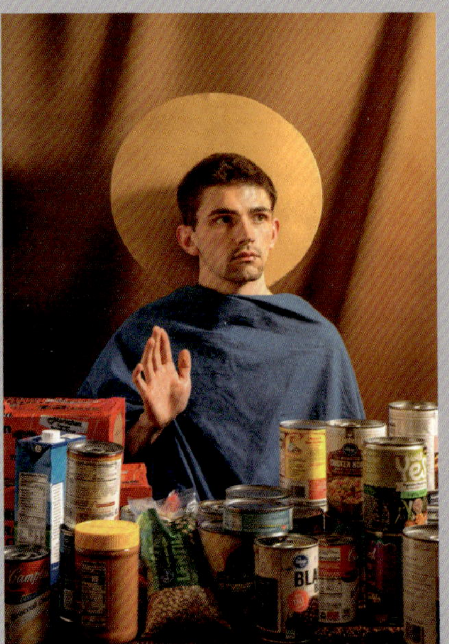

WELLS DOUGLAS, *Non-Perishable Saint* | During COVID-19, humanity's savior is now being prepared. BLOOMINGTON, IN, USA

04·20

APRIL

4_WHO Head Warns Worst of Virus Is Still Ahead *(AP)*

15_ Pourquoi l'OMS ne recommande-t-elle pas le port du masque a toute la population? *(Liberation)*

30_ Die Schweiz lernt, ohne Bargeld zu leben *(Swissinfo.ch)*

CARLOMAN MACIDIANO CÉSPEDES RIOJAS, A horseman in the lonely streets of quarentena in the city of Martinez. BUENOS AIRES, ARGENTINA

SOFÍA SEBASTIÁN, *The Ballet Class* | Day 19 of confinement. With schools and kids' activities closed, one of my daughters tries online ballet. WASHINGTON, DC, USA

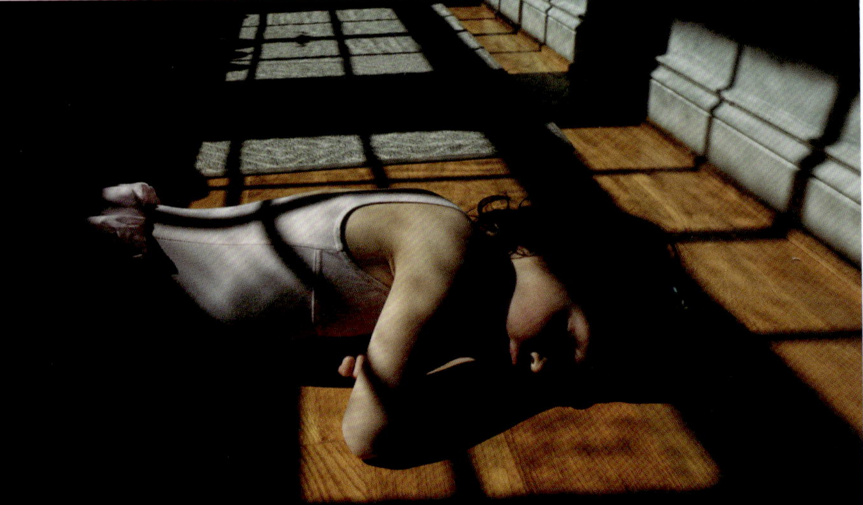

DORA SOMOSI, Amelia and Riley. NEW YORK, NY, USA

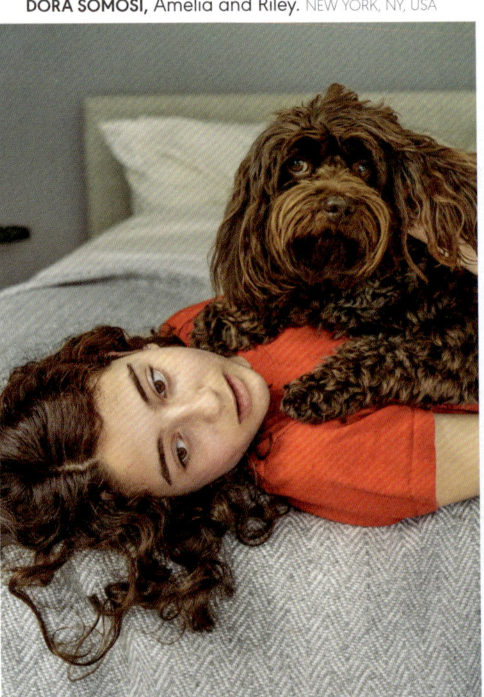

YONG ZHI YONG, *World's Best Airport |* An unprecedented sight at Changi Airport as flights around the world grind to a halt. SINGAPORE

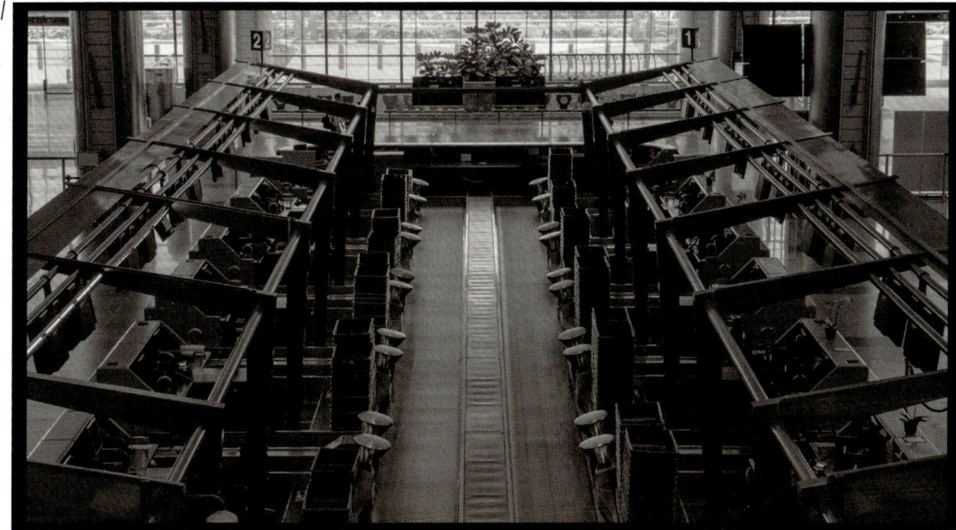

SCOTT SALEMBIER, In the air. WINDSOR TERRACE, BROOKLYN, NY, USA

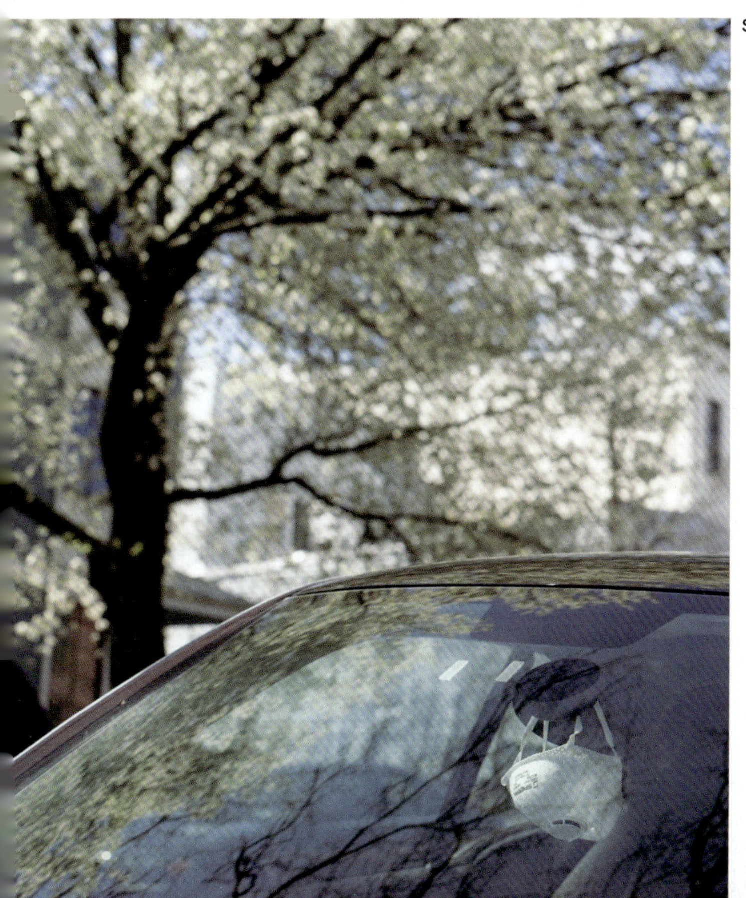

KAHORI FUJITA, Remember You at Home. JAPAN

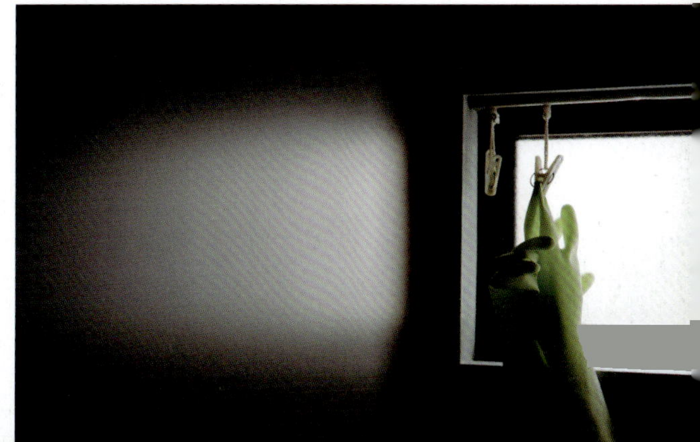

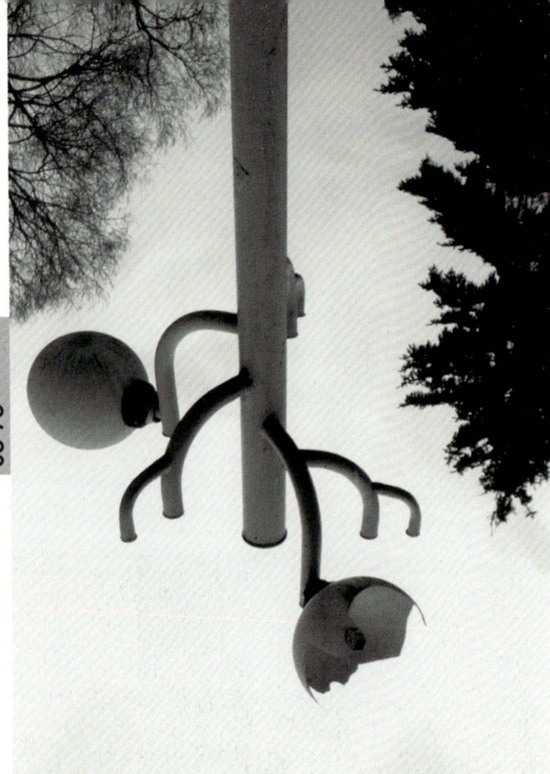

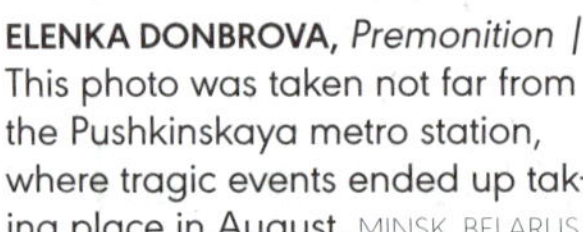

ELENKA DONBROVA, *Premonition* | This photo was taken not far from the Pushkinskaya metro station, where tragic events ended up taking place in August. MINSK, BELARUS

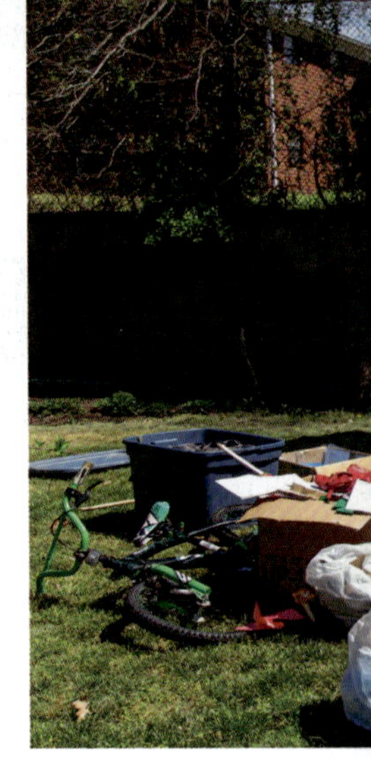

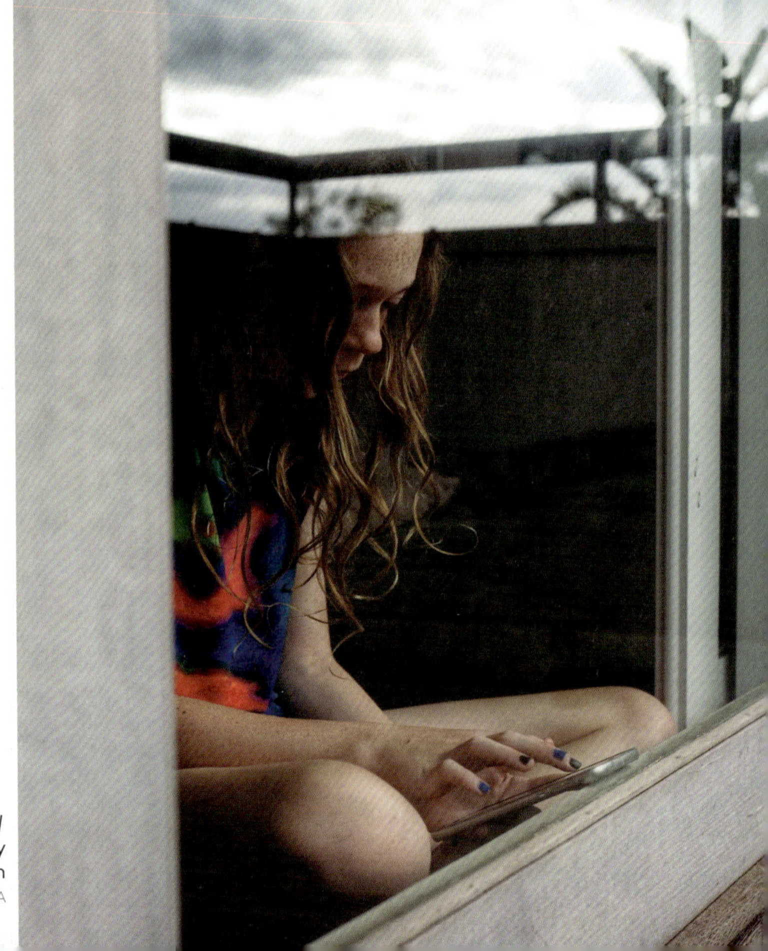

RACHEL DEVINE, *Another Friday inside* | My daughter playing online at the balcony door since going outside was no longer an option in lockdown. HAMPTON, VICTORIA, AUSTRALIA

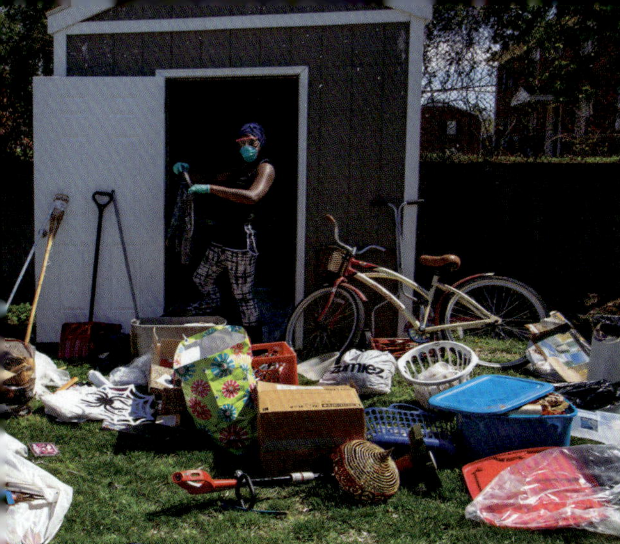

AMIRA KARAOUD, *Quarantine day #20* | Tammy Guy, a nurse's assistant in a Veteran hospital, took advantage of the sunny day to clean her shed. SHELBY PARK, LOUISVILLE, KY, USA

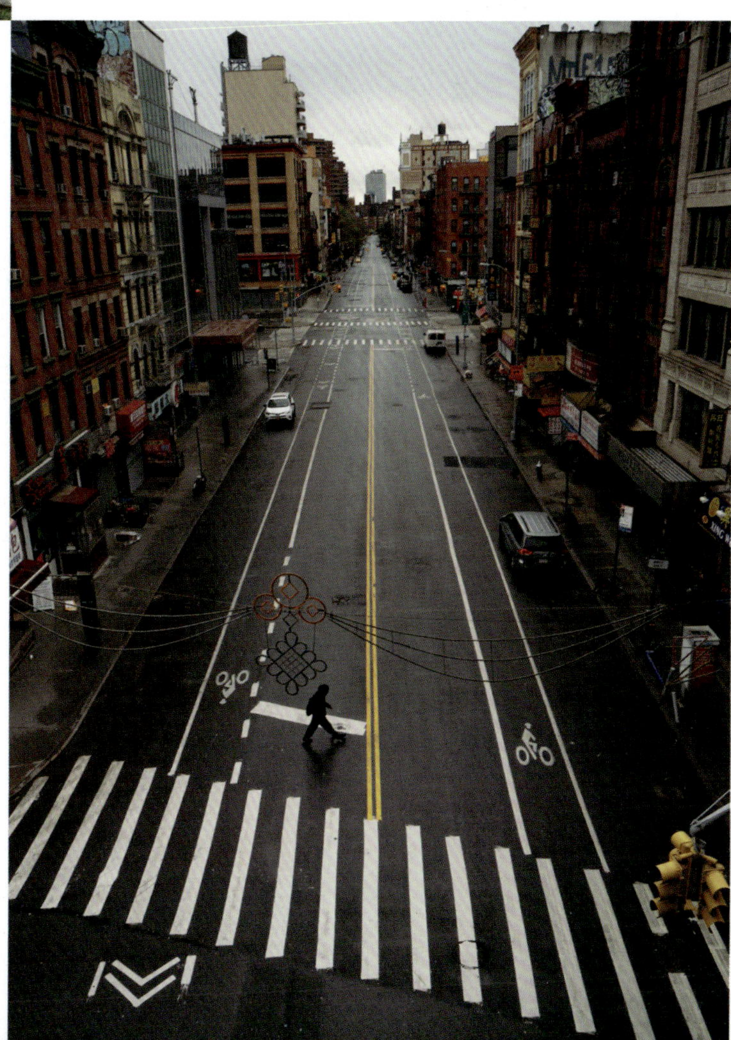

NATHAN KRAXBERGER, *These Empty Streets* | East Broadway, *Taken from* the Manhattan Bridge. NEW YORK, NY, USA

STUART COOPER, *The Coral Princess Docked in Miami |* Sadly, sick and dead people with the virus are aboard. PORT OF MIAMI, FL, USA

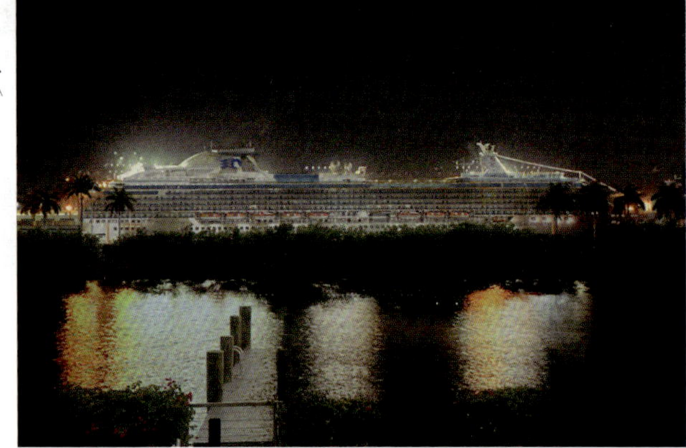

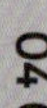

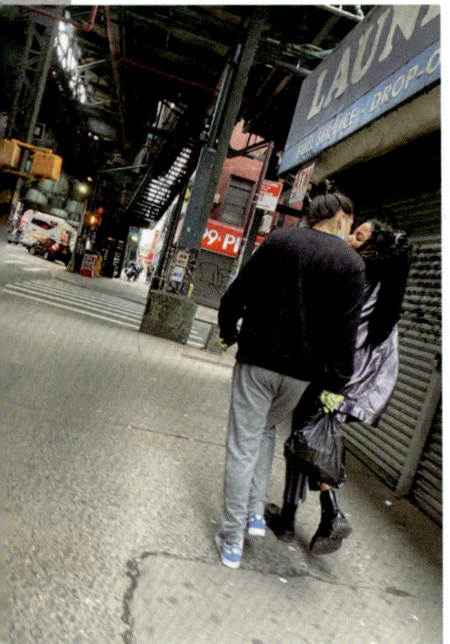

JASON HILL, Two lovers, BROOKLYN, NY, USA

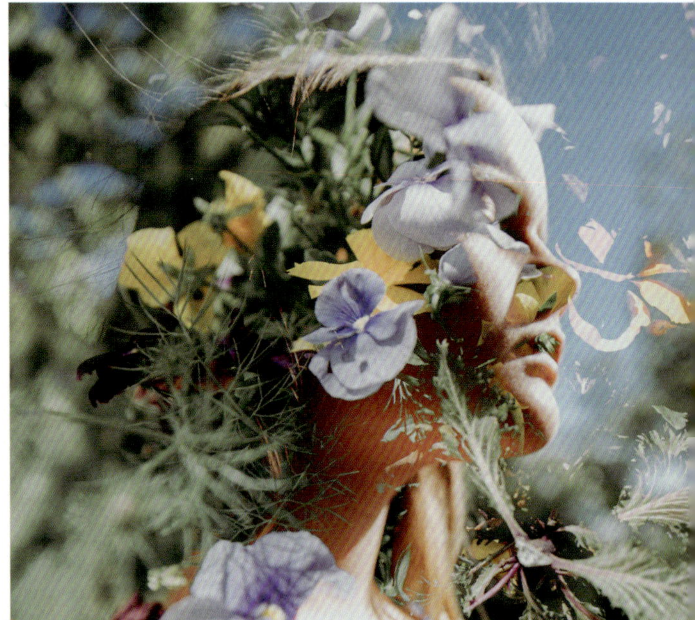

RENÉ TREECE ROBERTS, Double exposure of front yard blooms and my nine-year-old child. ASHEVILLE, NC, USA

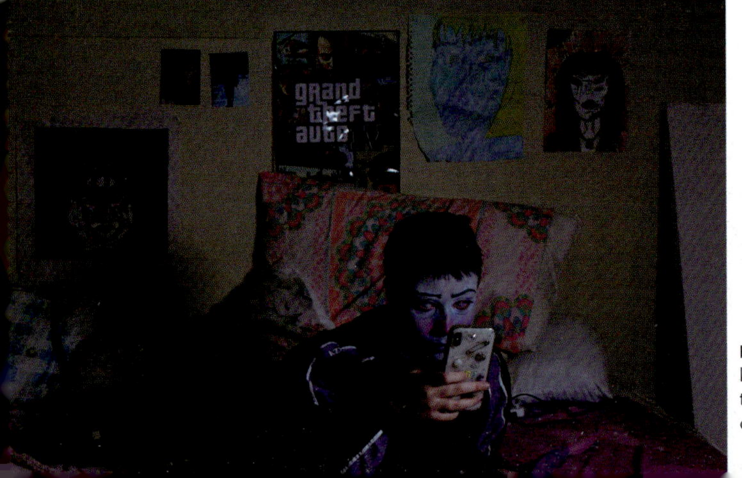

KITSCH DOOM, Maggots Quarantino has been forced to isolate during the COVID-19 pandemic. Maggots worries about the world alone in a small, overpriced studio apartment, with only the comfort of their phone. COUNTY WEXFORD, IRELAND

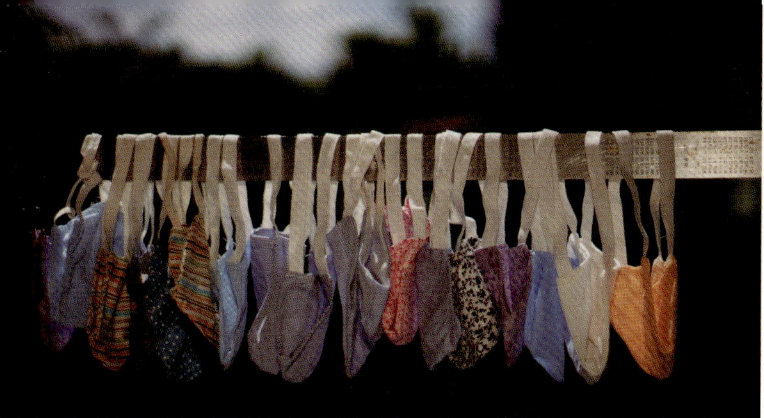

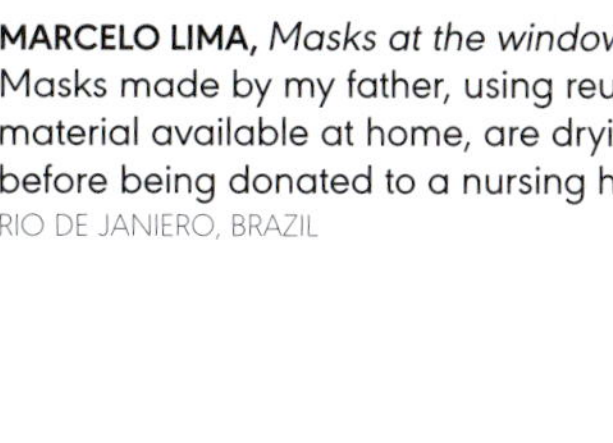

MARCELO LIMA, *Masks at the window |* Masks made by my father, using reused material available at home, are drying before being donated to a nursing home. RIO DE JANIERO, BRAZIL

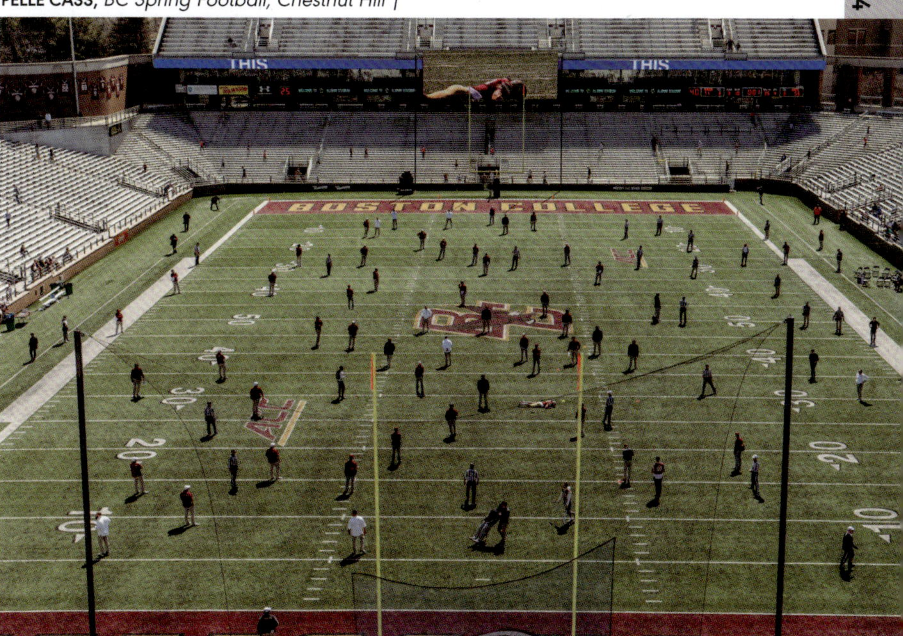

PELLE CASS, *BC Spring Football, Chestnut Hill |* A composite photo, originally completed in 2019 and reworked in 2020 during lockdown. MA, USA

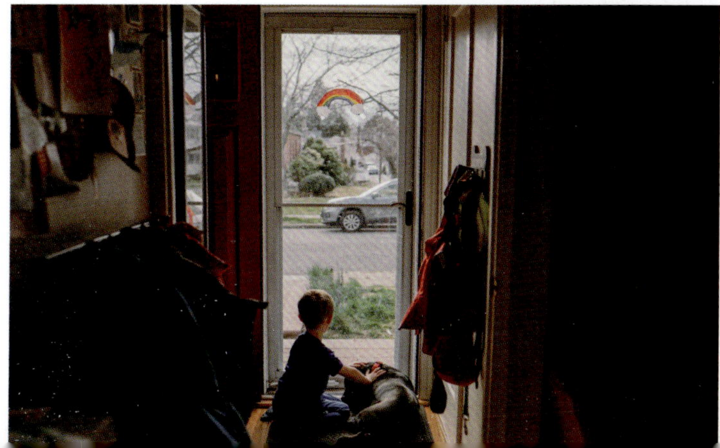

FRANCESCA RUSSELL, A little boy and his dog look out their front door to a world that is no longer safe. LONG ISLAND, NY, USA

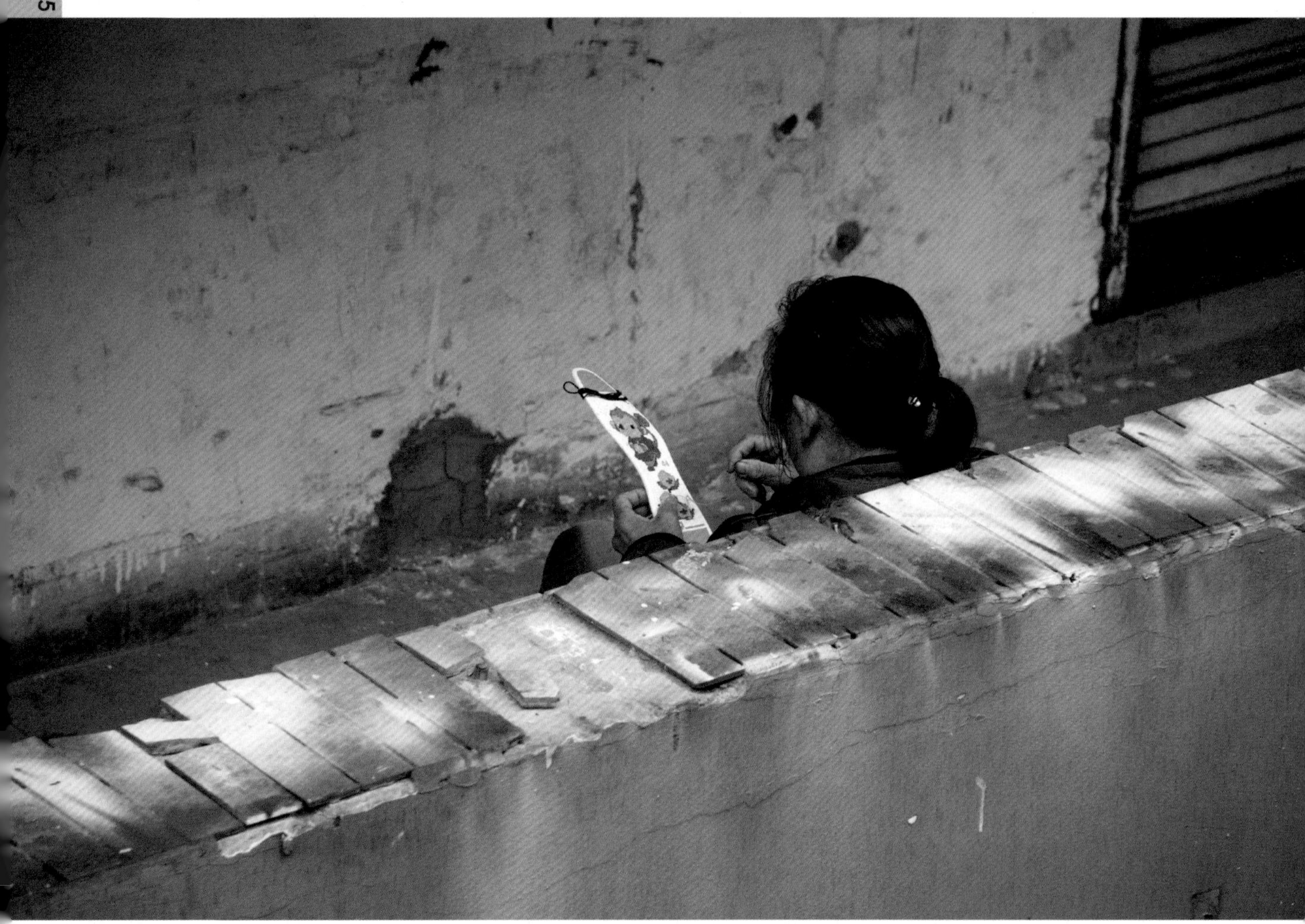

TINGLAN LI, *An Embroidered Insole* | On a rainy day, a woman sits alone making an embroidered insole. CHONGQING, CHINA

FIRDYA BADRUZZAMAN,
Carried by their mothers, girls shop at markets during the pandemic.
SUKOREJO TRADITIONAL MARKET, CENTRAL JAVA, INDONESIA

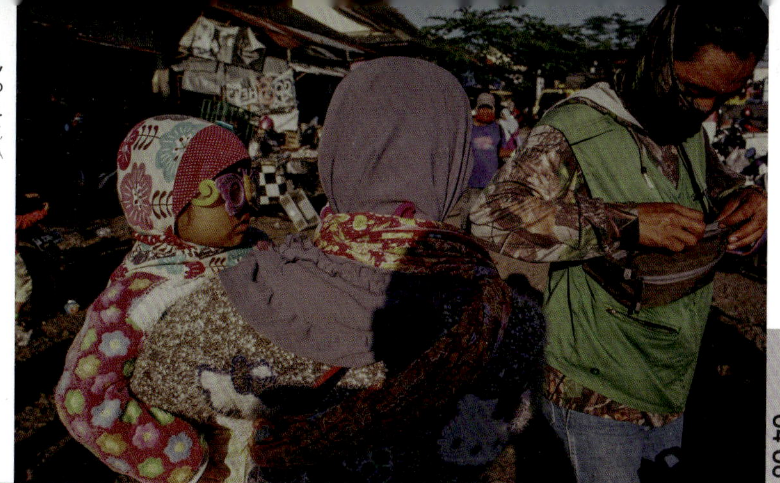

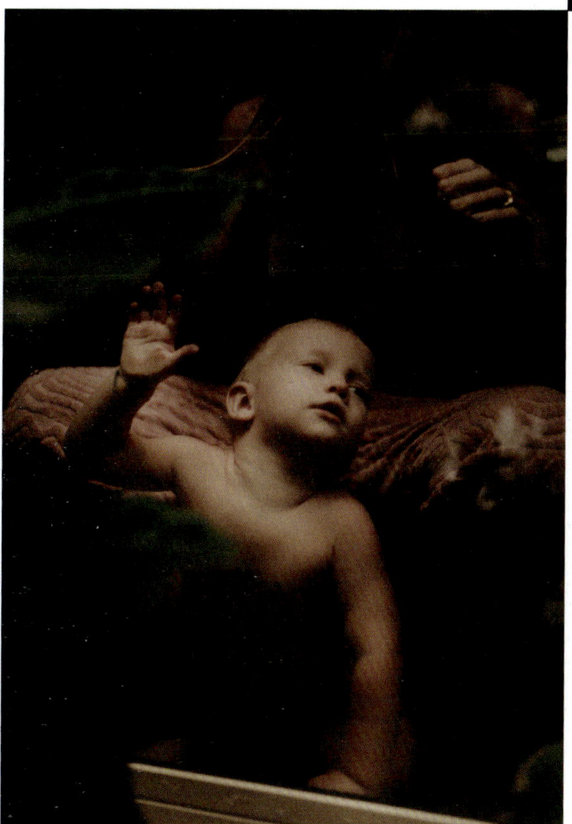

LISA SORGINI, Alby and Jules in the Dining Room. AUSTRALIA

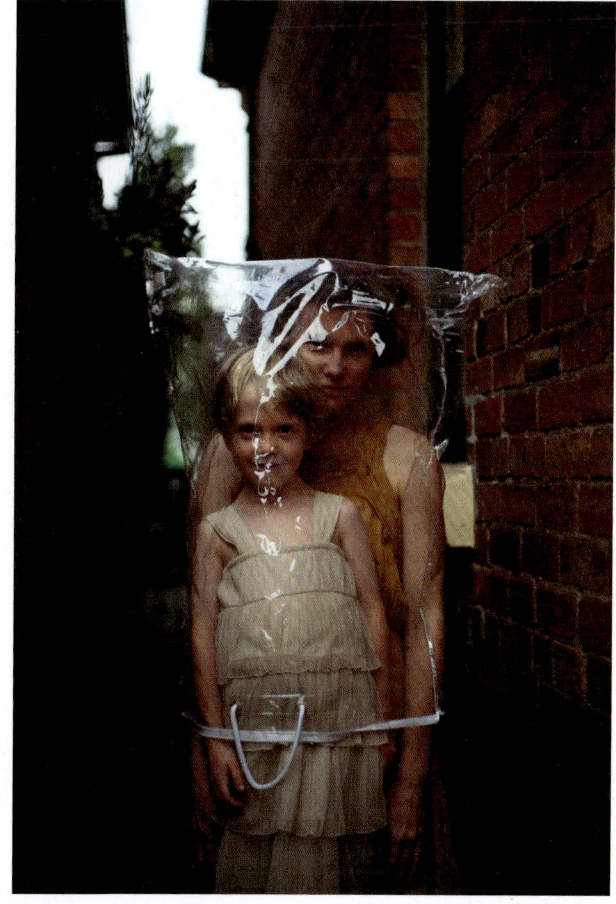

DAISY NOYES,
Exploring my four-year-old son's questions about the pandemic, self-isolation, and all the new rules. MELBOURNE, AUSTRALIA

ALICIA HABER, *Yearning* | In quarantine since March 17. I miss the city, the parks, urban life, being independent and autonomous, but above all I crave hugging my grandchildren. MONTEVIDEO, URUGUAY

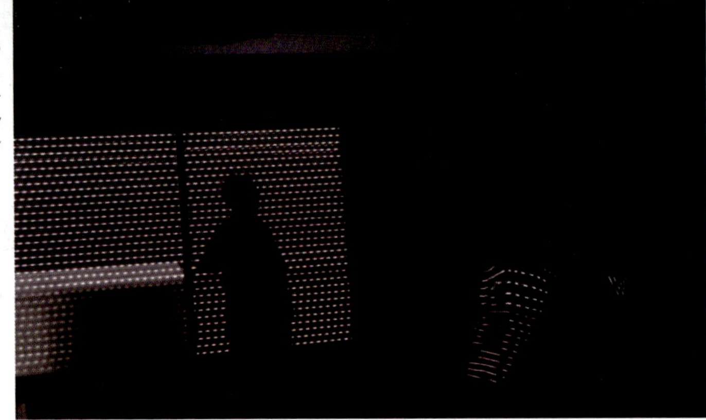

CRAIG MUNGAVIN, *I Wont Die for Wall Street* | Thinking about all those still working and getting out in the world. CROWN HEIGHTS, BROOKLYN, NY, USA

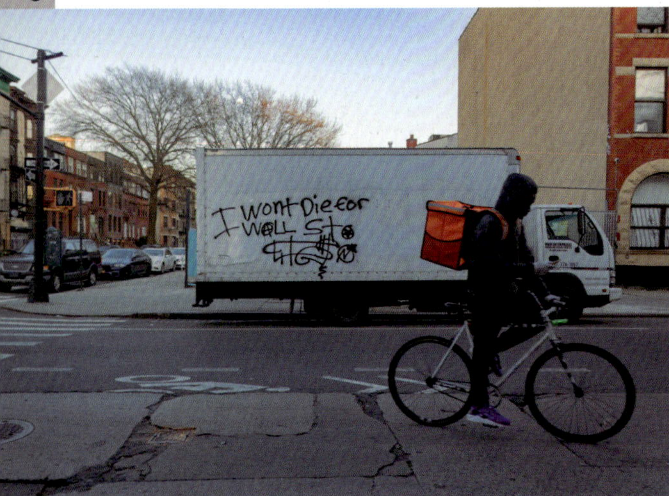

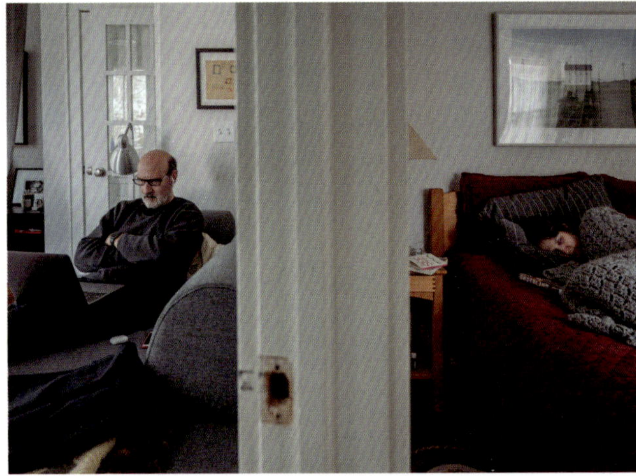

MATTHEW LUDAK, *Pandemic Portraits* | Mom and Dad practicing social distancing. USA

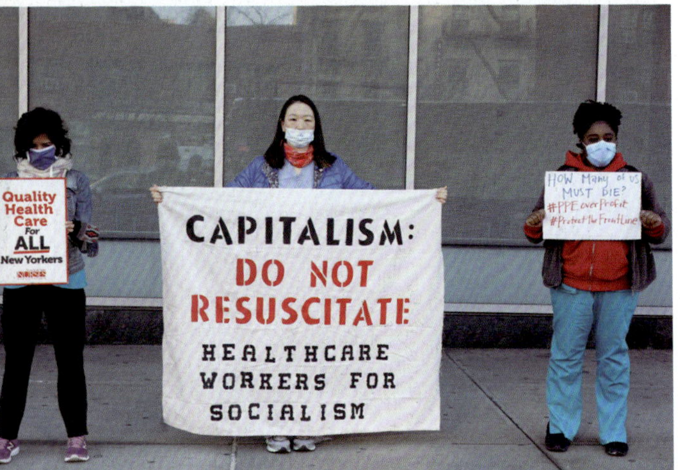

LUIGI MORRIS, Nurse activists at Harlem Hospital on the frontlines of the pandemic protest against the systematic failure of the state and profit-driven healthcare system to provide PPE. NEW YORK, NY, USA

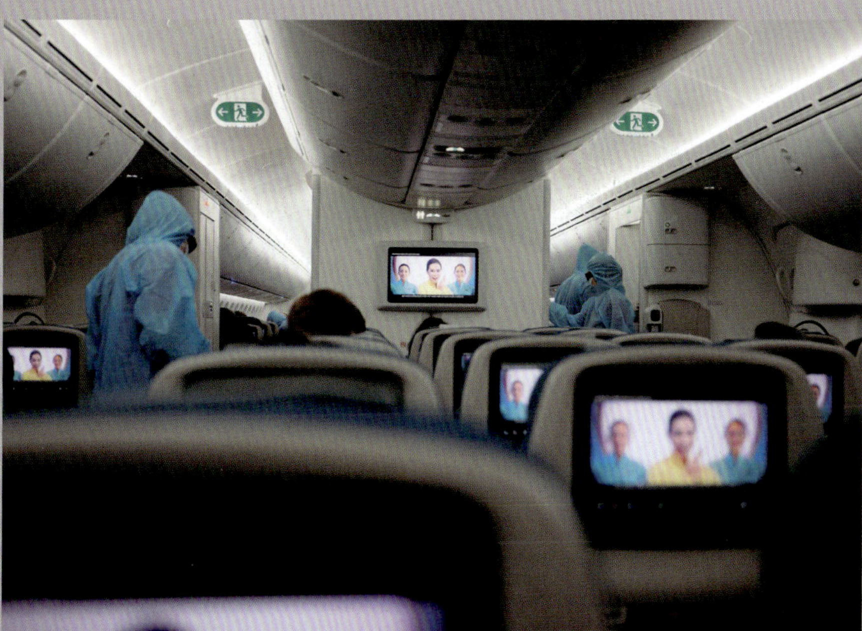

JAKOB SCHMITT, Finding our seats on the repatriation flight chartered by the German government, everyone around was nervous. As the safety instructions video started, I noticed how the colors on the screen matched perfectly with the PPE worn by the cabin crew. Meanwhile, the joyfulness in the safety instructions seemed absurd compared to the atmosphere around. For a moment, it seemed like we had just boarded a plane from a sci-fi movie. The flight attendants were friendly, yet they were afraid of us. Us, the European tourists who had brought the virus to their country. The crew took pride in bringing us home safely. VIETNAM/GERMANY

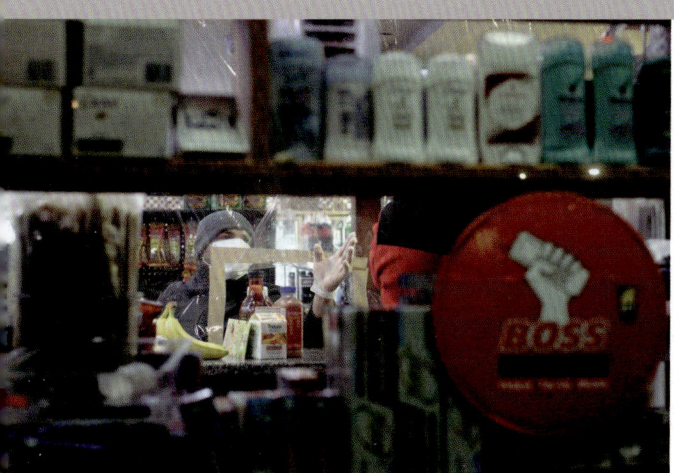

DOMINICK MASTRANGELO, A bodega worker in Washington Heights—clad in gloves and mask—reaches through the opening of a makeshift plastic window rigged to prevent the transmission of the coronavirus. NEW YORK, NY, USA

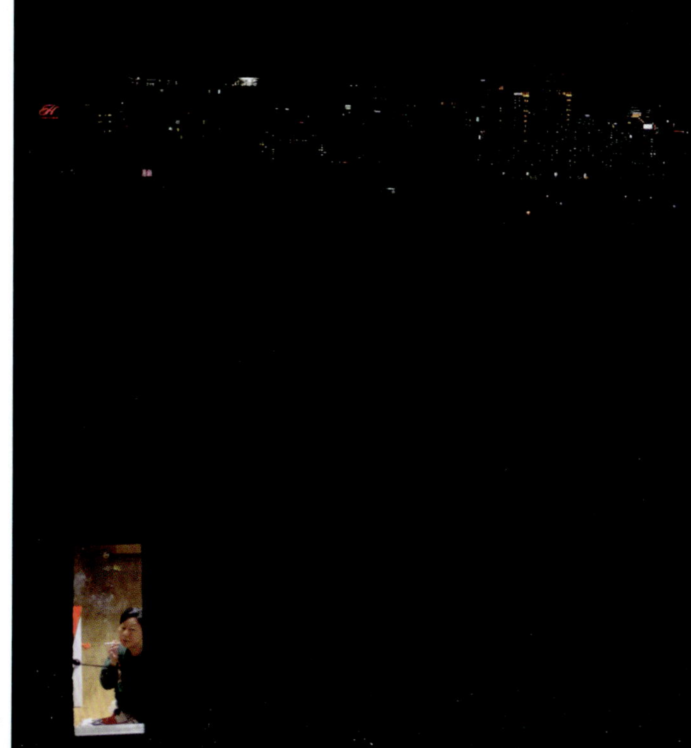

HENRY KNIGHT, *The Burnt Out Ends of Smoky Days* | borrowed from T.S. Eliot's "Preludes." SEOUL, SOUTH KOREA

REYAD ABEDIN, Going out after three weeks for groceries. MIRPIR, DHAKA, BANGLADESH

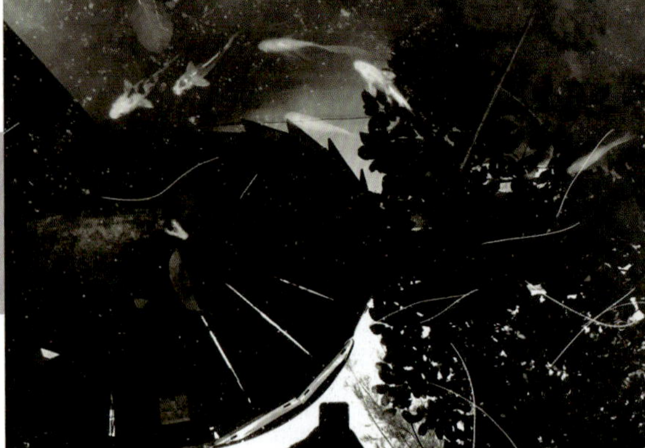

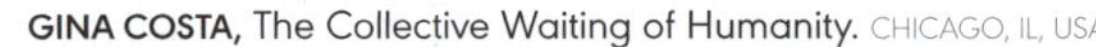

GINA COSTA, The Collective Waiting of Humanity. CHICAGO, IL, USA

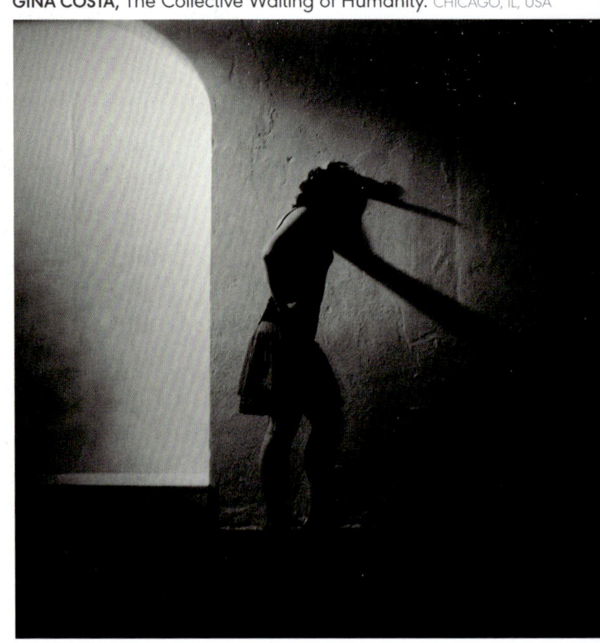

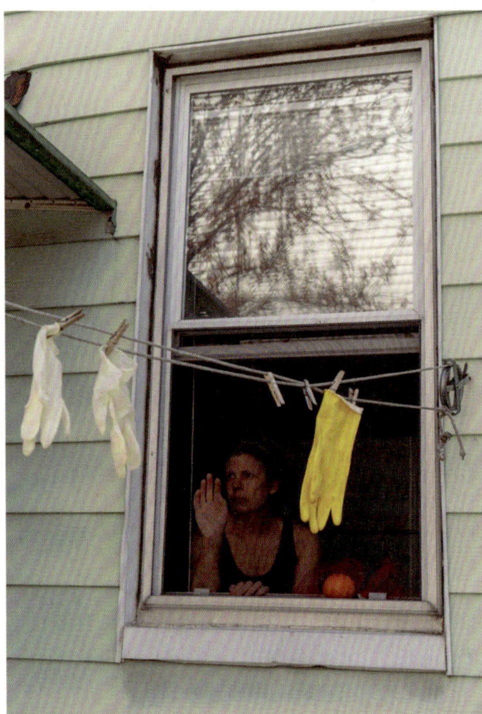

LORI PERBECK, Washing gloves. JERSEY CITY, NJ, USA

AISHAH KENTON, *Self-portrait in Isolation* | COOLAGOLITE, NEW SOUTH WALES, AUSTRALIA

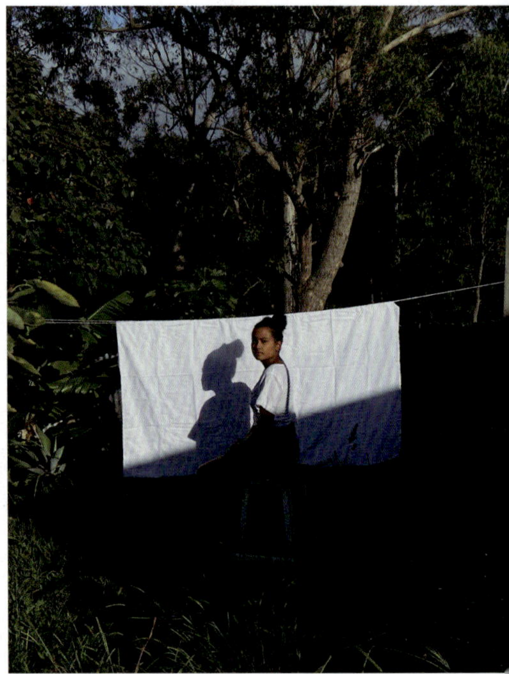

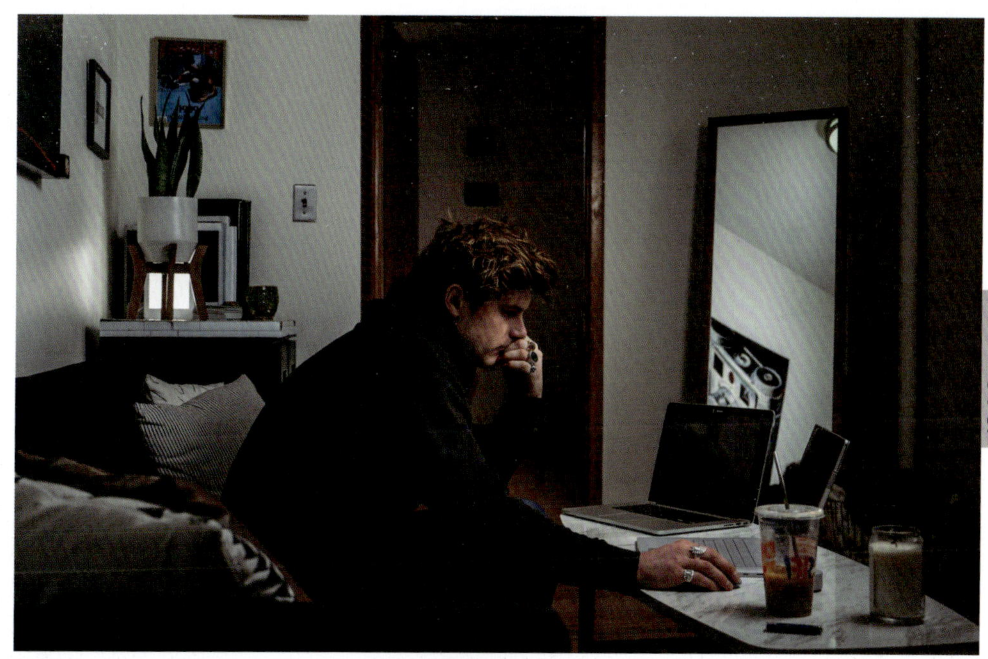

RYLAND WEST, *Working from home* | My company decided the city had gotten too dangerous to go outside and shoot. This was my life for months. Working out of a one-bedroom apartment on the Upper East Side. I traded button downs for hoodies, *and an office chair for a couch.* NEW YORK, NY, USA

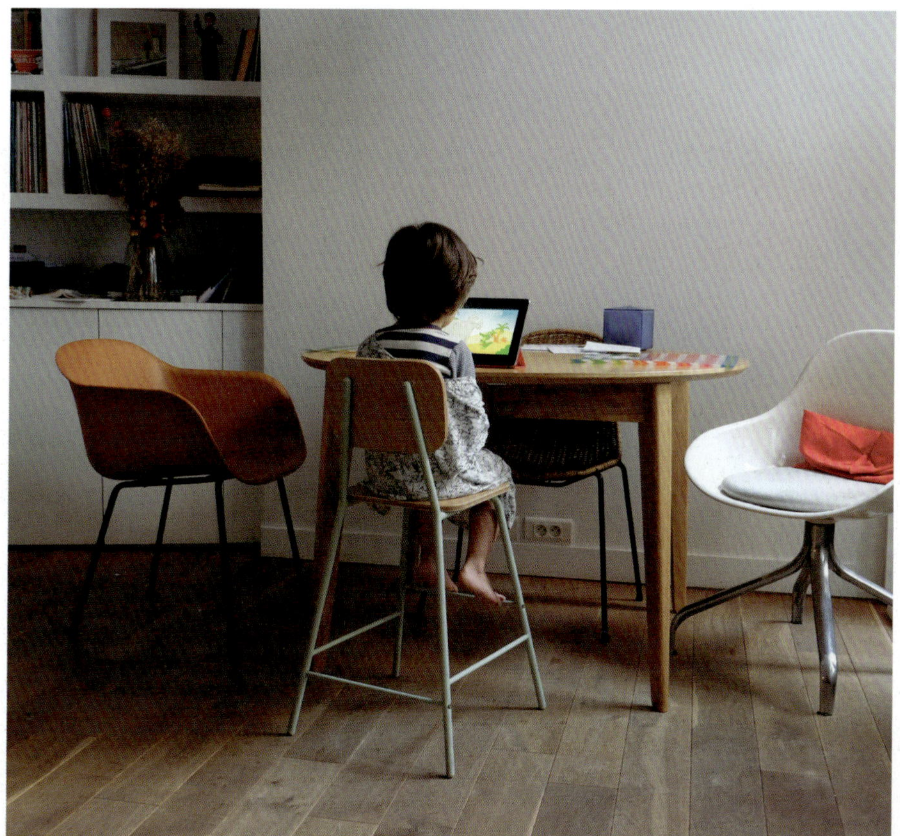

VINCENT MIGRENNE, A little quiet moment in the house. RUE PAJOL, PARIS, FRANCE

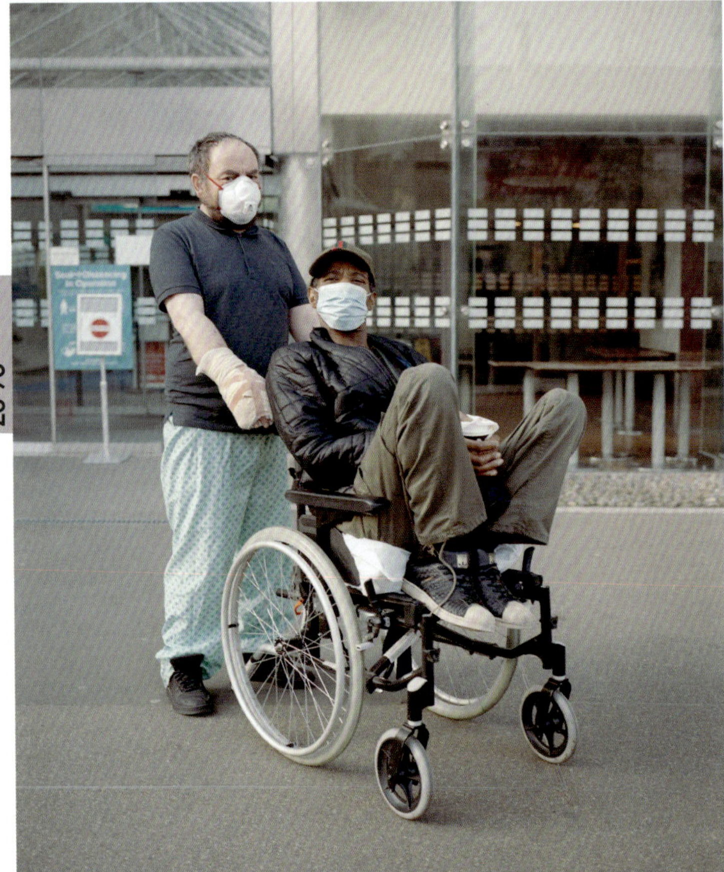

PAUL ROMANS, Front Entrance, Guy's and St Thomas' NHS Hospital. LONDON, UNITED KINGDOM

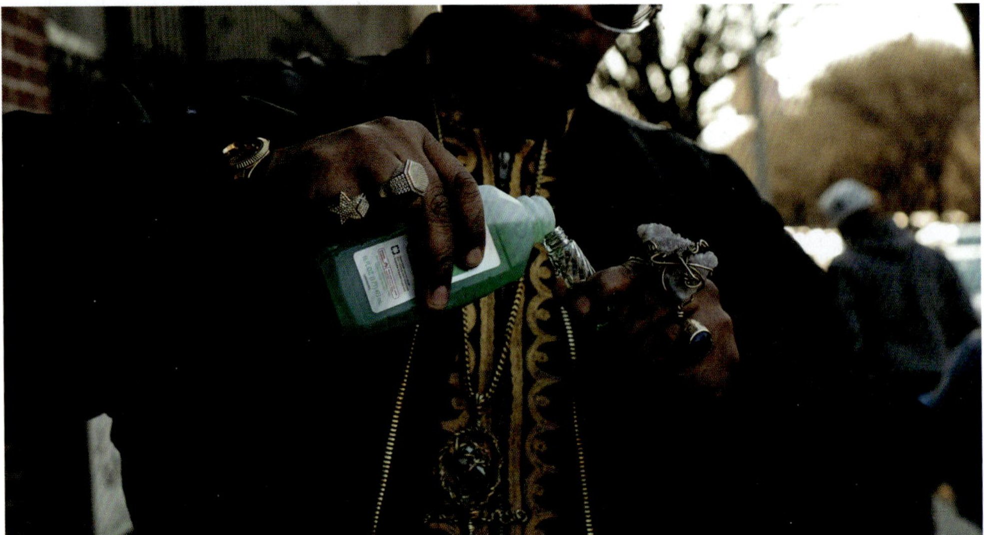

LAYLAH AMATULLAH BARRAYN, *The Hustle Don't Stop* | A vendor pours rubbing alcohol into a perfume bottle for customers waiting to purchase for $1. As stores are completely out of stock of products like alcohol, sanitizer, masks, and gloves, folks get creative. BROOKLYN, NY, USA

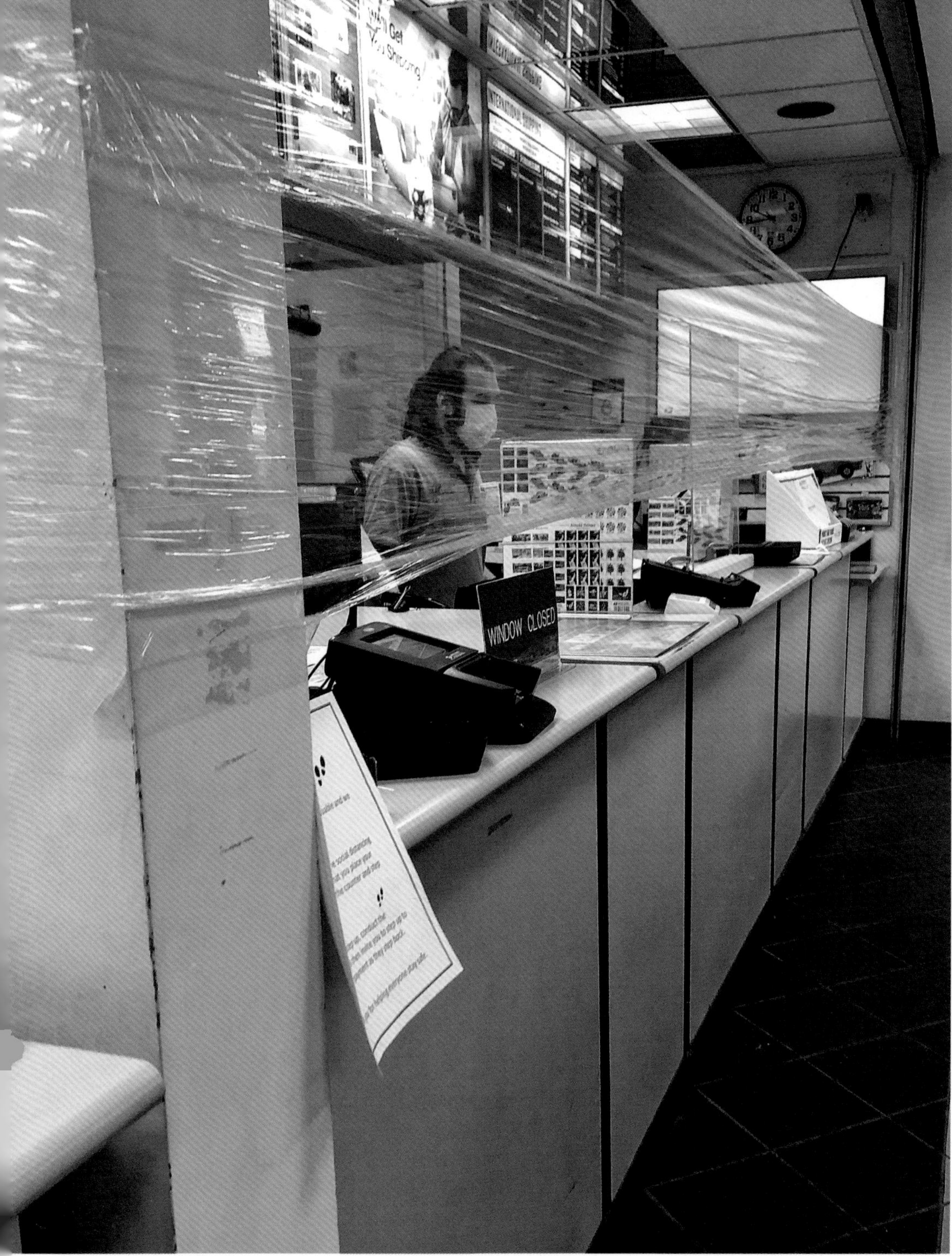

DARREN PORT, *USPS Essential Workers* | In the early days of the pandemic, USPS workers create their own barrier using plastic pallet wrap. NORTHAMPTON, MA, USA

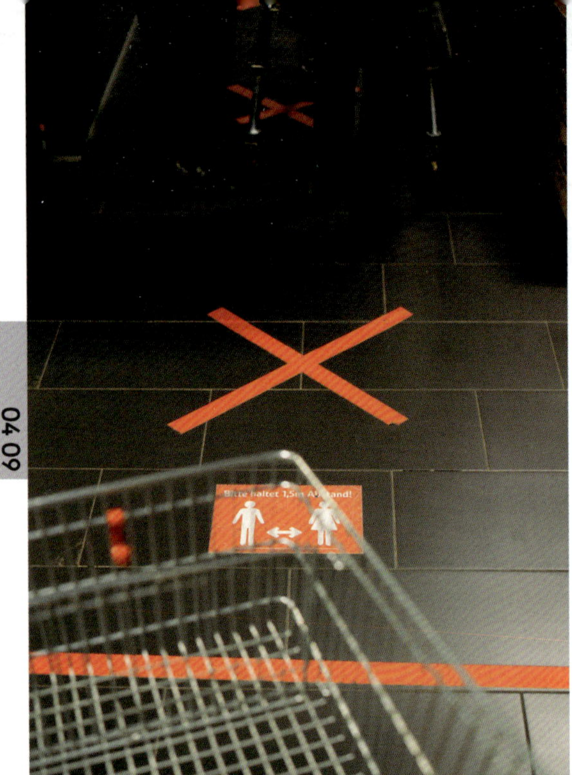

DANIEL BREITBACH, Shopping with distancing markings. GERMANY

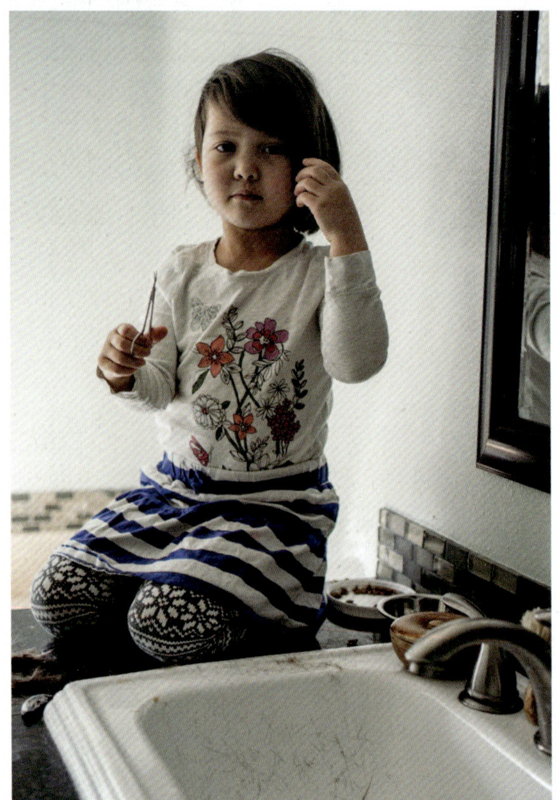

MARGARET ALBAUGH, *Portrait of a Hair Artist* | My 5-year-old took matters into her own hands when COVID-19 shut down salons. SPOKANE, WA, USA

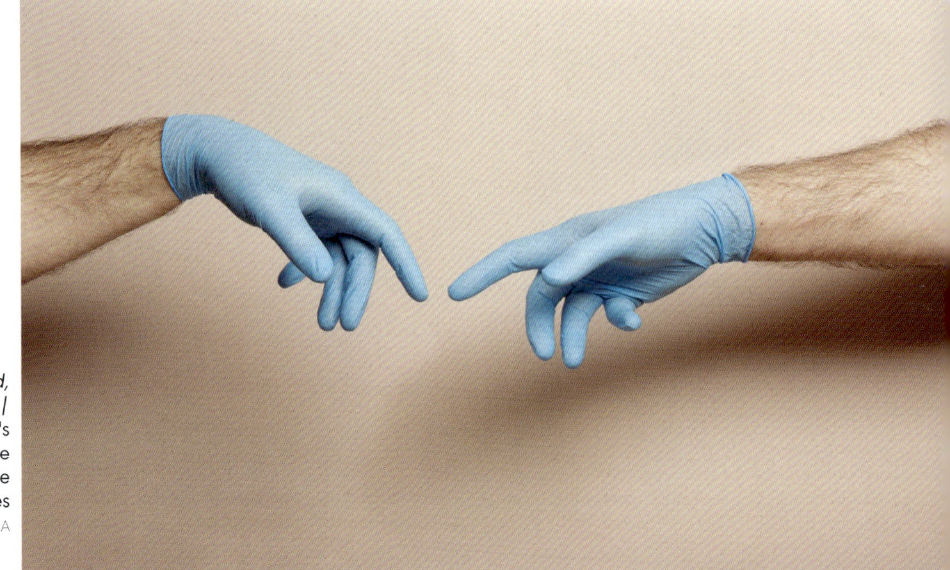

KAREN EPSTEIN, *Hand of God, in the midst of a Pandemic* | Inspired by Michelangelo's Creation of Adam fresco, the *photographer* (with creative director Linda Keil) reimagines the gift of life. KINGSTON, NY, USA

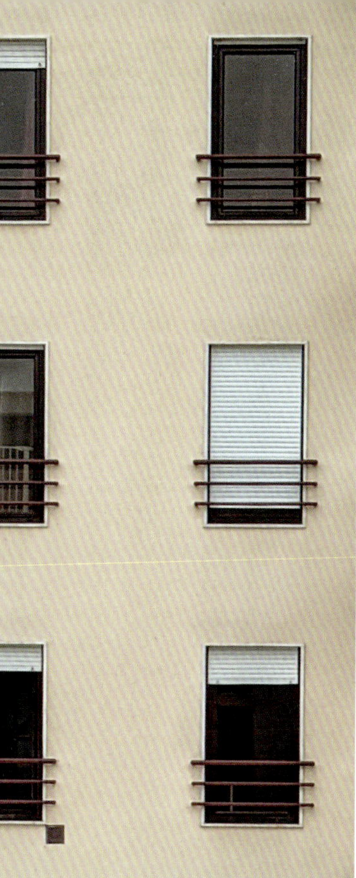

ANTÓNIO FONSECA, The Lone Smoker. PORTUGAL

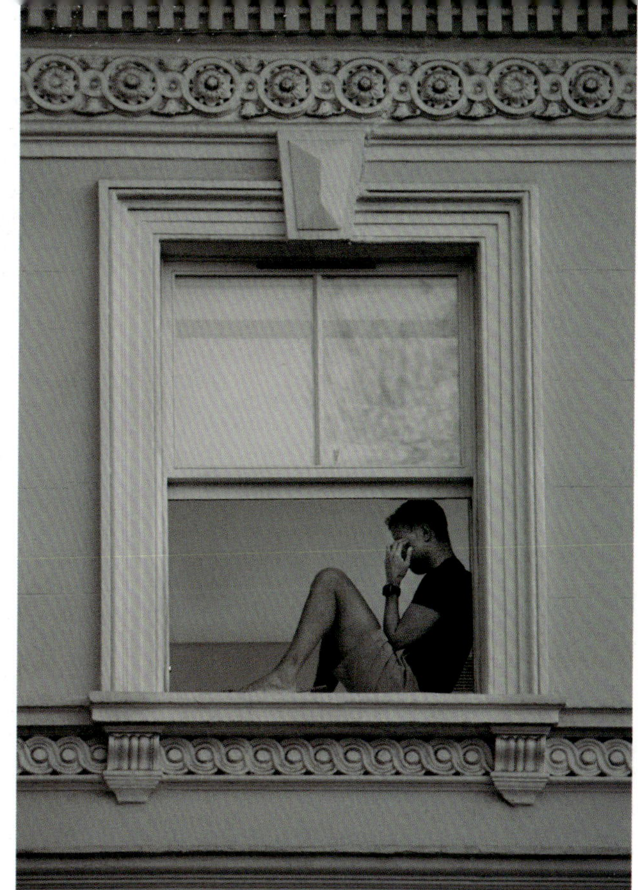

ANDREA BASTERIS, *Isolation Obsession* | I felt so nostalgic taking this picture of my neighbor. I did not know him at the time, now we are friends, and he was having a very difficult time dealing with the lockdown. ST. STEPHENS GARDEN, NOTTING HILL, LONDON, UNITED KINGDOM

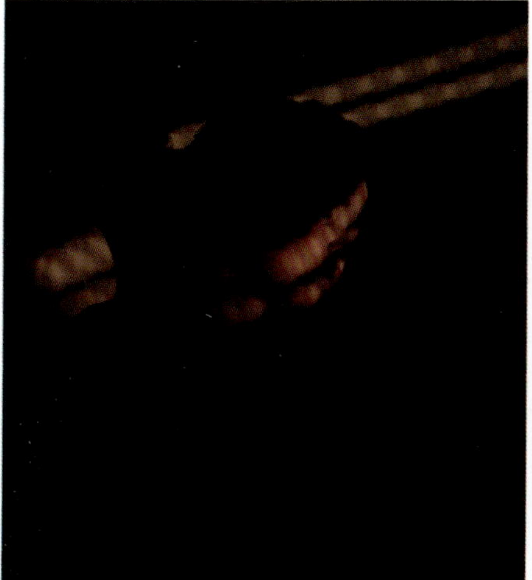

CHRYSTEL MUKEBA, *Une petite lueur malgré le chaos/A small glow despite the chaos* | Intimacy diary about quarantine with children. BRUSSELS, BELGIUM

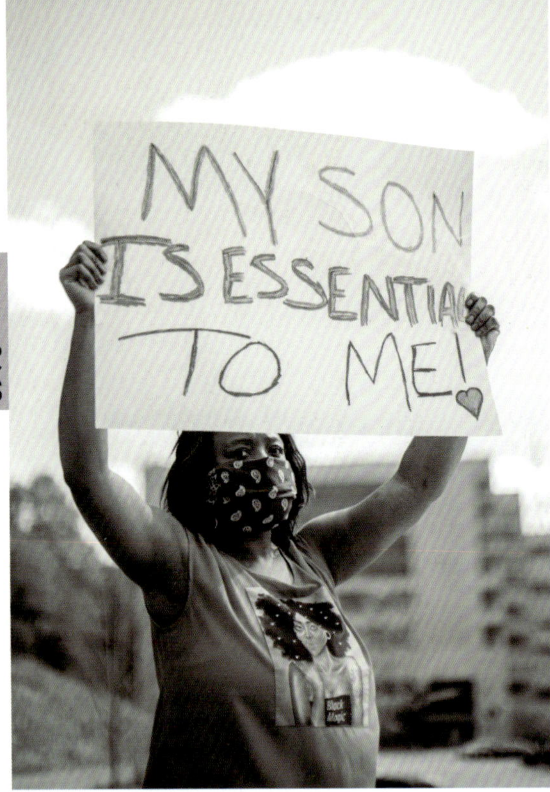

ALEX MATZKE, Doug's mom joins a socially distanced car rally outside of Richmond City jail. VA, USA

KEITH NG, I've come to realize every dystopia begins and ends with a queue. SEVENOAKS, KENT, UNITED KINGDOM

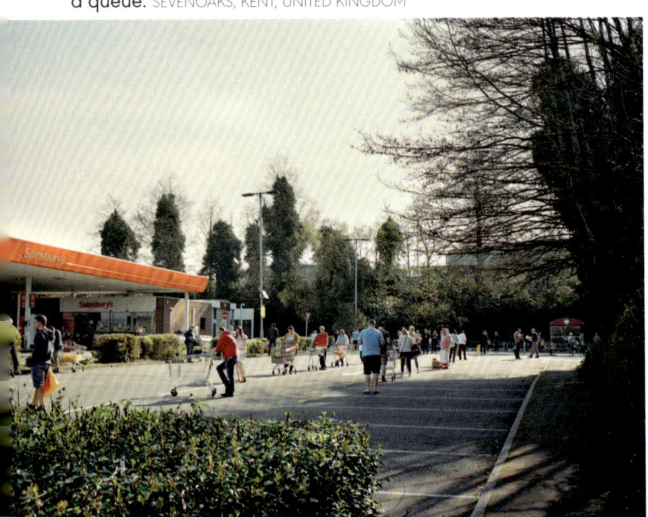

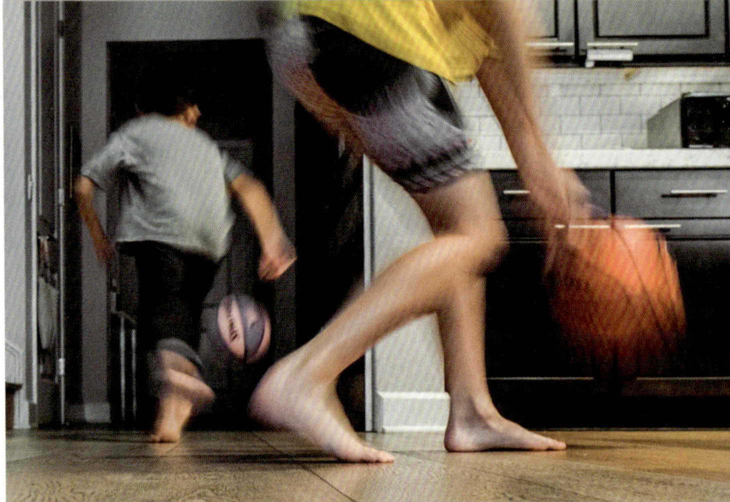

LISA HU CHEN,

I made this photo as a reminder of what life was like for my kids during quarantine. This was in the early days of our state's stay-at-home mandate and we were trying really hard to figure things out. Before COVID, my kids, like so many other kids, were busy with their recreational and club sports. Weekends were insanely hectic with tournaments and games. After school practices pretty much dominated our weekdays. Then all of a sudden everything stopped. No more practices, no more games, no more camaraderie. Poof! It was all gone. Soon after the mandate was issued, some of the coaches started offering free Instagram Live training sessions to keep the kids motivated and active at home. This photo was made on my belly on our living room floor during one of the first basketball live sessions. Between the rhythmic pounding of the balls, the muffled yet encouraging commands coming from the livestream on the iPhone, I decided to slow my shutter speed down to 1/15th of a second, because I wanted to capture the restless, frenetic energy that permeated throughout the early days of the pandemic. I wanted it to emote the dreamlike state we were in, having entered the unknown, uncharted territory of this mysterious virus and the path it was paving. Now, I can see that this photo represents a foreboding of what was to come for us. The chaotic unstructured routines, the days blurring together, the isolation, the sense of feeling trapped, and the failing disorganized efforts to end the pandemic. Now we are in our 20th week of quarantine. After two state shut downs my kids are happy and they are healthy, but I don't make photos like this anymore. I am just waiting patiently to move on.
ORANGE COUNTY, CA, USA

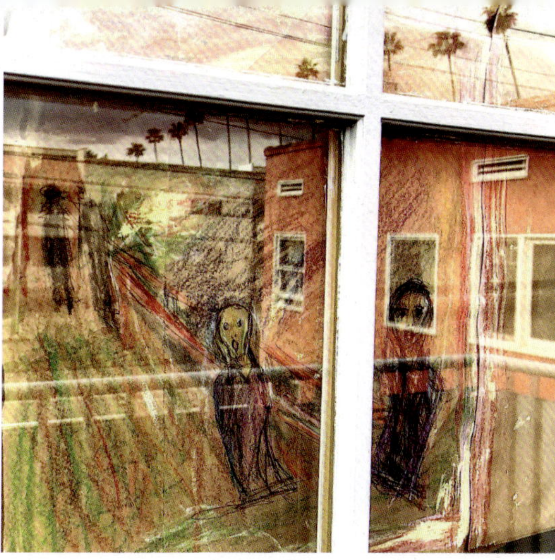

PATRICIA FARRELL, *Lost Selves, Screaming |* Drawn and photographed in LA, where I was stuck and knew no one. I started taping them in the window for the interesting effects of the glass and to share with my unknown neighbors. CA, USA

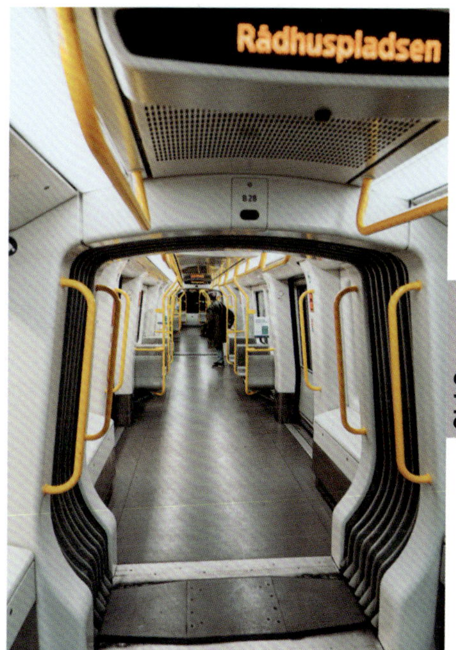

VLADAS CIZAS, Will the story be repeated again soon? What if this will be our new normal? Empty metro line during COVID-19 lockdown. COPENHAGEN, DENMARK

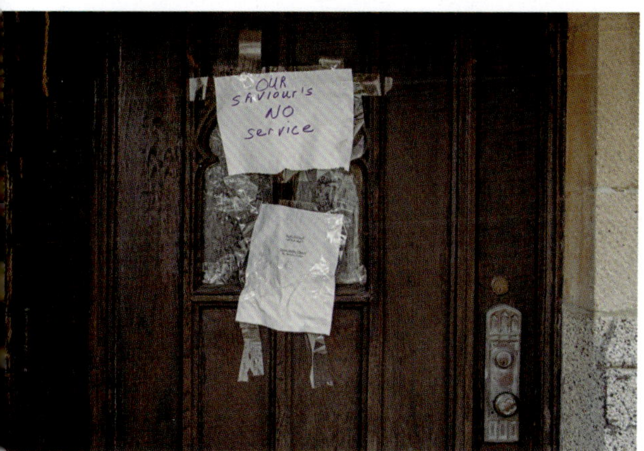

PETER ARCESE, *Good Friday 2020 |* Our Saviour's/ No Service. BROOKLYN, NY, USA

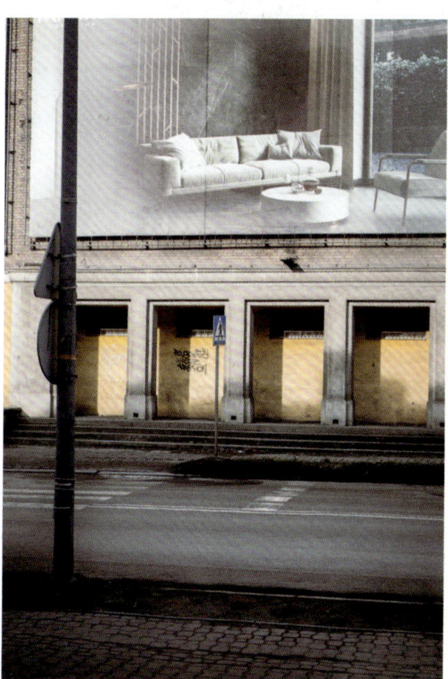

MAREK LOCHER, *Stay at Home |* Upper Silesia, the city of Bytom. POLAND

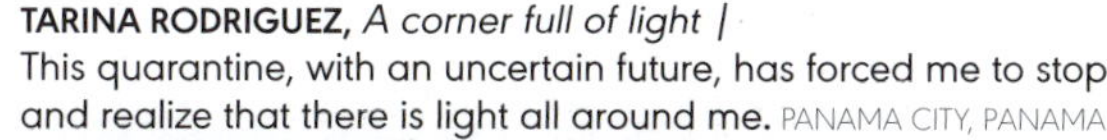

TARINA RODRIGUEZ, *A corner full of light |* This quarantine, with an uncertain future, has forced me to stop and realize that there is light all around me. PANAMA CITY, PANAMA

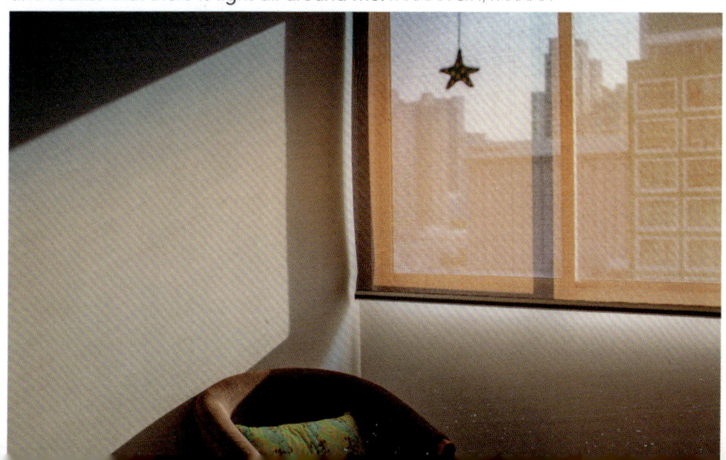

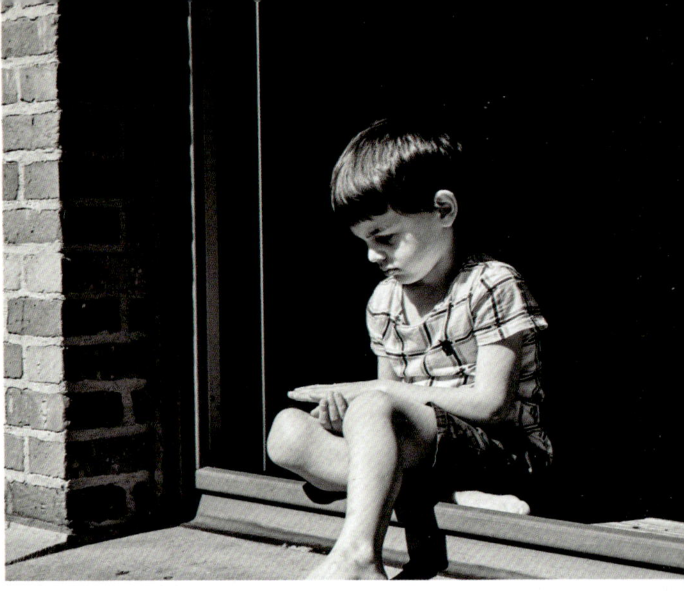

JULIAN HILLS, My confined neighbors. Unhappy kid *(he was laughing the next minute!)*. BRUSSELS, BELGIUM

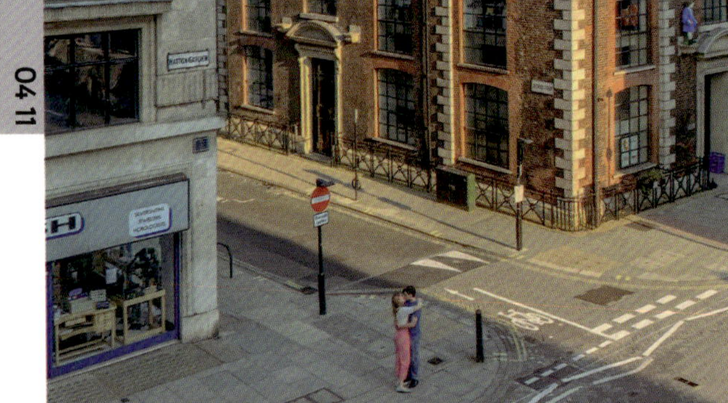

WILLIAM HALL, Compressed by emptiness, I saw them because there was no one else around. It felt like a distillation of love in the time of coronavirus. HATTON GARDEN, LONDON, UNITED KINGDOM

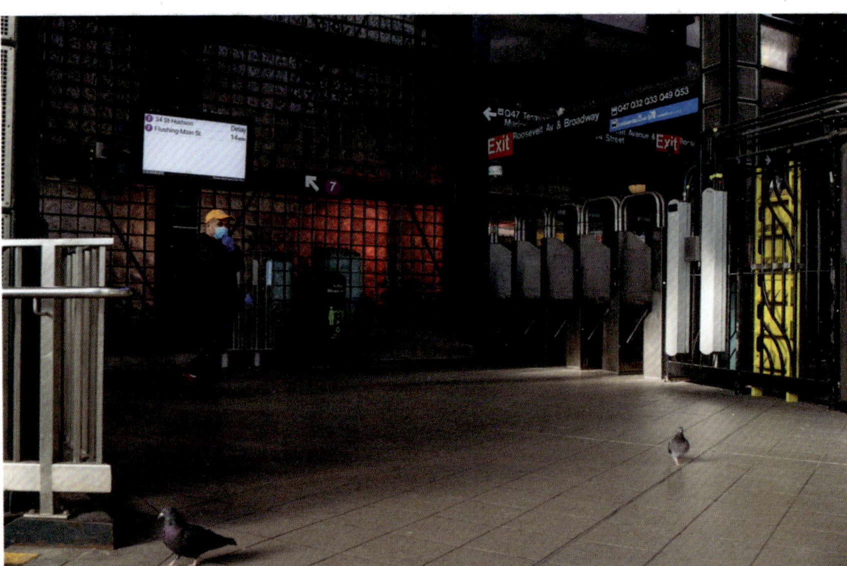

MICHAEL CHRISTOFFERSON, At the epicenter of the epicenter, the 74th Street/Roosevelt Avenue station complex in Jackson Heights, Queens. NEW YORK, NY, USA

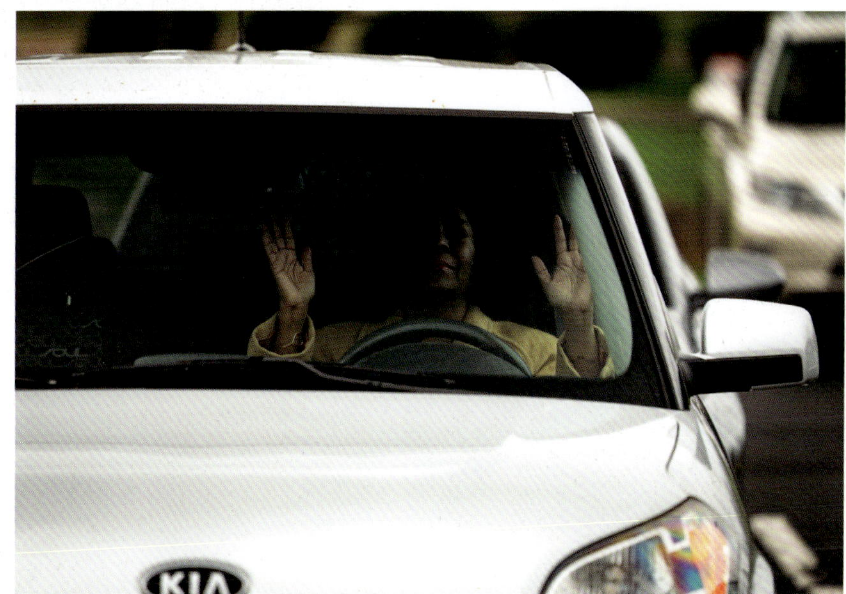

MATT SHIFFLER, Mt Zion Church had two drive-in church services on Easter morning 2020. Sandra Robinson, a 15-year congregation member, said "I'm blessed to be here. This is my church. I'm a caregiver and my parents both passed away recently. I needed this." OAKWOOD VILLAGE, OH, USA

OLGA TZIMOU, I meet them downstairs. Distant portraiture in the back yard. ATHENS, GREECE

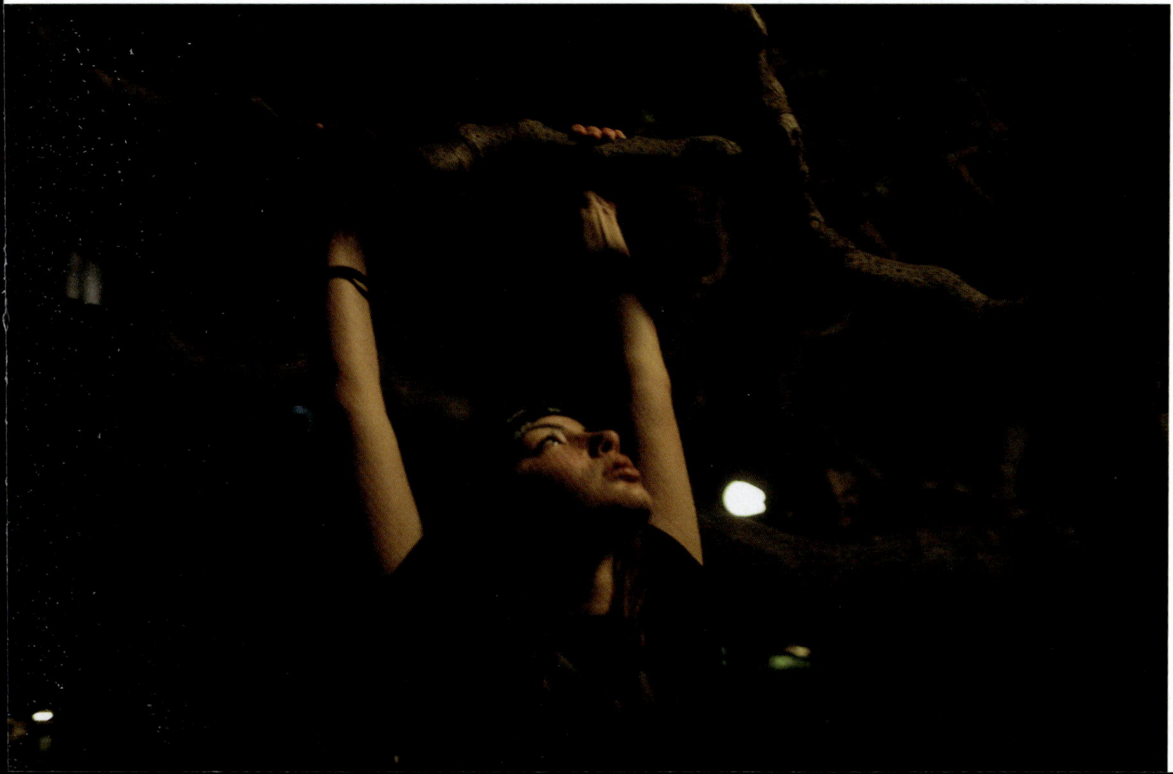

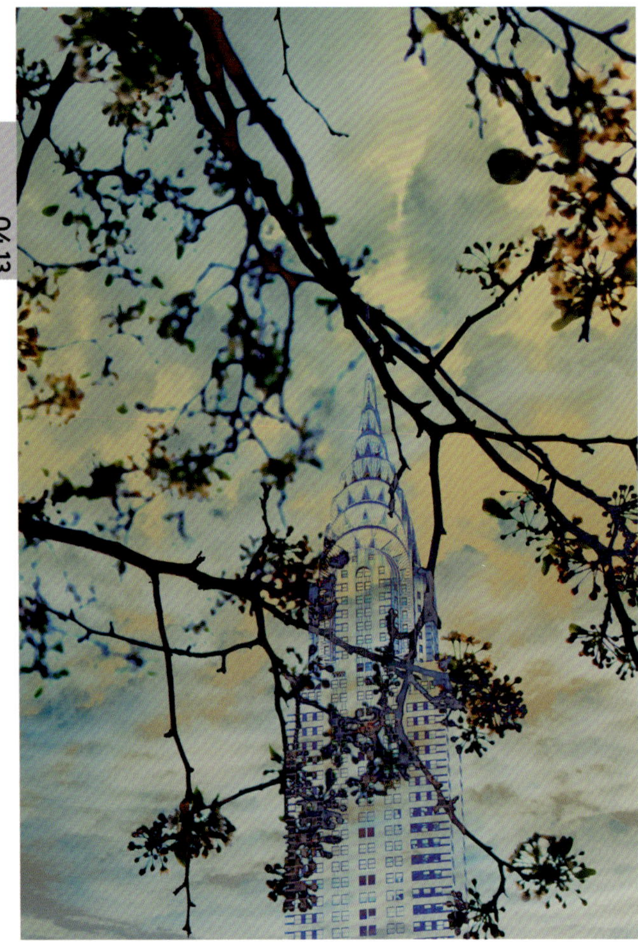

ROBERT A. RIPPS, *Untitled* | From my ongoing series, Negativityness. CHRYSLER BUILDING, NEW YORK, NY, USA

LAURENT THAREAU, The French president announced the lockdown's extension up to May 11 just after the applause in tribute to the caregivers at 8 PM. NICE, FRANCE

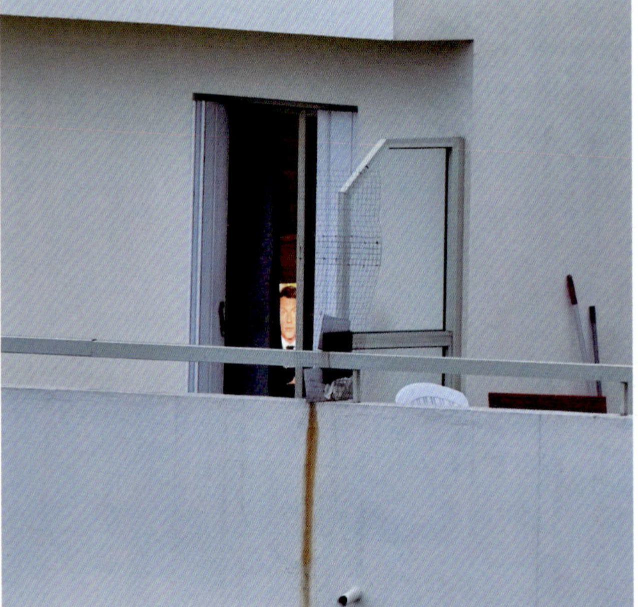

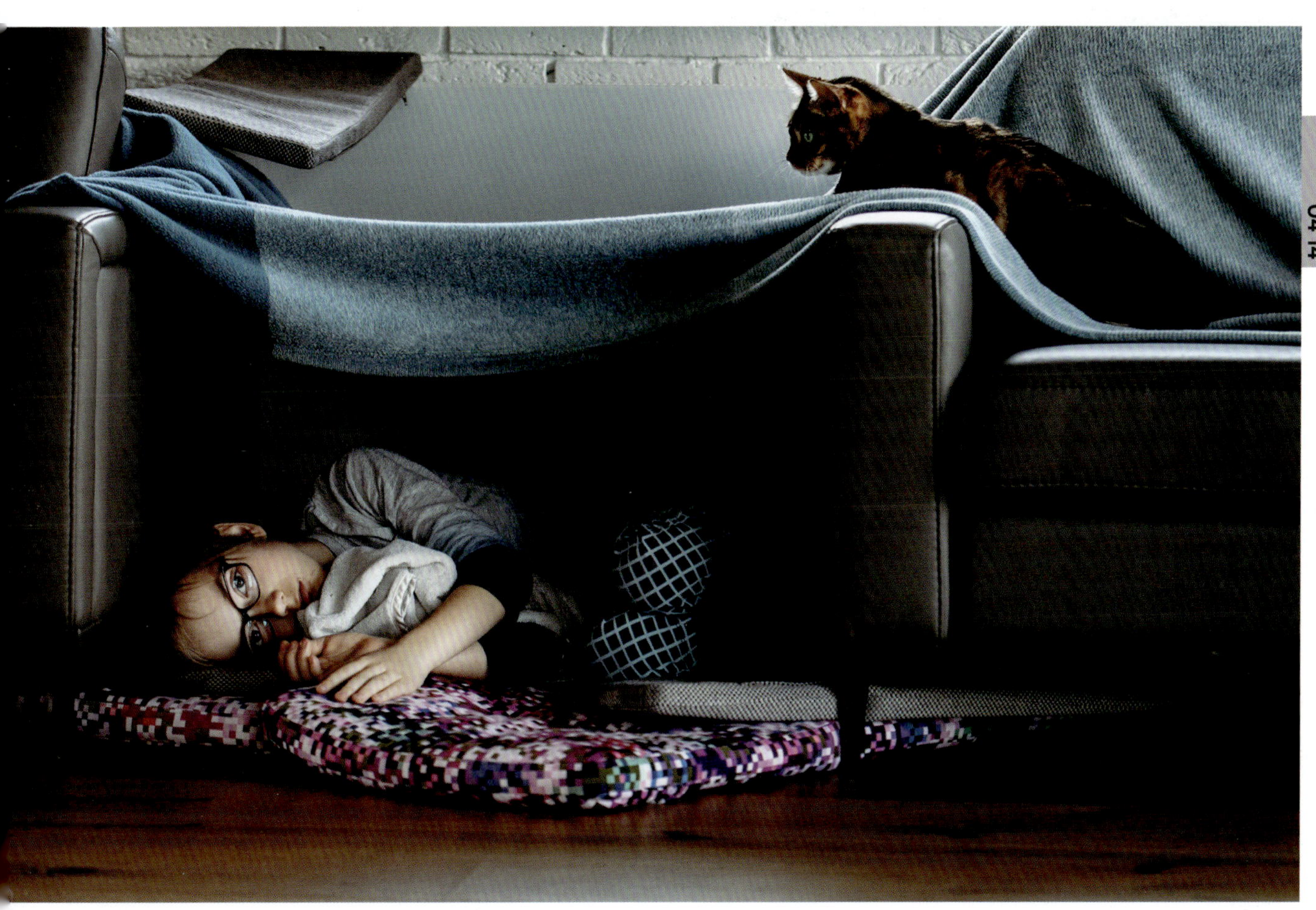

MALGORZATA SMIESZEK LESZCZYNSKA, *Lockdown* |

During the pandemic my son built a tent in which he sometimes stayed.

DYWITY, POLAND

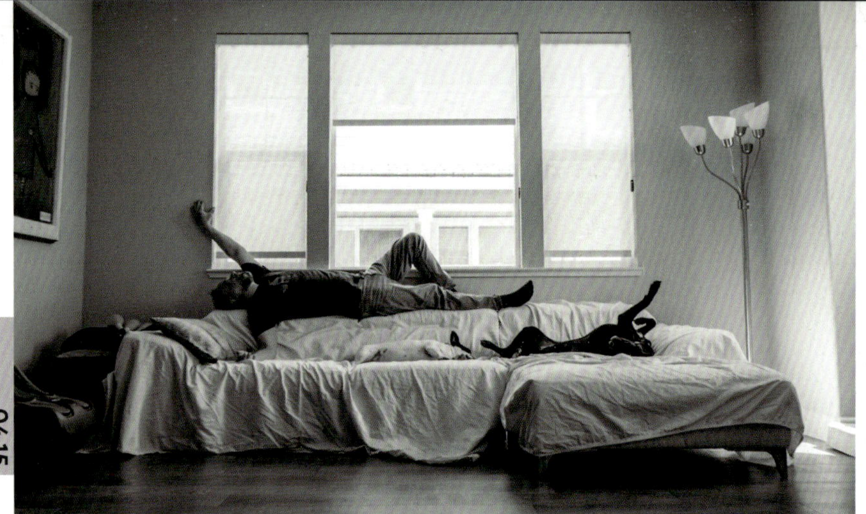

ERIC DAVIDOVE, *COVID-Fatigue |* Day 29 of the Shelter-in-Place order with no end in sight and feeling tired of staying at home. SUNNYVALE, CA, USA

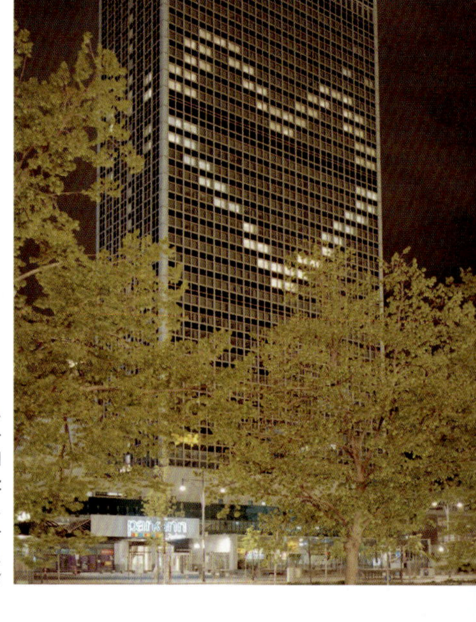

MARCUS GLAHN, Window light installation at Park Inn Hotel Berlin-Alexanderplatz during Corona times. Captured while strolling around at night. GERMANY

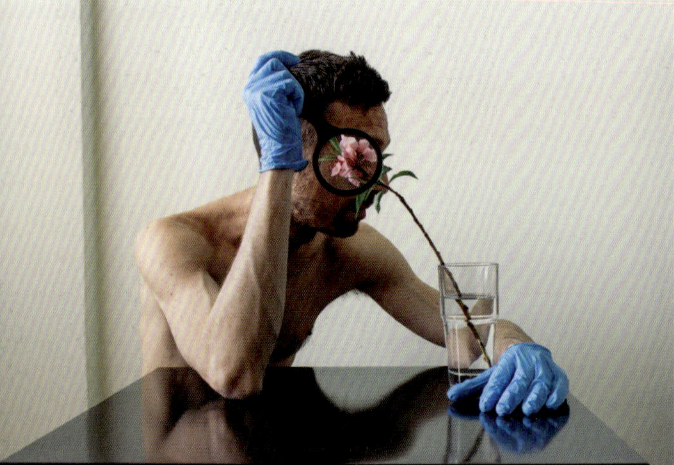

GEORGIOS KYLPASIS, This photo is a part of my project "'My COVID era-ἔαρ'' (ἔαρ in Ancient Greek language means Spring), taken during the Greek lockdown. PATRAS, GREECE

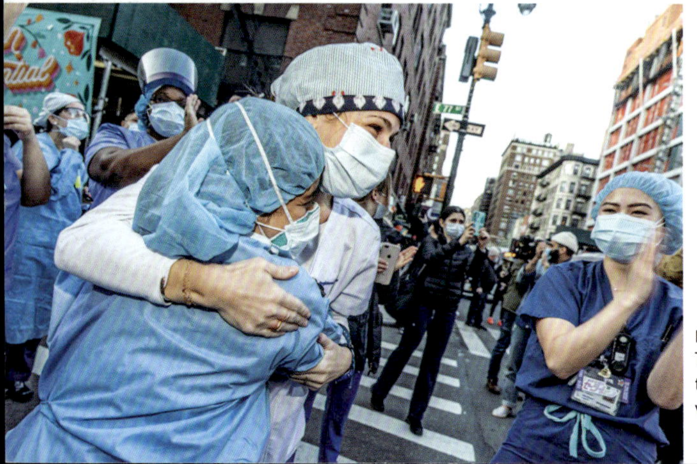

MARSHA LEBEDEV BERNSTEIN, *Essential Hug |* Two Lenox Hill healthcare workers hug during the citywide 7 PM clapping to honor essential workers. NEW YORK, NY, USA

MORFI JIMÉNEZ MERCADO, The (un)Real #4. LIMA, PERU

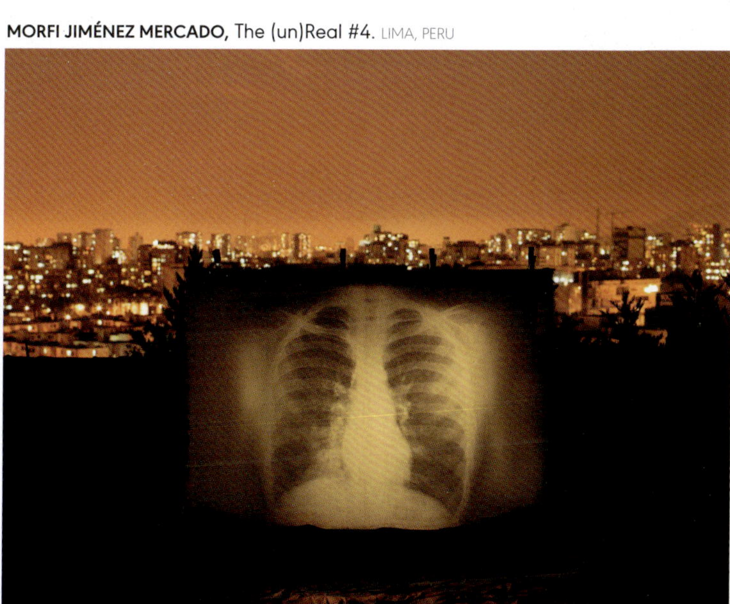

ANGELA DORAN, My happy place, also known as the place I go when I need to process. Water brings clarity. AUSTIN, TX, USA

SELINA SHIDA HACK, *Coffee with Caution |* Cafe on Ralph was open during the heat of the pandemic in Brooklyn, serving its community with freshly made coffee. NY, USA

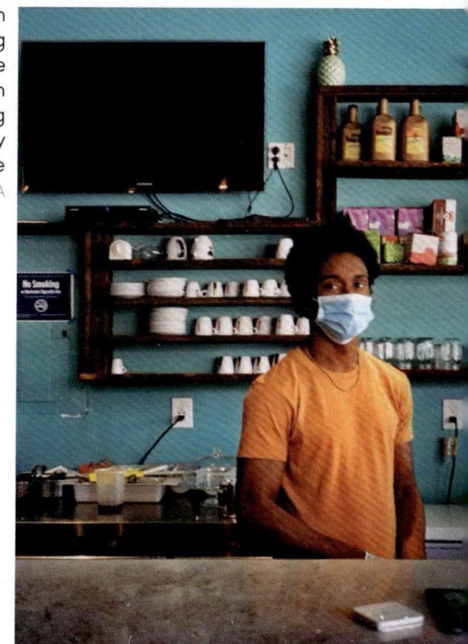

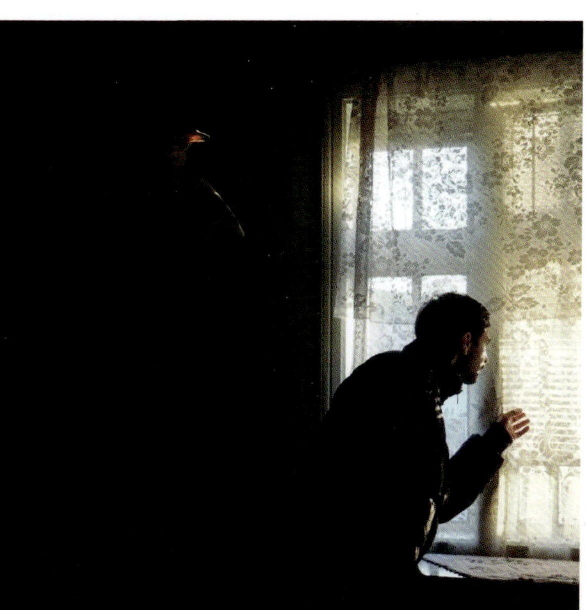

ALINA MOISE, Isolation in the countryside. Grandma's house. VALEA SEACĂ, ROMANIA

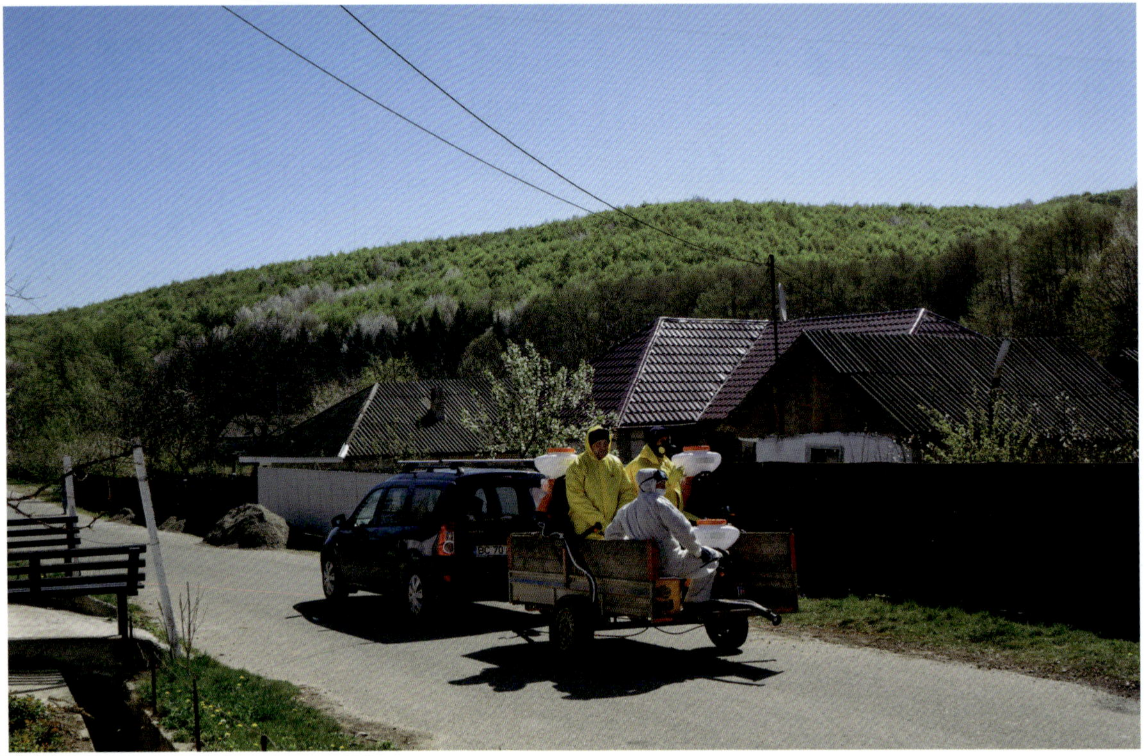

IUSTIN BĂISAN, The safety measures from big cities are applied also in rural areas. Three well-equipped people in a truck disinfect the main street of the village. One of them is sitting on a beer crate from a local beer. BACĂU, ROMANIA

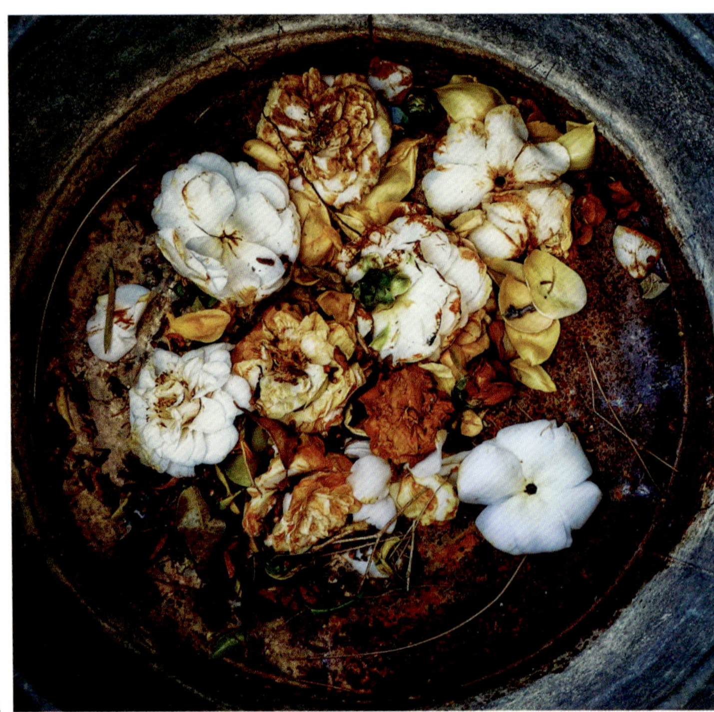

BETINA LA PLANTE, What Remains. LOS ANGELES, CA, USA

JAMES HOLE, *Muhala / Dubai, UAE |* Photographed through Zoom on an iPad in a makeshift lockdown home studio. UNITED KINGDOM

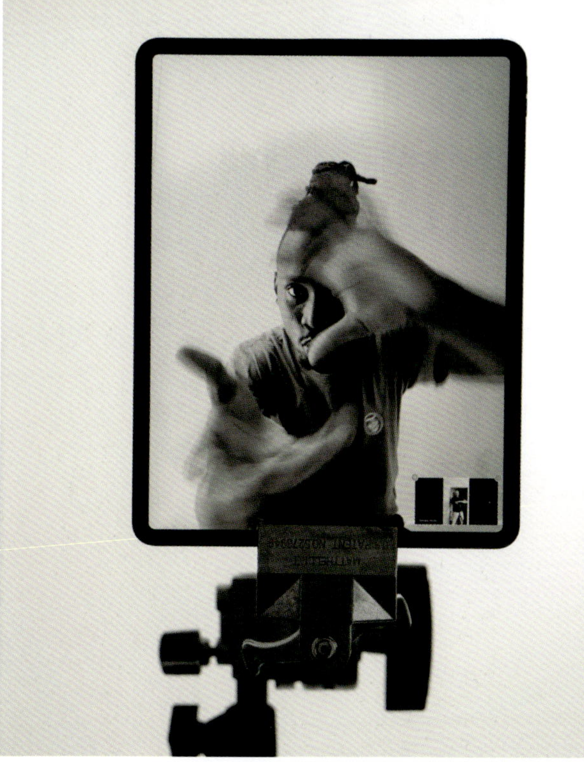

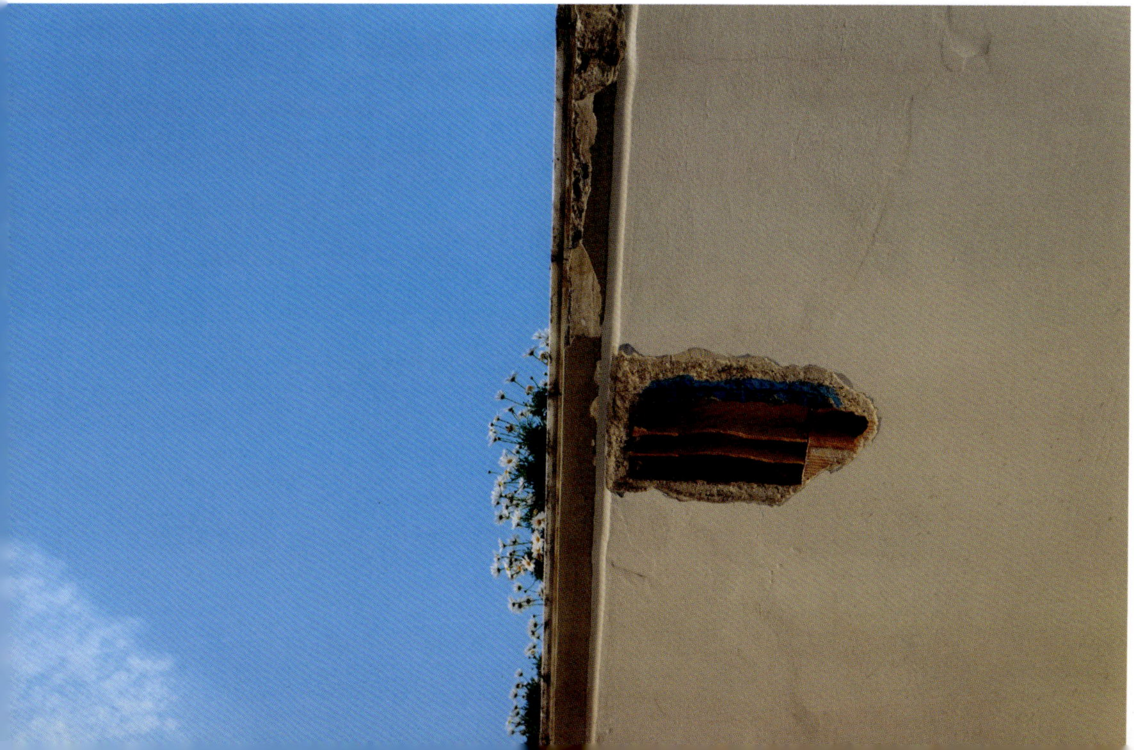

ANNA MARZIA SORIA, *HOPE |* Out on my balcony looking up at a wound, a pain that then still leads to life, to color. It is the vision of this tragic, dark period for the whole world with the hope of new light. BARI, PUGLIA, ITALY

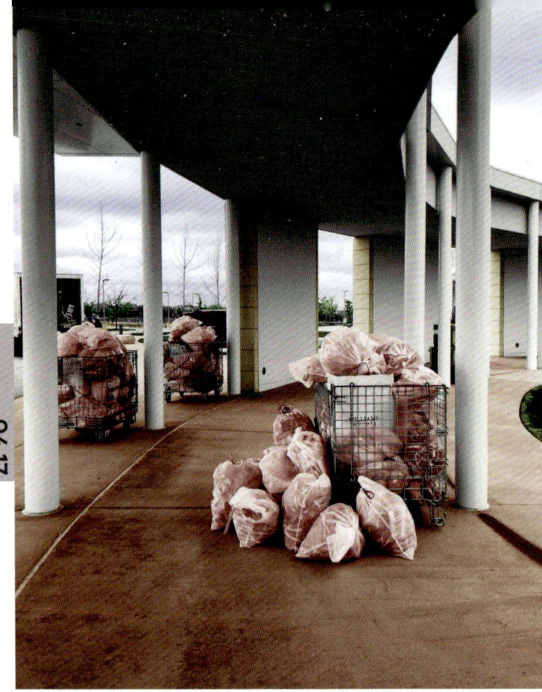

MADDIE MCBRATNEY, *Technicolor Wasteland* | A collaborative work with my mother. She works for Saint Luke's and has been organizing mask-making and collection of sanitary goods. USA

CHARITY RATTINER, *No More Rent* | On May 1st, to coincide with May Day, the #cancelrent movement called on states in the U.S. to freeze rent during the pandemic. BROOKLYN, NY, USA

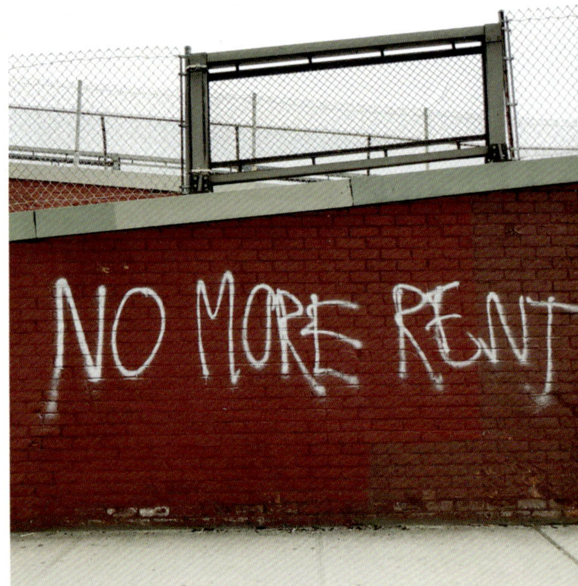

JENNIFER FORMICA, COVID-19 Discarded Glove with Spring Blossoms. LORIMER STREET, WILLIAMSBURG, BROOKLYN, NY, USA

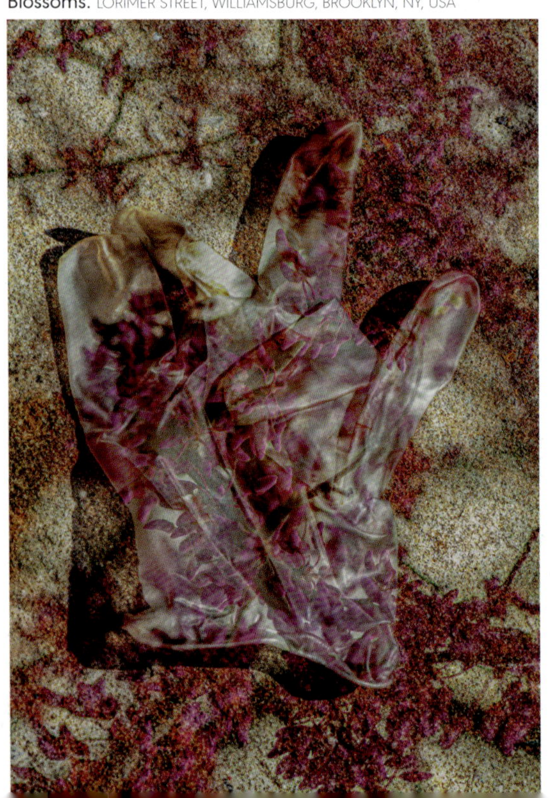

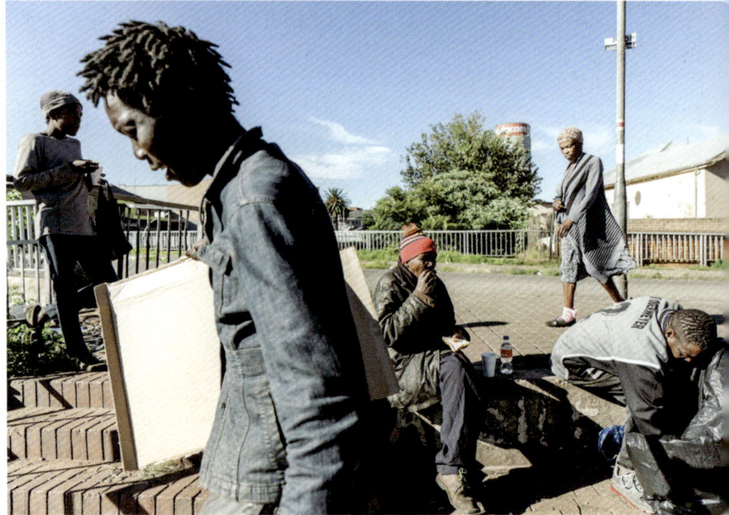

ILAN GODFREY, A hot cup of tea and a few slices of bread are the only provisions that could be shared by the local church this morning as the ongoing food crisis across South Africa continues. All provinces face unprecedented challenges in feeding an estimated 30 million people facing hunger during lockdown. BEREA, JOHANNESBURG, SOUTH AFRICA

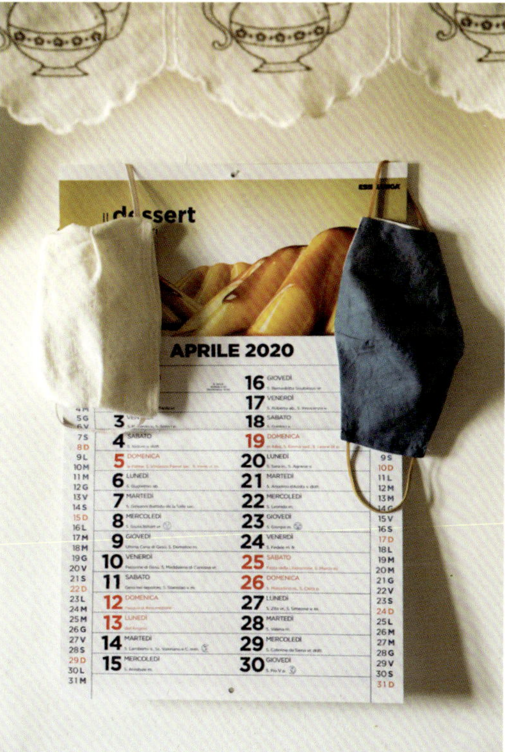

MEDISPROJECT PHOTOGRAPHY, Our 2020 calendar—a gift from our neighbors—and our homemade face masks. FLORENCE, ITALY

MAXIM SARYCHAU, *Carnations* | 16,387 dead / 418,169 sick. From the series "Where Have All the Flowers Gone?" VIENNA, AUSTRIA

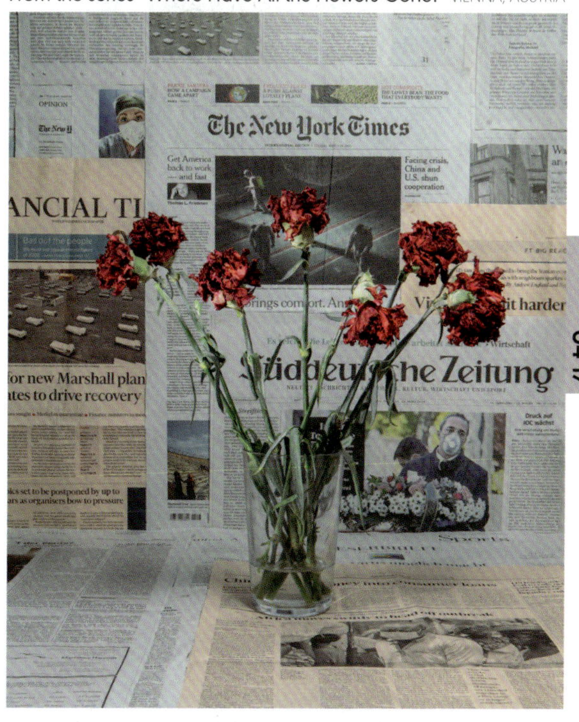

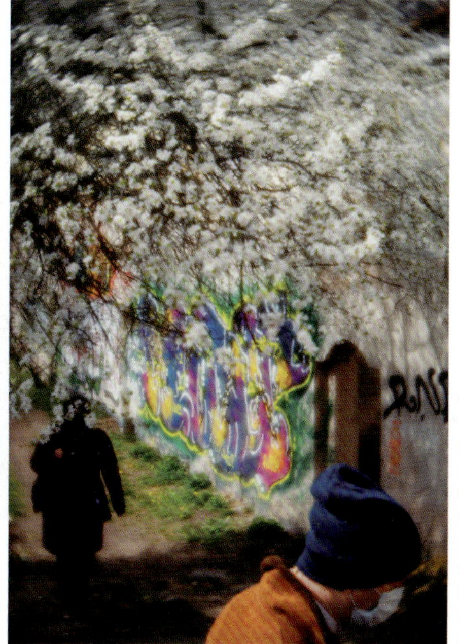

OLEG GANT, Vilnius was empty during the quarantine period. People tried not to leave the house. Tourists left the city. But sometimes residents left the house to walk along the river and breathe air. LITHUANIA

OMOTAYO TAJUDEEN, *No Visitors Allowed* | Photo of a man standing at his gate in Lagos. SOMOLU, LAGOS, NIGERIA

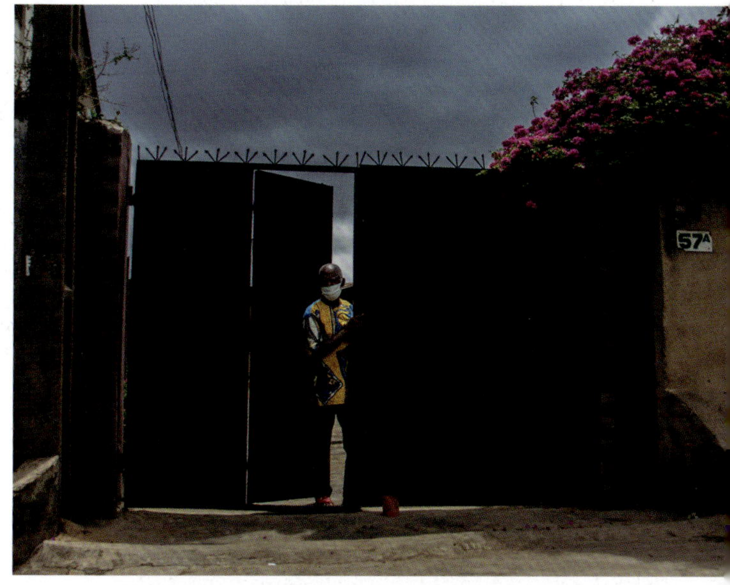

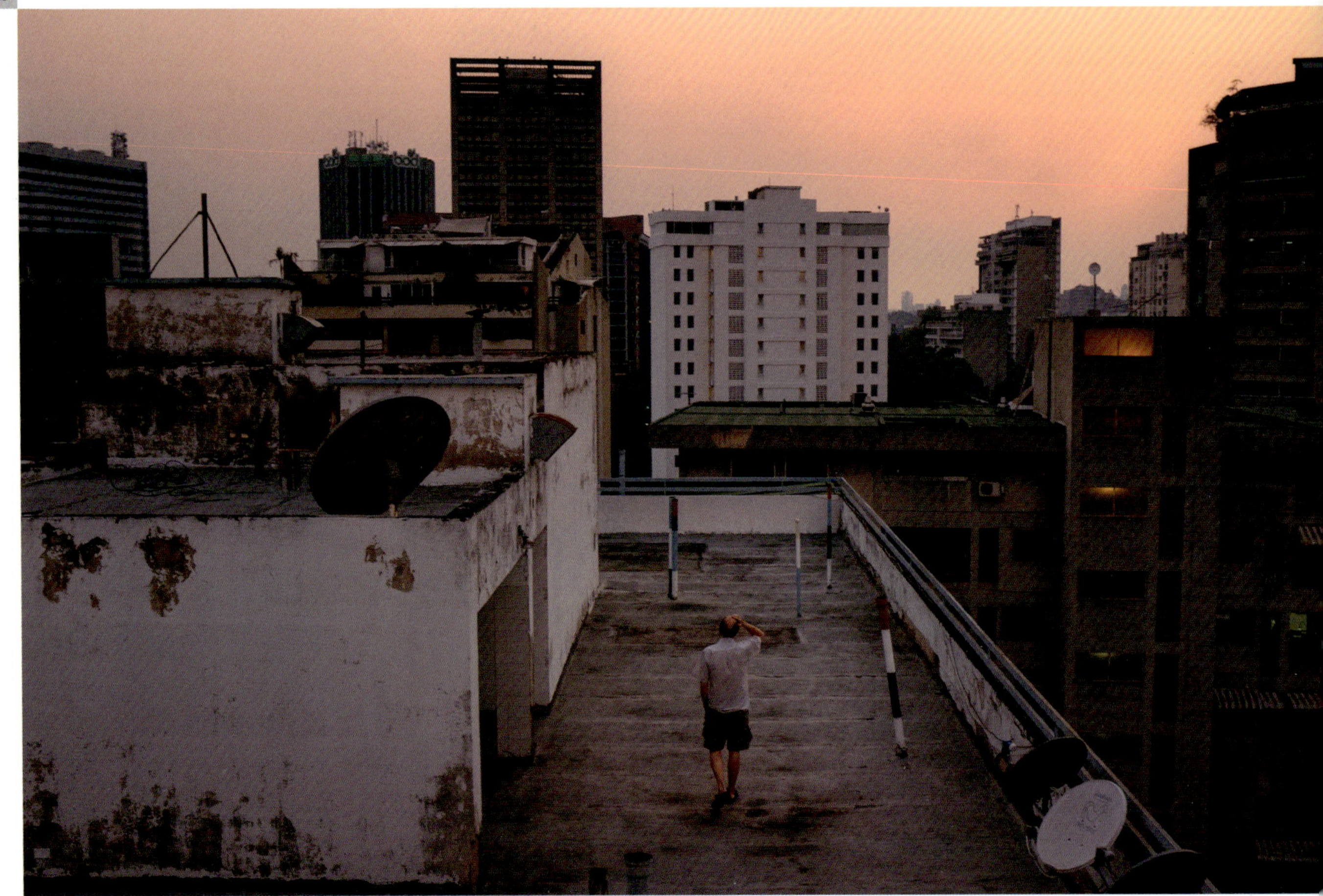

ANDREA HERNÁNDEZ BRICEÑO, A man scratches his head after exercising on his rooftop on a building in Caracas. VENEZUELA

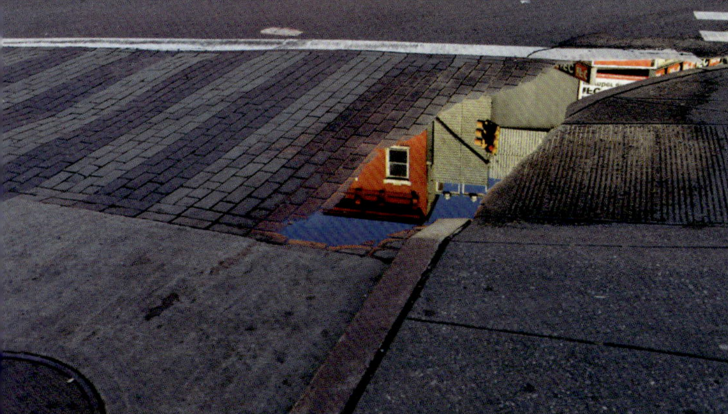

PAMELA BERKOVIC, *Heart* | New York in Coronavirus Time. NEW YORK, NY, USA

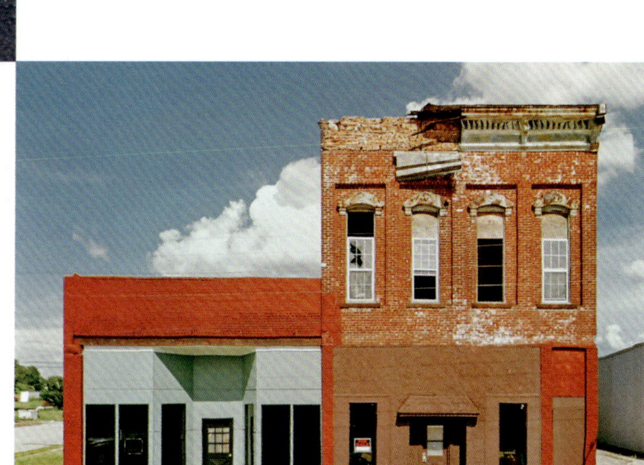

TIM MELIDEO, From "Road Trip in Quarantine" which features images captured with Google Earth Street View. GALENA, KS, USA

FLAVIA PIOLA, *Italy Stops for a While* | Maria is 82 years old, she is affected by the coronavirus. Nurses are the only people she has seen in a month. SAN FILIPPO NERI HOSPITAL, ROME, ITALY

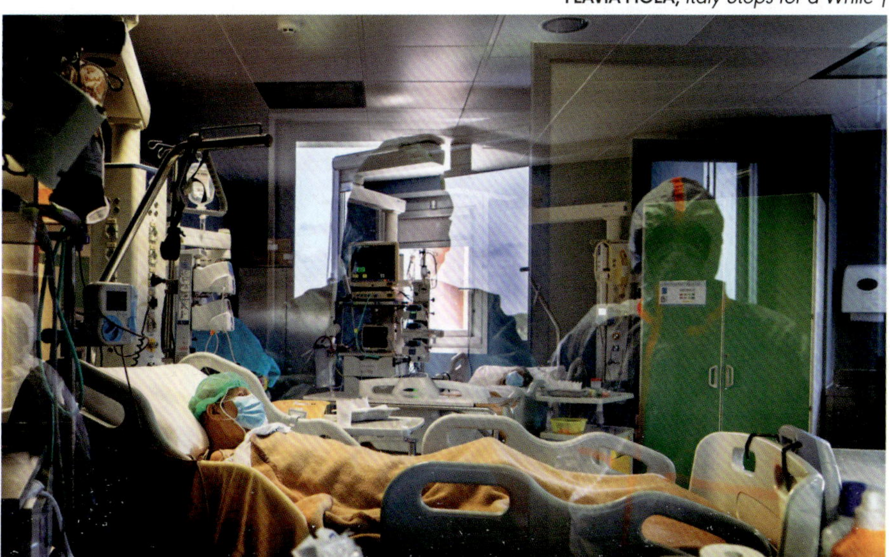

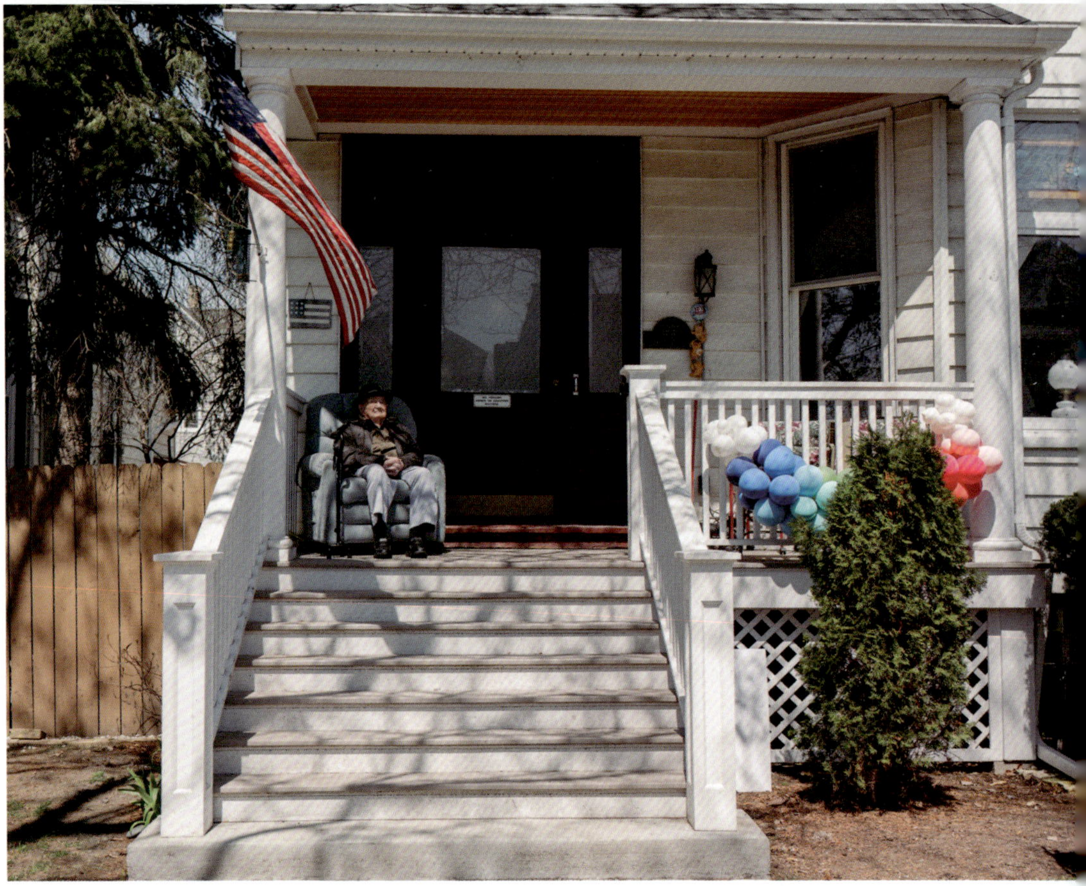

NATHAN BOBEY, Frank's 100th Birthday. CHICAGO, IL, USA

TYLER PEACOCK, *Ring Of Fire* |

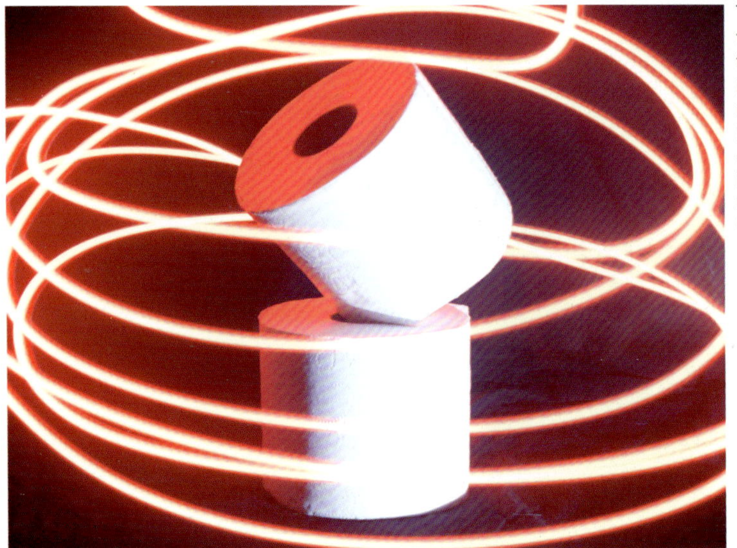

This photo was taken during the lockdown period in a makeshift studio I created out of black t-shirts in my kitchen. MAZARRÓN, MURCIA, SPAIN

LIAM LEE, Untitled. PROSPECT PARK, BROOKLYN, NY, USA

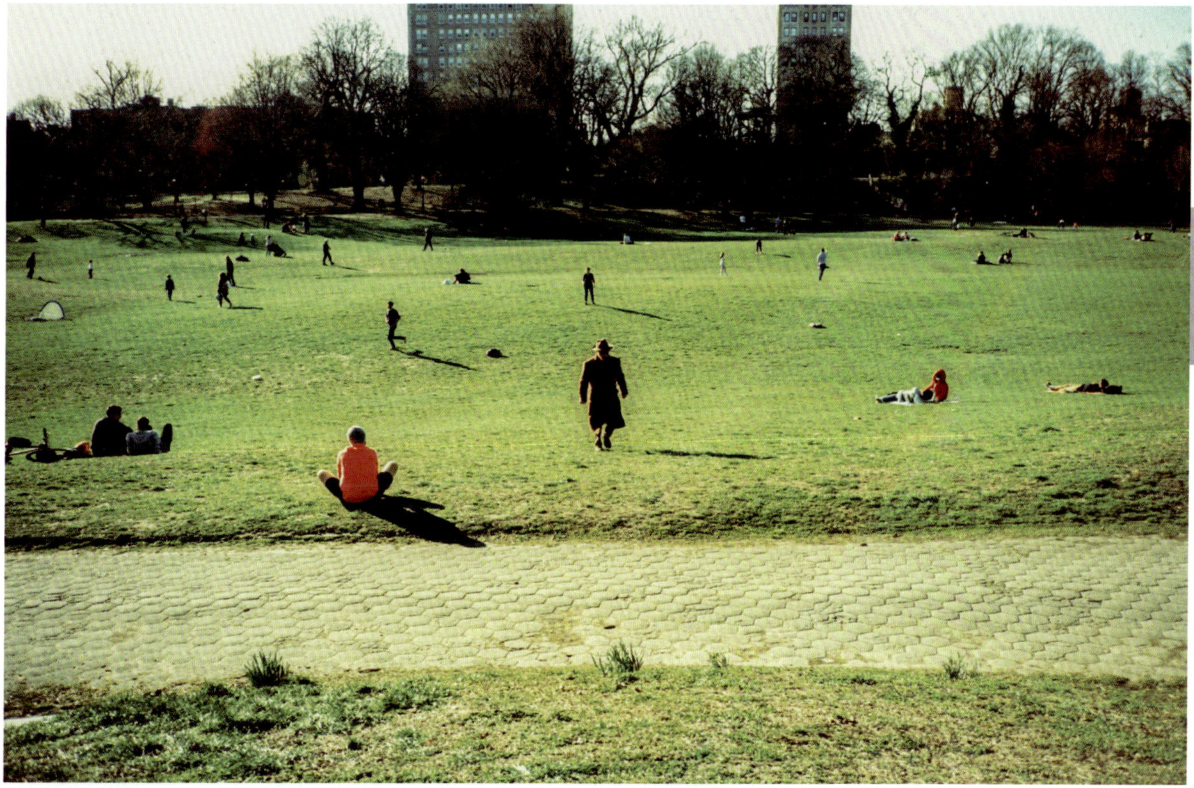

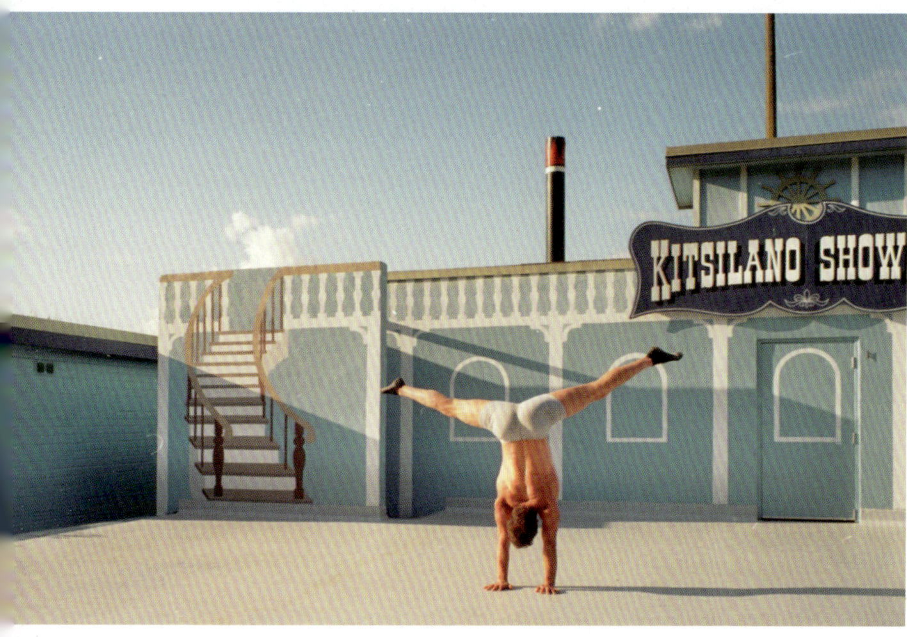

JASON CHENGCHEN GUAN,
A stunt performer practices on an empty stage in Kitsilano Beach. VANCOUVER, BC, CANADA

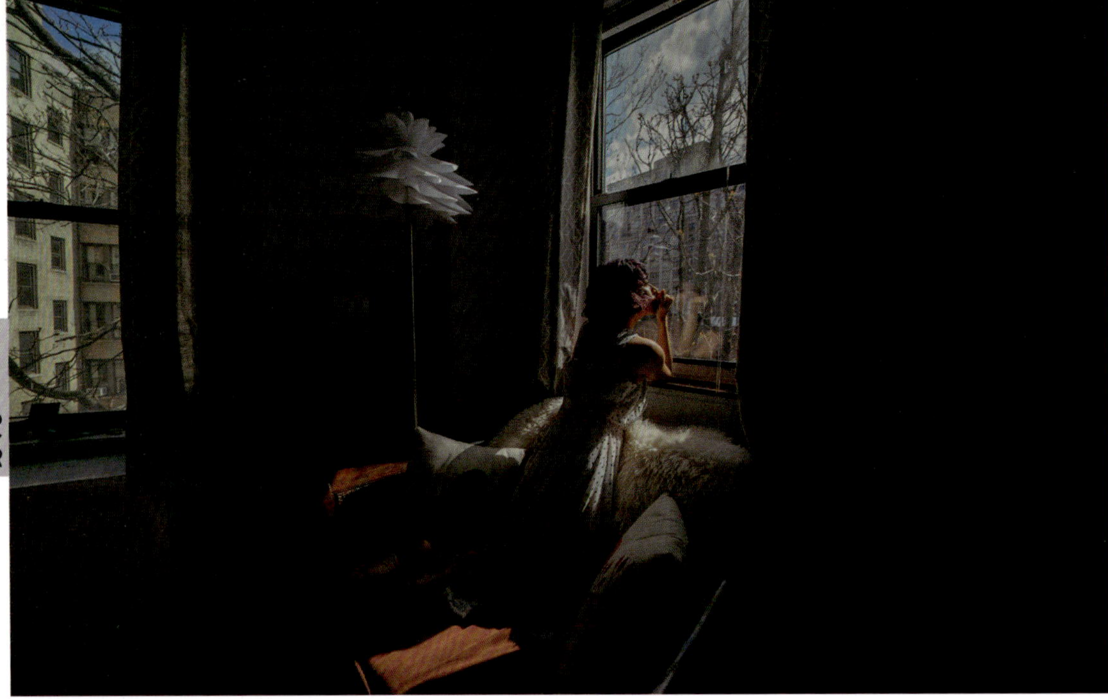

NALLIELI SANTAMARIA, Another day in quarantine. I am grateful for my windows and the beautiful sunshine.
UPPER WEST SIDE, MANHATTAN, NY, USA

MATTHEW DEVER, Touching Great-Grandma's Hands Through the Window. HOME, NORTH YORKSHIRE, ENGLAND, UNITED KINGDOM

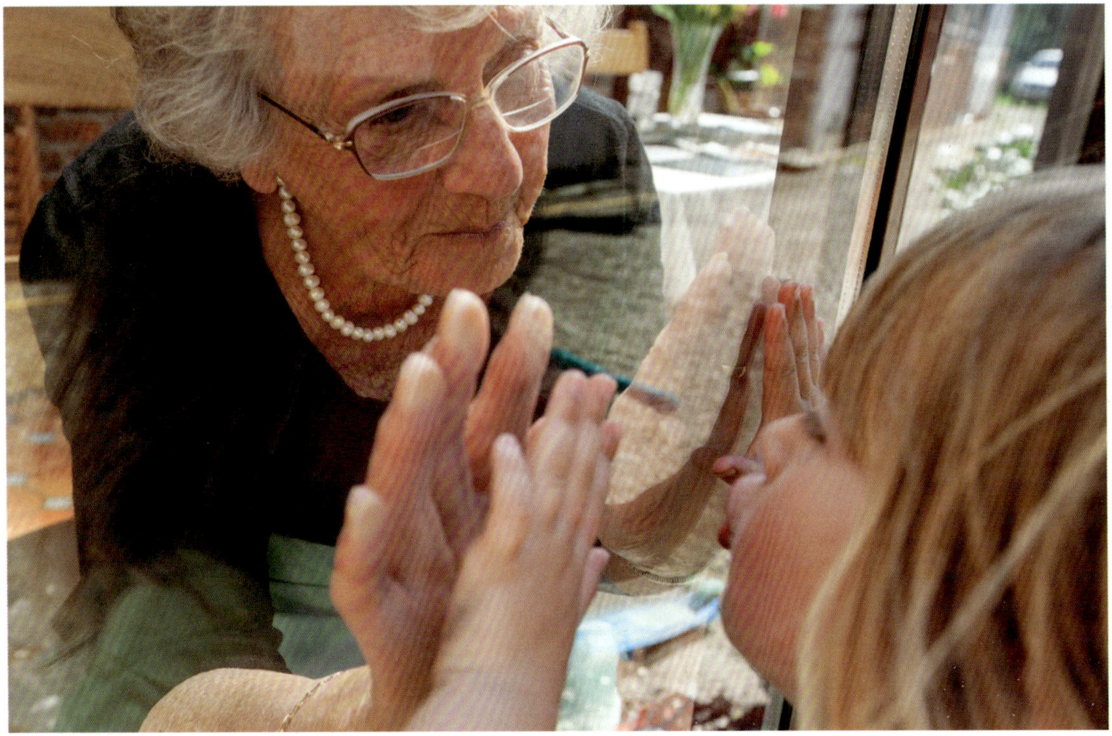

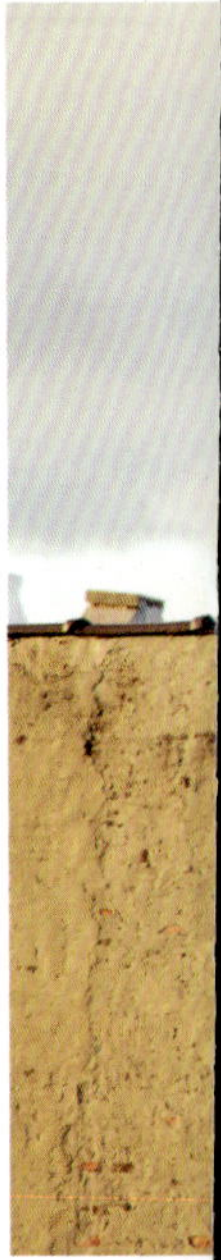

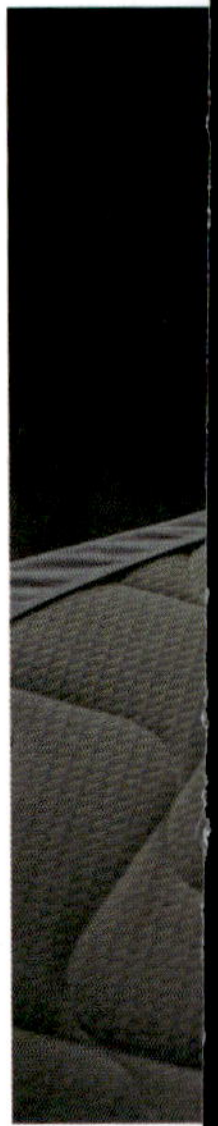

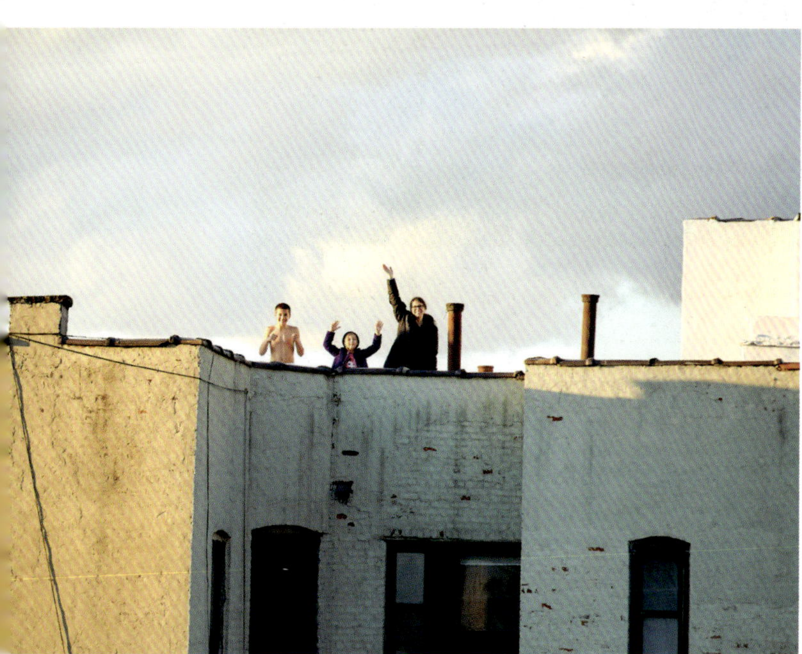

DAPHNE YOUREE, View from my roof with my Brooklyn friends doing the 7PM cheer for the frontline workers–we may not meet on the streets but we surely meet in the sky. NEW YORK, NY, USA

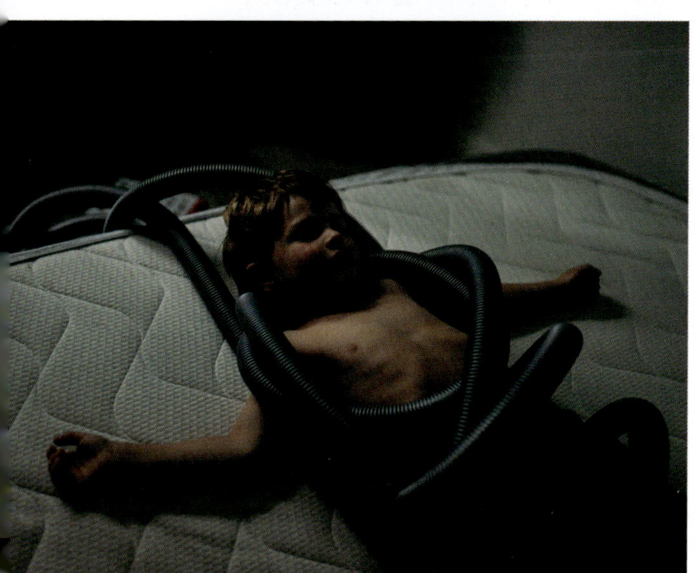

LEILA MACAIRE, Enyo during the cleaning. FRANCE

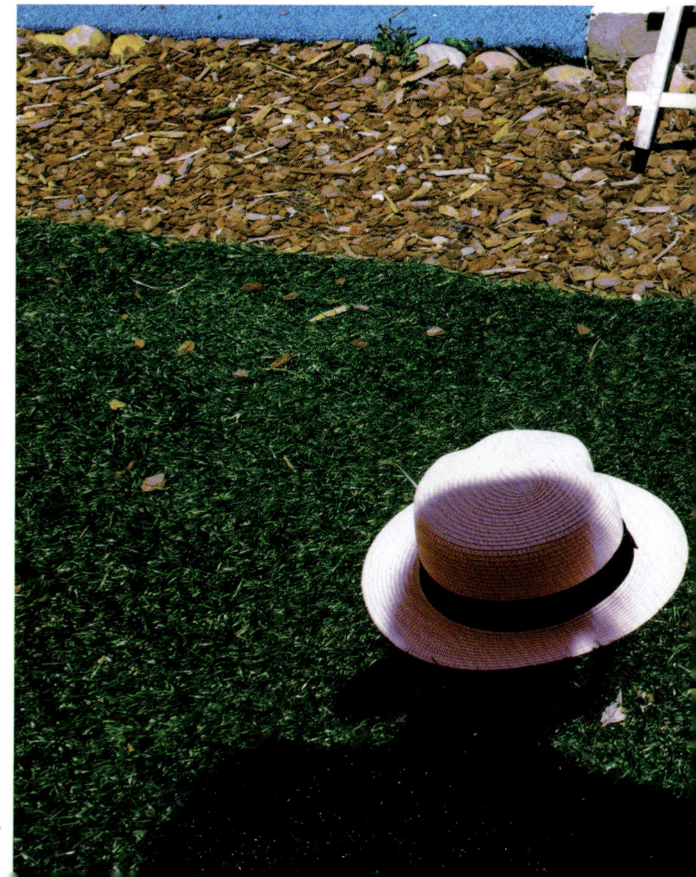

NASRAH OMAR, Quarantine self-portrait in the garden. QUEENS, NY, USA

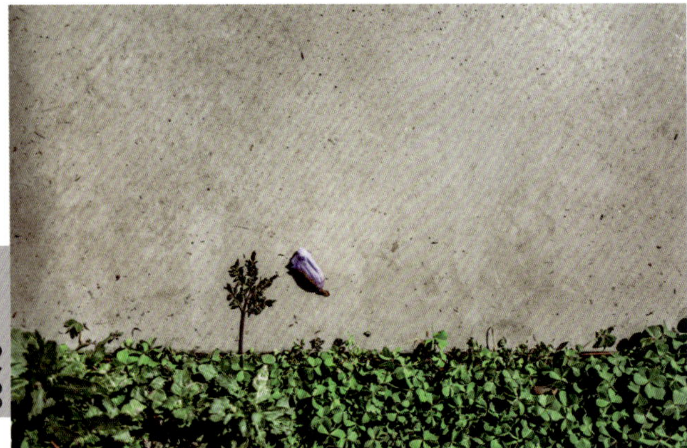

DIANA FEIL, *Day 38* | On this day Mother Nature demonstrated her incredible power to us Californians. Earthquake. Again. And I found the first bloom of our Jacaranda tree. Happy Earth Day! LOS ANGELES, CA, USA

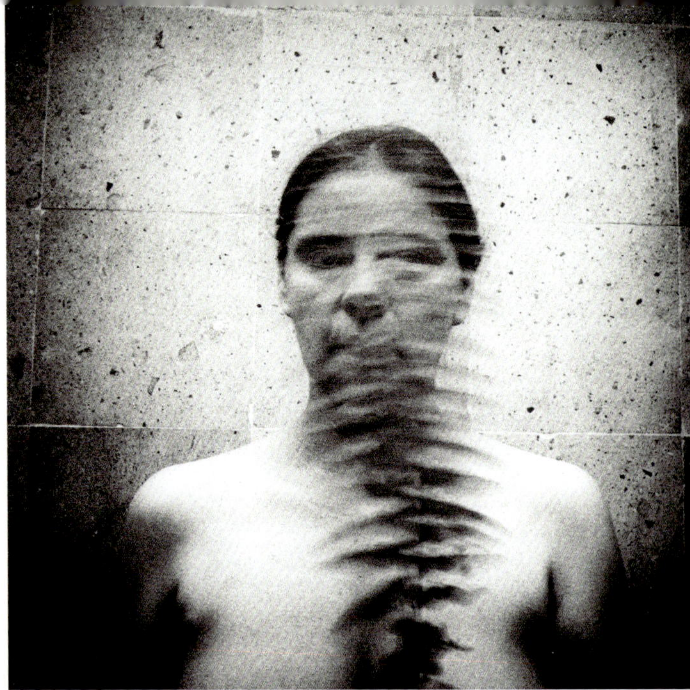

LILIÁN GUERRERO, *Madness* | From the series "Diary of an emotional state." 40 days of social distancing. Isolation feels surreal and it begins to hurt. QUERETARO CITY, MEXICO

SIJIA MA,

I wanted to make the experience of wearing a mask, physically permanent for a series of performances on both the Smith College campus and in China. As the pandemic weakened in my home country, I was eager to take off the airtight mask, revealing the wound on my skin. I painted the brownish color on my face and contoured my face with a brush until the muddy paint softly covers half of my face. My appearance looks strange, disgusting and familiar. Sitting under the hospital bus station, I was aware of the whispering, the staring and pointing as people pass by. Some look at me with curiosity. Some ignored me. Perhaps they thought I was merely another diseased hospital patient among thousands. I was anxious, of course. The awkwardness and ugliness I received with my seared face exposed me to a vulnerable position. I didn't know if I should feel fear or joy. Four...Three...Two...One. As the shutter closed, all my struggles quietly reconciled to this image. JIAXING, CHINA

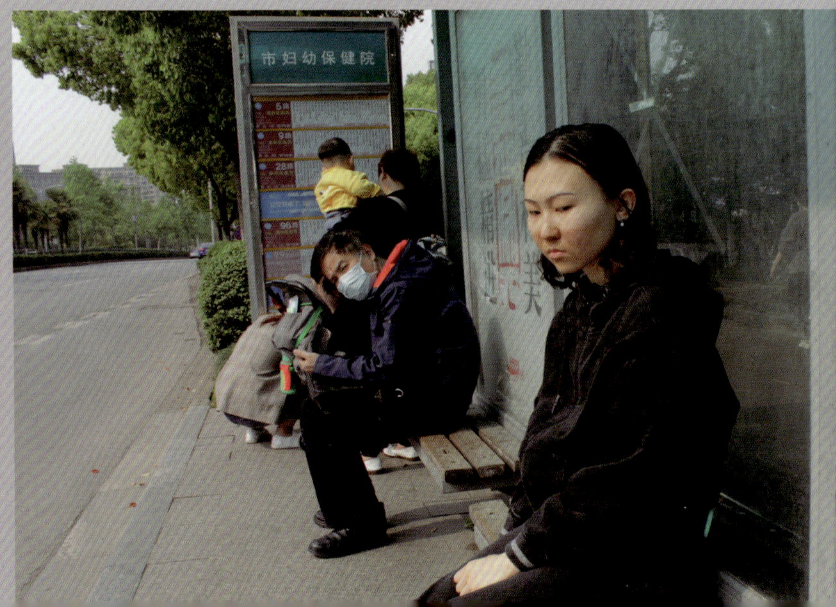

KATALIN SZÁRAZ, *Phases* | Going through several emotional phases during the lockdown, I turned my room into a camera obscura to project the outside world inside my bedroom. PARIS, FRANCE

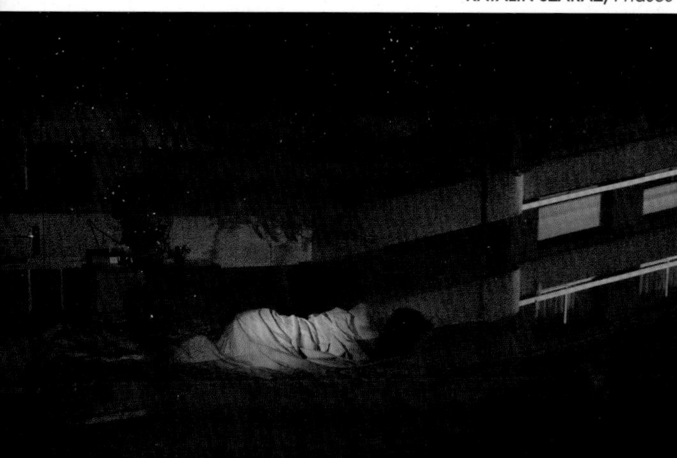

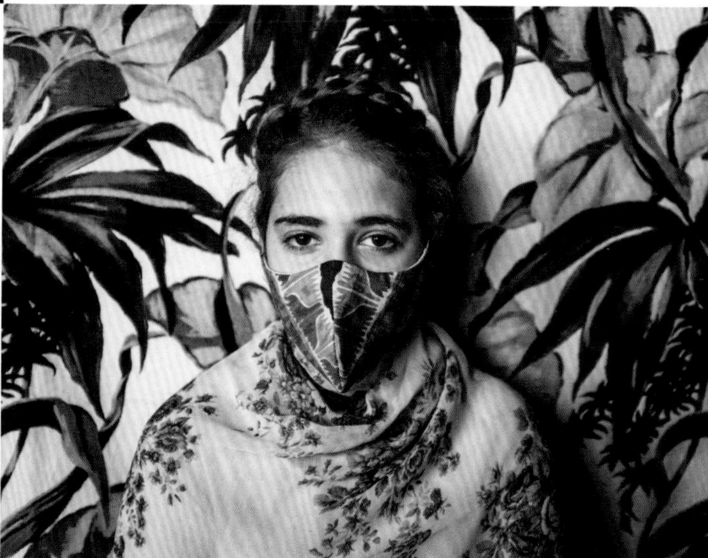

DOMINIK ŻYŁOWSKI, *Spring at home* | Portrait of my daughter Zosia during the lockdown. ELBLĄG, POLAND

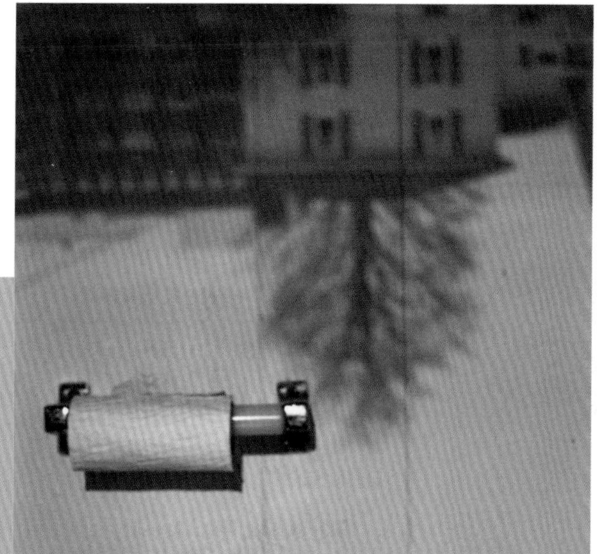

LAURA PANAGIS, *Discontinuance* | Conceptualizes camera obscura and emotions highlighting how the world is inside out and upside down. USA

WALID MOHANNA, *Untitled* | A portrait of An Duplan during lockdown. Image taken while we were social distancing together in my apartment in Ridgewood. QUEENS, NY, USA

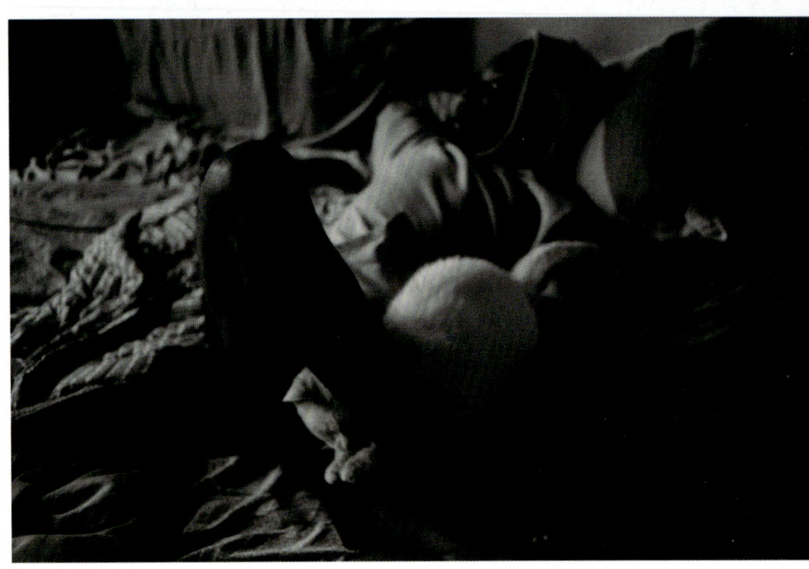

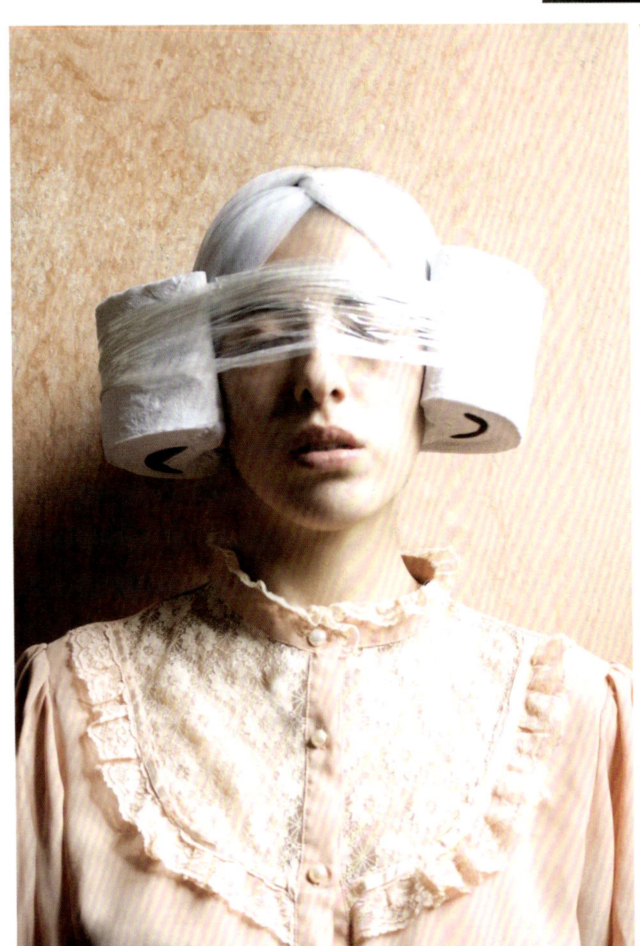

VERÓNICA LOMBEIDA, Who believes about herself what is insensitive? Characters in quarantine because of coronavirus. Self-portrait. QUITO, ECUADOR

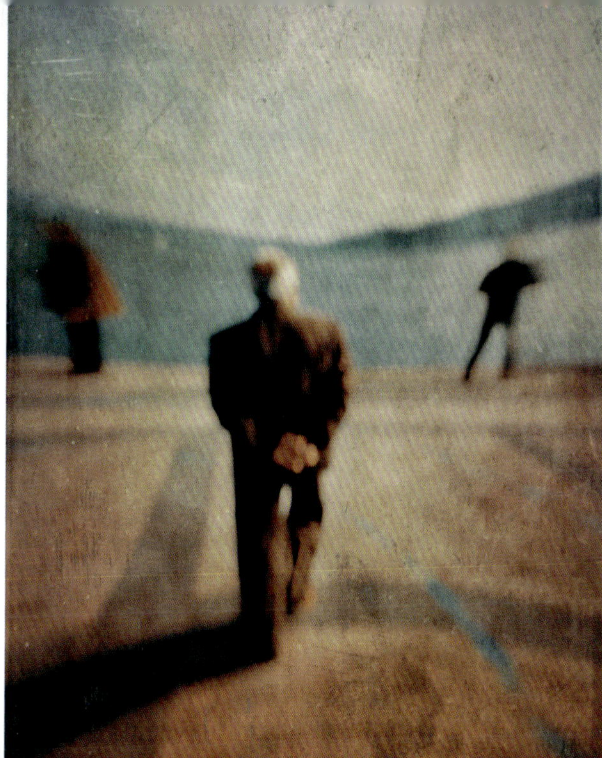

YALIM VURAL, Shot and edited on iPhone. ÇANAKKALE, TURKEY

JOSEPH GLASGOW, Home schooling sucks. I keep this cover of the New York Times magazine section around to remind me that things could be worse. VANCOUVER, WA, USA

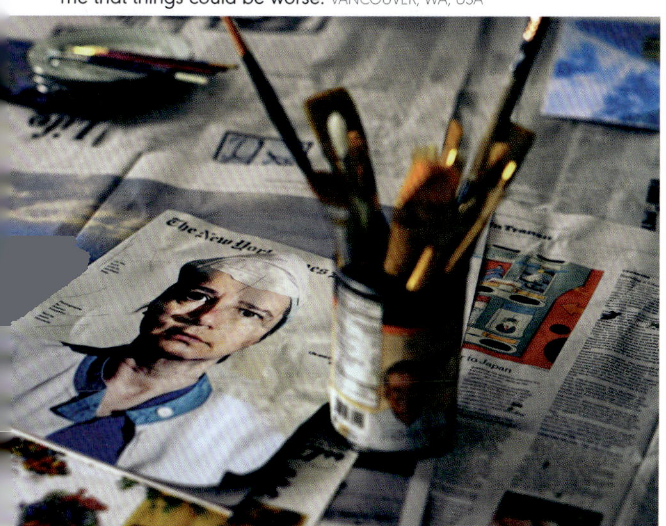

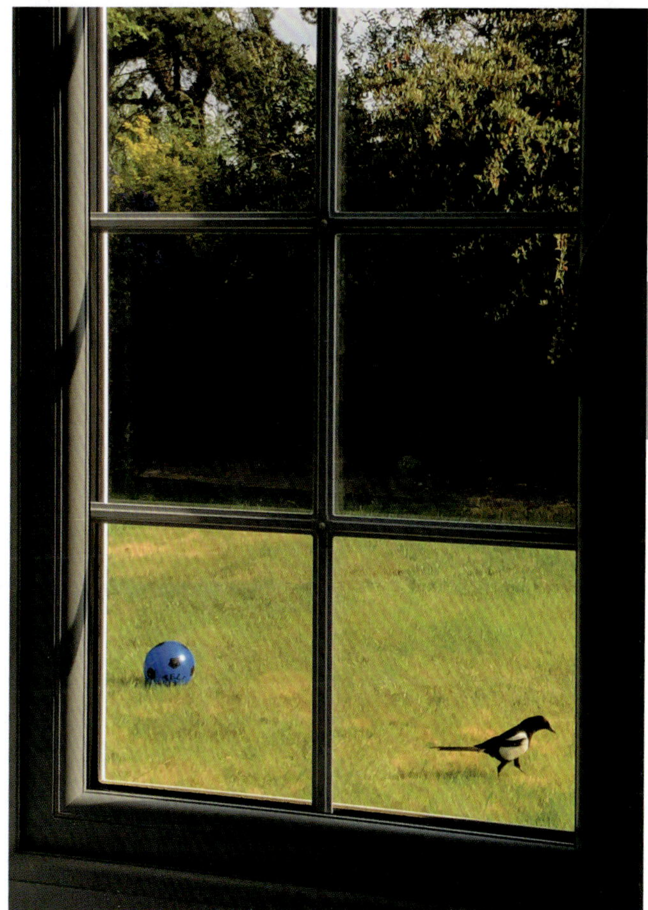

KAGAN BASTIMAR, *Offended* | While I cannot go out of my house, this bird kept visiting my backyard inviting me to play with it. ESSEX, UNITED KINGDOM

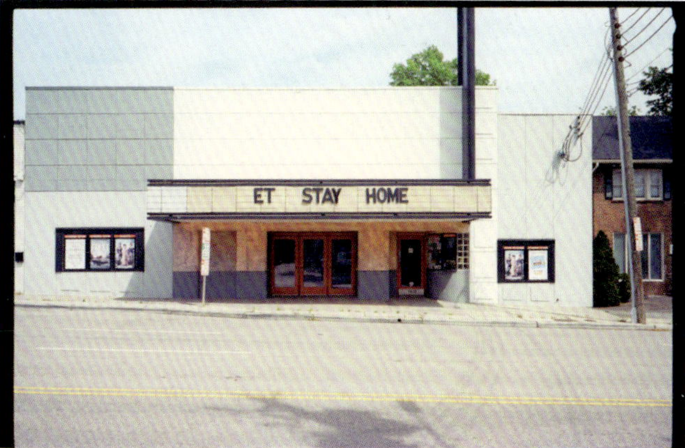

VANN POWELL, This marquee at the Rialto Theatre in Raleigh had been changing quips every few days. NC, USA

CECILIA REYNOSO, I wonder if our family gatherings will be something like this? This is an intervened photo from the "Flowers Family" series. BUENOS AIRES, ARGENTINA

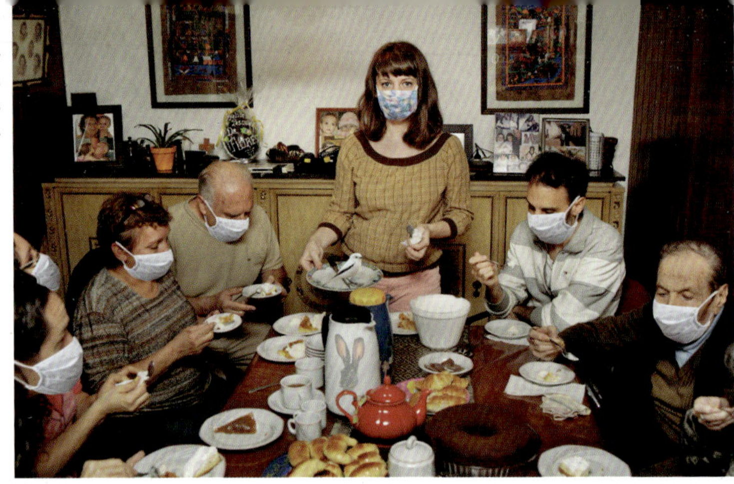

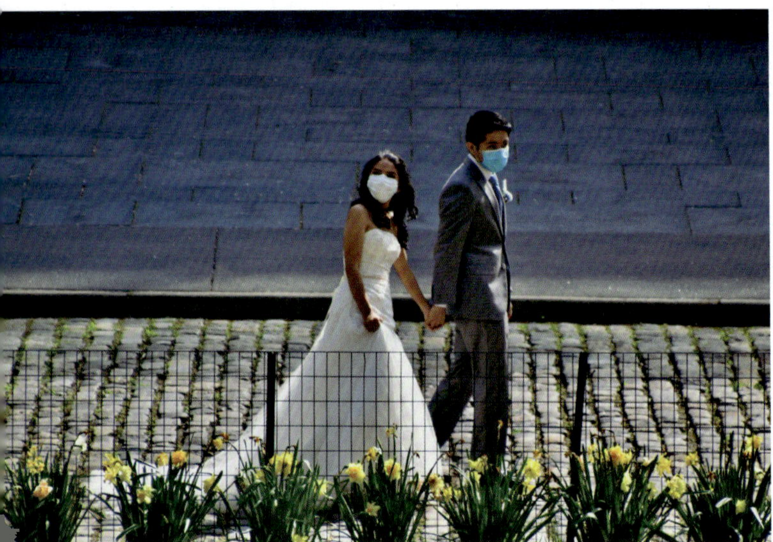

SLOANE SHELDON, *Corona Couple* | A bride and groom didn't let anything stop them from getting married. Taken on the Upper West Side of Manhattan. NEW YORK, NY, USA

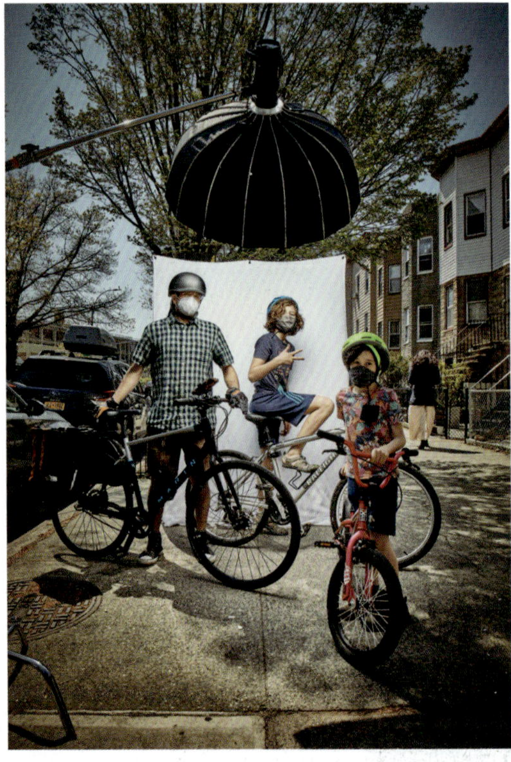

ASHTON WORTHINGTON, Julian, Ozkar, and Marco Buchanan. BROOKLYN, NY, USA

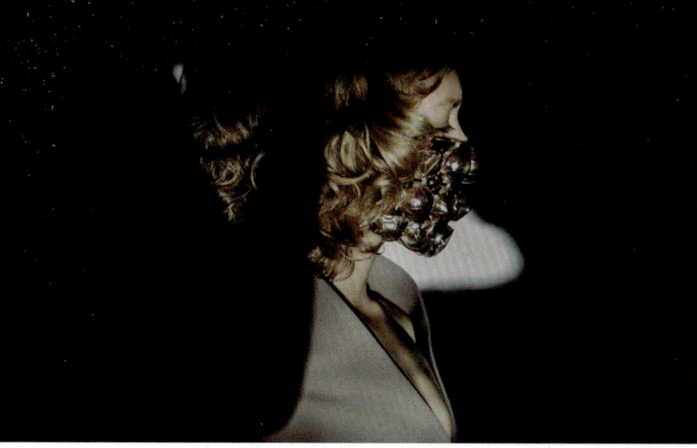

ANITA GRYZ, *The new normal?* | Muenster Nordrhein-Westfalen. Strange, bizarre, scary or exciting and challenging. We find an inspiring connection to the great fantasy films about distant galaxies and other worlds. GERMANY

JAIME CODY ROSMAN, We'll be Aight, NYC. NEW YORK, NY, USA

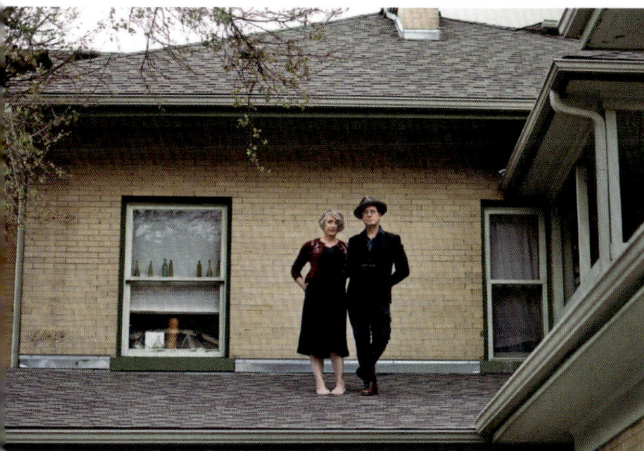

TINA HAGERLING, Social distancing, elevation style. DENVER, CO, USA

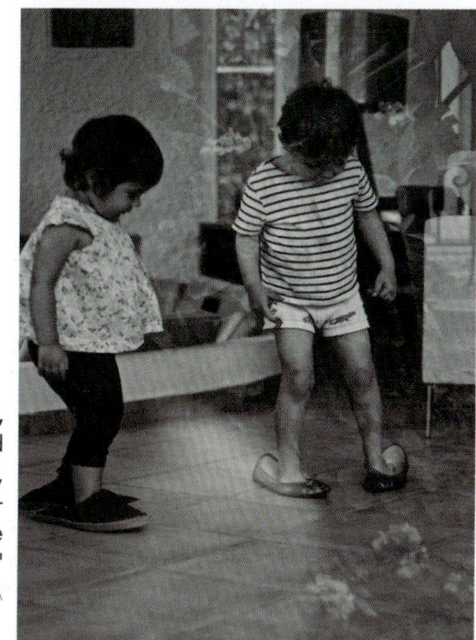

ADELINA COLUCCI, Salomé and big brother Gustave, on day 44 of self-isolation. From the series "Not Alone." TUNIS, TUNISIA

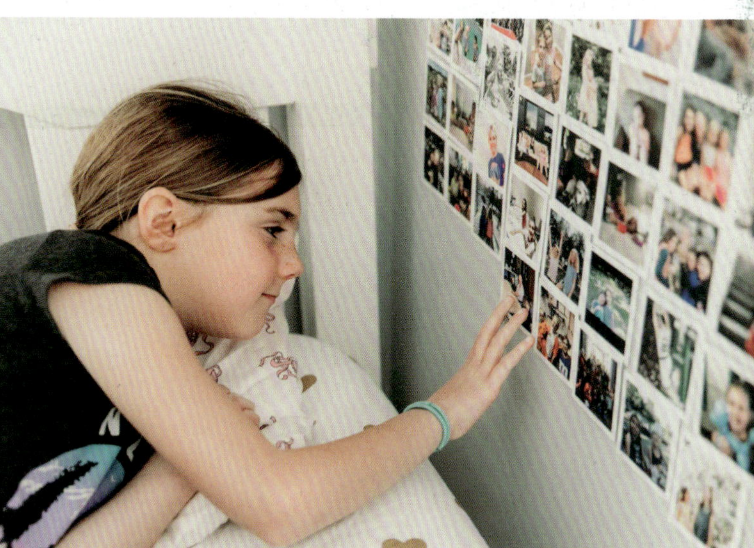

MEGHANN GREGORY, *Remembering* | Our daughters were desperately longing to see their friends and family. We created a photo wall dedicated to them. I caught my youngest daughter in a quiet moment after she hung the photos. BOSTON, MA, USA

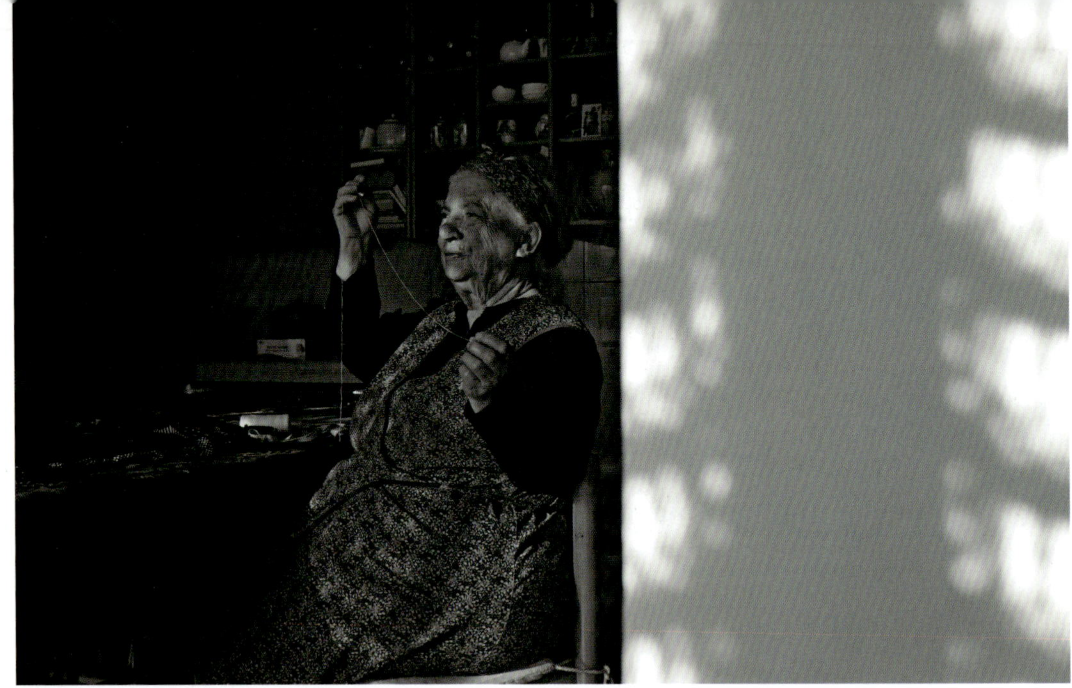

ANTONIO PELLICANO, *The Tailor* | Portrait of my mother. REGGIO CALABRIA, ITALY

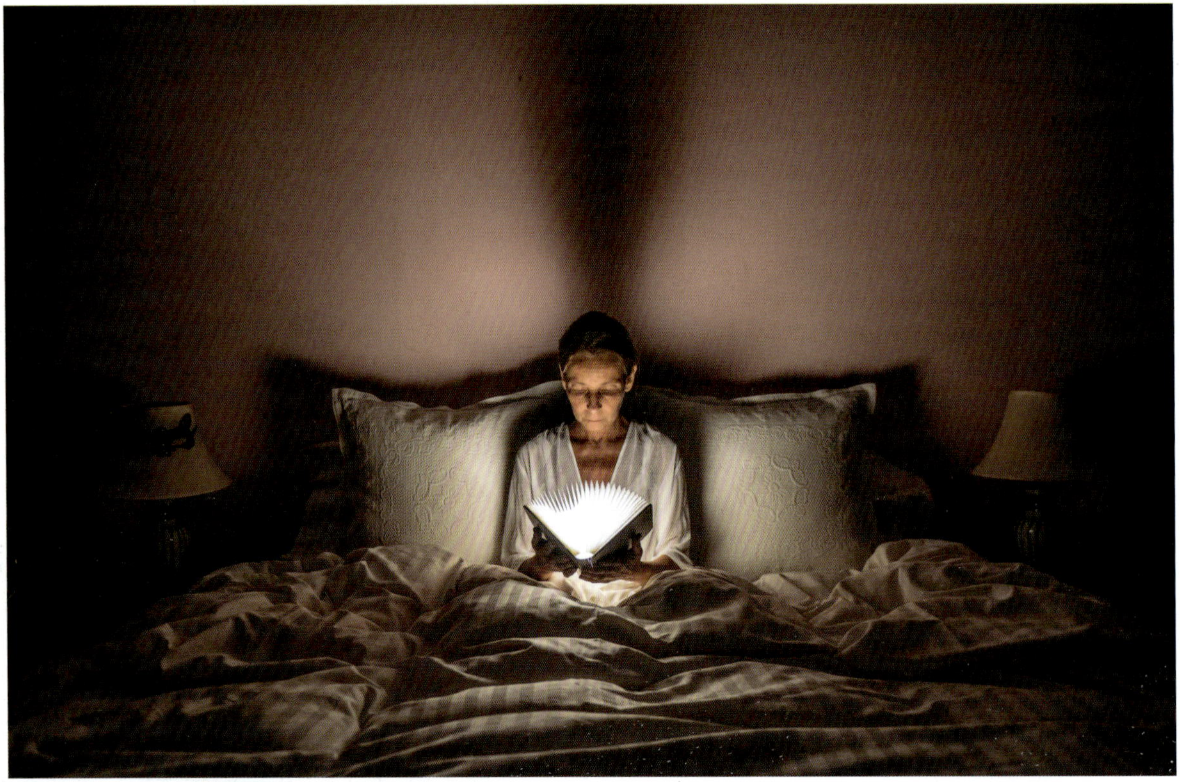

MARGARITA MAVROMICHALIS, Burning The Midnight Oil. LONDON, UNITED KINGDOM

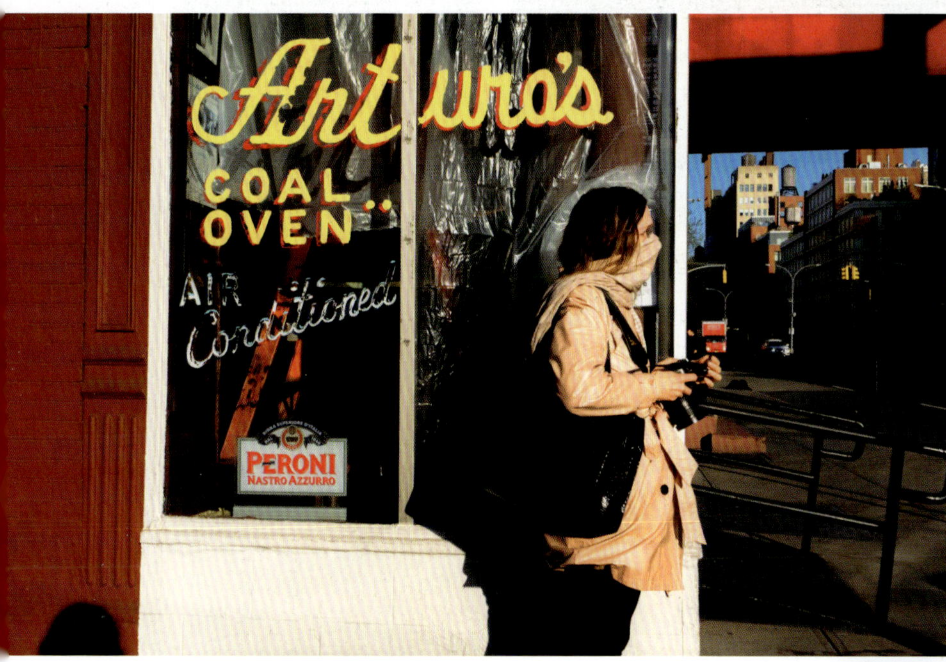

MICHELLE RICK, Outside Arturo's Pizzeria. GREENWICH VILLAGE, NEW YORK, NY, USA

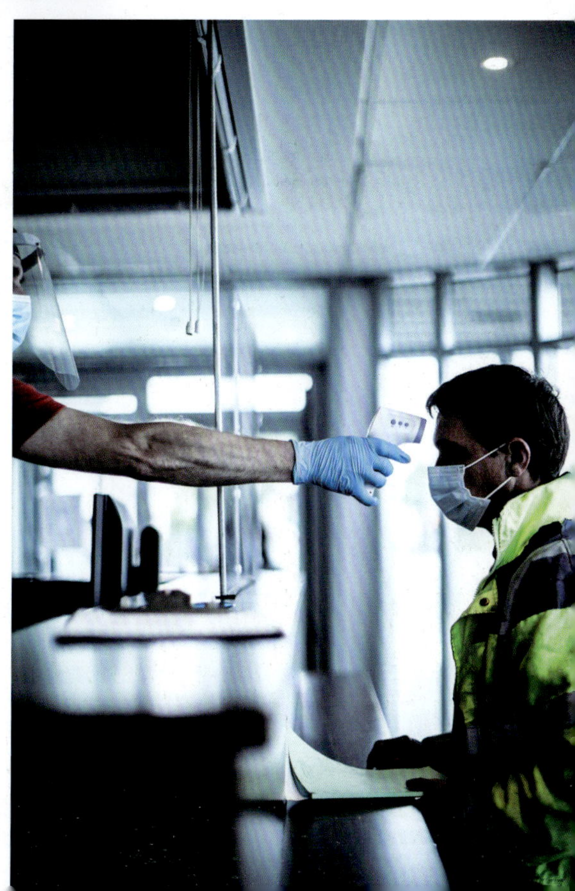

DENIS ALLARD, In the Oise, north of Paris, on the first day of the reopening of a factory after two months of confinement. BEAUVAIS, FRANCE

GHAYYAN AL AMINE, Several young South-east-Asian migrant workers hang out in a building entrance in Najada Street with the lights off to avoid the police. DOHA, QATAR

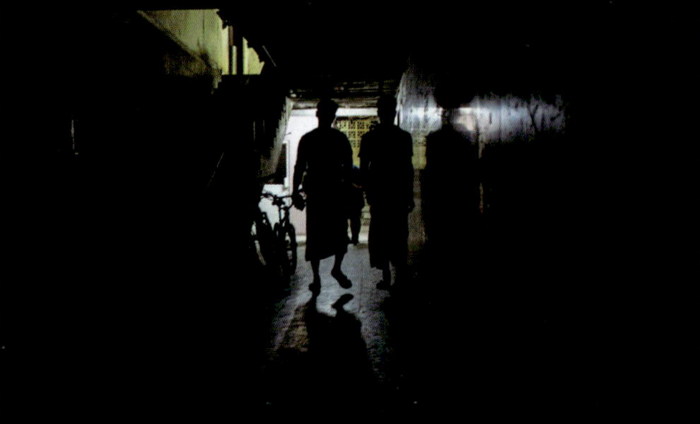

04 29

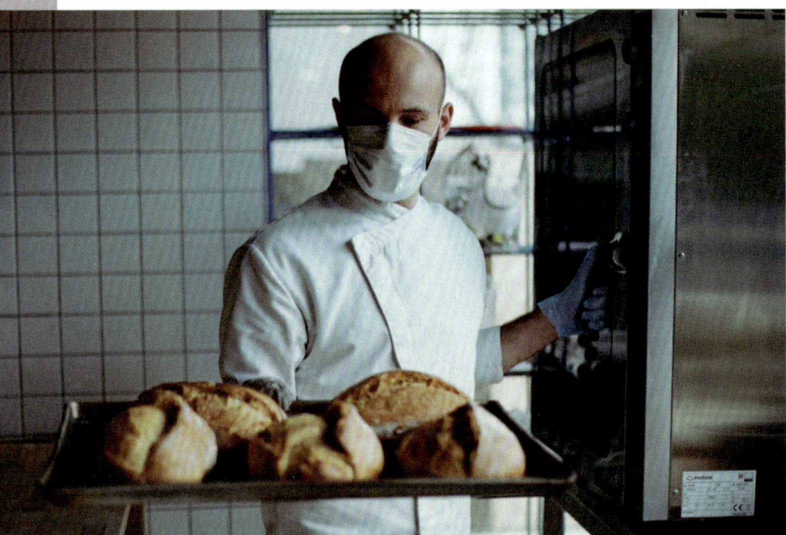

ZURAB CHACHANIDZE, Despite the current situation, the baker continues to work and provide for people's essential needs. TBILISI, GEORGIA

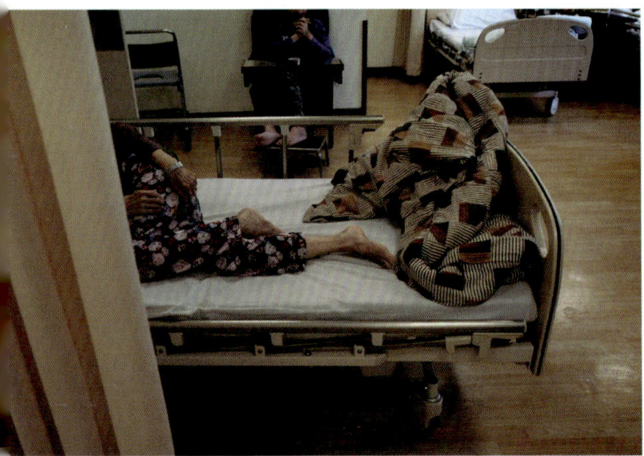

GONÇALO LOBO PINHEIRO, Nursing home life goes far beyond the pandemic in Santa Casa da Misericórdia of Macau, partial lockdown. CHINA

ALAN BEHR,

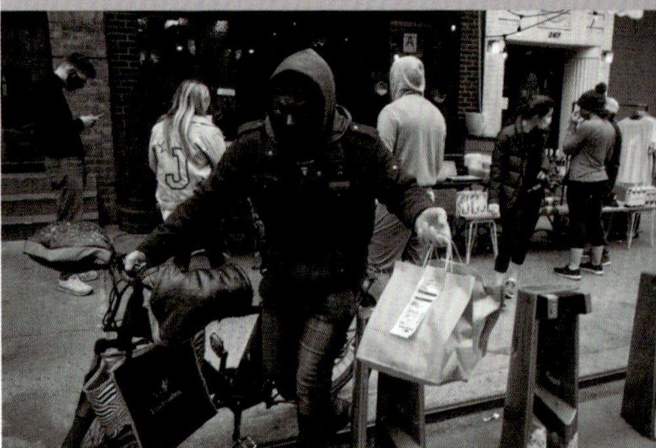

So many of my neighbors on the Upper East Side of Manhattan had fled. I felt left behind, expendable. But I'm a photographer, and when history is being made, photographers move toward the event. We're not first responders seeking to change the outcome, we chronicle the story in images, so that history will be revealed, truthfully. I moved through the neighborhood on foot, photographing a place known to me so well, but now become enigmatic. Neighbors hidden from contagion behind sullen doormen are passing each other furtively, hands pressing facemasks tight. About the only sustained movement was by bicycle delivery men, pizza boxes stacked over their rear wheels like bricks for a tomb built for no one. The man in this photograph has picked up food at a restaurant that doubled as an outdoor market, the last store open for blocks, vending snacks, clothes and citations to normalcy. I don't know if he was delivering what he collected or simply hungry, but he had to go, and I had the moment, sweet and anxious, to take his picture. For those unable to move, such as my mother and stepfather, confined to an elder care residence in Florida, there was nothing to do but hope. That ended for me in August when the virus entered the facility and took them both from me.
EAST 81ST STREET, NEW YORK, NY

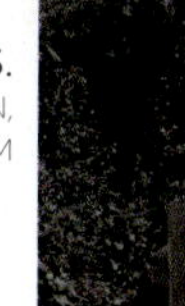

BEN MCCANN, NHS.
BALHAM, LONDON, UNITED KINGDOM

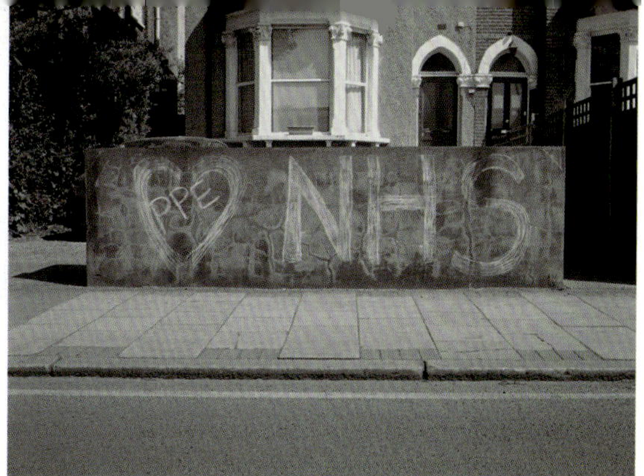

MANU TORRES, *Family Number 18* | Madrid.
My daughter Lara watching a video on the iPad. SPAIN

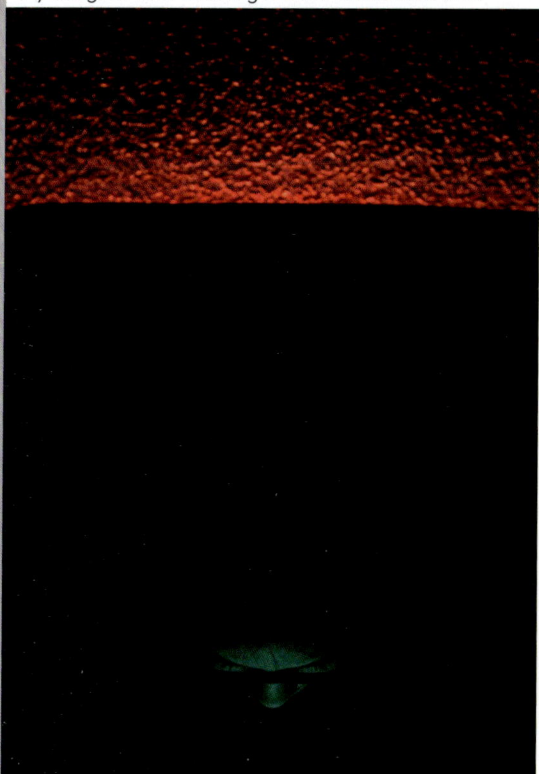

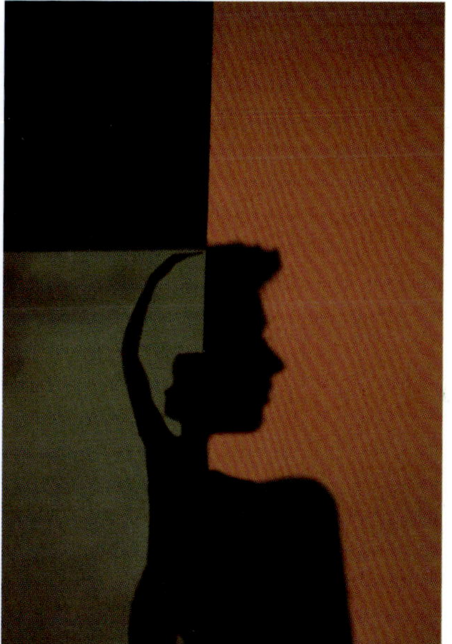

FEDERICA BELLI, Rediscovery of self.
MILLESIMO, LIGURIA, ITALY

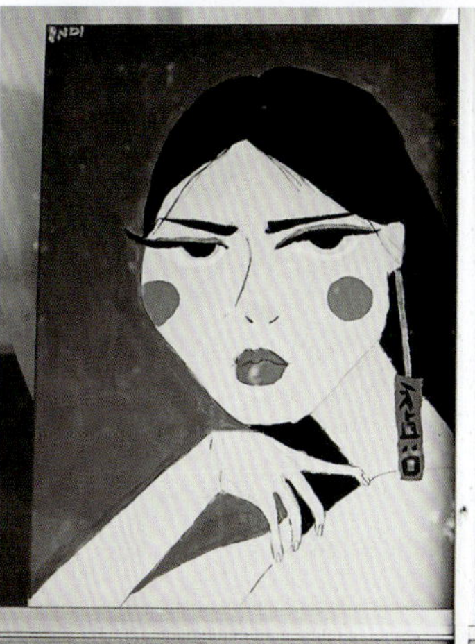

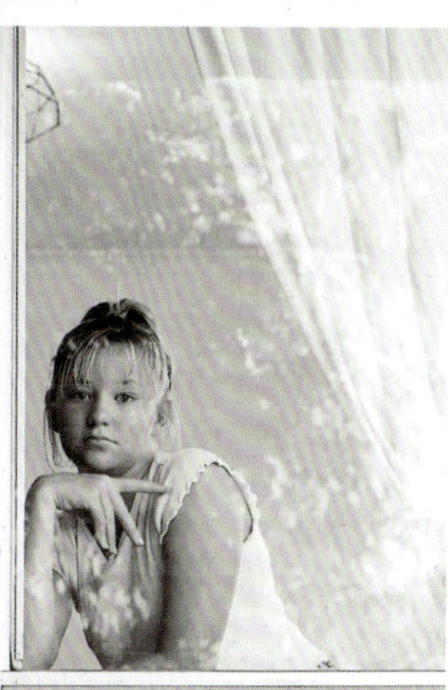

SHERI D'ROSARIO, *alter ego* |
From the series "In Captivity," exploring the experiences of young people in isolation during the pandemic. BYRON BAY, NEW SOUTH WALES, AUSTRALIA

JONAS JUNGBLUNT, *Apart/Together* | Portraits taken remotely via video chat. SANTA BARBARA AND GAVIOTA, CA, USA

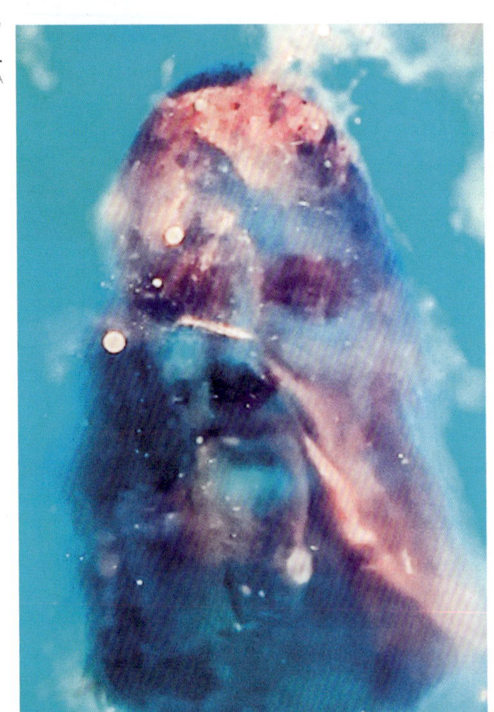

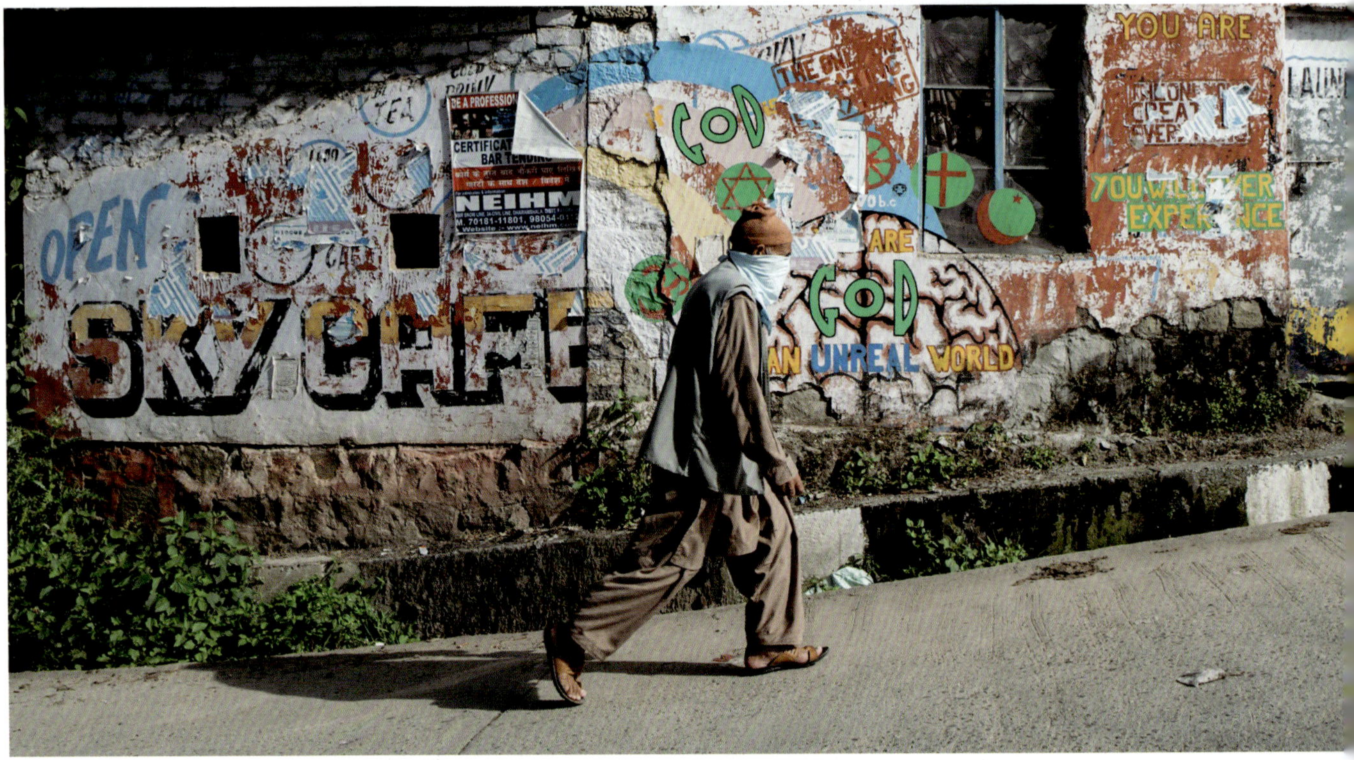

TENZIN DOLKER, An Unreal World. MCLOED GANJ, DHARAMSHALA, INDIA

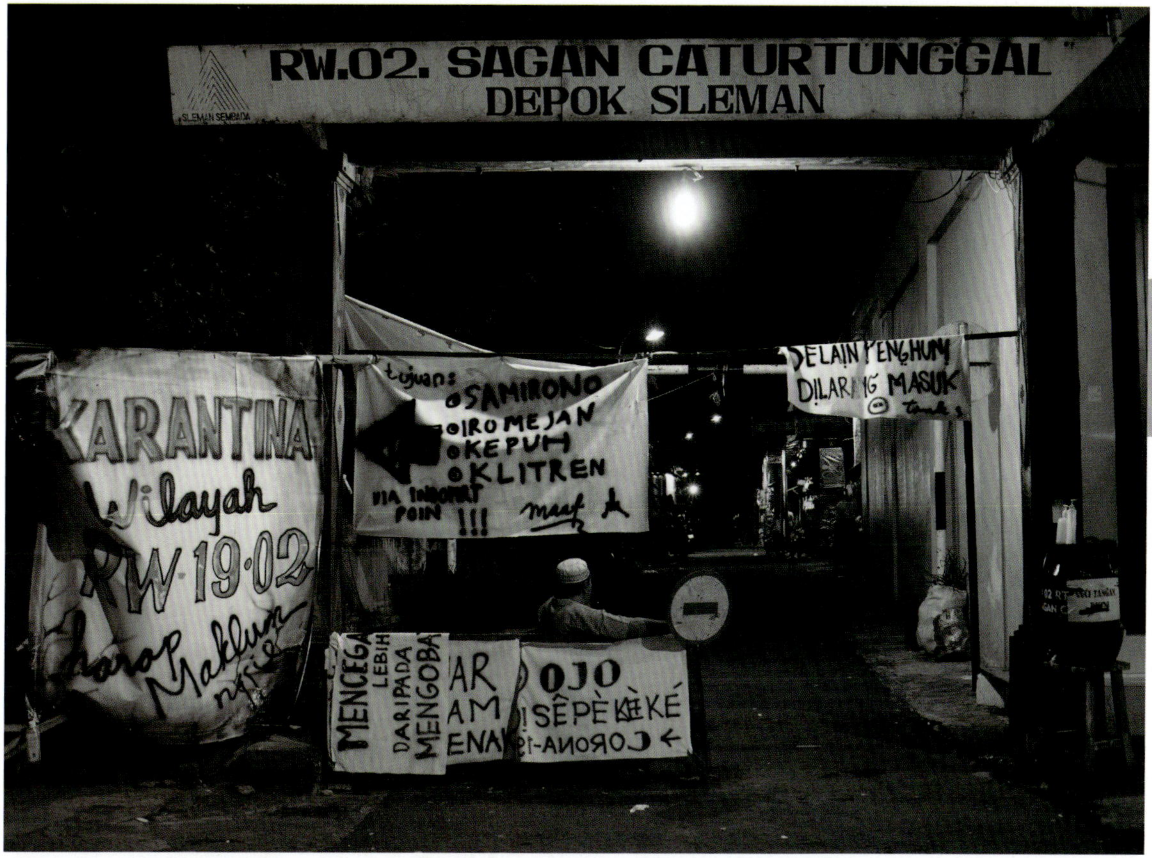

WIMO BAYANG, *Surat-surat Malam (Night Letters) series* | An entrance gate closed by the local community to self-quarantine their district in Yogyakarta to avoid the spread of COVID-19. JAVA, INDONESIA

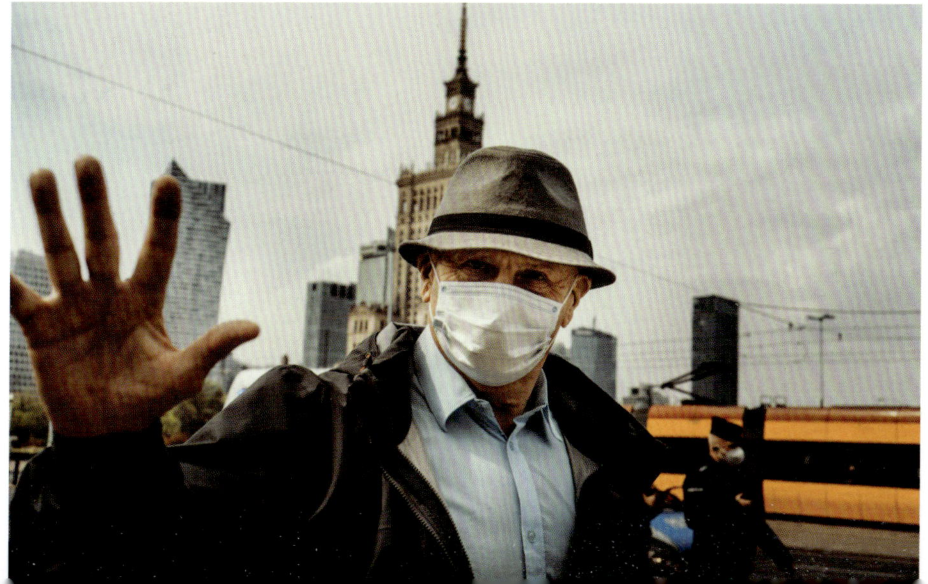

LUKASZ WASZAK, Elderly gentleman en route to an anti-government rally in central Warsaw. POLAND

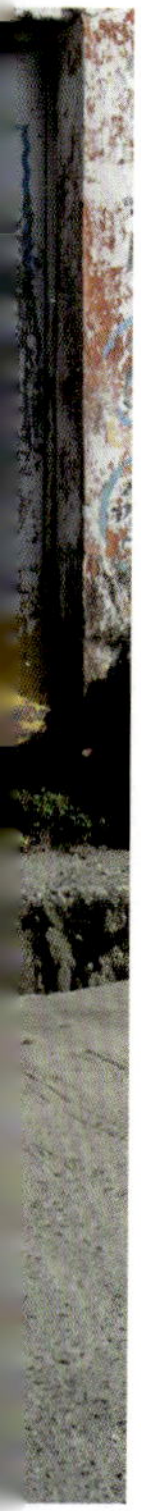

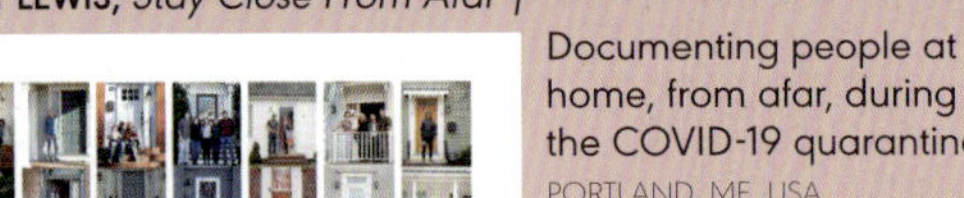

WINKY LEWIS, *Stay Close From Afar* | Documenting people at home, from afar, during the COVID-19 quarantine. PORTLAND, ME, USA

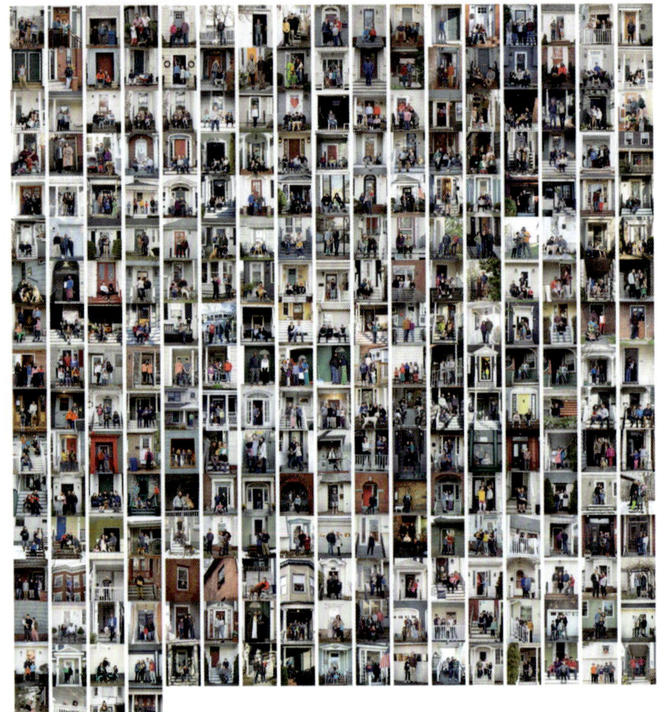

BETH CARON, My favorite puddle in Central Park. NEW YORK, NY, USA

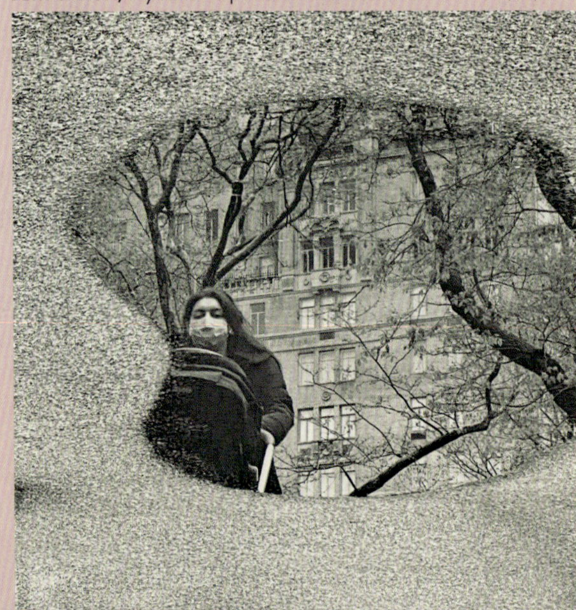

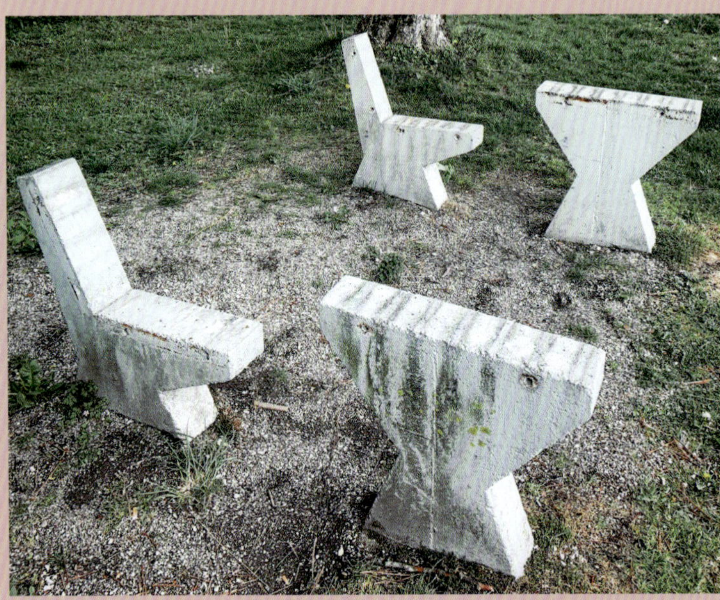

RENZO WELLINGER, *Something's Off* | Picnic bench without its wooden seat due to social-distancing regulations. Please don't sit down. MUNICH, GERMANY

05·20

MAY

2_Le site anti-«fake news» du gouvernement fait grincer des dents *(Le Parisien)*

10_ France to be Exempt from UK Quarantine Rules, Johnson and Macron agree *(The Guardian)*

4_Profile of a Killer: the Complex Biology Powering the Coronavirus Pandemic *(Nature)*

ELENA EROSHEVICH, *Market* | There is no quarantine here. There are a lot of people in the market, just like everywhere else. Sellers are forced to work in personal protective equipment. OSIPOVICHI, BELARUS

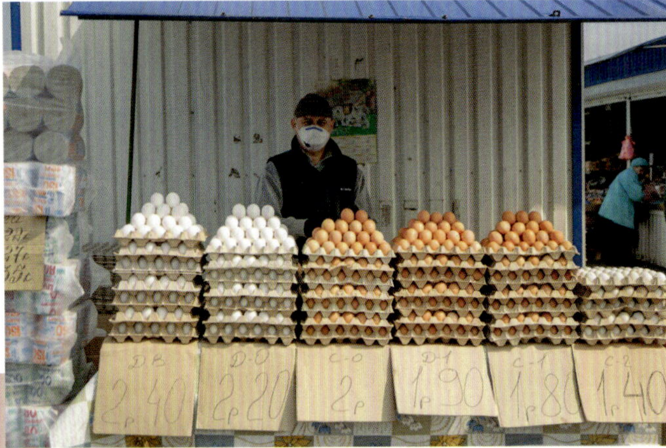

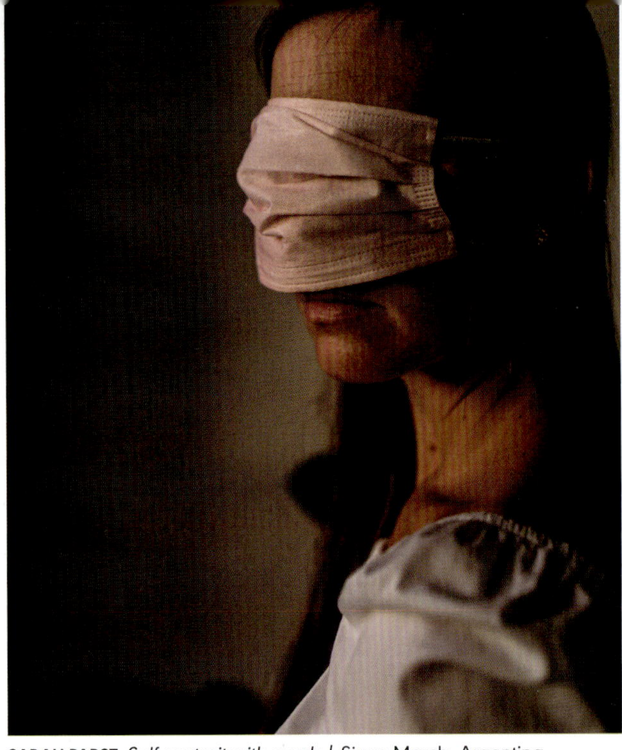

SARAH PABST, *Self-portrait with mask* | Since March, Argentina has been under a full lockdown due to the pandemic. The future feels uncertain. BUENOS AIRES, ARGENTINA

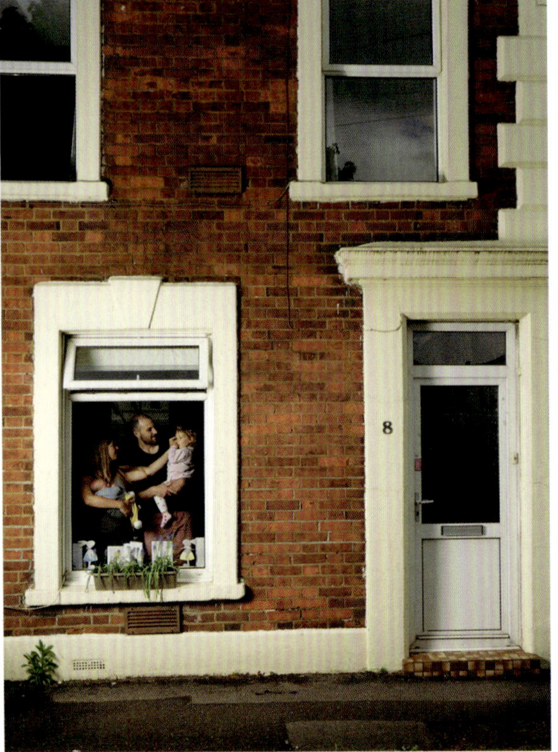

KIN HO, *Isolation–Portraits From An Unsociable Distance* | Arrival of Baby Charlie; born during lockdown, mum Harriet thanked the NHS staff for the "calm and relaxed" experience. SALISBURY, WHILTSHIRE, UNITED KINGDOM

CARME RIPOLLÉS MARTÍNEZ, *Hug confined* | After the video call, Cristina crumbles in the arms of her roommate. They are Latin American refugees who spend the confinement with six more people in an apartment in Castelló. SPAIN

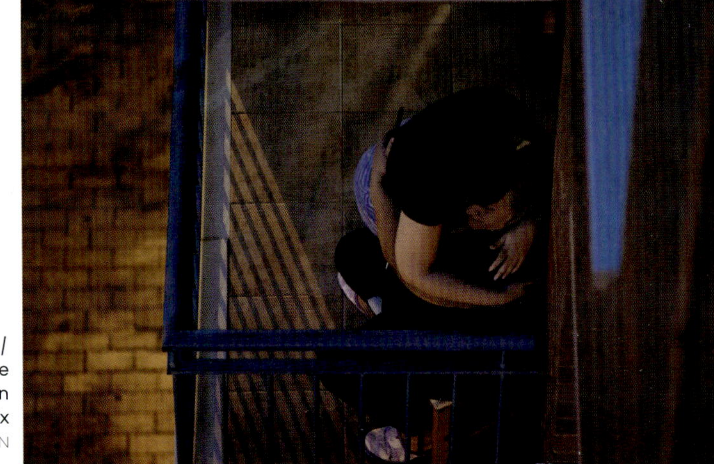

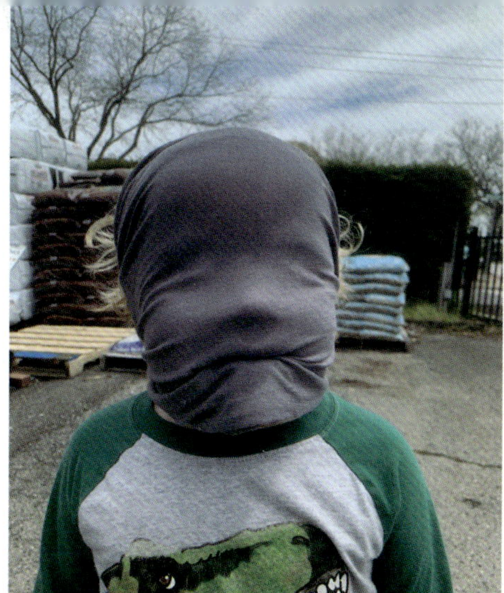

NICK WAPLINGTON, My son on our first trip out with masks to a garden center on Long Island, he is doing an impression of the Invisible Man. NEW YORK, NY, USA

FABIO RENZI, The kiss. ROME, ITALY

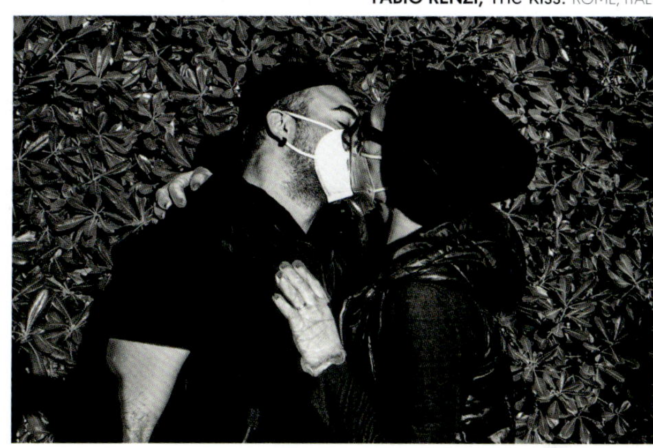

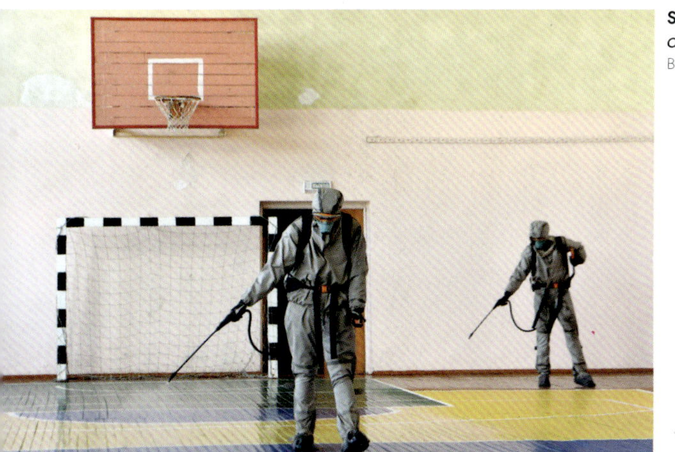

SERGEI GAPON, *Servicemen wearing protective gear disinfect a school gym in the village of Mikhanavichy, outside Minsk.* BELARUS

AMNA YASEEN, *Untitled |* Self-Portrait, "Being With The Self" Series. LAHORE, PAKISTAN

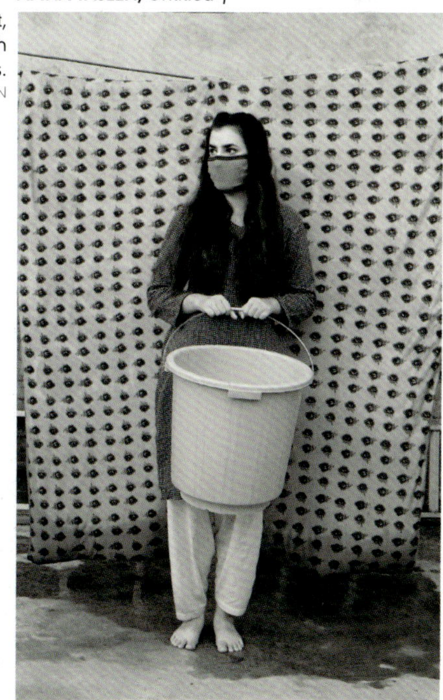

FIRDYA PUTRA JEHAN MUHAMMAD, Talking Without Speaking. SUKOREJO MARKET, INDONESIA

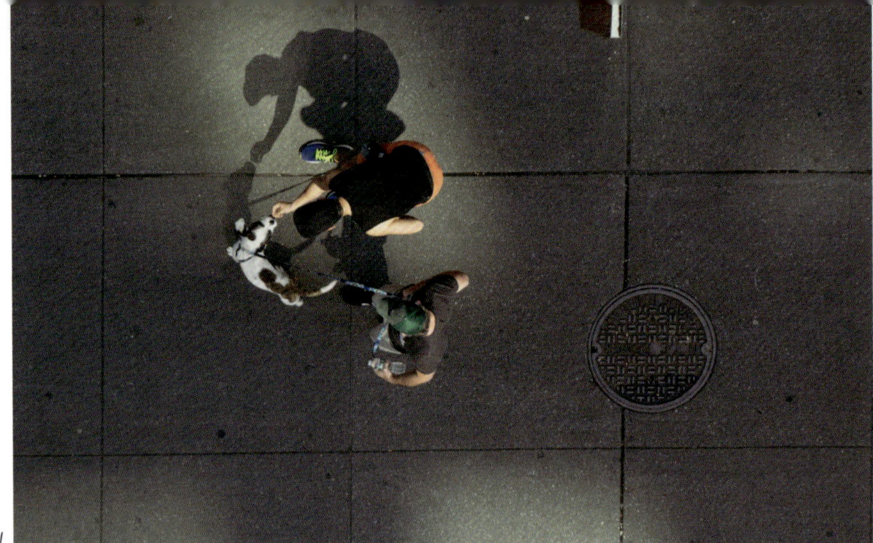

NATE BOZEMAN, *Day 44* | NYC Quarantine, seen from the 21st floor in Hell's Kitchen. NEW YORK, NY, USA

STEVE REEVES, Exhausted bus driver. LONDON, UNITED KINGDOM

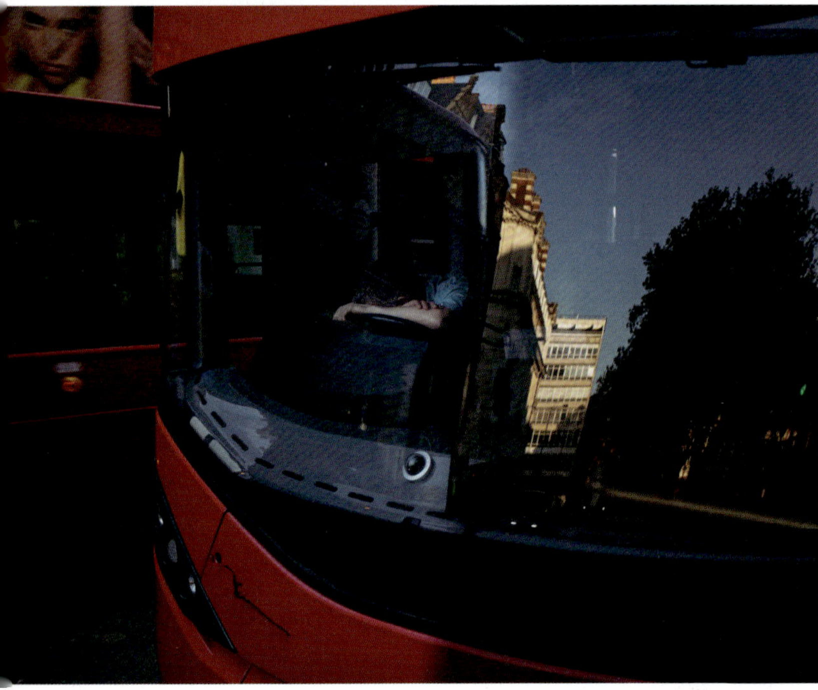

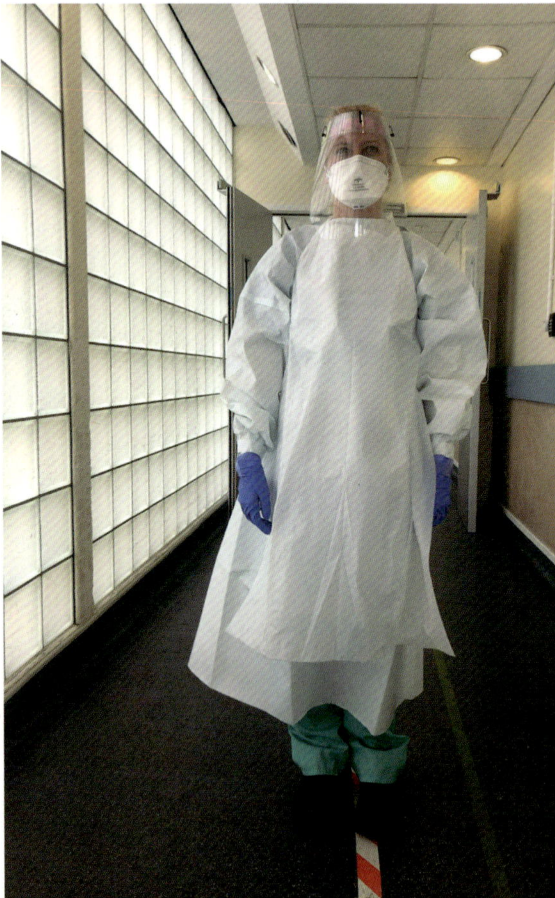

HANNAH GRACE DELLER, *Nurse Stephanie Perry* | Waiting for the arrival, St. Mary's Hospital Emergency Department. LONDON, UNITED KINGDOM

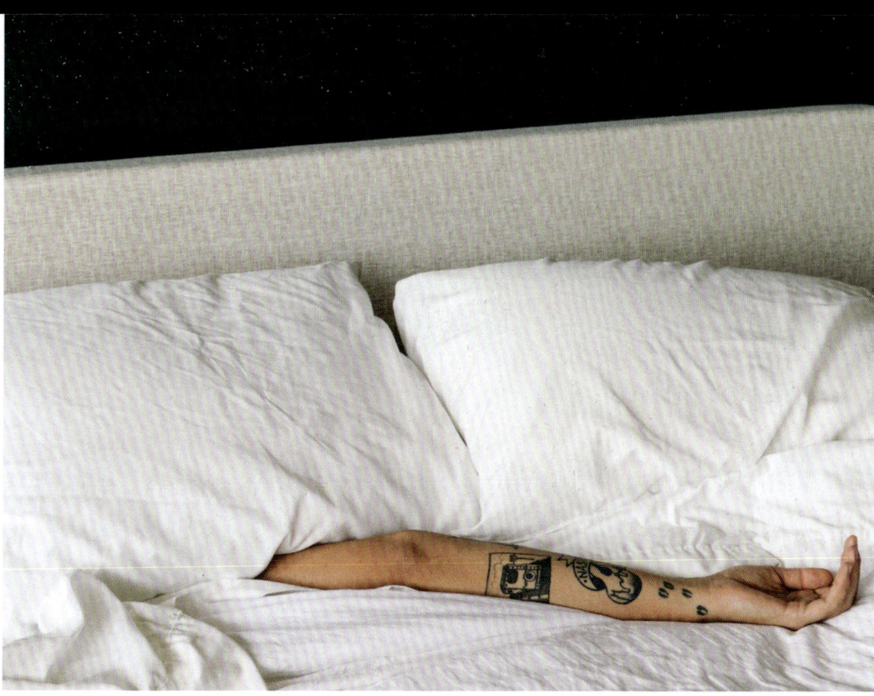

NATASHA MOUSTACHE, Untitled Self-Portrait. CHICAGO, IL, USA

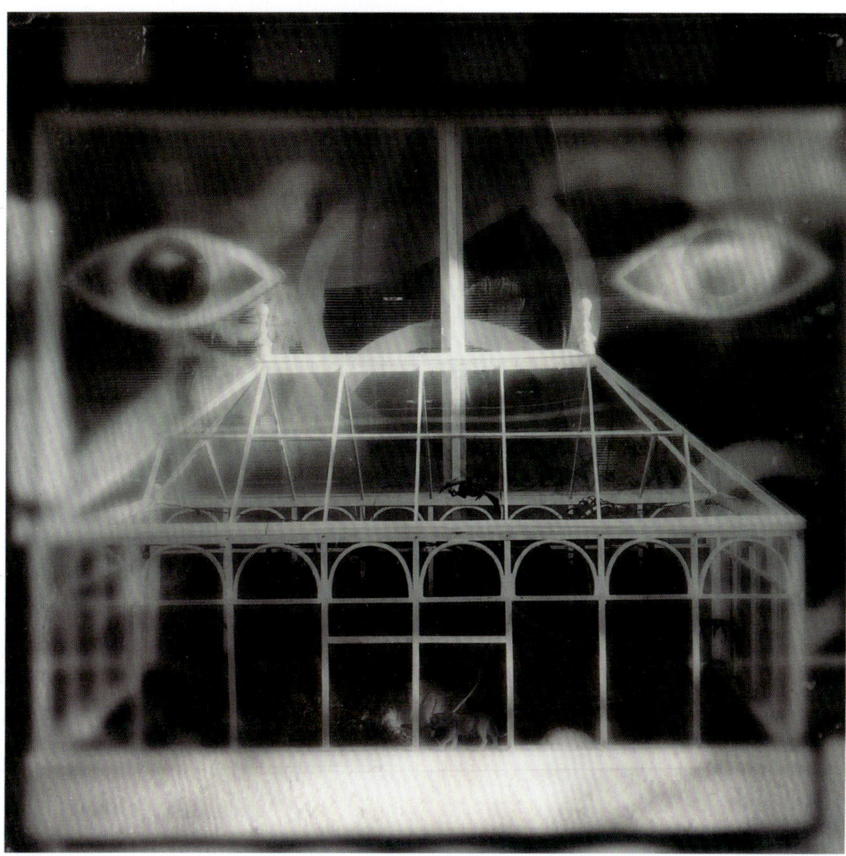

MELANIE WALKER, *Signs of Spring* | After winter we bring out our miniature plant conservatory. CO, USA

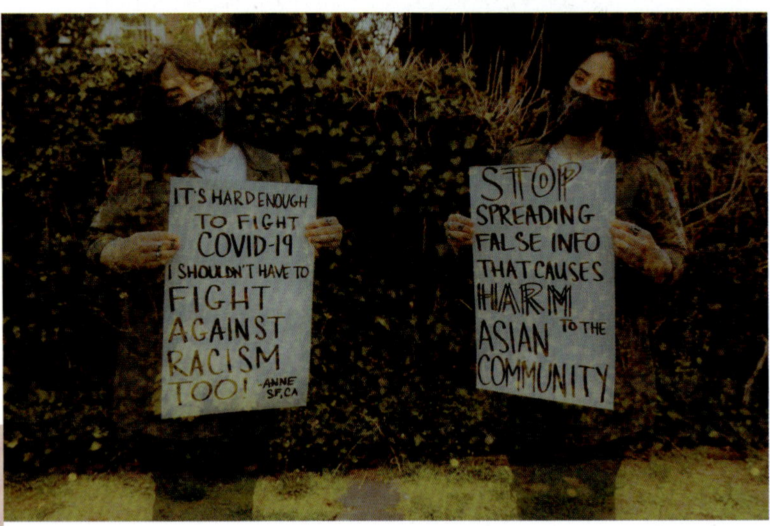

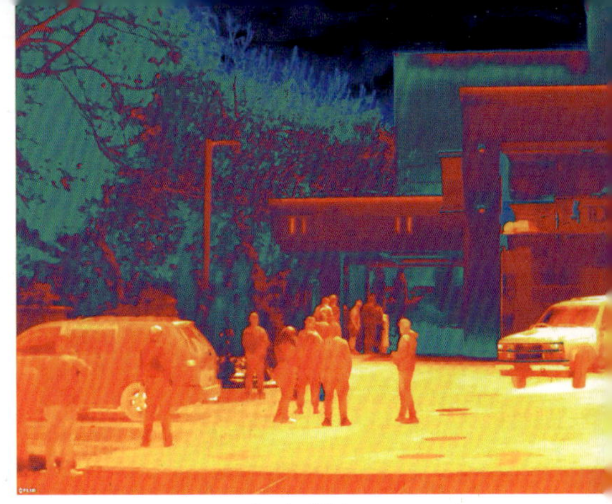

JUSTIN BRICE GUARIGLIA, Bank ATM queue, Sunset Park. Thermogram. BROOKLYN, NY, USA

ESTER SEGRETTO, *Isolation Demonstration 21* | From a project photographed at home in Queens. NY, USA

TAYLOR SESSELMAN, Marissa, Zenda and Alex Gimeno. #20 of the Pandemic Portrait Project. WILLIAMSBURG, BROOKLYN, NY, USA

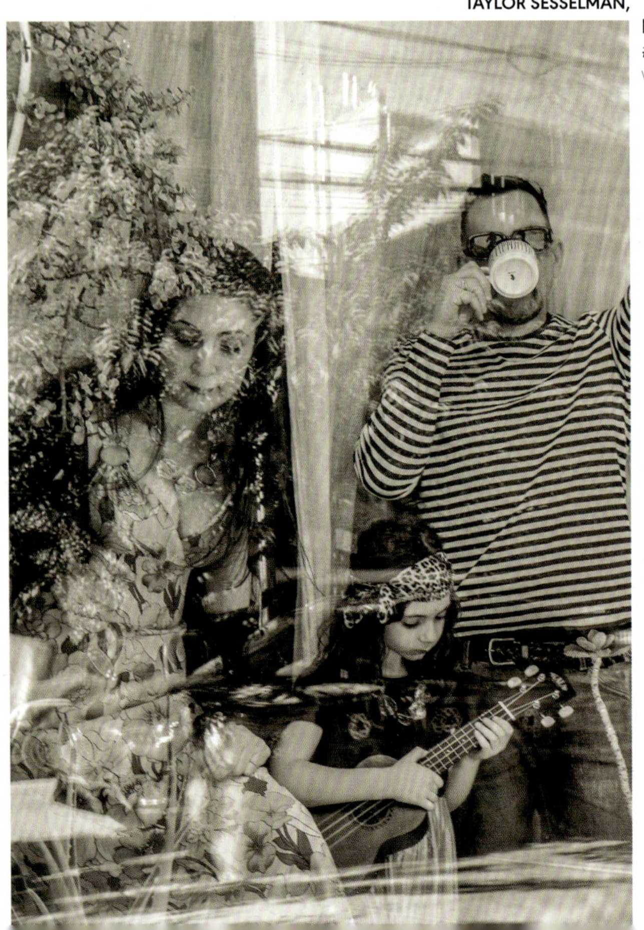

LINDA KLETNIECE, *Face Times* | Portrait of society in the digital age and at the time of pandemic. Blurred, exhausted, isolated. When the only way of meeting each other was through screens on our devices. LATVIA

LUCA PUCCI,
Drone portrait of artist Yohannah on her window. SÃO PAULO, BRAZIL

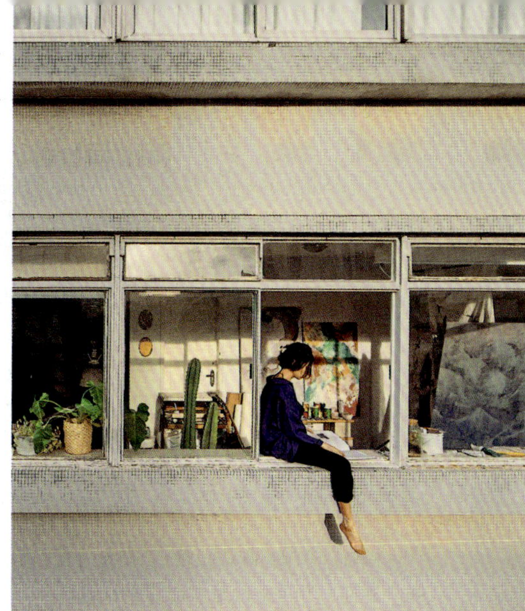

SANDRA HERNÁNDEZ, This morning, with the first rays of the sun, I asked for enlightenment to keep myself calm and wise. QUERÉTARO CITY, MEXICO

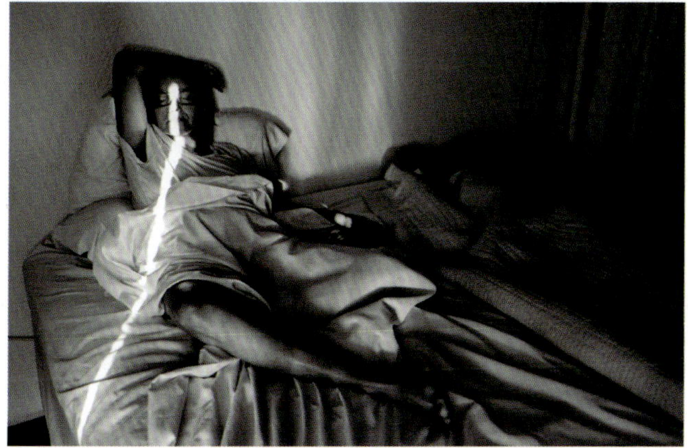

EMMA PERRY, *COVID Cast-offs* |
While on a walk during our first lockdown, I stumbled across a box of discarded "Buffy the Vampire Slayer" books. The book on the top was "Doomsday Deck." Seems appropriate for the cards we are being dealt this year! MELBOURNE, AUSTRALIA

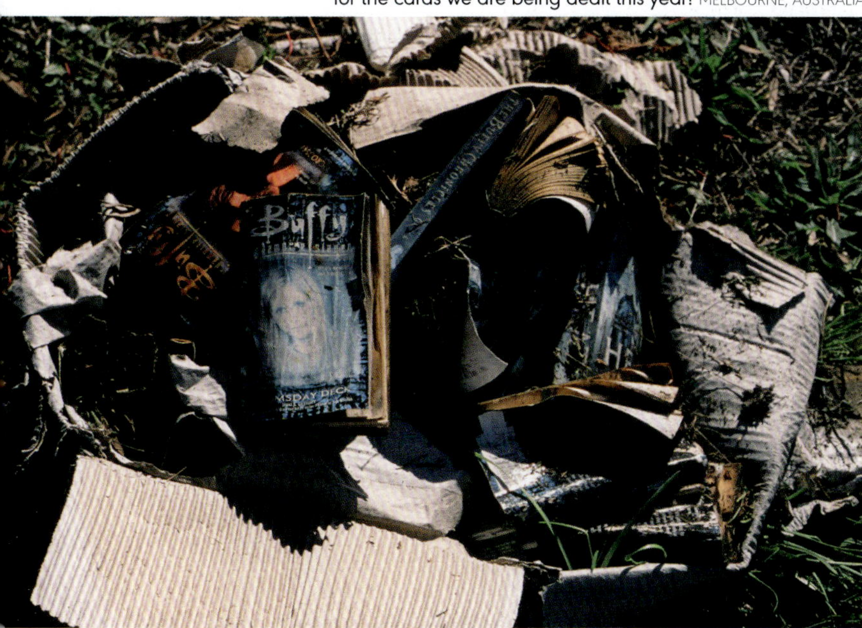

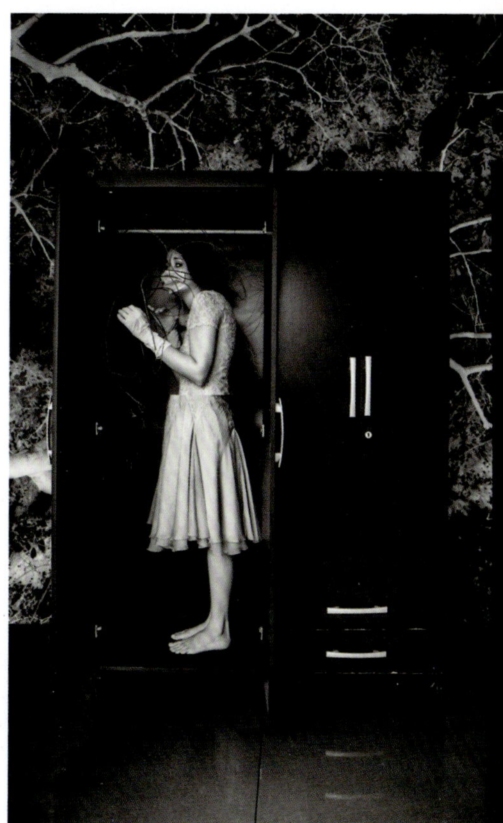

CAROLINA ZAMBRANO, *Isolation* |
Isolation runs through us, removes us, and places us in front of our deepest fears: uncertainty, loneliness, and frustration. GUAYAQUIL, ECUADOR

SARAH MCCLELLAND, *Pandemic Prom* | 2020 Prom Dress Photoshoot. HOLLYWOOD CEMETERY, RICHMOND, VA, USA

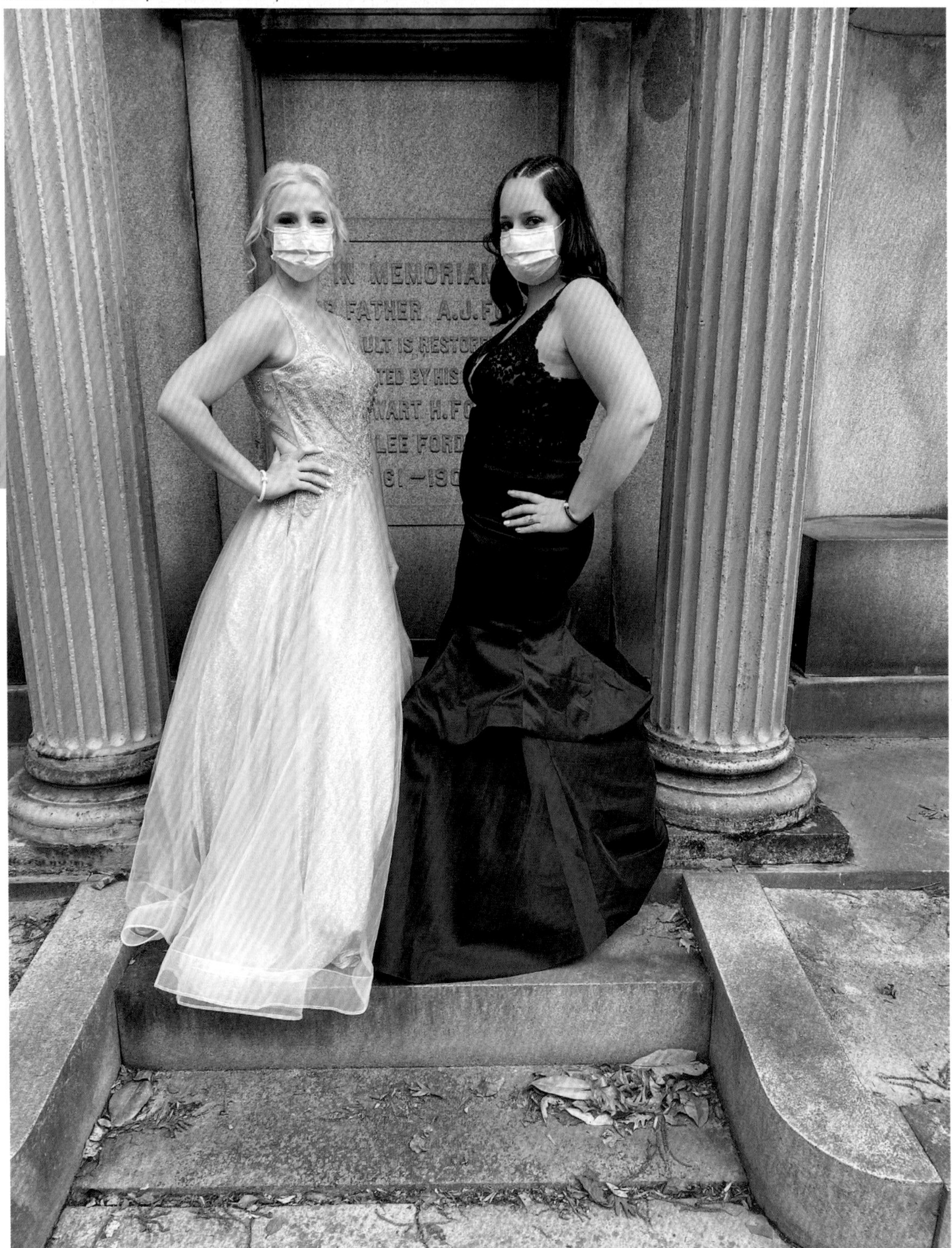

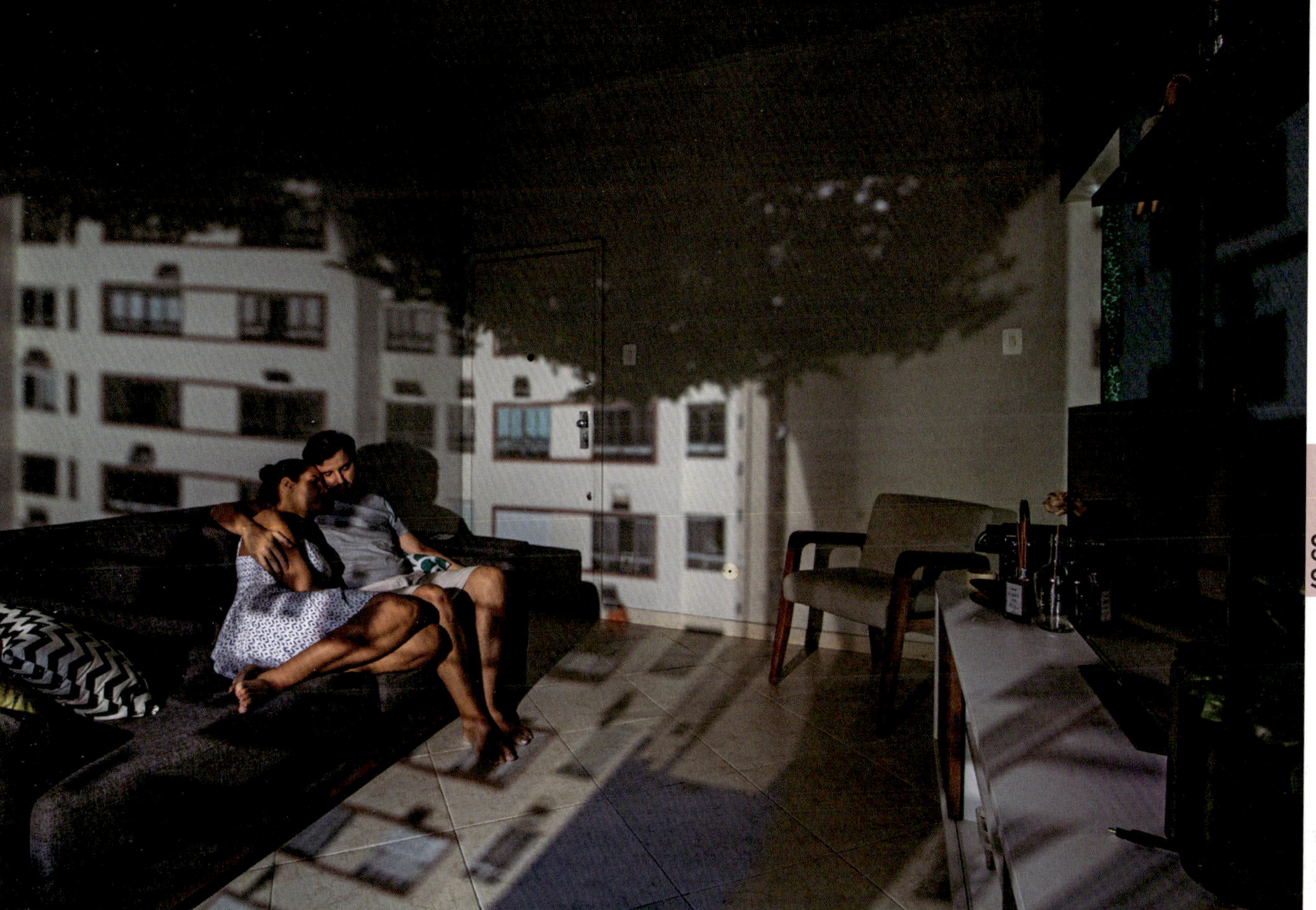

FELIPE MARTINI,

"We were going to get married and move abroad so I could enroll in a master's degree. 2020 ended up different from what we planned. The pandemic showed us that we have no control over anything." From the series Obs-cu-ra produced by Bruno Alencastro.

COPACABANA, RIO DE JANEIRO, BRAZIL

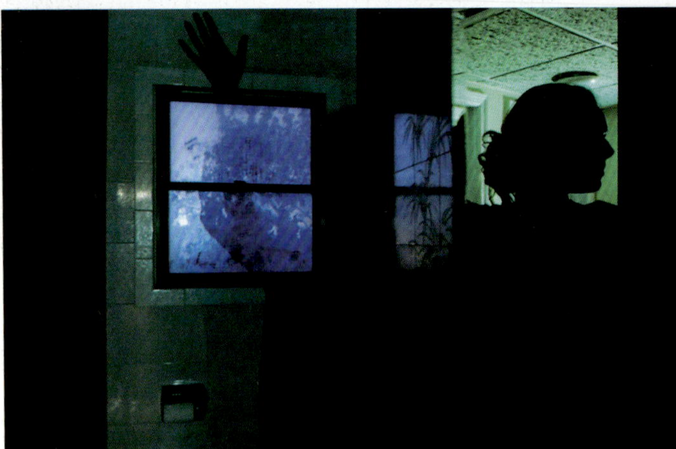

SONIA GOYDENKO, *Quarantine Chronicles* | Greetings from the beyond (my bathroom) on a dark and gloomy day. Playing with reflections and shadows as the light fades into night. Any day that we have toilet paper is a good one. PALISADES PARK, NJ, USA

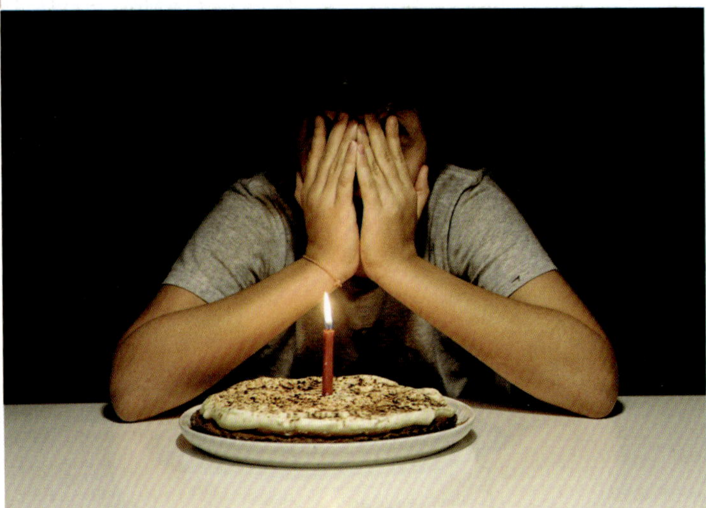

MARTÍN BONETTO, Joaquin Bonetto turning fifteen in quarantine. BUENOS AIRES, ARGENTINA

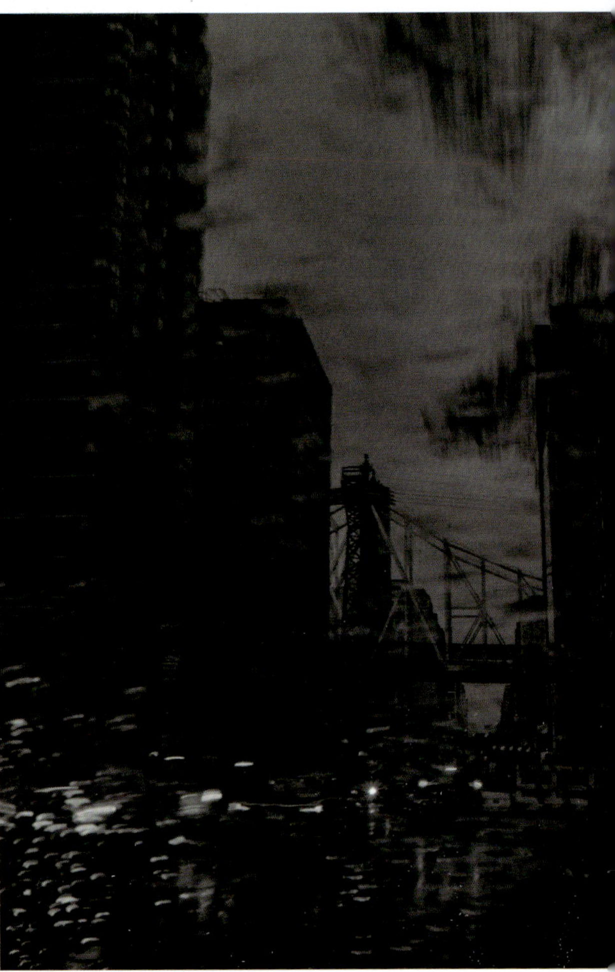

NINA WELCH-KLING, Untitled. NEW YORK, NY, USA

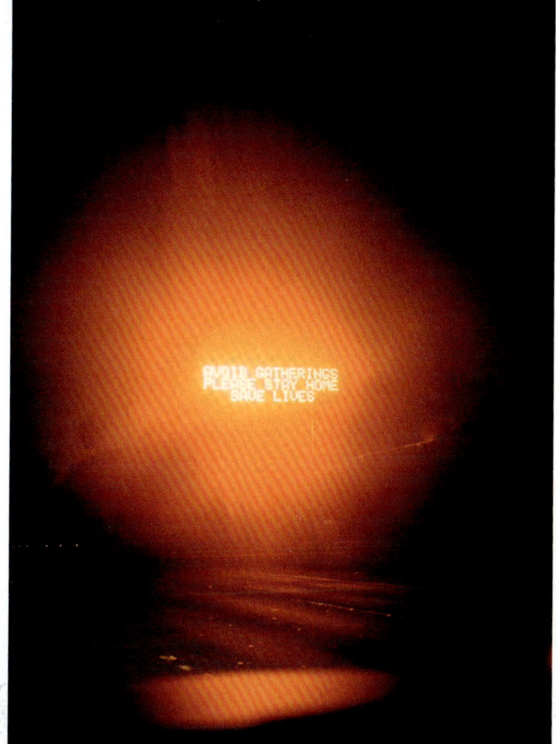

BRANDON TAYLOR, Late night drive on an empty freeway at 2AM. The 405 freeway is known for always having traffic, but not on this night. It was empty. SANTA MONICA, CA, USA

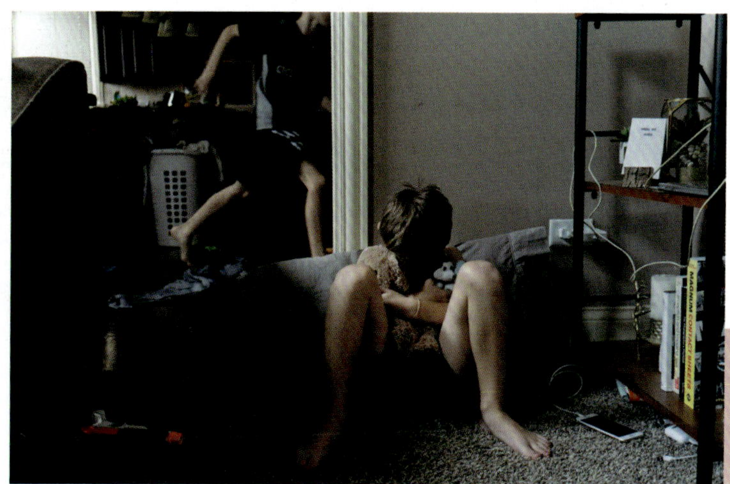

KAREN OSDIECK, My younger son, age 7, reaches a breaking point after six weeks of quarantine and homeschool. NEW LENOX, IL, USA

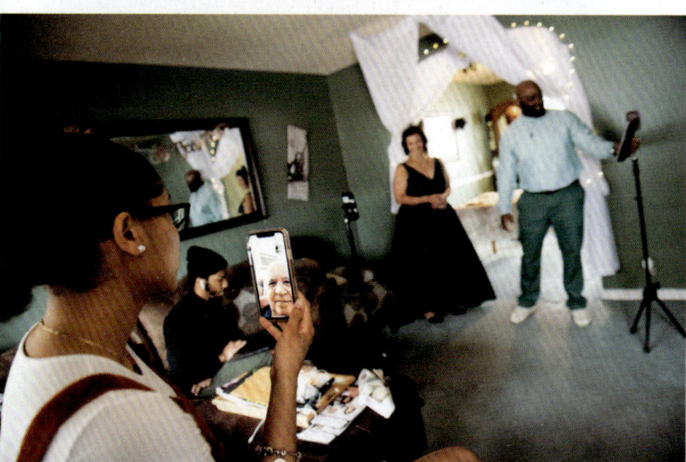

HEATHER SIZEMORE, As Vilma and Corey get married in their living room during the pandemic, Vilma's dad watches from his home via FaceTime. PHILADELPHIA, PA, USA

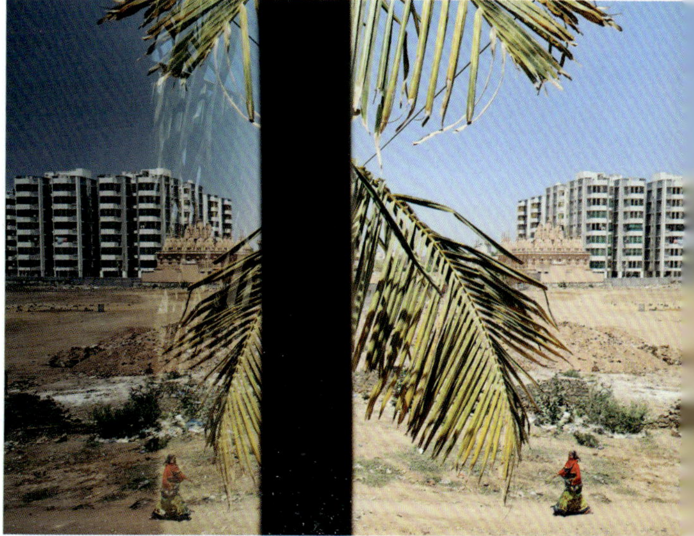

MANTHAN PATEL, This image was shot from the window of my room. SURENDRANAGAR, GUJARAT, INDIA

LOUISE HAWSON, *Inside* / During lockdown, I photographed people inside their homes, and then interviewed them about their experience of isolation. This portrait is of my nieces, April and Gina. SYDNEY, AUSTRALIA

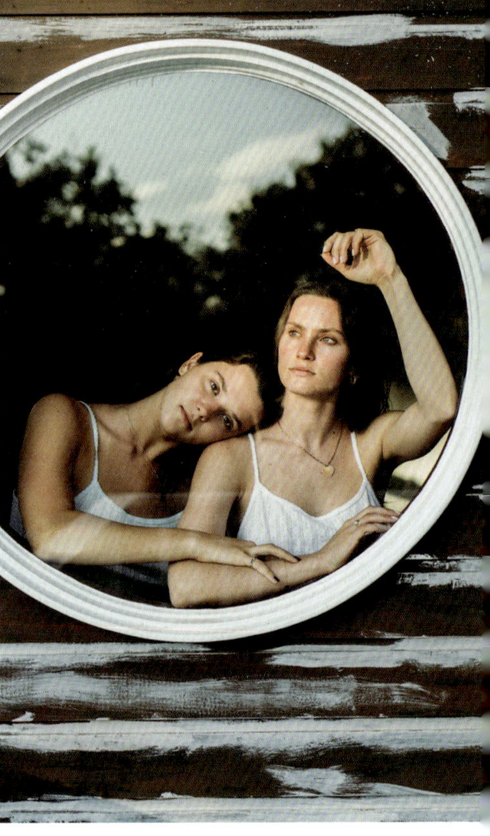

FRANCESCA MAGNANI, I saw Antonio walking down 10th Avenue while I was on the bus. I got off and ran to catch up with him. "I'm actually a lawyer," he said. "We are all looking for a way to make this situation a little bit more fun. And I had this caftan..." NEW YORK, NY, USA

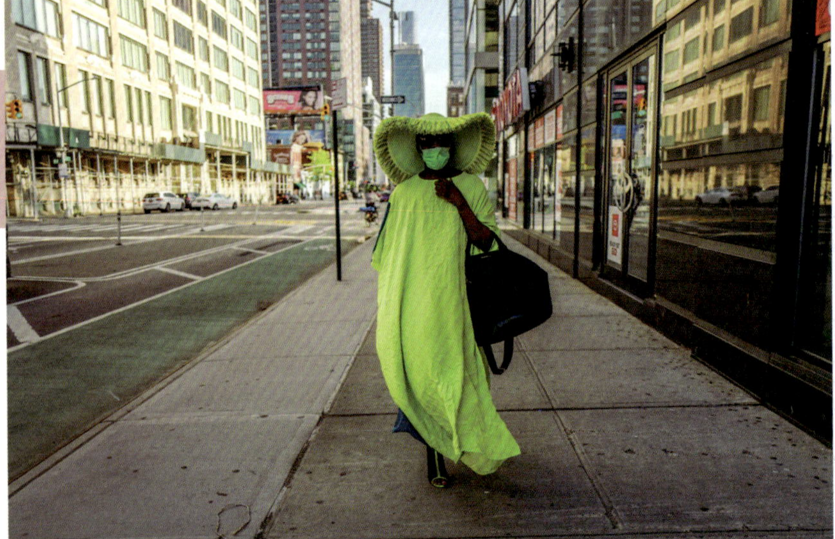

LUDOVICA BASTIANINI, COVID-19, a visual diary from Naples, Day 60, Mother's Day. ITALY

Day 60. 10.05.2020 It's Mother's day and I've been really undecided and worried about joining my parents for lunch, because they still isolating themselves from the outside, while I went out walking in the evening. I saw again the sanitary car in front of my house, so I imagine that there are new infection where I live. By the way I decided to go and I also cried for the strong and long hug of my sister. I didn't see her in 60 days. I spent the full day playing with my nephew. We were happy and sad at the same time. There is an unusual sense of precariousness and danger, in the future and even in the simplest things

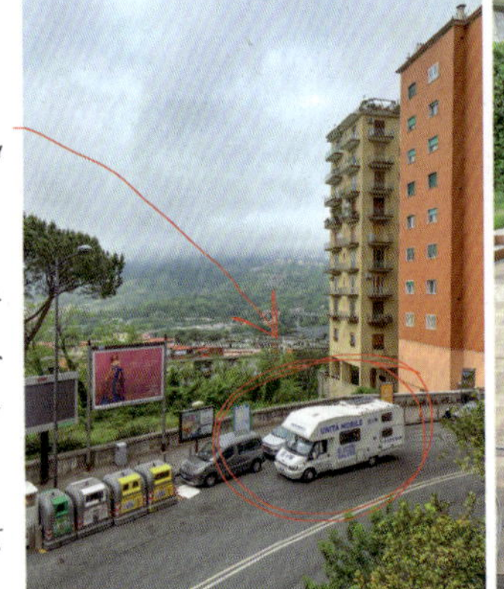

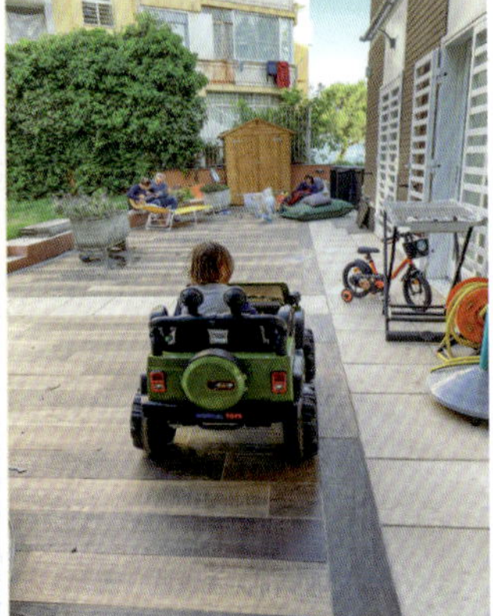

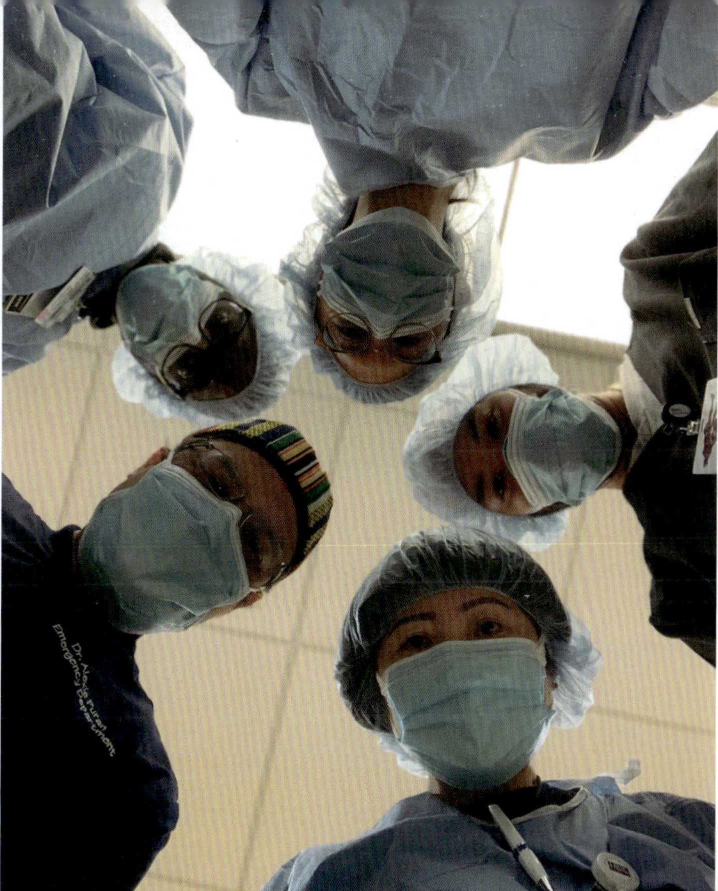

ALEXIE PURAN, *bettER togethER* | The collective power of a team of nurses and physicians in the Pediatric Emergency Department at NYC Health and Hospitals. HARLEM, NEW YORK, NY, USA

EDUARDO MARTINEZ, The Bronx Hustle. NEW YORK, NY, USA

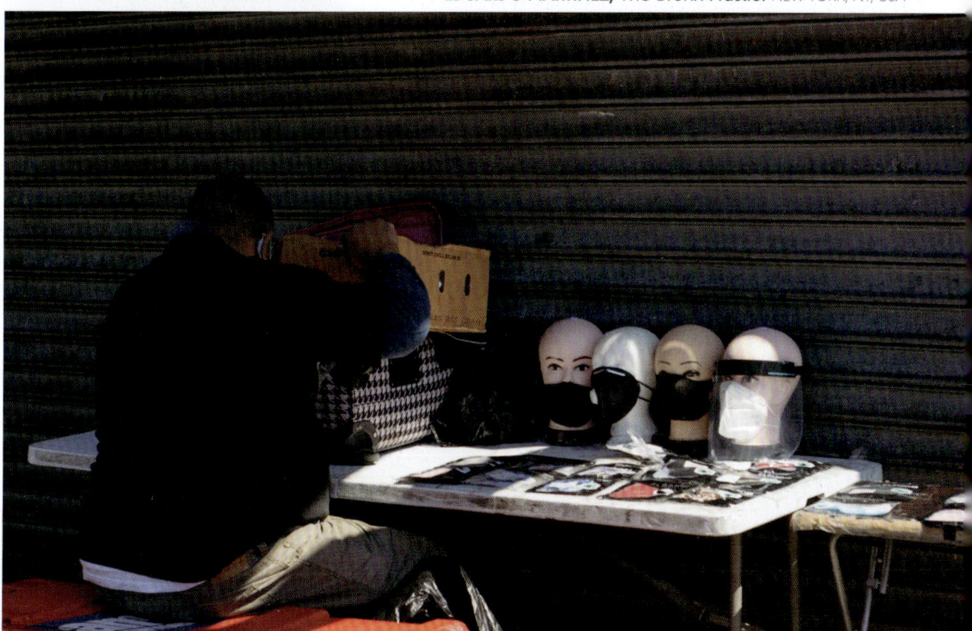

MARÍA DOLORES VILELA,
Me tomaría unos mates contigo cariño.
LAS FLORES, BUENOS AIRES, ARGENTINA

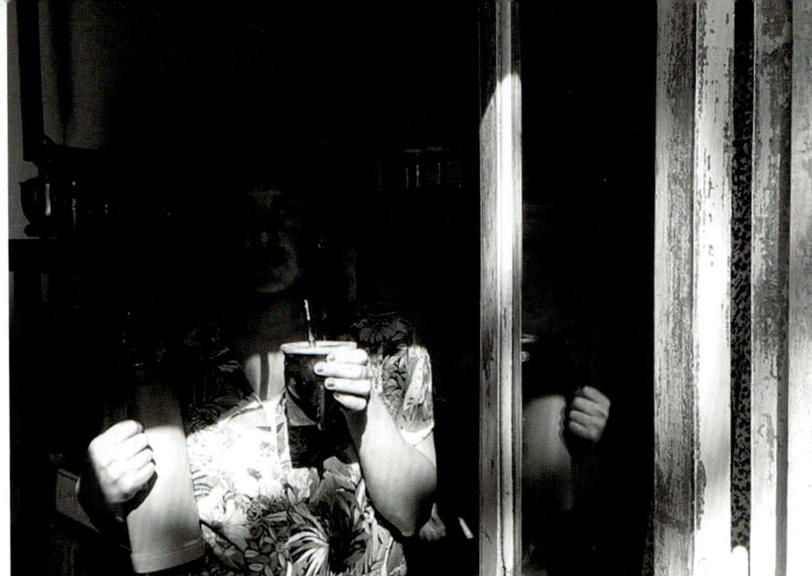

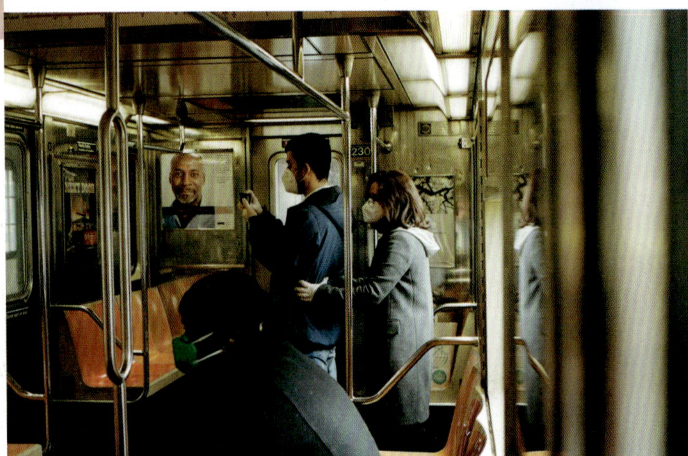

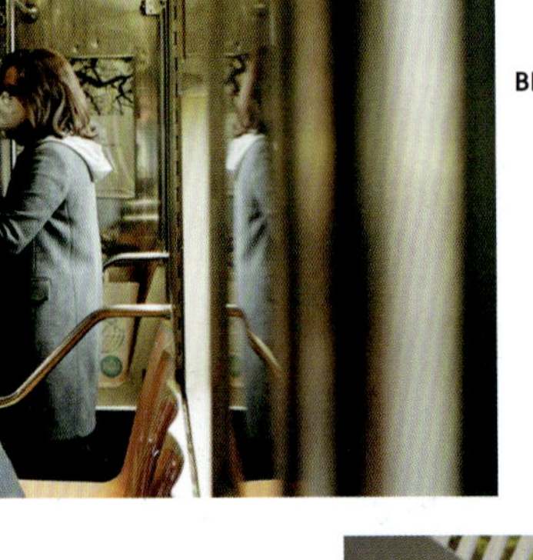

BRIANNA MANCINI, *Everything is Weird* |
Seen on the uptown 1 train at 125th St, Manhattan. Captured on my way home from the pharmacy.
NEW YORK, NY, USA

DAVID PLAKKE,
Nurse, Lenox Hospital, Greenwich Village. NYC AIDS Memorial, 7PM Clap.
NEW YORK, NY, USA

AIMEE ROSE, An individual attempt to reverse environmental damage by returning what was taken. MEATH, IRELAND

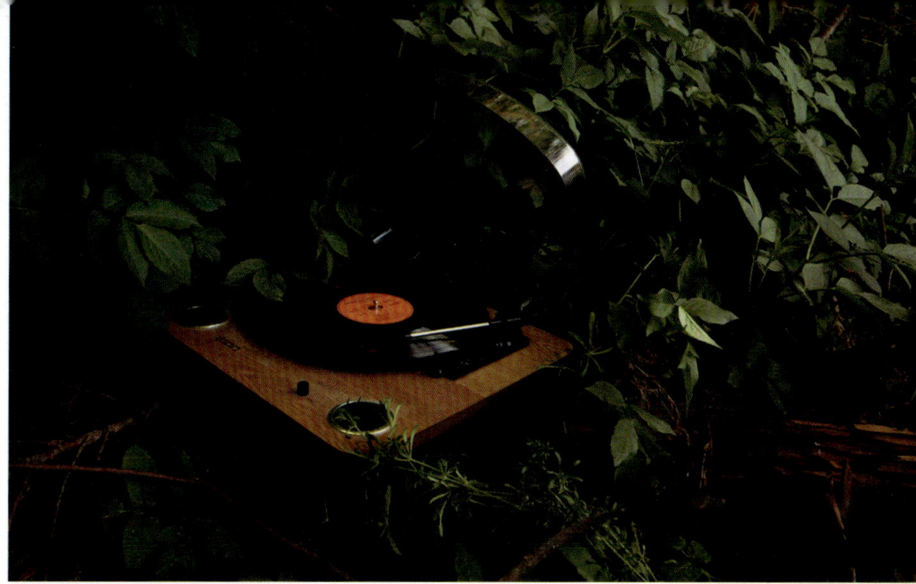

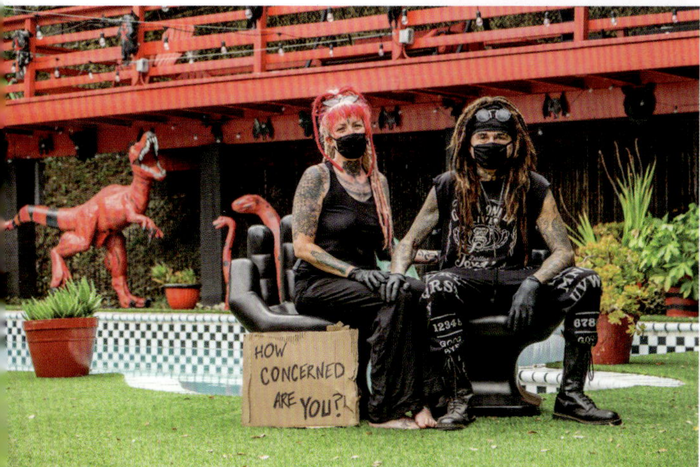

ANDREW PUTSCHOEGL, Liz Walton and Al Jourgensen. LOS ANGELES, CA, USA

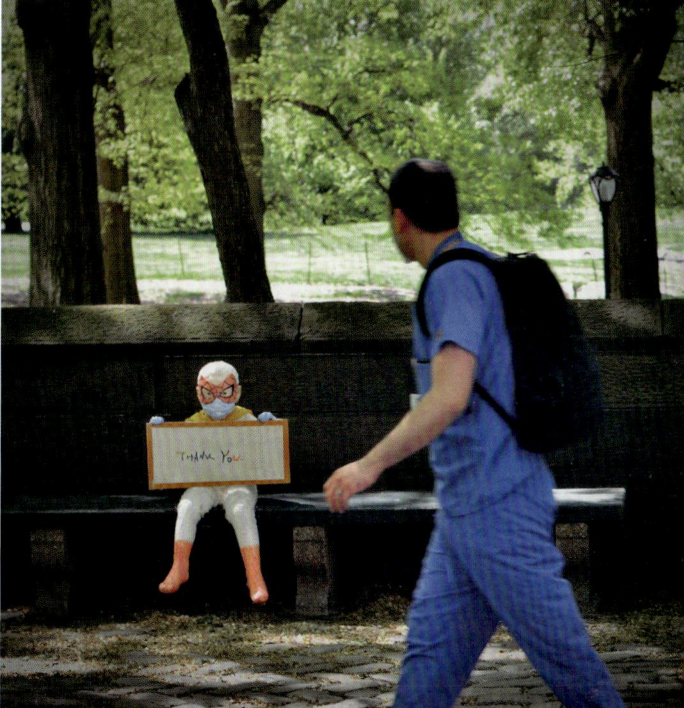

BEÑAT INGLESIAS LOPEZ, *Thank You* | Sculpture installation across Mt. Sinai Hospital in Central Park. NEW YORK, NY, USA

MO GELBER, I wasn't sure if this man was trying to protect himself from the virus or escape New York City by submarine. BROOKLYN, NY, USA

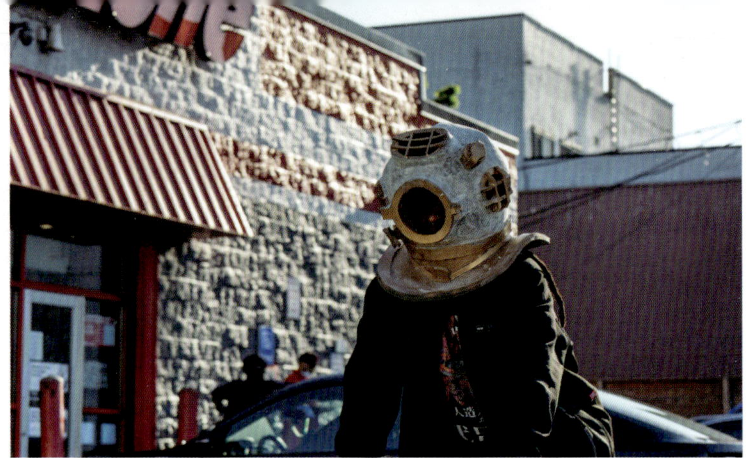

05 13

GEOFFREY BLACK,

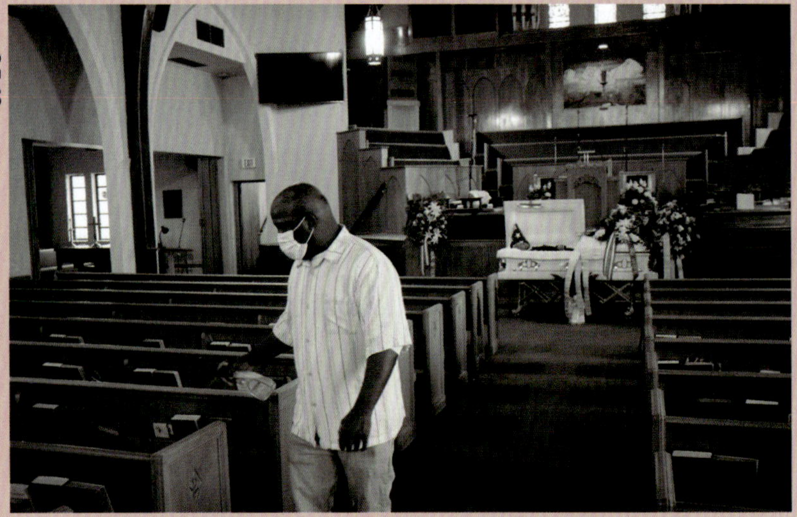

At this time, the city of Gary was in the middle of a COVID-19 lock down. You could only leave your house for essential services. Schools, restaurants and public spaces were shut down. The city was allowing home going services but no more than 25 people could attend and only if social distancing and facemasks were used as a way to flatten the curve. What struck me about this particular moment, is finding peace and dignity and how we publicly grieve passages during the pandemic. The gentleman in the photo is spraying disinfected and wiping down pews in the sanctuary before the family hour. The scene represents an overall change 2020 has had for the most vulnerable. Once a place of joy and praise, the church has become a place of fear and uncertainty. GARY, IN, USA

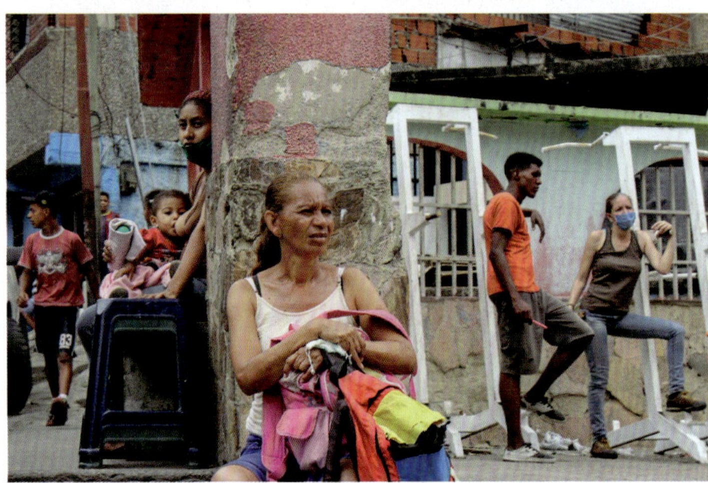

YADIRA PEREZ, A teenage girl breastfeeds her baby while others wait for the water cisterns to fill their pots at the entrance of La Parrila in Petare. Some protect themselves others don't. CARACAS, VENEZUELA

B JANE LEVINE, Falling Down the Rabbit Hole! USA

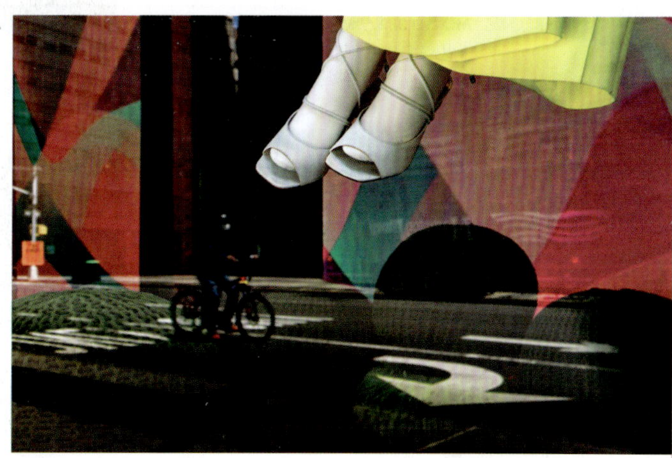

BARBARA COLEMAN, *Transitu* | This photograph was taken during the coronavirus pandemic, when the streets in Chicago were empty. The lone, masked figure speaks to my feeling of isolation at a time full of uncertainty. The patinaed colonnade suggests a faraway place, the Parthenon, or a Roman ruin. IL, USA

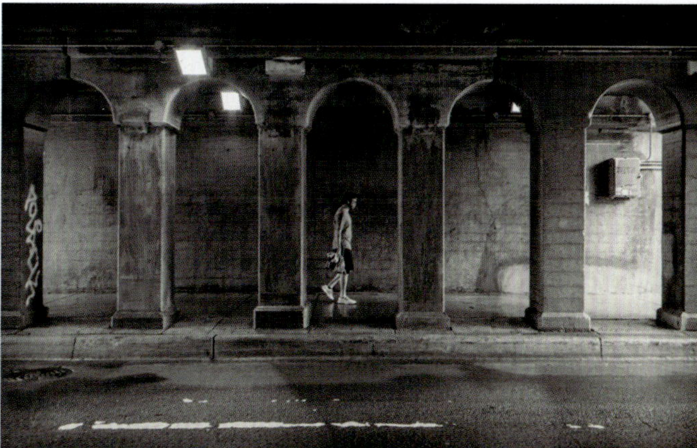

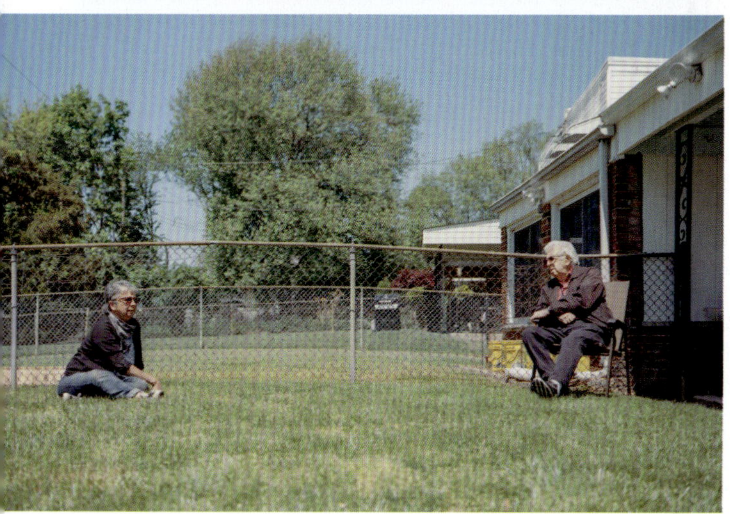

JAKE DUNDERDALE, A 92-year-old father and his 61-year-old daughter keep socially distant in the backyard of the home she grew up in. PHILADELPHIA, PA, USA

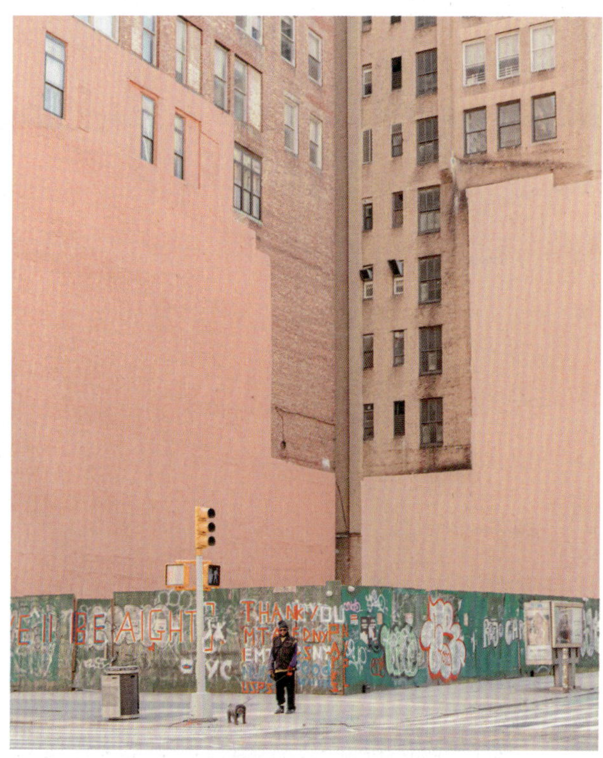

DIMITRI MAIS, Socially distant. NEW YORK, NY, USA

SHARI YANTRA MARCACCI, Family, Lockdown Day 63. LOS ANGELES, CA, USA

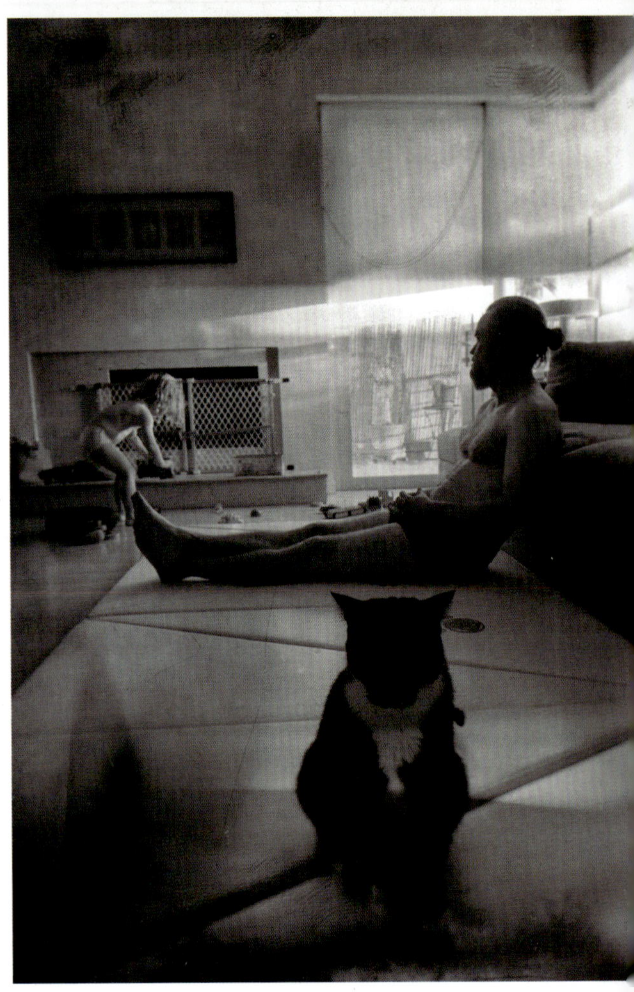

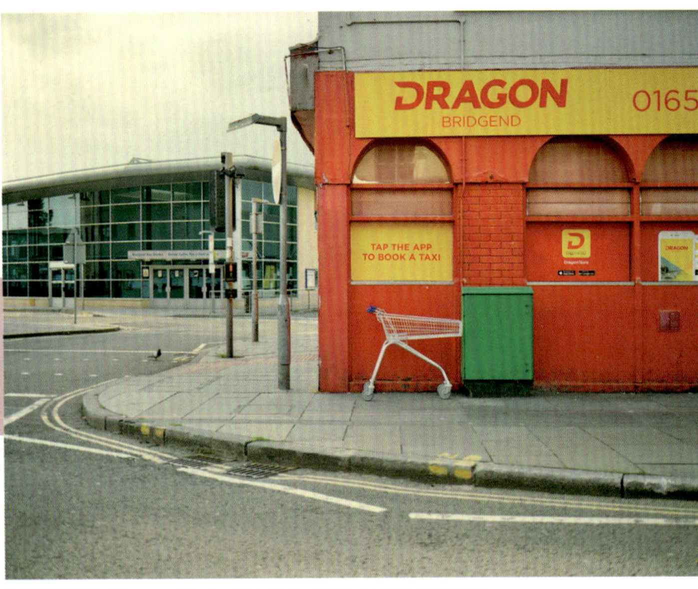

DAN WOOD, Dragon Taxis. BRIDGEND, WALES, UNITED KINGDOM

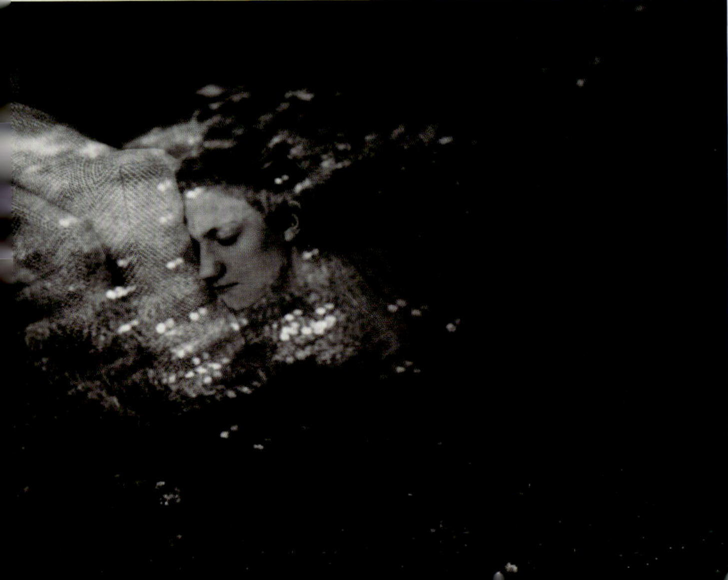

SIGRID DEBUSSCHERE,
Still stuck at home. Two months in isolation. Schools are closed. Not being able to see her friends is very difficult for my youngest daughter.
BRUSSELS, BELGIUM

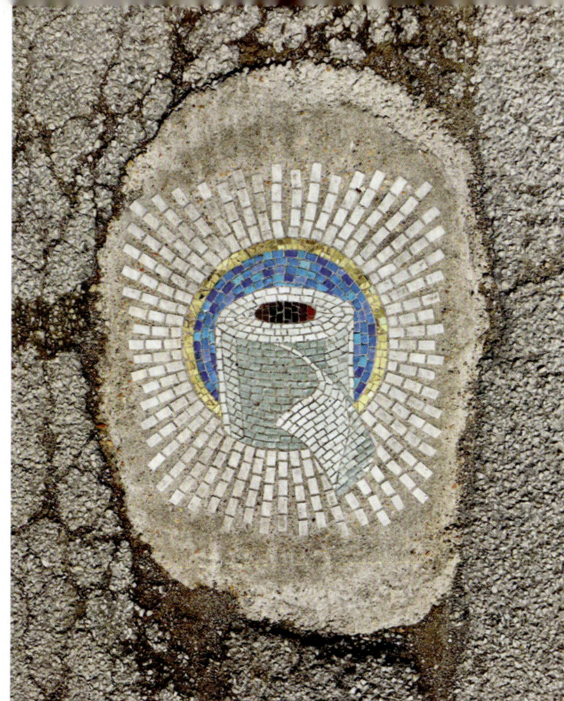

LOLITA BECKWITH, Spotted at Coney Island, this "Who will survive in America?" sticker struck a painful chord during these unprecedented times. Rooting & praying for us all. BROOKLYN, NY, USA

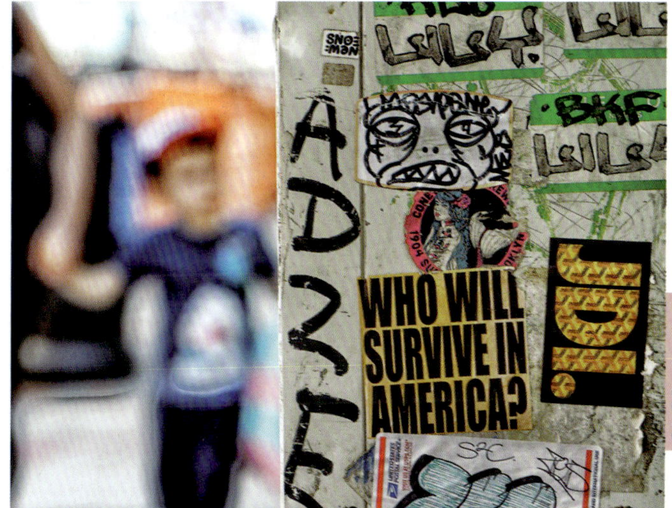

SPIRO BOLOS,
This is one of a series of pothole installations that artist Jim Bachor has scattered through the city. CHICAGO, IL, USA

PAMELA CASTILLO, *Instinctive sense of color order |*

When the pandemic started, I was living in downtown Mexico City. From that month, I lived through lockdown working online every day. At the time this photo was taken, I had decided to go outside for an afternoon break. Living in that building during the day, I began to witness the lives of my neighbors and I was able to capture quiet moments of their days. I wanted to capture the soul in the small things. As a witness to the evenings in my city during lockdown, I was forced to slow down too. By doing so, these small moments feel like a breath of fresh air. Watching the light change and connecting with what is happening around me. CENTRO HISTÓRICO, MEXICO CITY, MEXICO

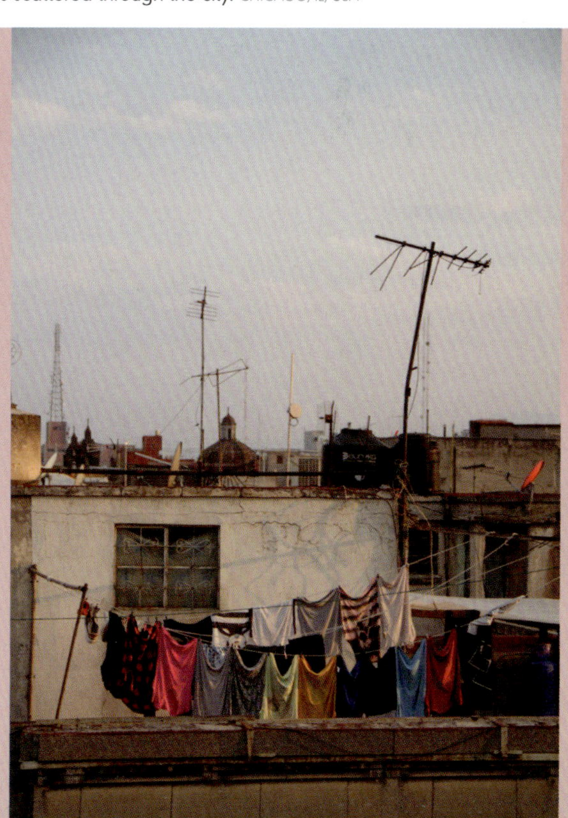

DANIELLE L. GOLDSTEIN, *From My Window* | My neighbors emerging from their apartments at 7 PM to clap for our essential workers. NEW YORK, NY, USA

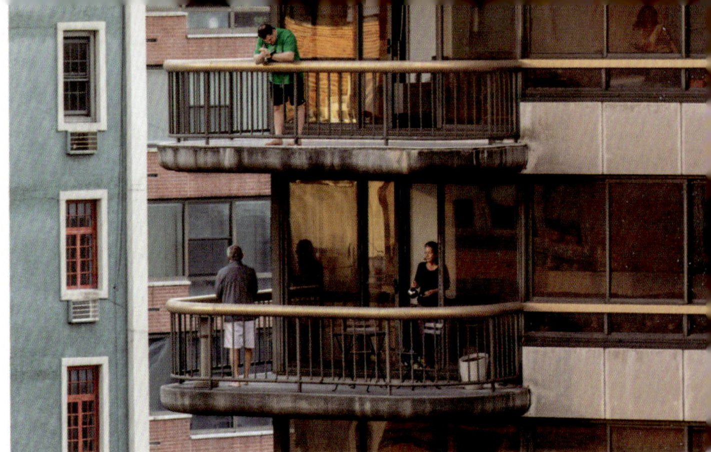

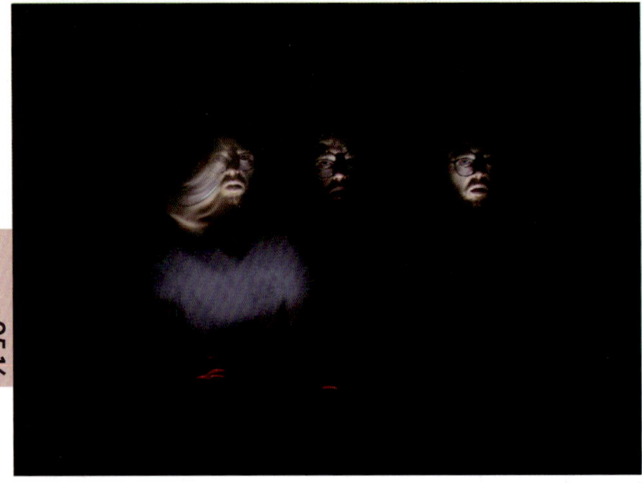

BLO CARO, *Routine* | The routine begins to get a little repetitive. BUENOS AIRES, ARGENTINA

BOB COOLEY, Pandemic Pastiche. MEATPACKING DISTRICT, NEW YORK CITY, NY, USA

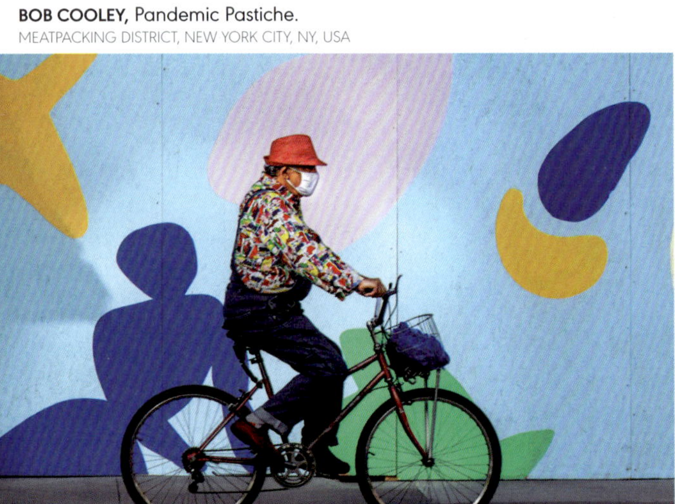

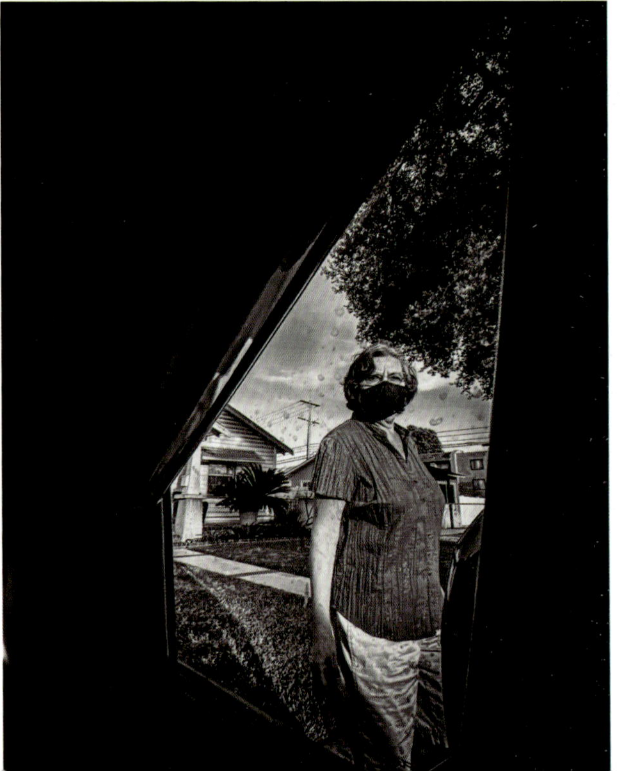

AMANDA VILLEGAS, Visiting Nana through window greetings is difficult. I want to hug her, but keeping her and my Ampa safe supersedes all of my longings for reunion. AZUSA, CA, USA

CYRUS GILMARTIN, *Home Experiment 7* | Reanimated childhood toys and other nearby objects, two months into UK lockdown. LONDON, UNITED KINGDOM,

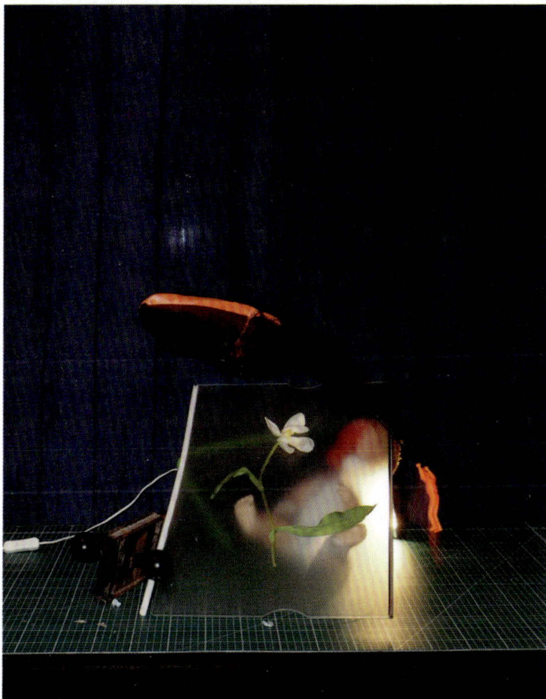

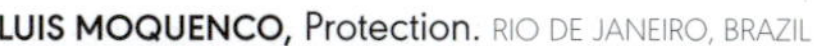

LUIS MOQUENCO, Protection. RIO DE JANEIRO, BRAZIL

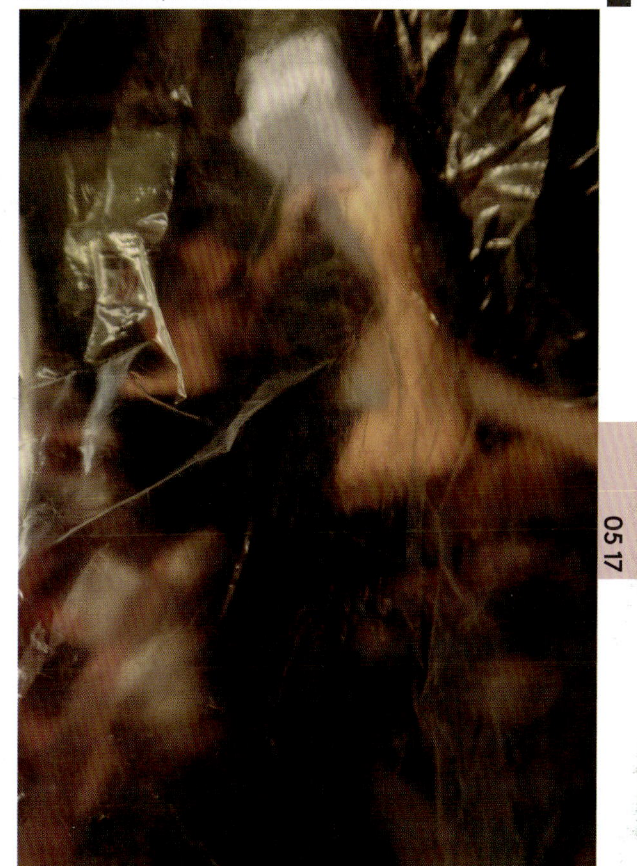

SHARON DRAGHI, *Some Days are Just Too Hard* | Part of an ongoing project about the pandemic and its effect on me. Being confined is terrifying, but it has helped me to see and appreciate what surrounds me with a new clarity. NEW YORK, NY, USA

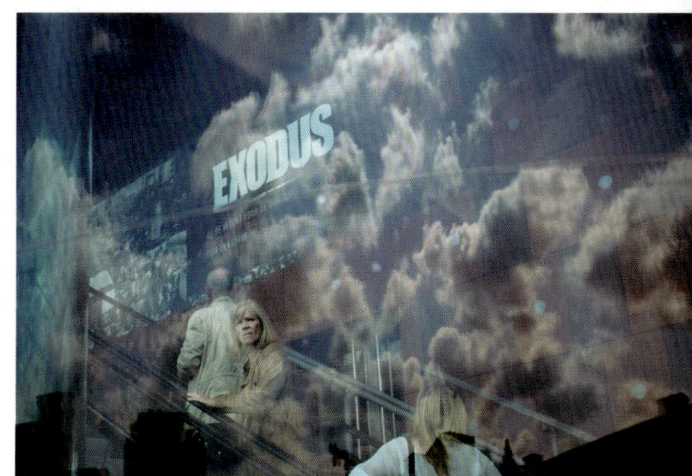

KRISTIN VAN DEN EEDE, Untitled. ANTWERP, BELGIUM

MICHAEL BACH, Instruction manual for protective air mask found lying next to a parked car on Washington Street. TROY, NY, USA

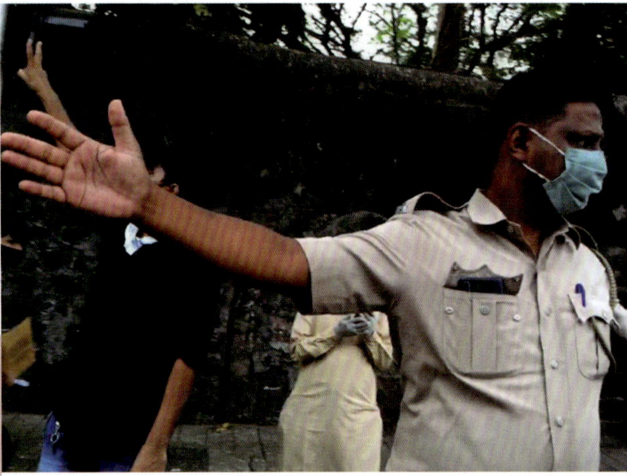

PRIYANKA GOWA, *Is your city a Great Place To Live? |* Mumbai police arranged a special train for migrant workers to their hometown.
CHHATRAPATI SHIVAJI TERMINUS, MUMBAI, MAHARASHTRA, INDIA

ANGELA DOUGLAS RAMSEY, *The Green Room |* An exploration of loosing one's identity during quarantine.
NORFOLK, VA, USA

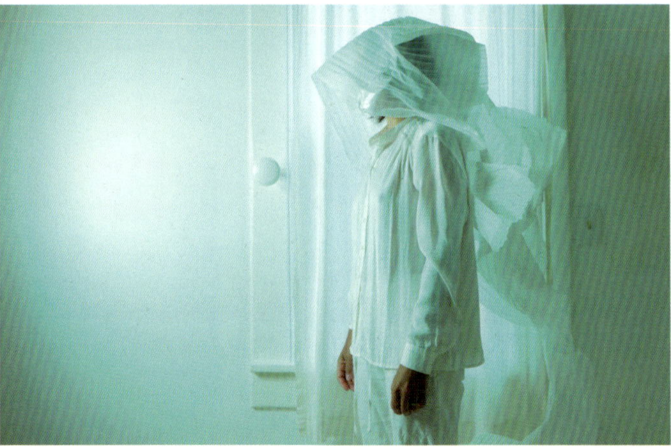

ANGELA GORDON, Self-portrait, in quarantine. OTTOWA, CANADA

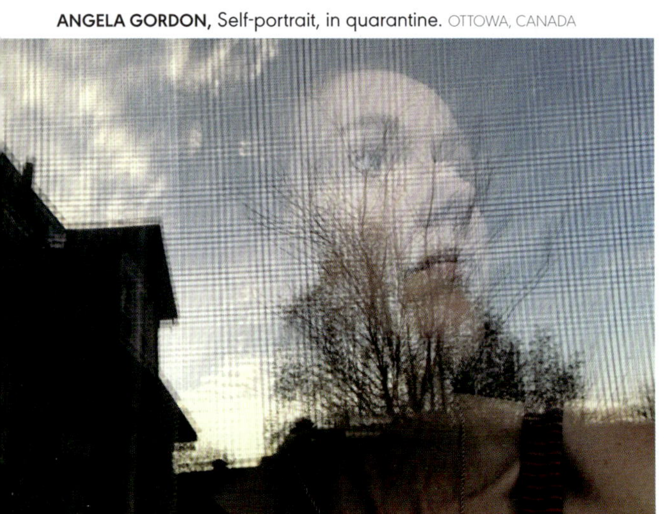

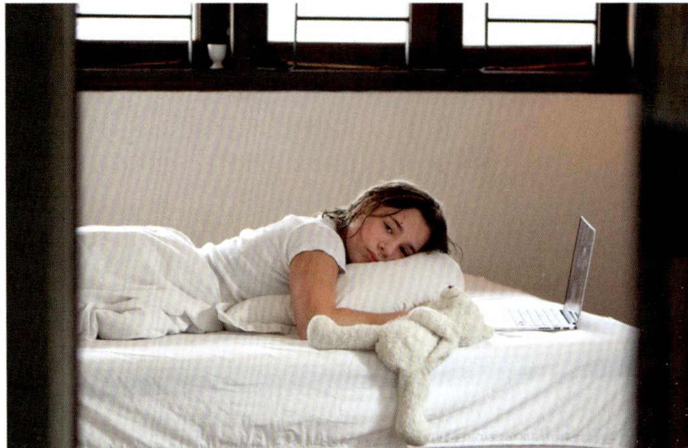

MARIKA POQUET, *Confinement Day 43 |* I started this family album as a means to document this extraordinary period. SINGAPORE

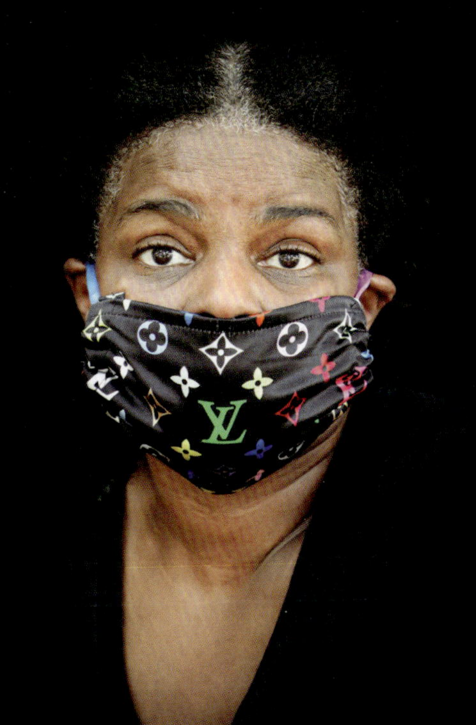

CYNTHIA ISAKSON, I felt the need to show the many reactions and emotions that stand out in the middle of the pandemic—desolation, fight, darkness, sadness, hope, fear and anger—that could only be noted in a fragment of the face—in the eyes. The rest is the denied, hidden, at least sometimes. With limited contact, my obsession with not being guilty of passing the disease to anyone, and of course, my fear of catching the virus myself, I took my studio to the street—to my front door to be more specific. With a black background in front of the door and a stool for the model to sit on. Just that. A black background, a stool, something to say, and someone who wanted to say with me. USA

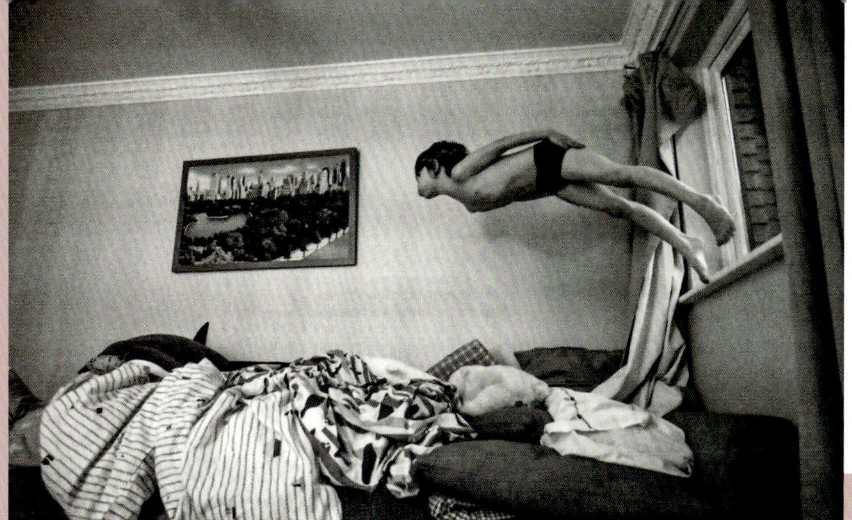

MARISA PRIVITERA MURDOCH, *Denny Dolphin* | Six-year-old Denny dives into the air like a dolphin. In lockdown, our house has become an adventure park and playground for his endless imagination.
GLASGOW, SCOTLAND, UNITED KINGDOM

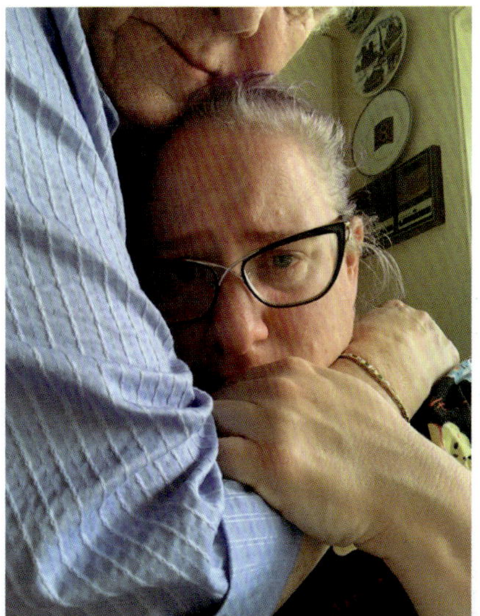

DAFNA STEINBERG,
Tuesday is for therapy. At my childhood home in McLean.
VA, USA

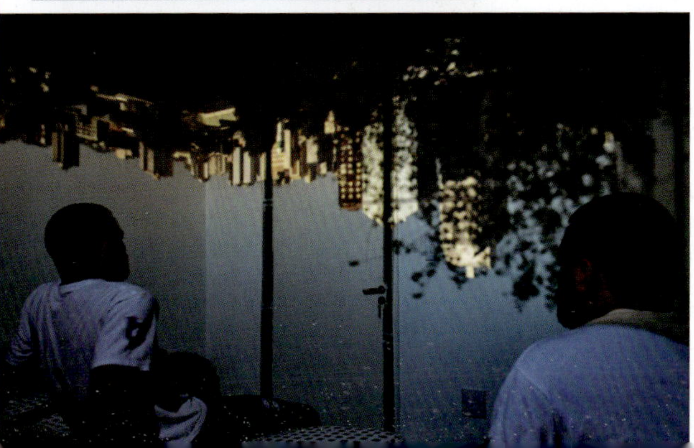

JÚNIOR CÉSAR WEISS,
Photo captured for Bruno Alencastro's Obs-cu-ra Camera project. Freedom and confinement through this limited framework of reality—the window—and its representation of a changing life.
RIO GRANDE DO SUL, BRAZIL

ROBINSON GERMAIN, Thankful Nun. NEW YORK, NY, USA

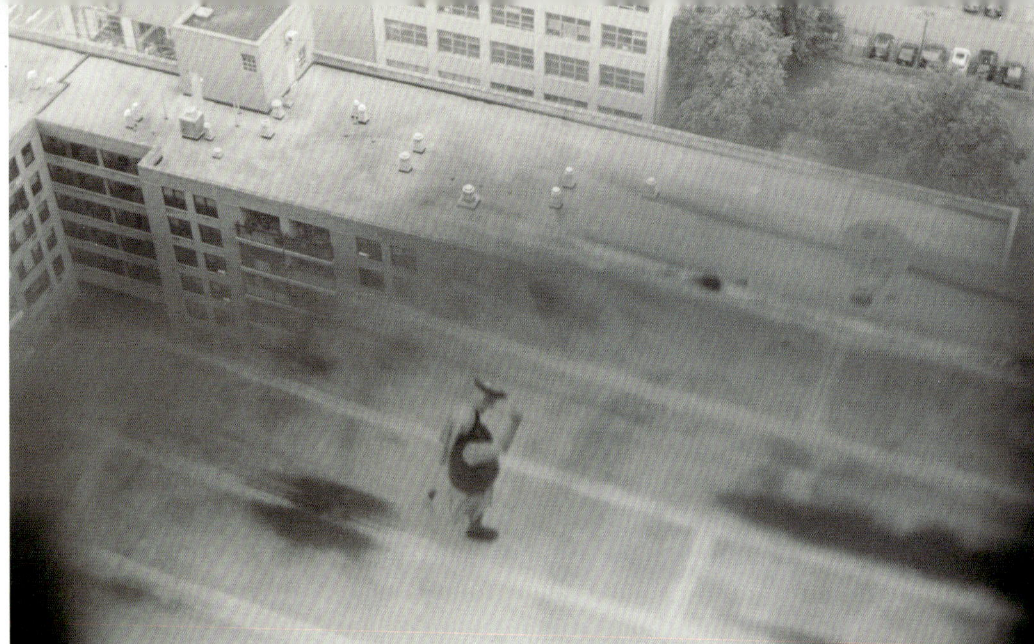

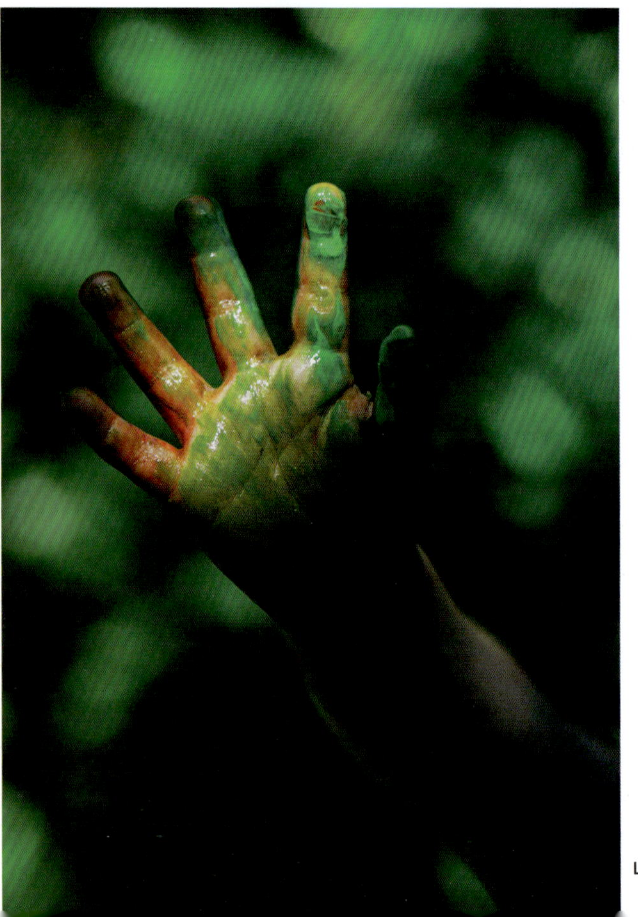

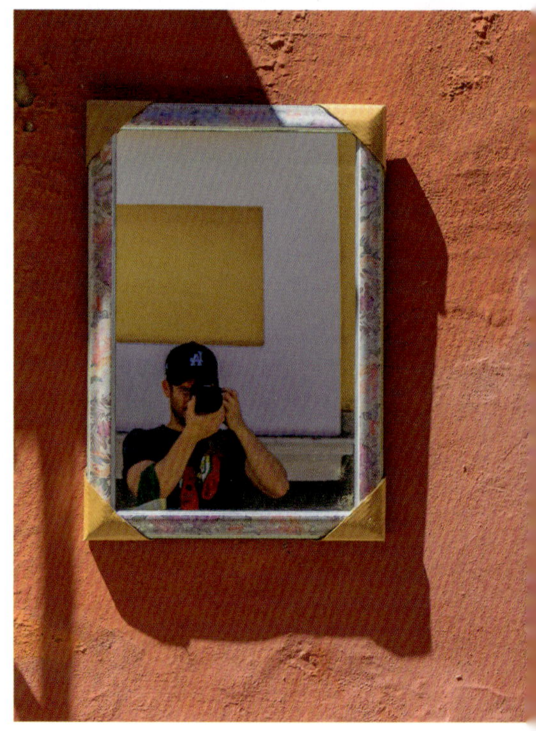

LAUREN PISANO, West Finger Painting During Quarantine. ALTADENA, CA, USA

CLAUDIA HERNANDEZ, *HOPE* | Hope, at this time, is essential. Having the aspiration of a world where everyone matters. NJ, USA

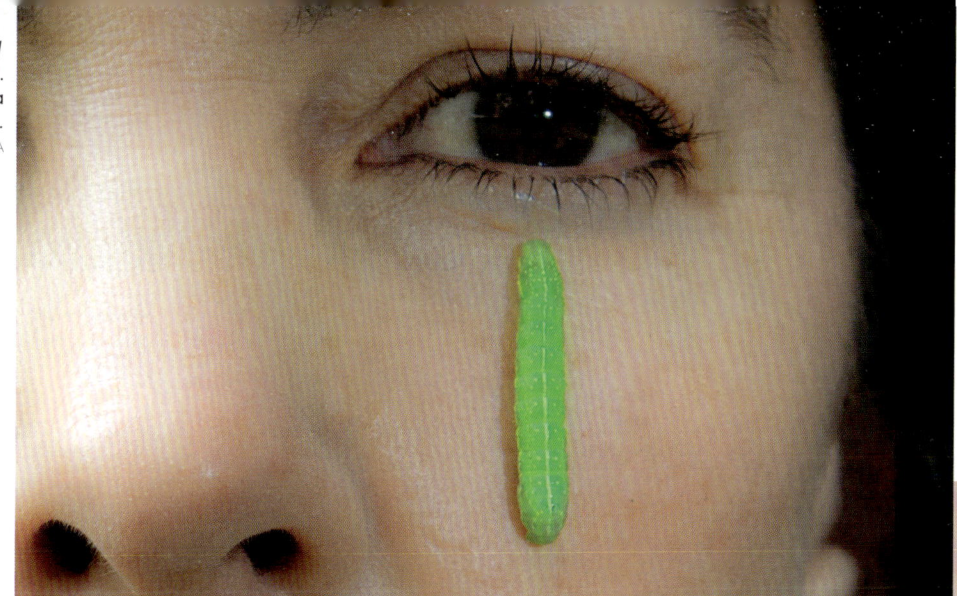

JOSE ANTONIO SILVA GOMEZ, *New look* |

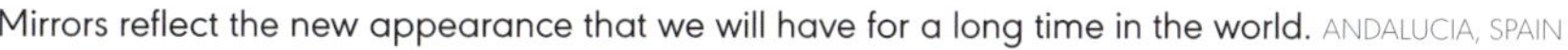

Mirrors reflect the new appearance that we will have for a long time in the world. ANDALUCIA, SPAIN

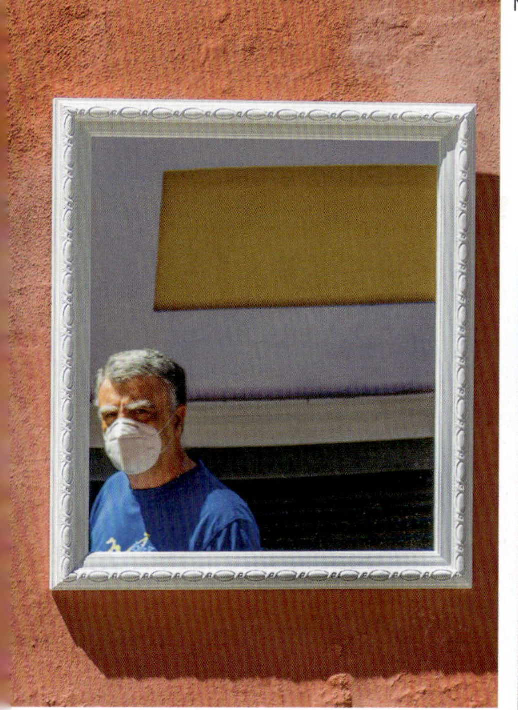

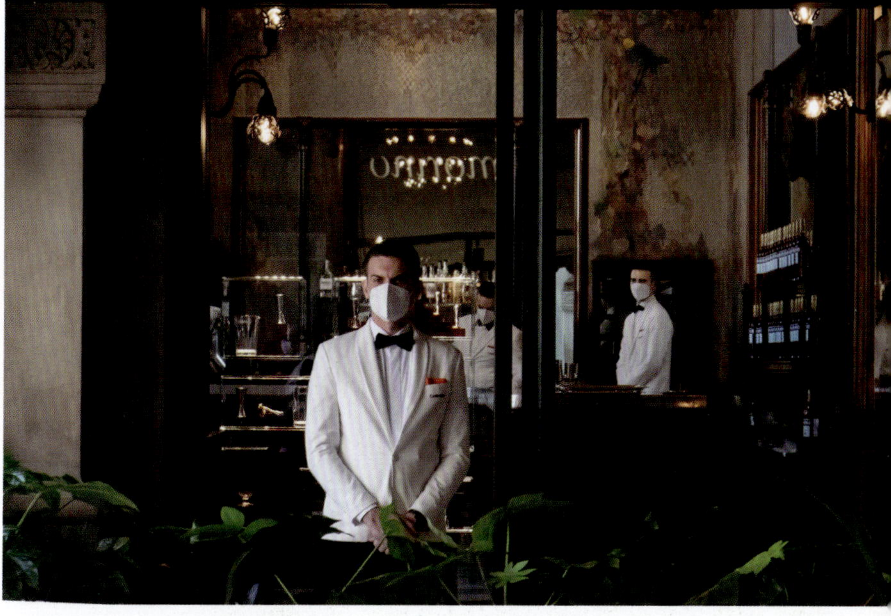

VALERIA CAMMARERI, *The way we are* | Camparino in Galleria Vittorio Emanuele is a historic bar in Milan. It is an icon for citizens and tourists. Its re-opening was a symbol of going back to normality. ITALY

ANGÉLICA ARBULÚ, *The world in my world* |

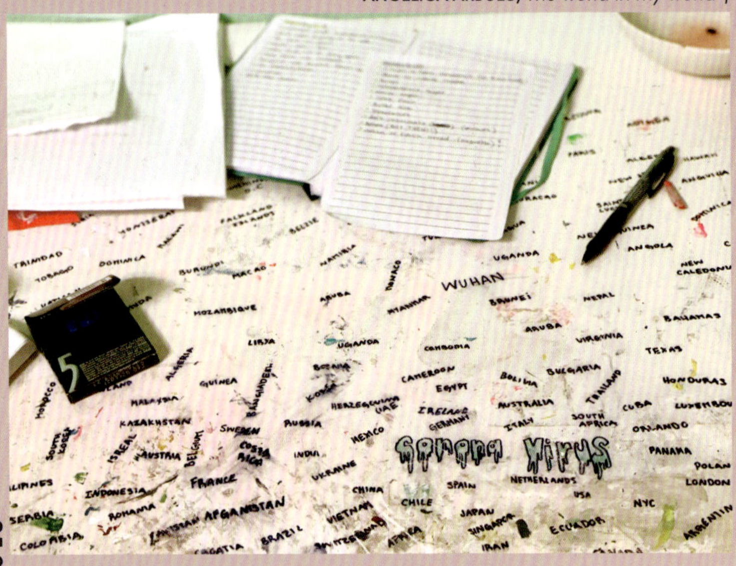

My daughter has written the names of all the countries affected by COVID on her desk. I spent much of my teen years drawing bubble letters in my diary, big and colorful bubble letters with my name, that of my crush or the band I loved most of the time. Tagging, the act of writing your graffiti name with spray paint, was a cornerstone of graffiti culture when it emerged as a form of self assertion in the sixties. First came the name, then came the mural. Just like them, prehistoric men drew animals of their hunting practices on cave walls. Their survival at the mercy of the beast, the caveman drew them in an attempt to both honor and possess them. It's human nature. By drawing on a surface, we're acknowledging the importance and the power of something in our lives. At the same time, we were seeking to affect our environment, to transform it with our interpretation of reality. It broke my heart to walk into my daughter's room to see her work desk, now converted into her home school, covered with hundreds of names of countries, many of which she'd probably never even heard of before. She had painstakingly written one by one to record the expansion of the virus across the world, bleeding ice blue bubble letters in the center, spelling out what mattered most in her world now. Not a crush, not a band, not the assertion of her own name but the coronavirus. PANAMA

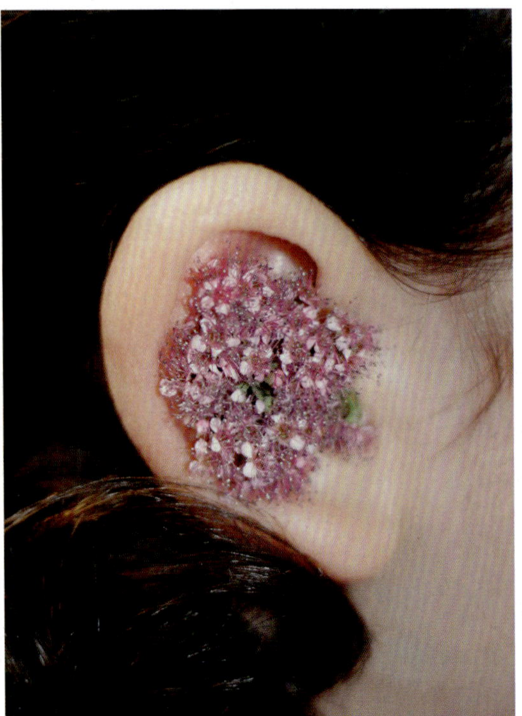

SABRINA SARTORI, *Perceptible symphonies* |
In times of coronavirus, nature recaptures its spaces in the silence of everyday. MILAN, ITALY

PASCALE ROUX DE BEZIEUX, *Where are the Quarantined?* |
From my rooftop quarantine series on the Upper East Side. NEW YORK, NY, USA

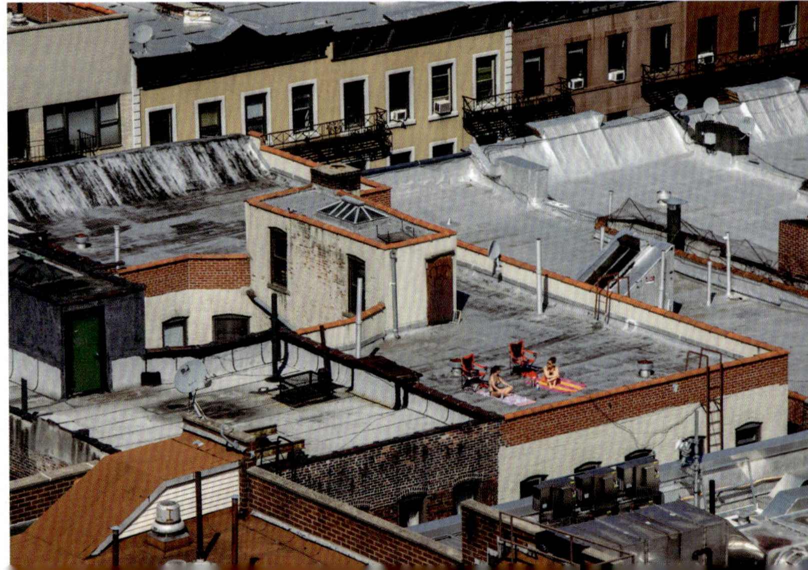

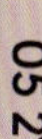

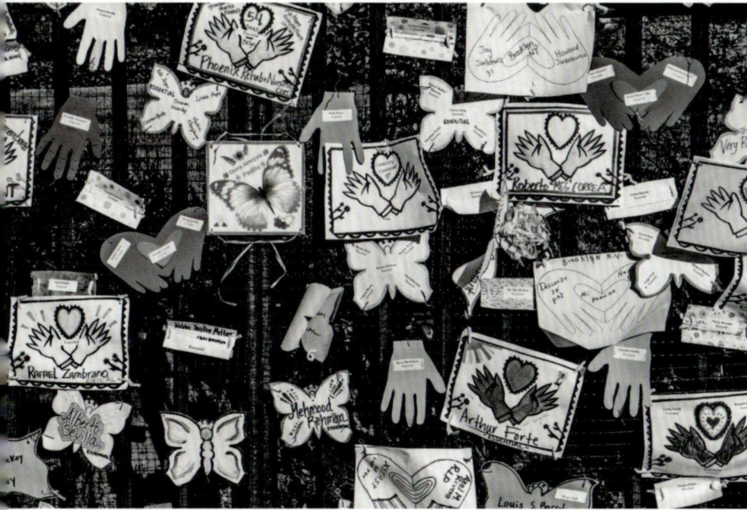

JEAN ROSS, *Naming the Lost |*
At the entrance to Green-Wood Cemetery in Brooklyn. NEW YORK, NY, USA

AMY TOUCHETTE, West 125th Street. HARLEM, MANHATTAN, NY, USA

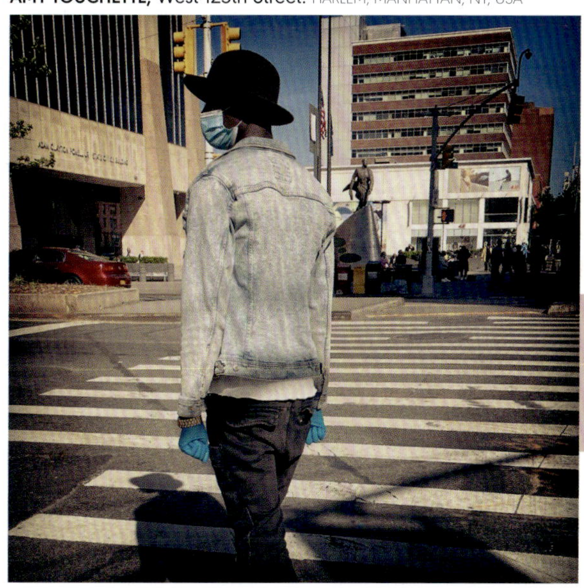

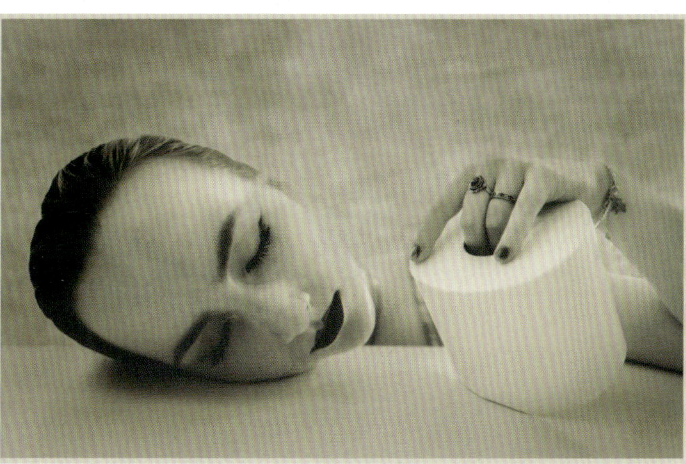

CHRISTY MCDONALD, *Rolls & Tubes Collective, Photo Noir et Blanc, 2020 |*
After Man Ray, Noir et Blanche, 1926. USA

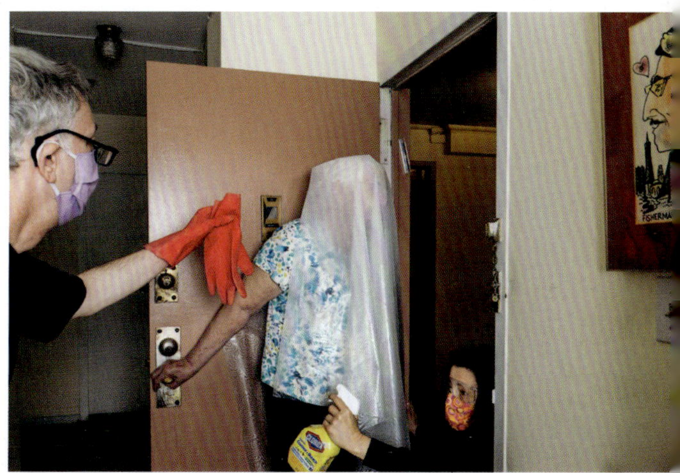

NEIL KRAMER, My mother leaving the house alone for the first time in three months. QUEENS, NY, USA

FAITH NINIVAGGI, Gwyn McLear, 17, a Beaver Country Day graduate lies in the grass in what she would have worn to the prom. Part of a pandemic prom project, an opportunity for high school seniors to get dressed up and be seen and heard. CHESTNUT HILL, MA, USA

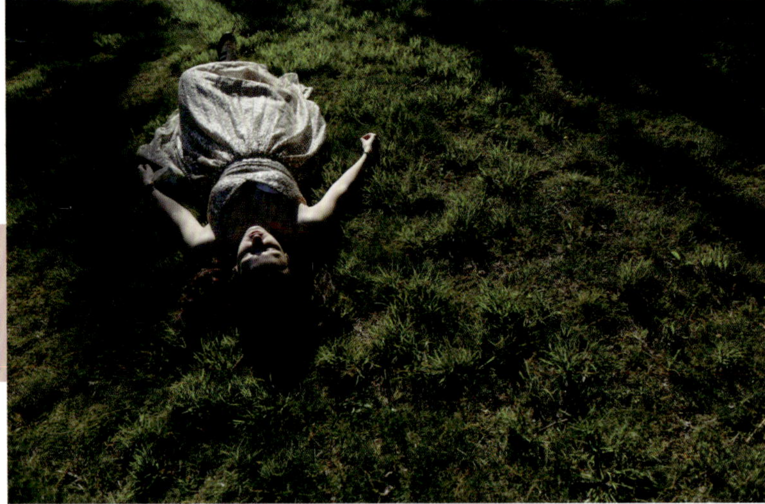

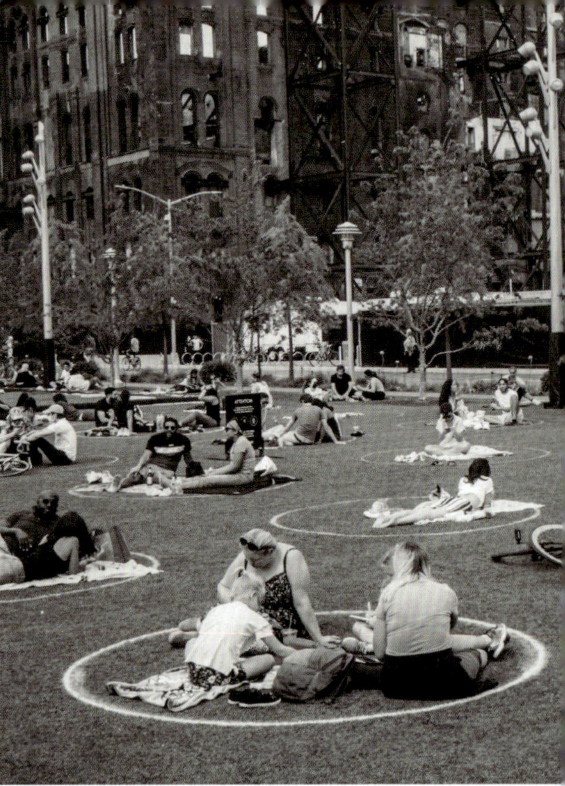

VALERIYA NURGALIEVA, *Disproportion* | Ufa embankment. REPUBLIC OF BASHKORTOSTAN, RUSSIA

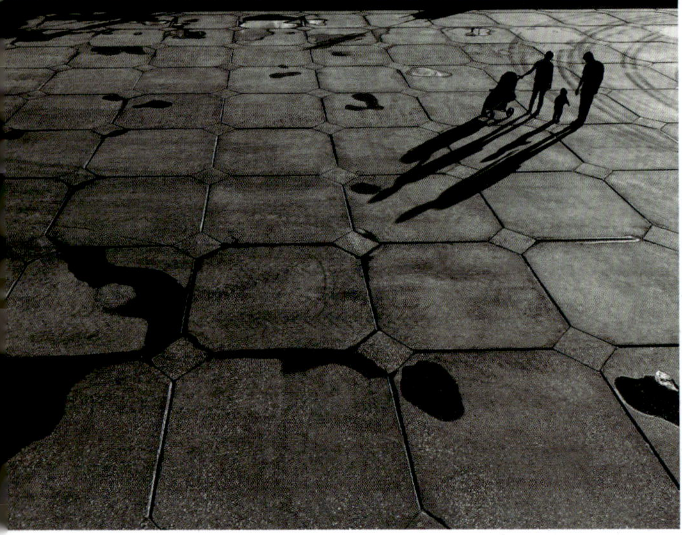

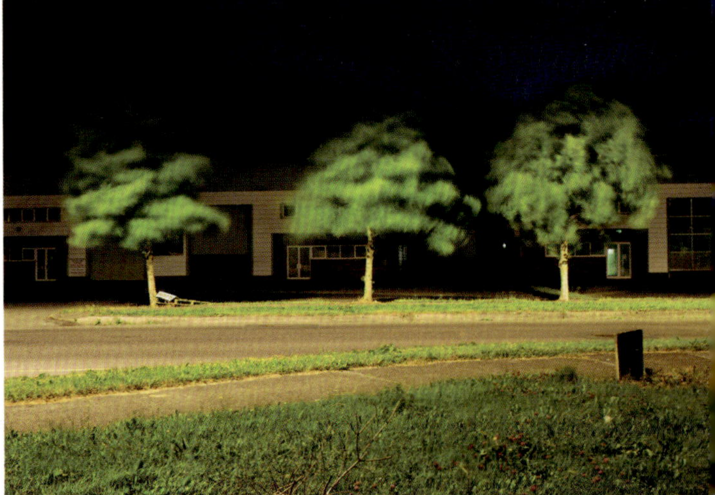

MICHAEL CROGHAN, The air we don't see. LONGFORD TOWN, IRELAND

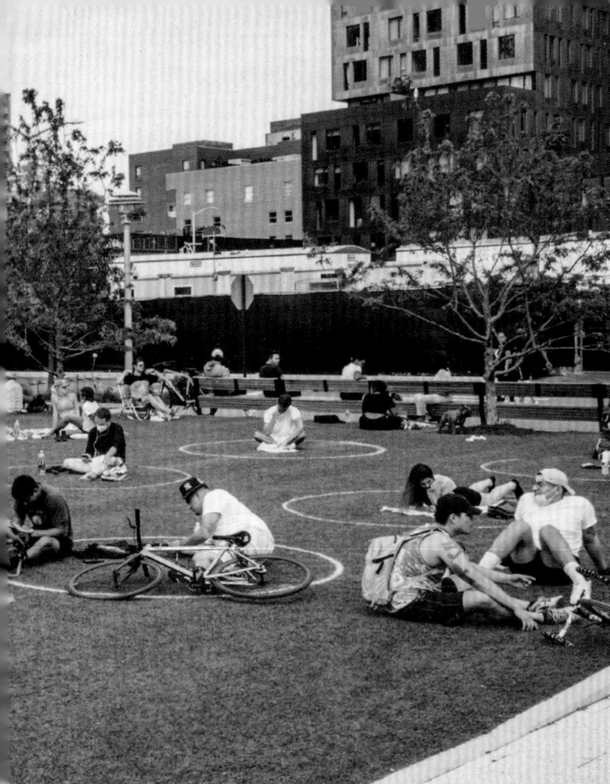

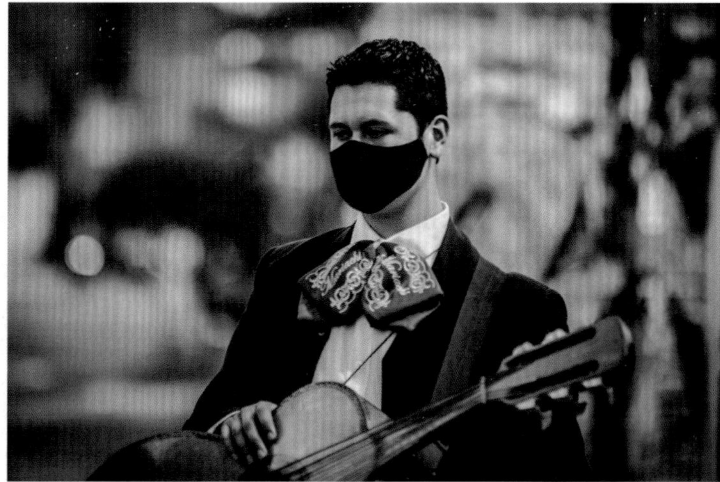

ANDRÉS HERRERA PÉREZ, @andresherreraperez. Colombian mariachi who cannot play at social events due to COVID-19. Now, he must play on the street for money. BOGOTÁ, COLOMBIA

TAJ HOWE, *Social Circles* | Brooklynites gather in Domino Park in Williamsburg. BROOKLYN, NY, USA

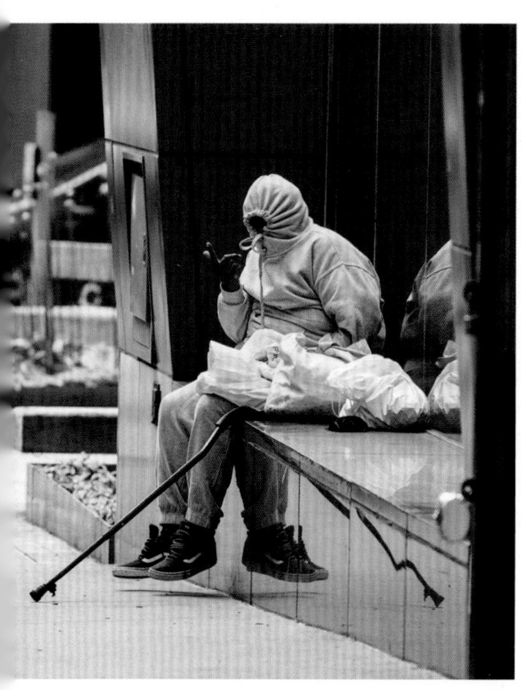

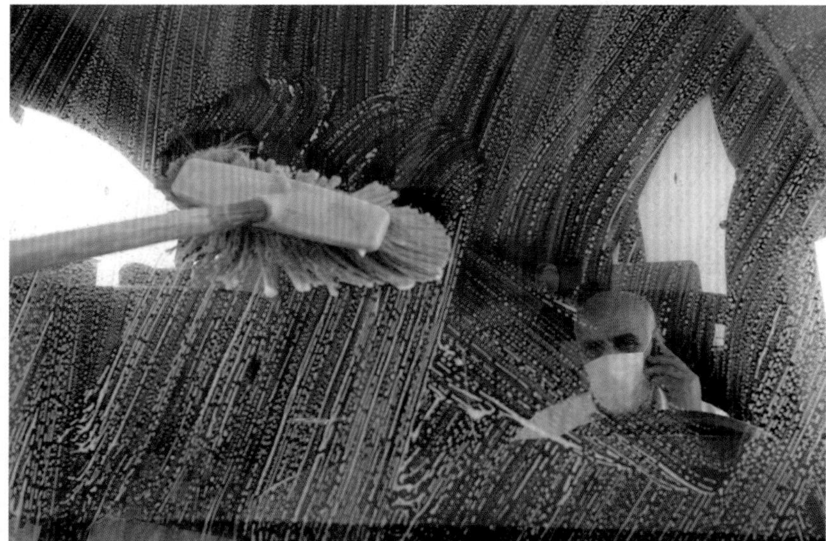

MEMMET ERHAN GURKAN, Last Bus Before Lockdown, Bus Terminal Adana. TURKEY

PATRICK MACLEOD, If it Works it Ain't Stupid. FINANCIAL DISTRICT, NEW YORK, NY, USA

RAJAÂ KHENOUSSI, *Serious crisis* | Closed shops in Tangier's old Medina provide an uncertain state due to the economic paralysis brought on by COVID-19. MOROCCO.

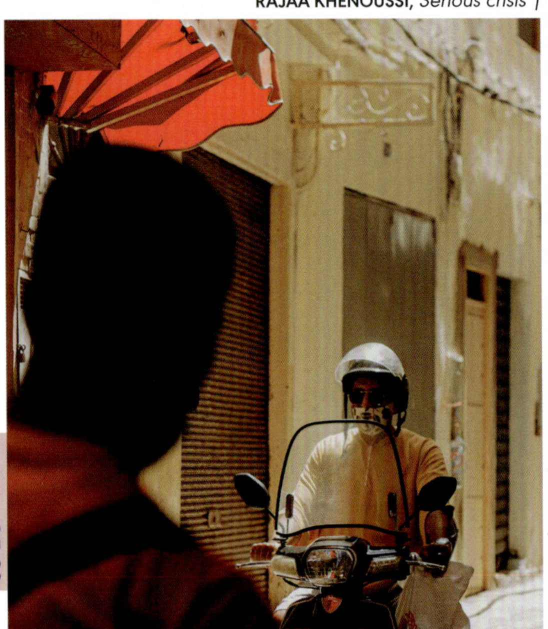

FRANK SCHRAMM, Presby Memorial Iris Garden. MONTCLAIR, NJ, USA

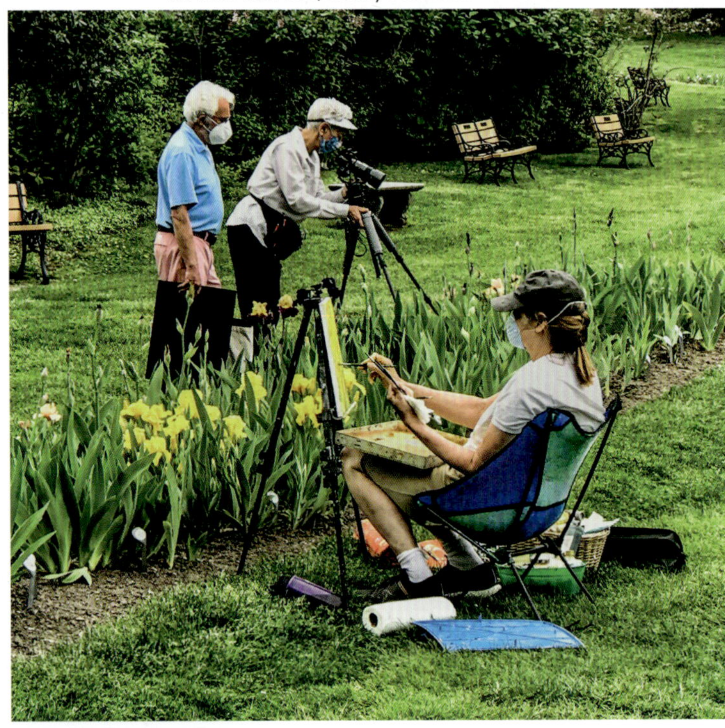

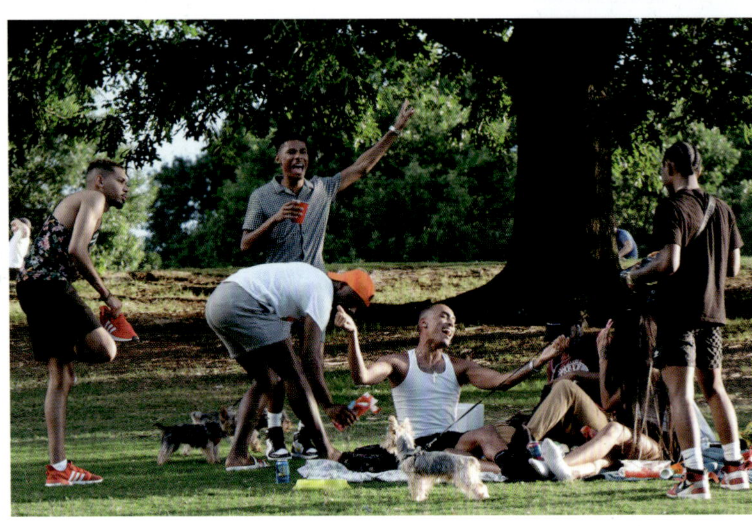

ARVIN TEMKAR, Memorial Day weekend 2020 at Piedmont Park. ATLANTA, GA, USA

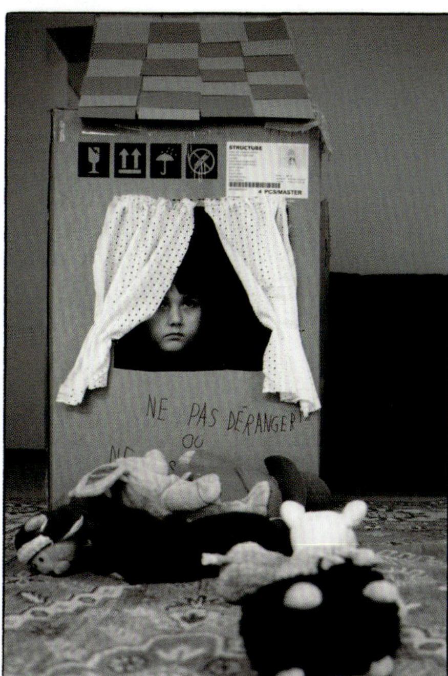

NICOLAS ST-PIERRE, During confinement, my nine-year-old daughter Camille is playing with her gaming console sitting in the cardboard house she built for her stuffed animals. OTTOWA, ONTARIO, CANADA

GARRY LOTULUNG, Muslim women wearing face masks pray to celebrate Eid al-Fitr, the festival marking the end of Ramadan, at a residential area amid the spread of COVID-19. BEKASI, INDONESIA

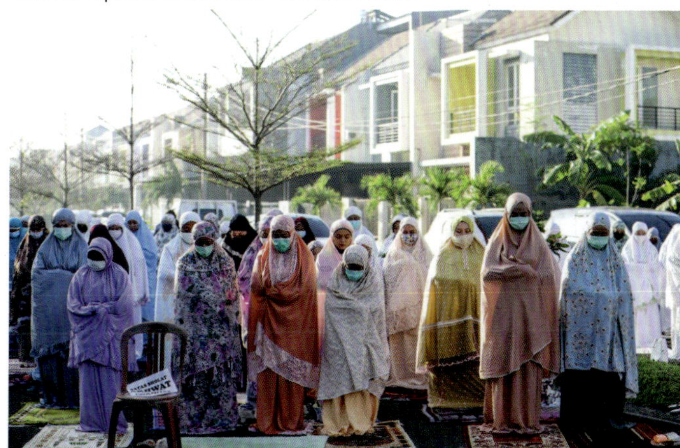

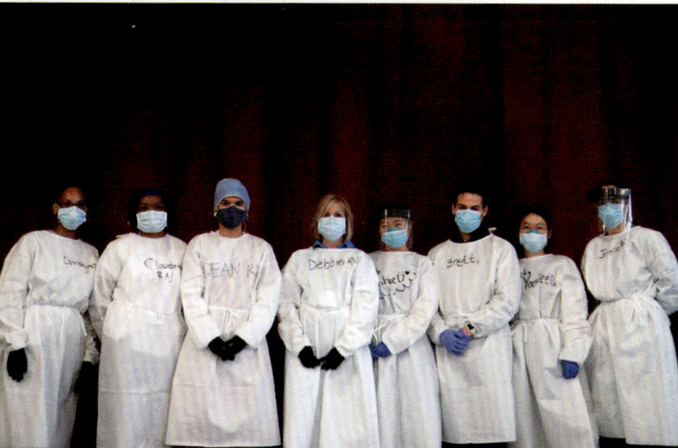

RUSS ROWLAND, *The Graduate* | Ran into this young kindergarten graduate in Brooklyn Bridge Park who offered a glimmer of hope for the future. NEW YORK, NY, USA

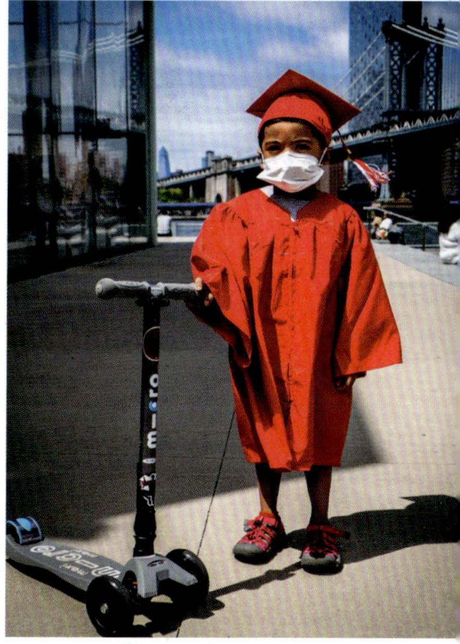

DEEDEE DEGELIA, *Heroes: COVID-19 Testing* | Team of healthcare workers administering swab and antibody testing at First Baptist Church of Corona. QUEENS, NY, USA

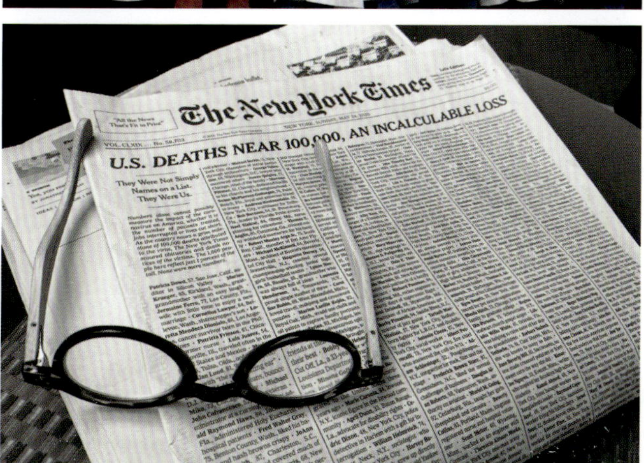
The New York Times

U.S. DEATHS NEAR 100,000, AN INCALCULABLE LOSS

They Were Not Simply Names on a List. They Were Us.

ORESTES GONZALEZ, I drove to the closest bodega to pick up this Sunday New York Times, but it was sold out. It took three more tries in Astoria to find it. I got back in my car, read that first page, and lost it. I laid it on the passenger seat, and removed my glasses to wipe my tears. QUEENS, NY, USA

JAMES ENGLISH, Photography became a therapy for dealing with the pandemic, sometimes it let me talk, and sometimes it asked questions I didn't know the answers to. LONDON, UNITED KINGDOM

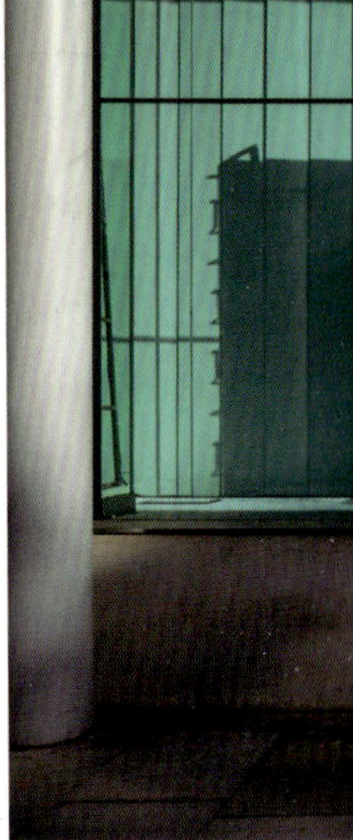

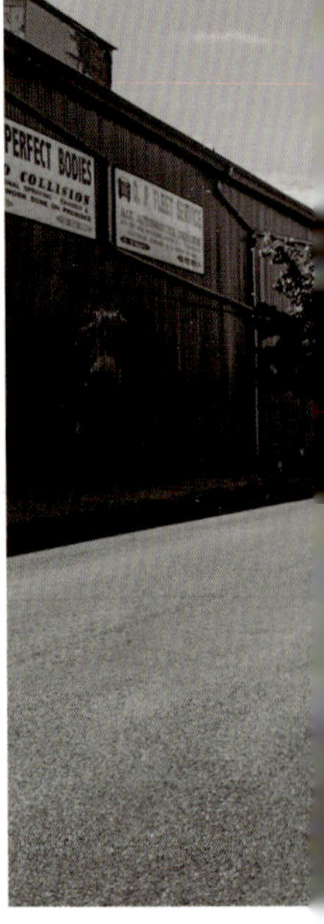

MERAV MAROODY, *Photokabine* | Berlin during the pandemic. What used to be an essential part of tourism, the photo booth, is now standing empty, reflecting our new masked identities. GERMANY

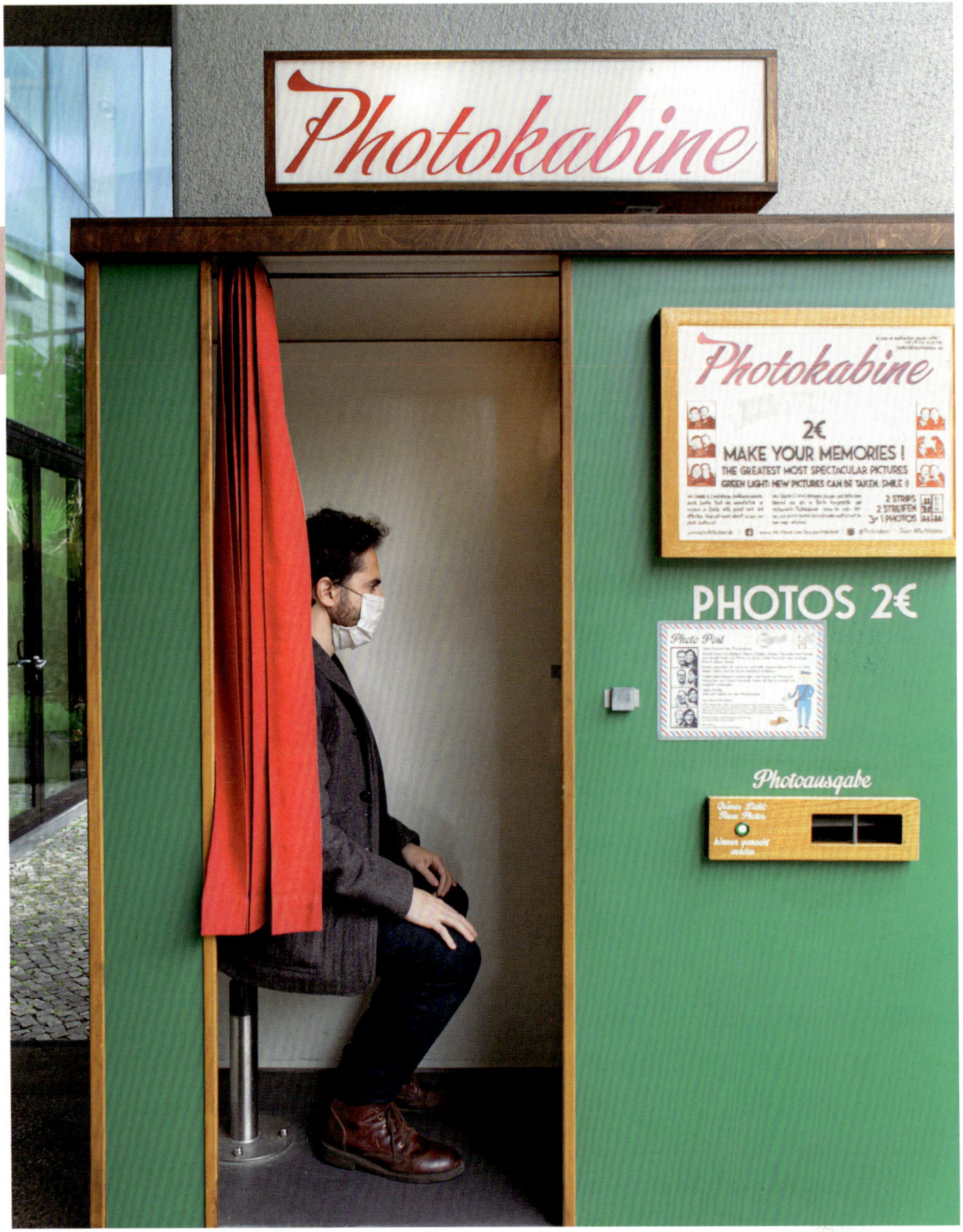

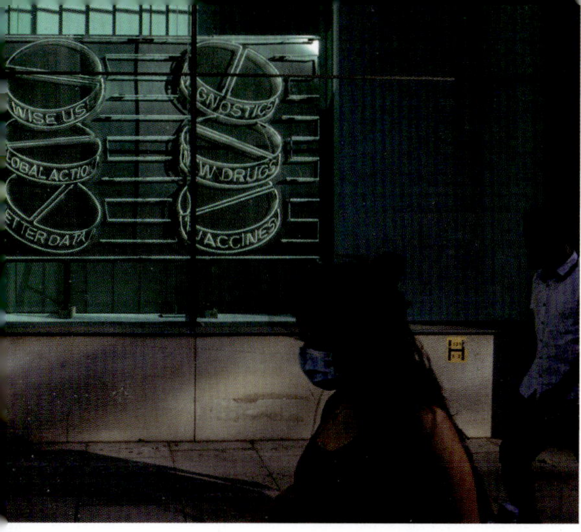

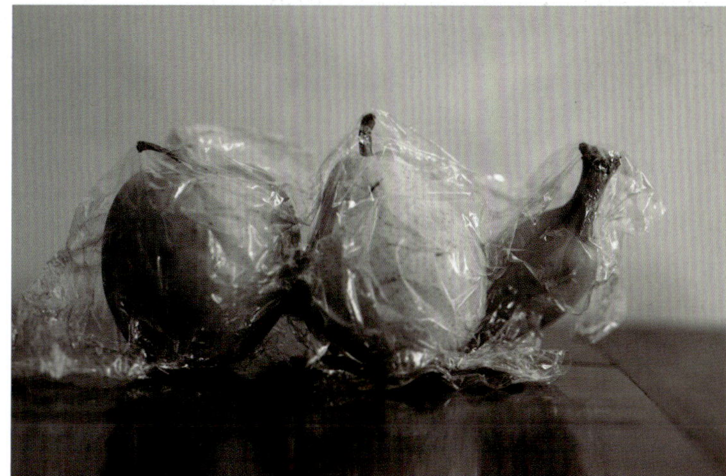

CLAUDIA IOAN, *SET ME FREE* | Vacuum-sealed life in the time of coronavirus. In need of breath, longing to go ahead. PERUGIA, ITALY

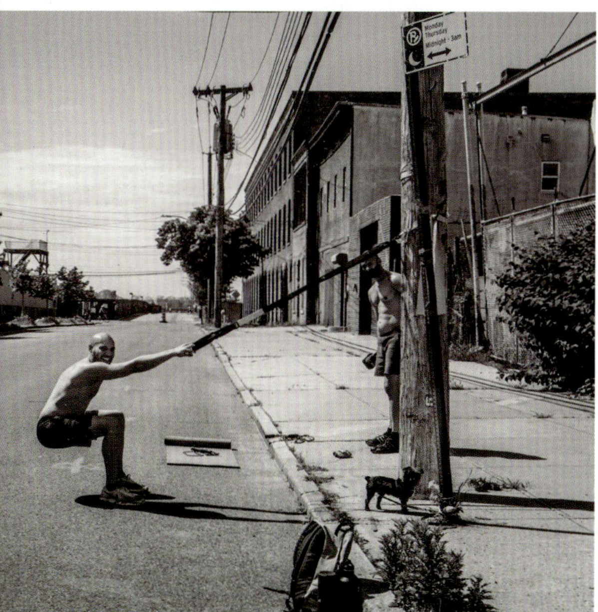

GRAHAM MACINDOE, Two men and a dog, working out during the COVID-19 lockdown and gym closures. REDHOOK, BROOKLYN, NY, USA

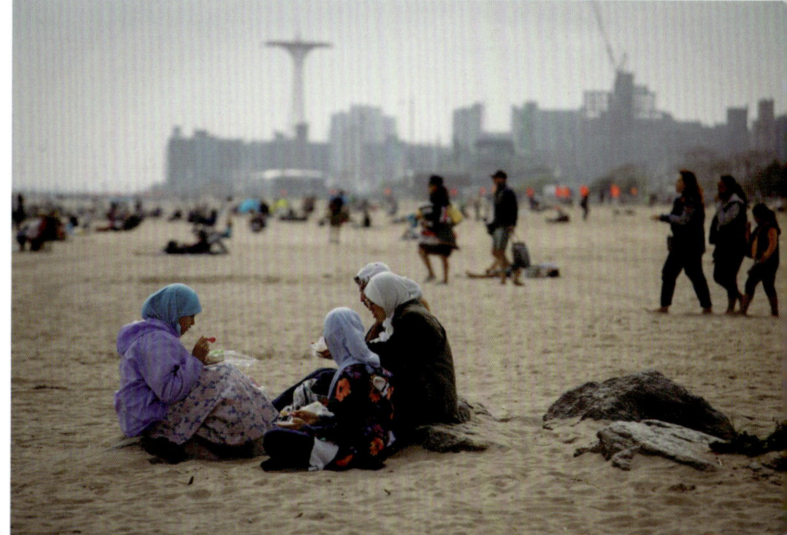

ERICA LANSNER,
A Muslim family (Nizar from Syria and Seiju from Japan) celebrate Eid with lunch at Brighton Beach with their two daughters. CONEY ISLAND, NY, USA

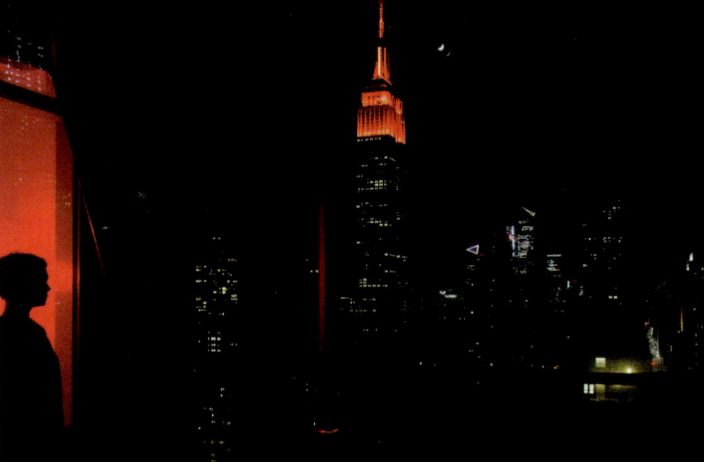

XIMENA ECHAGUE, *Street Photographer Without Streets* | The new plague has confined all of us indoors, allowing only for introspection, imagination and symbolism to capture the new fuzzy reality, the invisible risk, the permanent fear. MANHATTAN, NY, USA

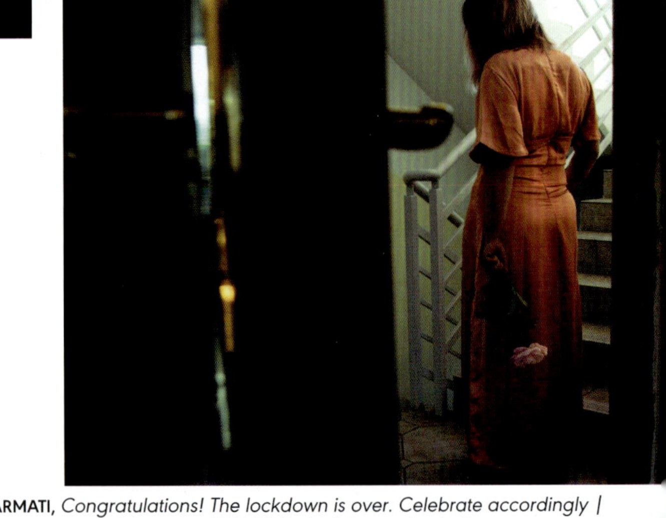

LILI GYARMATI, *Congratulations! The lockdown is over. Celebrate accordingly* | Part of the series "PAUSE," which is my visual diary of the COVID-19 pandemic. BUDAPEST, HUNGARY

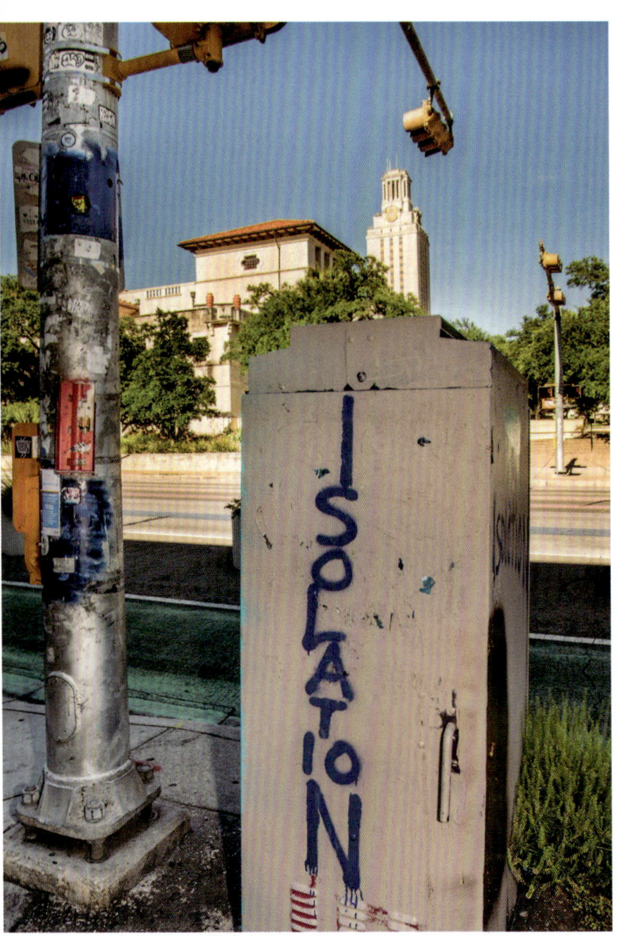

ED MALCIK, Isolated. Stay home. No work. No touch. No future. AUSTIN, TX, USA

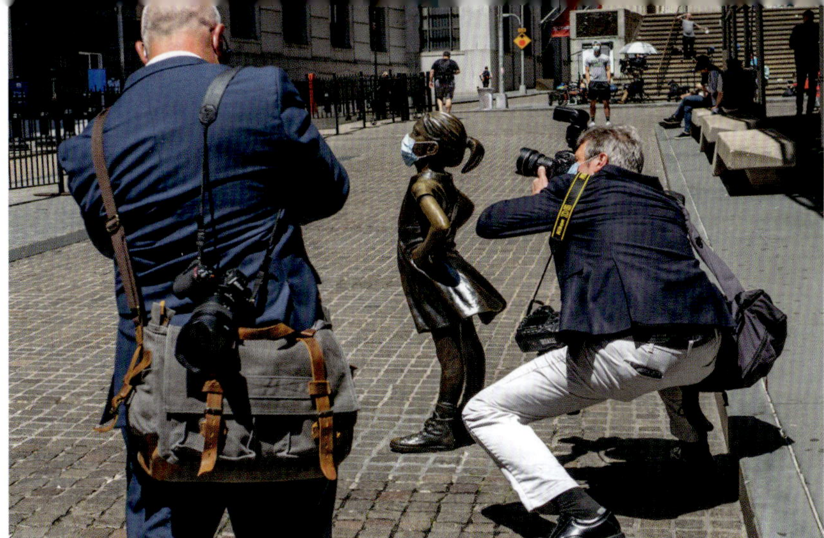

MILO HESS, Fearless Girl on Wall Street being safe with a mask while being photographed by two unmasked photographers. NEW YORK, NY, USA

MOLLIE SCHAIDT, Searching for God. KING GEORGE, VA, USA

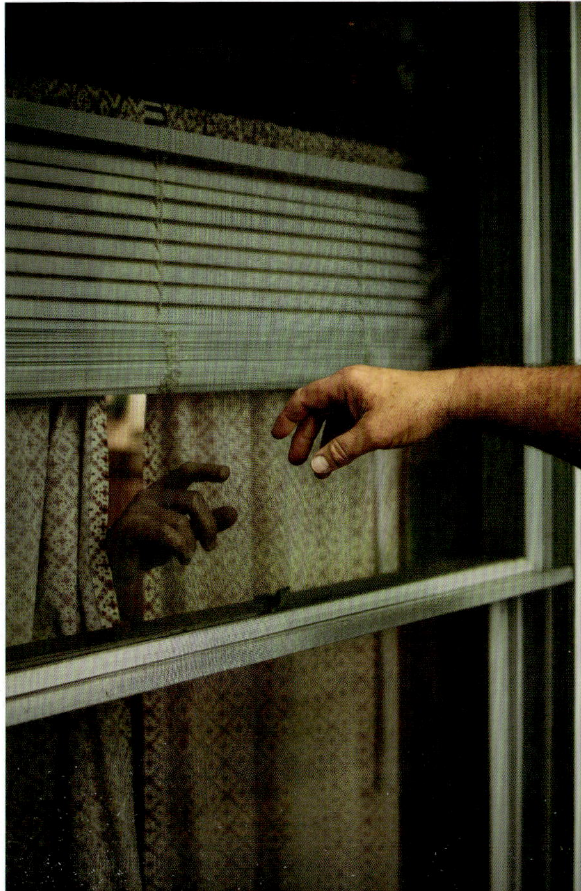

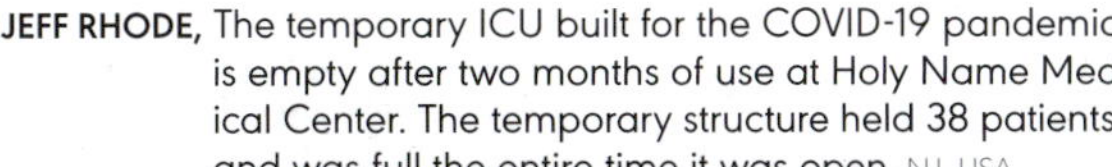

JEFF RHODE, The temporary ICU built for the COVID-19 pandemic is empty after two months of use at Holy Name Medical Center. The temporary structure held 38 patients and was full the entire time it was open. NJ, USA

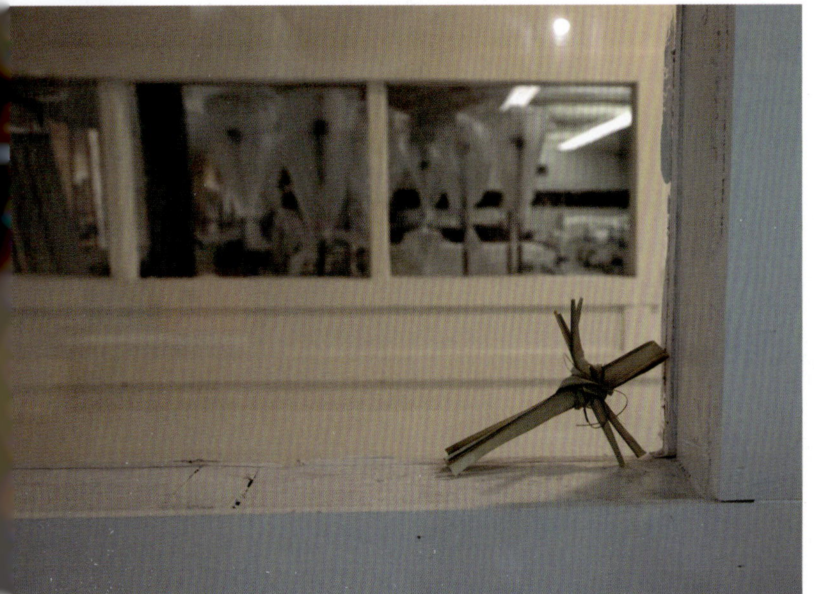

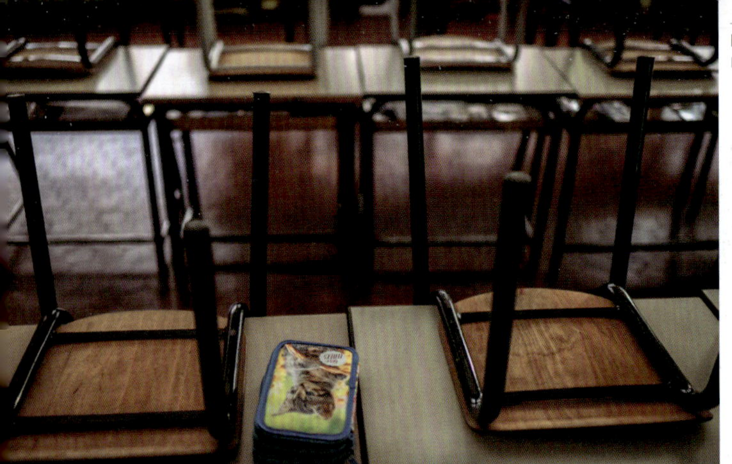

MAURIZIO GJIVOVICH, An elementary school in Turin during the lockdown. ITALY

GEORGE KAMPER, *Happiness Comes in Waves* | So happy to sea the beach again. Expanding our bubble with our first outing. Staying safe and self-distancing, please do the same! FORT LAUDERDALE, FL, USA

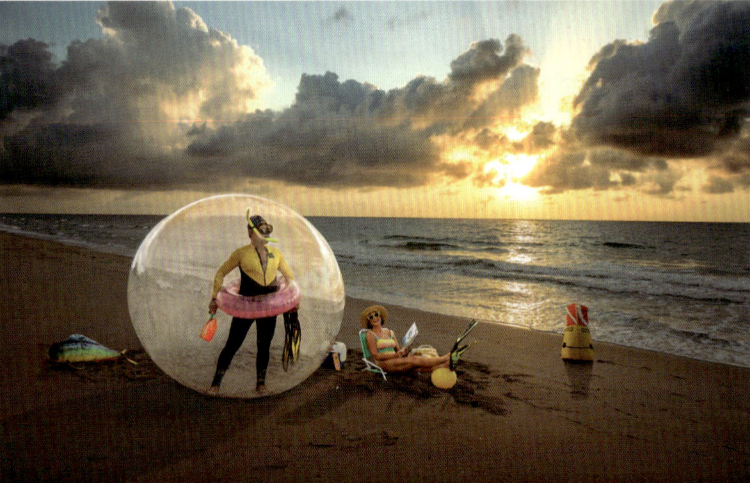

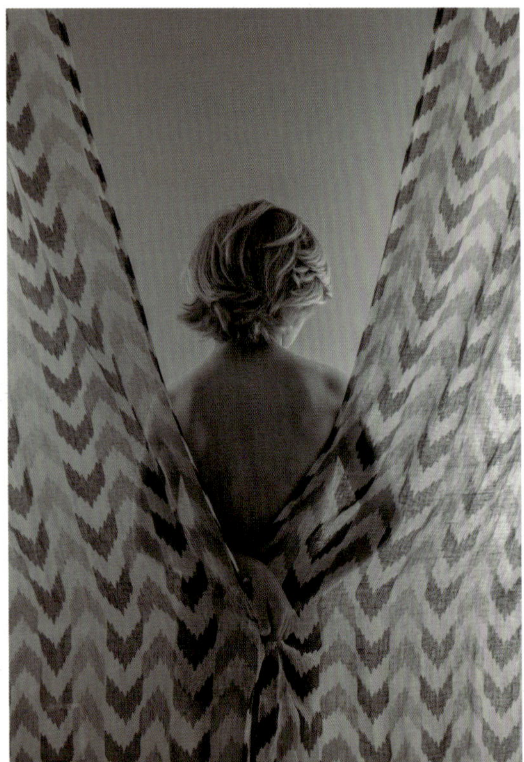

SARAH STACKE, *The Bookmark Portraits, Lockdown Week 11* | To process the lockdown and ease tension from homeschooling, my first-grade son and I collaborate on portraits about our pandemic experience. BROOKLYN, NY, USA

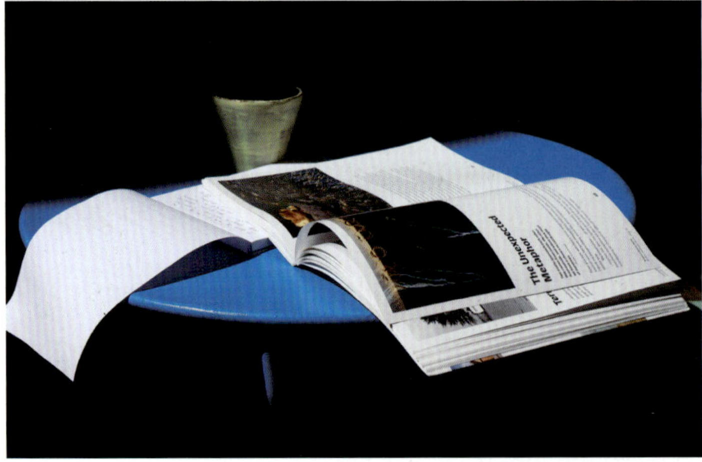

NOELIA NICOLÁS, *Blue* | In my garden in Amsterdam during the lockdown. I had just painted an old table in blue, the color of the Mediterranean where I am from. NETHERLANDS

MICHAEL GEBEYHU, *Waiting for Me |* The title references the day-to-day struggles people face in fighting COVID-19 as they work to meet their daily needs, their dreams and find their way to their loved ones. ADDIS ABABA, ETHIOPIA

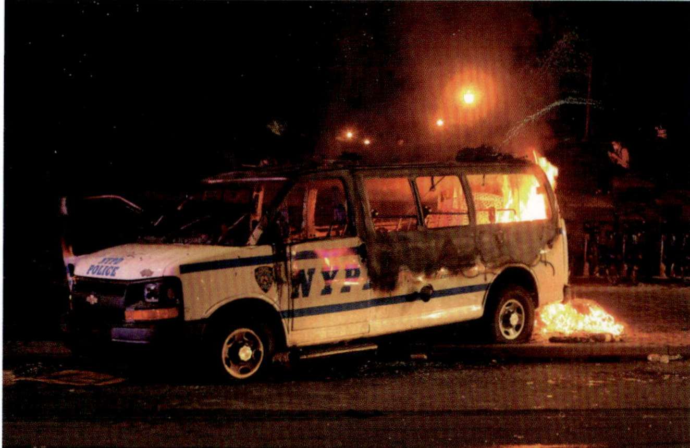

JOSHUA MOISE, The corner of South Portland and Dekalb Ave on one of the worst weeks in American history. BROOKLYN, NY, USA

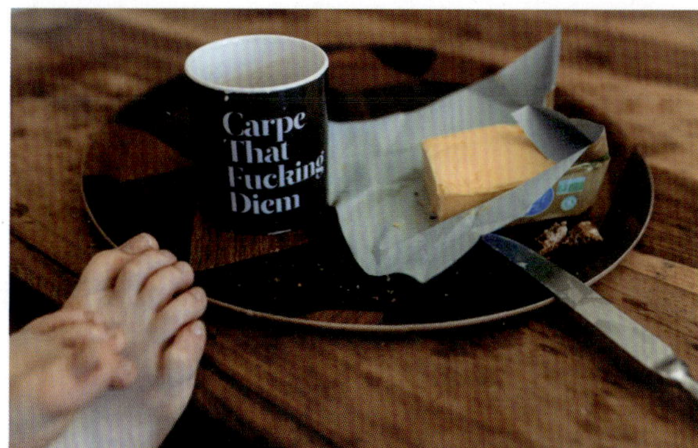

MARINE PORON, Every moment of this strange period reminds us of how much we should enjoy life. PARIS, FRANCE

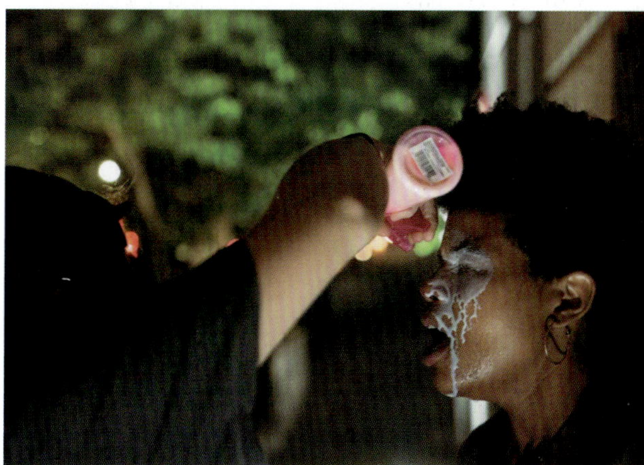

NOLAN SEPTER, A protester gets milk sprayed into her eyes after being tear-gassed. DENVER, CO, USA

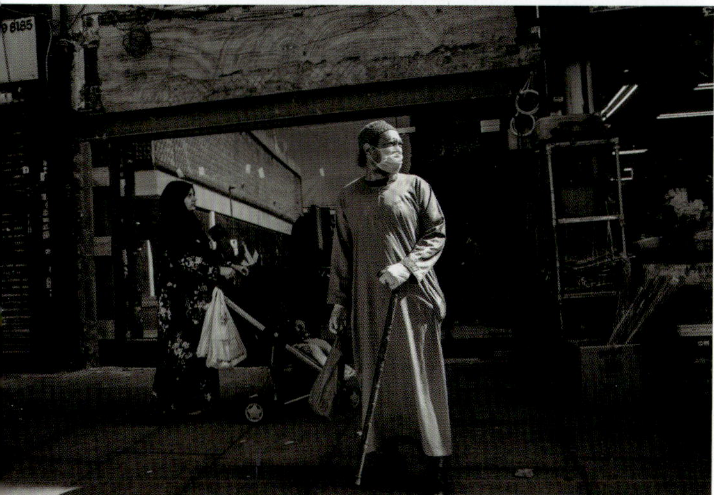

JEFF MOORE, As London starts to reopen, shoppers return to the streets. BETHAL GREEN, UNITED KINGDOM

FRANCIS YBANEZ, Hands up. FAIRFAX, LOS ANGELES, CA, USA

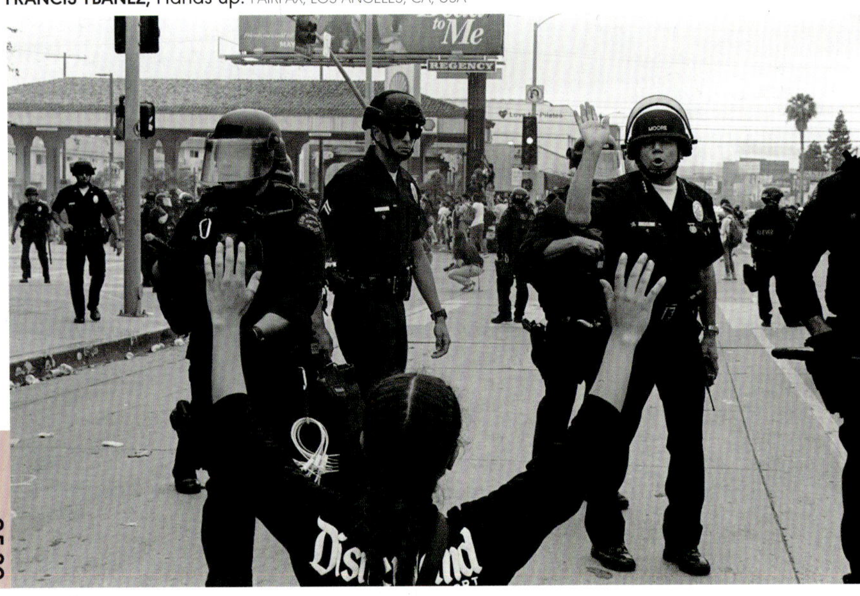

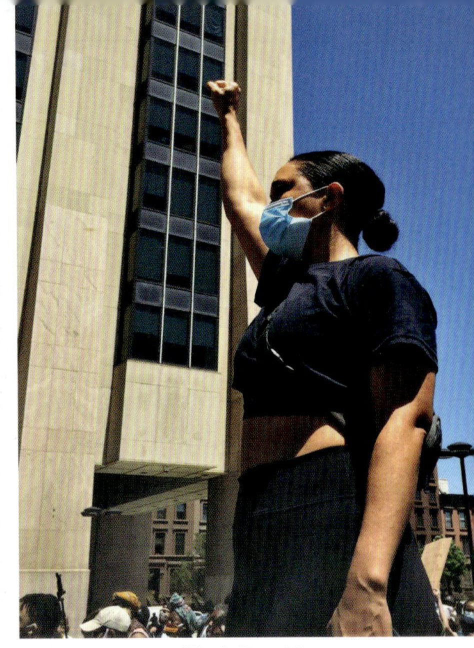

PATRICIA BELLUCCI, Black Lives Matter protest on 125th Street in Harlem. NEW YORK, NY, USA

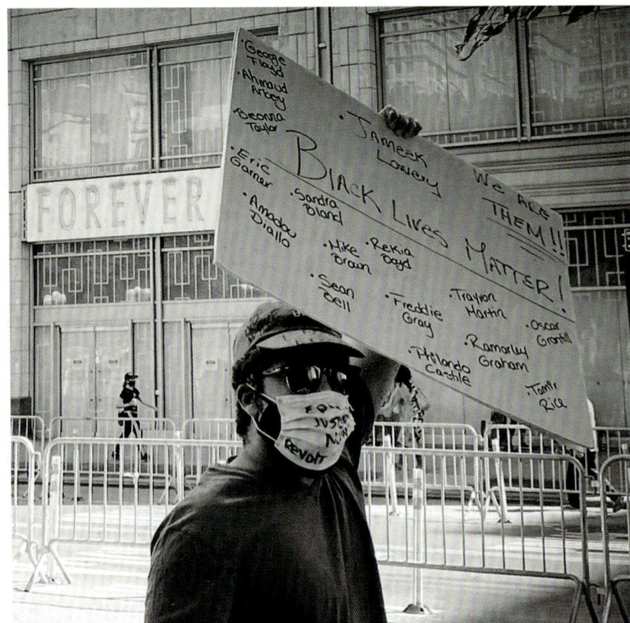

NIKKI JOHNSON, Forever, NYC. NEW YORK, NY, USA

RICKY VALENTE, Resist. PITTSBURGH, PA, USA

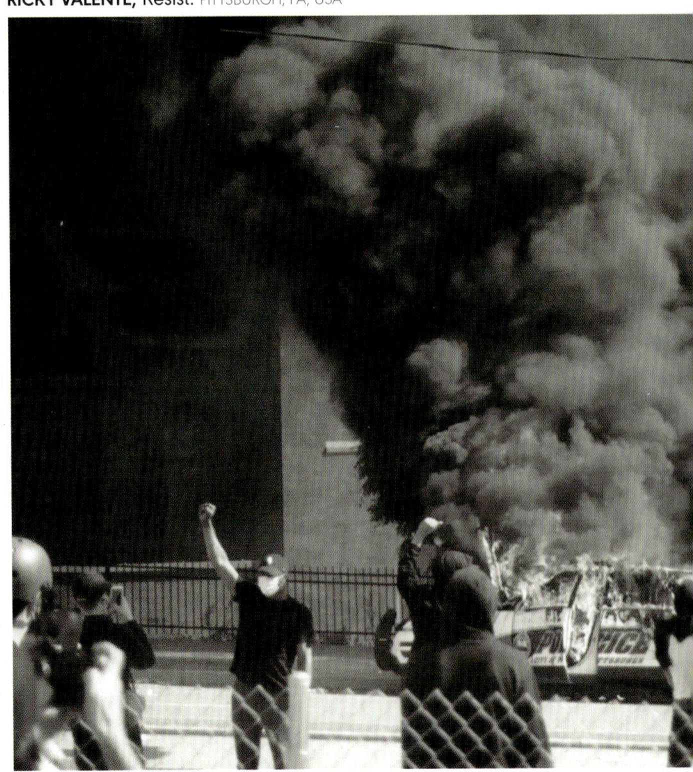

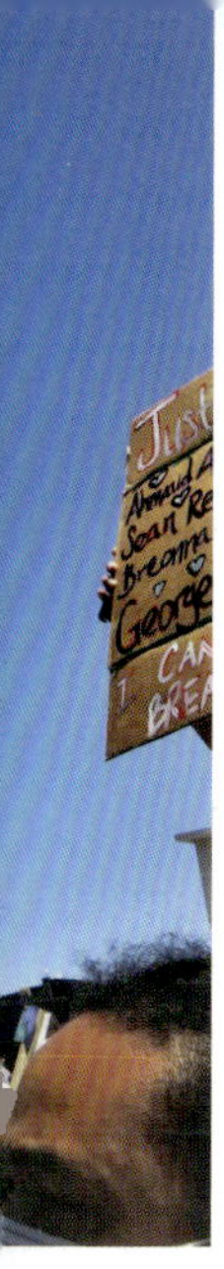

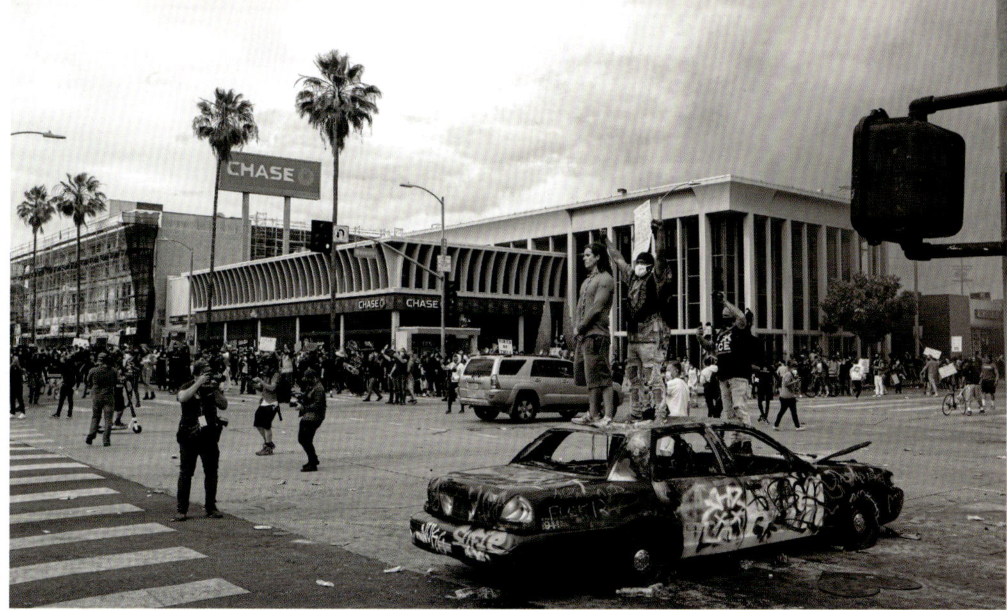

JAHNNY LEE, *Liberation* | The uprising in honor of George Floyd and the movement for Black lives was met with violent force by riot police. The term riot implies meaningless violence and has long been used by a culture of systemic racism to signify the image of Black people wreaking senseless chaos. LOS ANGELES, CA, USA

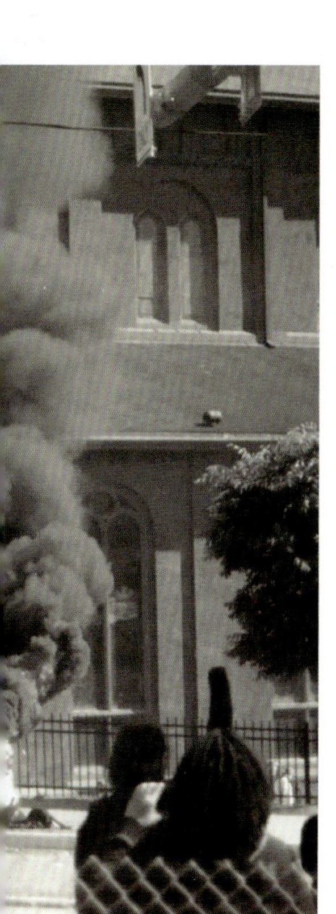

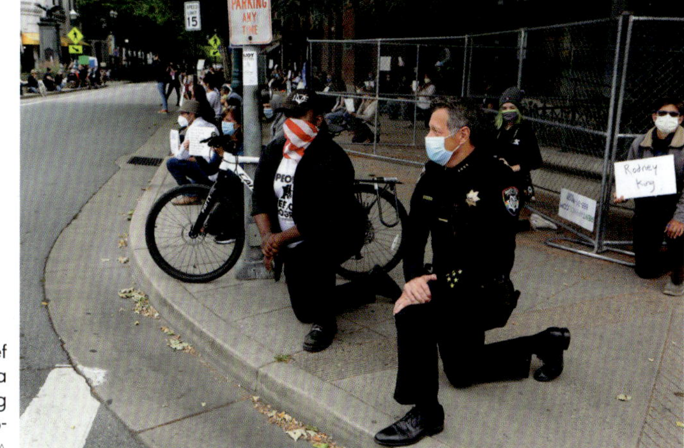

SHMUEL THALER, Santa Cruz Police Chief Andy Mills takes a knee next to Santa Cruz Mayor Justin Cummings, bringing attention to institutionalized police violence against Black people. CA, USA

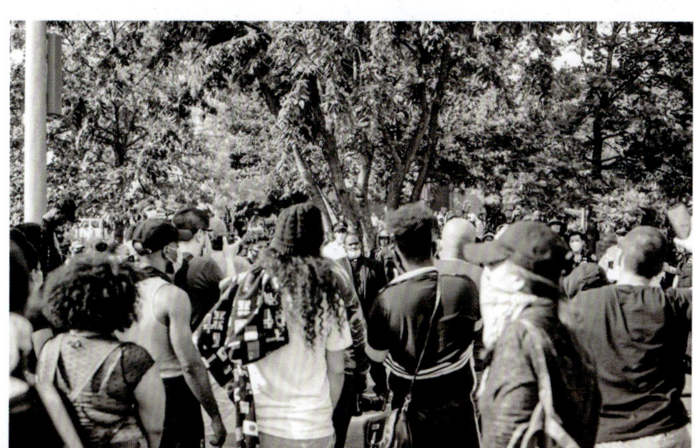

PHILLIP JUNOR, Everyone was as peaceful as this preacher spoke. BRONX, NY, USA

05 30

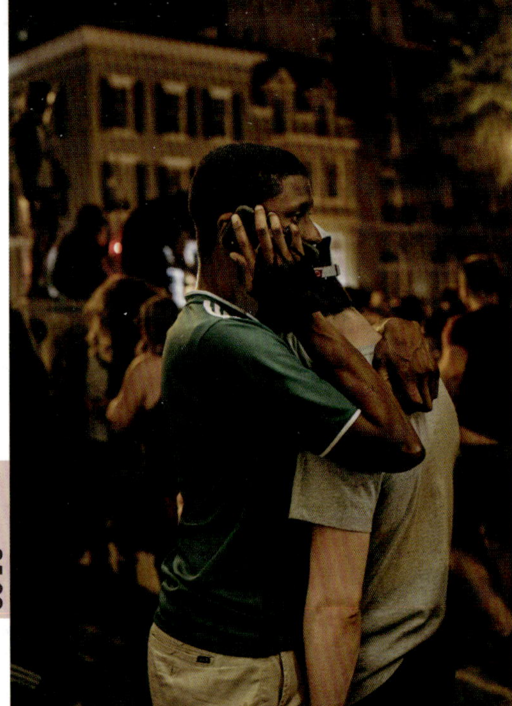

JASON ANDREW, Two young men embrace following tear gas canisters and flash bangs being thrown at protesters outside of the White House. WASHINGTON, DC, USA

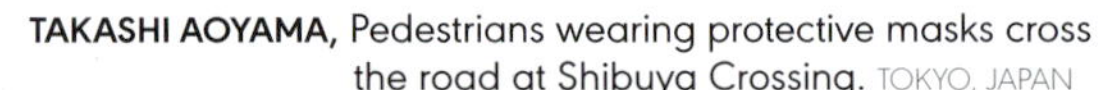

TAKASHI AOYAMA, Pedestrians wearing protective masks cross the road at Shibuya Crossing. TOKYO, JAPAN

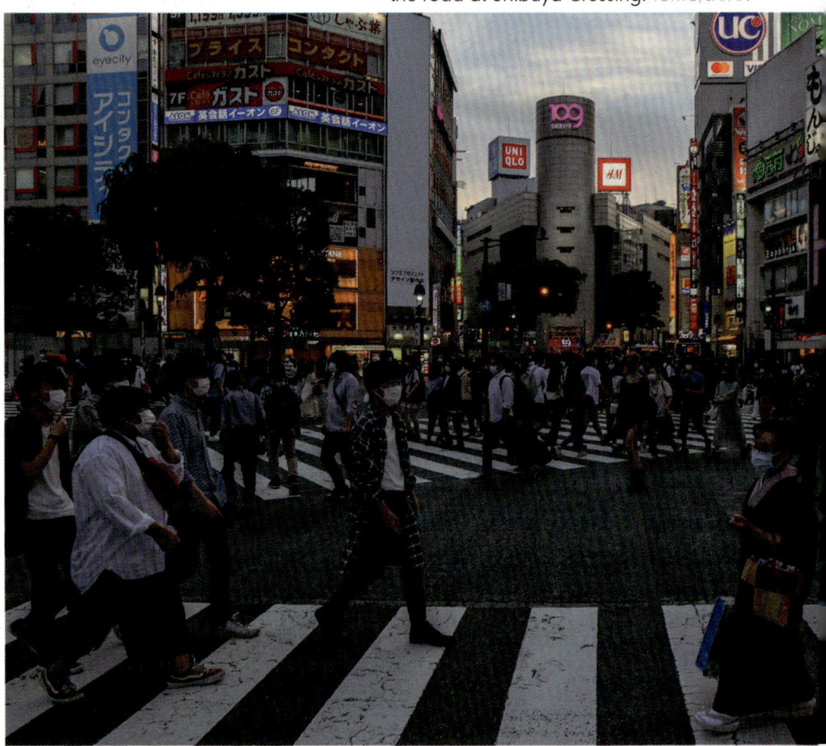

MAYNOR ORLANDO VALENZUELA CISNEROS, In the Sierras de Paz private cemetery in Managua, an express or hurried burial is carried out for a 65-year-old woman who died of COVID-19 on Mother's Day. NICARAGUA

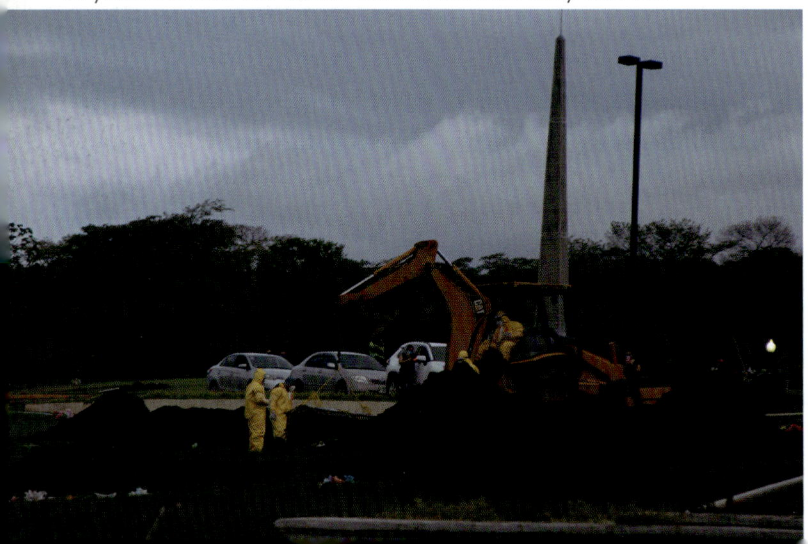

RYAN LEYBA, Labor and Delivery, birth of our fourth child, COVID precautions required. PHOENIZ, AZ, USA

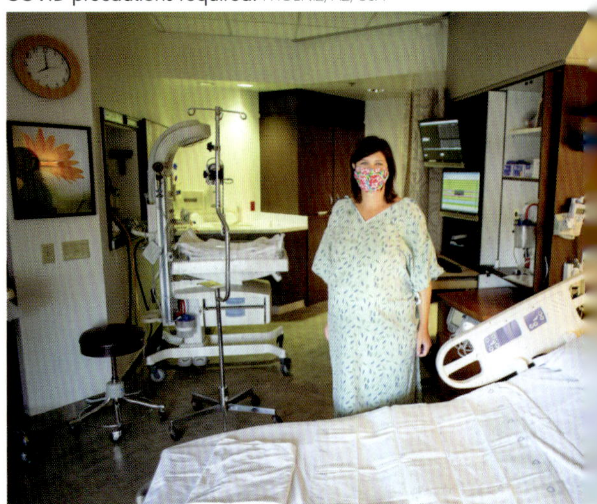

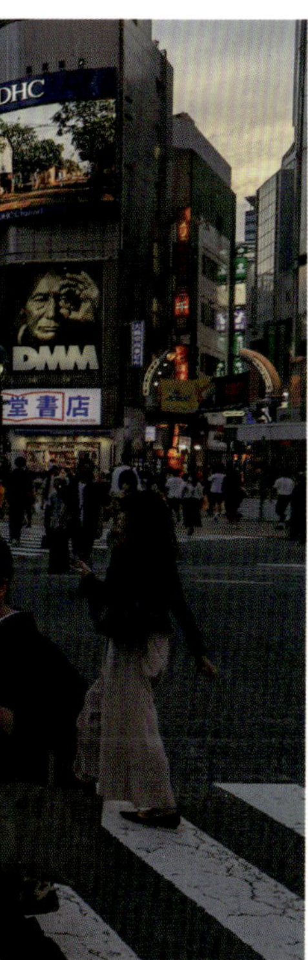

JOHN PUGA, *Line in the Sand* |

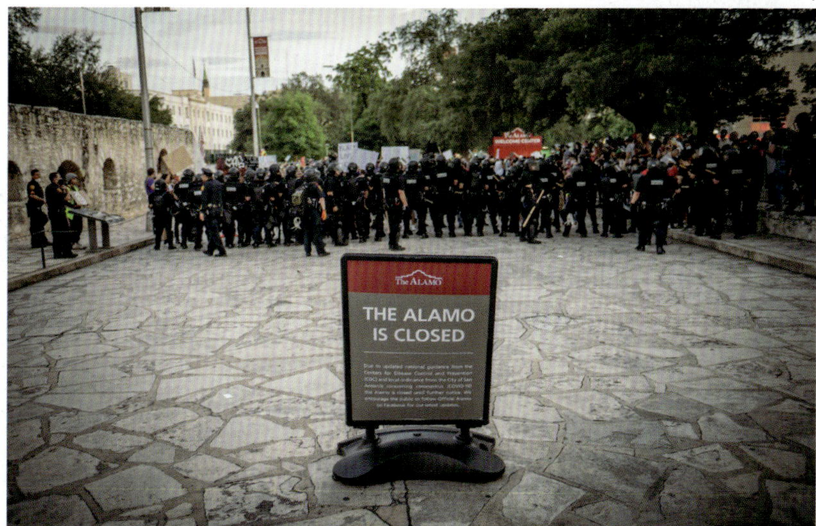

184-years later a new line is being drawn at The Alamo between police and protesters. Does history always repeat itself? SAN ANTONIO, TX, USA

ADAM SCHLESINGER, Protestors head south on Madison Avenue in New York City. NY, USA

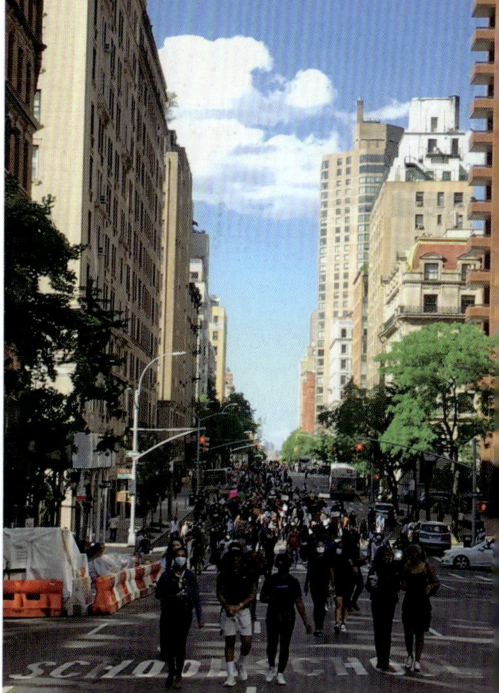

TWINKLE BANERJEE, *Characters of Memorial Park, Calgary* | As the day progresses, my mother usually will narrate the interesting stories unfolding in the park in front of our apartment. I picked up her binoculars and decided to record these stories. CANADA

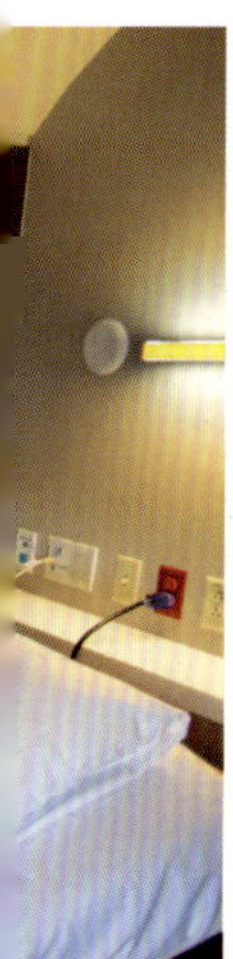

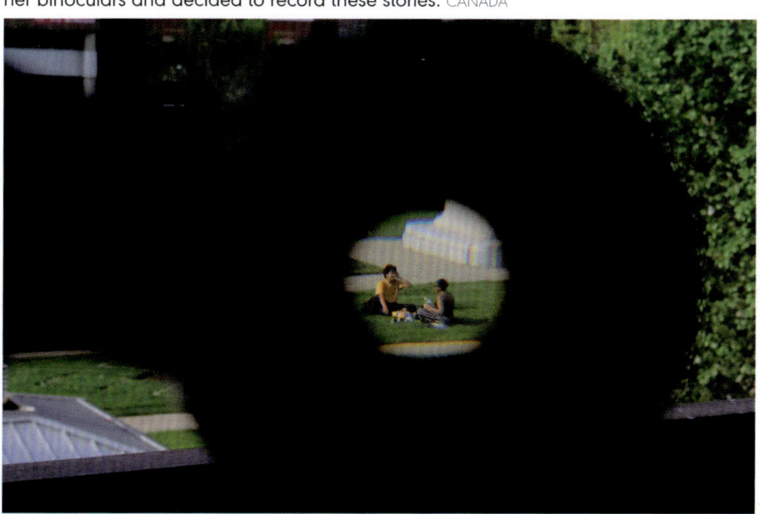

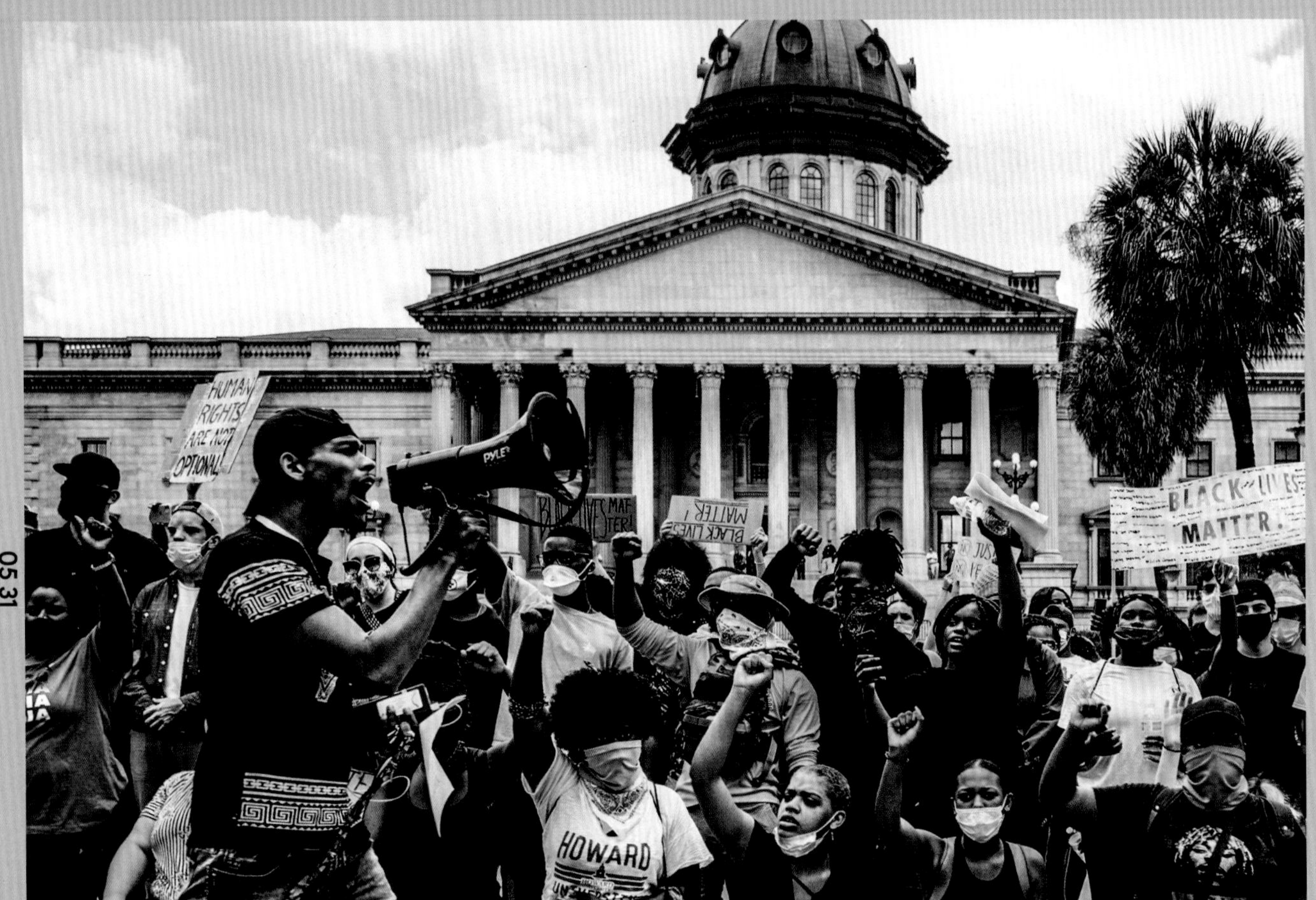

ANNA MORALES,

Peaceful protestors advocating for Black lives at the South Carolina State House. I captured this moment at a Black Lives Matter protest at the South Carolina Statehouse. There, hundreds of participants lined the block to hold hands and share a moment of silence for George Floyd. Torn between being a part of this beautiful moment or using my power as a photographer to capture and share it, I made my way into the middle of the empty road, sat down and began photographing. I watched through my lens as people of all different backgrounds and colors came together, raising their fists and signs with might. At this moment the silence was broken as the man with the megaphone led the crowd in a chant. "I can't breathe," he said. And the crowd answered. "I can't breath!" "I can't breath!" "I can't breath!" "I can't breath!" Kneeling on the concrete in front of the scene, I felt overwhelmed with emotion and empowered to make a change. CA, USA

CEDRIC ROUX, Paris Unconfined. FRANCE

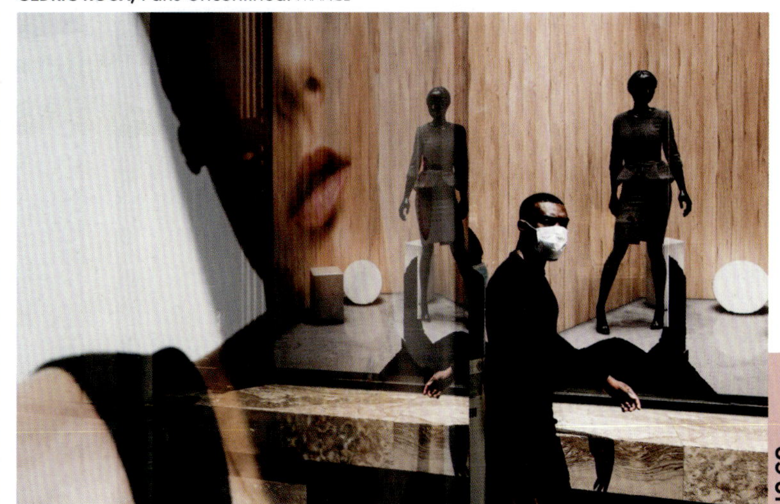

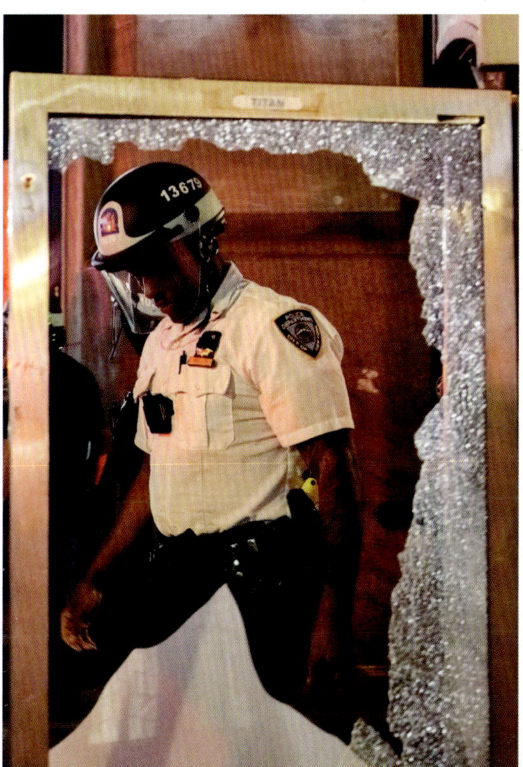

ALEX GOLSHANI, NYPD officer stands amid broken glass in Union Square. NEW YORK, NY, USA

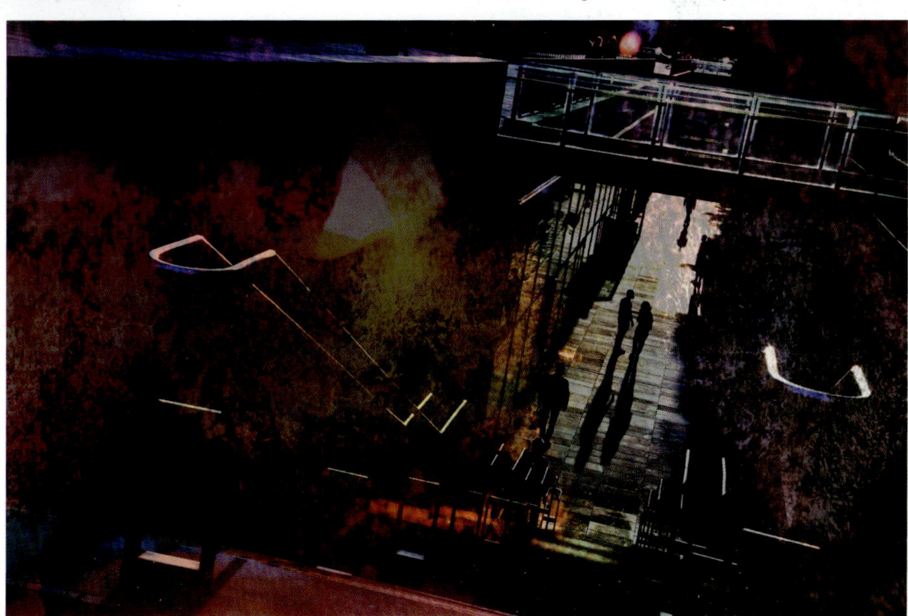

ENZO REDAELLI, *Contaminated Landscape* | The color has contaminated the picture. The virus has contaminated cities and nations. The anguish has contaminated our souls. MILAN, ITALY

AMIR HAMJA,
A couple watches a protest for George Floyd pass by from a window in the West Village.
NEW YORK, NY, USA

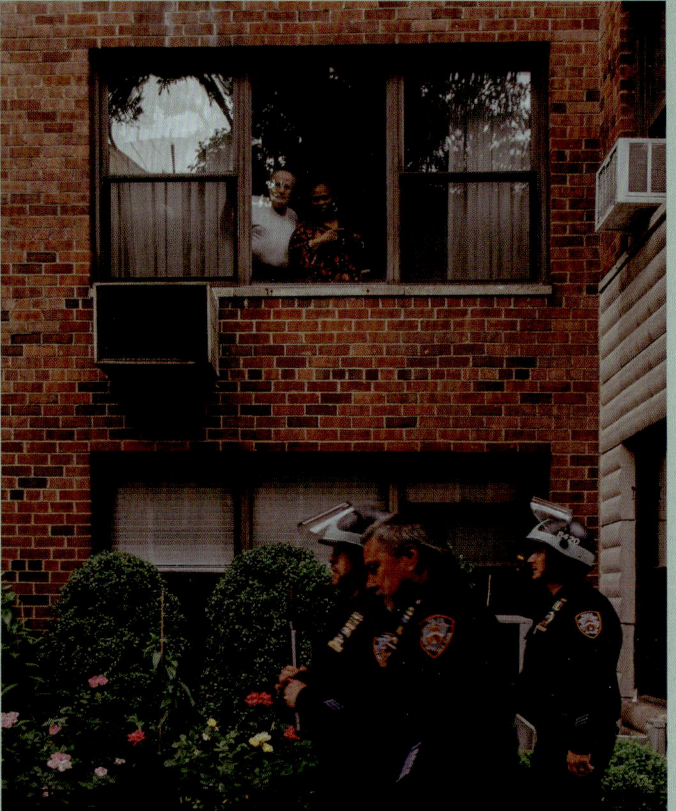

06 01

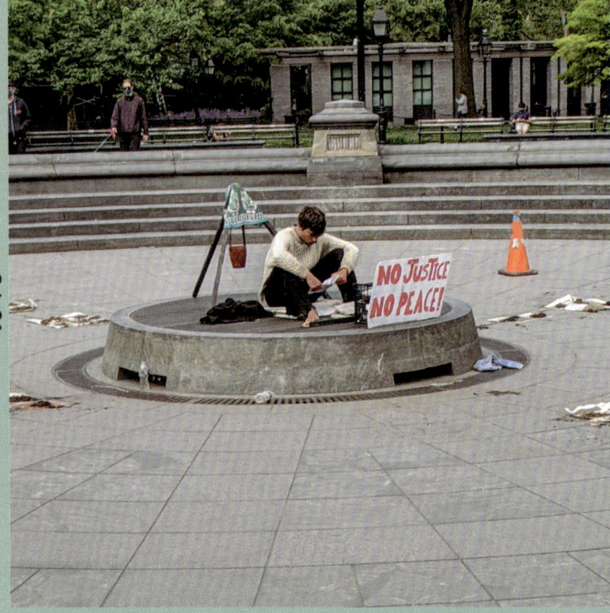

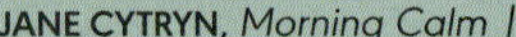

JANE CYTRYN, *Morning Calm* |
Washington Square Park, New York City, the morning after the riots and fires.
NEW YORK, NY, USA

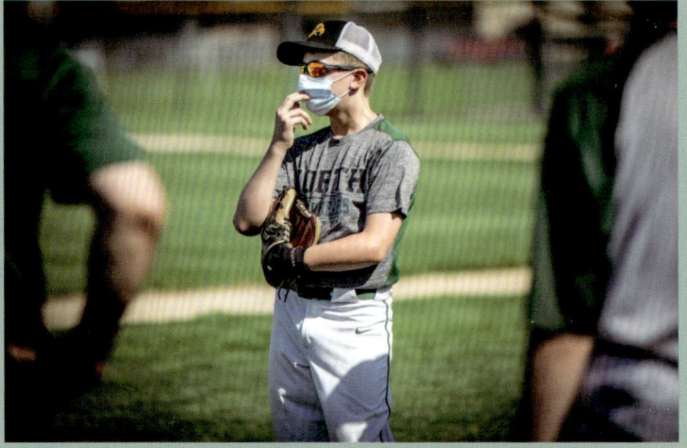

PHIL ROEDER,
A North High student adjusts his mask on opening day of baseball practice. Iowa was the first state to resume high school sports during the pandemic. DES MOINS, IA, USA

06·20

JUNE

6_FDA Withdraws Emergency Use Authorization for Hydroxychloroquine *(The Hill)*

11_تعطیلی موقت بخش روادید سفارت آلمان در تهران برای مراجعین *(teheran.dipolo.de)*

15_„МИД Нидерландов снял ограничения на поездки в 16 европейских стран" *(ria Новости)*

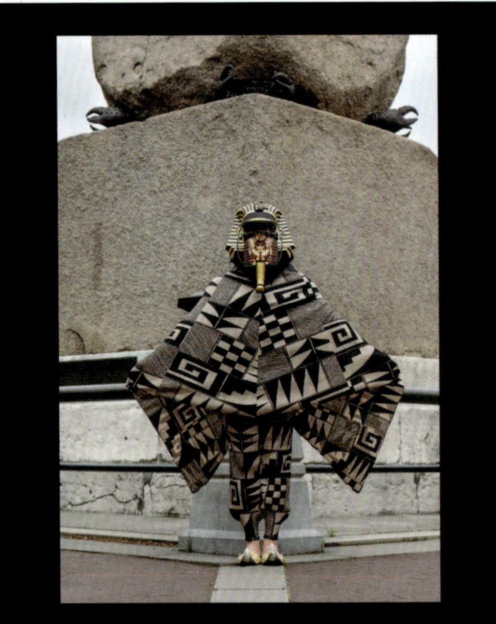

KAREN SMUL, *Davey in his PPE* | Art by Davey wears his Egyptian-themed deconstructed shield and facemask PPE paired with tribal fabrics at the Central Park obelisk. NEW YORK, NY, USA

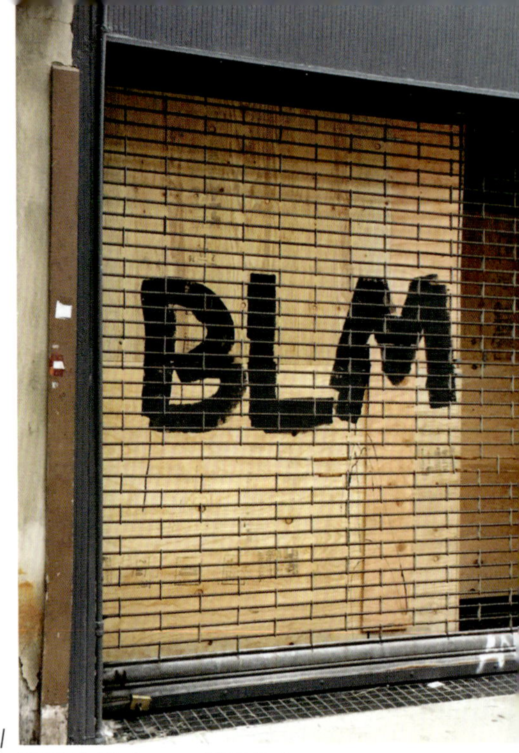

VALA KJARVAL, *One of Many New Normals* | 7:27 PM, 7th Avenue, NYC. Eerie moment 30 minutes before the 8 PM (police-enforced) curfew, every business in sight has closed unusually early and boarded up. NEW YORK, NY, USA

ALEX BAGUIO, *Safeguarding Liberty* | In these times of chaos and turmoil, freedom prevails! NEW YORK, NY, USA

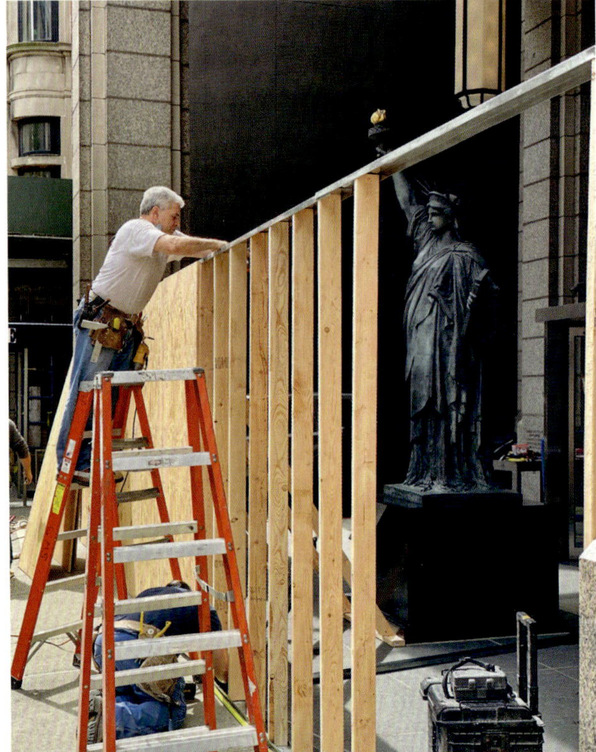

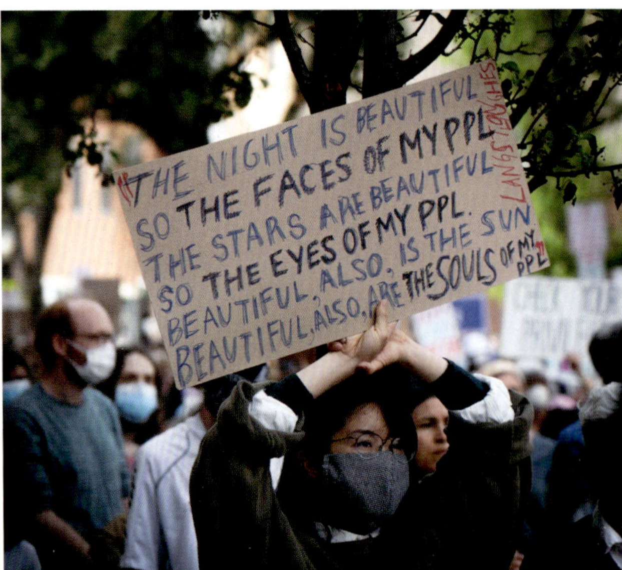

MAGDA RITTENHOUSE, Peaceful "Kneel for Justice" protest in Princeton. NJ, USA

EVELINE SCHNEIDER, *Black Trans Lives Matter* | Stonewall Inn. NEW YORK, NY, USA

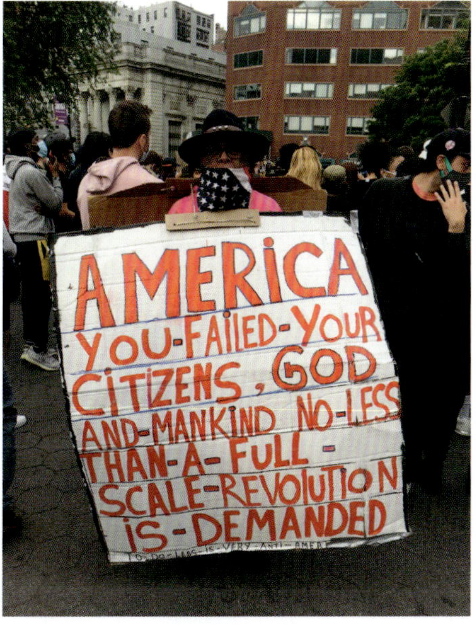

KURT BOONE,
A man wears an American Flag scarf over his face and full body sign around his neck at a Black Lives Matter protest rally in Union Square.
NEW YORK, NY, USA

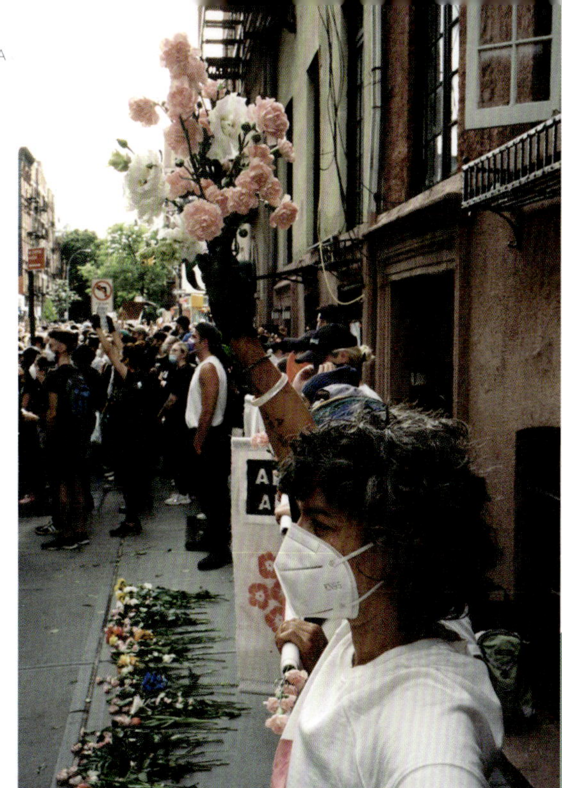

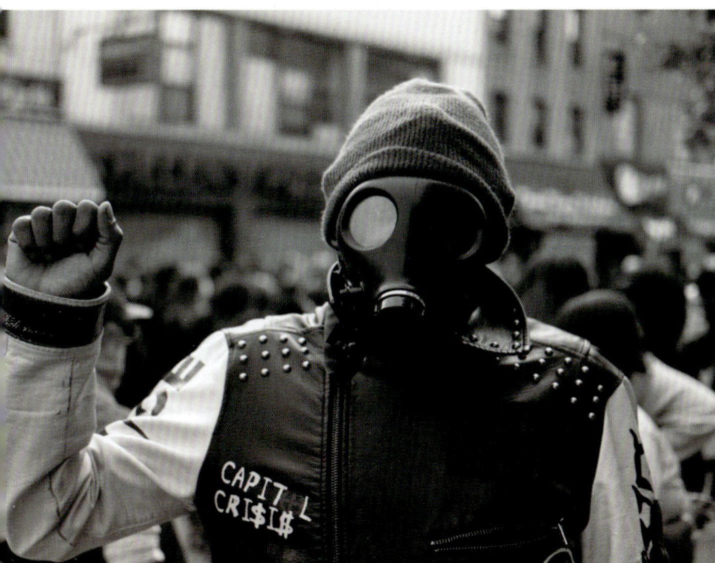

ALASTAIR ARTHUR, Protestor at an anti-racism demonstration in Jersey City following the death of George Floyd. NJ, USA

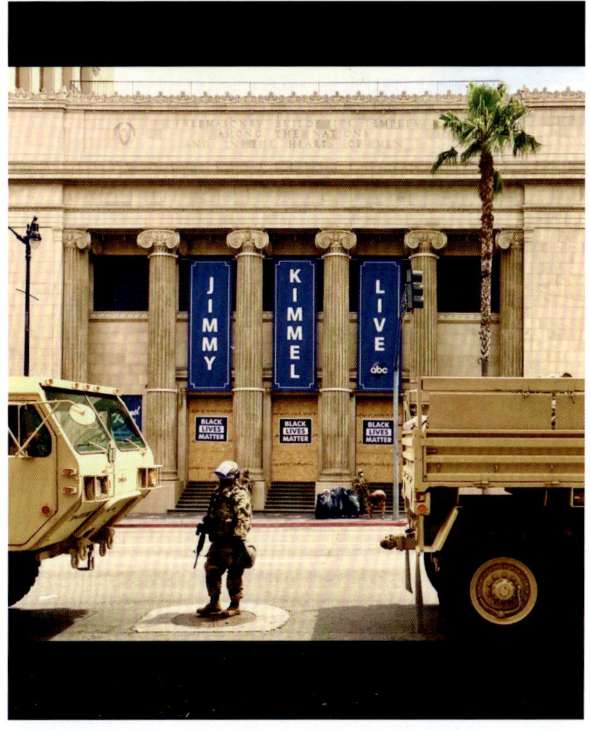

ANNE GRAUSO, *Surprise Guests* | The US National Guard deploys in front of the boarded up Jimmy Kimmel Live theater on Hollywood Boulevard, papered with Black Lives Matters posters. LOS ANGELES, CA, USA

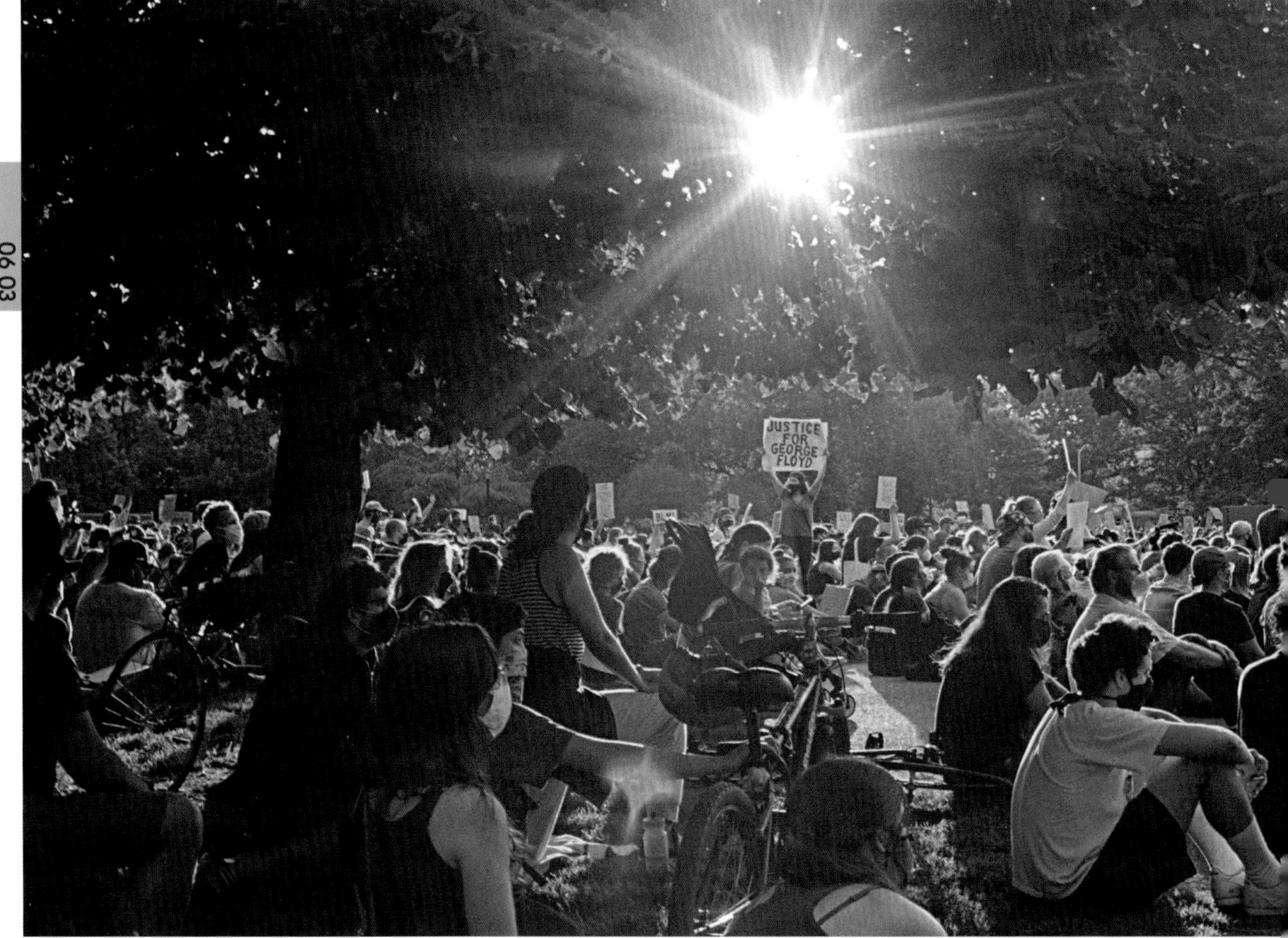

LILY RESZI ROTHMAN, *Bringing Injustice to Light* |

Silent, masked protest, early in the movement spurred by George Floyd's death. About 7 PM, when New York City's 8 PM curfew was still in effect. NEW YORK, NY, USA

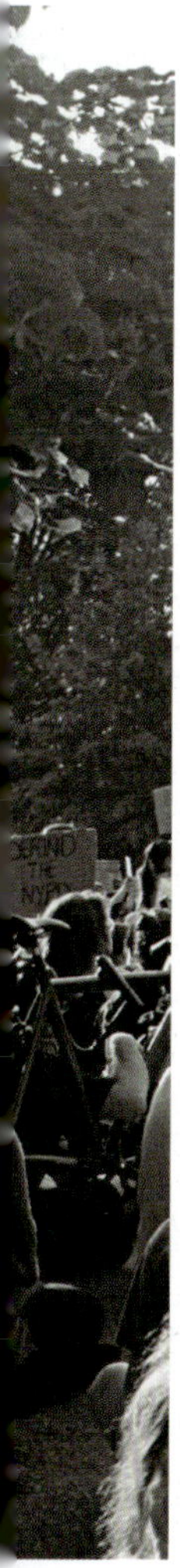

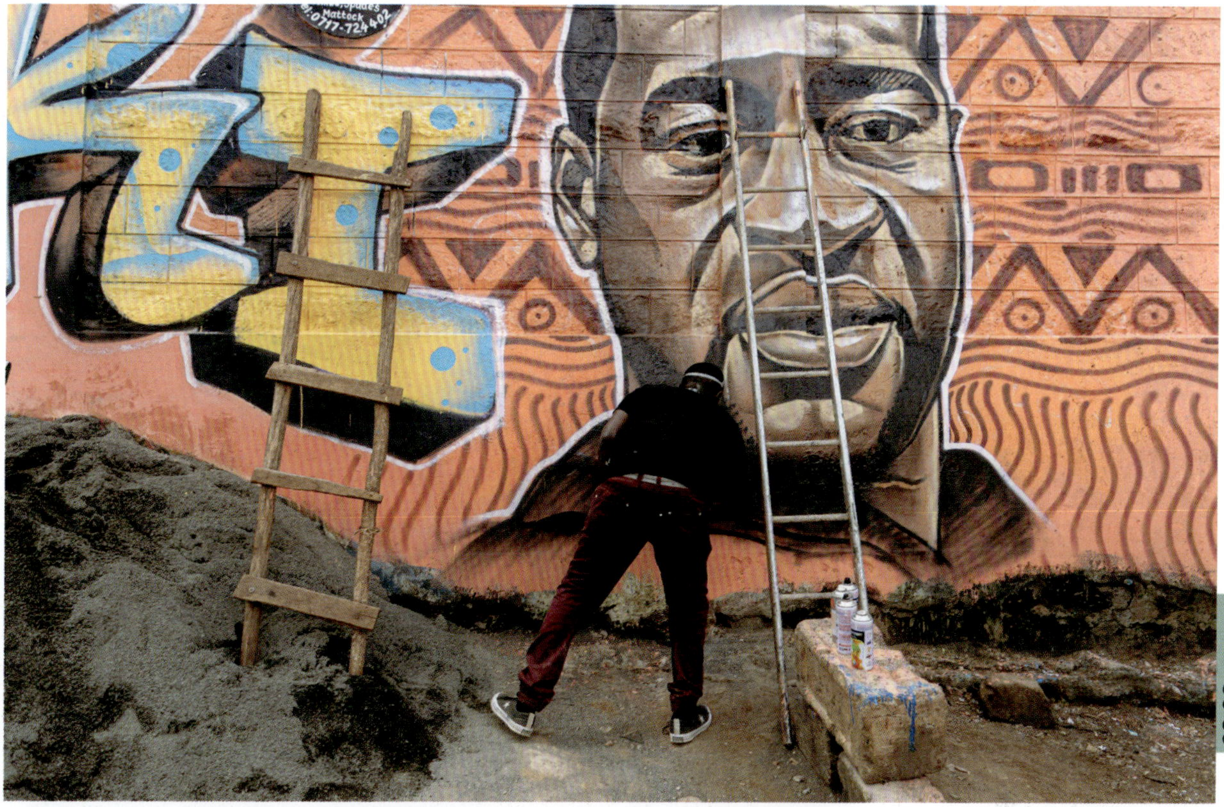

KESH NTHAMBA, *Racial Abuse and Police Brutality, Kibra, Kamukunji* | A mural depicts George Floyd. In Kenya, thousands have died at the hands of the police. Police brutality has long needed attention. Officers guilty of these crimes are never held accountable, introducing yet another grave concern of the impunity lurking deep in Kenya's judicial system. KENYA

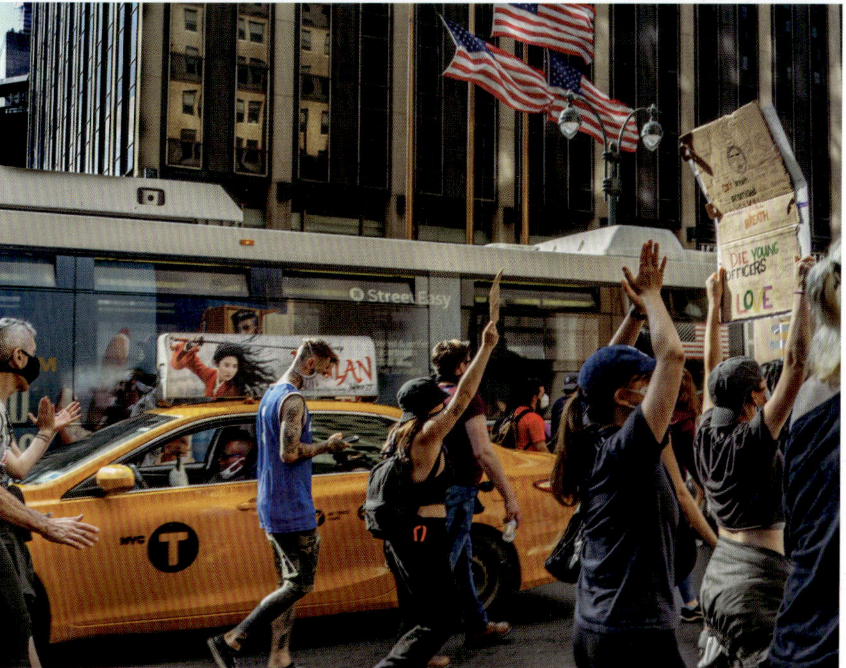

ALLISON PLASS, Uprising. NEW YORK, NY, USA

ANNA RATHKOPF, Two friends elbow bump in solidarity at the George Floyd Memorial at Cadman Plaza in Brooklyn. NEW YORK, NY, USA

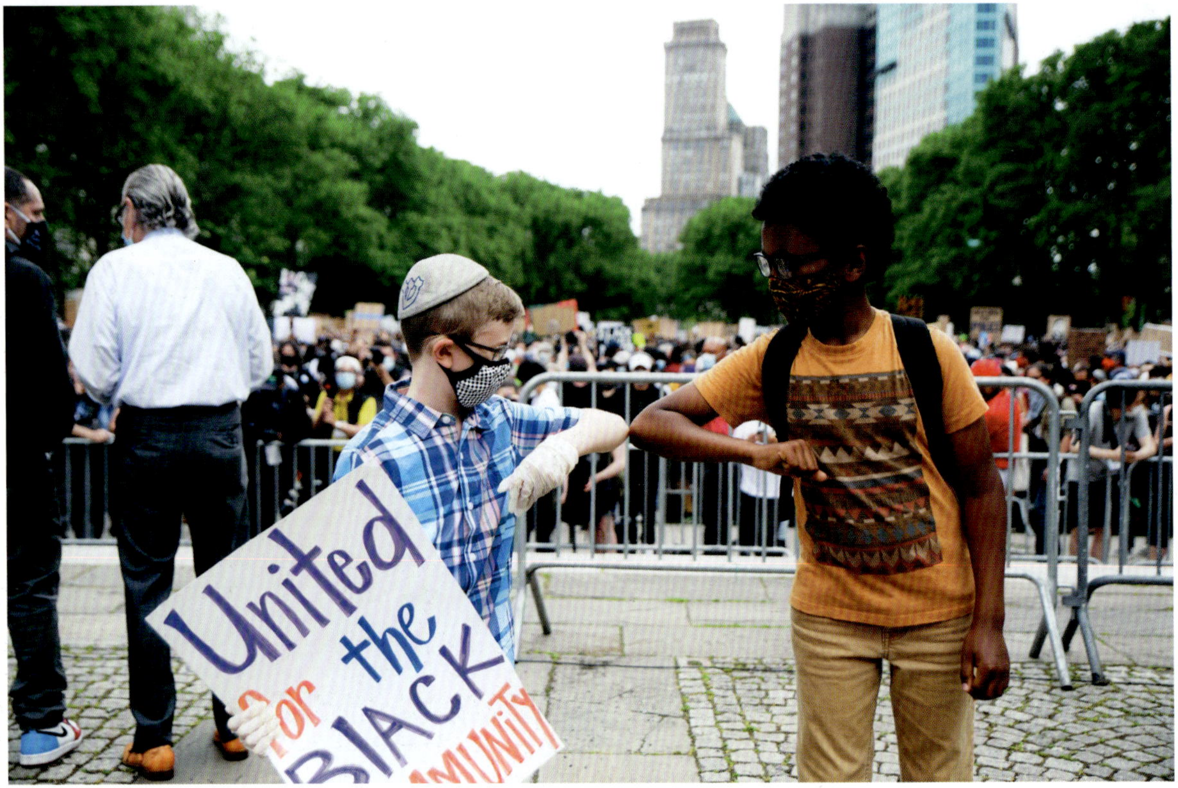

MG VANDER ELST, George Floyd's Memorial in Brooklyn. NEW YORK, NY, USA

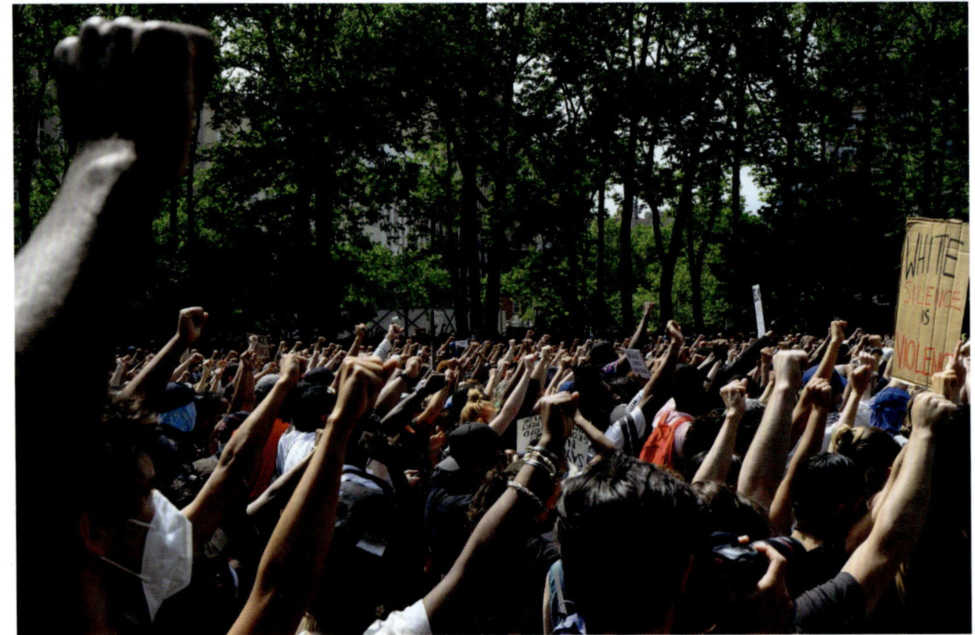

DANIELE VIVIANO, Since 2015, the Cathedral of Monreale has been a World Heritage Site (UNESCO) as part of the Arab-Norman itinerary of Palermo, Cefalù and Monreale. ITALY

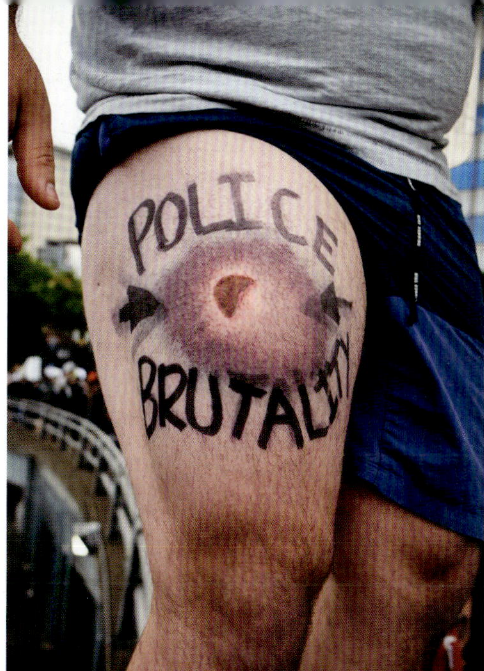

CHRIS NESSETH, Police Brutality. PORTLAND, OR, USA

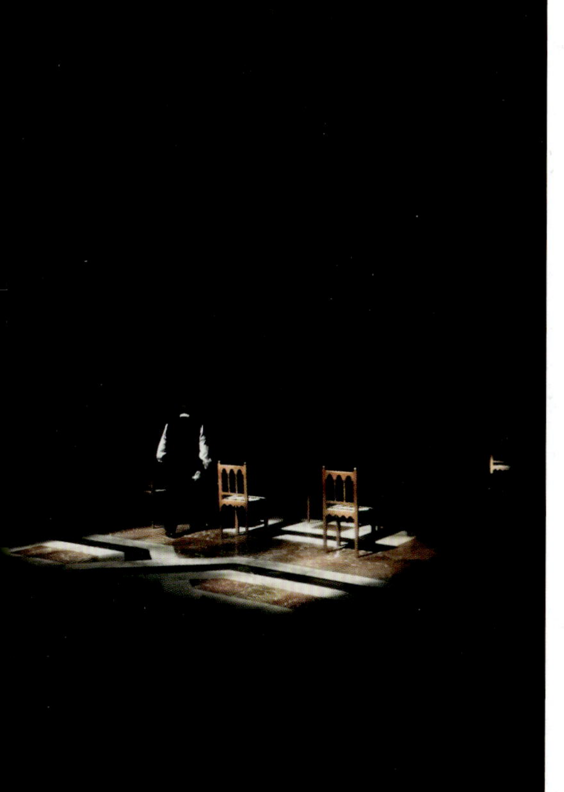

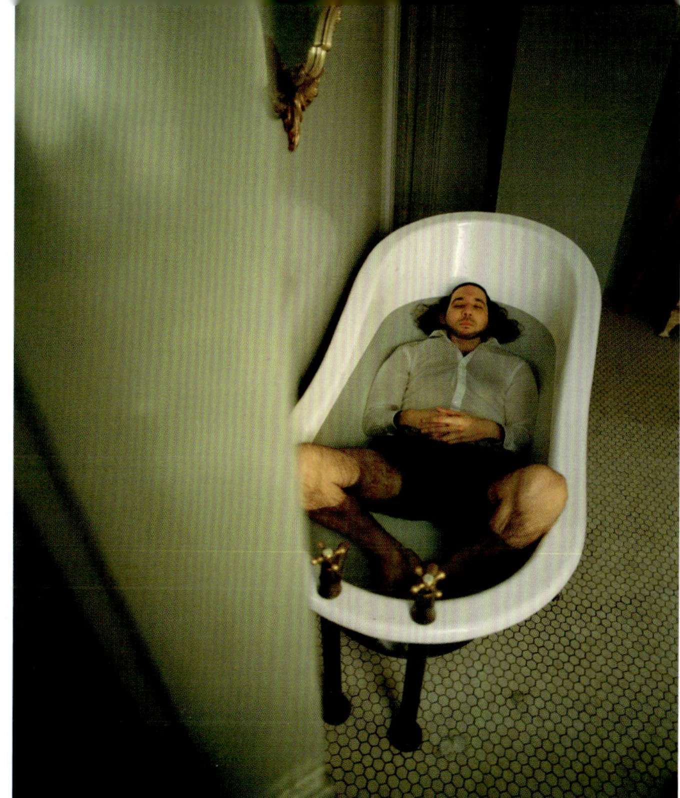

LILLI WATERS, *Friends on Film #2* | This series was inspired by isolation and the need for human connection and sharing of our own individual experiences of this strange time. MELBOURNE, AUSTRALIA

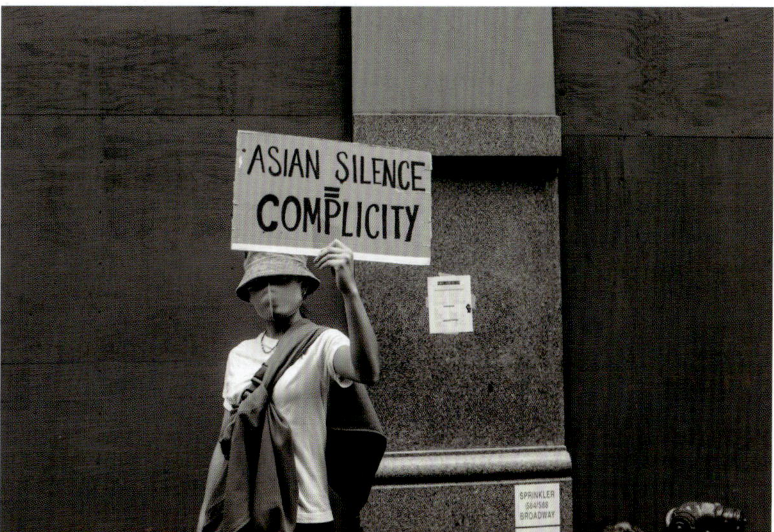

GUDRUN GEORGES, *Asian Silence* |
I encountered this protestor after that day's protest. NEW YORK, NY, USA

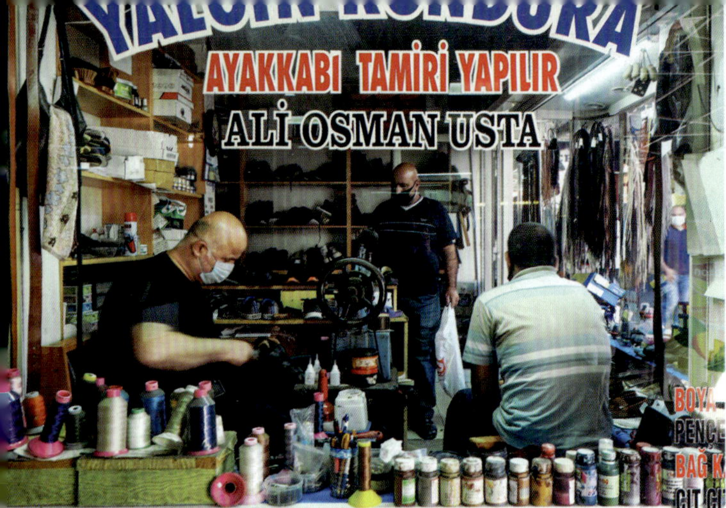

HÜSEYIN CAN, Shoe repairman in the historic market. He opened his shop after a long break during the pandemic. In this small shop, customers and shopkeeper take care to obey all the rules. Shoe repair is one of the traditional professions in Turkey that is disappearing. ADAPAZARI, SAKARYA, TURKEY

ZENZELÉ MOORE-YSAGUIRRE, *The Anger, the Pain, the Unity* | Artists for Change, Los Angeles. CA, USA

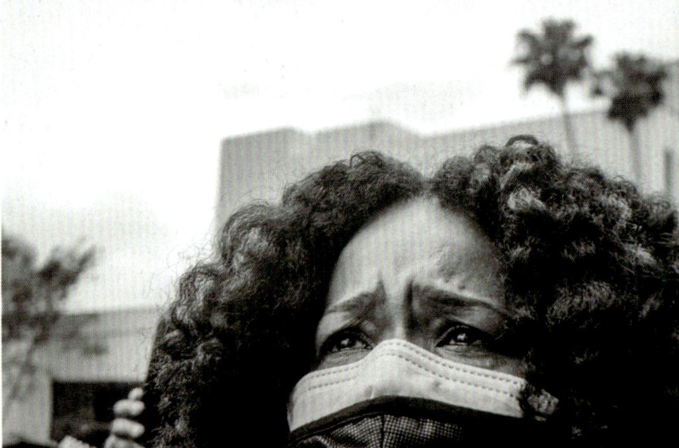

MARC OHREM-LECLEF, After weeks of isolating, I marched in the streets of New York City to protest against police brutality inflicted on Black communities. NEW YORK, NY, USA

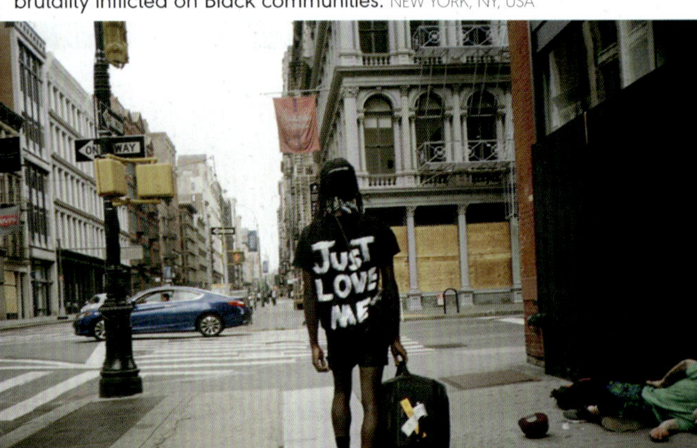

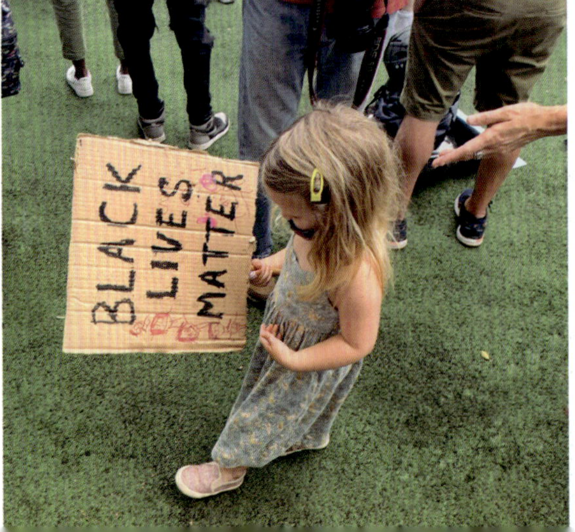

EAMON DOLAN, Pointing to the future. BROOKLYN, NY, USA

NICOLE FREEZER RUBENS,

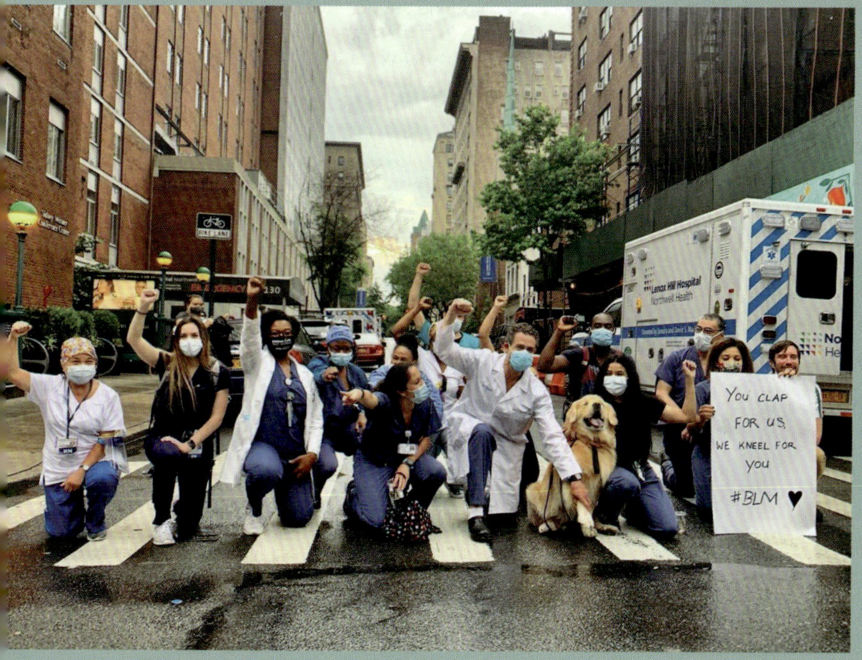

I will never forget the first night of the "Clap Because We Care" ritual. It was March 27th. My family was at home together and hunkered down. Word got out that at 7 PM daily, New Yorkers would open their windows, and their hearts, and applaud for our essential workers. It started quietly and gained momentum around New York City, but that first night was highly emotional for me. It was not only an expression of gratitude for those who risked their lives without proper PPE or any hesitation, but also relief for me to yell and scream. It became a daily means to release some stress. Doctors, nurses, orderlies and others appeared daily as their shift changed. NYPD on horses, FDNY, on top of their trucks came together. Religiously night after night, we waved to our neighbors, and to the workers and scrubs who knew to look up at us. With signs, pots, musical instruments and simple clapping and cheering, a new ritual was solidified. We all counted on it. We did not miss a single night for the duration, which ended in June, shortly after this photo was taken. After George Floyd was murdered on May 25th, the marches for racial equality took over our streets. Peacefully and mostly masked, people began to protest and take a knee together in solidarity. On June 5th, when this photo was taken, marches were constant. Diverse people move together. On this night, even though it was drizzling, my family decided to go outside at seven and be on the street with the hospital workers. It was the only night we left our balcony. This is what I found. NEW YORK, NY, USA

BEN LURIE, I'm Human. CHICAGO, IL, USA

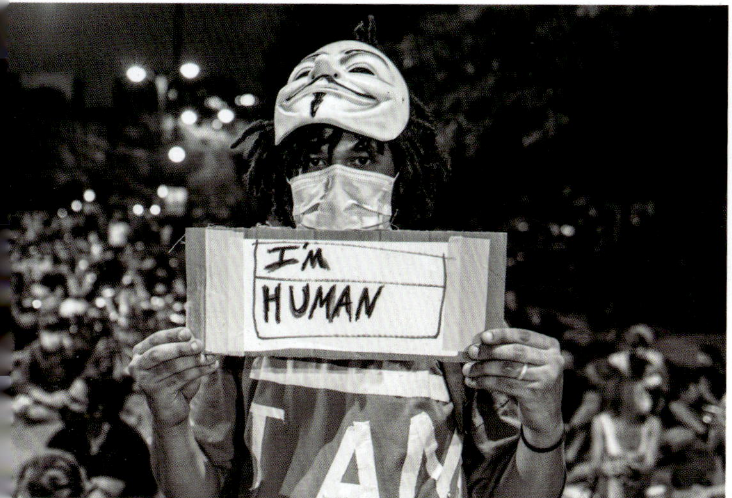

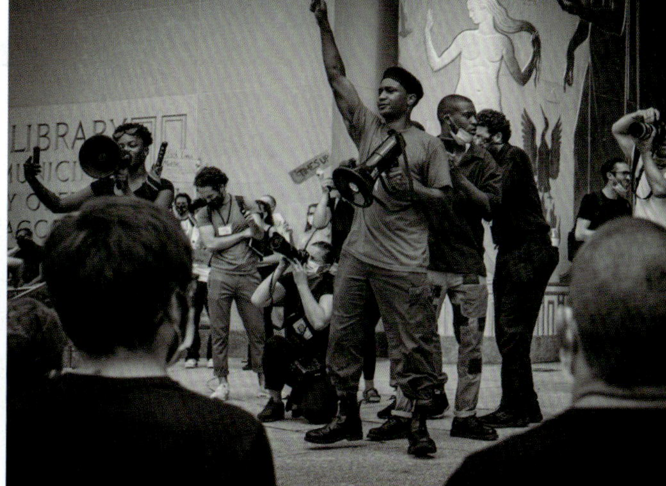

SHAWN PRIDGEN, *Power to the People* | Chi Ossé on the steps of the Brooklyn Public Library main branch. NEW YORK, NY, USA

LILLIAN AVILA MEDRANO, *Rest in Power* |

George Floyd's memorial site, a city burning, an entire community mourning and one powerful, fervent demand: no justice, no peace. These murals, created by local artist Peyton Scott Russell, were right next to the place where George Floyd was murdered by three Minneapolis police officers on the evening of May 25th of 2020. This intersection of Chicago in 38th became a sacred space field with balloons, letters, signs, thousands of flowers, tears and grief. And while hundreds of people gathered around his memorial, quietness stood out. A profound quietness that represented the palpable pain and respect that people felt well being there. People were mourning, kneeling, crying, honoring, hurting and during my effort to capture it all through photos, a visitor walking by stood next to me and said, "It feels as if the whole world was here right now," and it truly did feel that way. MINNEAPOLIS, MN, USA

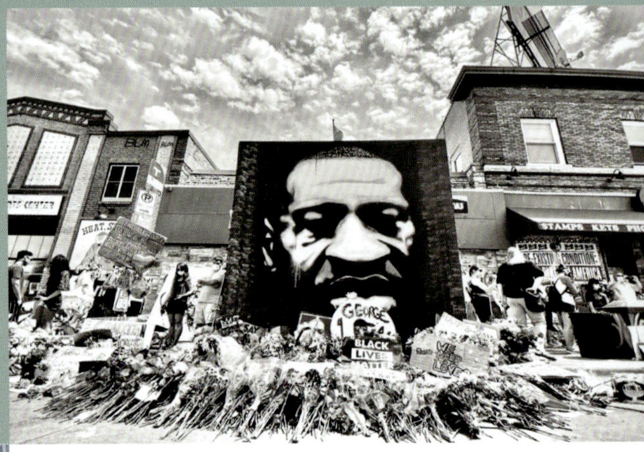

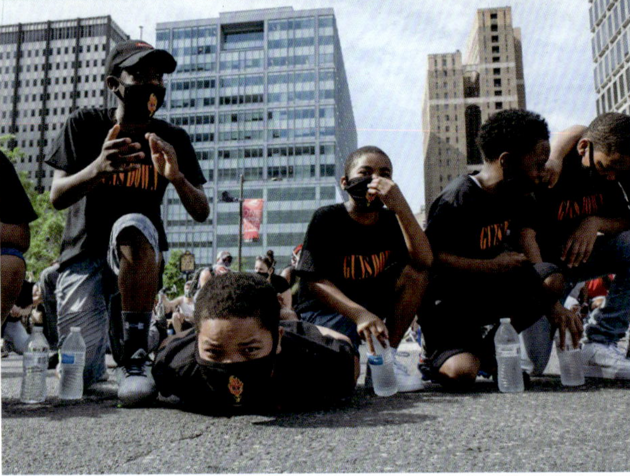

SHANTANU SAHA, *Young Flames* |

A child lies down on the ground in Philadelphia as a gesture of solidarity against police brutality in the aftermath of the death of George Floyd. PA, USA

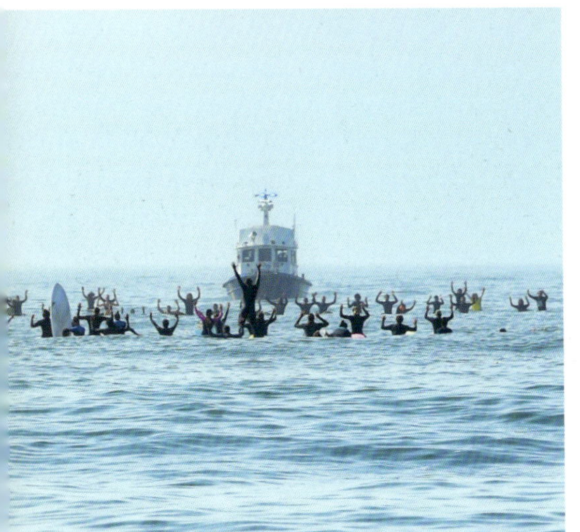

SOLANGE CROCI, *About Peace* |
Paddle Out Memorial, Rockaway Beach. NEW YORK, NY, USA

GÜZIN MUT, More than 15,000 people protested peacefully against racism and for Black Lives Matter on Alexanderplatz in Berlin. GERMANY

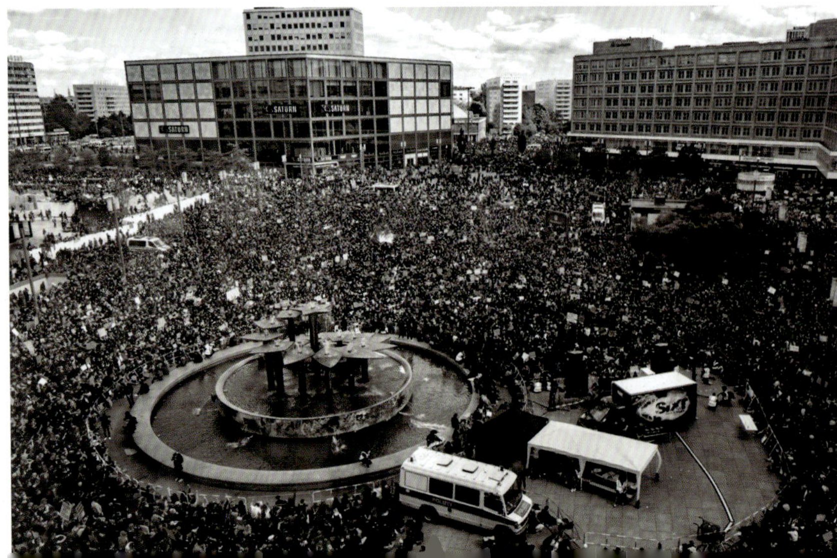

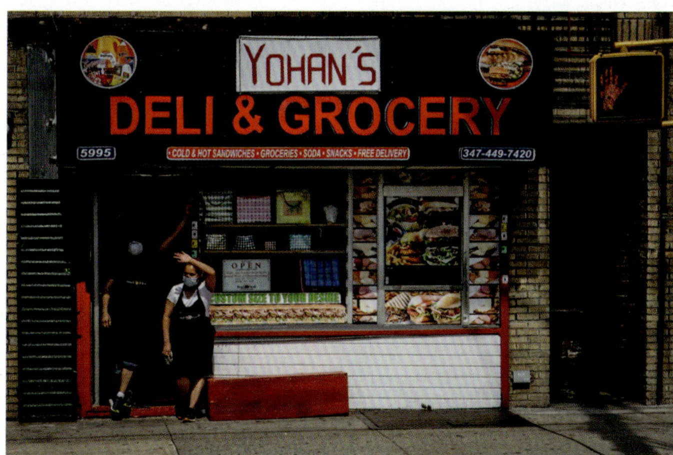

REBECCA WESTON, This was taken as I participated in a Black Lives Matter demonstration for racial justice. I was very moved by the level of engagement and support shown by people along the street. BRONX, NY, USA

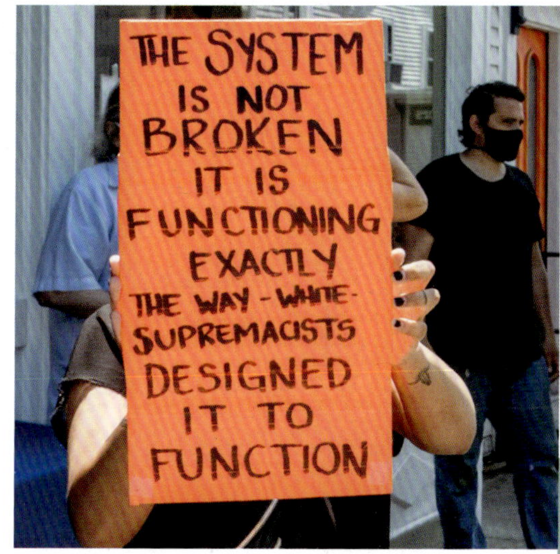

ROBERT JOHNSON, Working As Designed. PROVINCETOWN, MA, USA

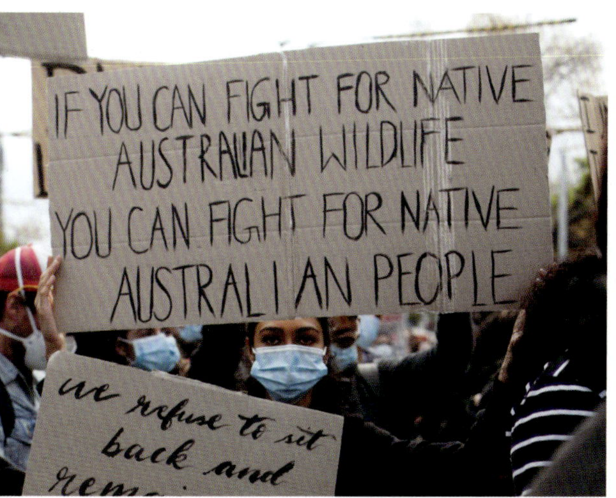

MARIA COLAIDIS, BLM. MELBOURNE, AUSTRALIA

SAM SALGANIK, Family at the Brooklyn Promenade. NY, USA

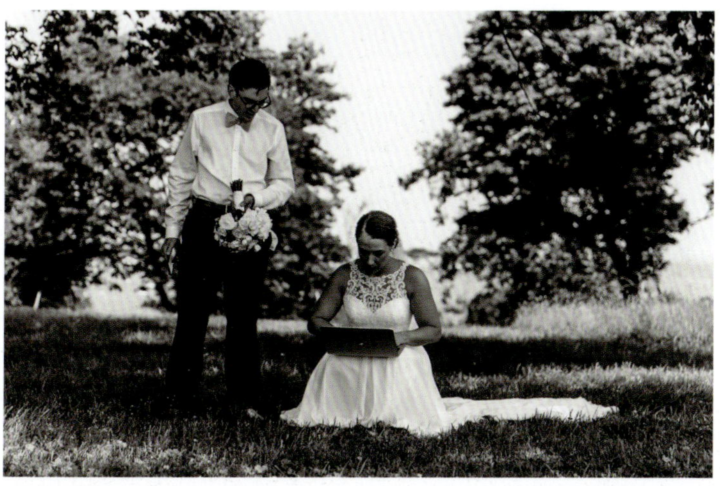

BROOKE BARTLETTA, Bride and Groom try to problem solve technical issues with the livestream during their socially-distanced wedding at World's End park. HINGHAM, MA, USA

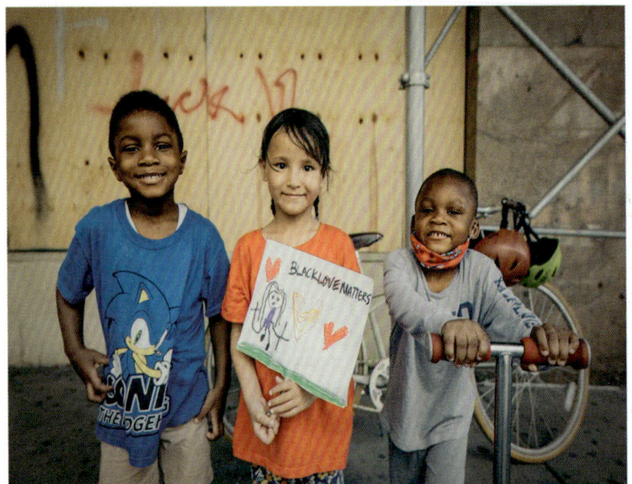

GIUSEPPE MALPASSO, *Black Loves Matter* | Broadway and Canal street. NEW YORK, NY, USA

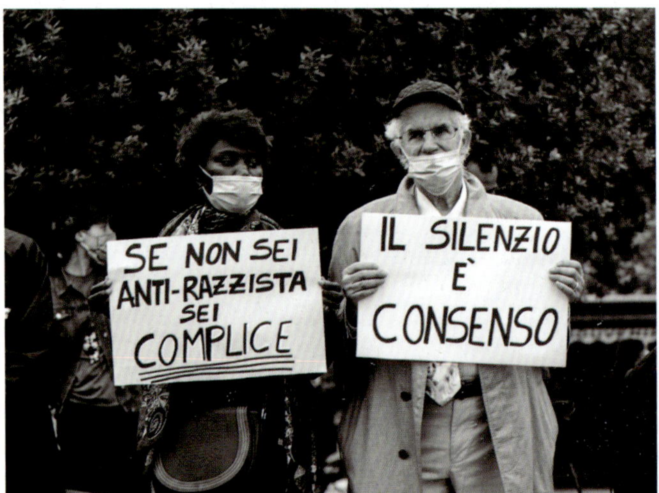

ALESSANDRA MARINOZZI, *RESPIRO* | Milan Black Lives Matter Rally. ITALY

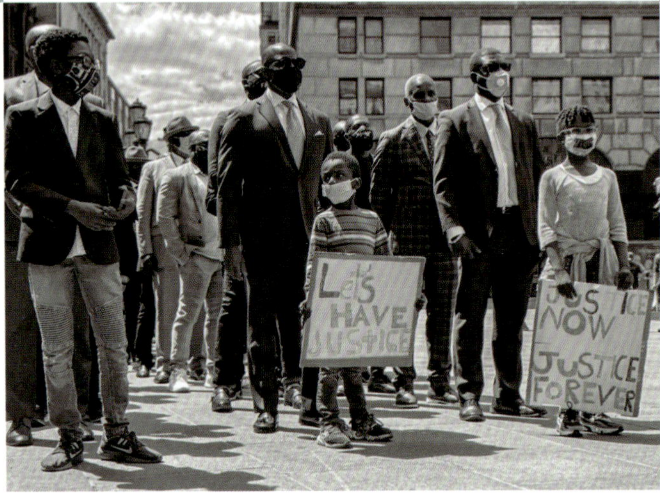

ANTHONY FIELDMAN, *Brooklyn Strong* |
Borough Hall, Downtown Brooklyn. NEW YORK, NY, USA

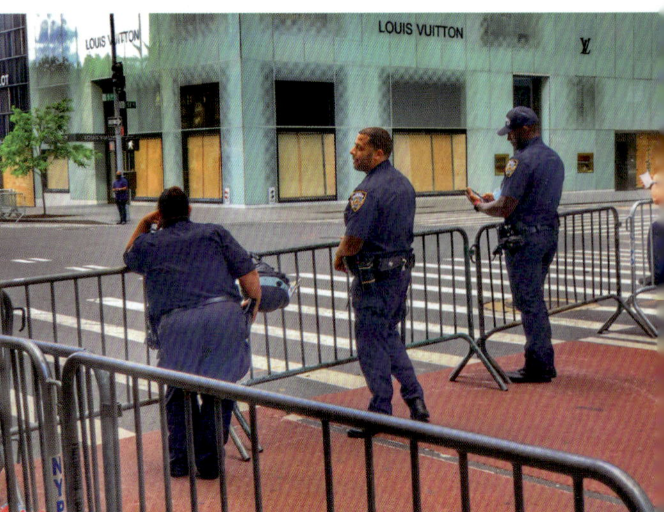

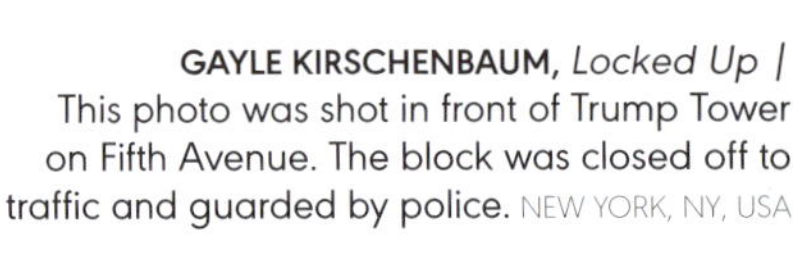

GAYLE KIRSCHENBAUM, *Locked Up* |
This photo was shot in front of Trump Tower on Fifth Avenue. The block was closed off to traffic and guarded by police. NEW YORK, NY, USA

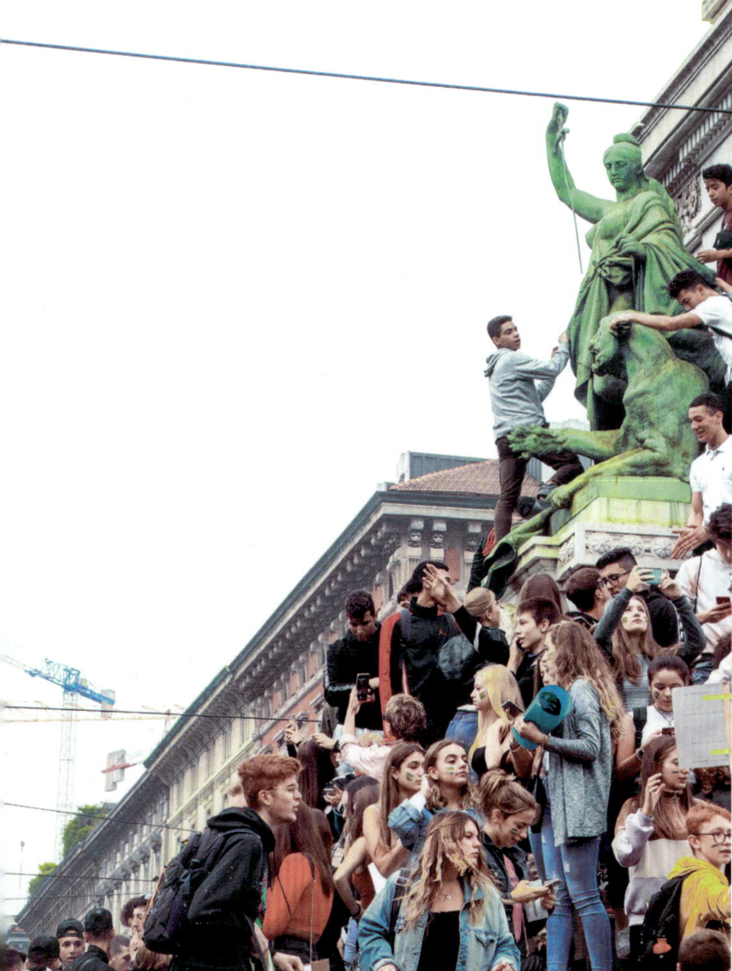

GABRIELE PUGLISI, Pindaric statues. MILAN, ITALY

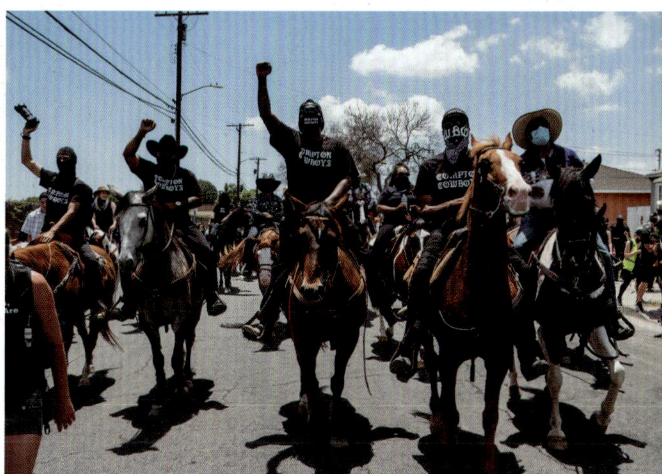

NICHOLAS SLOBIN, Thousands of people took to the streets again this weekend. Joining them in solidarity were The Compton Cowboys. COMPTON, CA, USA

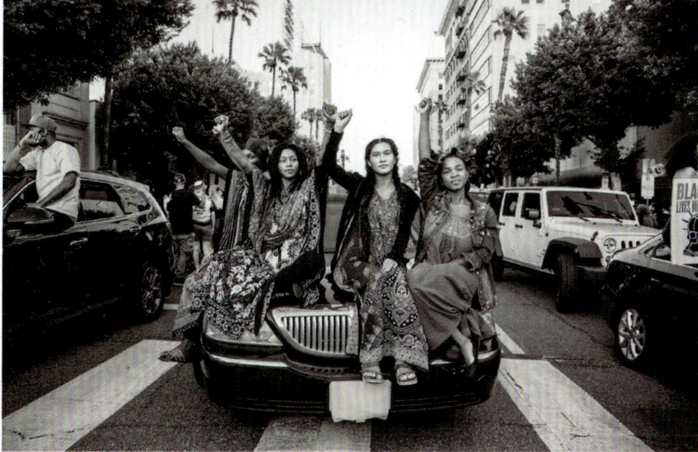

TAZ ESSA, *Strength* |

Women raise their fists in unity during a Black Lives Matter protest in Hollywood. CA, USA

ERI MORITA, Surfers Raising Surfboards as BLM Signs at "Paddle Out for Peace" protest, Windansea Beach. CA, USA

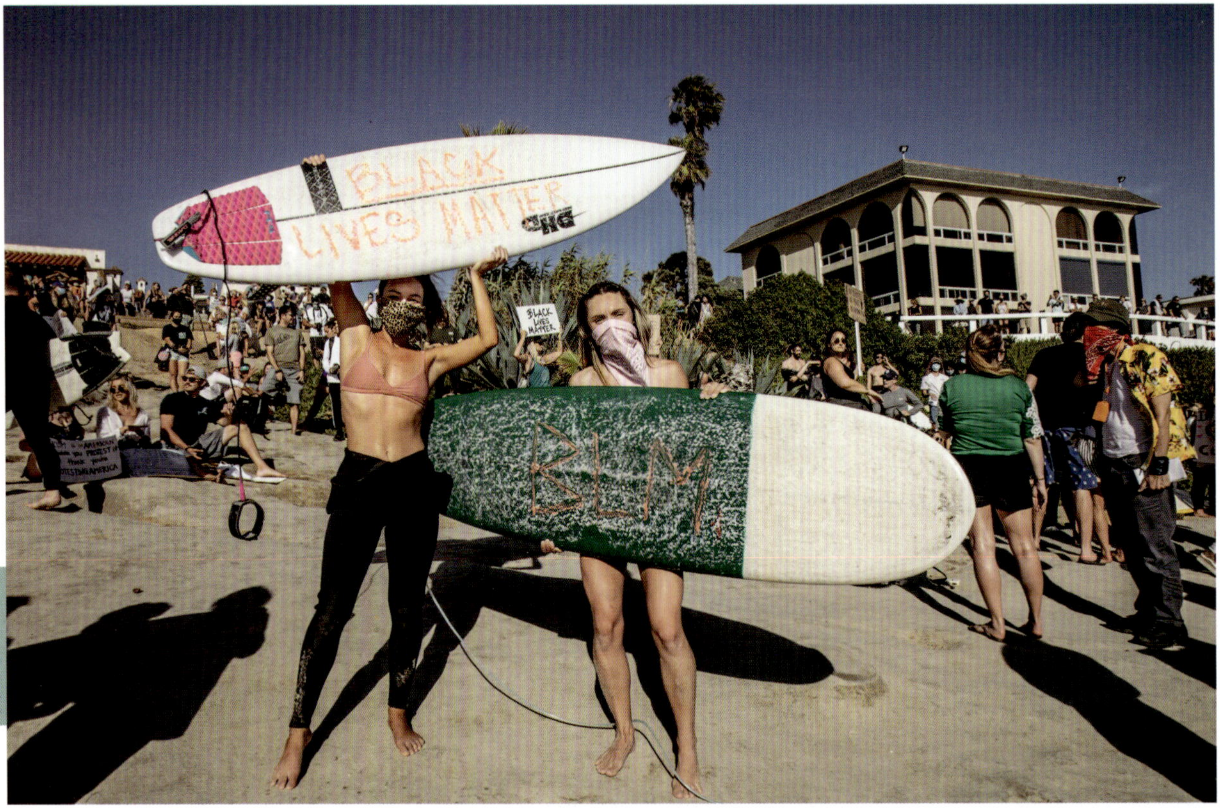

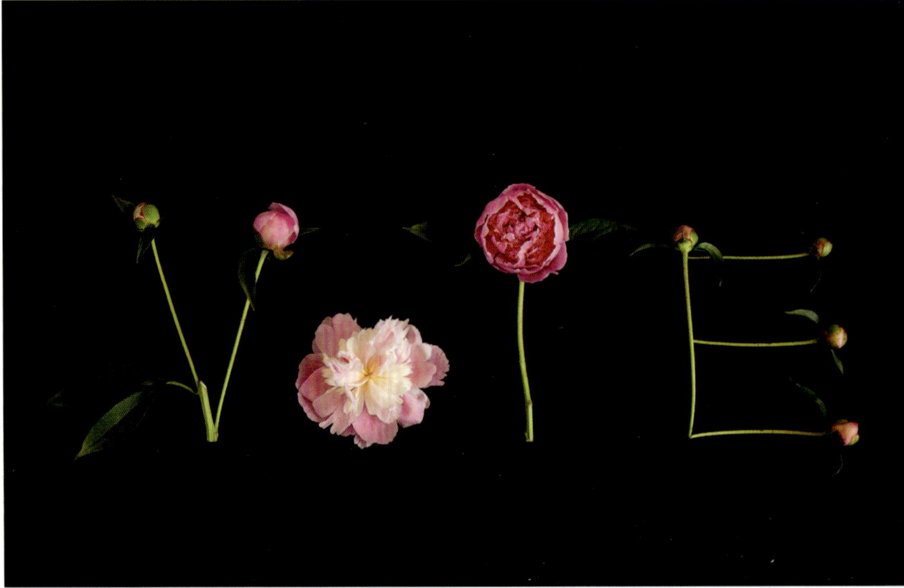

CONSTANCE KELLER, *VOTE* |
For a flower to thrive and bloom, a garden must be tended. For a country to thrive and have hope, its citizens must be heard. CT, USA

ELIZABETH SOBIESKI, Dr. Fauci Said So. NEW YORK, NY, USA

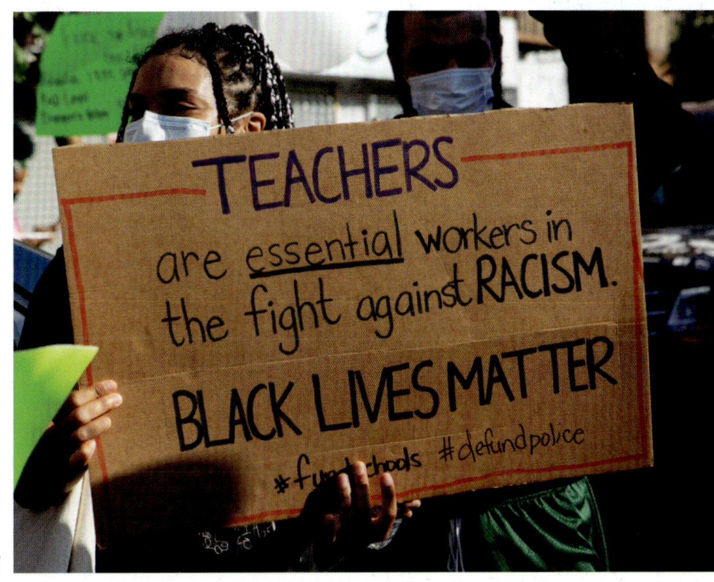

KRISTIN SLABY, *Essential* | A sign in one of the many protests throughout New York City stating the obvious: to incorporate a dialogue and curriculum in our educational institutions. THE BRONX, NY, USA

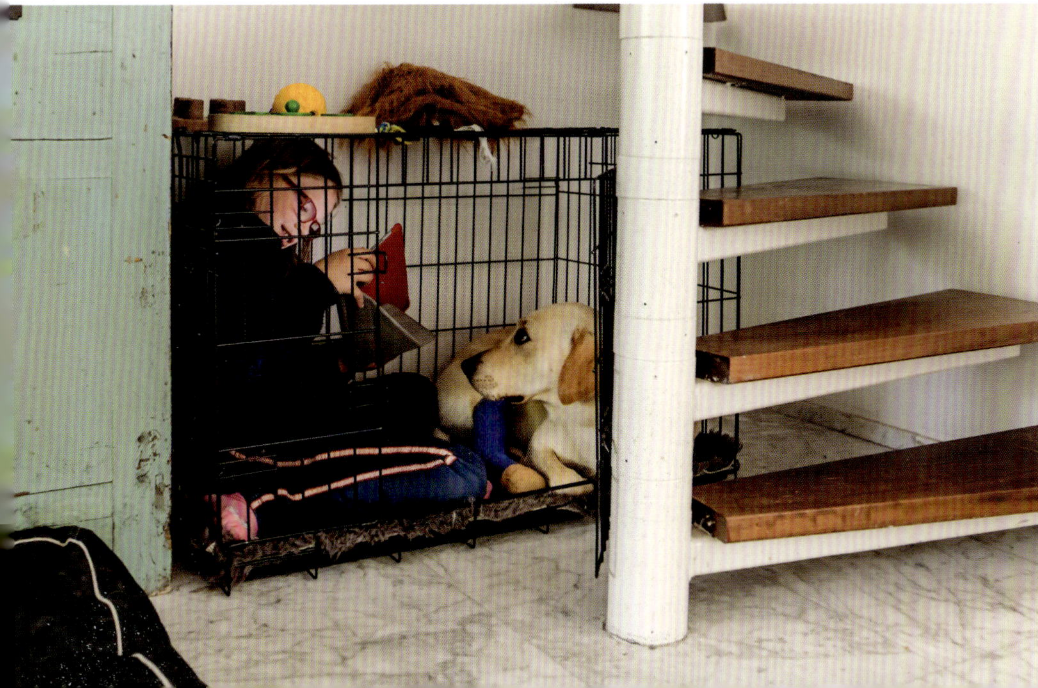

SANDRA STOKMANS,
When the dog is hurting, you keep him company, even if you're doing school work.
MAARSSEN, UTRECHT, NETHERLANDS

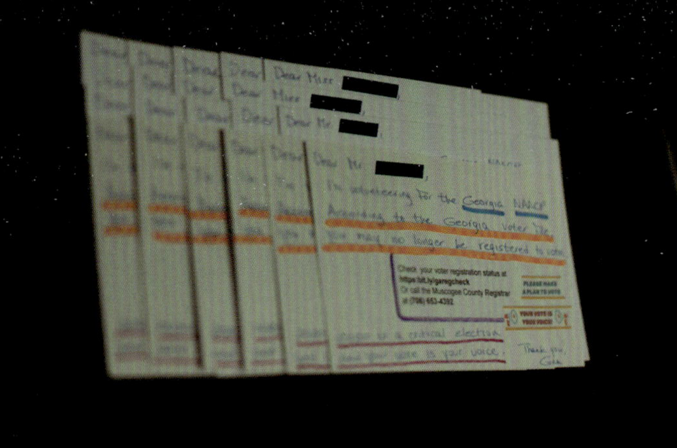

GINA RANDAZZO, *You May No Longer Be Registered To Vote |* From "Postcards for Reclaim Our Vote" series. HASTINGS-ON-HUDSON, NY, USA

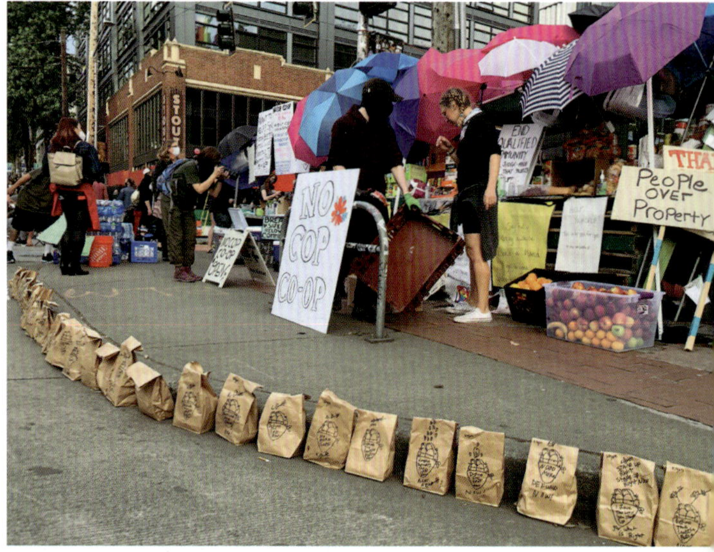

TIFFANY JIANG,
Local volunteers of the "No Cop Co-op" redistribute food and resources to visitors of the Capitol Hill Autonomous Zone. SEATTLE, WA, USA

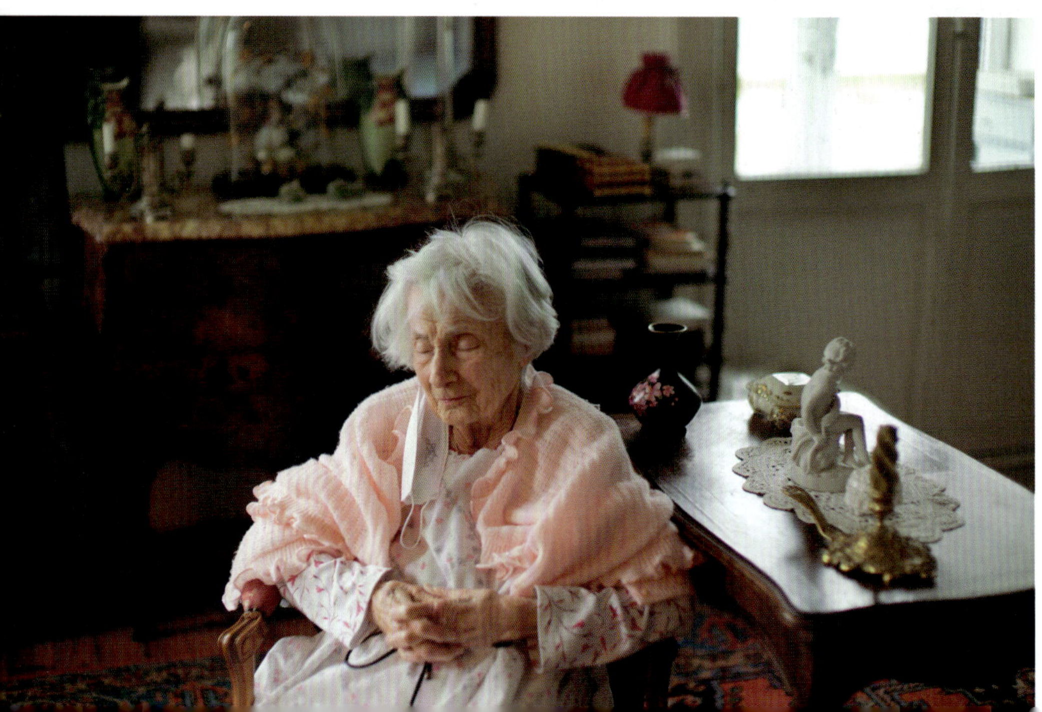

OLIVIA FERNANDEZ,
Mamydette is my grandmother. She is 96 years old. She wants to go out and yet she is scared to go out. The pandemic brought me back to France and it has been a blessing to spend time with her.
BIARRITZ, FRANCE

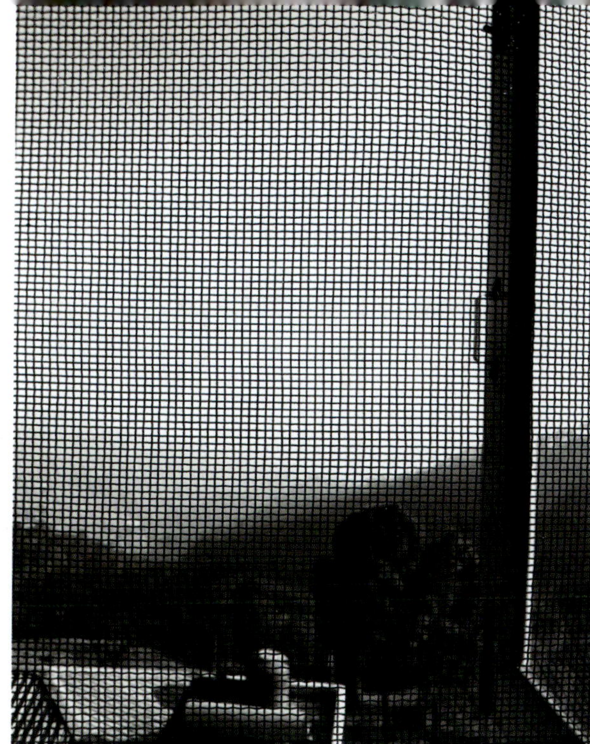

VIPIN BALONI, We are in a great trap inside our minds. There is sheer beauty outside to be seen but we are trapped in the cages created by none other than our own minds. LANSDOWNE, UTTARAKHAND, INDIA

JIMMY DOMINGO, *Junk Terror Bill |* Protest at the University of the Philippines on Independence Day against an anti-terrorism bill. QUEZON CITY, PHILIPPINES

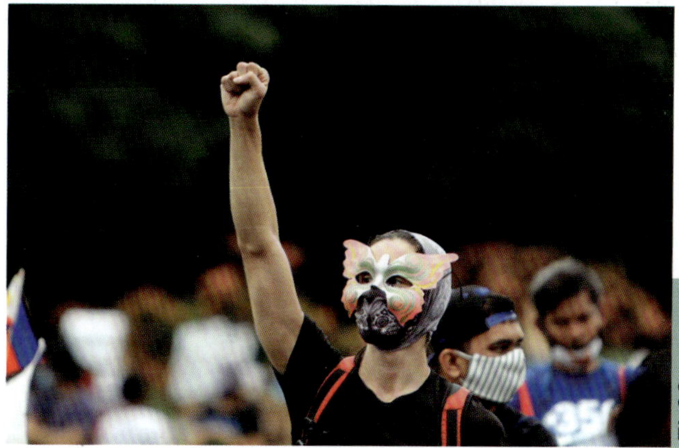

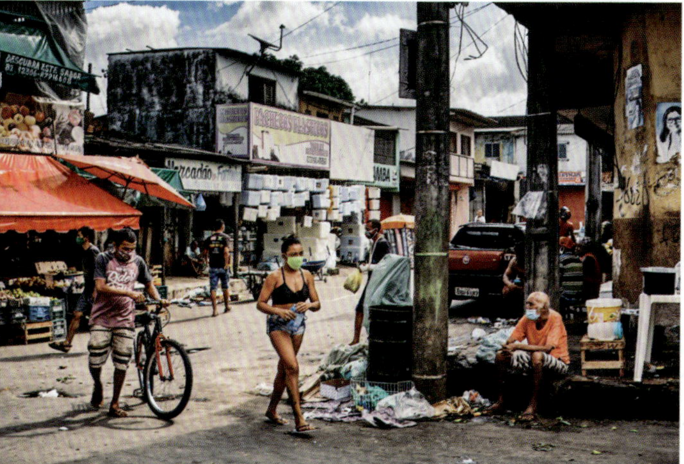

GUSTAVO MINAS, Scene close to a street market in João Paulo neighborhood, in São Luis. (for Businessweek). BRAZIL

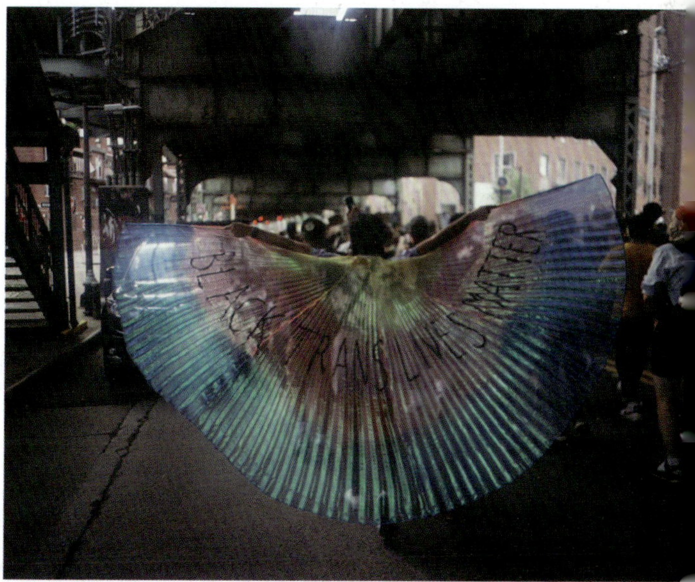

BRIAN KARLSSON, Brooklyn, 2020. NEW YORK, NY, USA

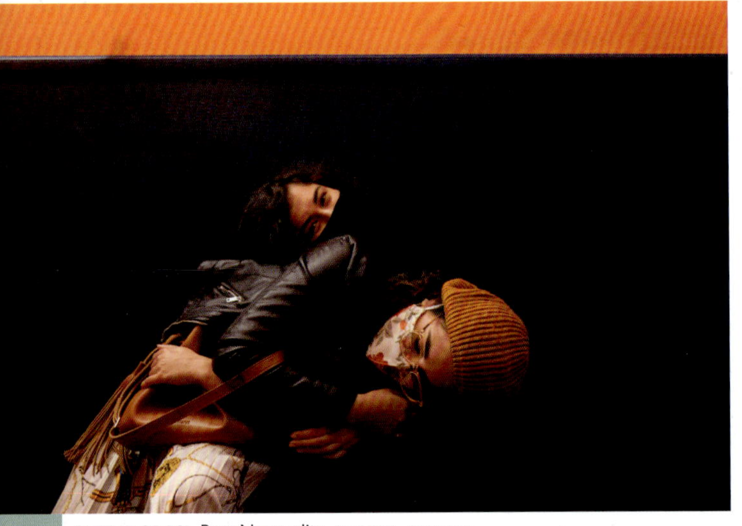

SATTVA ORASI, Post Normality. COIMBRA, PORTUGAL

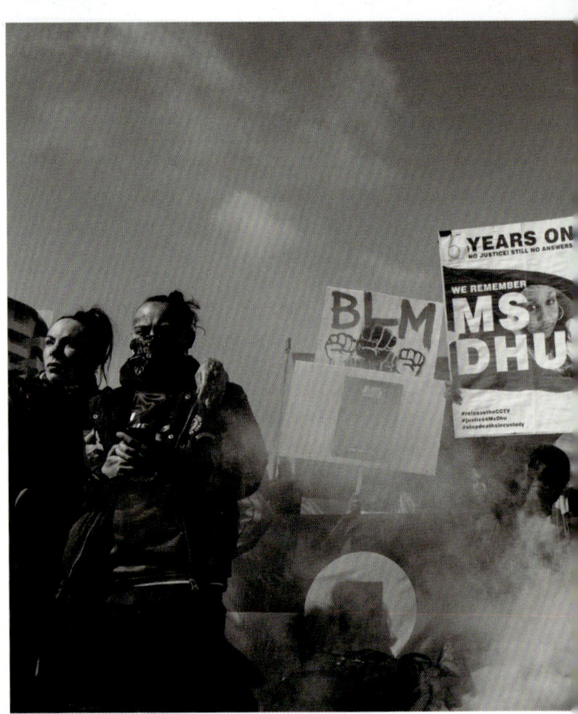

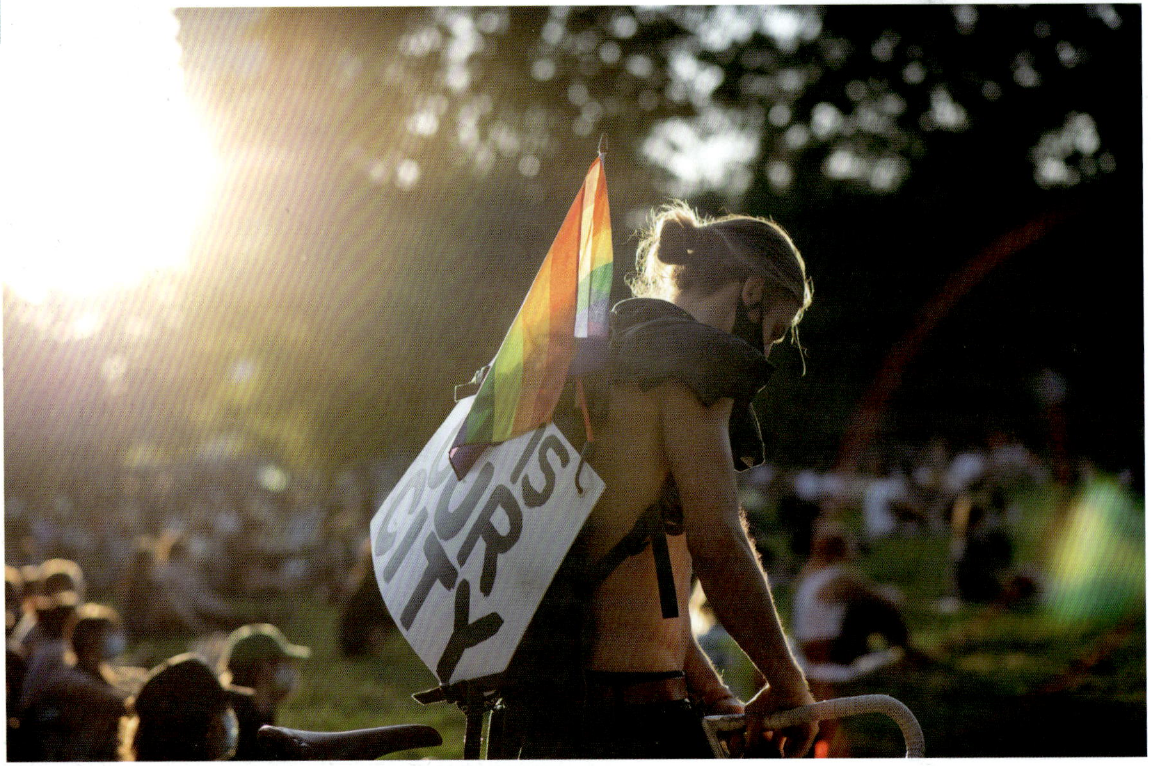

GLORIA SALGADO GISPERT, Waking up, because like many, I've been "asleep" to this most of my life. PERTH, AUSTRALIA

HILARY BENAS, The McCarren Park Vigil, at the intersection of the Black Lives Matter movement, Pride month, and COVID. BROOKLYN, NY, USA

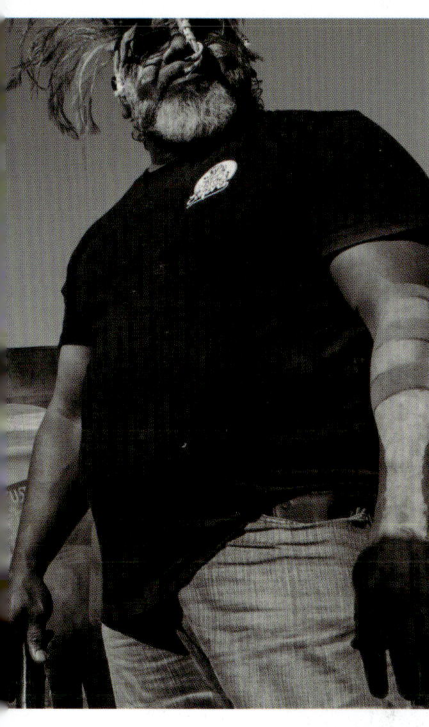

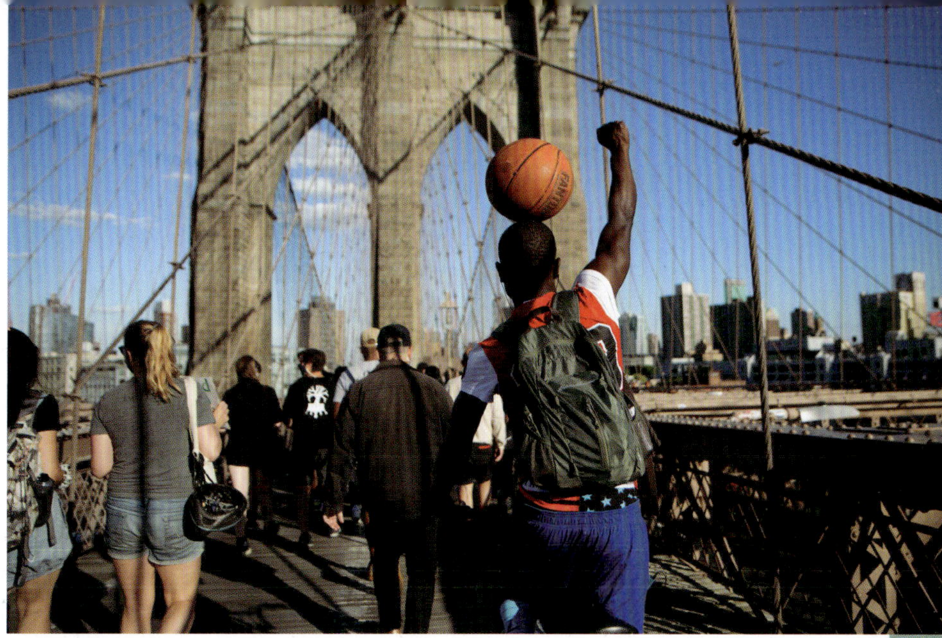

SYDNEY KORNEGAY, A Black Lives Matter protestor balances his bike and a basketball while riding across the Brooklyn Bridge. NEW YORK, NY, USA

JULIA FULLERTON-BATTEN, *Otto, Lockdown Day 82* |

People at home in self-isolation. Imprisoned in their homes, they gaze forlornly out of their windows onto a different desolate world outside. LONDON, UNITED KINGDOM

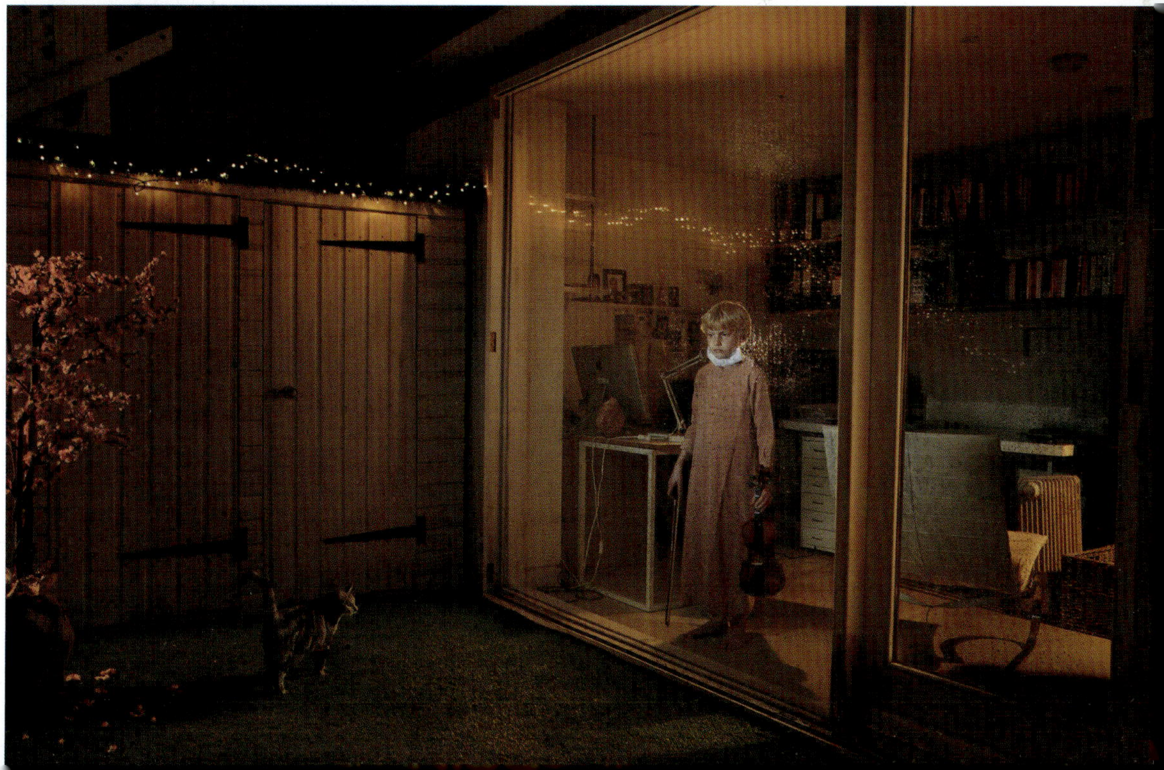

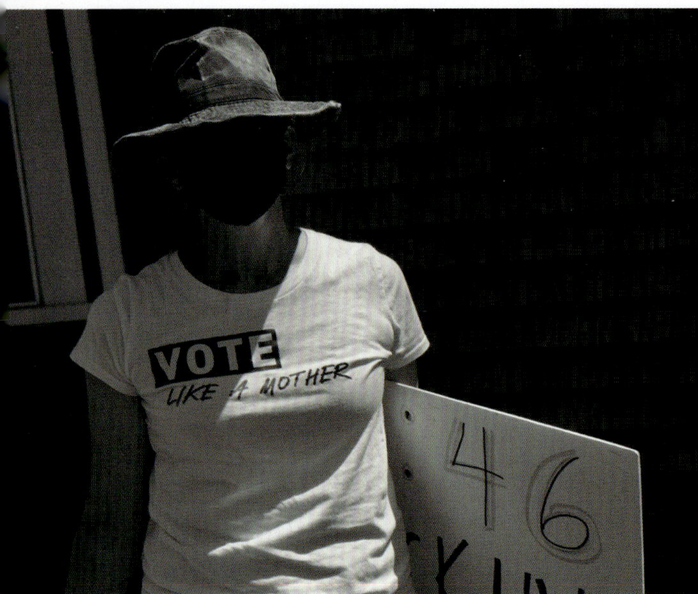

DOUGLAS ALLEN, Young Activists for Social Justice of Martha's Vineyard March. MA, USA

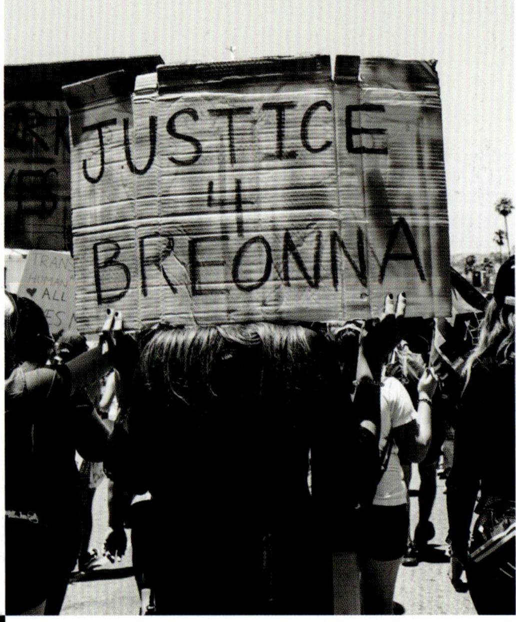

SOPHIE LARGHI, *Justice For Breonna Taylor* | Black LGBTQ leaders organized the "All Black Lives Matter March" in Los Angeles to protest racial injustice and oppression. An estimated 40,000 people gathered and peacefully walked from Hollywood to West Hollywood. CA, USA

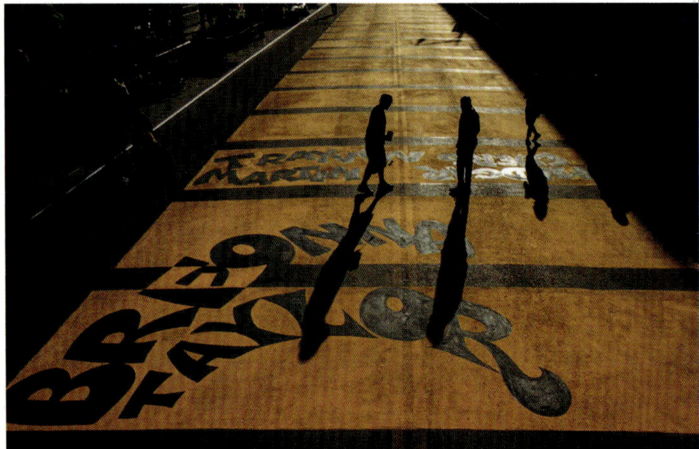

DANIELA CRUZ-CHARLOT, Justice for Breonna, bring criminal charges against the cops involved in her killing. BEDFORD-STUYVESANT, BROOKLYN, NY, USA

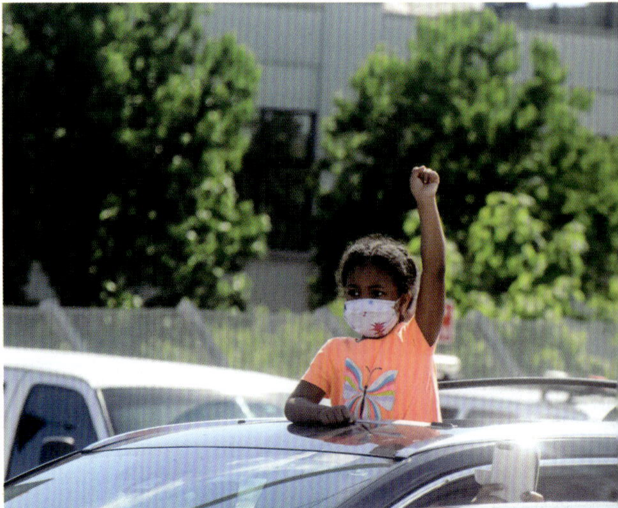

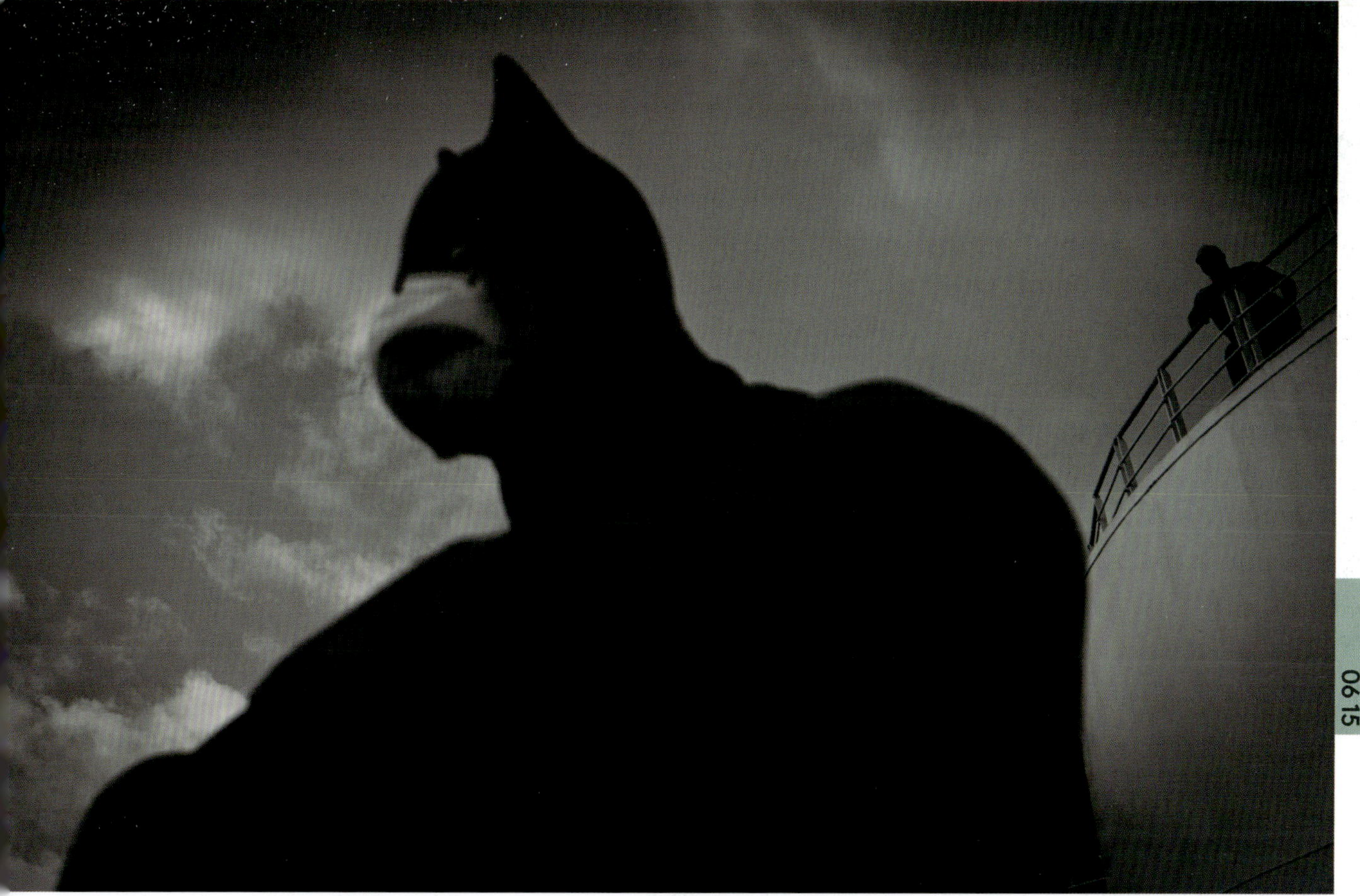

JANA RAJCOVÁ, *Even superheroes wear masks* | Taken during the ferry ride between Lugano and Olbia (Sardinia). ITALY

KIMBERLY ANDERSON, *Untitled* | Atlantic Avenue, Brooklyn. NEW YORK, NY, USA

DANIELA RIVERA ANTARA,

Lindsay, five, with her puppy inside the living room of her 80-year-old family house where she lives with her fourteen family members.
CHORRILLOS, LIMA, PERU

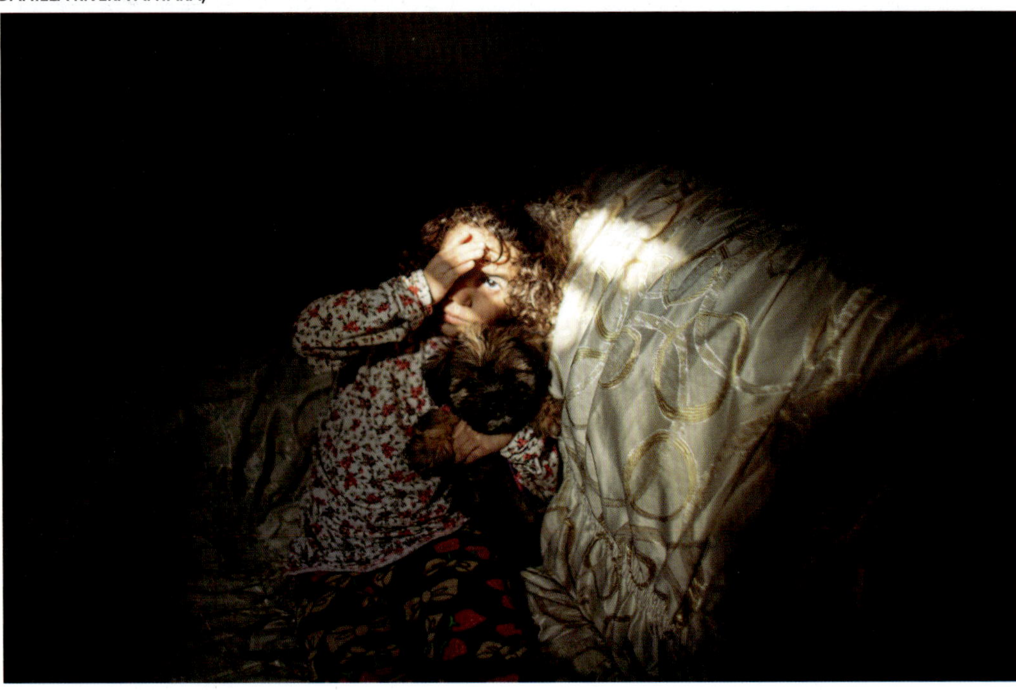

NINA DRAPACZ, *Kirk Beach* |

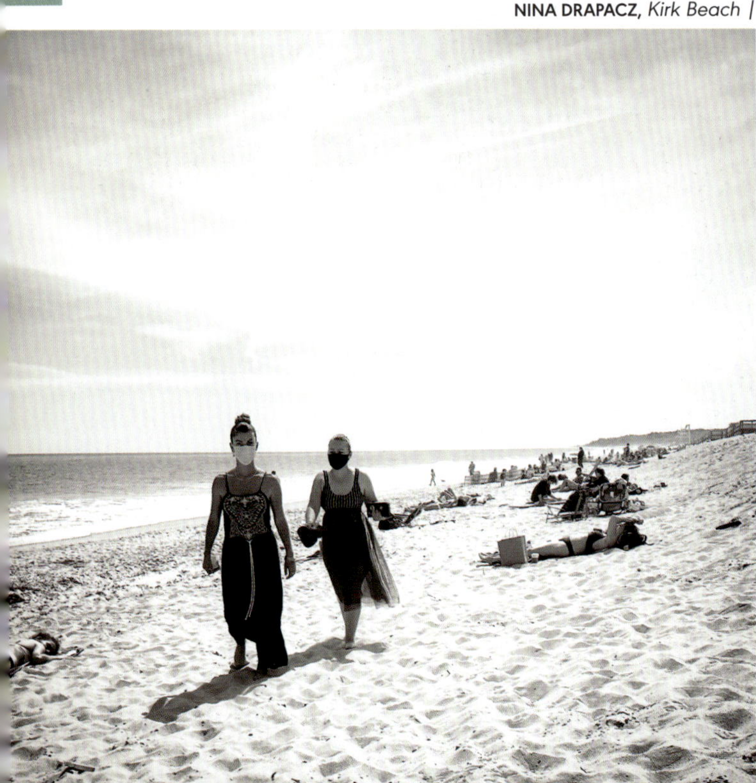

After three months of isolation in NYC, I drove to the beach to find only these two women wearing masks. It was surreal, both the denial and the reality.
MONTAUK, NY, USA

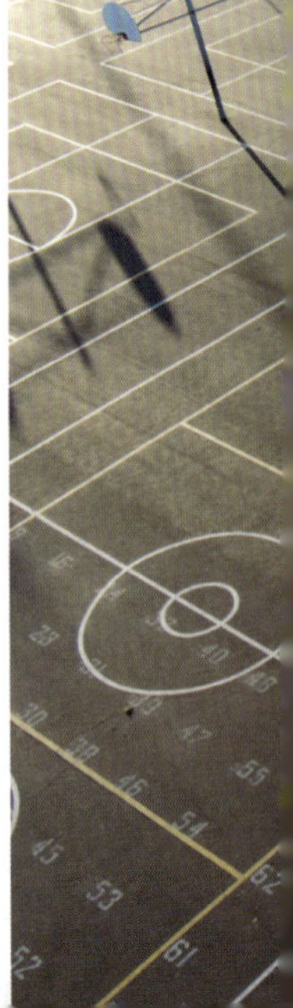

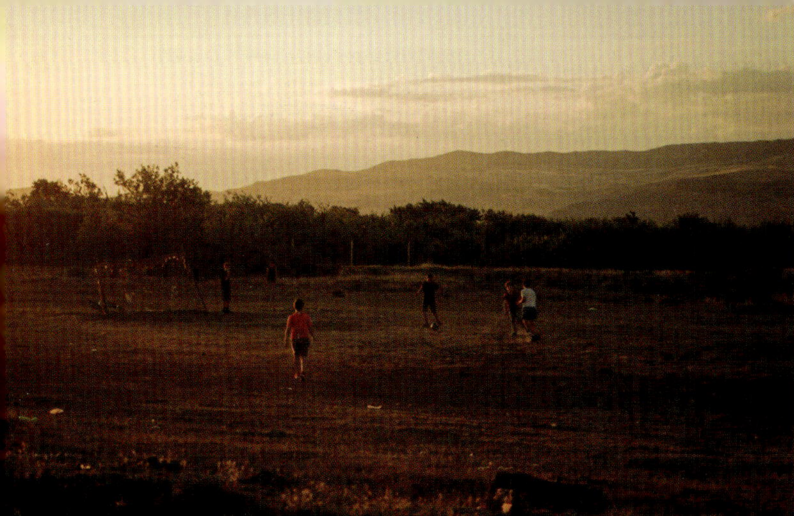

NICOLO VINCENZO MALVESTUTO, This picture was taken in a Georgian village called Gori. Some residents of the village enjoy outside time amidst the pandemic. GA, USA

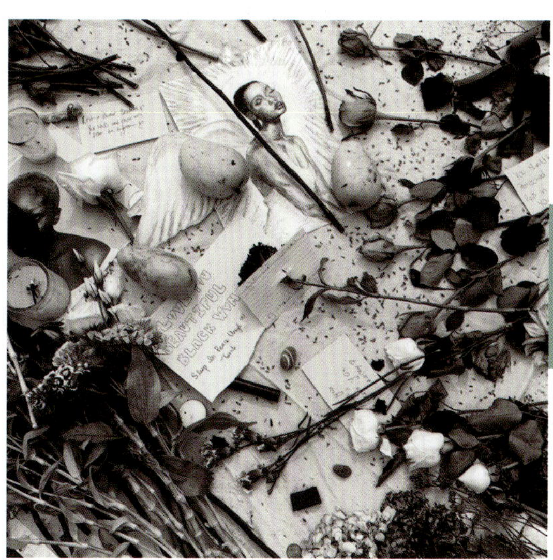

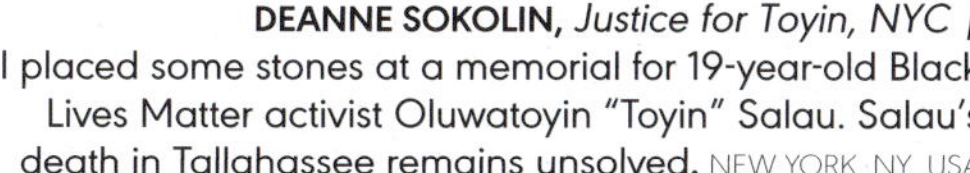

DEANNE SOKOLIN, *Justice for Toyin, NYC* | I placed some stones at a memorial for 19-year-old Black Lives Matter activist Oluwatoyin "Toyin" Salau. Salau's death in Tallahassee remains unsolved. NEW YORK, NY, USA

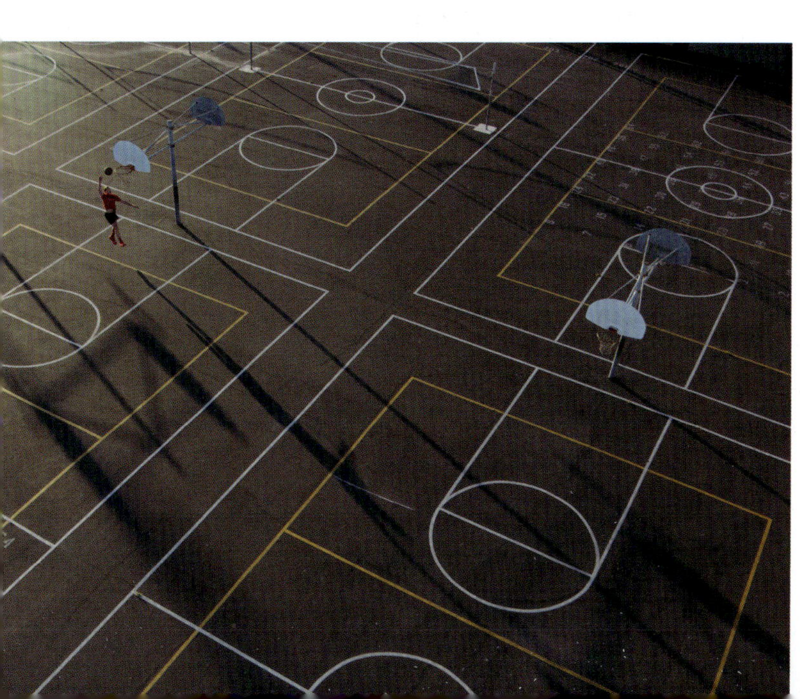

TRACY BOULIAN AND DAVID AHNTHOLZ, *Athlete Persisting* | Without his team, a dedicated high school basketball player trains alone. SAN JUAN CAPISTRANO, CA, USA

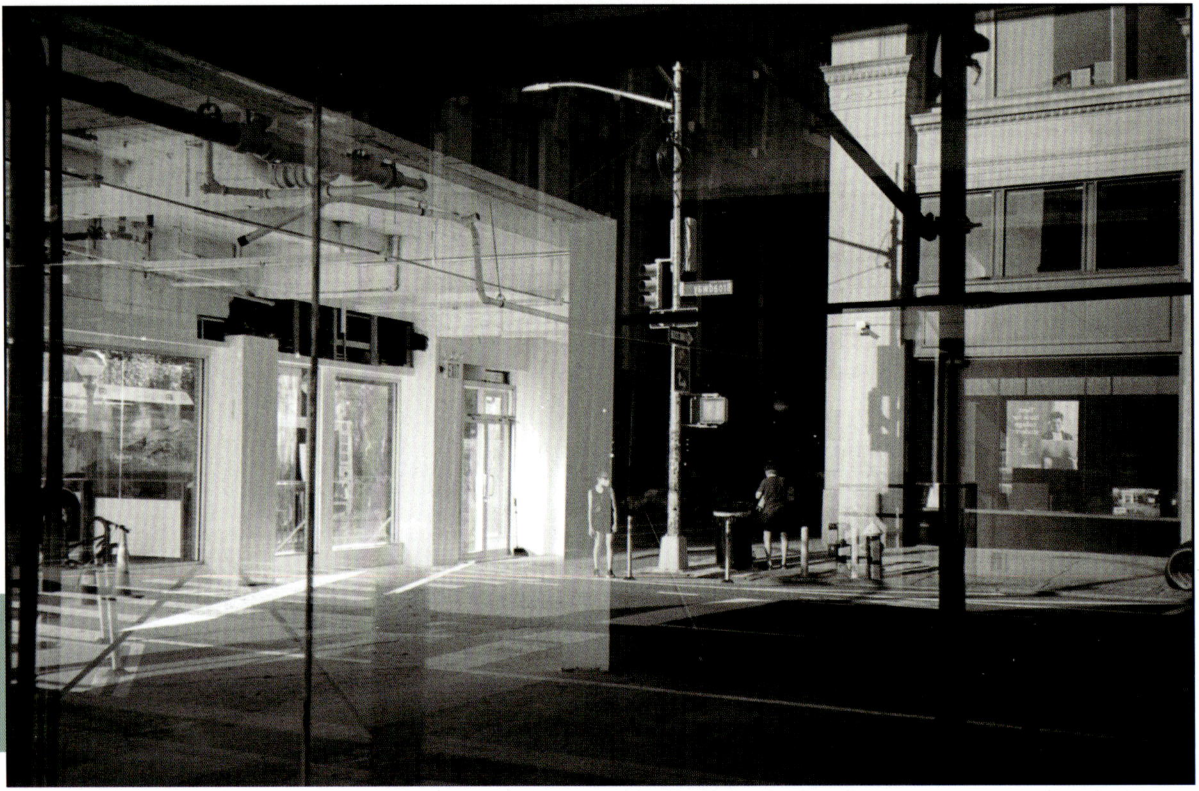

RYAN SCOTT, *Broadway Prism* | Light fractures around the empty city and each human encounter takes on a special significance. NEW YORK, NY, USA

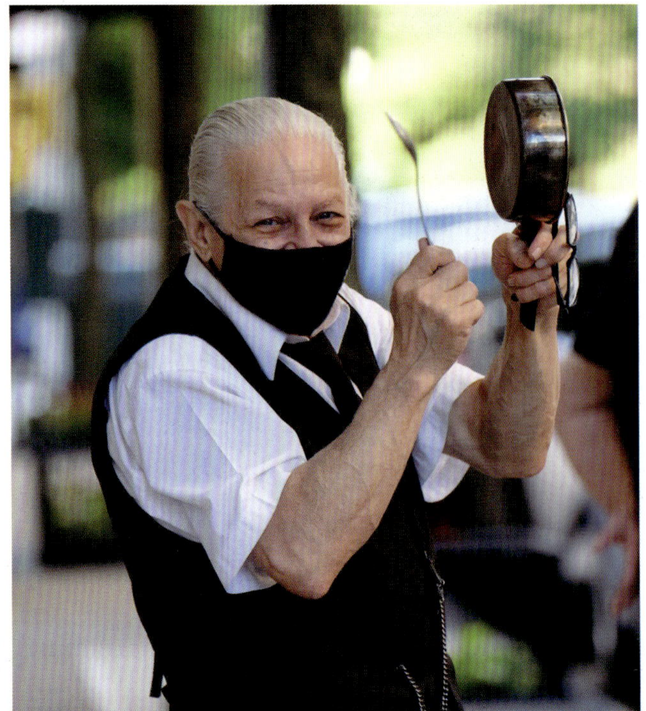

DEBORAH SHAPIRO, A Manhattan doorman on West End Avenue applauding front line workers with a spoon and pan. NY, USA

CARLOS DONADUZZI, Emanuel Monteiro, Curitiba/Brazil (FaceTime). SANTA MARIA, BRAZIL

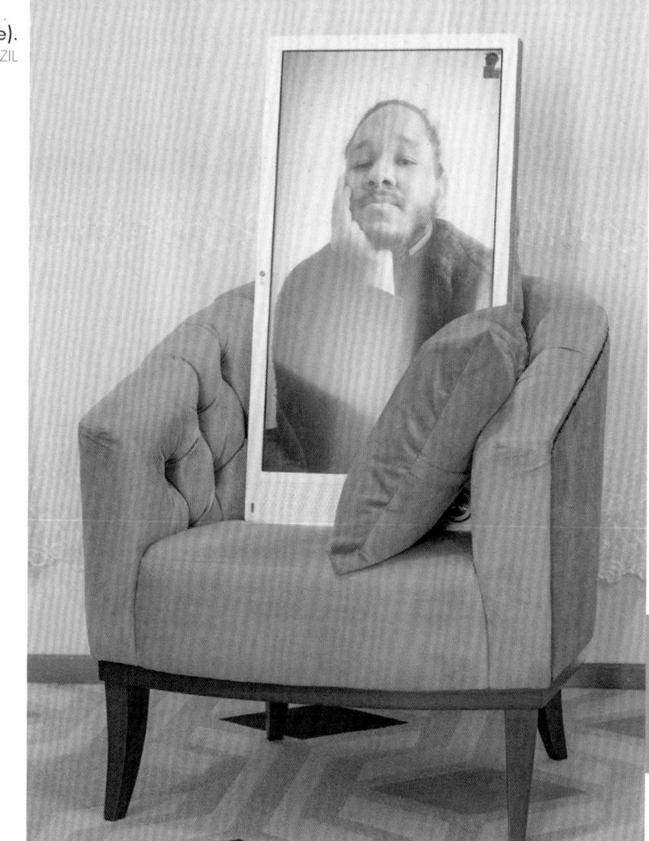

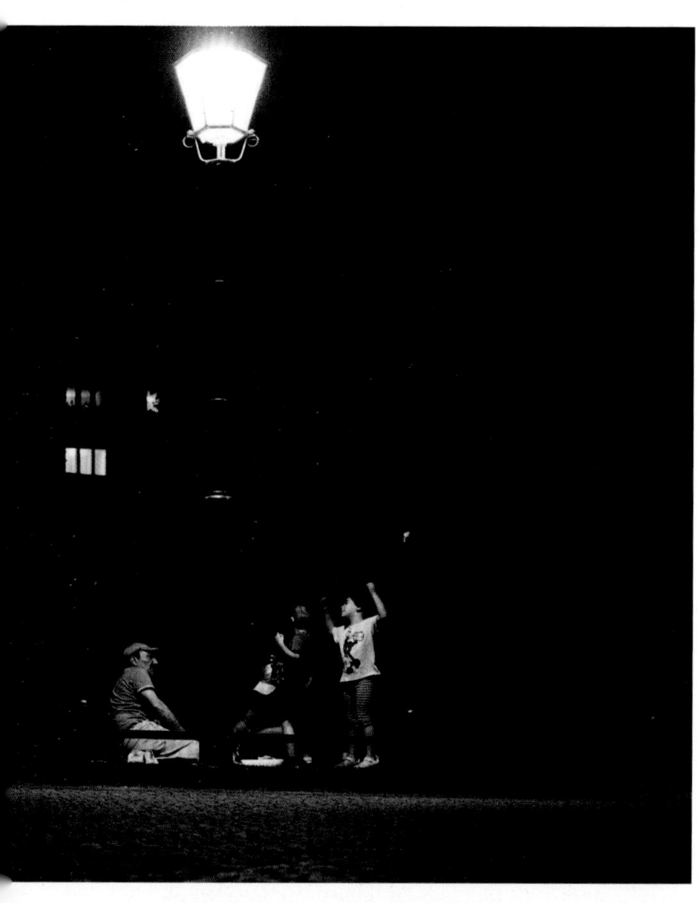

SAE HAN KIL KIM, HOPE 2020. BERLIN, GERMANY

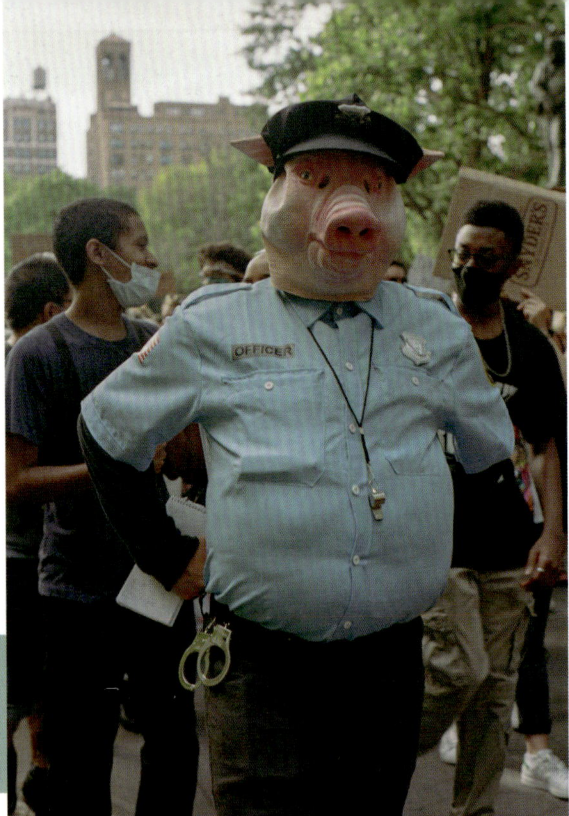

SOPHIA KALINOWSKA-WERTER, Juneteenth Manifestation and BLM Protest. WASHINGTON SQUARE PARK, NEW YORK, NY, USA

LAURA PROCTOR, A young boy stands with his father in the shade of a tree, watching a Black Lives Matter protest in Toronto. CANADA

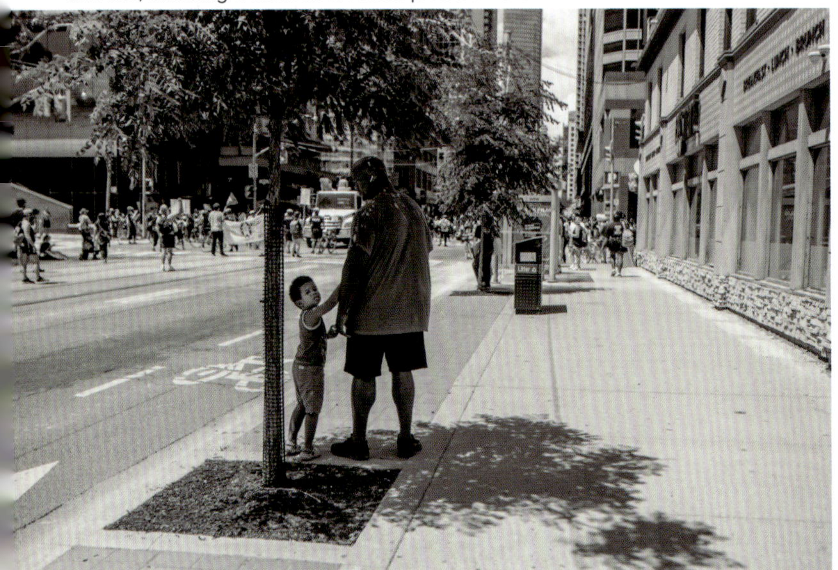

MIRACLE UKEJE, The New Normal. OYINBO BRIDGE, OYINBO, LAGOS, NIGERIA

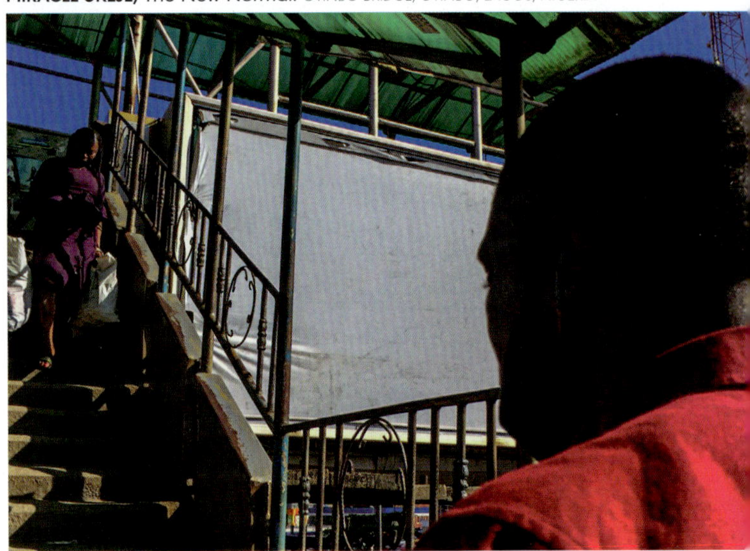

NORMAN BORDEN, Fashion-conscious masked protester in African-themed dress holds a George Floyd poster while marching up Sixth Avenue. NEW YORK, NY, USA

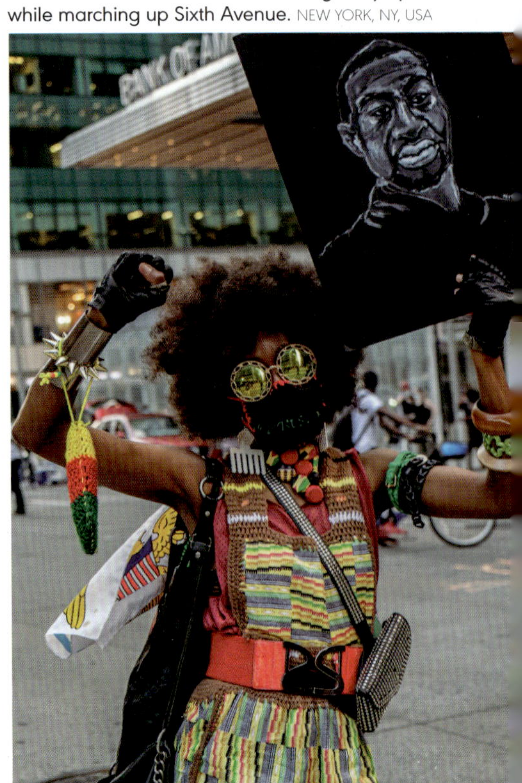

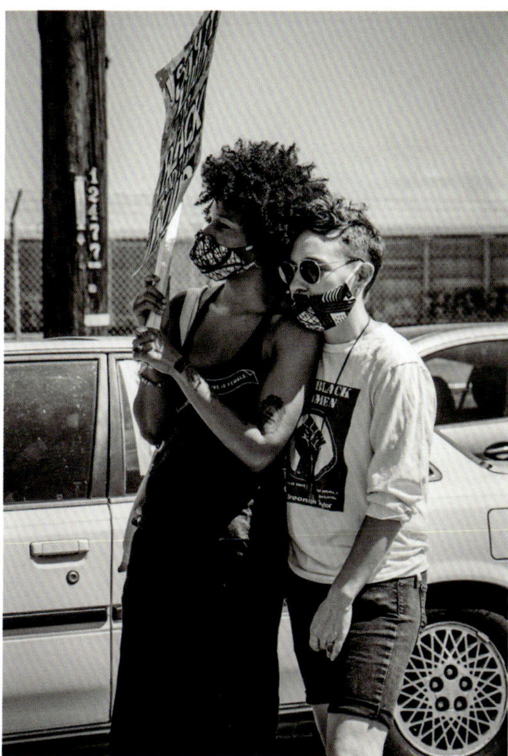

CHRIS PARTIN, Someone to Lean On. OAKLAND, CA, USA

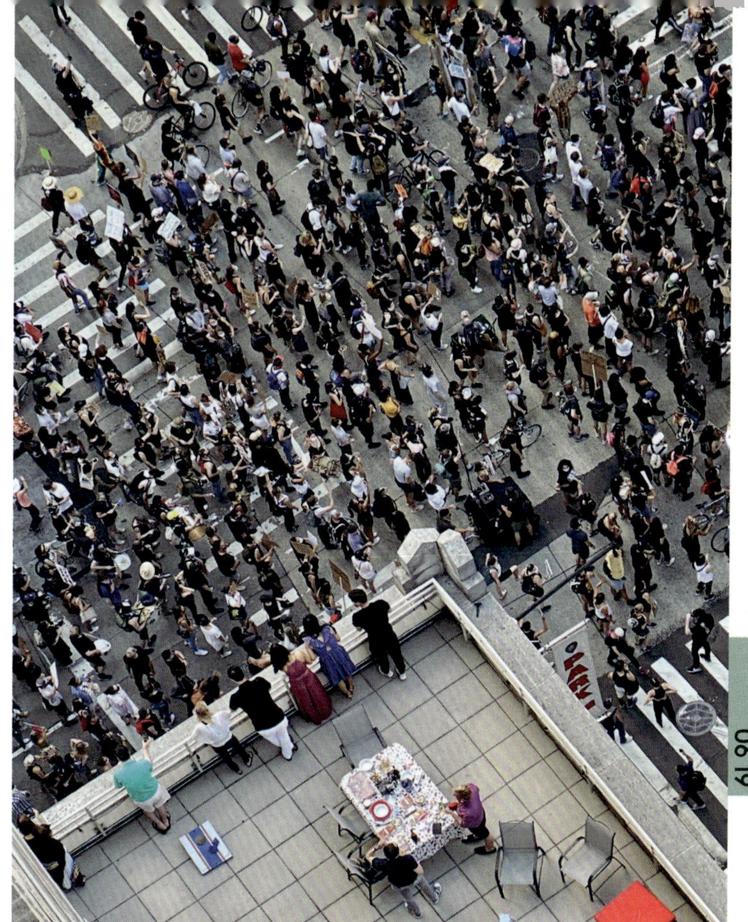

SOPHIA MICHELEN, The two types of summer 2020. MIDTOWN MANHATTAN, NY, USA

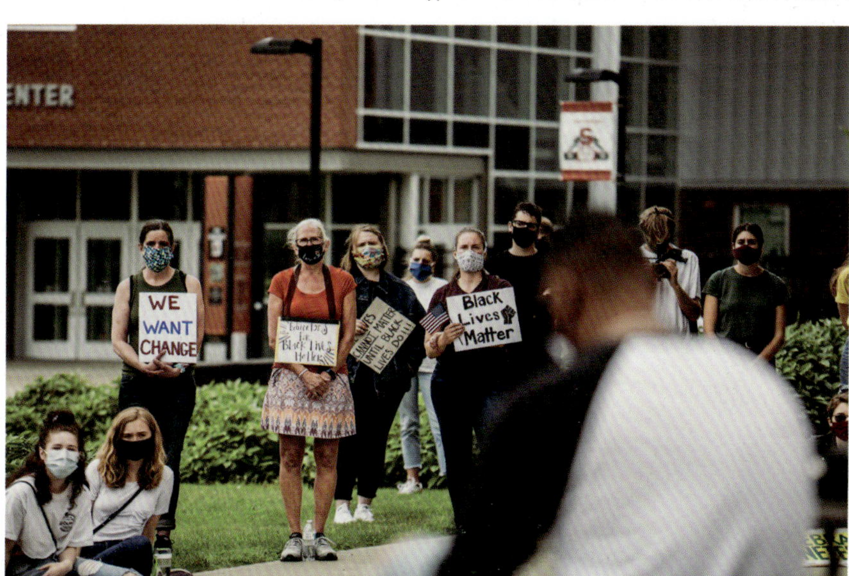

WILLIAM KING, Juneteenth. SNOHOMISH HIGH SCHOOL, WA, USA

DANE MANARY, This Machine. WASHINGTON SQUARE PARK, NEW YORK, NY, USA

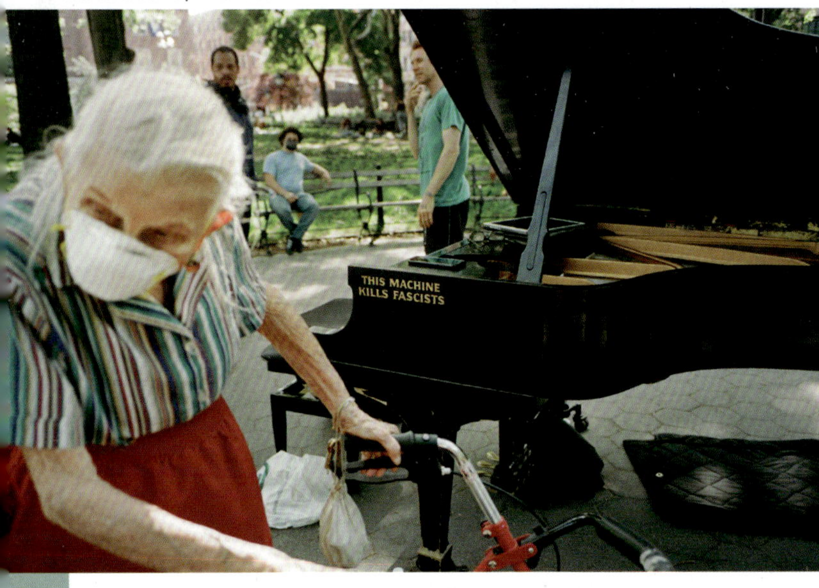

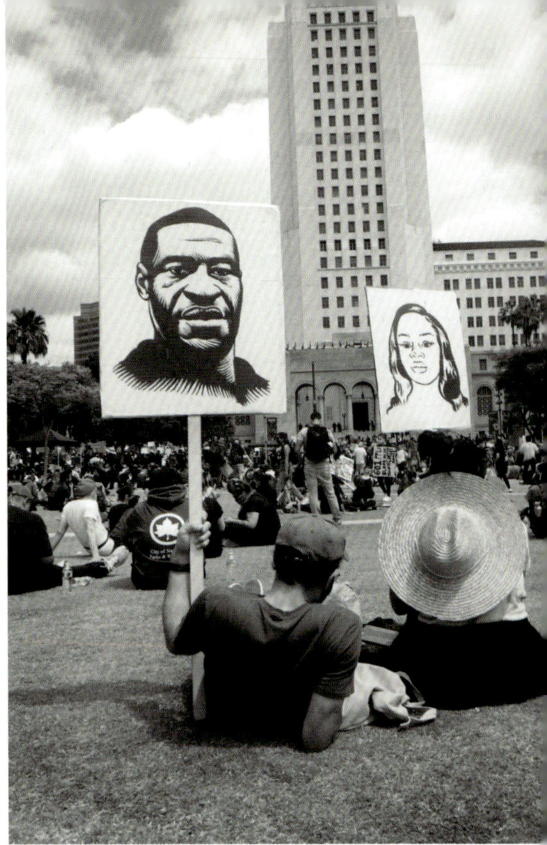

ALICE DISON, Black Lives Matter!
LOS ANGELES CITY HALL, CA, USA

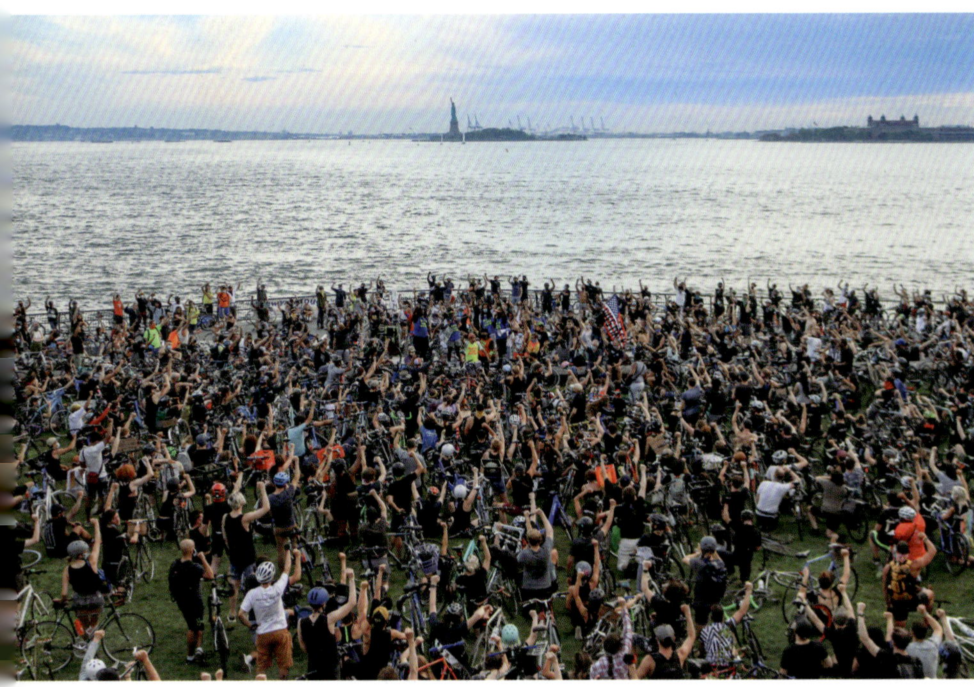

ILARIA D'ALESSANDRO,
Say hello to a new Miss America.
We can't breathe. Justice ride 3.
BATTERY PARK, NEW YORK, NY, USA

KAREN S. BELLEVUE, *The Kiss* | Photo taken on the ferry from Amsterdam station to Amsterdam North. NETHERLANDS

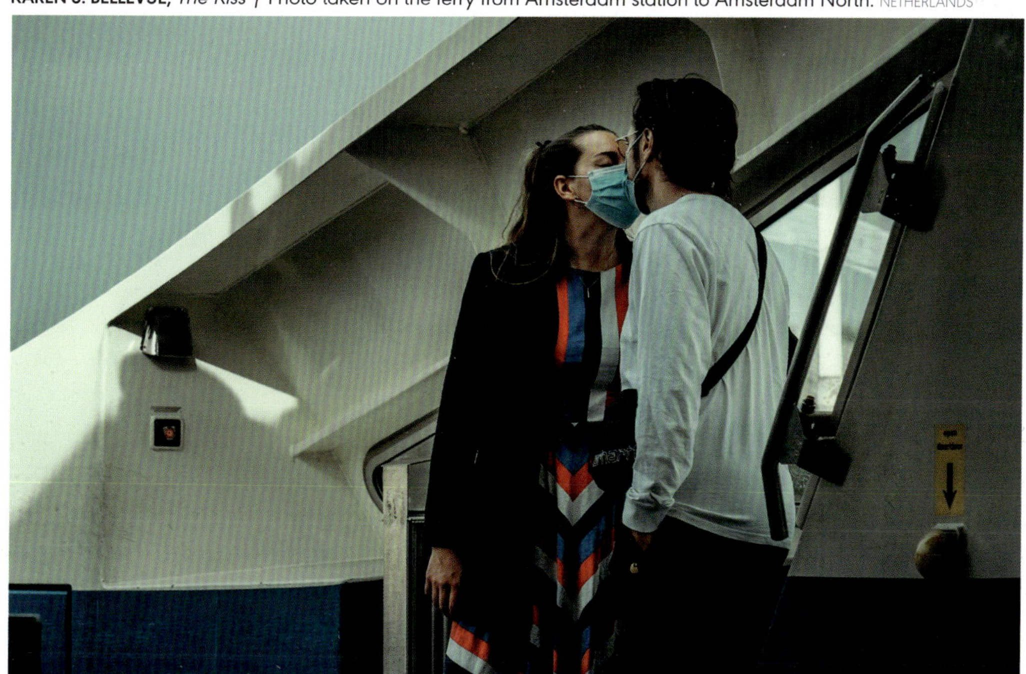

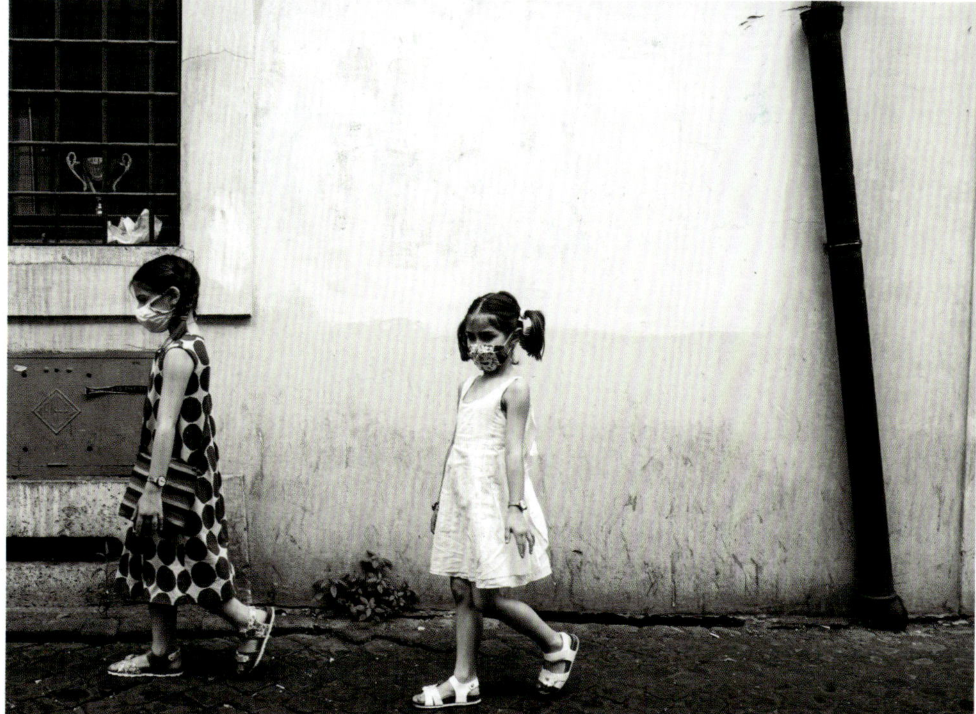

ANDREA TORREI, *Street life under COVID-19* |
Social distancing and mask wearing are the few tools we have to curb the spread of the virus. ROME, ITALY

BESAT EMAMI, *Hands* | Tehran city center, Naser-khosro Street, near Tehran Grand Bazaar. IRAN

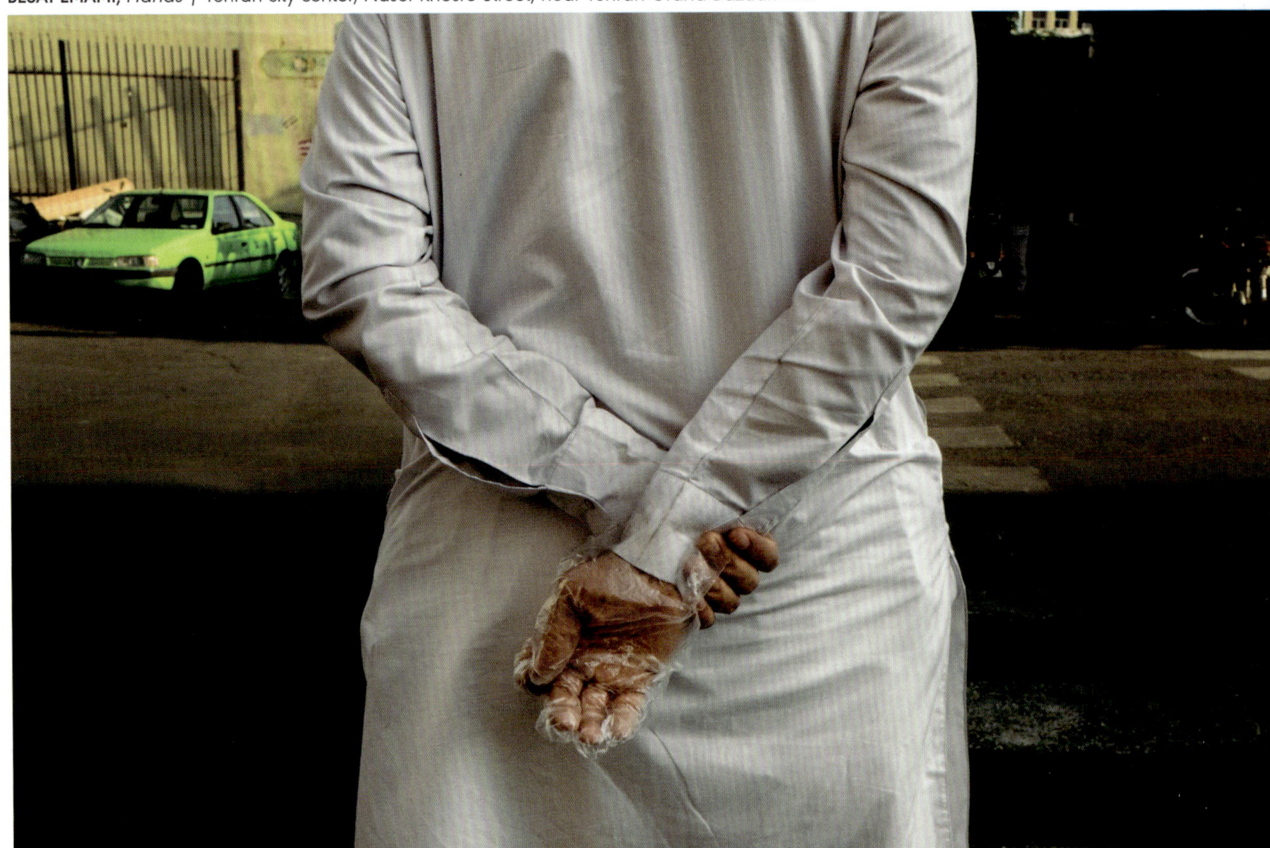

LAWRENCE LEVI, Bedford-Stuyvesant, Brooklyn. NEW YORK, NY, USA

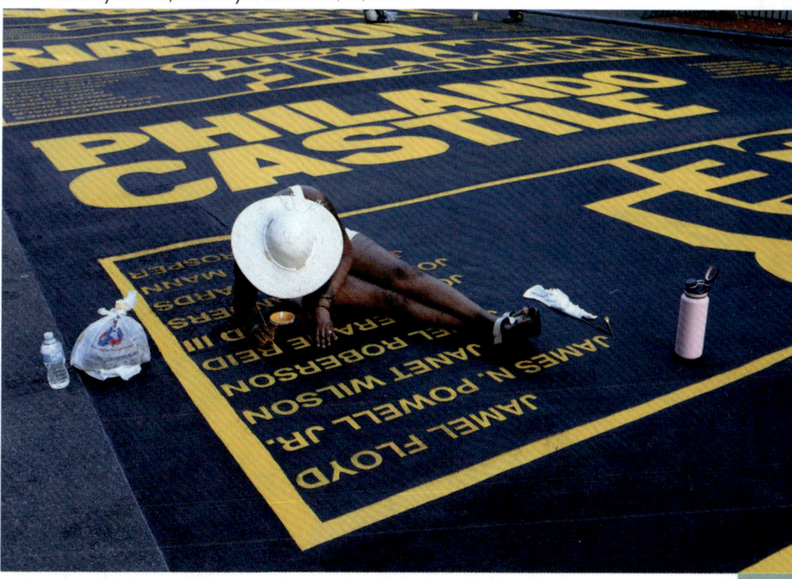

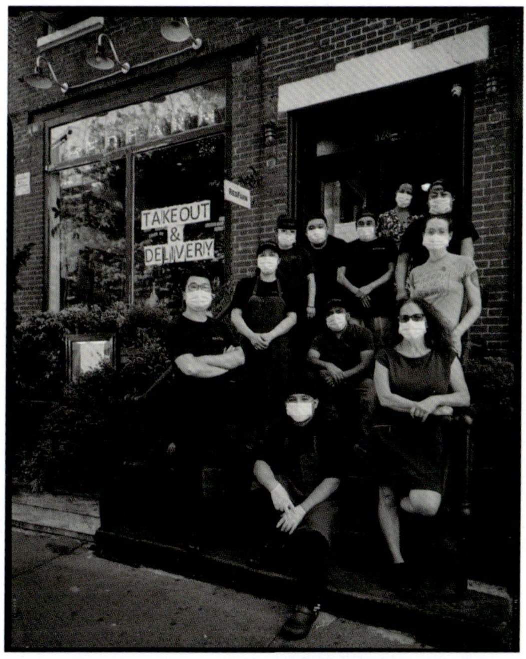

GEOFF GREEN, *Open, RedFarm* | RedFarm has been open and providing to the community throughout the pandemic. WEST VILLAGE. NEW YORK, NY, USA

AUTUMN MORAN, *Black Lives Matter Sit In at City Hall* | Police look from a safe distance as protesters push to defund the police ahead of the budget review. NEW YORK, NY, USA

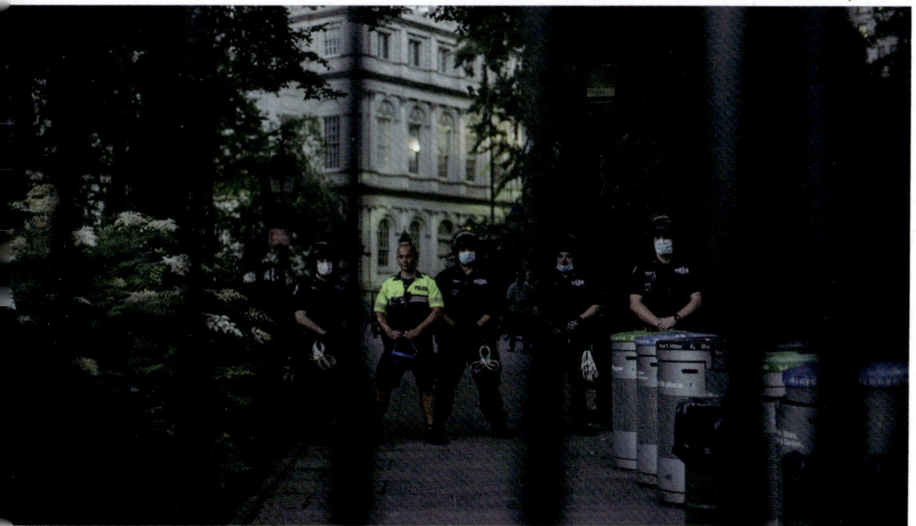

MARCI LINDSAY, Reading Material at Black Lives Matter Plaza. WASHINGTON, DC, USA

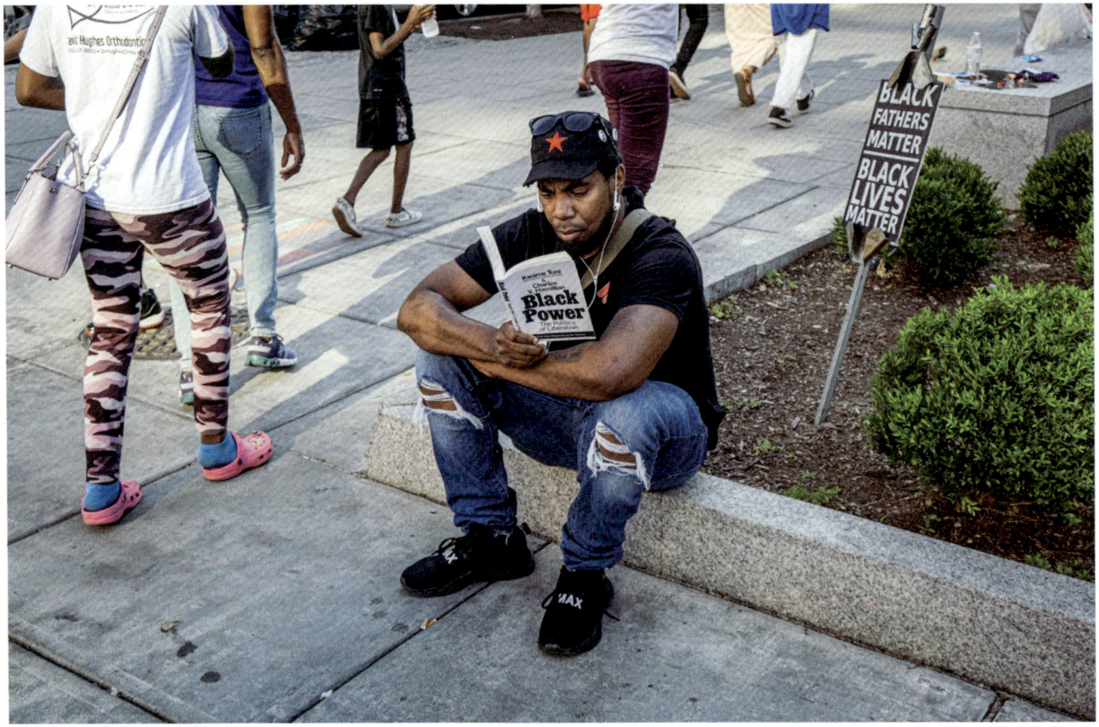

06 25

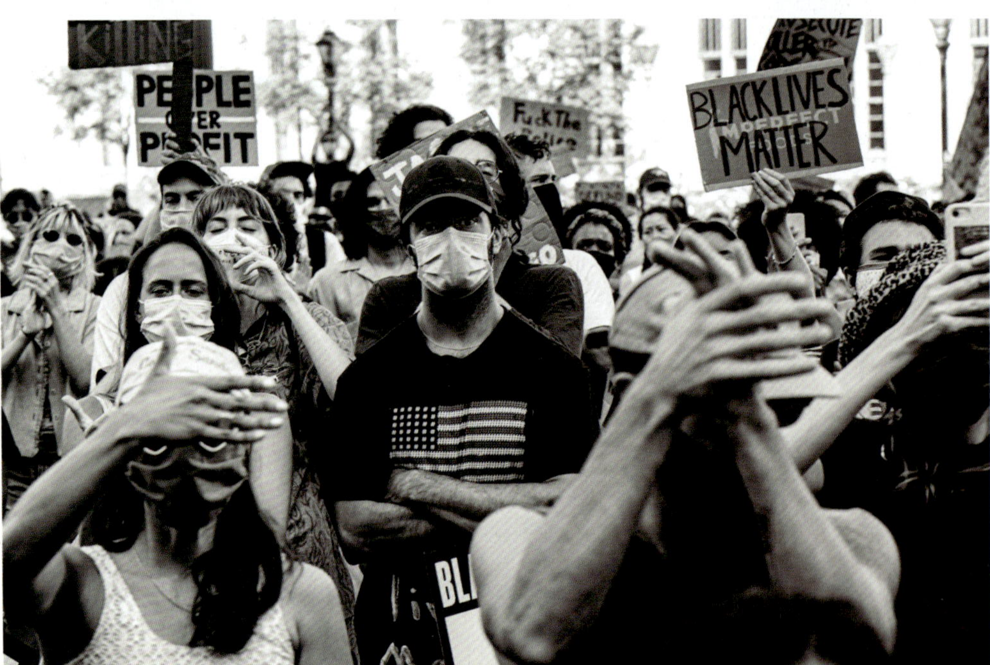

KATE STERLIN, *Black Lives Matter Protest, Los Angeles* | Weekly protest at the Hall of Justice to ask for the firing of Jackie Lacey, the district attorney. CA, USA

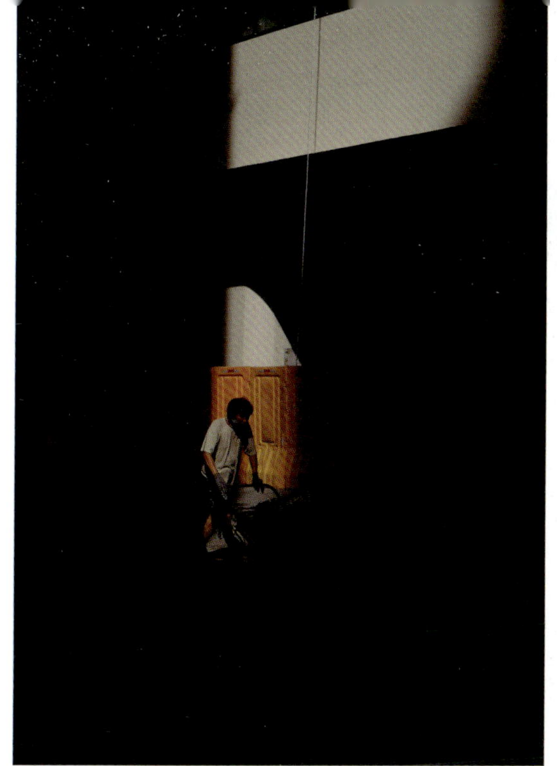

JIMMY CHAN, Under the Shadow. HONG KONG

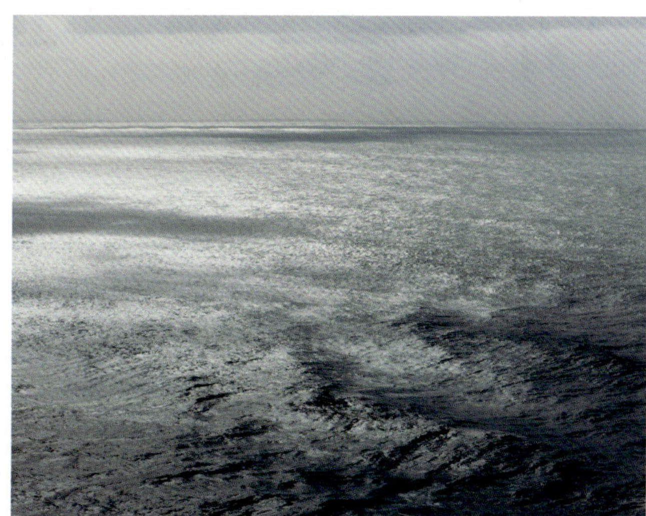

ALESSANDRO PUCCINELLI, *Summer, Mare 461* | This image is part of an endless series, "Mare," depicting the ocean that I started more than ten years ago. CABO SARDÃO, ALENTEJO, PORTUGAL

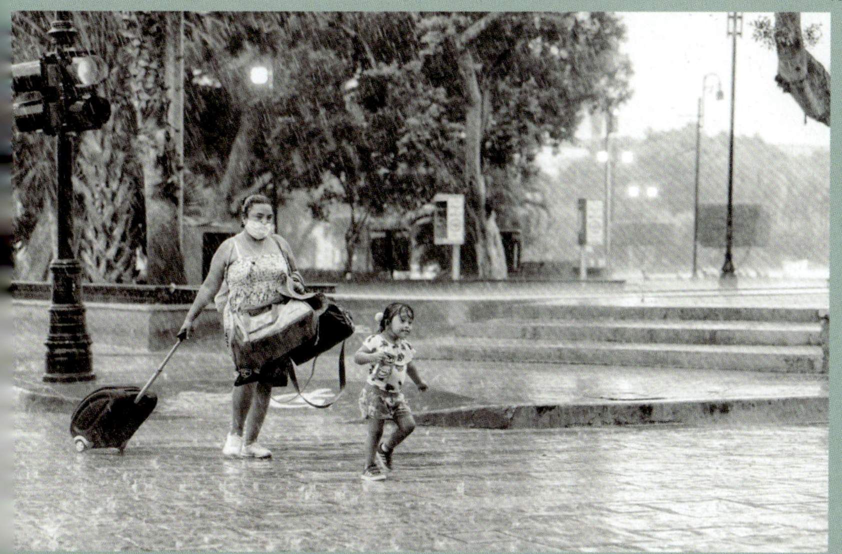

IVAN GABALSON,

To me, this image represents my experience of the current moment because in a way it embodies a contradiction. That is, it shows both the desolation of a city that is usually full of life and the resilience and energy of human beings. It was raining very hard and few people were outside because all non-essential activities had been stopped. I saw this woman and child as they started to cross the street in my direction, completely oblivious to the rain, almost as if they were playing in a park somewhere. The woman was wearing a mask, the sign of the times we're living. But the child was not. I made several frames before they finished crossing and took shelter close to me, where I could see the woman using a small towel to carefully dry the girl. It made me think that she wasn't really being reckless, but rather they were just being alive. They may have been scared off COVID-19, as we all are, but they were certainly not afraid of the rain. MÉRIDA, YUCATÁN, MEXICO

JOSH WINDSOR, *Recasting the Crisis* |
A protester holds up a sign during a Black Lives Matter protest in London. UNITED KINGDOM

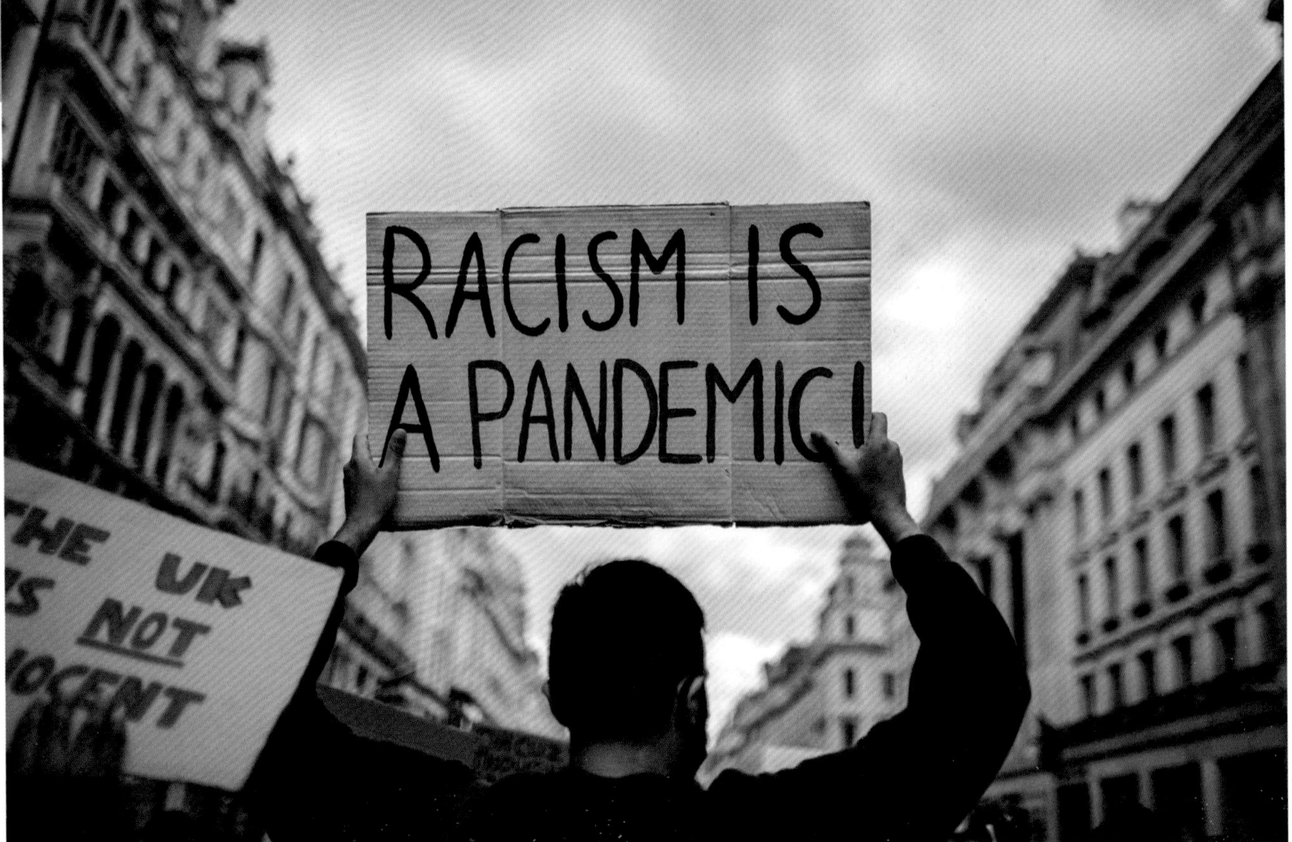

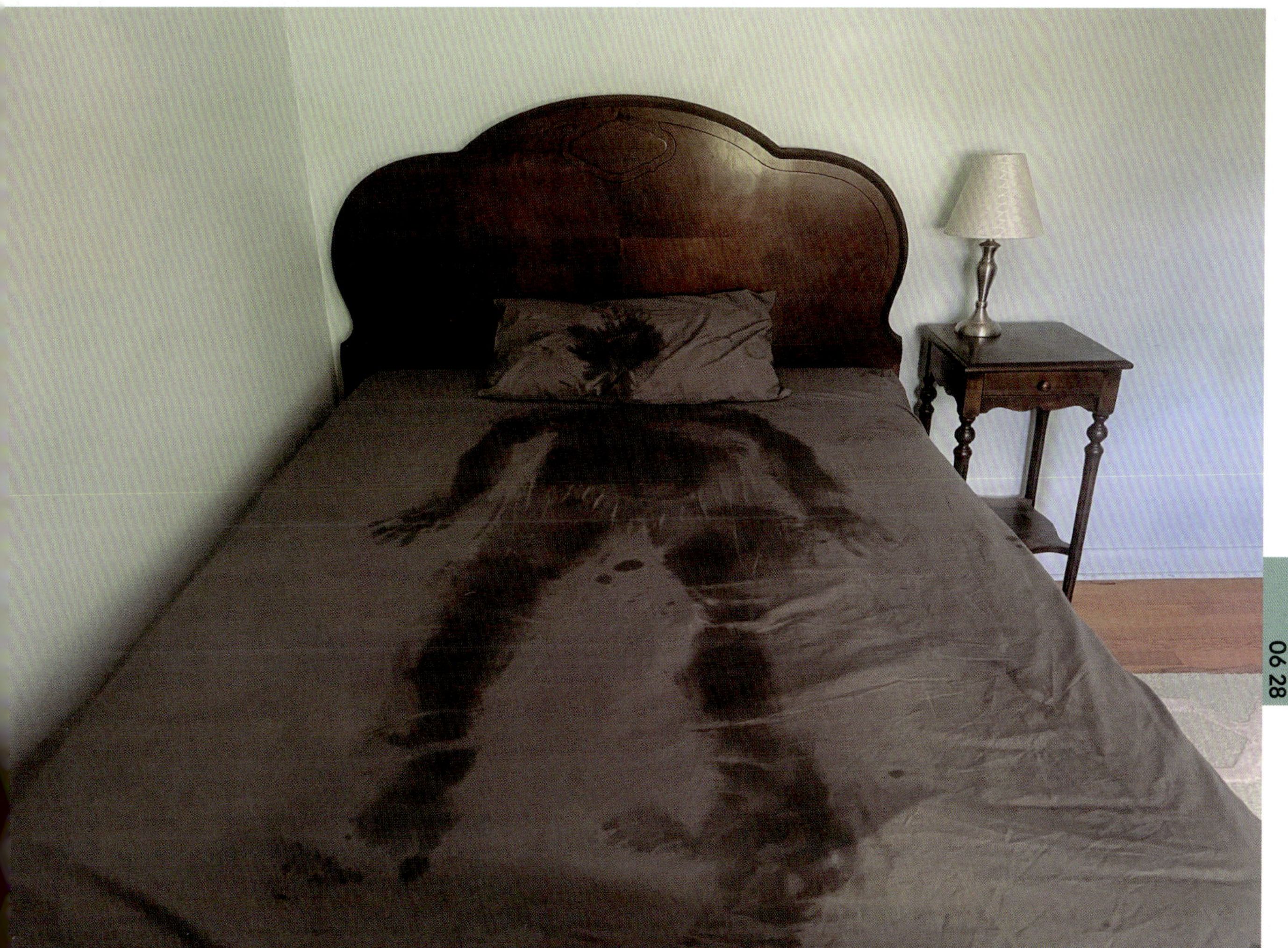

KAITLIN SANTORO, *Absence* |
Oil Body Print on Cotton Sheets. CT, USA

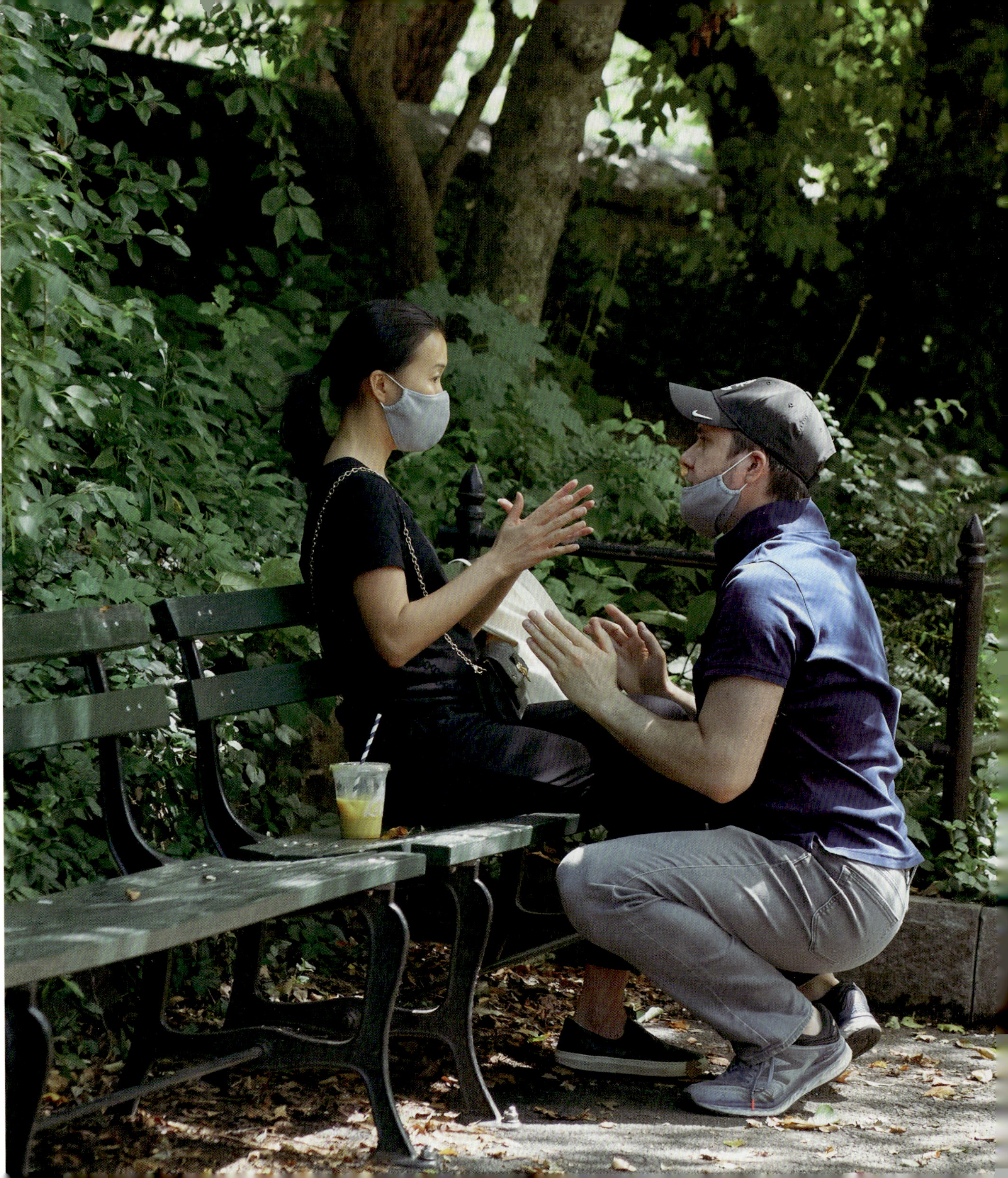

MONICA LORD, *Eavesdropping* | A pleasure lost to COVID-19. CENTRAL PARK, NEW YORK, NY, USA

IRIS EPSTEIN, *Dentro* |

This photo is part of a project called "Dentro," or "Inside," where I photograph close friends and family via Zoom. After months of worry and isolation, I wanted to feel connected again to the people I love, to find meaning through creativity and collaboration. I also wanted to have a record of this time away from time. This is a photograph of a childhood friend of mine who was visiting her family in Houston. Watching her take care of her children along with her cousin, I thought about the invisible and hard work mothers and caretakers do, one that now during the pandemic has become even more complicated but perhaps less invisible. Because this picture is a snapshot of my computer screen, it has a certain texture, and it's best seen from a distance—a distance being something we have become very familiar with during these strange times. MEXICO

07 01

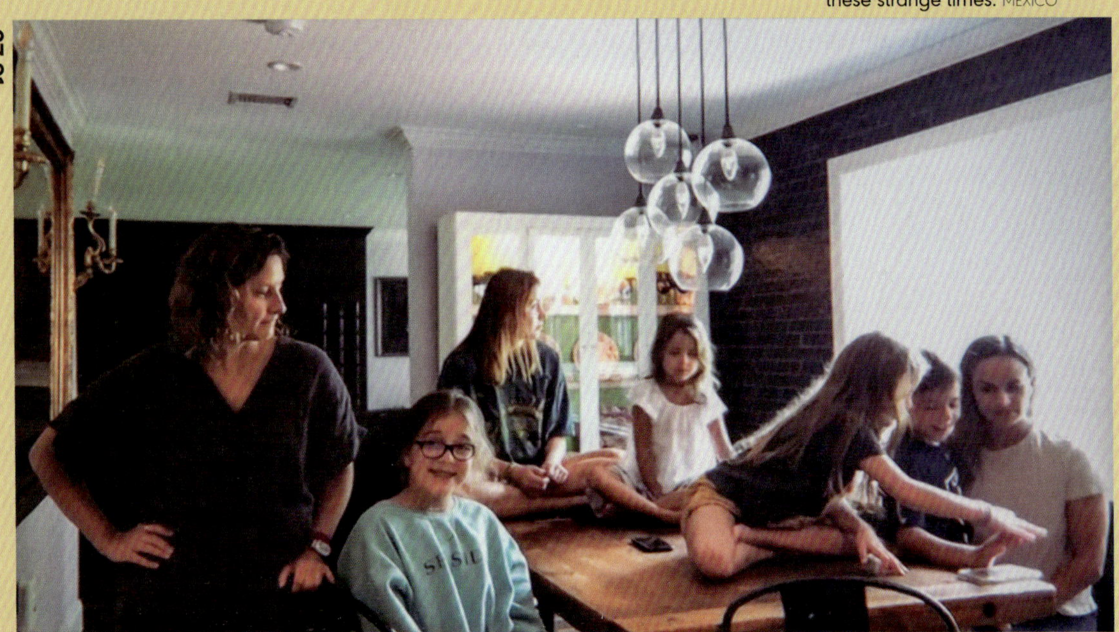

07·20

JULY

1_Coronavirus : plus de 160 000 nouveaux cas quotidiens depuis une semaine dans le monde *(Le Monde)*

13_ Rivals Dubai and Abu Dhabi Tackle Coronavirus in Very Different Ways *(Washington Post)*

22_ Pfizer Gets $1.95 Billion to Produce Coronavirus Vaccine by Year's End *(The New York Times)*

RAYMI FRANCISCO JEREZ, I'm glad you're back home. MILAN, ITALY

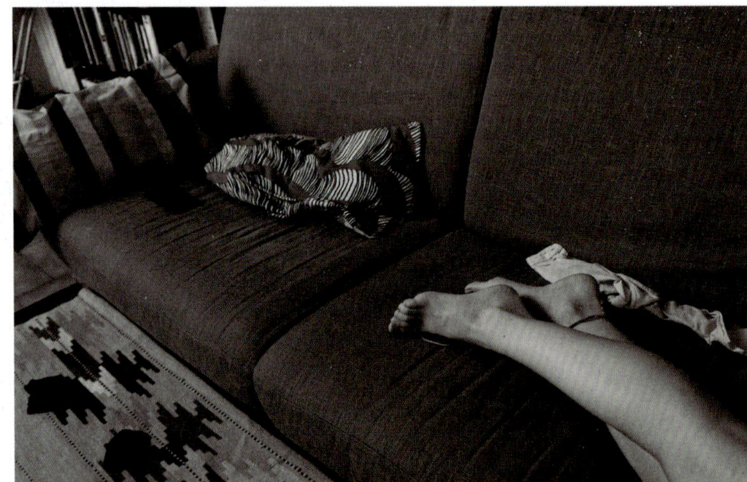

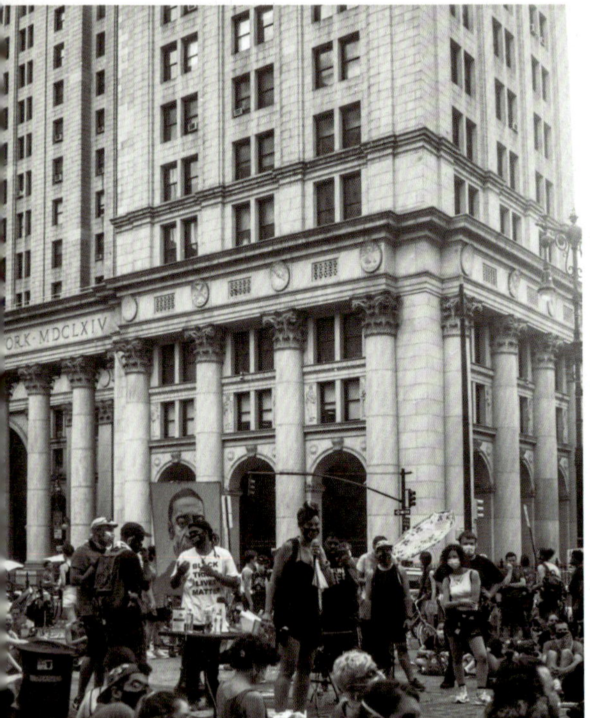

WASI FERDUS, Community Gathering at Occupy City Hall in New York City. NY, USA

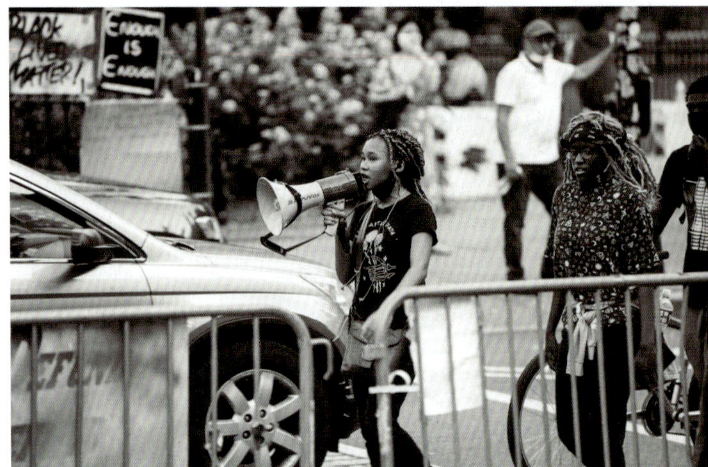

PETER PRICE, *Young Black Leaders |*

Young Black leaders with a group of protestors emerge off the Brooklyn Bridge to meet the protestors of Occupy City Hall, a movement fighting for justice and calling awareness to the continued acts of police violence towards black and brown communities. NEW YORK, NY, USA

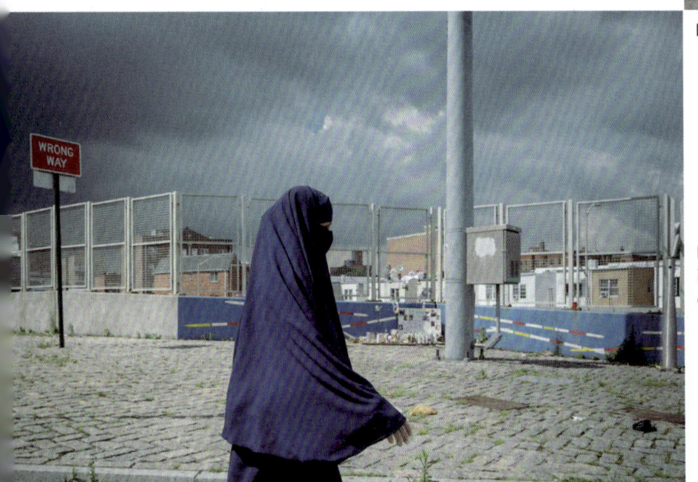

MASSIMO GIACHETTI, A woman wearing a facemask and a hijab walks in front of the exit of the Brooklyn Queens Expressway in Woodside. QUEENS, NEW YORK, NY, USA

GEORGIAN PARCHMENT, *No Sleep Til' Equality* | The band played for hours amongst a great, peaceful crowd in the sun, rallying and marching for justice and change. NEW YORK, NY

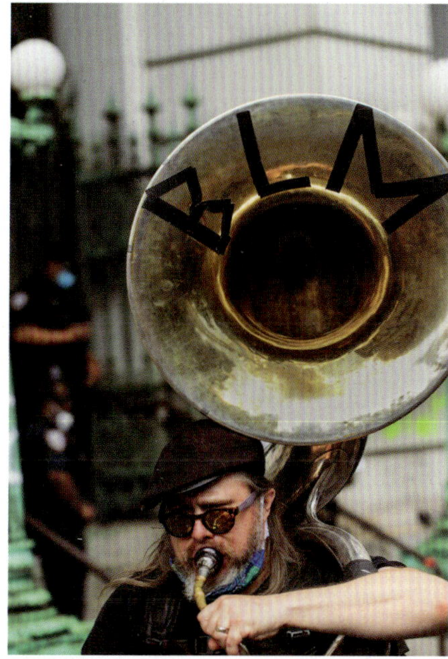

GERMAN ADRASTI, The medical staff of the SAME (Emergency Medical Attention System) evicted seventeen older adults from the geriatric Hospital Israelita Ezrah in the Flores neighborhood of Buenos Aires. ARGENTINA

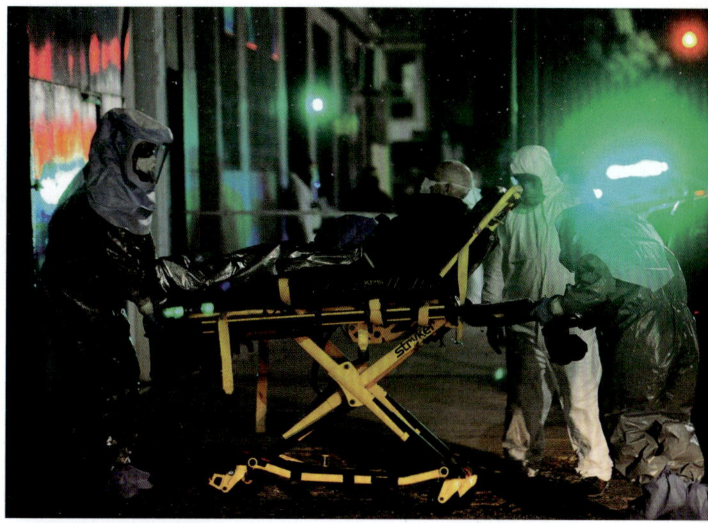

STEFANIE DWORKIN, *Fractured* | Limited to brief outings during early months of COVID-19, I took this photo while walking my dog in my neighborhood. BROOKLYN, NY, USA

KARL BADEN, Untitled. CAMBRIDGE, MA, USA

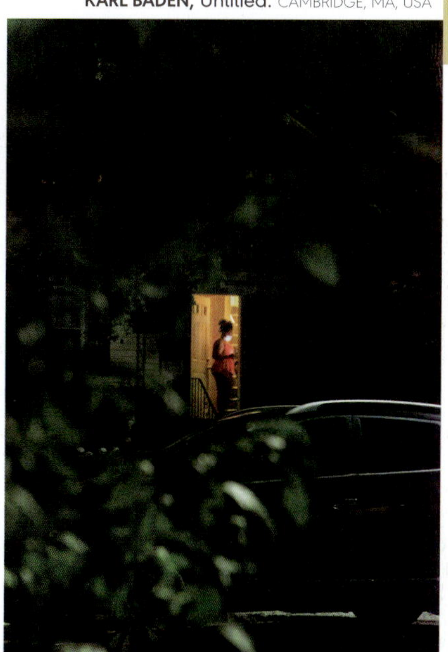

SANTIAGO FILIPUZZI, Ezequiel checks his four daughters' temperatures. He works as a sanitary agent in the neighborhood and earns $56 per month. BUENOS AIRES, ARGENTINA

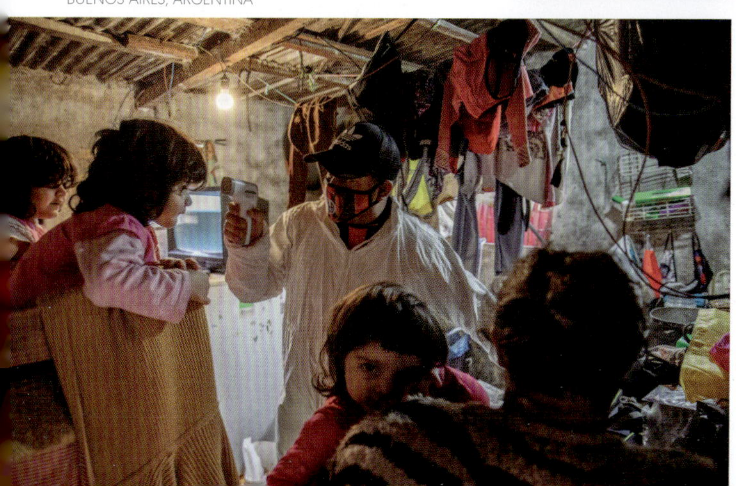

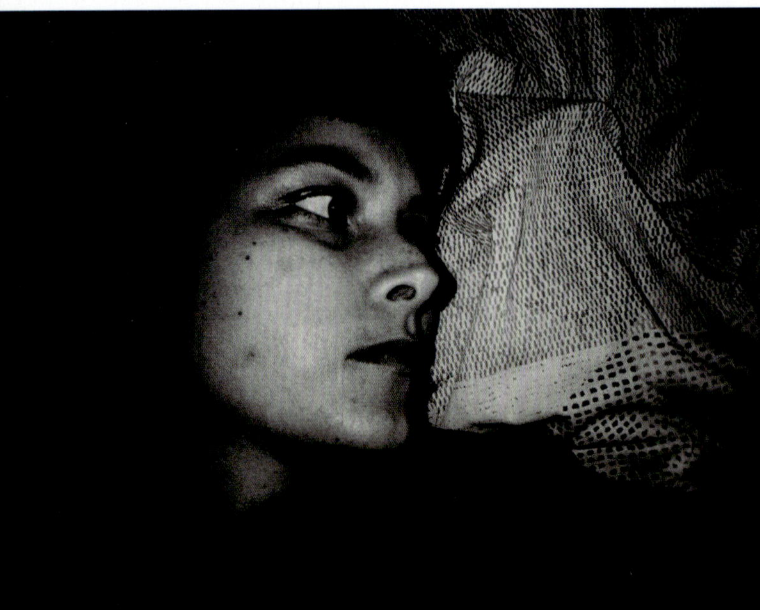

ARIANNA CAVALENSI, Untitled Lock Down Project. LONDON, UNITED KINGDOM

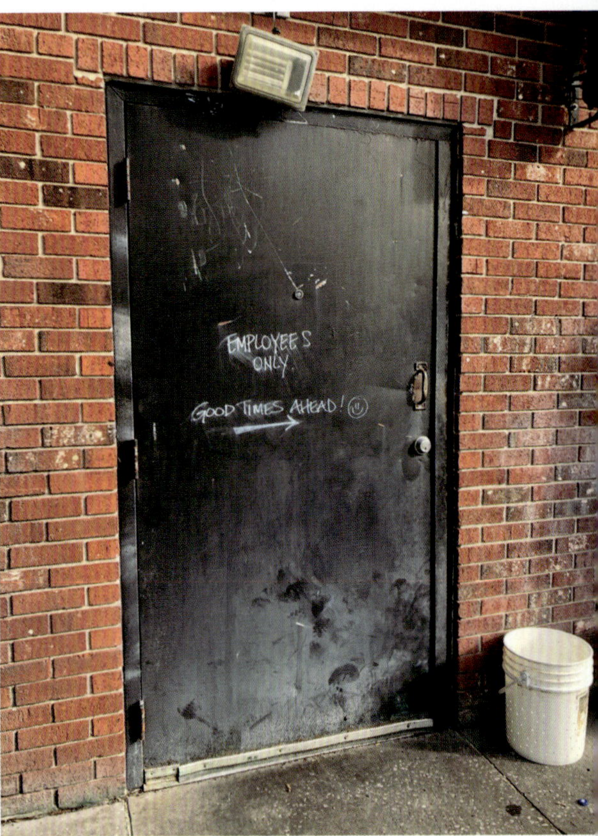

CINDY MURRAY, "Good Times Ahead," scrawled on a restaurant back door in Orlando. FL, USA

FIONA ABOUD, "This Fourth of July is yours, not mine. You may rejoice, I must mourn." - Frederick Douglass, July 5, 1852. From "Heart Series 2020." Photographic emulsion on Plexiglass. NEW YORK, NY, USA

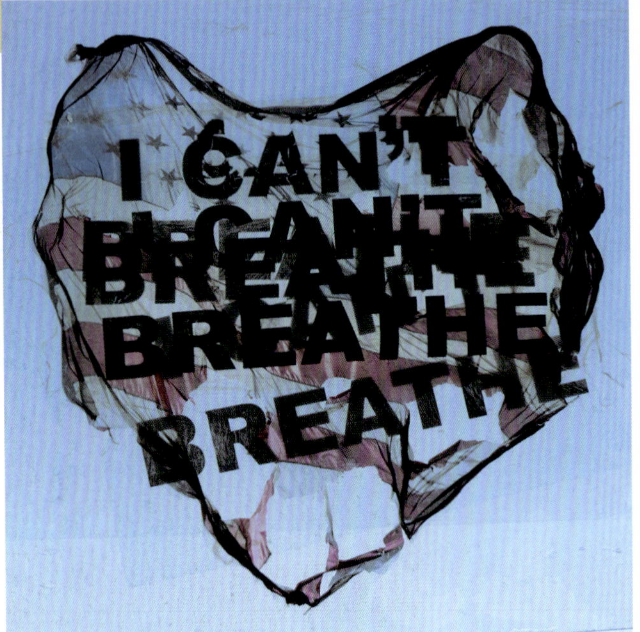

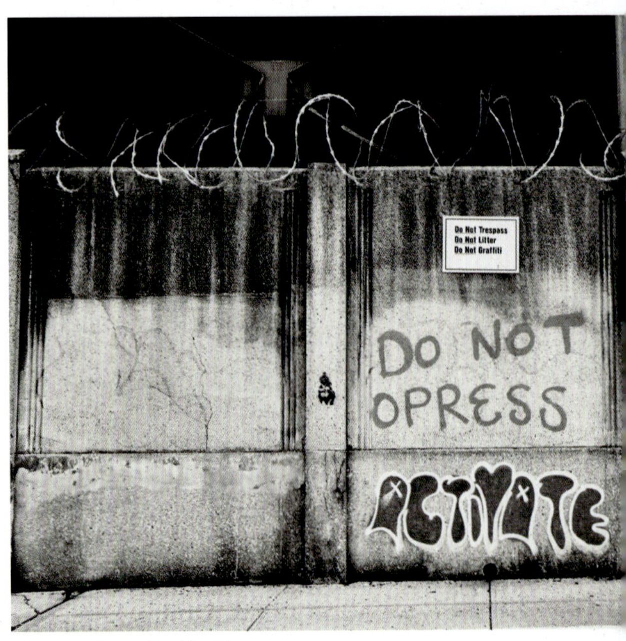

JOSHUA JANKE, Do Not Oppress. BROOKLYN, NY, USA

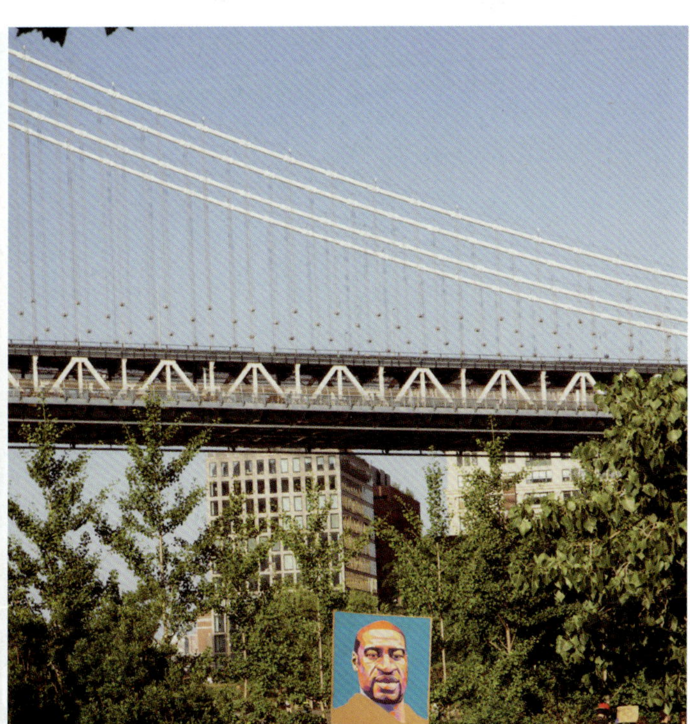

ZHAN TEH, Brisbane Black Lives Matter March. AUSTRALIA

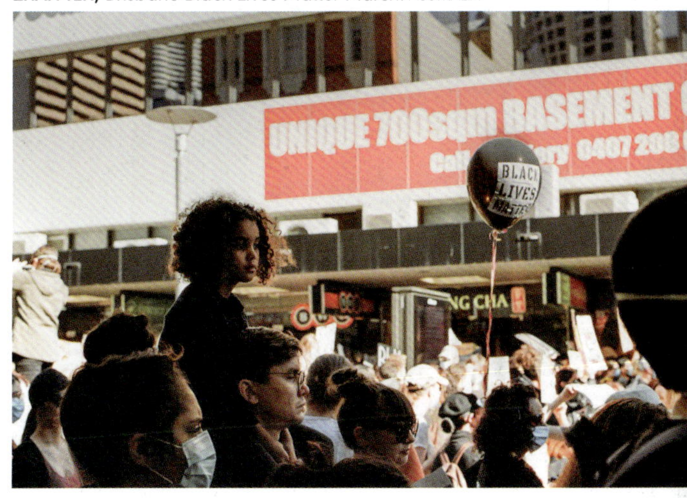

JAMES RUSSELL, Black Lives Matter protest stemming from murder of George Floyd.
BROOKLYN, NY, USA

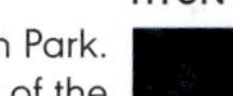

HYUN SUK KIM, *Holiday |*

Fort Totten Park. Because of the pandemic, a family celebrated the holiday outdoors.
QUEENS, NY, USA

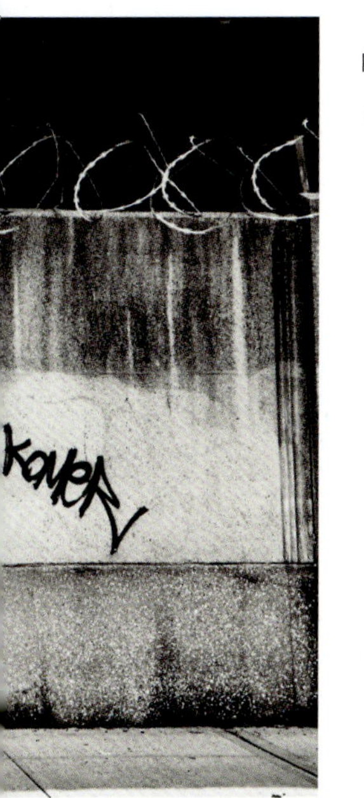

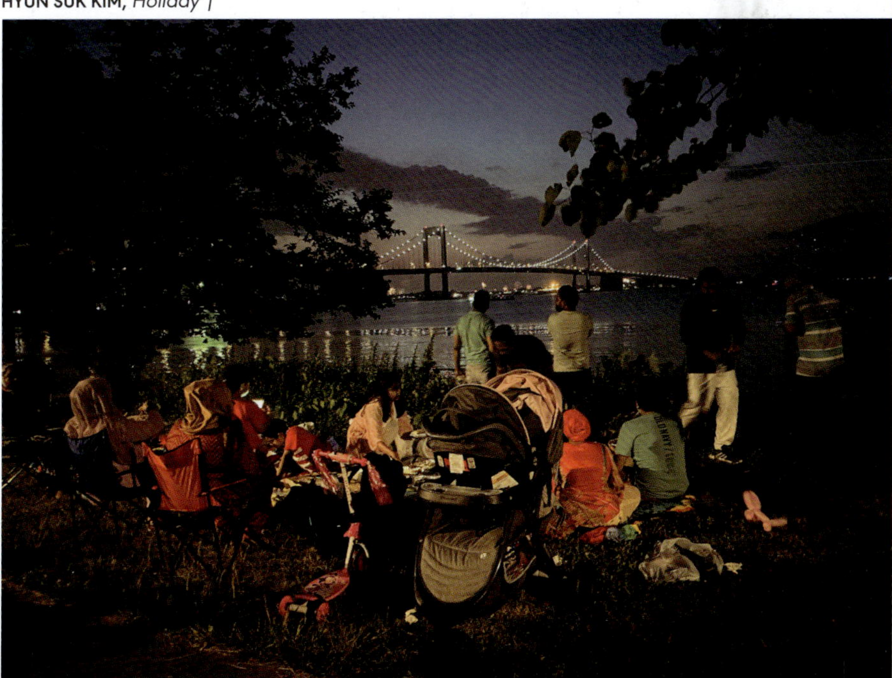

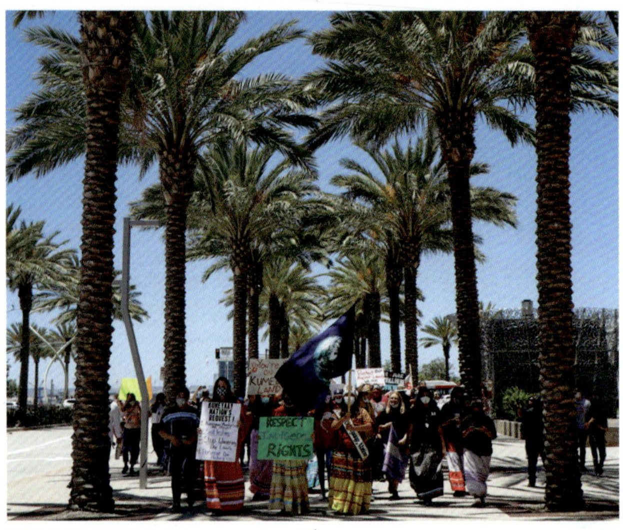

ZAYDEE SANCHEZ, *Kumeyaay Land* | The Kumeyaay Tribe protest in San Diego against the building of a wall on their indigenous land. CA, USA

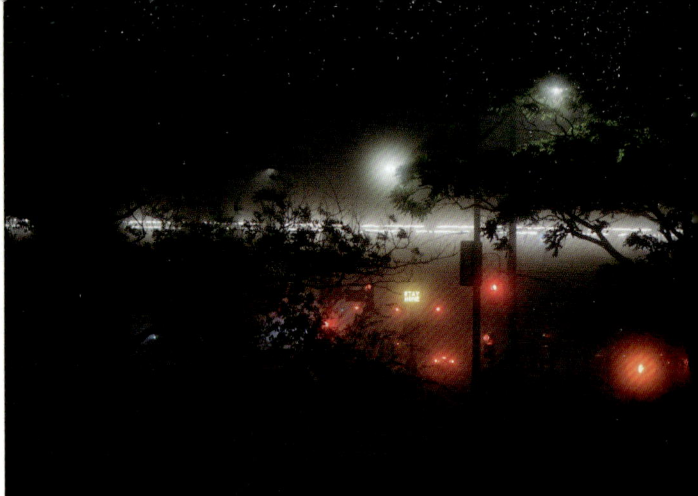

ALEXANDER KALUZHSKY, Stay Home. BRIGHTON BEACH, BROOKLYN, NY, USA

LINGFEI REN, Picnic on the Grass. CENTRAL PARK, NEW YORK, NY

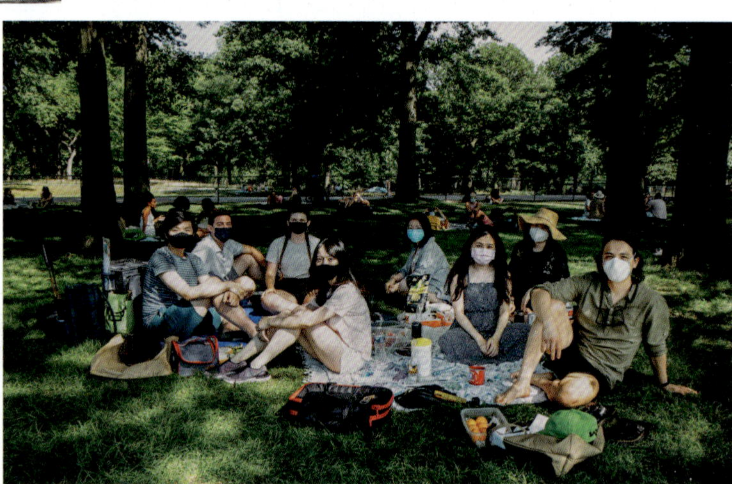

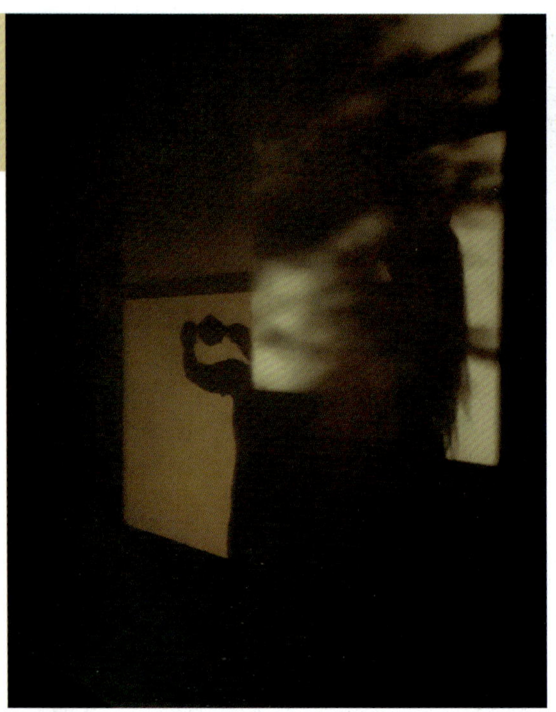

UNDINE GROEGER, *Corona Episodes: The Walls I Face and Embrace* | A self-portrait by a Berliner residing in New York City. NY, USA

PAUL MEYLER, Walking Past an Angel. SHOREDITCH, LONDON, UNITED KINGDOM

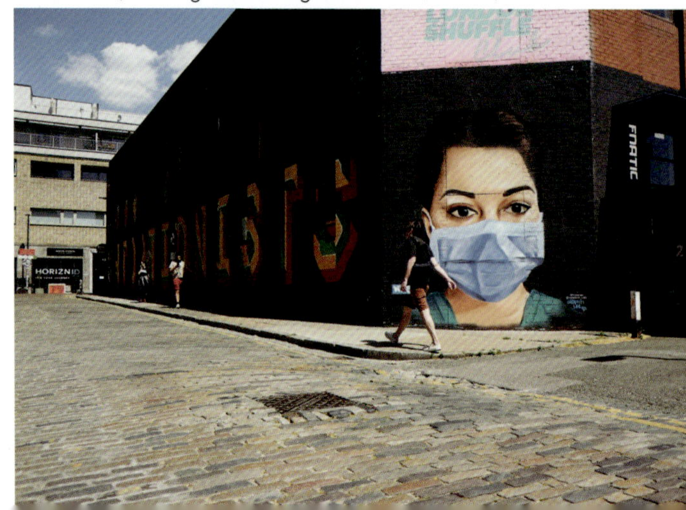

RITA TRAVERS, The Invisible Divide. CHELSEA, NEW YORK, NY, USA

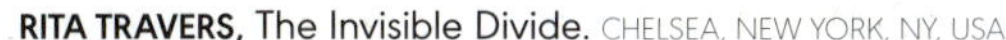

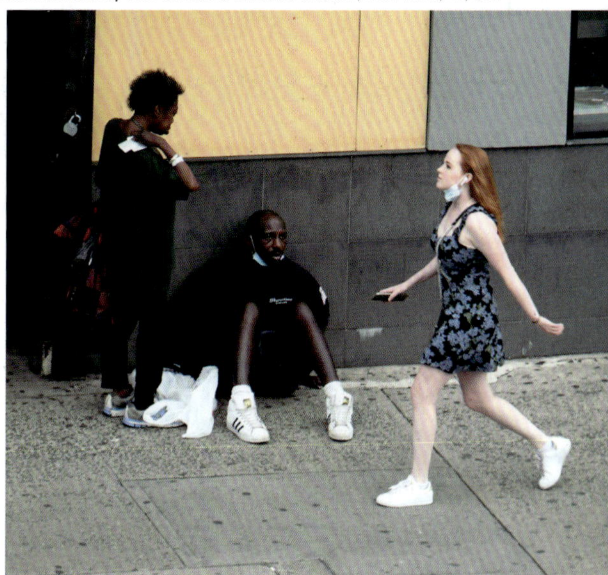

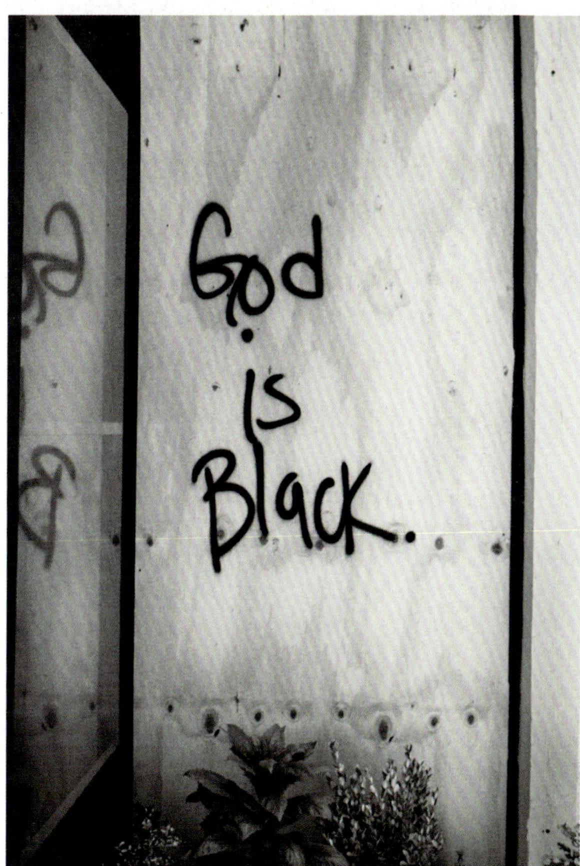

ELIZA RINN, *God is Black* | Taken in New York City. NY, USA

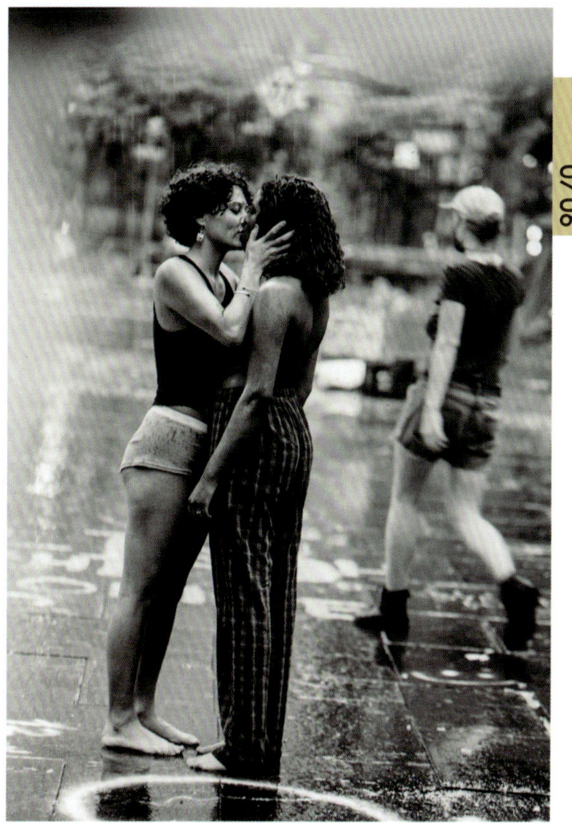

CARLOS VON DER HEYDE,
Souls of a Movement |
Occupy City Hall camp at New York City Hall.
NY, USA

MARKO RODRIGUEZ,

Eduardo started his Taqueria twelve years ago, and hasn't stopped working on the same corner ever since, despite the pandemic. He adopted technology in an effort to keep his business afloat, but has no experience in e-commerce. VILLA CORONA, MEXICO

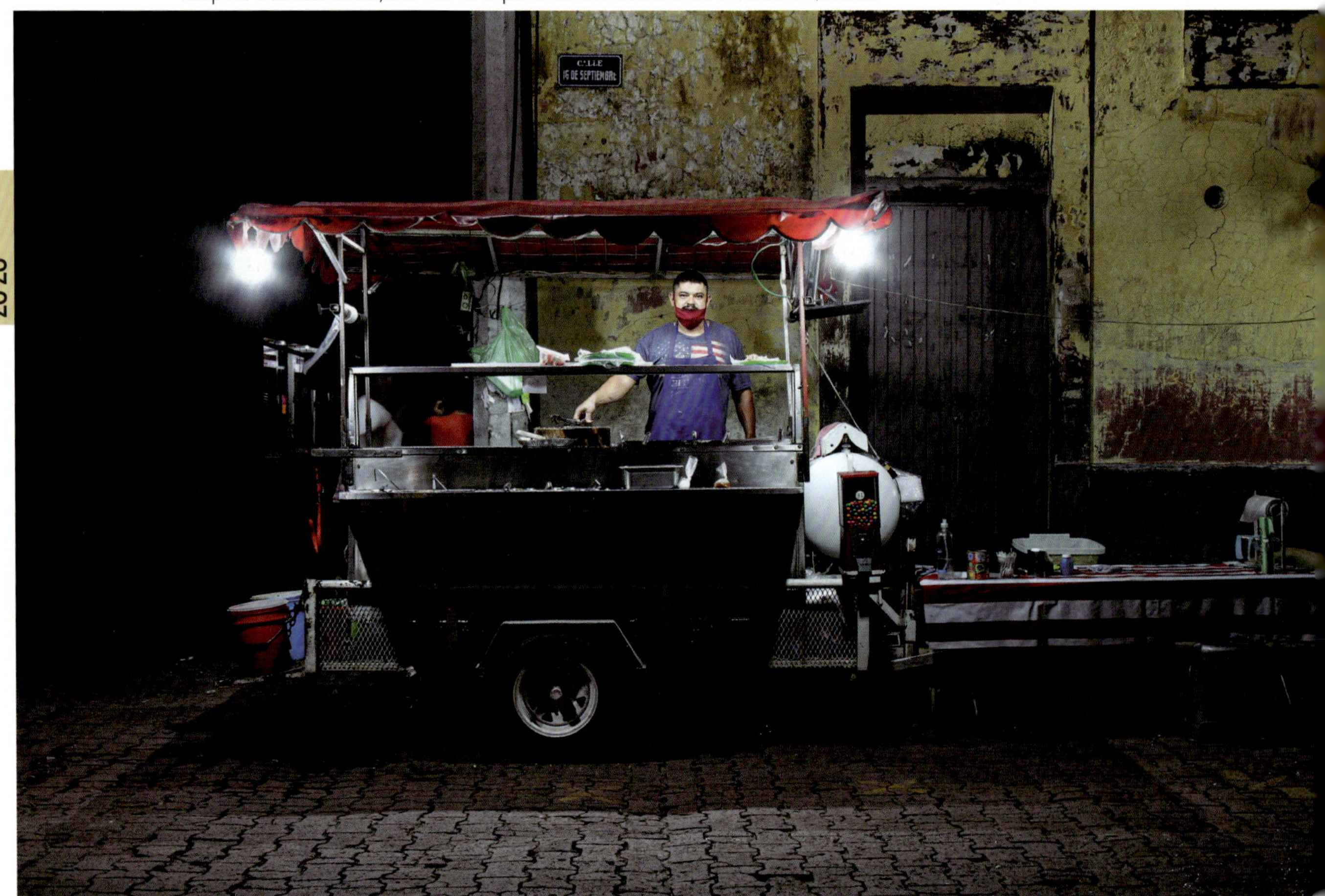

VICKI HUNT, Black Lives Matter. BIRMINGHAM, AL, USA

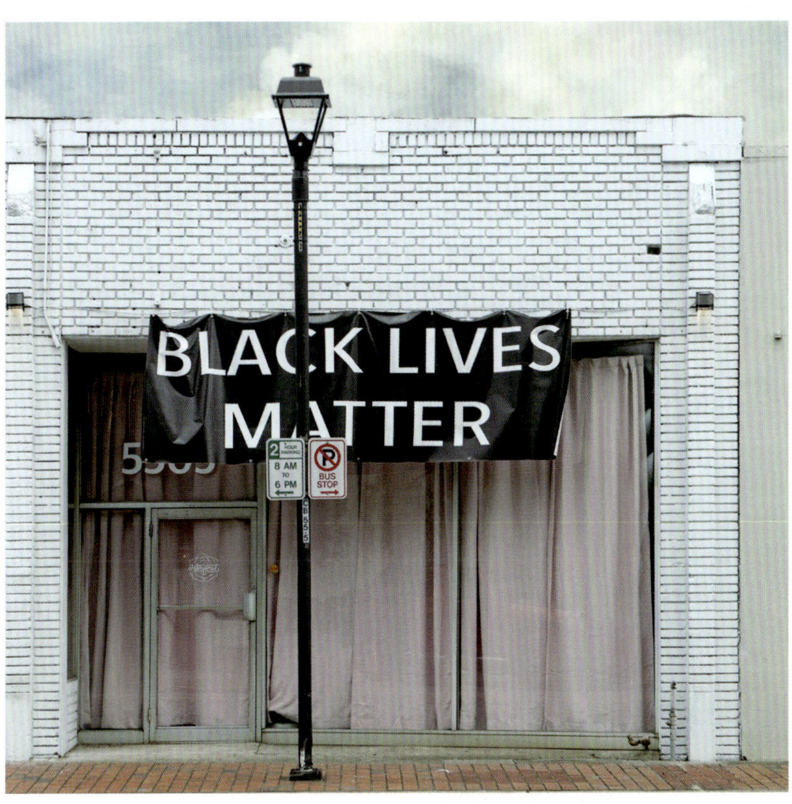

JERMAINE FRANCIS,

Something that was so familiar becomes distant.
LONDON, UNITED KINGDOM

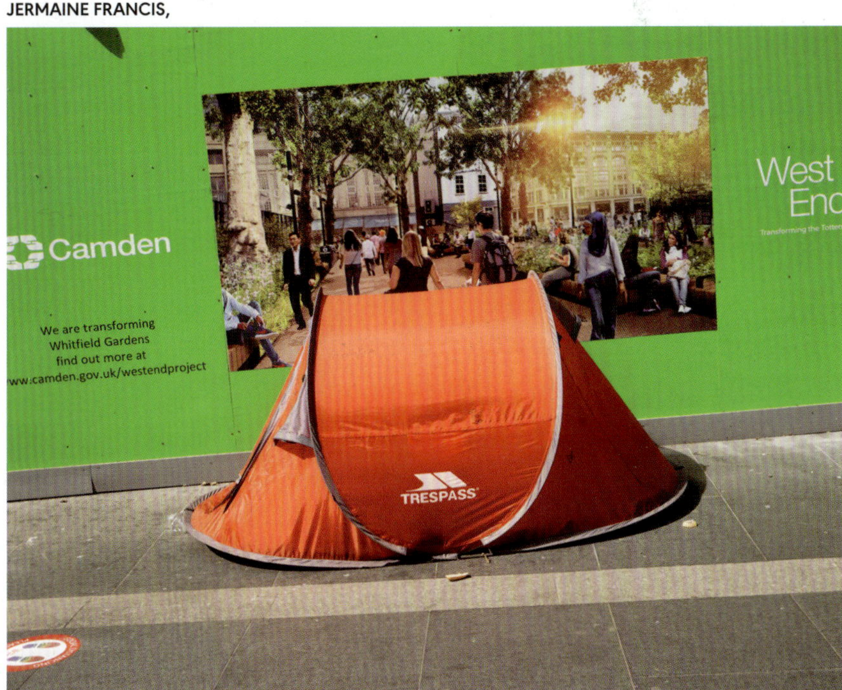

VALERIA BOVE, *Phase III, Graduation Time* |
Each student gets their own ceremony, one by one, social distancing. EAST VILLAGE, MANHATTAN, NY, USA

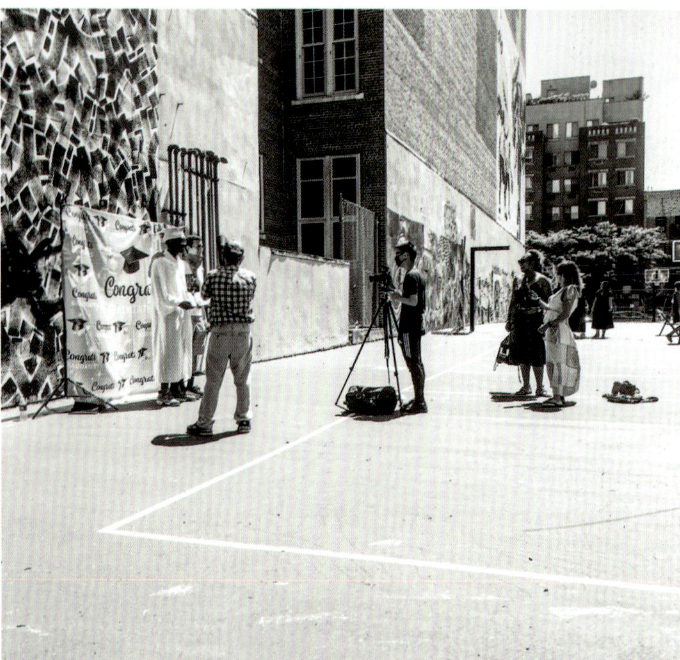

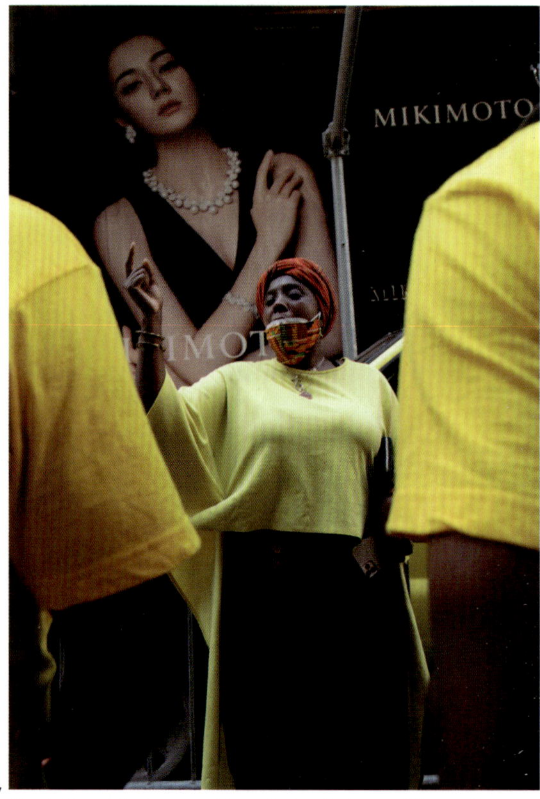

JUDIT GERMAN-HEINS,

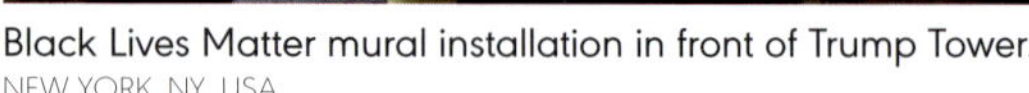
Black Lives Matter mural installation in front of Trump Tower.
NEW YORK, NY, USA

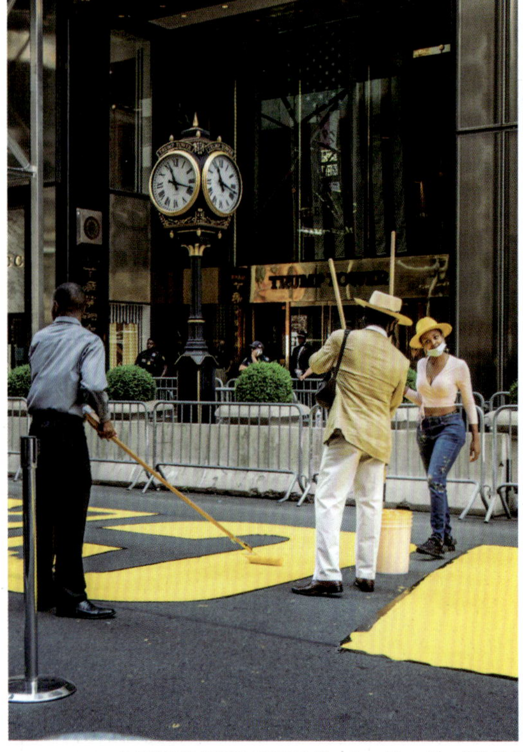

This image captures a Black Lives Matter mural being painted in front of Trump Tower.
NEW YORK, NY, USA

COLLEEN CAVANAUGH, *Tipping Hats (for BLM)* |

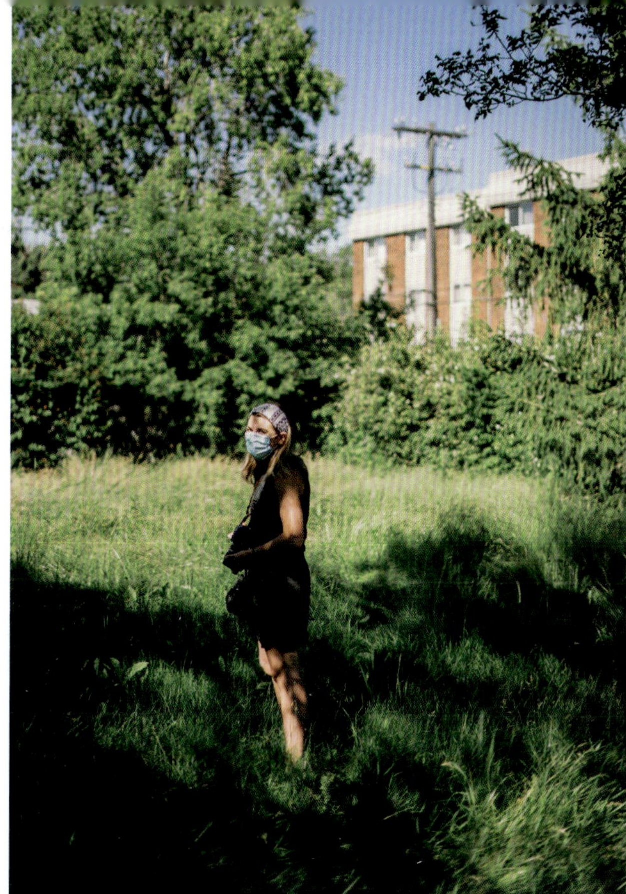

Our first meet up happened during this extraordinary time. Photograph captured in a neighborhood park. The parks are usually well maintained—not this year.
EDMONTON, ALBERTA, CANADA

DASH ZHONG, *Hannah* |

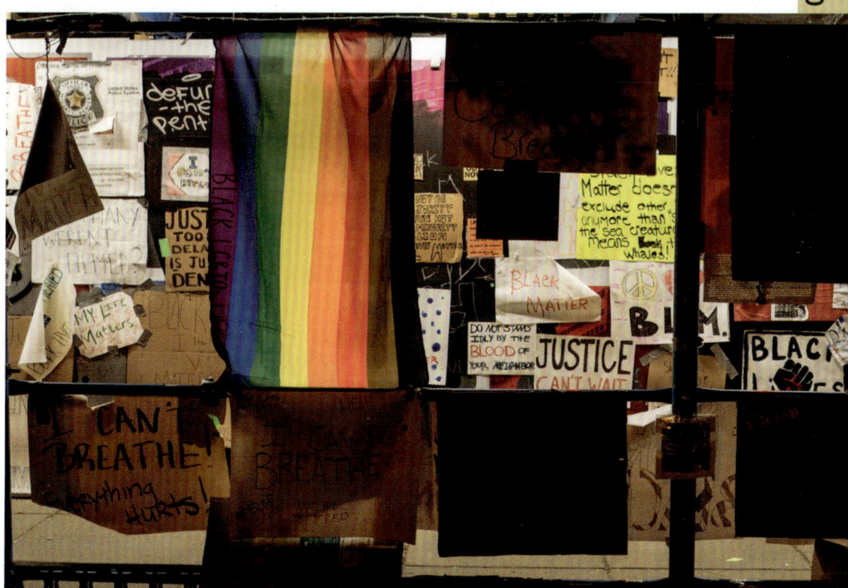

CATIANA GARCIA-KILROY,
Black Lives Matter in Washington DC. H Street, opposite the White House. USA

ALEXANDRA AVLONITIS, In front of Trump Tower, 725 Fifth Ave, New York City. NY, USA

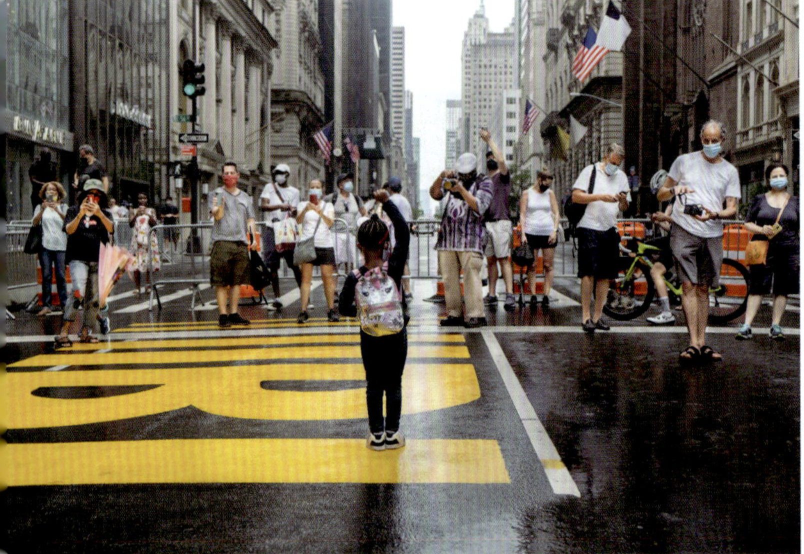

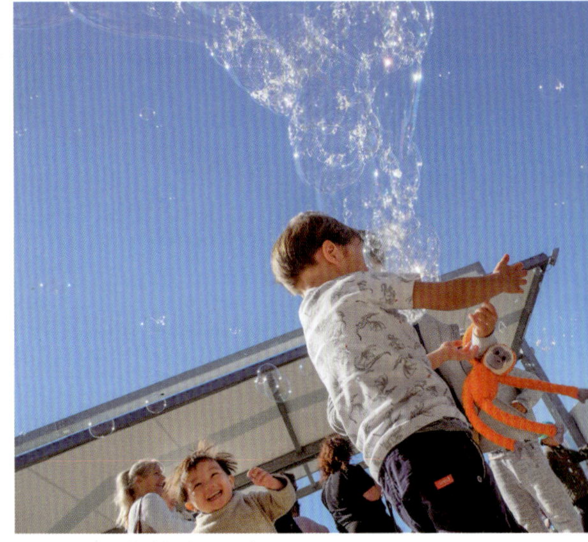

JULIE KERBEL, *Bubbalicious* |

Hillary's Boat Harbour, Perth. A bubble festival that was held soon after stage 3 lock-down was eased. AUSTRALIA

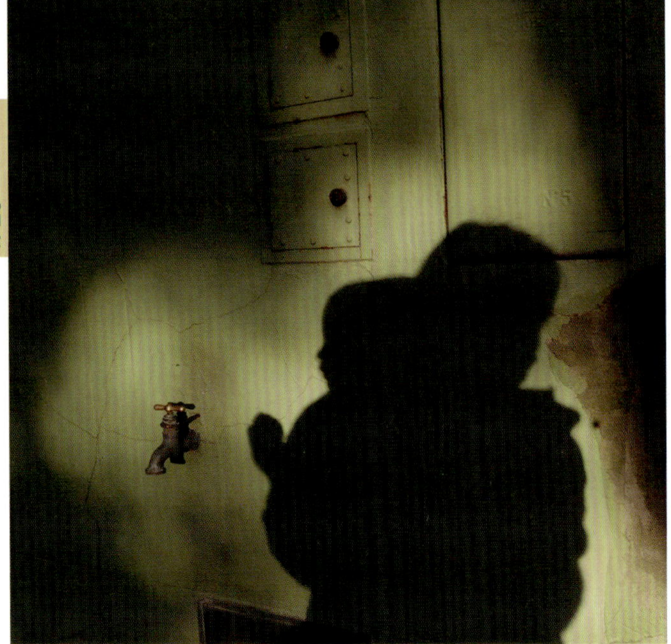

SOLEDAD BORCHES, *Recreational Outings* |

From the series "Diary of a Mother During Quarantine." BUENOS AIRES, ARGENTINA

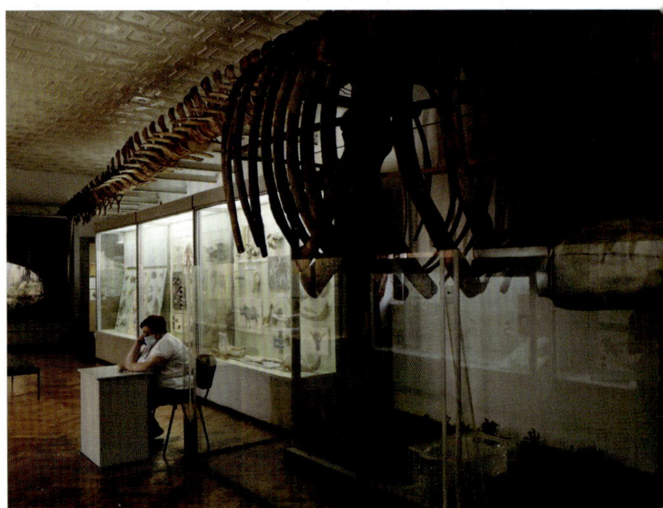

YELYZAVETA BUKREIEVA, Natural History Museum. KYIV, UKRAINE

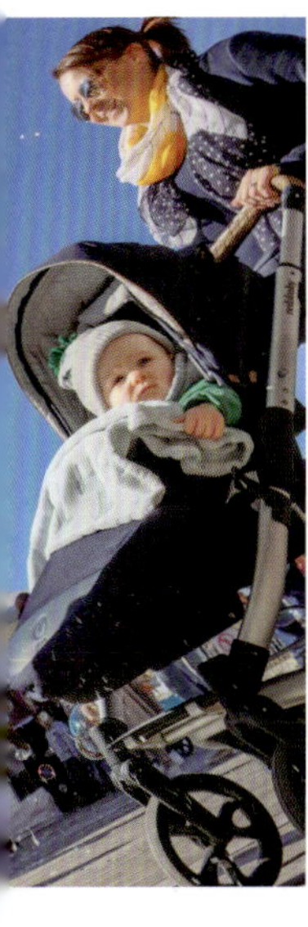

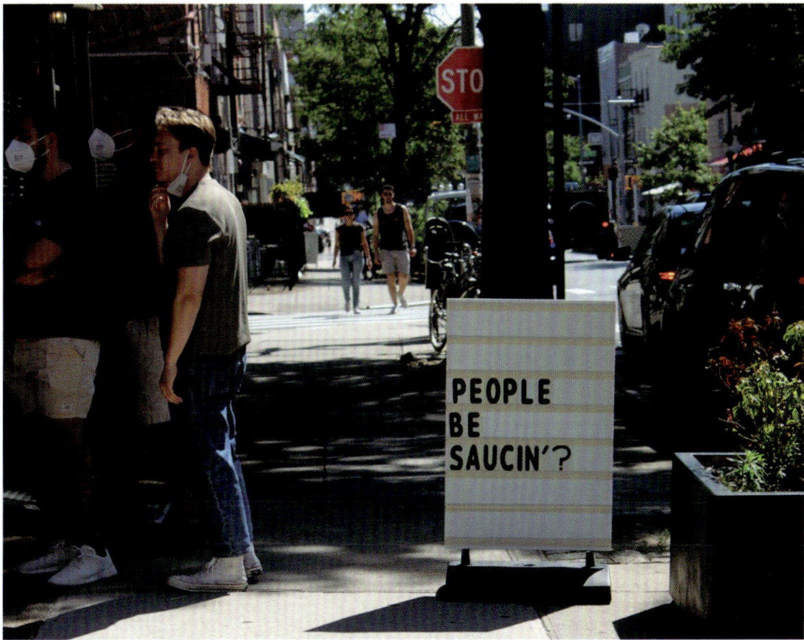

MICHAEL TRIMBOLI, A takeout line at a restaurant in Williamsburg. BROOKLYN, NY, USA

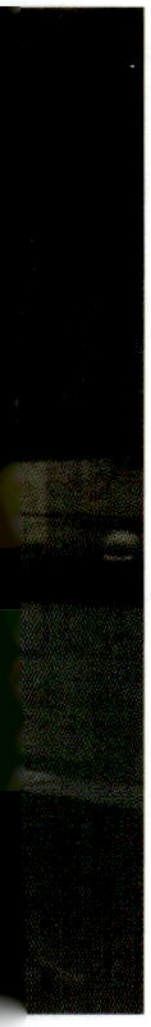

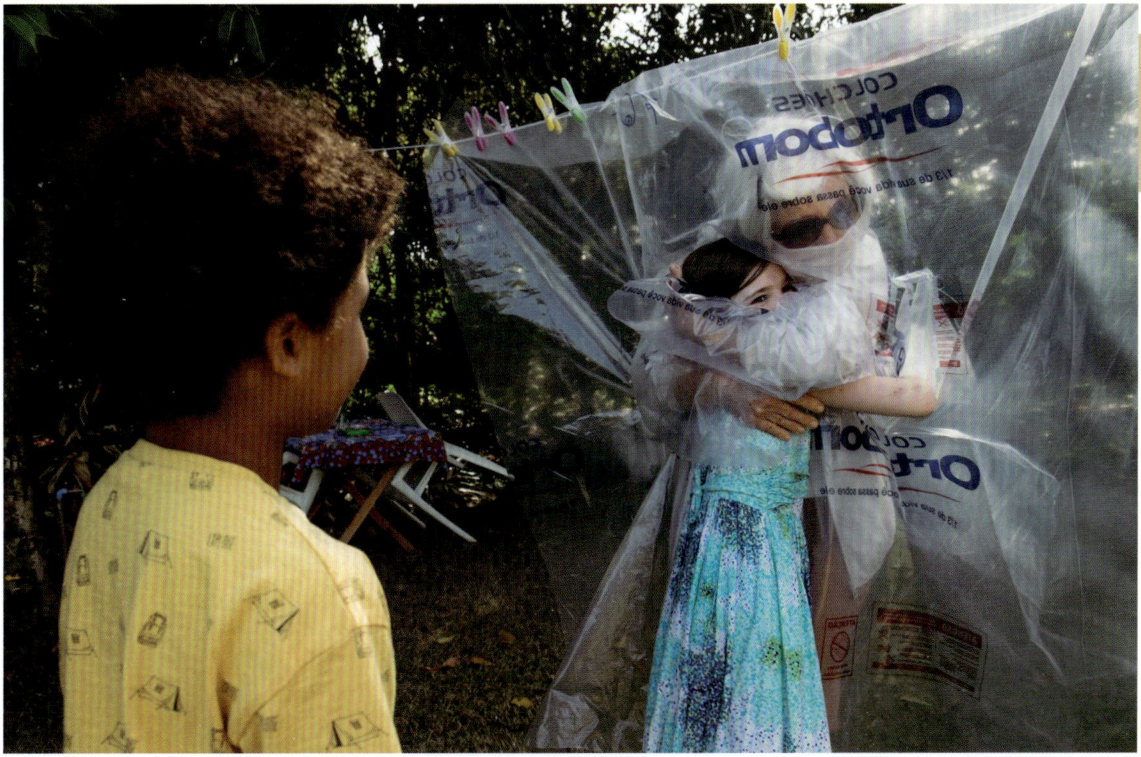

CRIS VEIT, Igor and Alice see and hug their grandma for the first time in four months. INDAIATUBA, SÃO PAULO, BRAZIL.

ANDREA MANUSCHEVICH, *The Presence, Self-Portrait* |

It was winter. It was cool and dark. Those were lonely months. We had been locked down since March because of COVID-19. I love taking pictures of other people and telling their stories, but as I live by myself in my apartment, and this has been a self-quarantine, I had no other choice than to stand in front of the lens and for this time tell my own story. I started a series of self-portraits, for the first time, which not only allowed me to learn, but also register this historic moment, and stay active by creating new work. Also, it has been kind of a therapy, that made me focus and stay present, paying attention to every detail in my own house, looking for inspiration. This has been also a time for being just with myself—a time to stop, to breathe, work shyness and to love who I am and what I do. SANTIAGO, CHILE

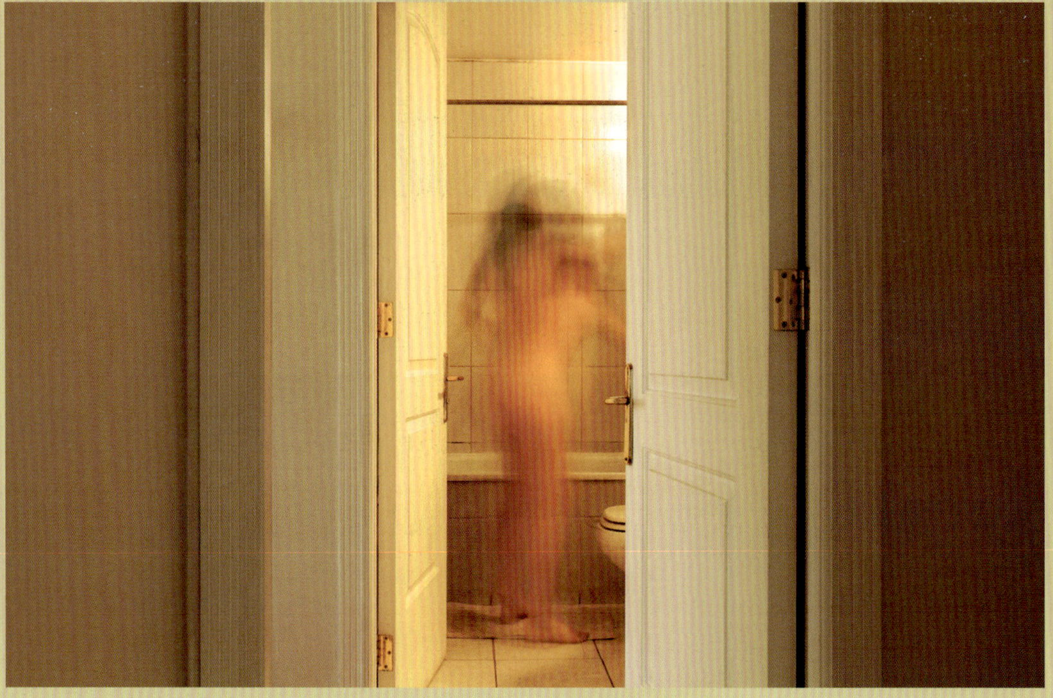

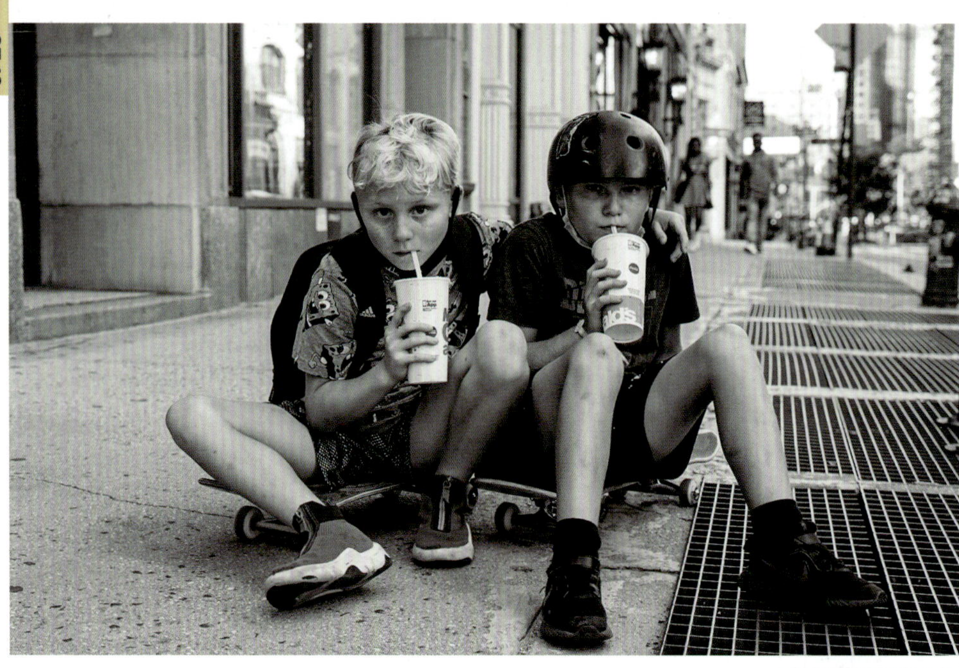

DOMINIQUE MISRAHI, Pandemic Staycation. NEW YORK, NY, USA

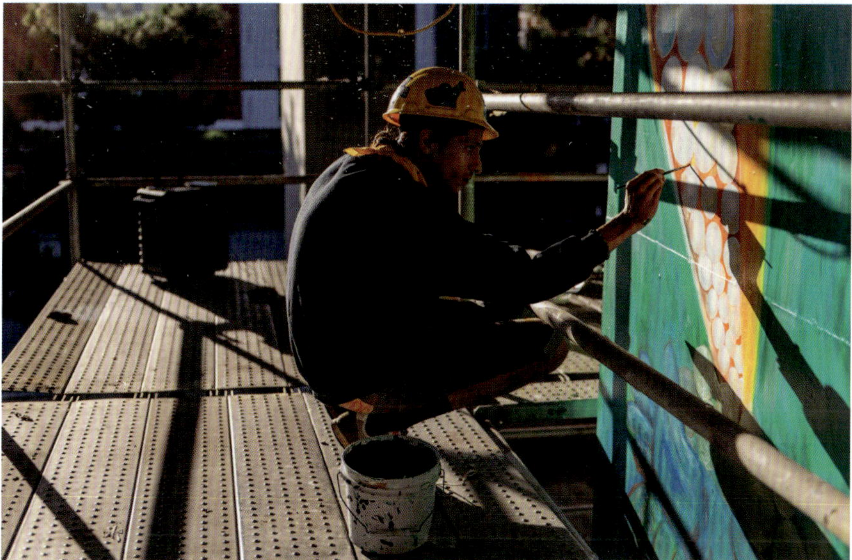

SCOTT BENNETT, Artist German Corrales paints a section of the Anastasio Hernández Rojas mural in Chicano Park, which honors Rojas on the tenth anniversary of his death. SAN DIEGO, CA, USA

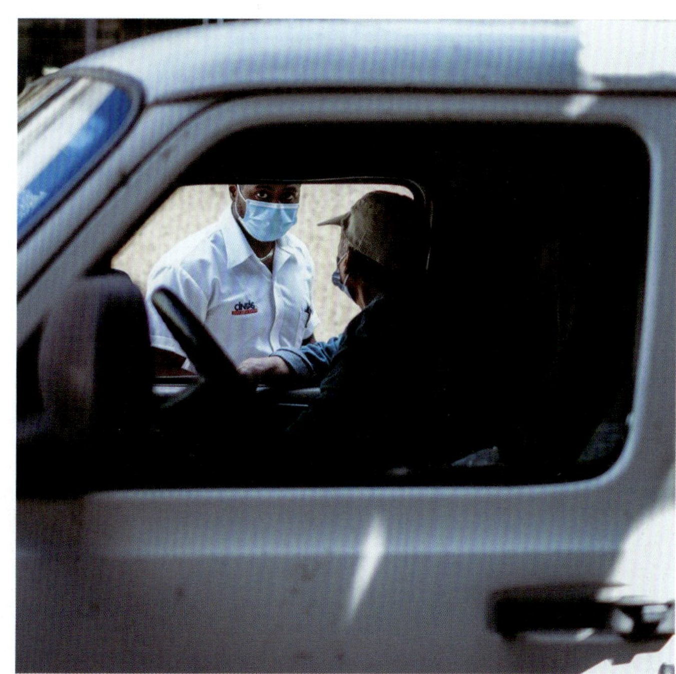

ANTONIO DI CATERINA, Stare Down. ASTORIA, NEW YORK, NY, USA

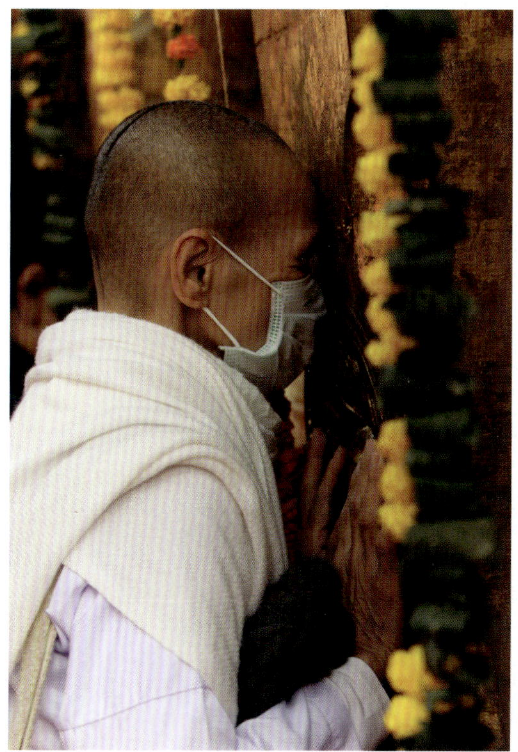

KHANDO THAR, *Faith is the powerful root of living!* | Mahabodhi temple in Bodhgaya Bihar. INDIA

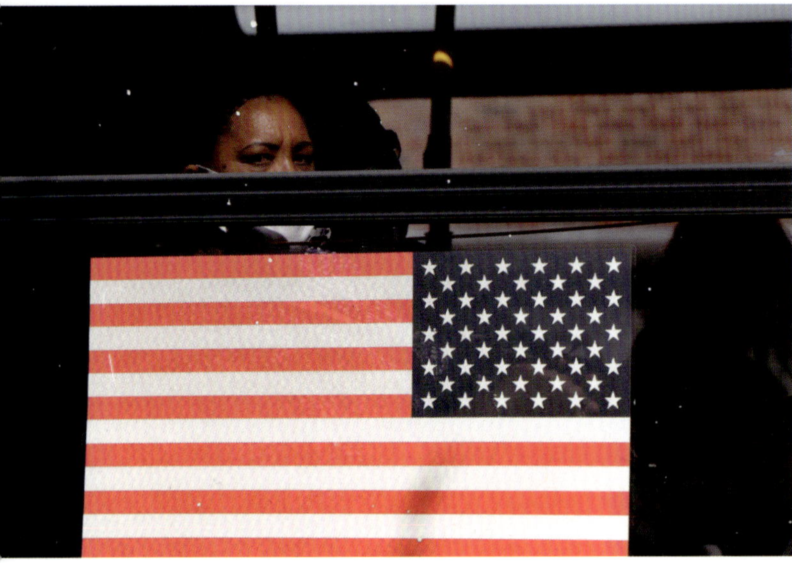

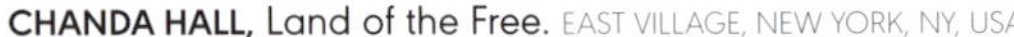

CHANDA HALL, Land of the Free. EAST VILLAGE, NEW YORK, NY, USA

BRIDGET MCQUILLAN, Pandemic coffee crew at Burger King. They let me know that their husbands were having breakfast inside. COLUMBUS, NE, USA

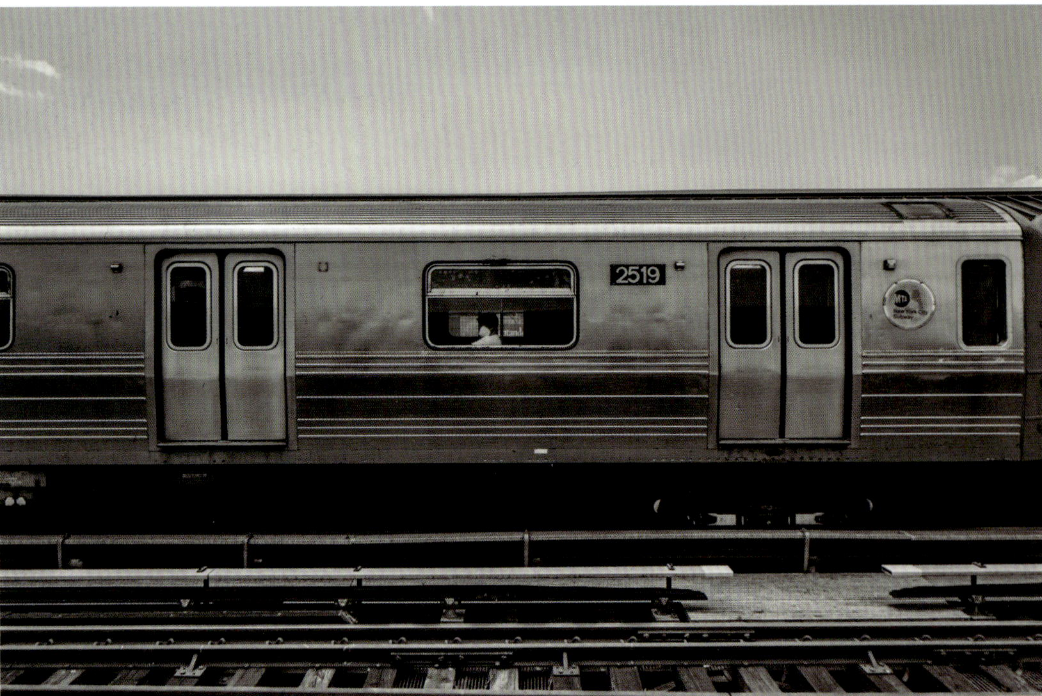

STEPHEN JESS, Despite the ever-present sense of isolation, a familiar energy begins to return as New Yorkers leave lockdown. NEW YORK, NY, USA

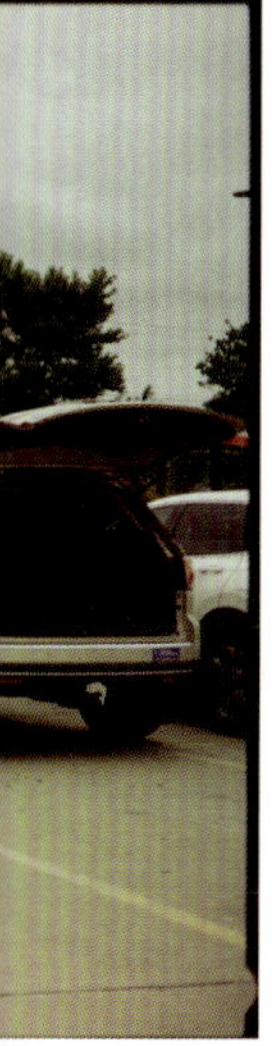

ALISON CROUSE,

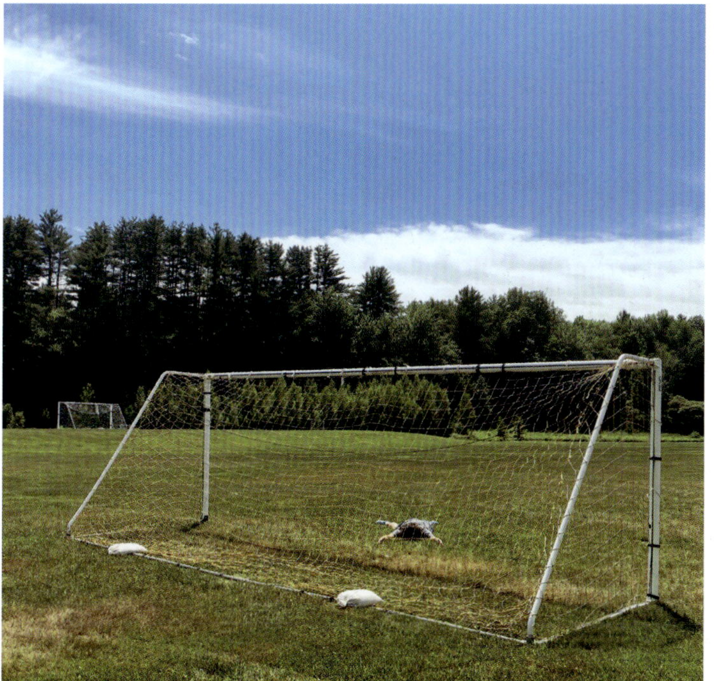

Devastation Portrait no. 296.
UNDERHILL, VT, USA

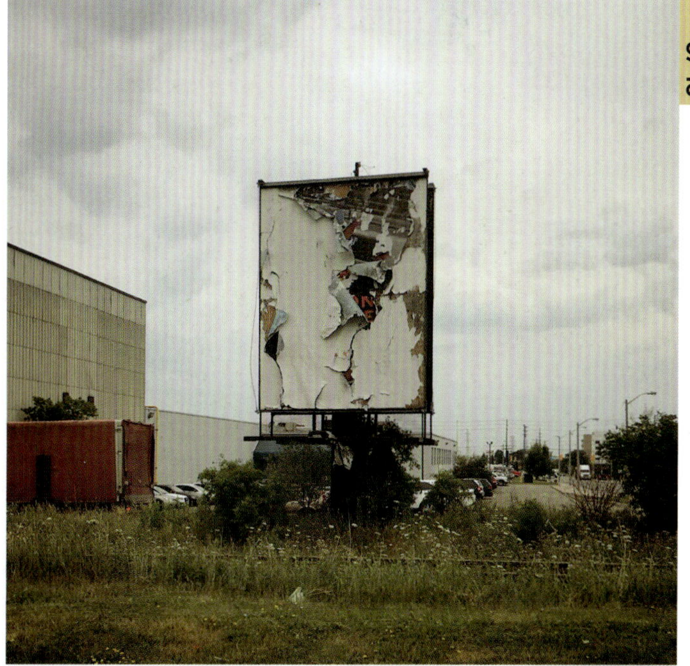

Layers of ads peeling away from a billboard, in Ontario. An unexpected visual byproduct of the pandemic, as ad money moves online. CANADA

DEREK SHAPTON,

SONJA STICH,
My son, niece and nephew help to prepare a party my parents throw for their birthdays. This is first time family and friends have gathered since March. BONN, GERMANY

MICHELE LAPINI, *I'm Here for You* |
A site-specific performance conceived as a symbolic path that will bring a single spectator to meet four artists using acoustic and electronic instruments, installations, voices, bodies and space, and words. BOLOGNA, ITALY

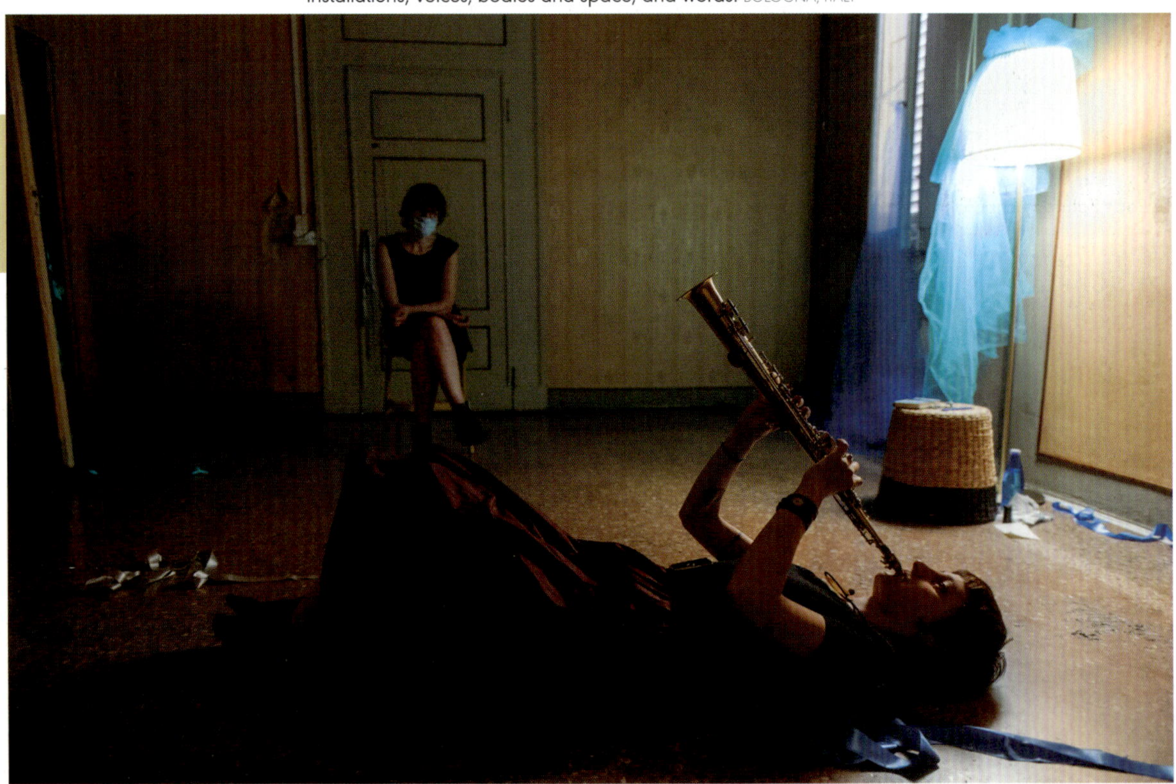

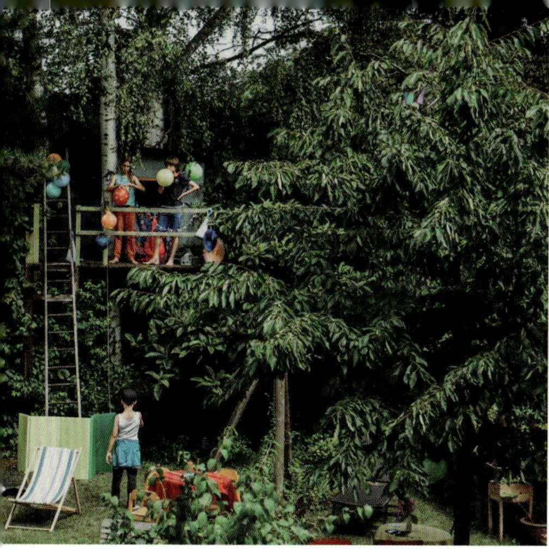

AAISHA SHAIKH, In the months since COVID began we have found a routine, but a sense of agitation remains. Slowness does not always bring a sense of calm. USA

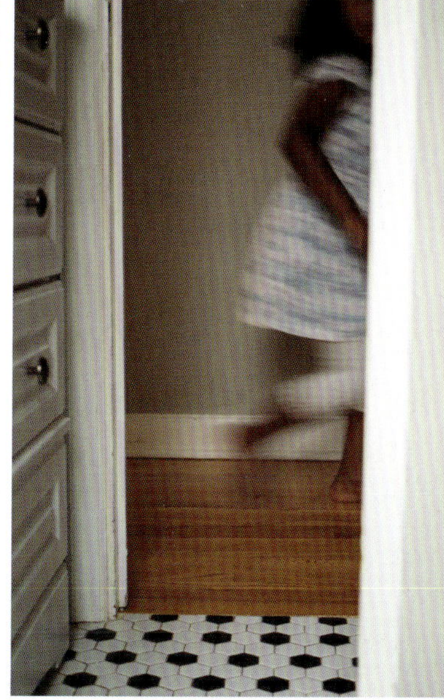

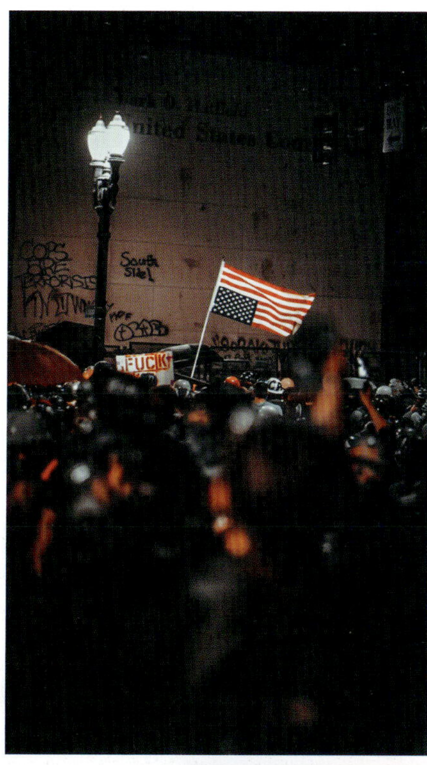

LUCAS DIAZ, In Distress. DOWNTOWN PORTLAND, OR, USA

KAREN ZUSMAN, Each Saturday, thousands of cyclists ride to demand an end to systemic racism with Street Riders NYC. This was at the start of our Justice Ride VI. FLUSHING MEADOWS, QUEENS, NY, USA

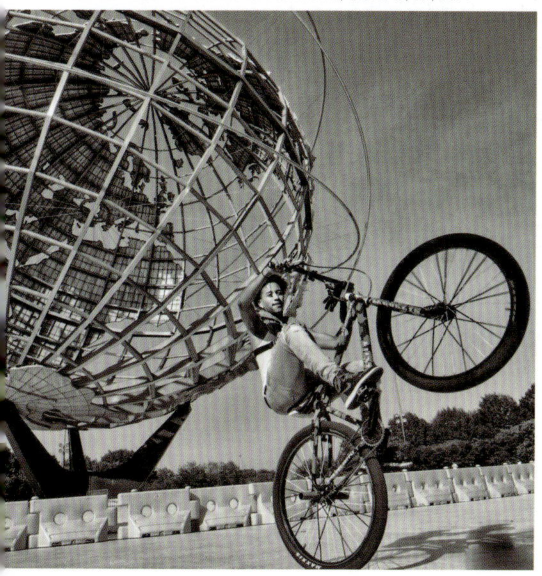

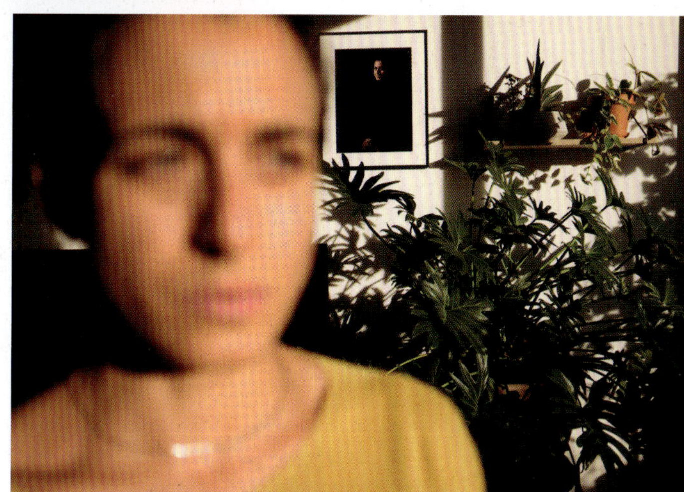

CRISTIAN DI CACCAMO, The COVID-19 pandemic is giving me the chance to observe expats' lives. What makes a place feel like home for an expat? To feel at home, Lucia surrounds herself with plants. ZURICH, SWITZERLAND

HANJING WANG,
After All, Tomorrow is Another Day.
THE HIGH LINE, NEW YORK, NY, USA

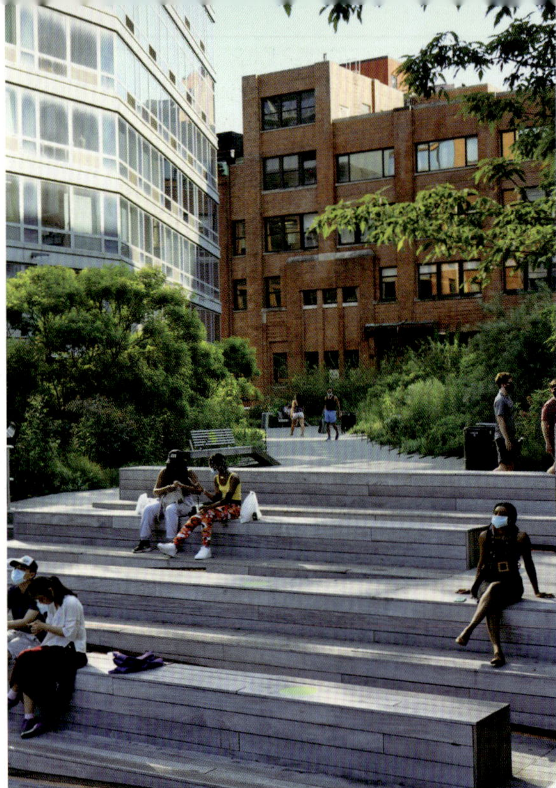

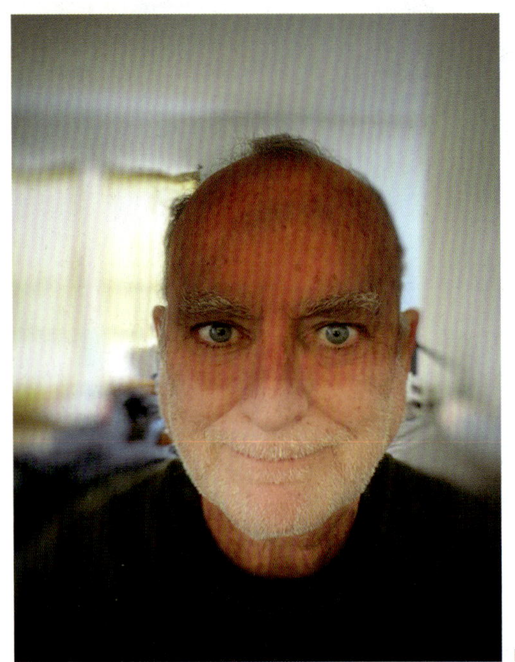

MITCHELL SINOWAY, Face mask fail! USA

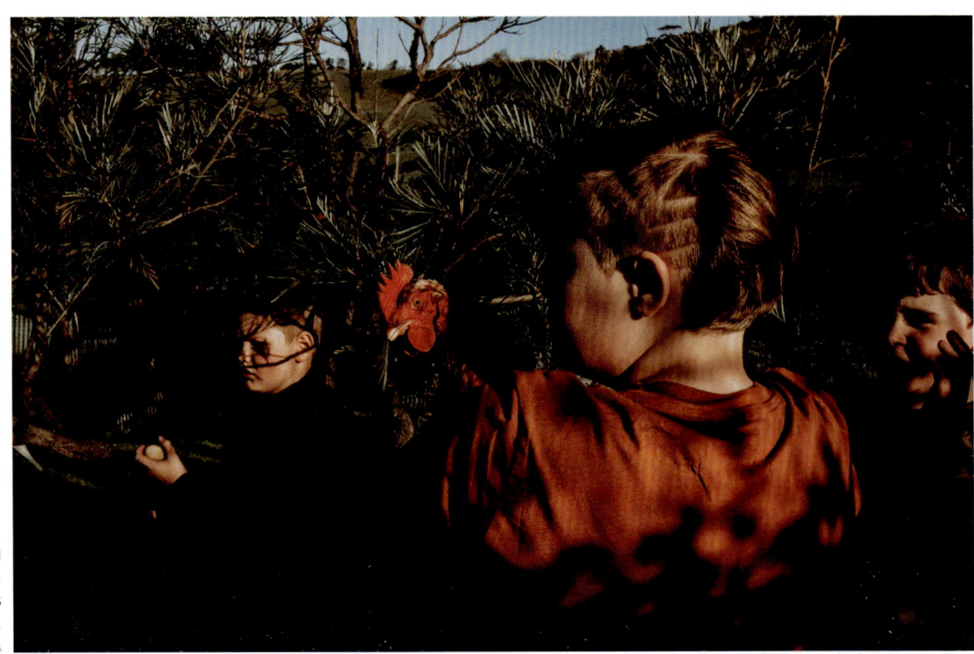

KATELYN SYLER, Kids reconnecting with the land during isolation. Creating long-lasting memories and spending quality family time.
KIAMA, NEW SOUTH WALES, AUSTRALIA

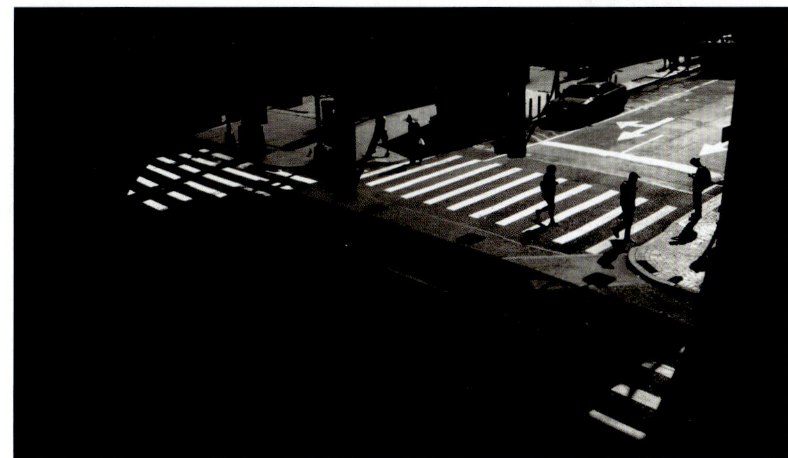

THEODORE A. SICKELS II, The Bronx. NEW YORK, NY, USA

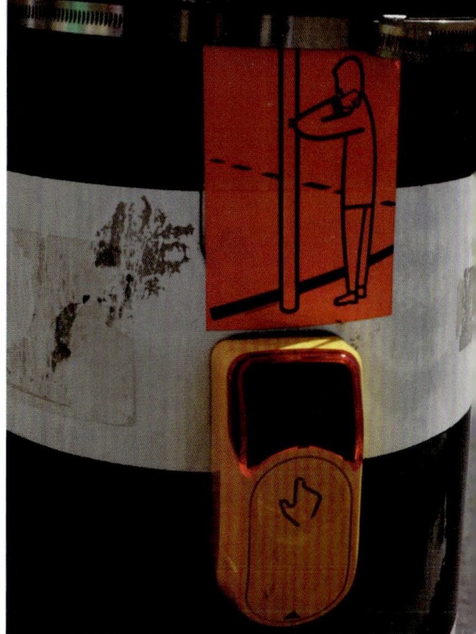

SYLVAIN DIEHL, Waiting to cross the street. ROTTERDAMN, NETHERLANDS

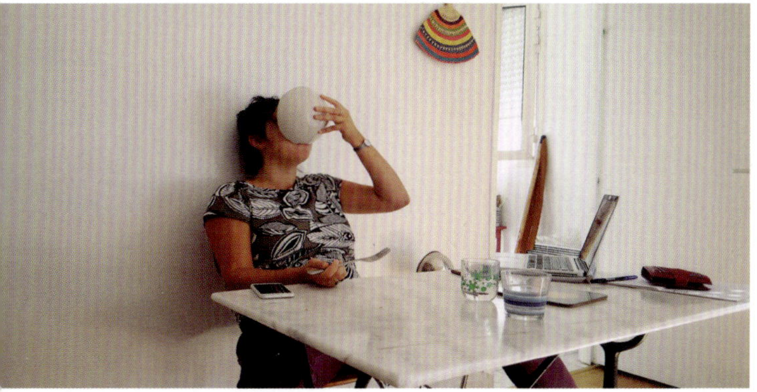

RAUL AMARU LINARES, *Télétravail |* Agathe Torres, 27, finishing her lunch while not finishing her labor day at home. PARIS, FRANCE

VINCENS SÁEZ, Collblanc-la Torrassa. Hospitalet de llobregat. The most densely populated neighborhood in Europe with more than 54,000 people per square kilometer. SPAIN

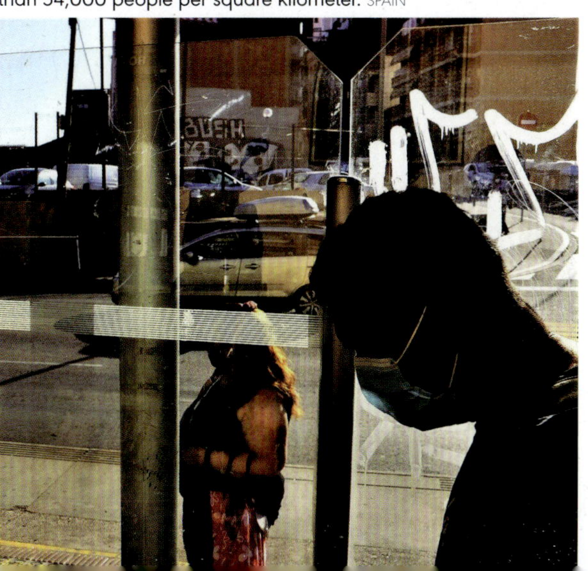

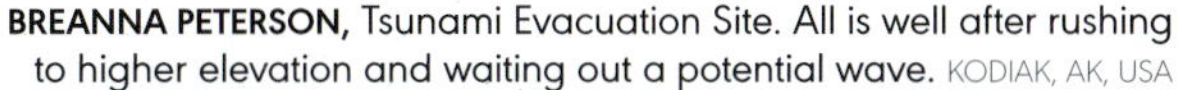

BREANNA PETERSON, Tsunami Evacuation Site. All is well after rushing to higher elevation and waiting out a potential wave. KODIAK, AK, USA

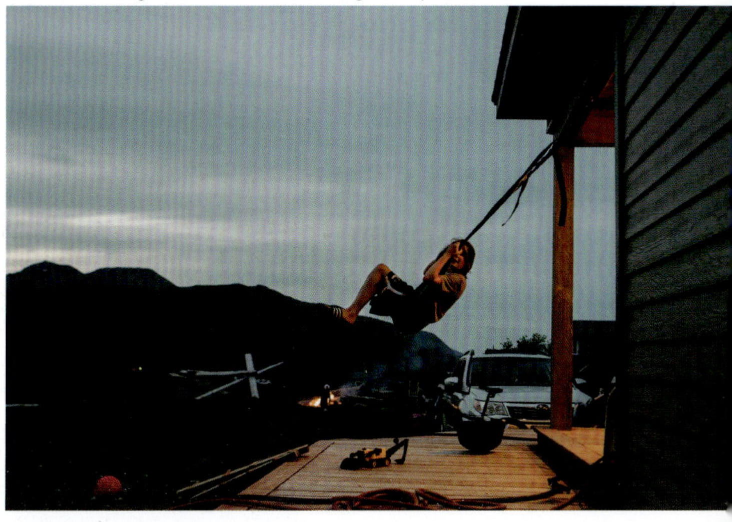

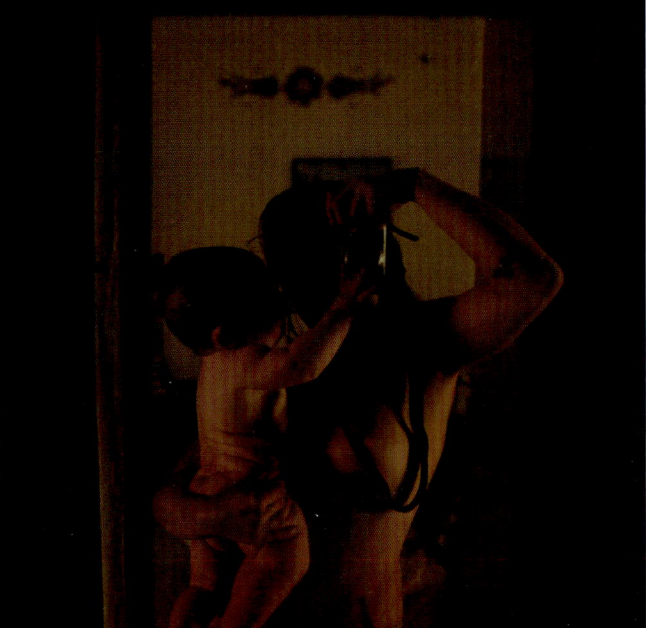

SANDRA GONZALEZ, *The Mirror* |

My six-month-old and I passing some time with my parents for first time after the COVID-19 quarantine. He was six weeks old when everything started. We were at old house that my grand-parents parents built. The mirror we are reflected in belonged to my baby's great-grandmother. SPAIN

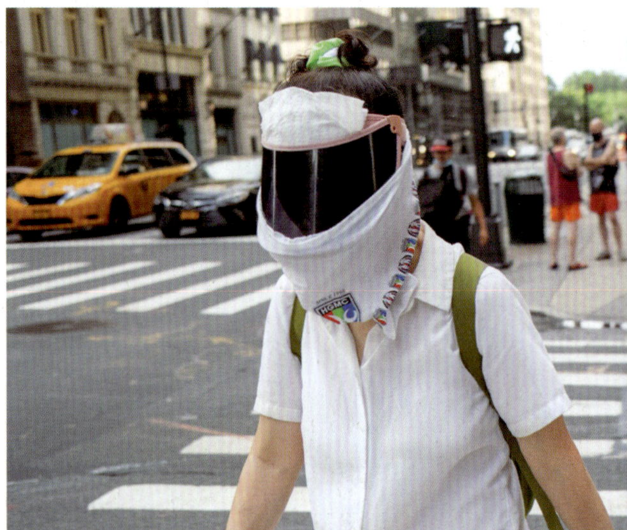

ILYA NIKOLAYEV, Wear a Mask! NEW YORK, NY, USA

LUCA JARDIM,

Iporanga is a gated community of vacation houses owned by wealthy families built inside the Atlantic Forest, two hours away from São Paulo. BRAZIL

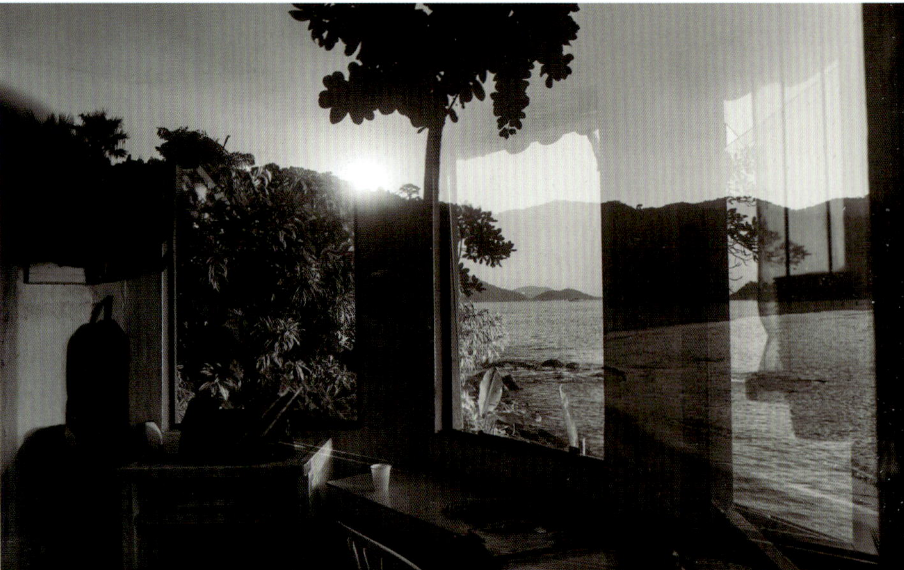

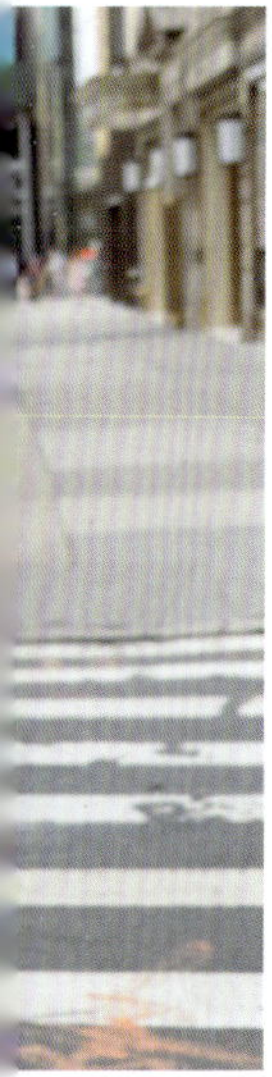

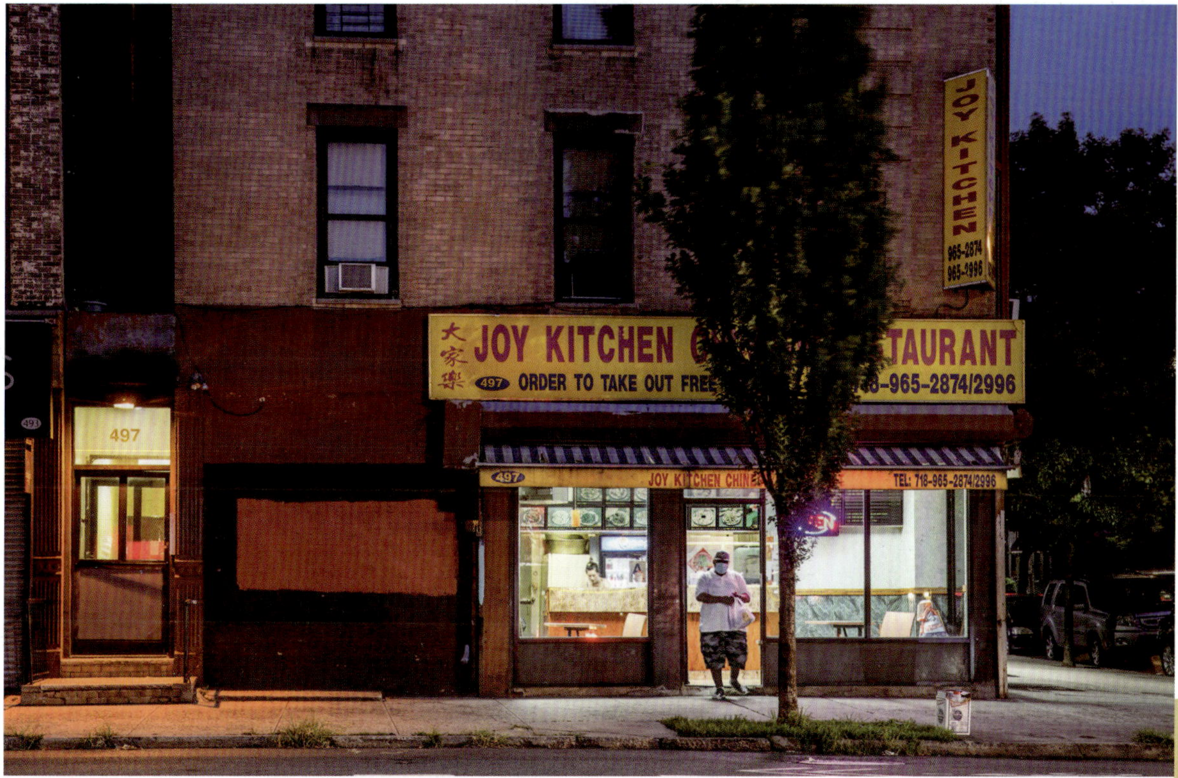

ROBIN MICHALS, Joy Kitchen resumes late hours for take out. BROOKLYN, NY, USA

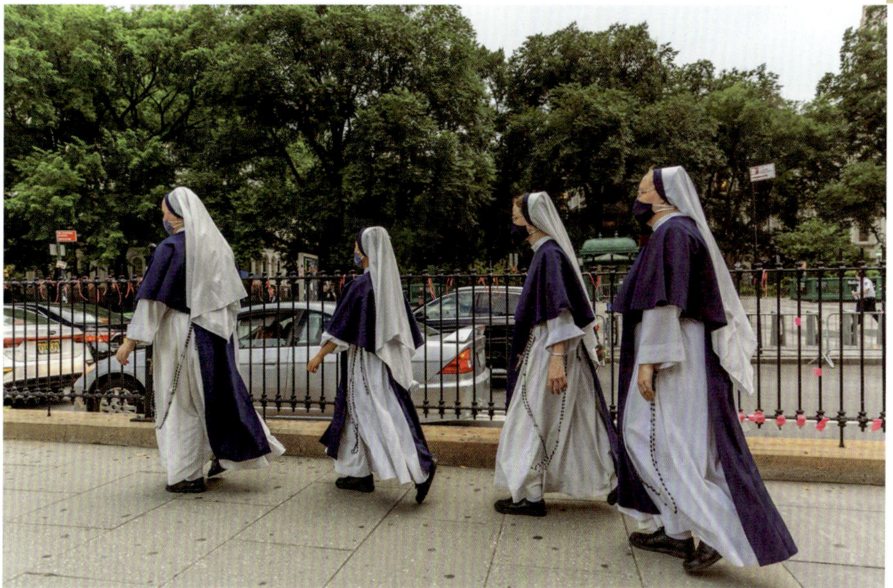

NETNARIN PADUNGJIRAPUNTIP,
New York Walkabout. NEW YORK, NY, USA

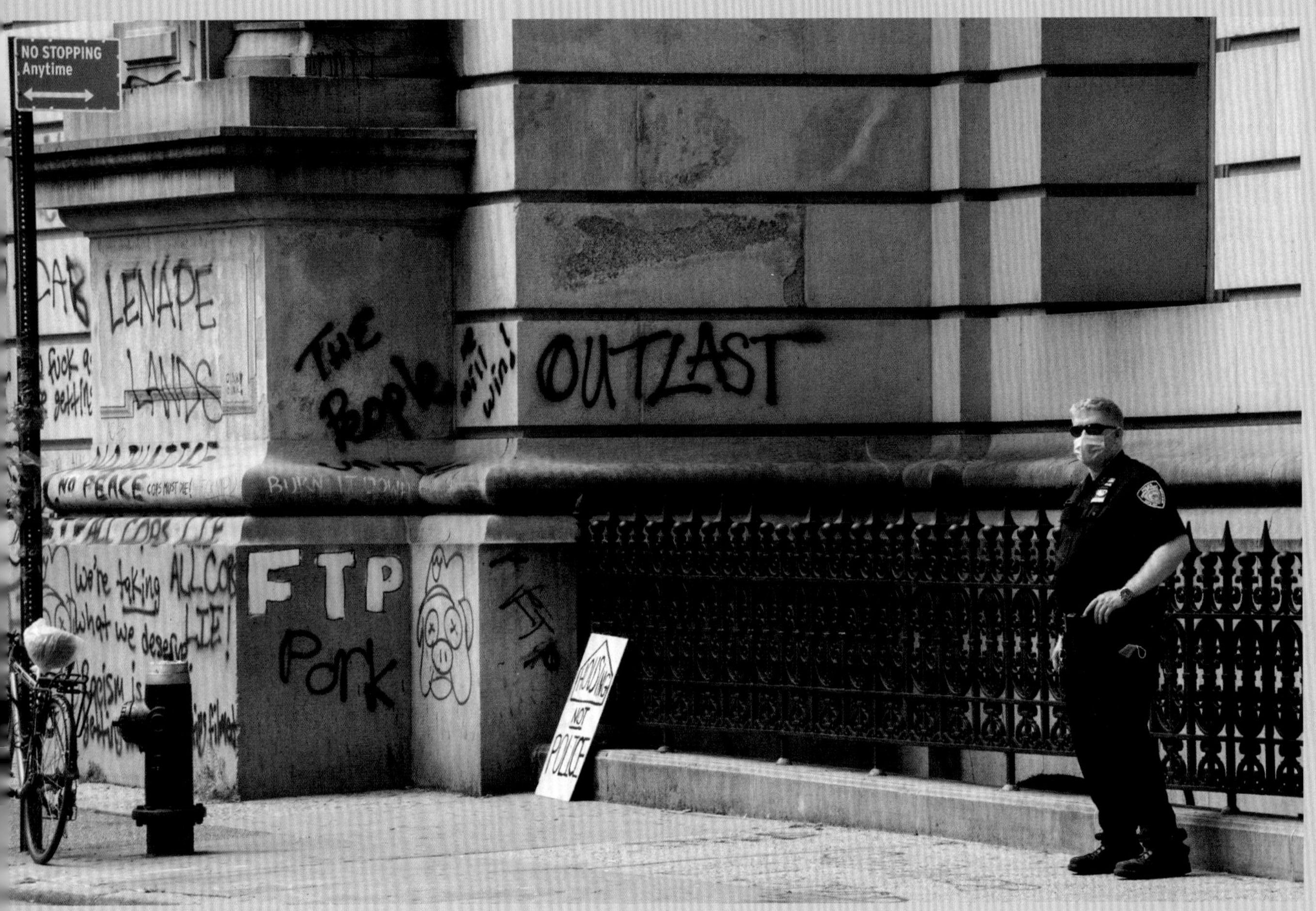

JULIANA MUCHINYI, *The Writing on the Wall* |

This photograph is part of my "Black Stories by Black People" series. This image was created at the height of the Occupy City Hall movement, whose focus was on urging the city officials that were working on the city budget at the time to reduce the amount of funds allocated to the New York Police Department and instead redirect that money towards investing in underfunded social programs in disadvantaged neighborhoods. Those emotions written on the wall right next to the police officer are due to the direct result of the killing of countless unarmed black men by law enforcement over the years. Events that subsequently led to numerous Black Lives Matter protests and marches seen all around the world in the summer of 2020. This image is part of a series that underscores the important role that black photographers like myself play in documenting and telling stories directly affecting our communities. NEW YORK, NY, USA

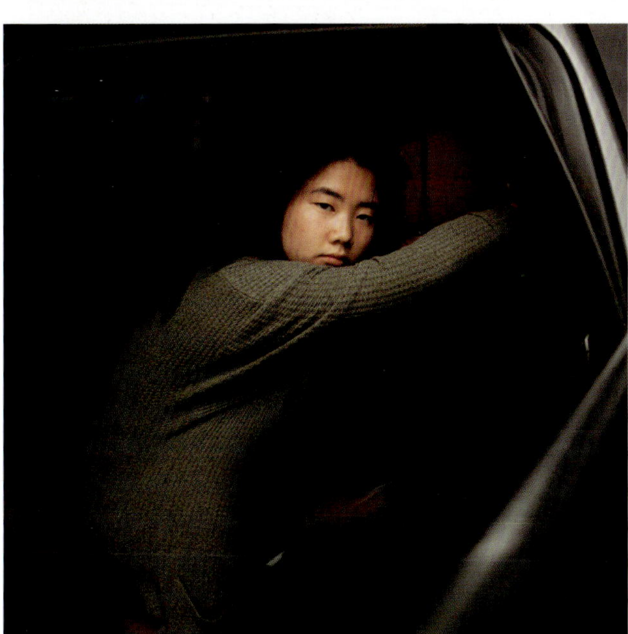

LINDSAY MORRIS, Teens living under New York State's "stay-at-home" order and the everyday happenings, coping mechanisms, and escape modes while living through this historic moment. EAST HAMPTON, NY, USA

DREW LEVIN, Onlookers at Old Faithful. YELLOWSTONE, WY, USA

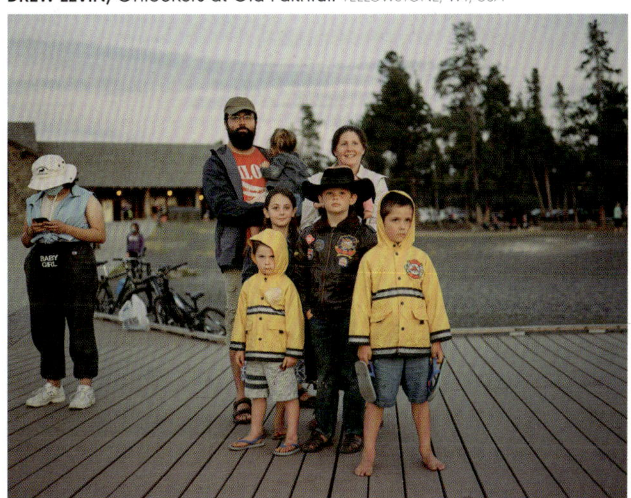

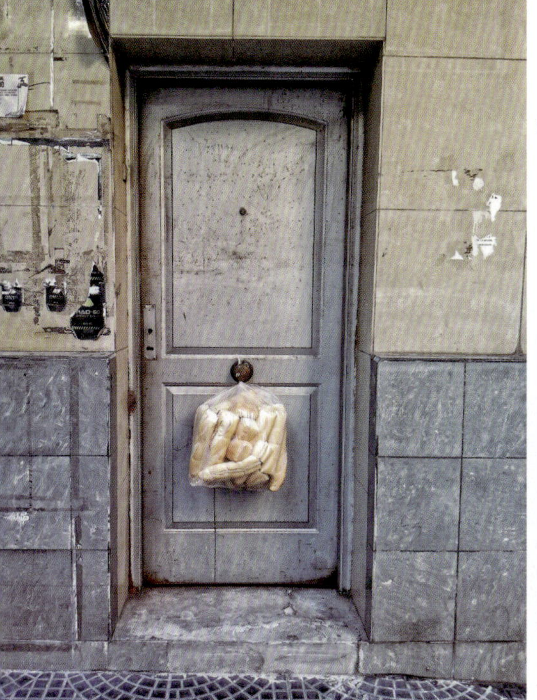

MATIAS SCHEINIG, The bread of everyday take away. BUENOS AIRES, ARGENTINA

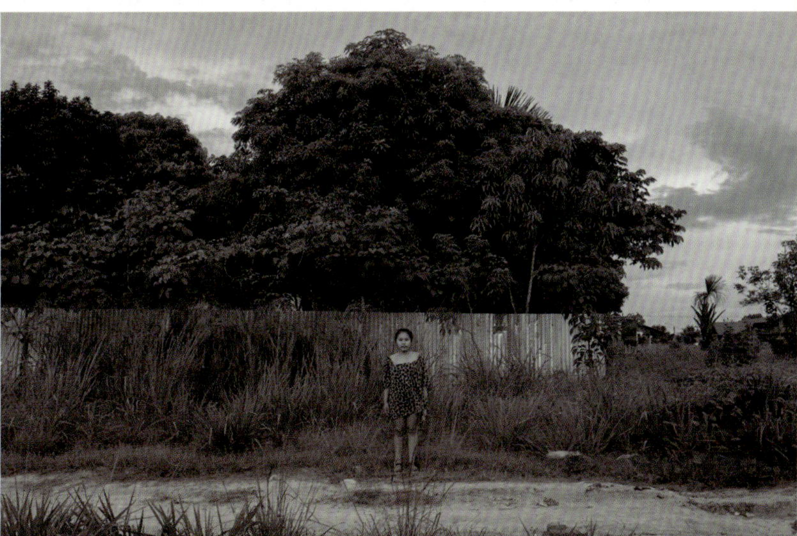

FLORENCE GOUPIL, Pamela Cahuaza stands in front of the house where her grandfather Carlos Guimaraes, 64, just died of COVID-19. This pandemic has taken away wise elders and indigenous leaders, leaving the new generations in solitude. From the project "Shipibo-Konibo: an indigenous community resists with medicinal plants against the COVID-19 virus." UCAYALI, PERU

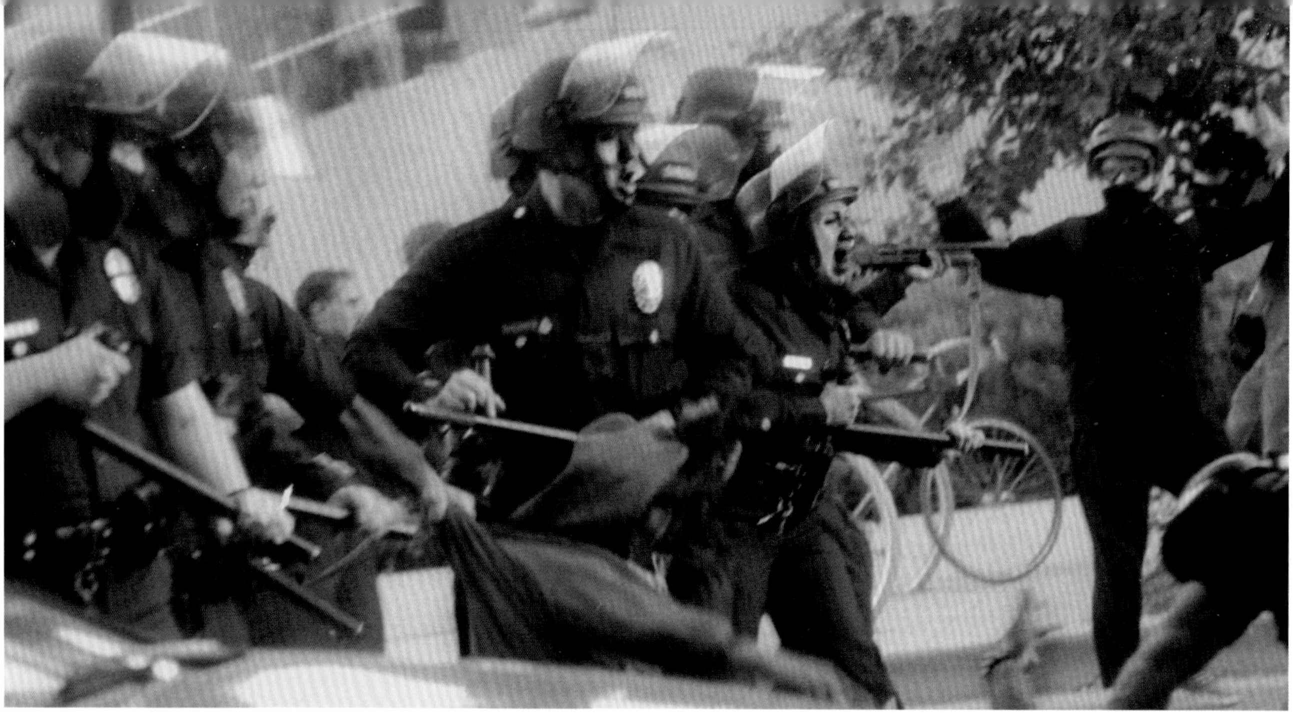

ORSON OBLOWITZ, Rage. DOWNTOWN LOS ANGELES, CA, USA

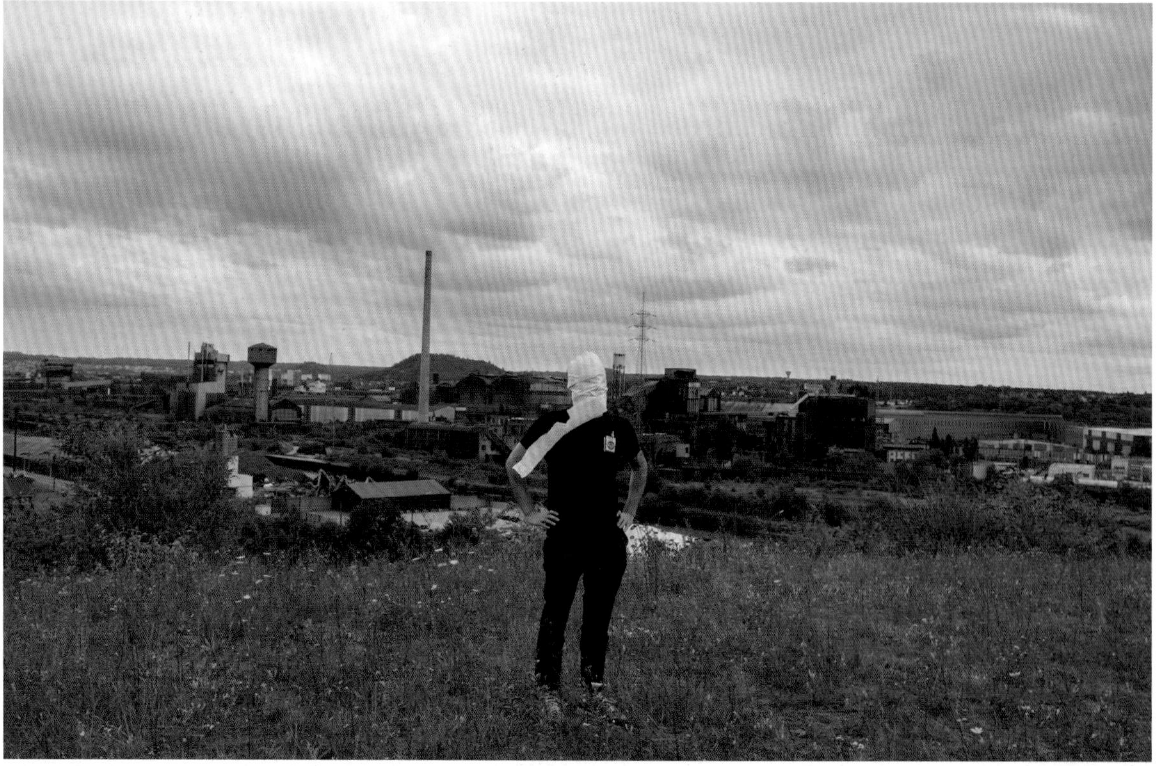

MONSIEUR PECU, Monsieur Pecu explores the world. CHARLEROI, BELGIUM

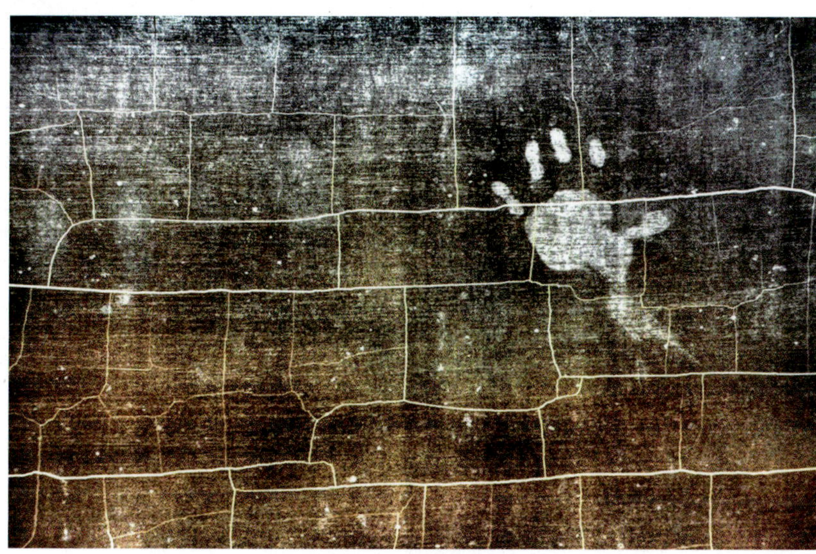

MARGARET WAAGE, *How Does It Feel |* A hand impression appears to reach for something, perhaps the truth. NEW BRITAIN, CT, USA

DADE MANN, Yesterday, Today, Tomorrow, Minneapolis, Dreams and Pain. MINNEAPOLIS, MN, USA

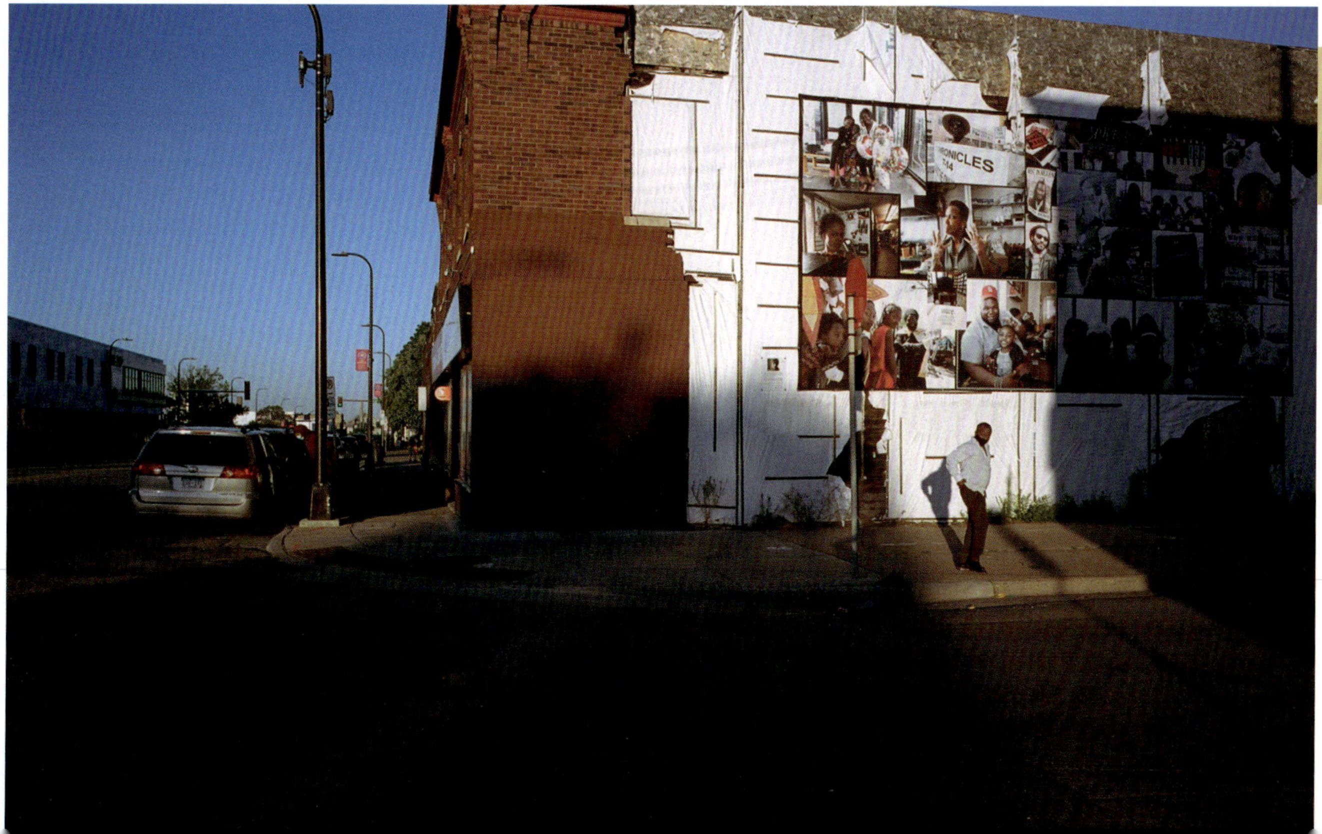

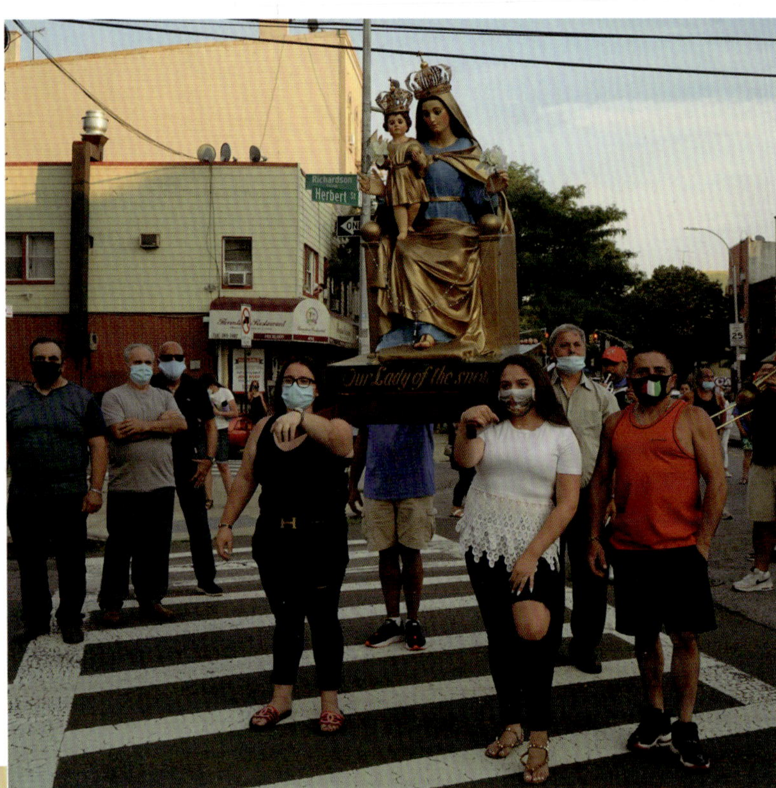

KEVIN D'ANGELO, *Il nuovo normale* | The Italian-American community in Williamsburg wore masks and practiced social distancing while celebrating the 132nd feast of Our Lady of the Snow. BROOKLYN, NY, USA

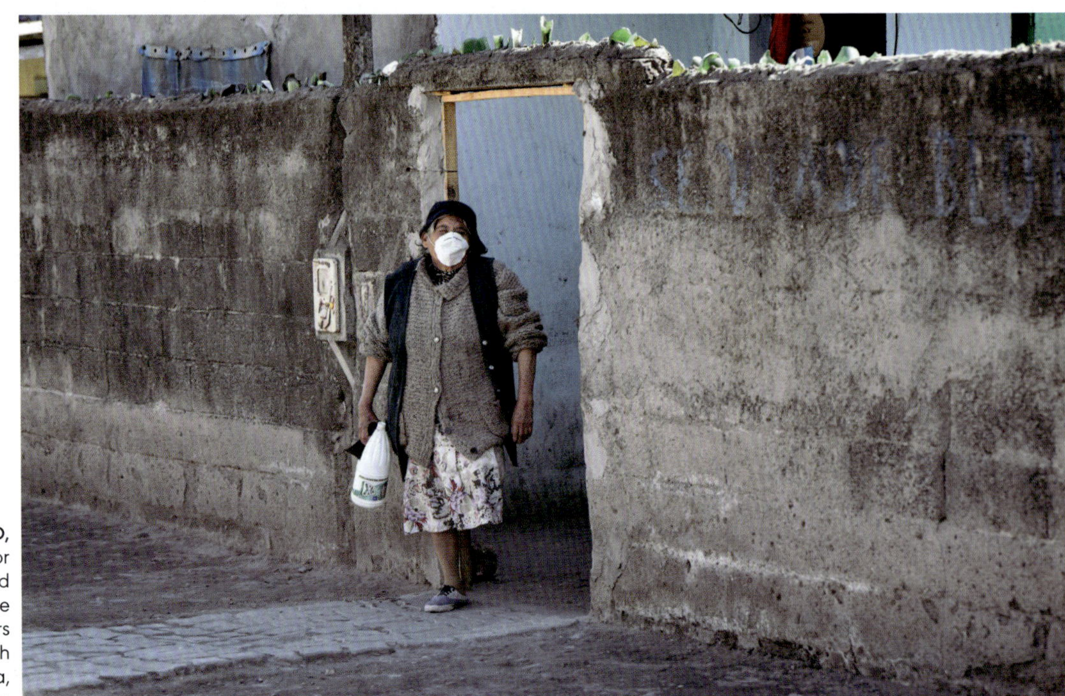

INÉS QUINTEROS ORIO, An old lady asking for help while doctors and police officers struggle to assist many neighbors who were infected with coronavirus in Lastenia, Tucumán. ARGENTINA

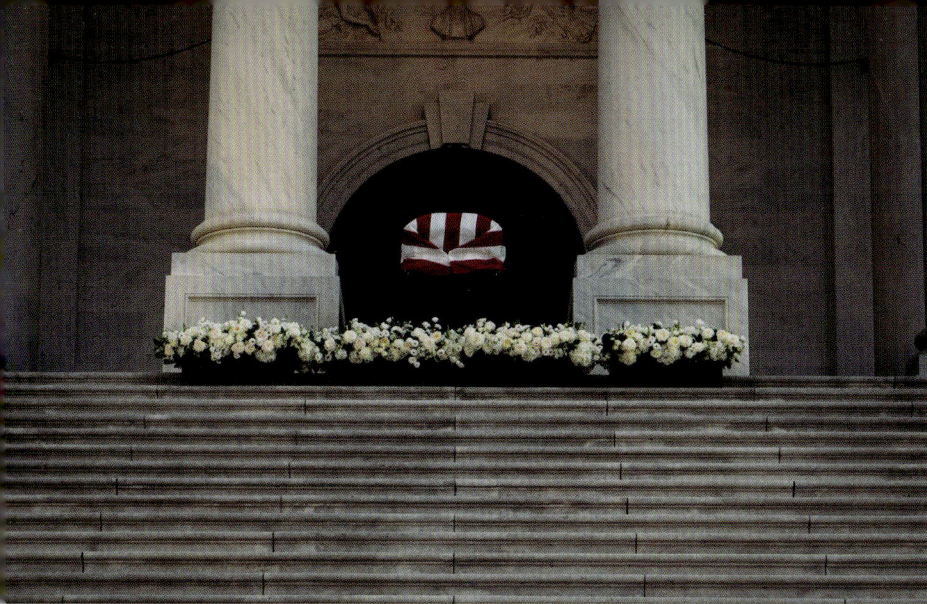

BECKY DAVIS, Civil rights leader John Lewis's public viewing on the East front steps of the United States Capitol. WASHINGTON, DC, USA

BRIDGET MCKENNA, Late July 2020. PITTSBURGH, PA, USA

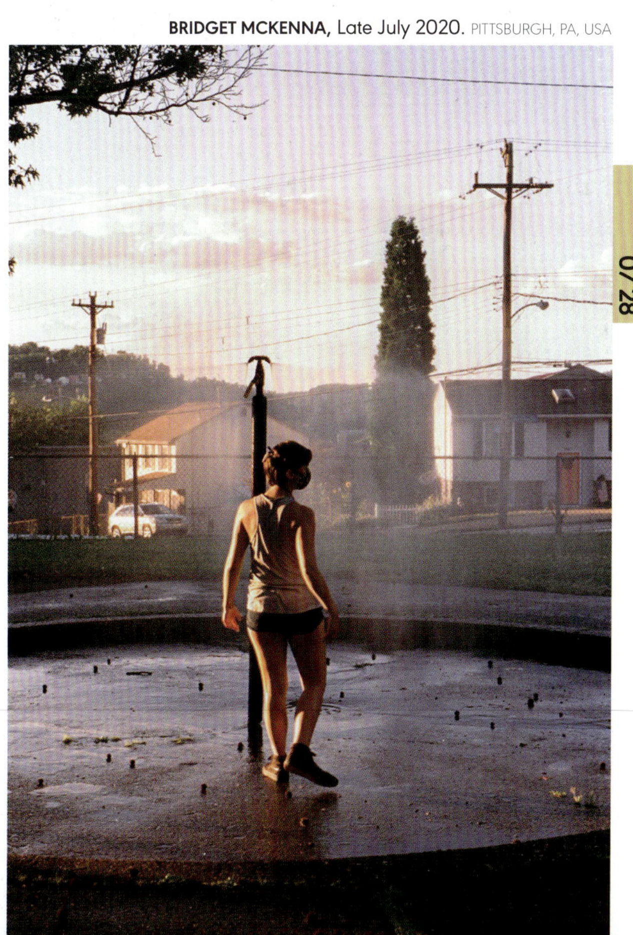

CARLOS RIVERA, New York City 2020. TOMKINS SQUARE PARK, NY, USA

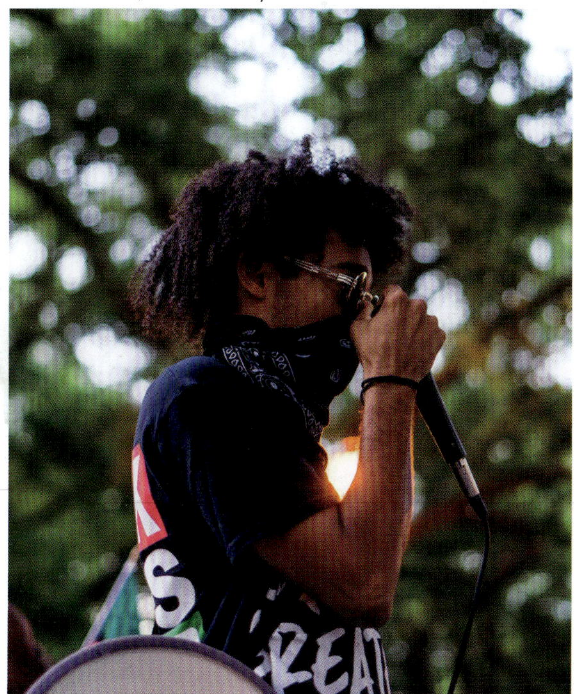

COLLEEN MULLINS, *Peephole/People* | Documenting delivery workers approaching my fortress. Often these are paired with the delivery person's "proof" image that the items were delivered.
SAN FRANCISCO, CA, USA

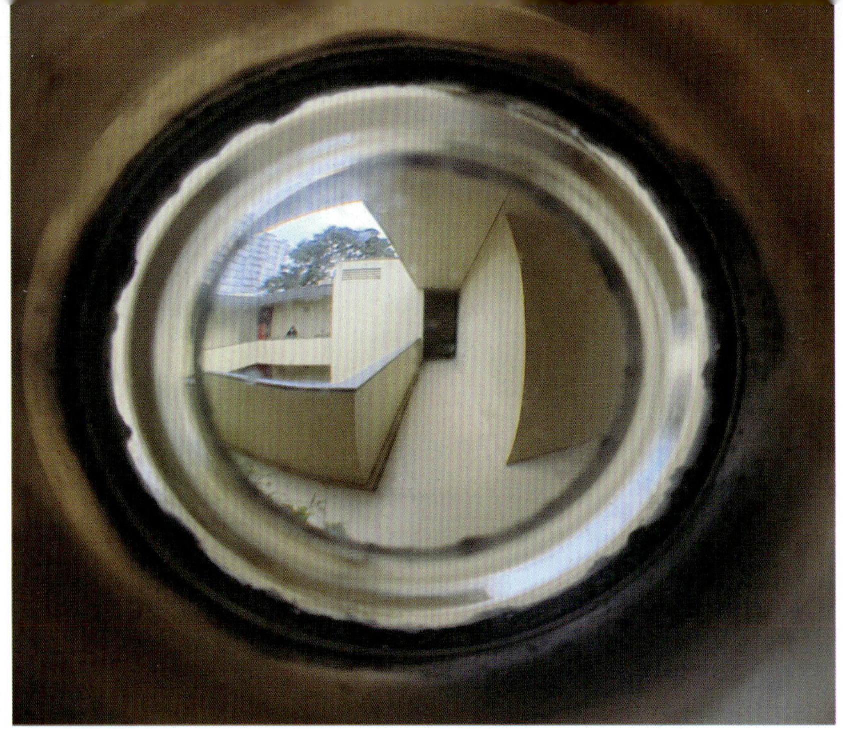

JAMIE ALVAREZ, *COVID Birthday* | While still in a pandemic, aging a year is an accomplishment that should be celebrated.
FISHTOWN, PHILADELPHIA, PA, USA

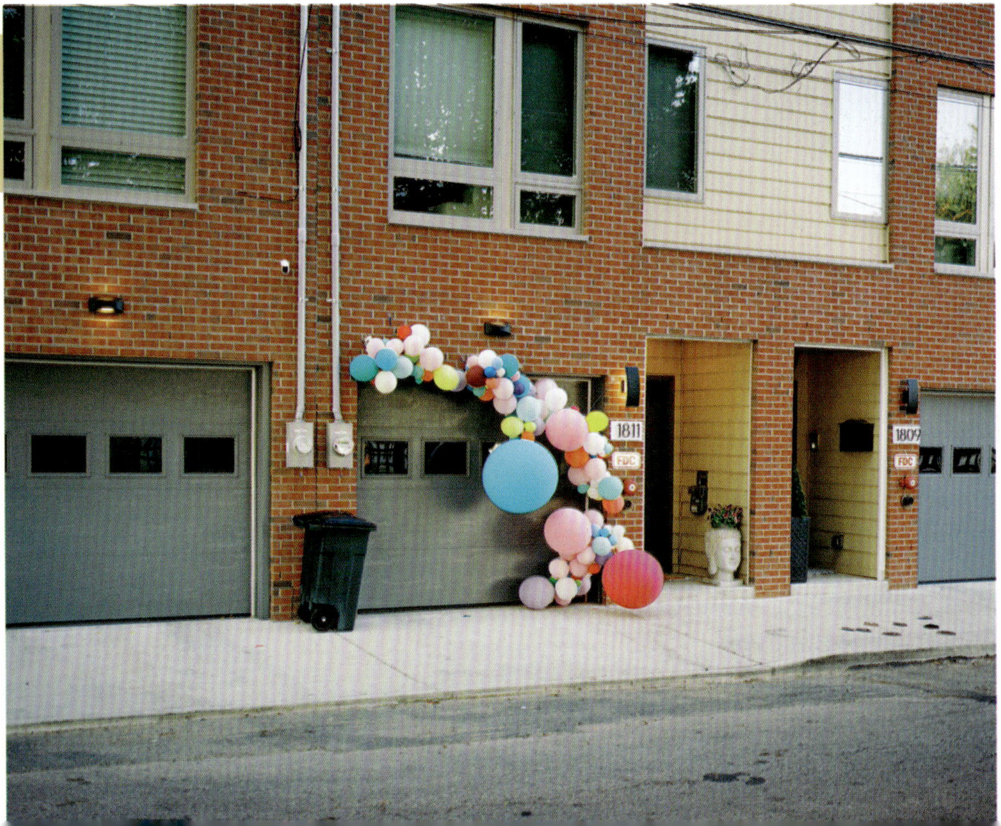

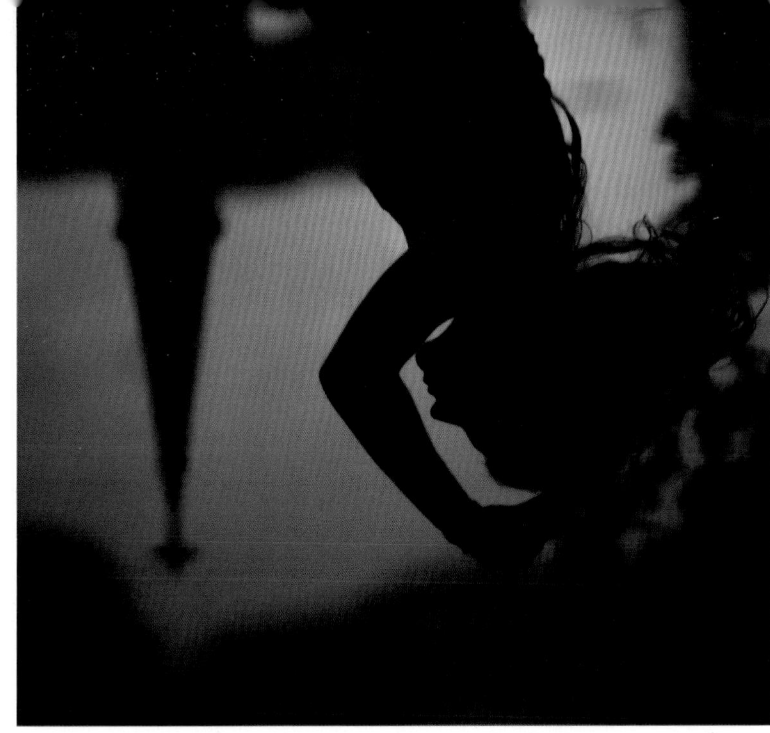

WILL ALLEN-DUPRAW, Under(the)world. CHARLESTON, SC, USA

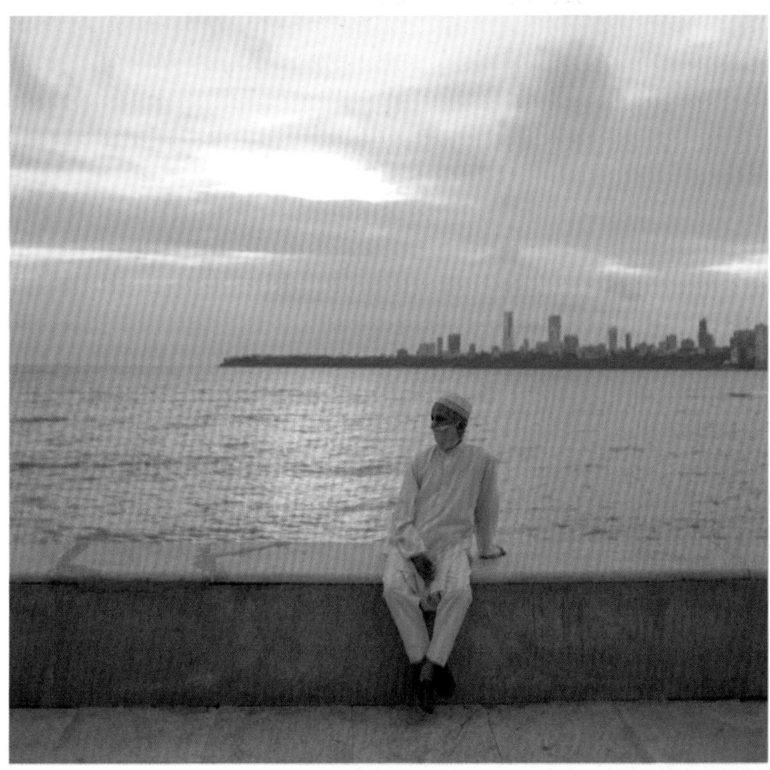

JANARDHAN IYER, A virus knows no religion. AT MARINE DRIVE, MUMBAI, INDIA

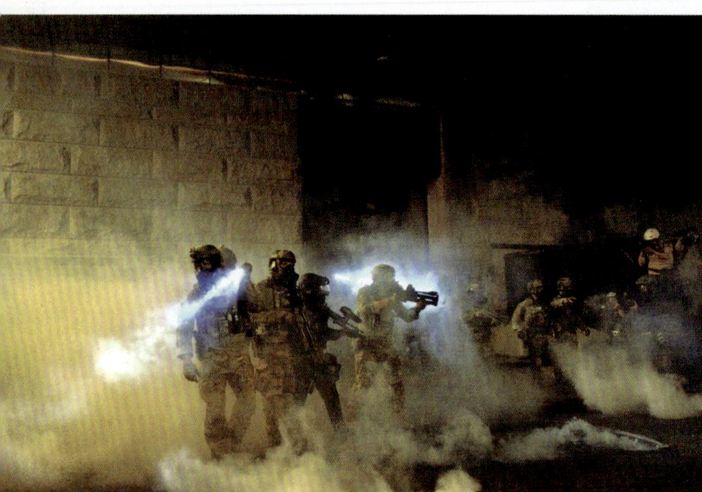

KENNETH BOWEN, The National Guard appears, concealing themselves with tear gas before making arrests. PORTLAND, OR, USA

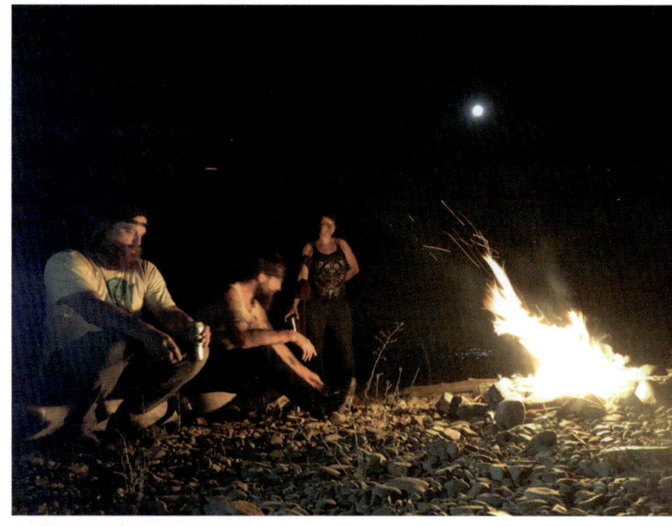

HEATHER MURRAY, River Rats. WILLAMETTE RIVER, OR, USA

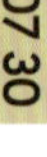

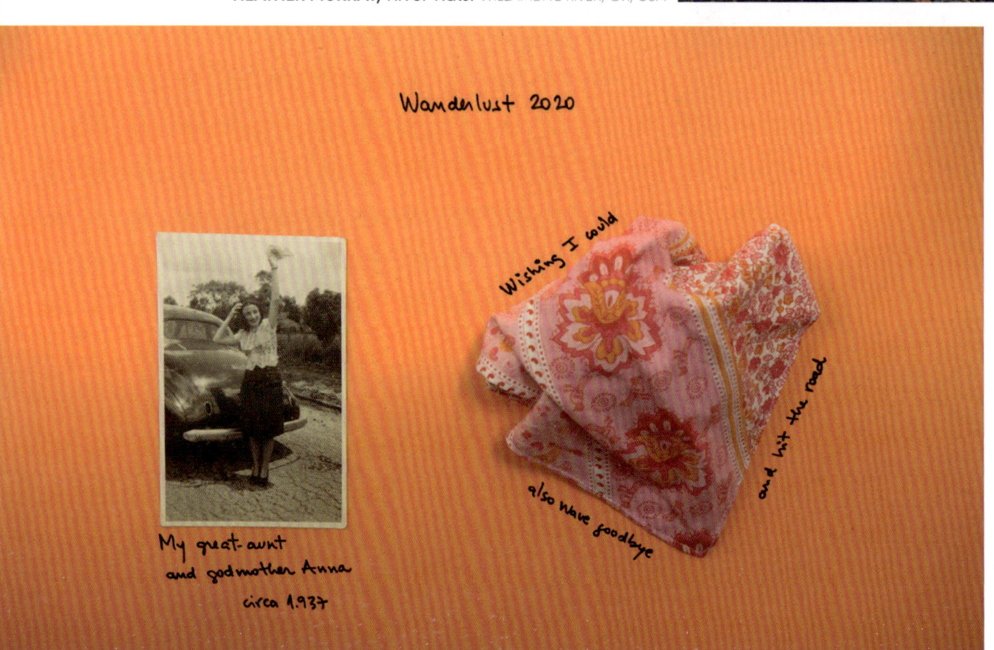

MARISTELA COLUCCI, My beloved godmother Anna, circa 1937. My wanderlust in 2020. SÃO PAULO, BRAZIL

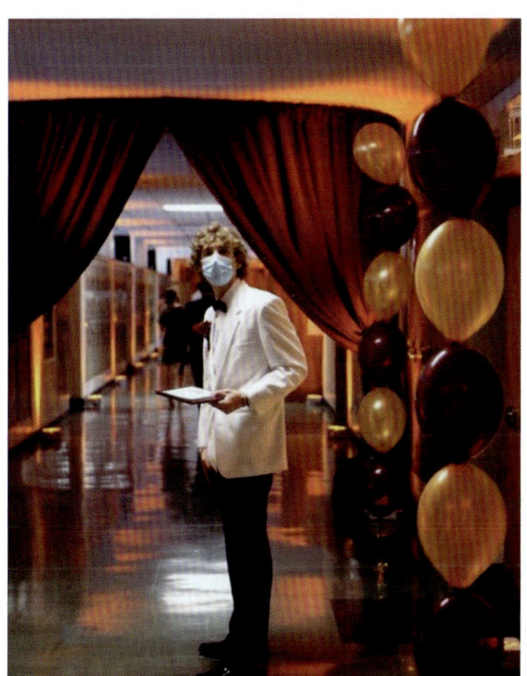

NANCY GIAMPIETRO, High school graduation during the global pandemic. WILMETTE, IL, USA

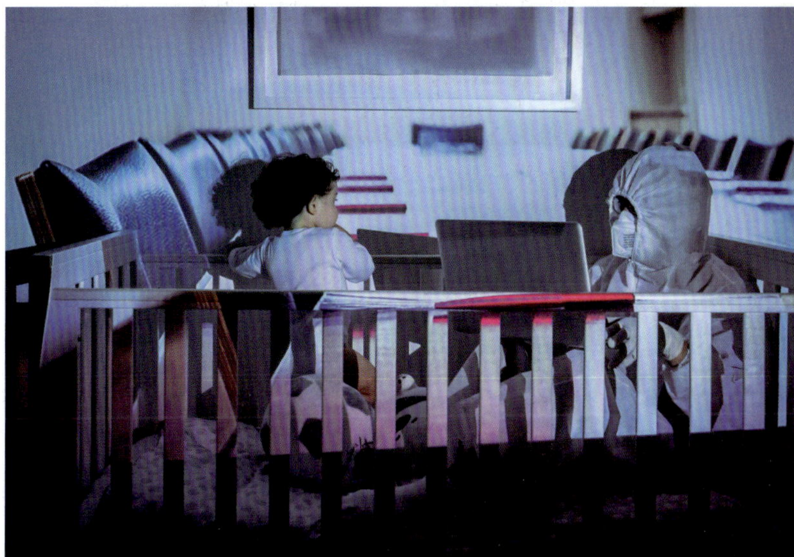

JUAN SEBASTIAN PINILLA, Catharsis 2020. Invaded by uncertainty, news, the obligatory pause, the digital virality of isolation, I create self-portraits by staging pandemic icons and personal concerns, capturing my visual catharsis. BOGOTÁ, COLOMBIA

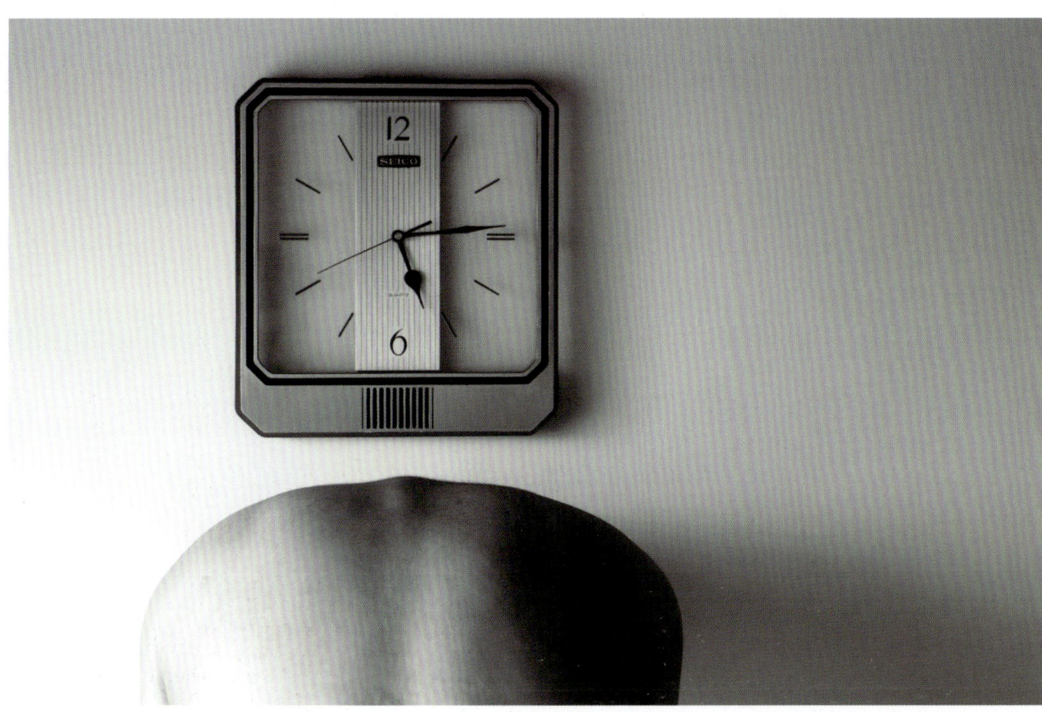

JUAN JOSE MENESES, *Origin |* We are carrying on our past and overthinking our future. The time consumes us, as long it remains. MEDELLÍN, ANTIOQUIA, COLOMBIA

TANYA AHMED, *Phase 4, Outdoor Dining* | 1st Avenue between 1st and 14th Streets. NEW YORK, NY, USA

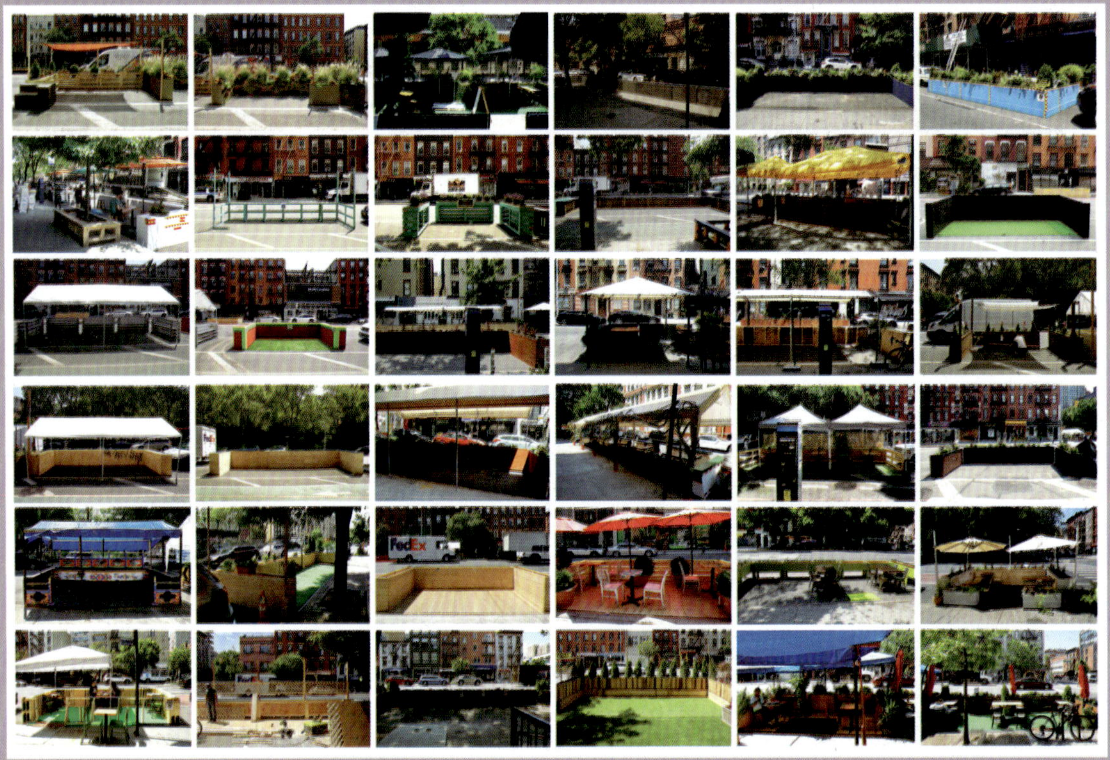

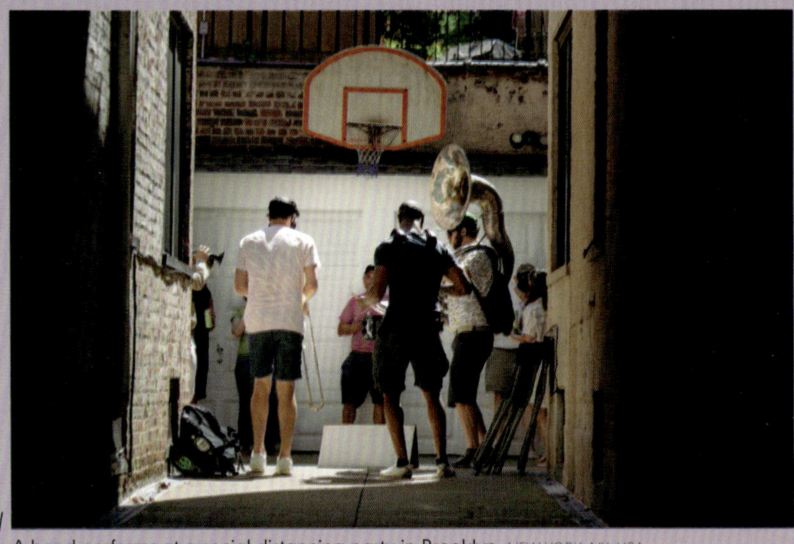

DANIEL ALBANESE, *When the Saints* | A band performs at a social-distancing party in Brooklyn. NEW YORK, NY, USA

08·20

AUGUST

3_WHO Chied Warns: There Might Never Be a "Silver Bullet" for Coronavirus *(NPR)*

6_France Records Two-Month High in Cases *(BBC NEWS)*

31_ Asi operan bares clandestinos en CDMX *(chilango)*

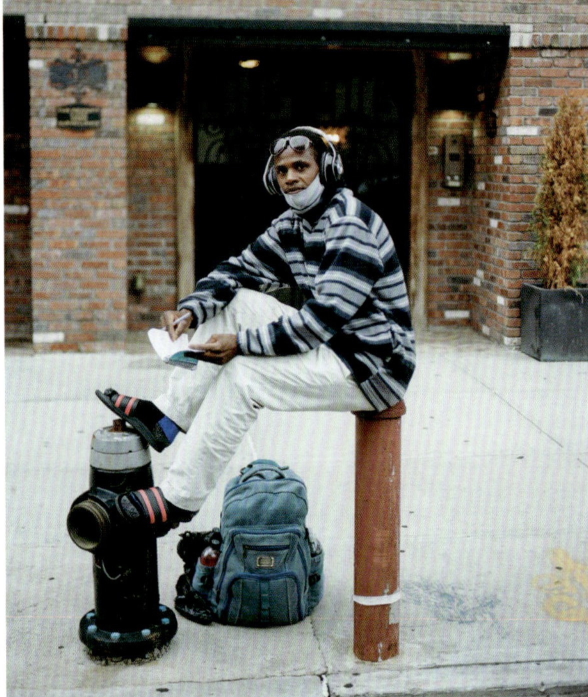

ADAM BANKS, Balancing Act.
BEDFORD-STUYVESANT, BROOKLYN, NEW YORK, NY, USA

KIRA PURNELL,
Intersection near the Frank Crowley Criminal Courts Building.
DALLAS, TX, USA

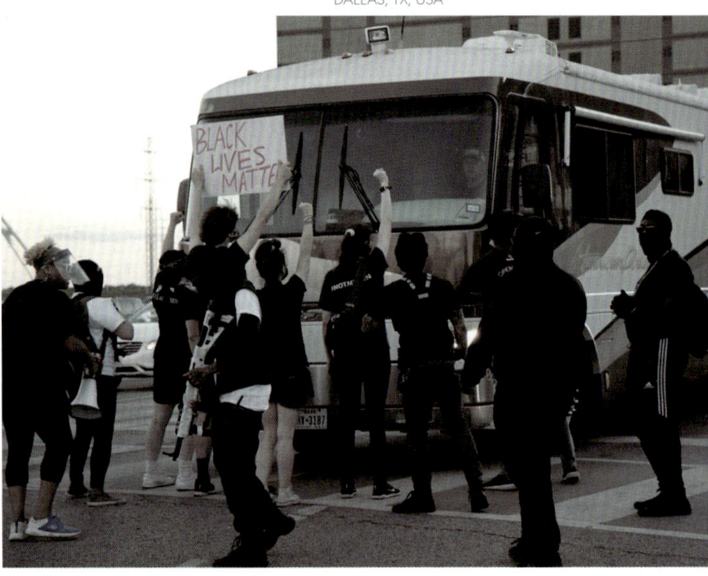

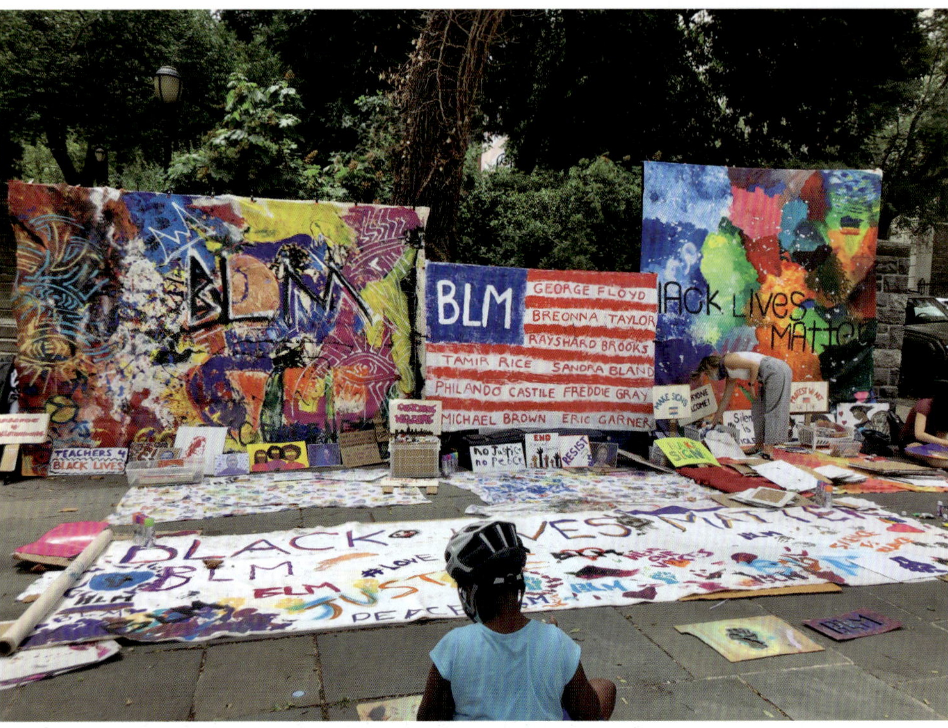

PENNELOPE GOODFRIEND, When you see something that isn't right, not just, not fair, you have a moral obligation to do something. Our children will ask us, "What did you do? What did you say?"
NEW YORK, NY, USA

JUAN VICENTE CENTELLES, *Bailando entre nubes* | Atardecer en el museo Guggenheim de Bilbao. SPAIN

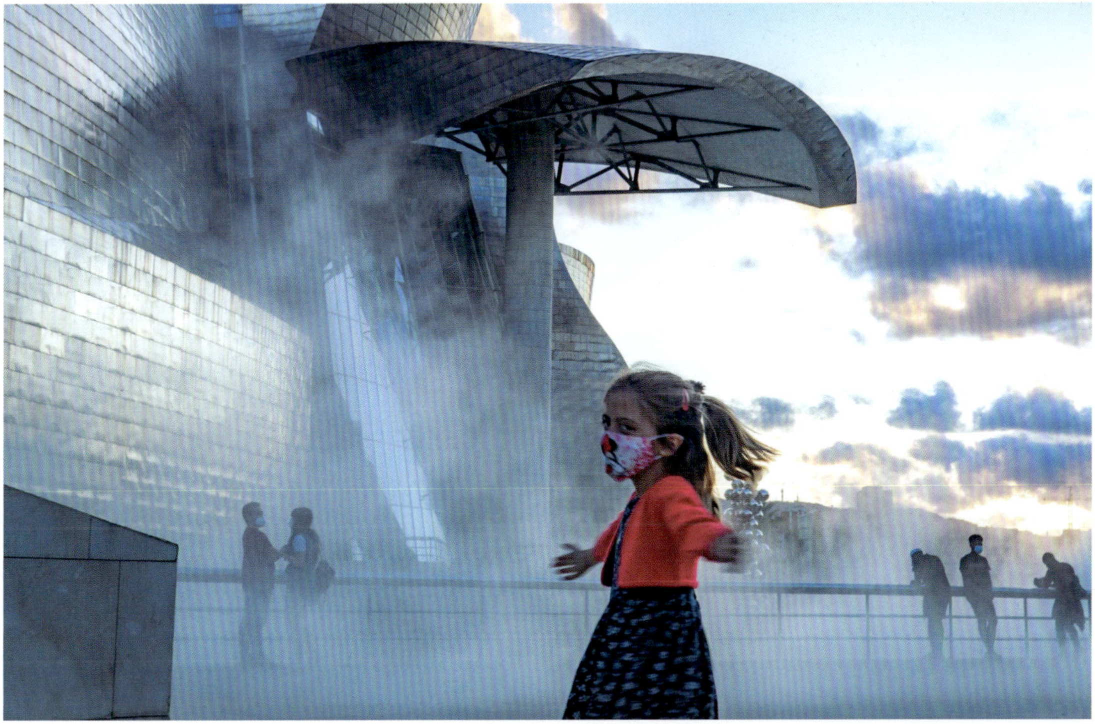

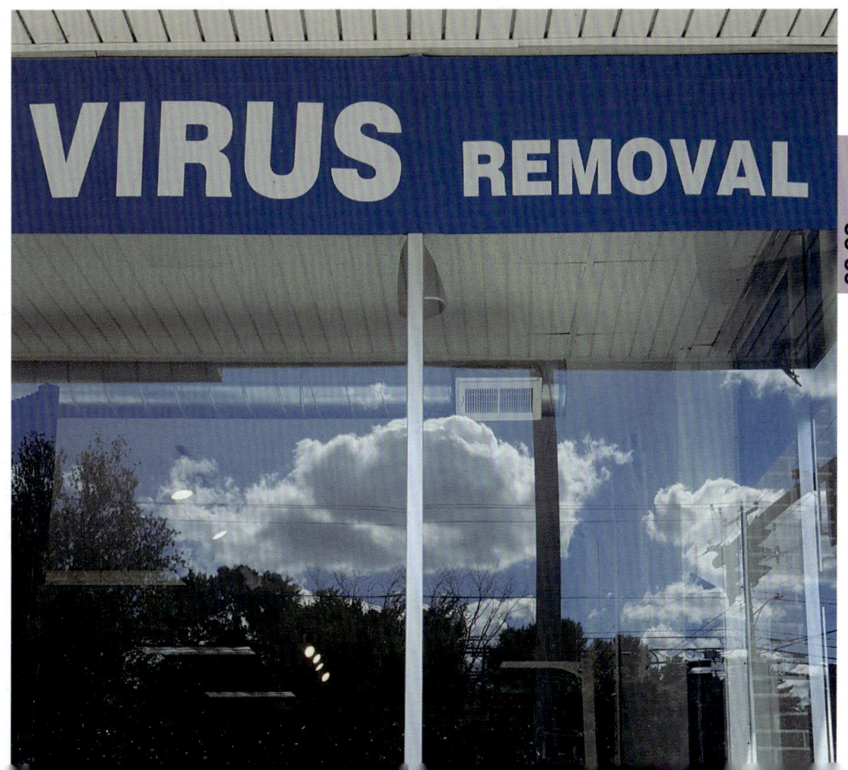

JENN WOOD, *Virus Removal* | New England on a hot, masked day. This struck me as poignant, simple—wishing it could be so easy. BOSTON, MA, USA

VICTORIA GONZÁLEZ GARCÍA, *Intervenida* | Esta fotografia es parte de una pequeña serie de fotos que realicé durante el mes de abril, en plena pandemia madrileña. Mi cuerpo añoraba la libertad, necesitaba de la naturaleza y un poco del caos del mundo exterior. MADRID, SPAIN

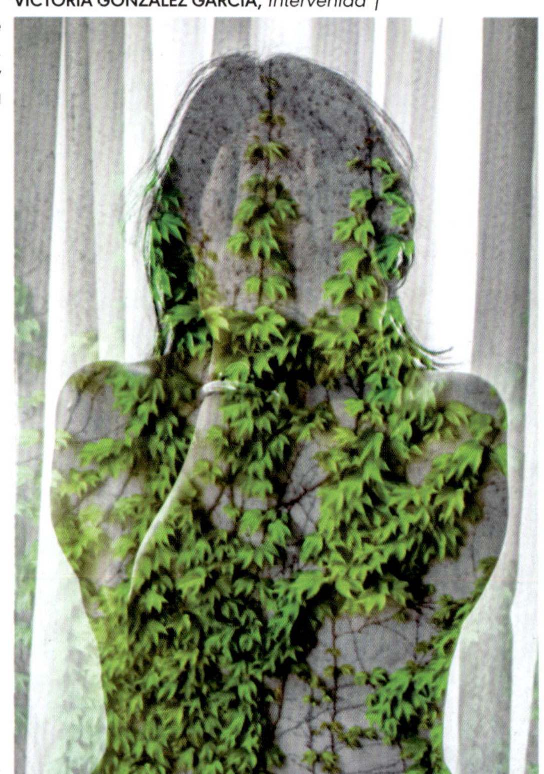

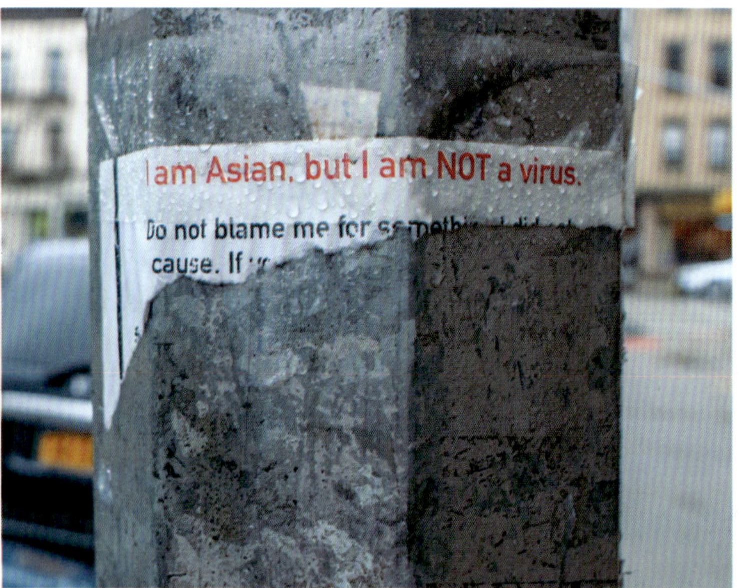

ED BARNAS, "I am Asian, but I am NOT a virus." Torn flyer seen on a light pole in Bay Ridge, Brooklyn. NEW YORK, NY, USA

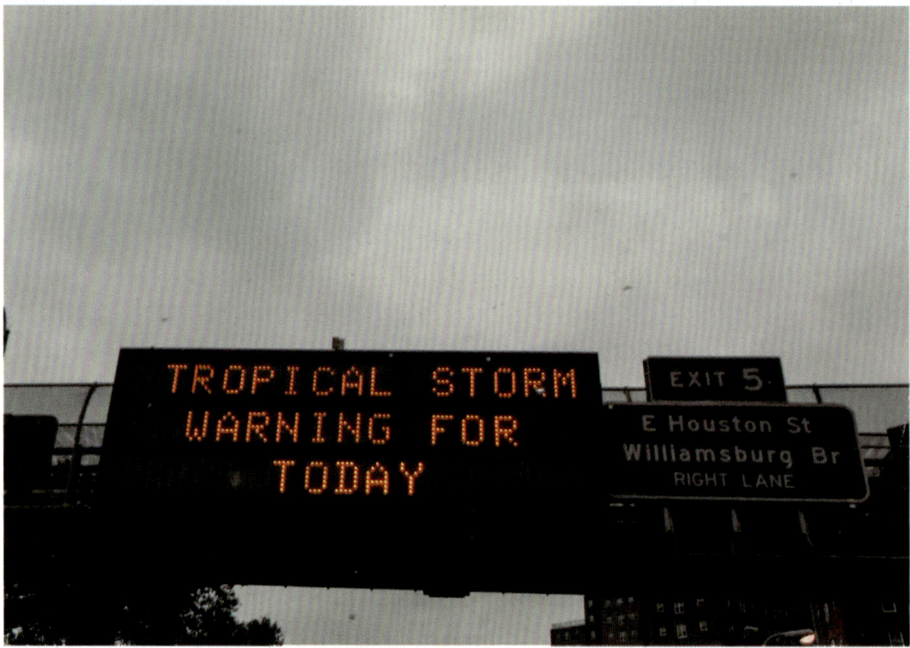

SEAN CUSHING, *Storm Warning* | Pandemic Shutdown Day 140. Tropical Storm Isaias hits New York City. NY, USA

LISA STROUT BEARD, Quincey at Bates Park. WOODSTOCK, IL, USA

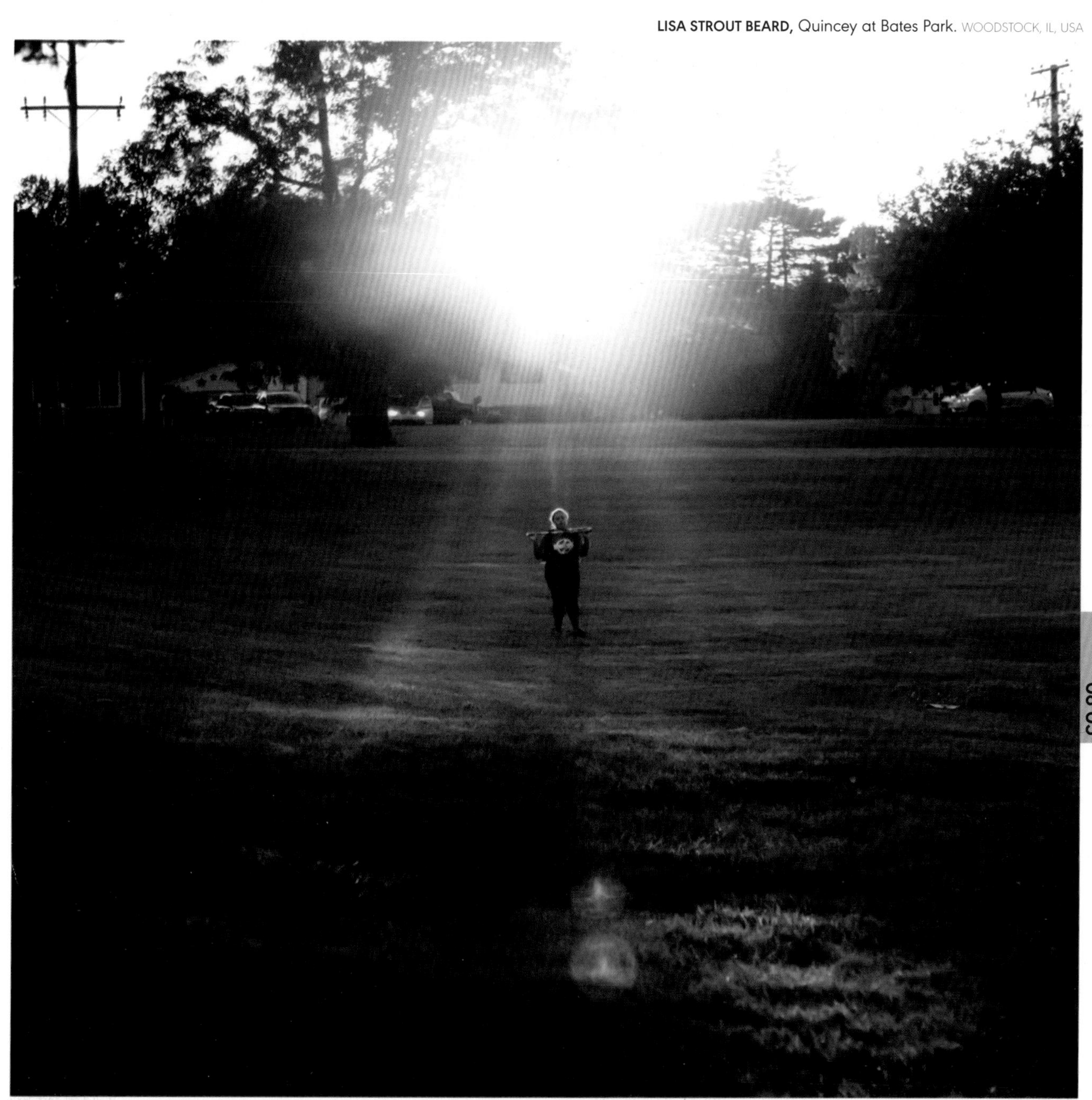

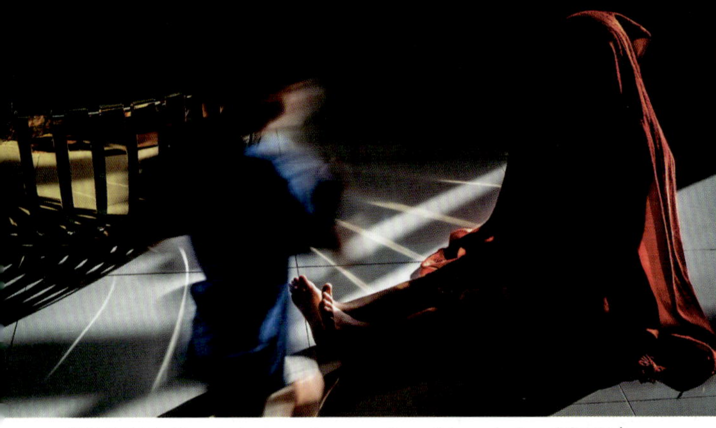

SAIF ASSAM, *Beauty in everyday mundane things during COVID |* My children playing in our living room. ABU DHABI, UNITED ARAB EMIRATES

ISSAM CHORRIB, South African men sell some local clothes. BAB MARAKECH, ESSAOUIRA, MOROCCO

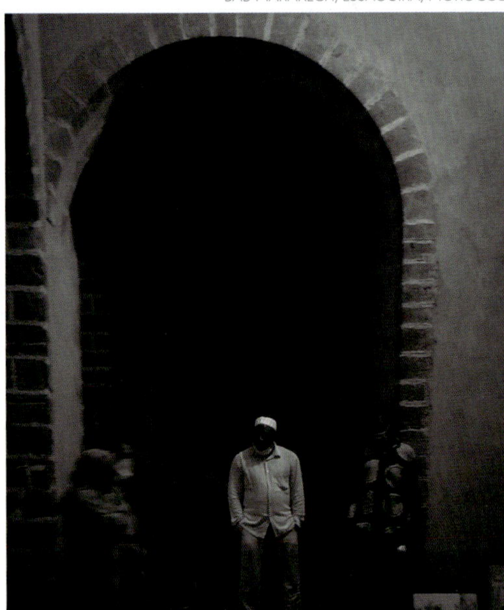

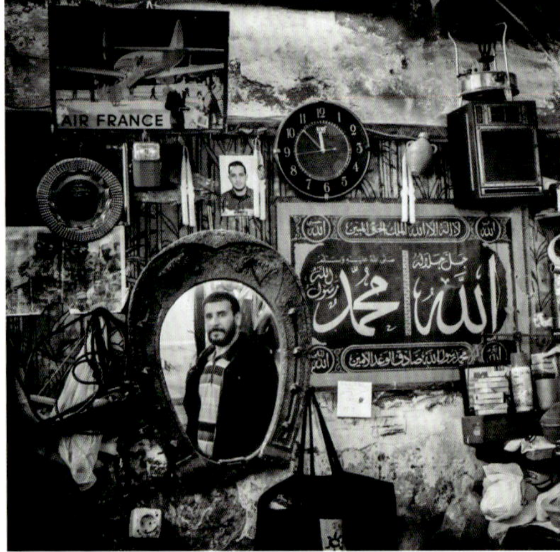

NORA ZAÏR, *Casbah of Algiers |* Part of a photo project on the Casbah, a heritage district classified by UNESCO. ALGIERS, ALGERIA

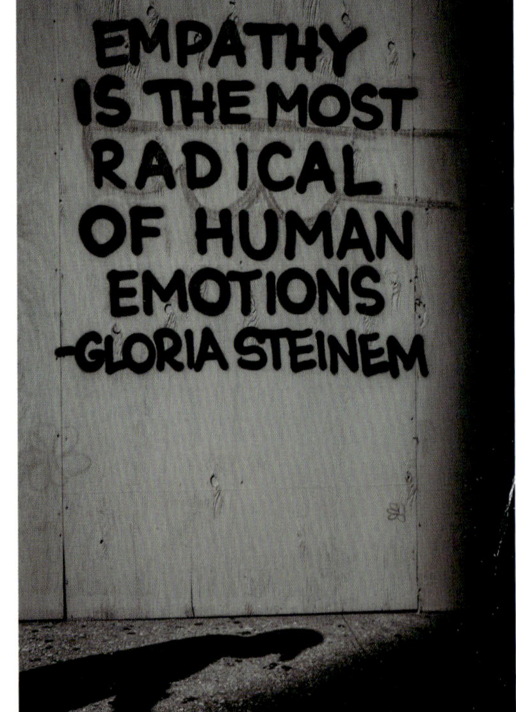

CHRISTINE L. MACE, Empathy. UNION SQUARE EAST & 16TH ST, NEW YORK, NY, USA

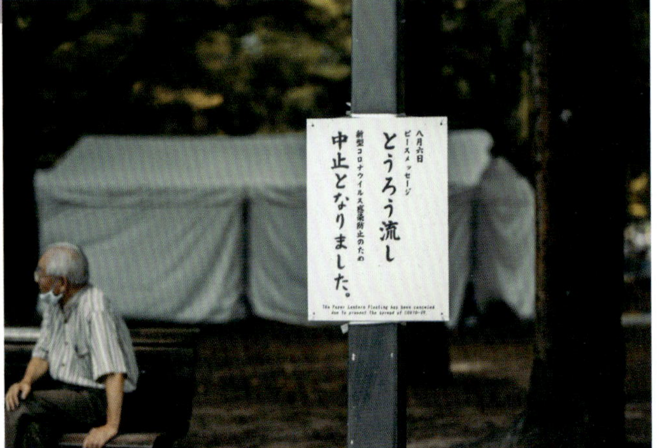

YOSHIHIKO SHIKADA, "The Paper Lantern Floating has been canceled due to prevent the spread of COVID-19." HIROSHIMA, JAPAN

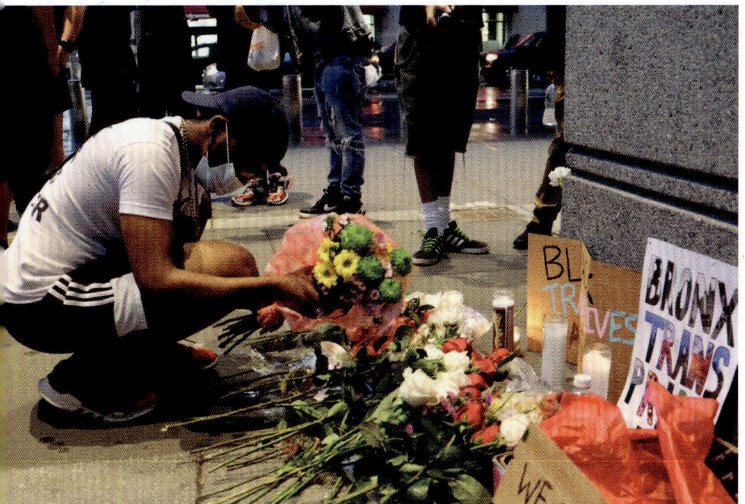

GERARDO ROMO, Vigil in honor of Tiffany "Dior" Harris. BRONX, NY, USA

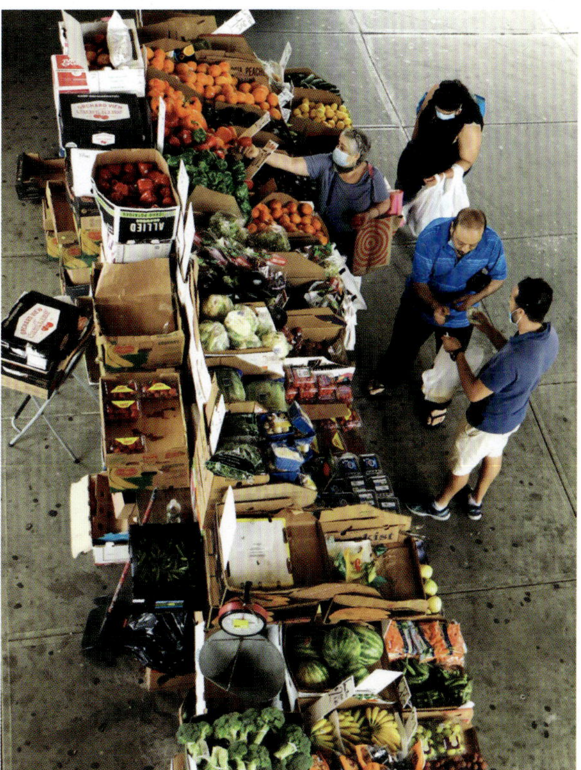

SEUNGJAE SEO,
Venders are selling vegetables under the 7 train 40st-Lowery station in Sunnyside, Queens, one of the most diverse counties in the United States.
NEW YORK, NY, USA

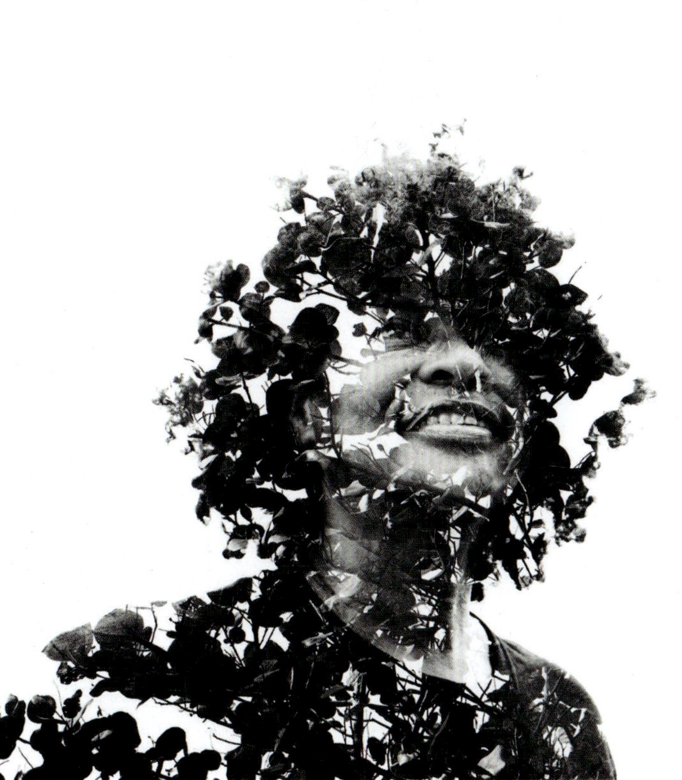

MEREDITH ANDREWS,
A portrait of Doreen Williams-James who promotes a plant-based life and is incredibly knowledgeable about our island's natural environment.
SMITHS PARISH, BERMUDA

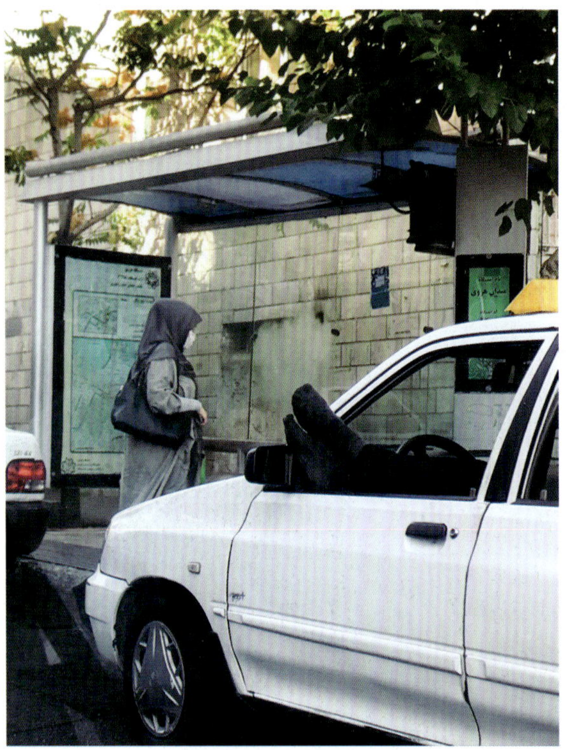

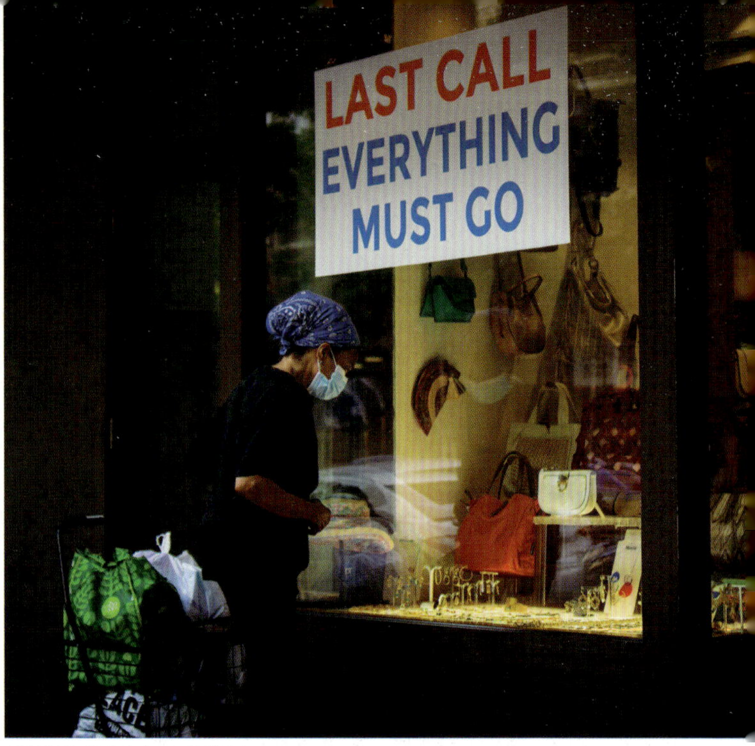

LORI HILLSBERG, Last Call. UPPER WEST SIDE, NEW YORK, NY, USA

SETAREH ESMAEILZADEH, *Easy from the world* | This image is of a taxi driver in Tehran, resting from the global concern. IRAN

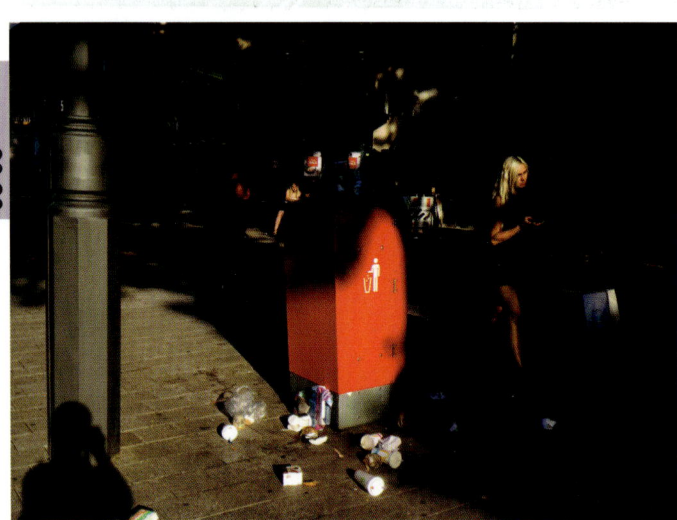

EDUARD MAITERTH, *Exploring Light 2* |
With this series, I want to show how the light could transform ordinary urban places into wonderful, poetic locations.
HAMBURG, GERMANY

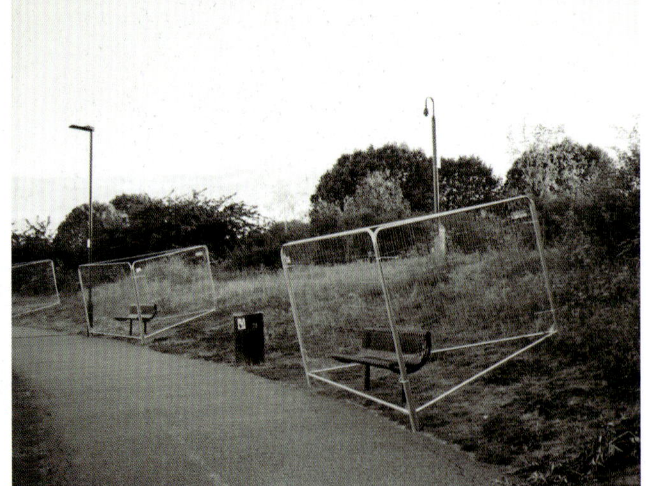

IOANA MARINCA, Benches temporarily fenced off in Millwall Park, Isle of Dogs. EAST LONDON, UNITED KINGDOM

DIANA ZULUAGA, Under Pressure. SPANISH HARLEM, NEW YORK, NY, USA

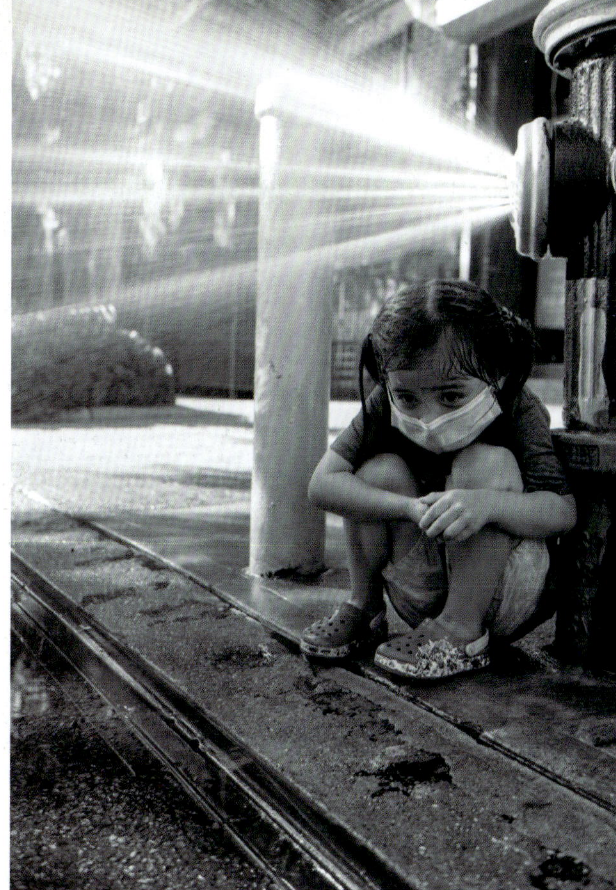

SHAWN REID, Reflecting On The Message. PHILADELPHIA, PA, USA

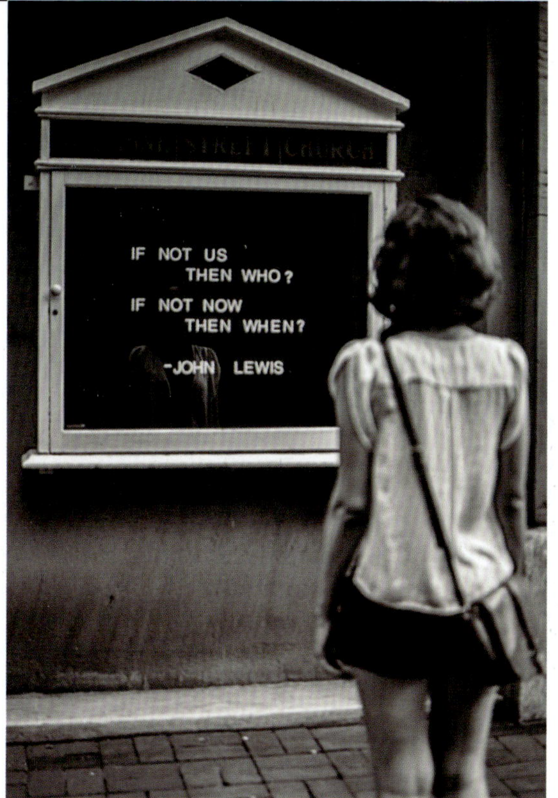

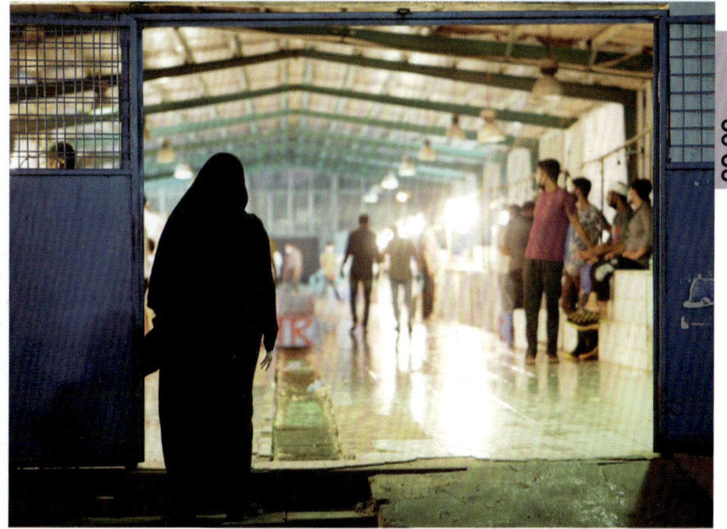

BATOOL ALKHALAF, A woman waits at the entrance of the Qatif Fish Market wearing vinyl gloves to receive her order from the local fishmonger and avoid crowds. SAUDI ARABIA

GIOVANNA ROSSELLI, *How Many More, New York* | After George Floyd's death, protests against police violence and racism flourished. Young, passionate and charismatic leaders are educating and encouraging protesters to condemn violence and take action for social justice. NEW YORK, NY, USA

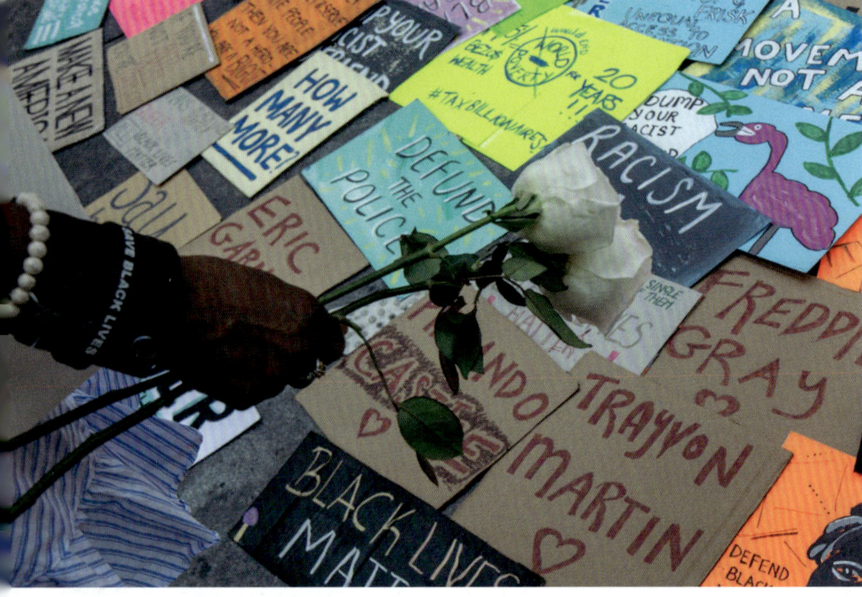

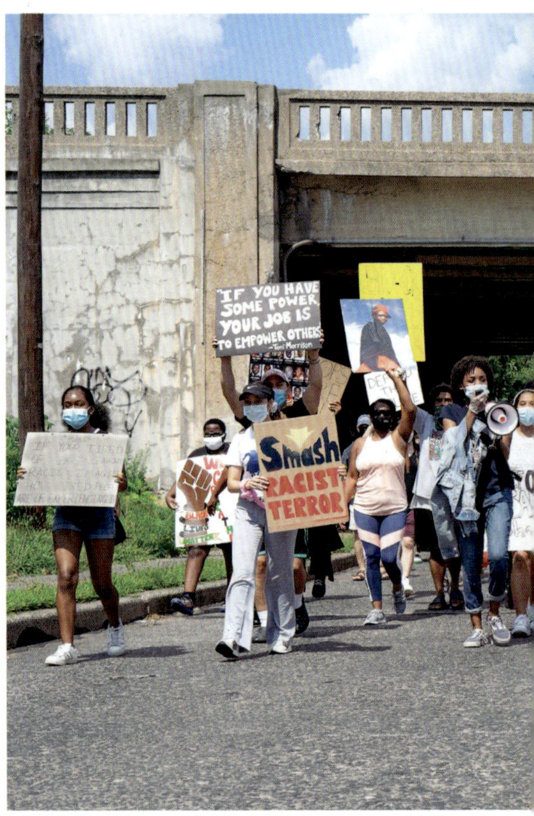

MARA TRILLA, Flowers for Miguel. BUENOS AIRES, ARGENTINA

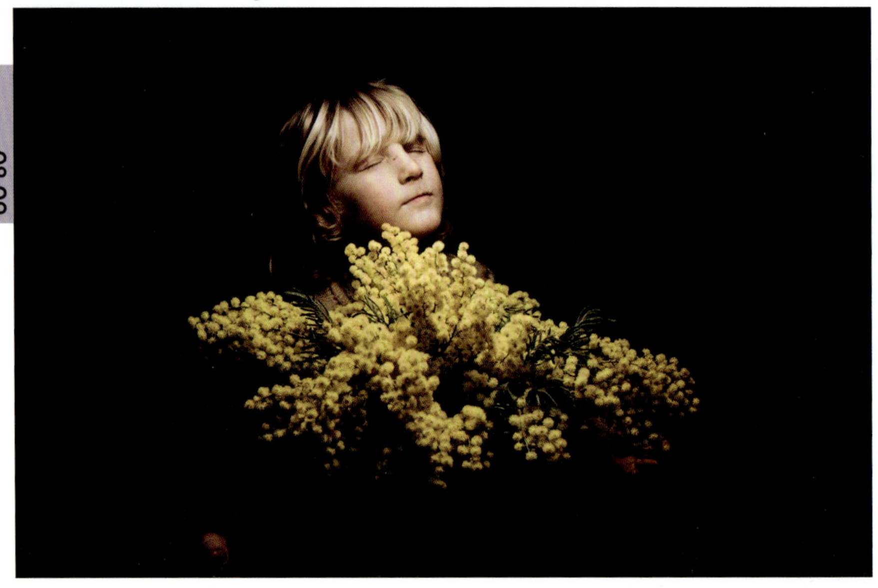

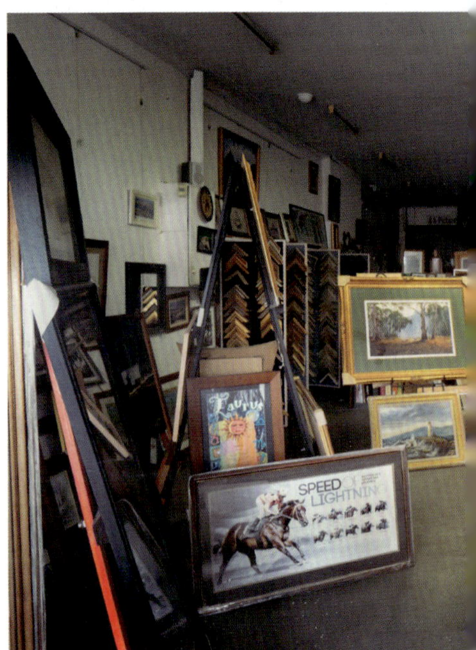

DAVID WADELTON, High Street shop in the time of COVID-19. AUSTRALIA

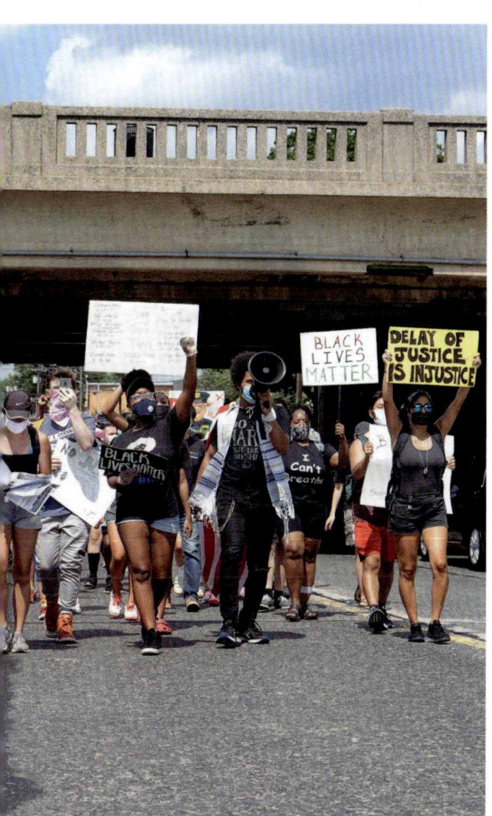

BRIAN JOHNSON,
The March of the Youth.
TEANECK, NJ, USA

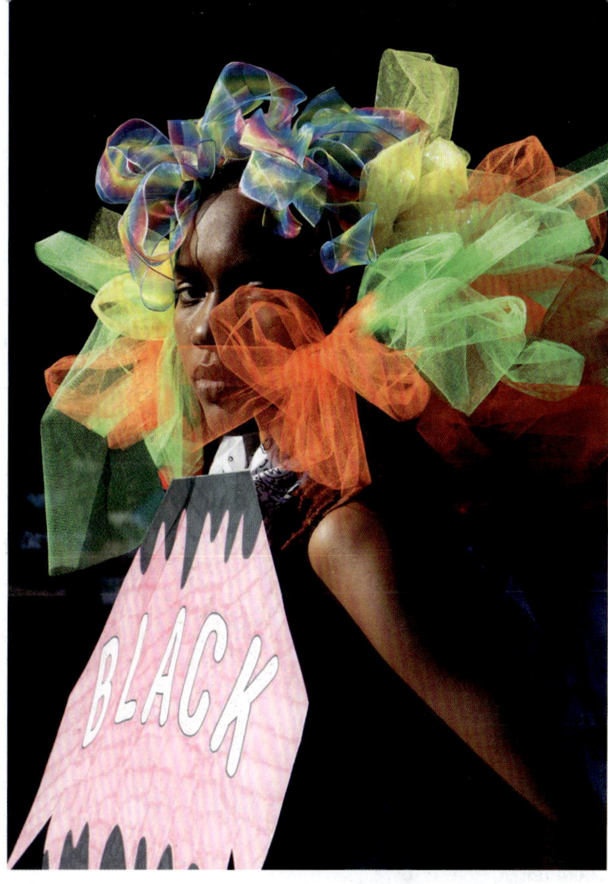

DEB FONG,
Za'Myai and Jason | Model Za'Myai Elliott, styled by designer Jason C. Peters at this Black Lives Matter march, merging activism, art, fashion, dance, and music.
NEW YORK, NY, USA

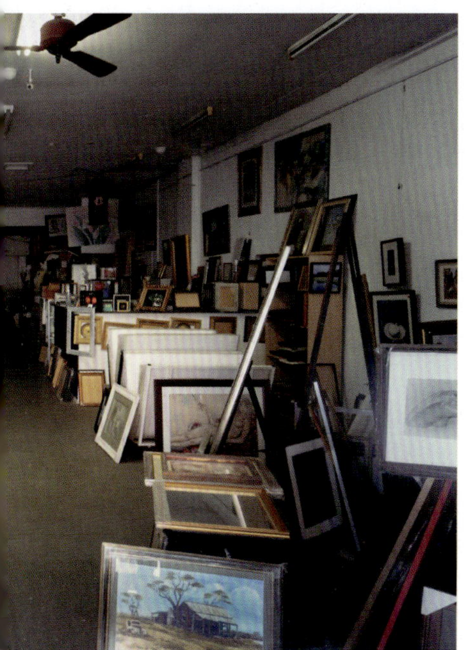

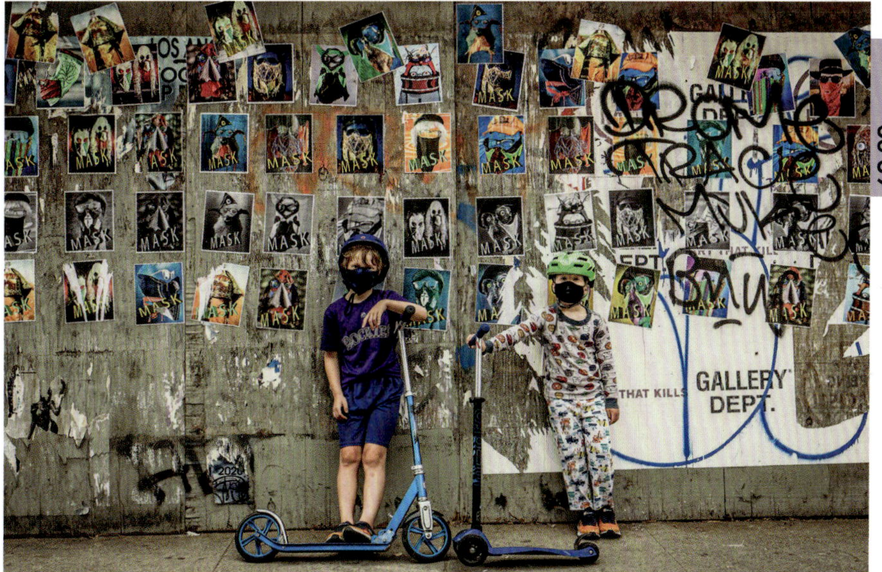

ERICKA KREUTZ, *Protect* | Protecting my kids while we scooter around the neighborhood. A local shop out of business and boarded up with "Mask" signs. LOS ANGELES, CA, USA

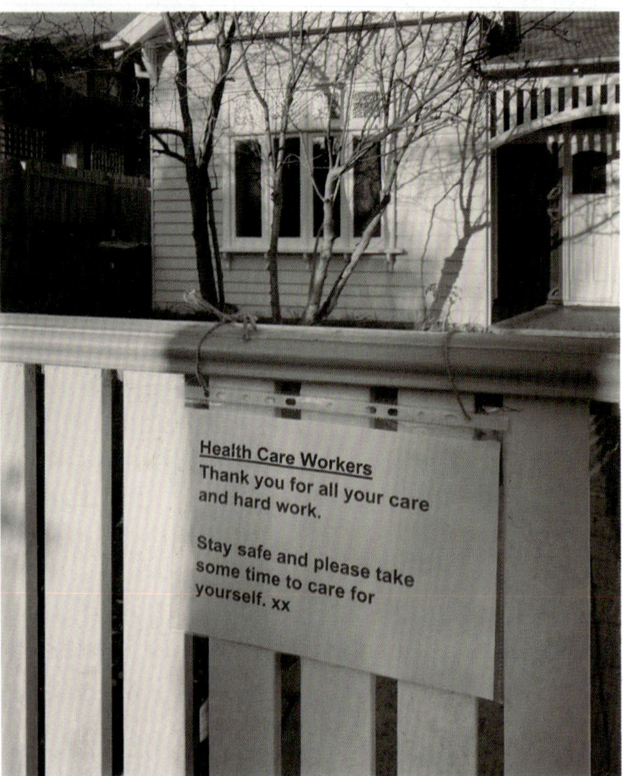

LESLIE ARNOTT, On my one-hour walk during Melbourne Lockdown. AUSTRALIA

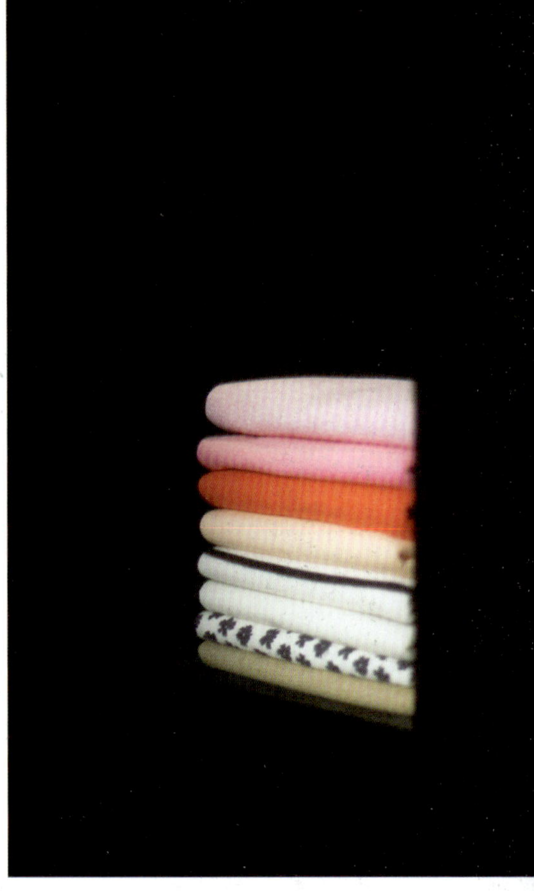

MATHIEU CLADIDIER, Poetic of the mundane. NEW YORK, NY, USA

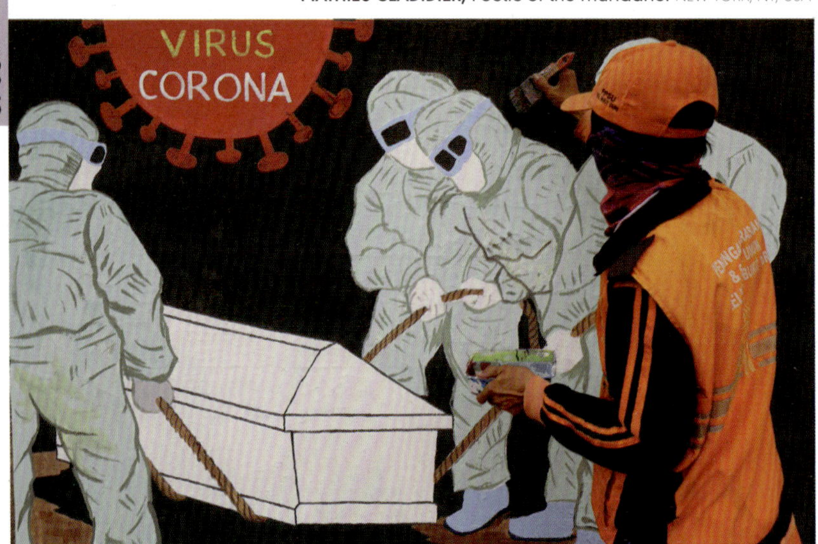

MIFTAHUL HAYAT, Mural Lawan COVID. JAKARTA, INDONESIA

PENNY STEPHENS,

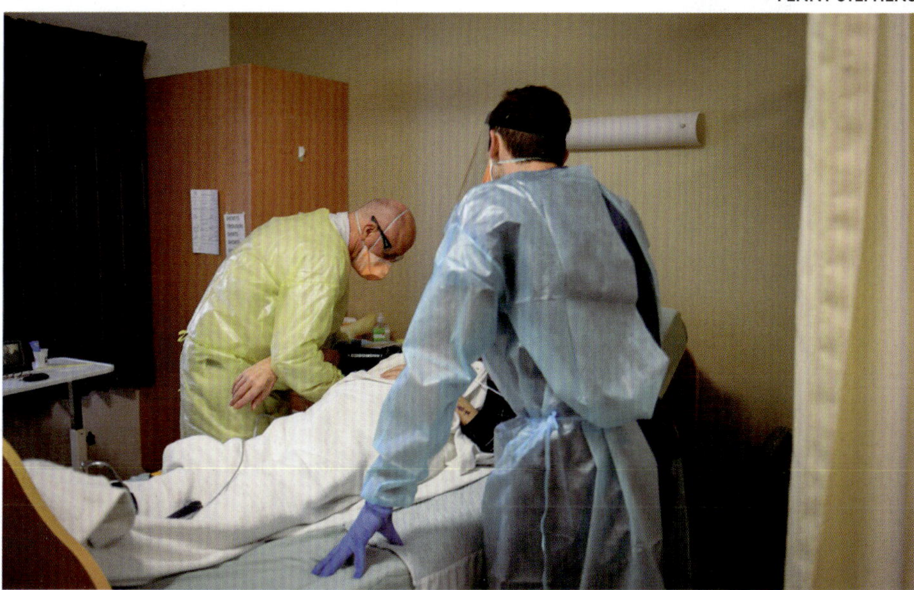

Nurse Shane Durance and Geriatrician Jesse Zanker, working in Melbourne's western suburbs, respond to a call from an aged care home overwhelmed with COVID-19 cases. AUSTRALIA

NICHOLAS COBB, *Untitled* |

I use a dichroic mirror to distort colour and can bend and dent it to distort space. The result is an expressionistic photography for these troubled times. PICADILLY CIRCUS, LONDON, UNITED KINGDOM

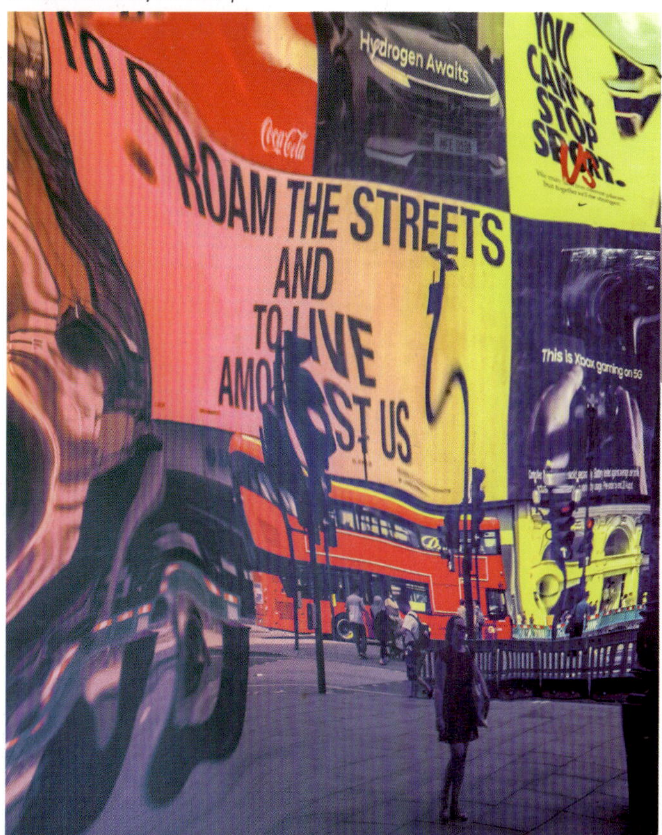

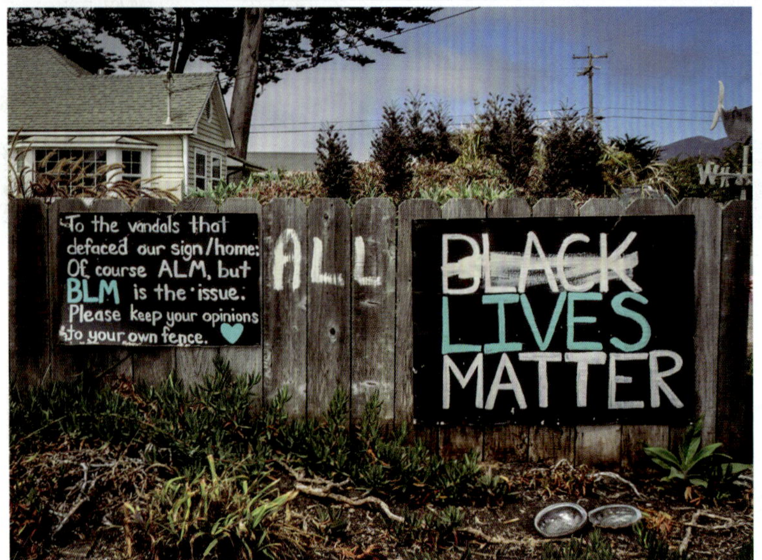

JEANNETTE FERRARY,

In the small town of Princeton-by-the-Sea, this image represents a dialog of sorts and a lesson in the adage that "good fences make good neighbors." CA, LA

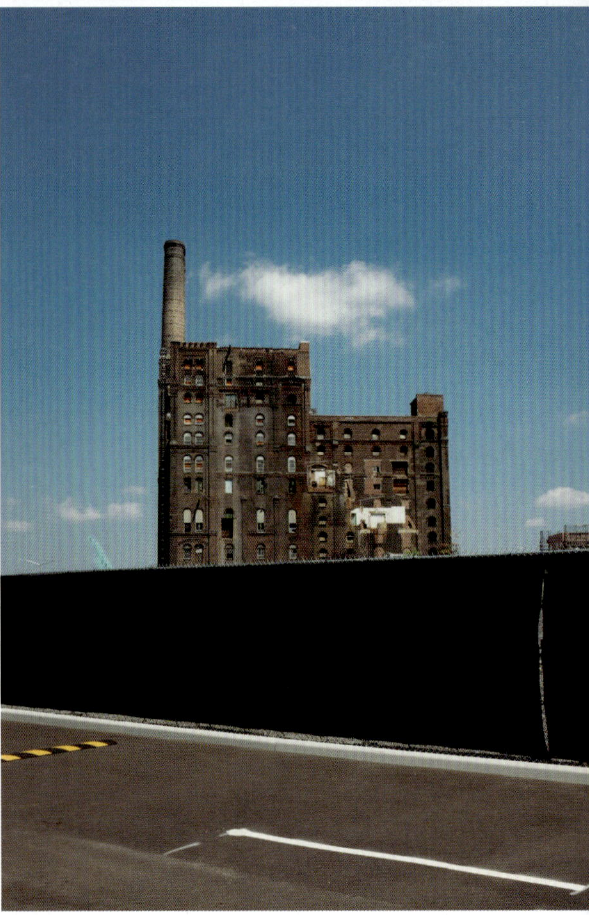

MATTHEW LESMAN, Domino Sugar Factory. BROOKLYN, NY, USA

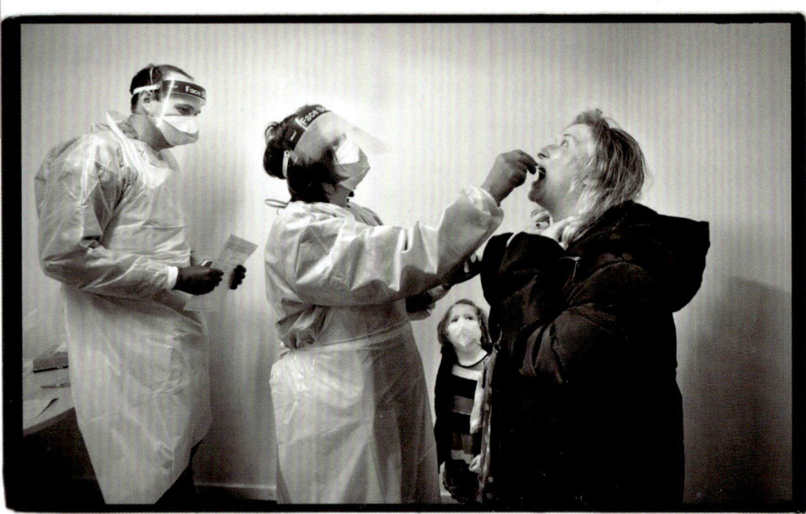

SANDY SCHELTEMA,

A young child watches apprehensively as her mother is tested at Kyneton Health's COVID-19 screening clinic. The nurse is assisted by an Australian Defence Force member. AUSTRALIA

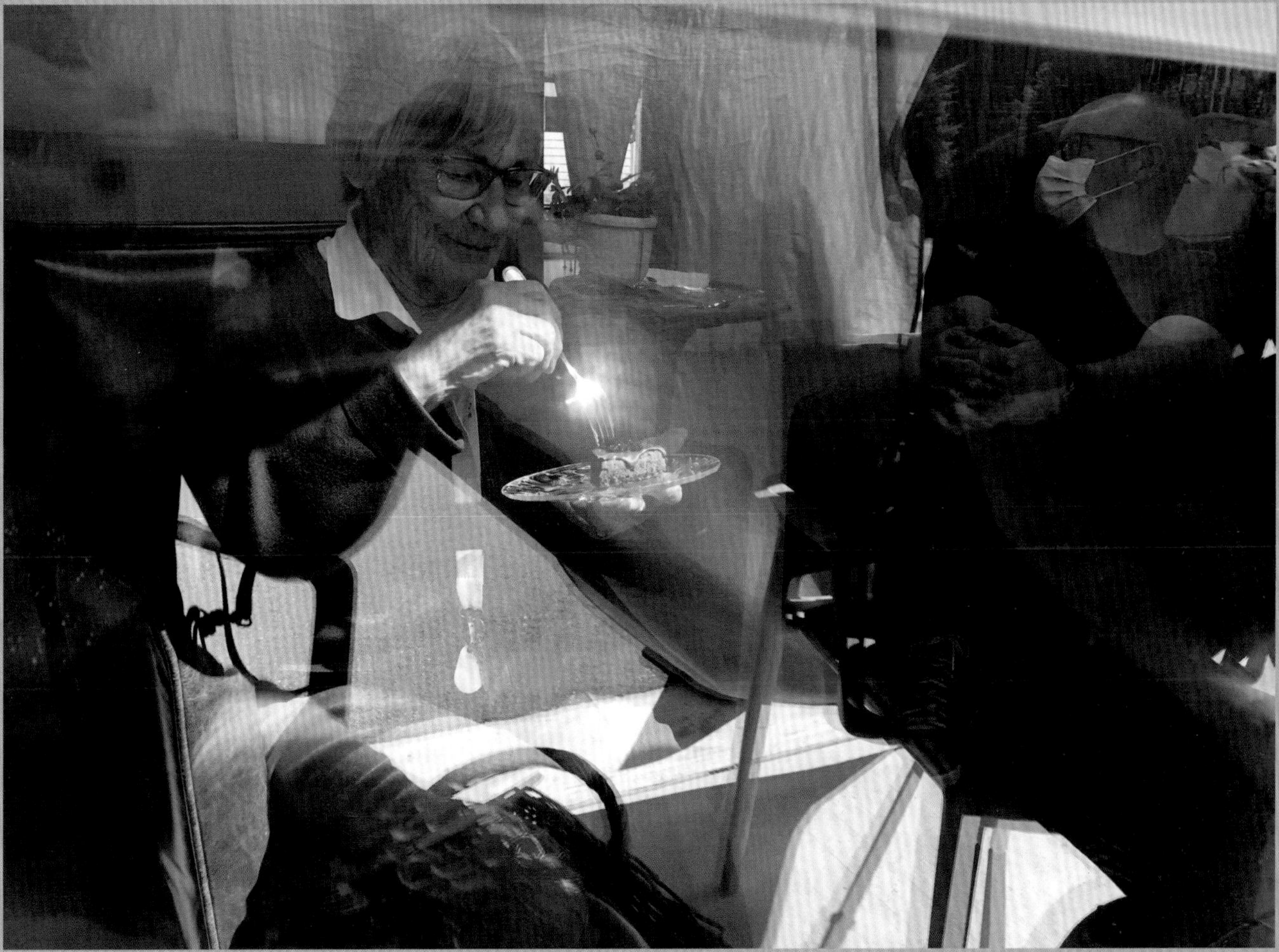

CHRISTINE LEVICZKY RIEK, *Care home birthday* |

08 13

My husband's mother is in a dementia care home. It was her 89th birthday. This was our family party. Our temperatures were normal. Still, I don't know what I'm seeing. Unsure what I'm hearing. I bake the sachertorte, one of her favorites. My husband took two slices into the visiting room. My daughter and I are in the parking lot with our slices. We sit under a tarp on hard chairs placed outside the visiting room window. There's no opening. Can you communicate through a closed window? We try singing Happy Birthday through our phones. Can anyone hear it? It's hot. The blue tarp flaps in the breeze. Light shadow, reflections all blinding. My daughter tries to show photos on her phone by holding it against the glass. The sun dances off a fork. 30 scheduled minutes and it's over. When you read this, I'll still be waiting for the heartbreak to pass, trying to find some meaning. If you ask me how my visit was, I'll tell you it was okay because I'm learning how to lie. BRITISH COLUMBIA, CANADA

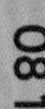

VALERIA FERRARO, An old lady seen crossing the street in Catanzaro Lido. Poor sanitary conditions and lack of services increase concerns for elders' health. ITALY

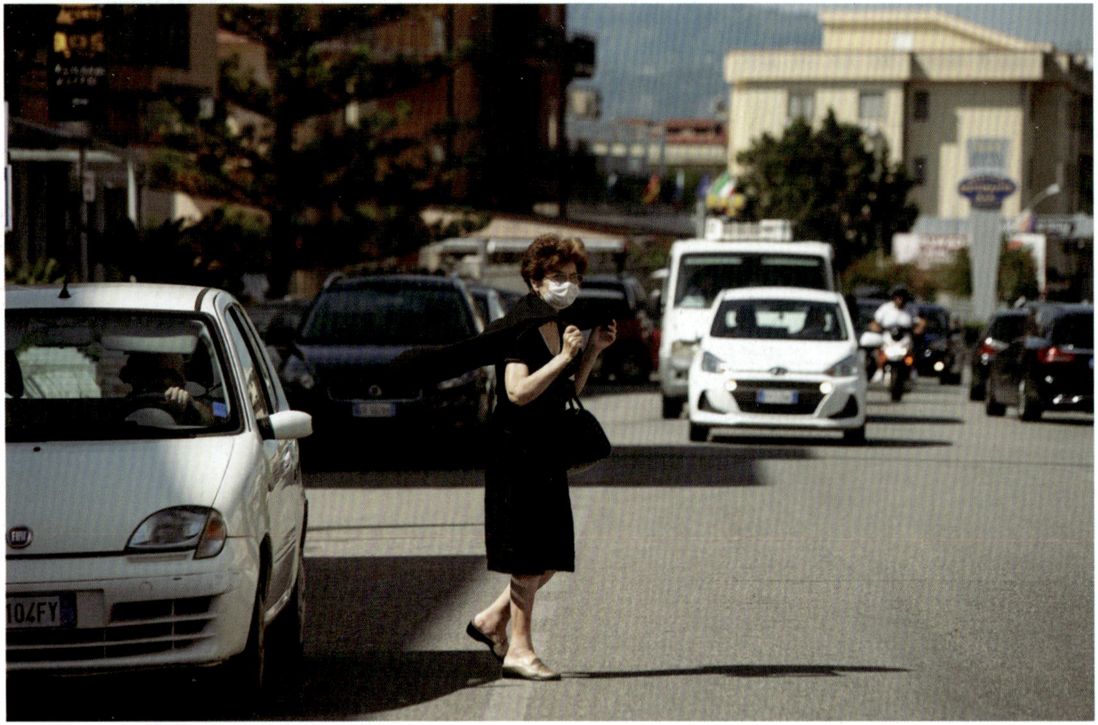

08 14

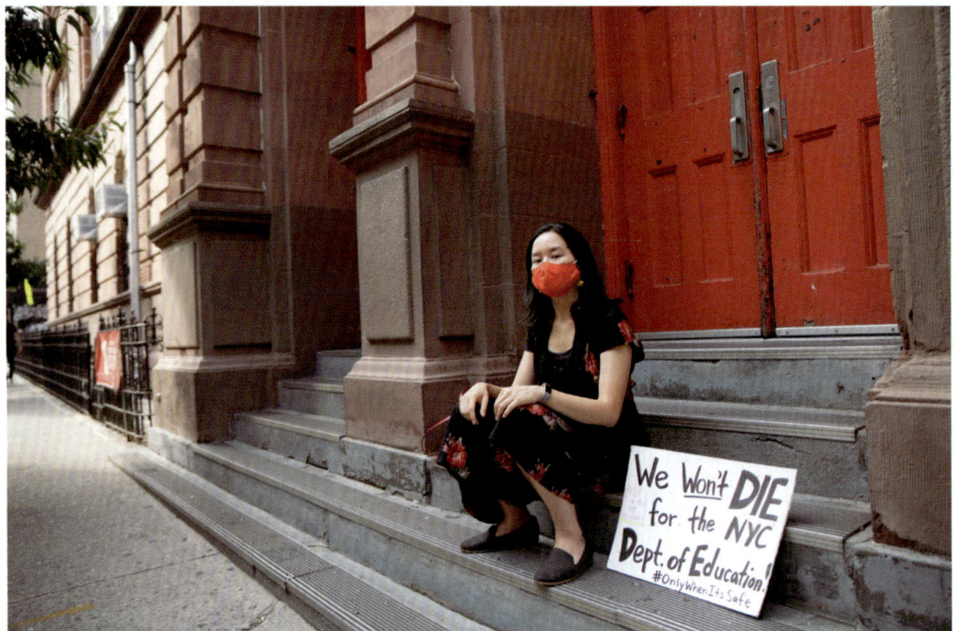

MARJ KLEINMAN, Annie Tan, a teacher in Chinatown, is an active voice against returning to unsafe school conditions in the largest school system in the country. NEW YORK, NY, USA

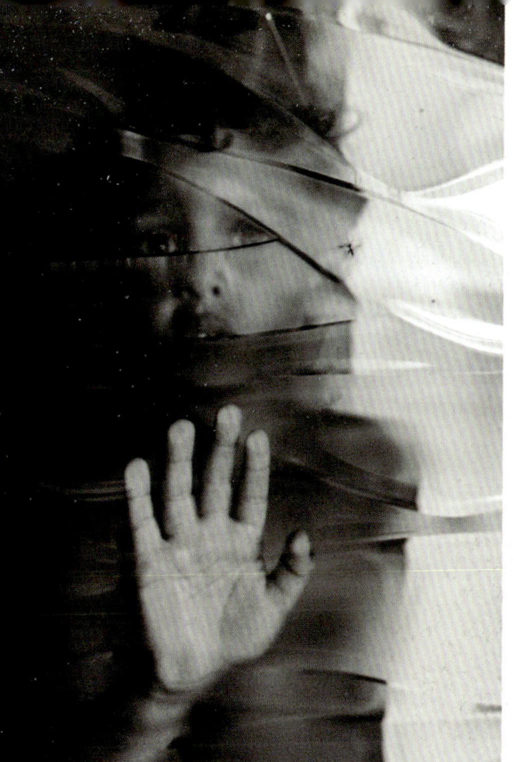

JONĖ REED, *In Limbo* | A touch-and-go visit to the grandparents when there was a short window of provisional travel between the UK and Lithuania with a big risk of being stuck there. LITHUANIA

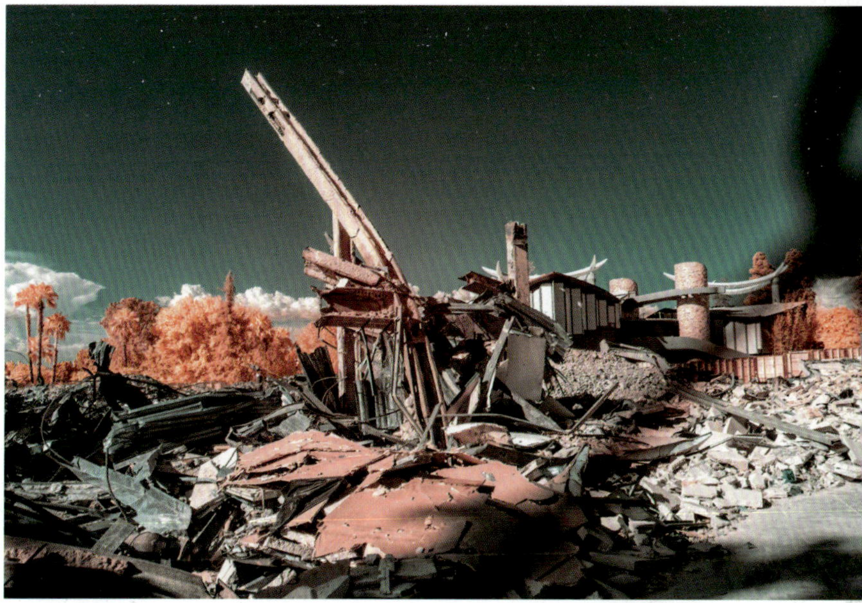

KAREN CONSTINE, *COVID LA, Day 149* | From the series, "(Un)real Landscapes." The stay-at-home order continues, as does the demolition of Los Angeles County Museum of Art's buildings, altering the landscape in Miracle Mile. LOS ANGELES, CA, USA

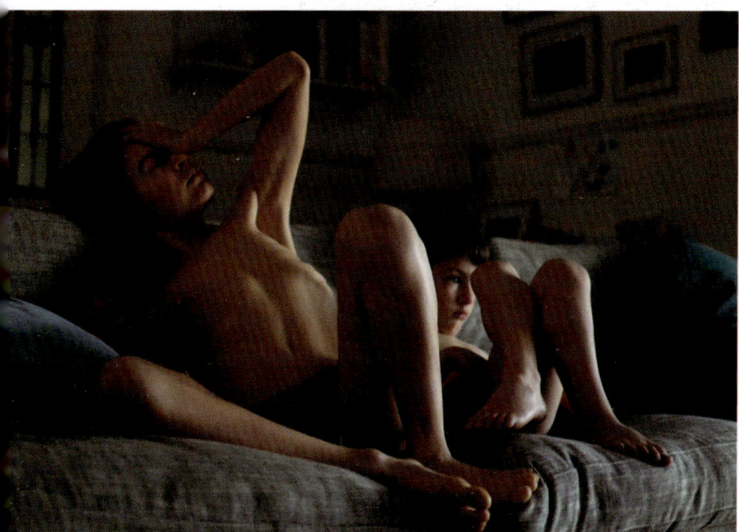

JILL VELINOS, *Sunday Morning, Melbourne* | Despite Stage 4 restrictions, Sunday morning still has the same slow feeling it did before COVID-19. AUSTRALIA

RONG JIANG, A sign calling for building a beloved community in the Petworth neighborhood. WASHINGTON, DC, USA

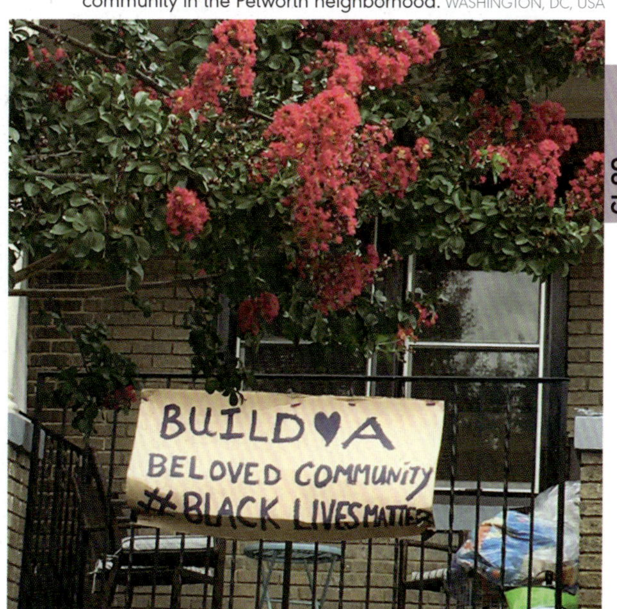

HERSLEY-VEN CASERO, *Plastic Crown* |

A woman walks towards the Dumaguete City Sunday market one morning with her basket in hand and adorned with a colorful face shield. PHILIPPINES

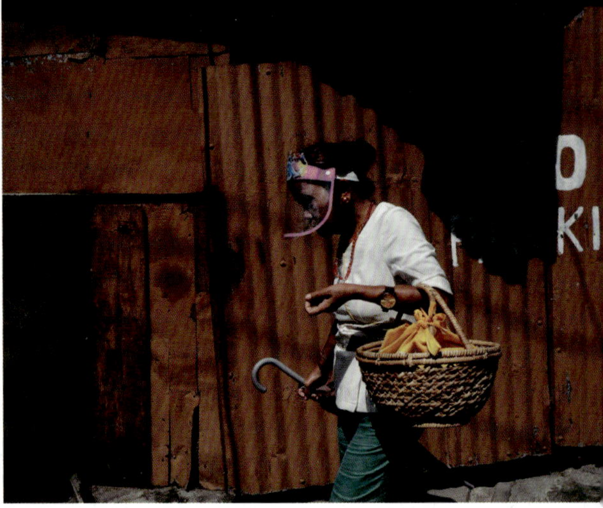

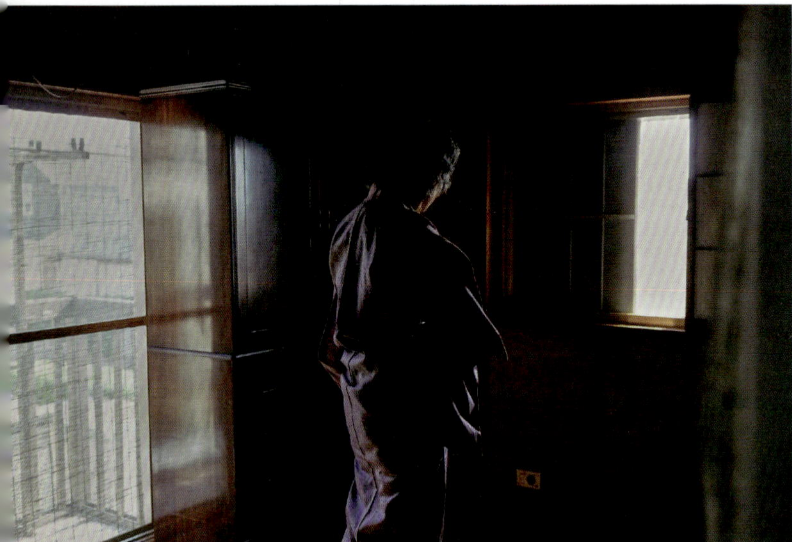

KAI YOKOYAMA, My mother doesn't go out, but she wears the kimono of her dead mother at home. SAKURA, CHIBA, JAPAN

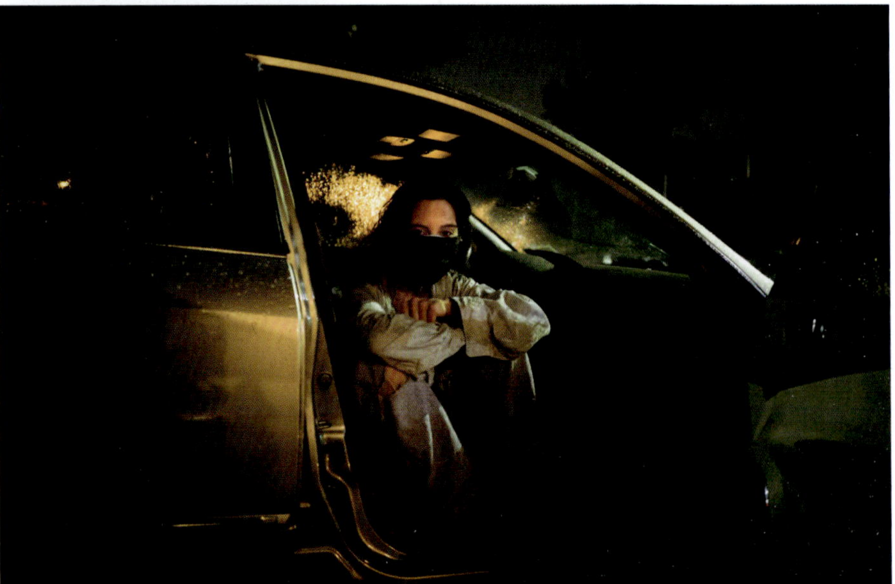

SUAN LIN, *Red Hook Jam* |

Poet NoLand takes shelter from the rain during an outdoor music jam. BROOKLYN, NY, USA

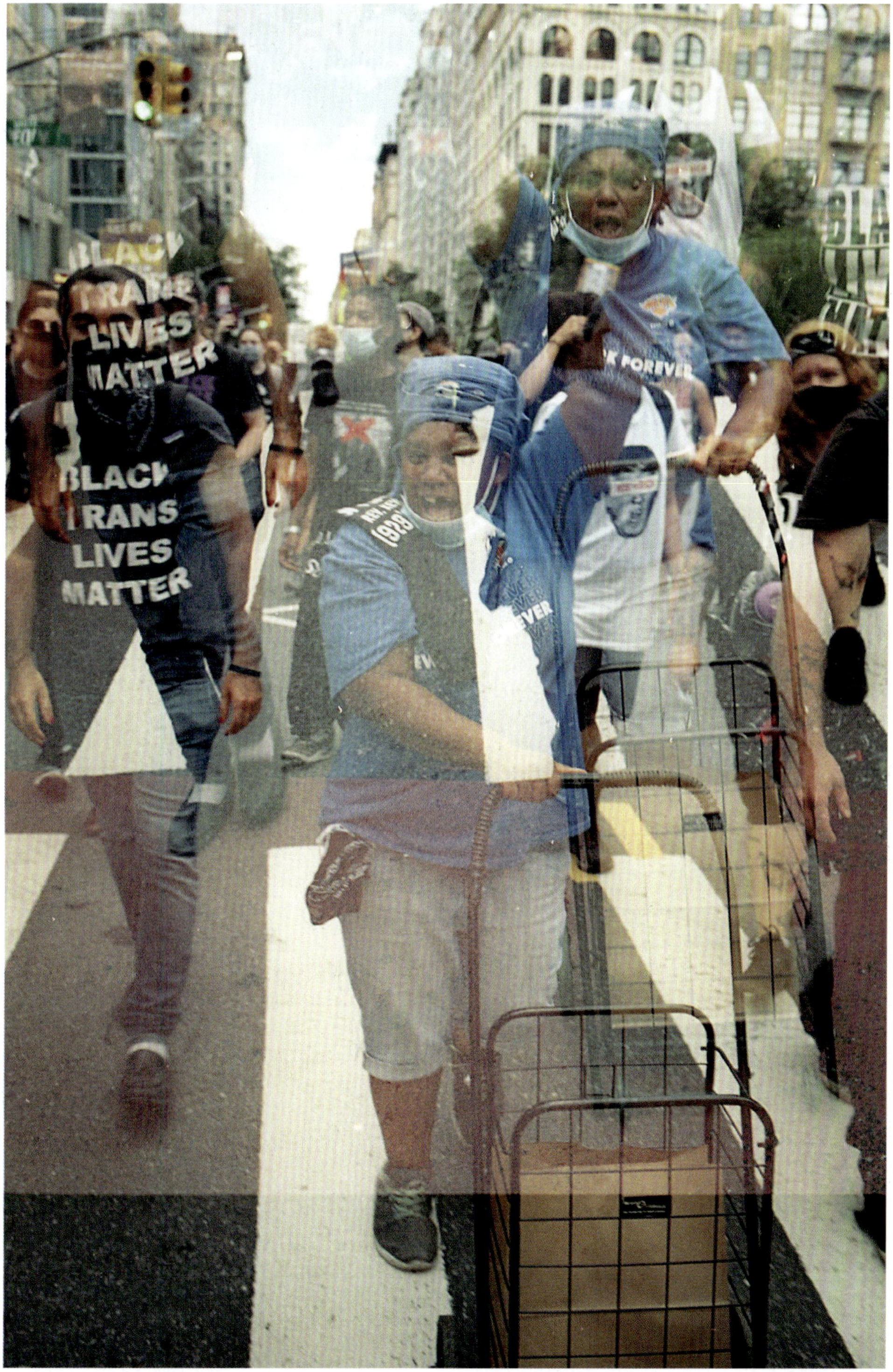

08 17

Accidental double exposure of a Black Lives Matter march in honor of John Lewis.
NEW YORK, NY, USA

BEN CHERTOFF,

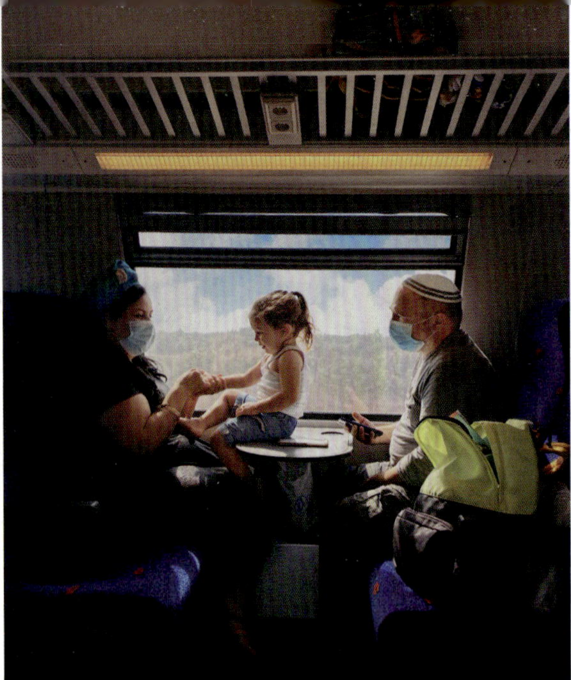

DINA ALFASI, Family Moments. HAIFA, ISRAEL

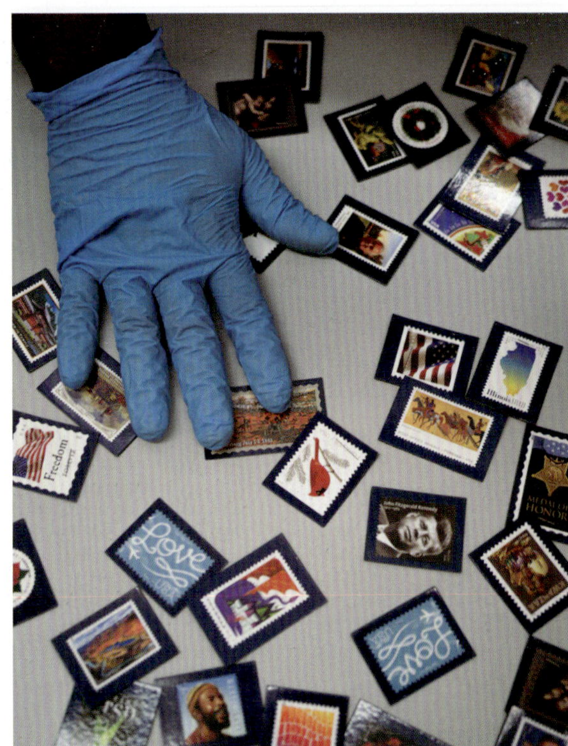

JOANNA KNUTSEN, Essential Service. WOODACRE, CA, USA

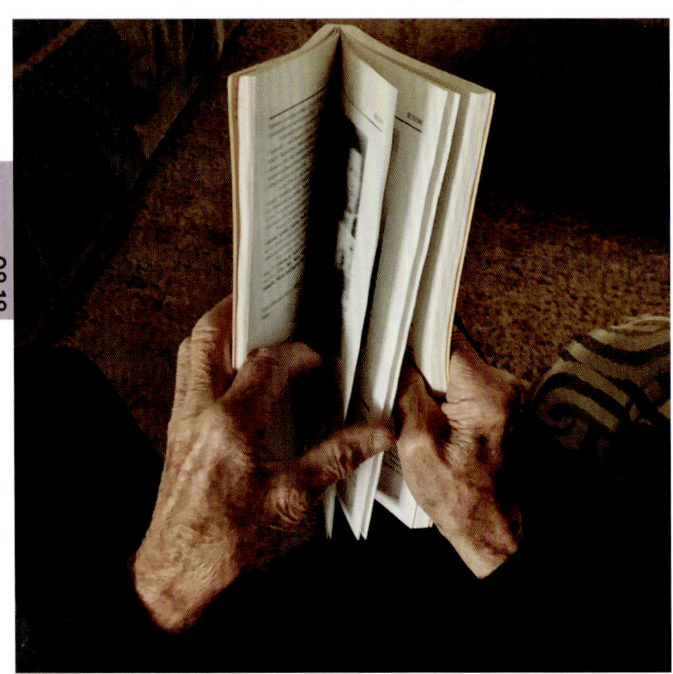

LIZ PEROBELLI, *The Memory Box, Itatiba, São Paulo |*
My family came from Verona, Italy to Brazil, and this is my grandfather reading the history of Italian immigration in the small town where I was born. BRAZIL

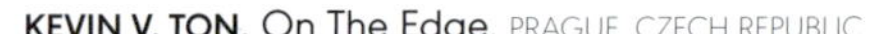

KEVIN V. TON, On The Edge. PRAGUE, CZECH REPUBLIC

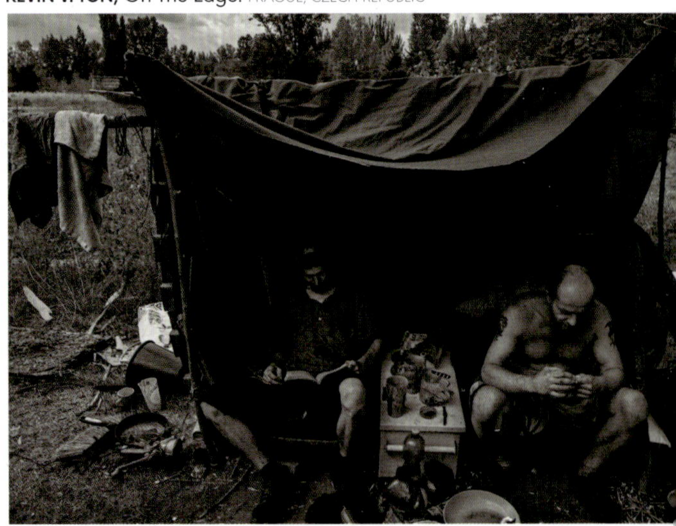

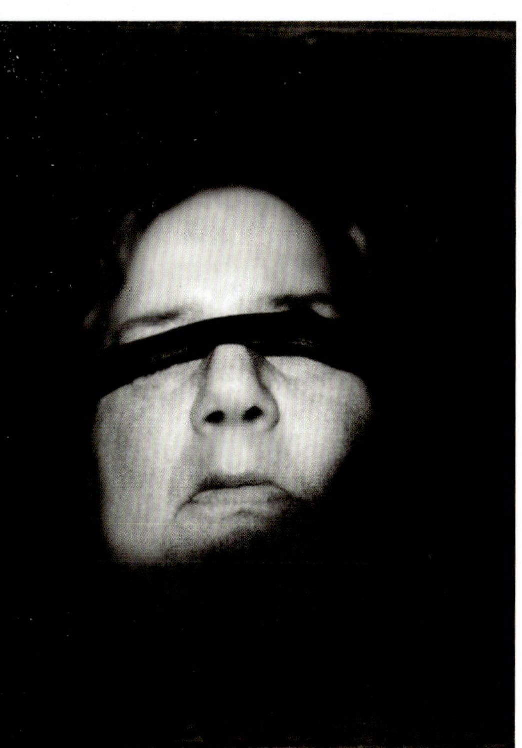

YUUKI TOYOSHIMA, *Money or Life* | The Japanese government is prioritizing the economy over the health of the people. SHINJUKU, JAPAN

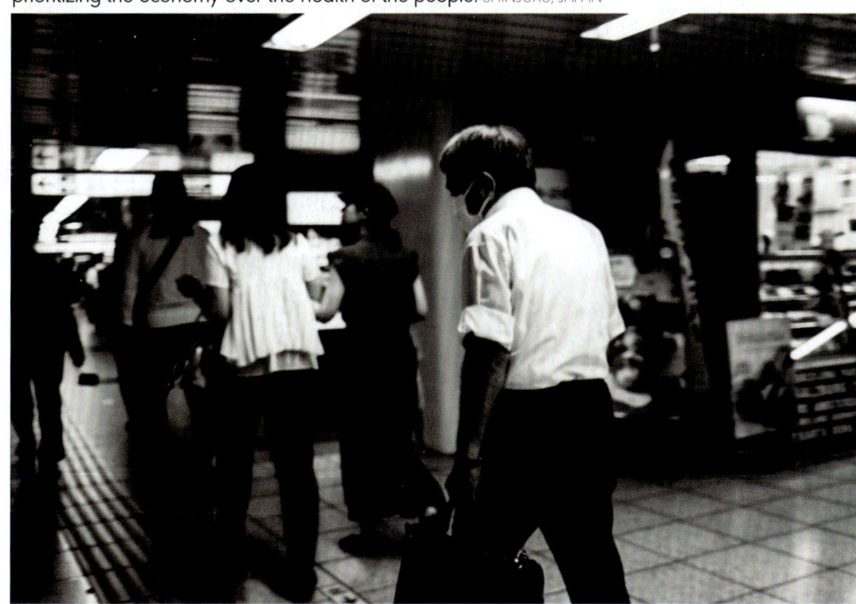

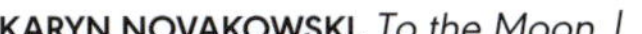

DIANE FENSTER, COVID-19.38. PACIFICA, CA, USA

KARYN NOVAKOWSKI, *To the Moon* | Using plastic toys and a vintage sheet, four-year-old Fennec wears an astronaut helmet while building a rocket ship in his backyard. ARLINGTON, MA, USA

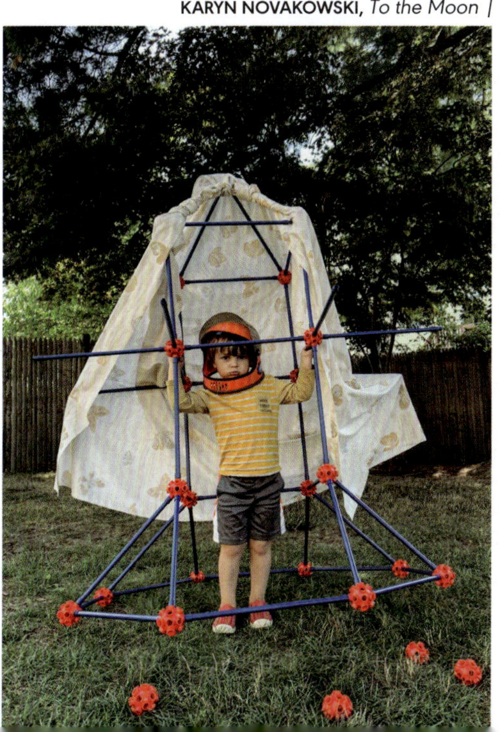

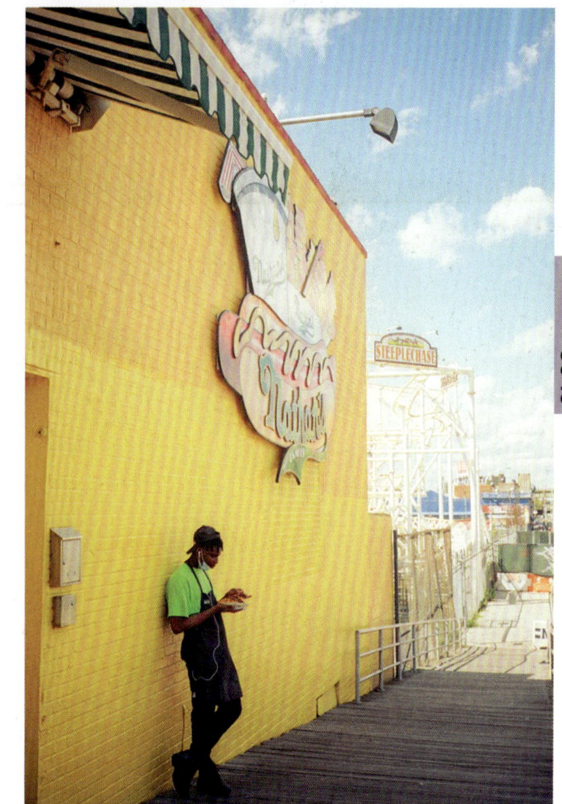

HAITAO ZENG, A guy taking a lunch break in Coney Island. BROOKLYN, NY, USA

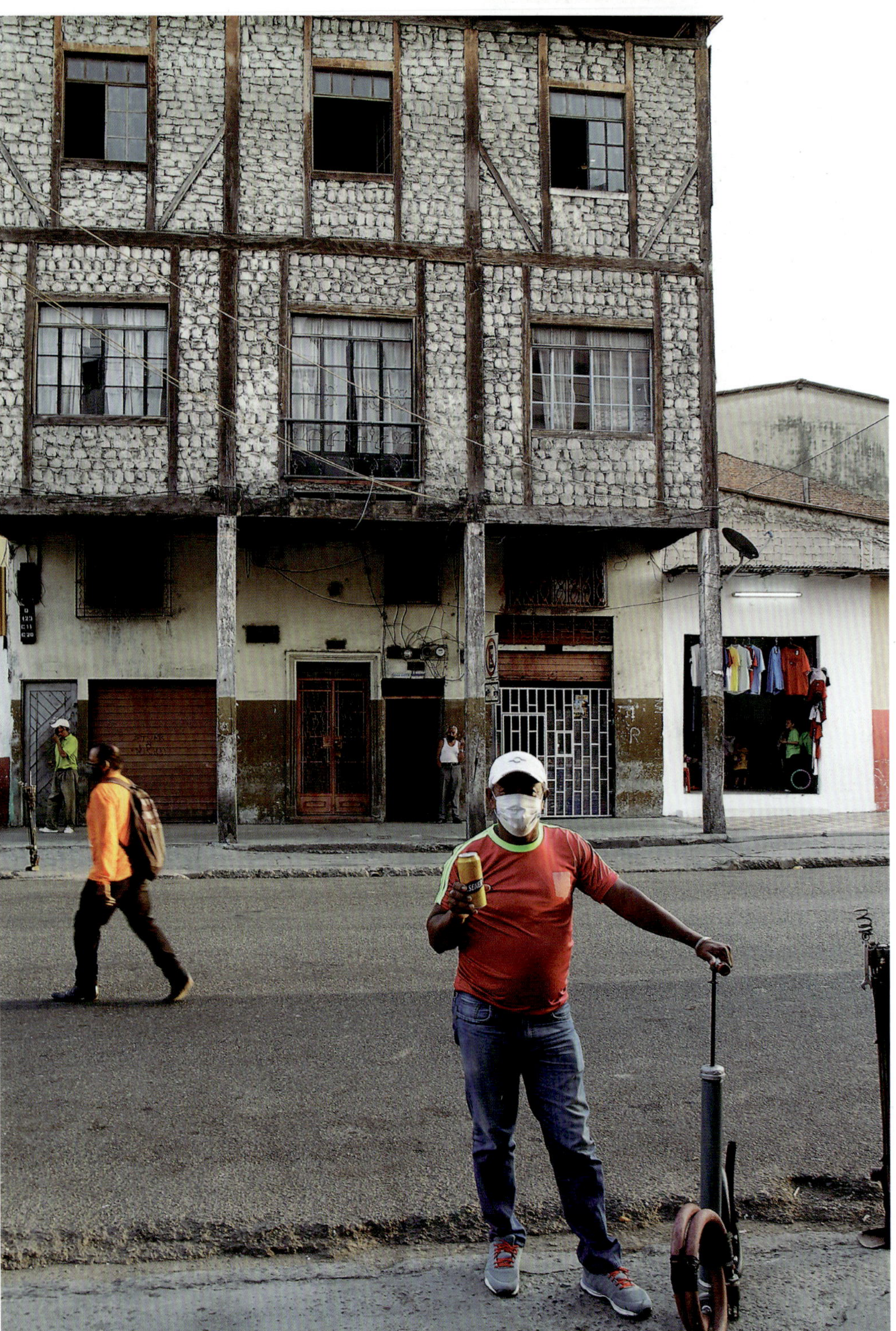

SANTIAGO POZA, *The Plumber* | Rodolfo's life has changed since the outbreak. Now he has just four busy days per week. Self-employment makes him feel free. GUAYAQUIL, GUAYAS, ECUADOR

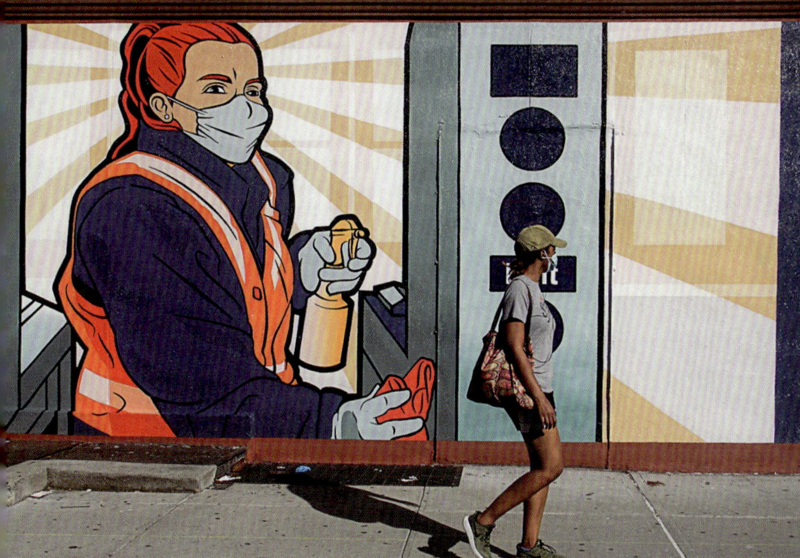

NURIA MENDOZA,
Thank you, essential workers.
HARLEM. NEW YORK, NY, USA

KAT BAWDEN, *Haircut* | This self-portrait is from my ongoing series, "Perceptual Isolation," which visualizes my spiral of anxiety, depression, and insomnia during quarantine. LOS ANGELES, CA, USA

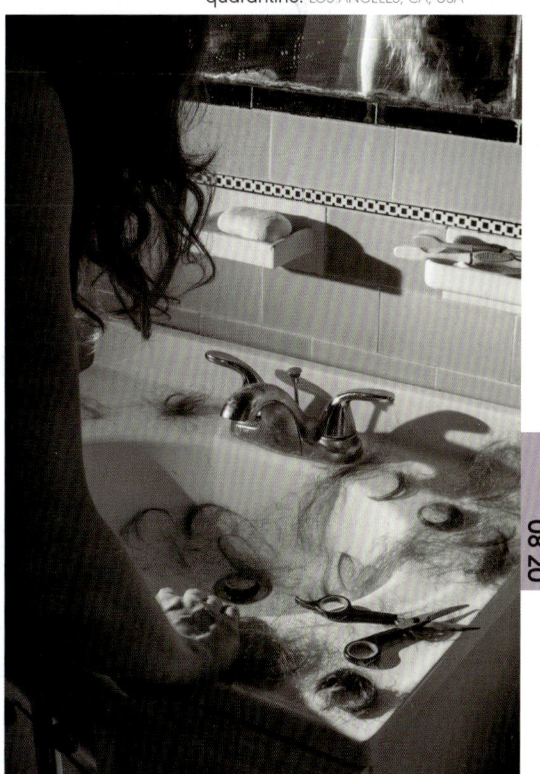

BRUCE SAILLE, *God's Army* | Black Lives Matter protestors confront a right wing religious group at the beginning of the March on the Democratic National Convention. MILWAUKEE, WI, USA

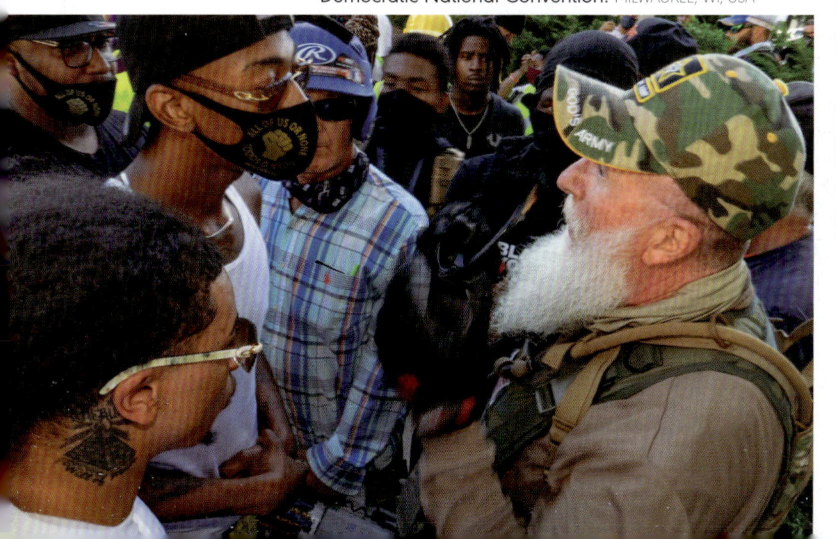

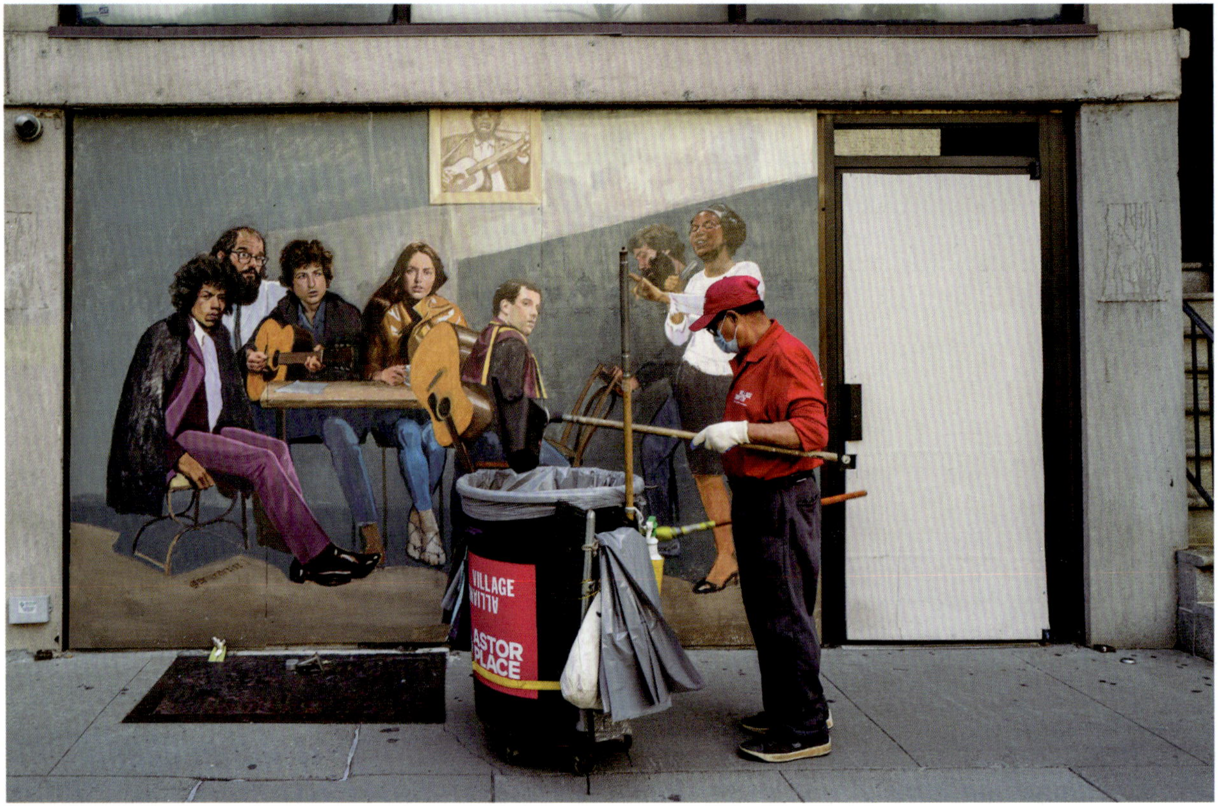

ANNE ROSEN, Greenwich Village Then and Now. NEW YORK, NY, USA

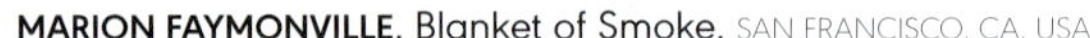

MARION FAYMONVILLE, Blanket of Smoke. SAN FRANCISCO, CA, USA

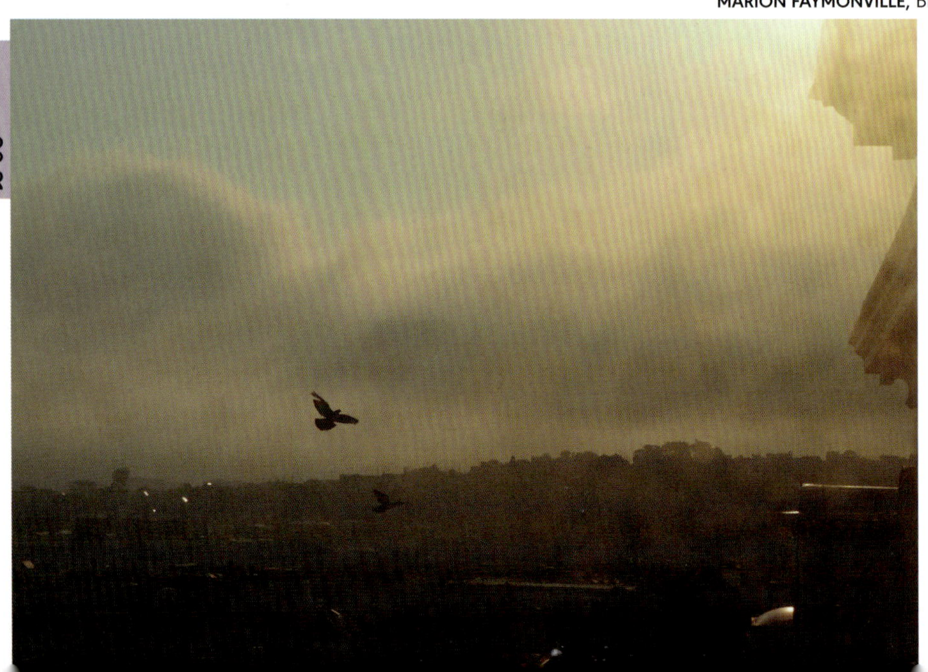

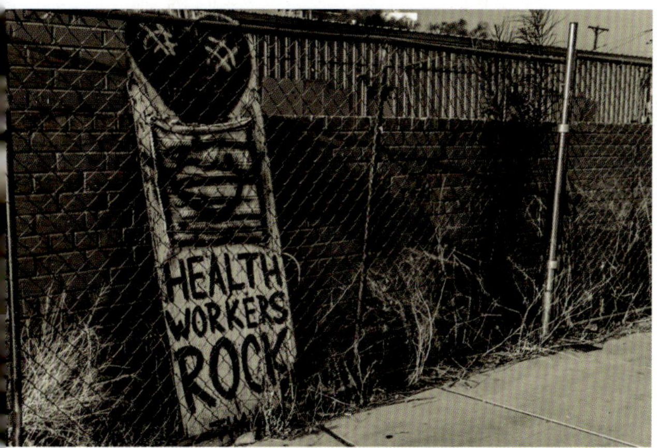

LESLIE J. YERMAN, *Health Workers Rock |* Seen on my walks through the downtown area of Tucson to document the effects of COVID-19. AZ, USA

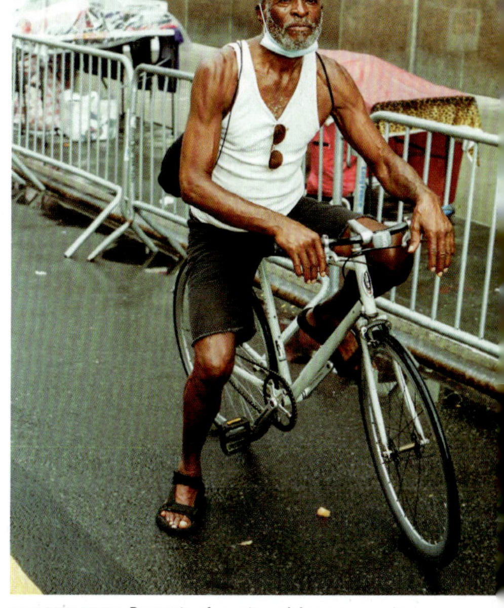

ALASSANE SY, Portrait of a wise elder supporting the Black Lives Movement. BROOKLYN, NY, USA

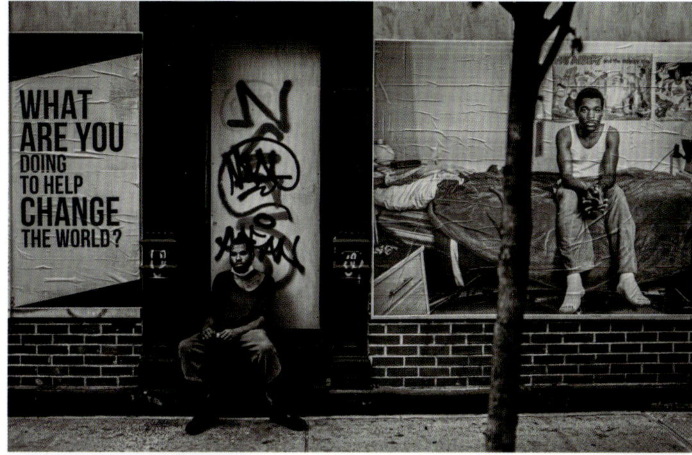

LEVENT KANIK, *Change |* It's been a long, a long time coming but I know a change gonna come, oh yes it will. NEW YORK, NY, USA

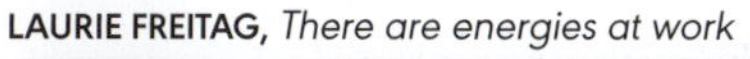

LAURIE FREITAG, *There are energies at work |* Every night I look out of my bedroom window to where a five-story condo was supposed to stand. COVID-19 stopped construction so every night I get the view of a lifetime. LOS ANGELES, CA, USA

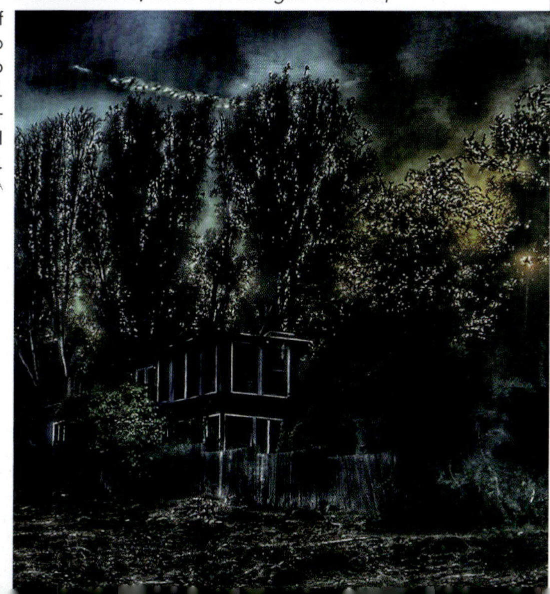

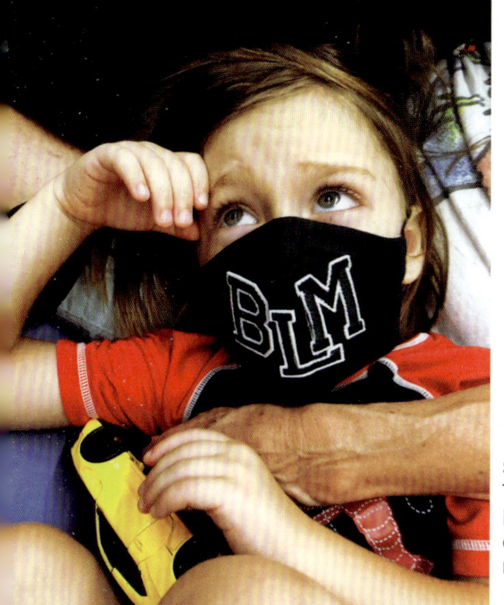

SAUL ROBBINS, Theodore on the N-Train during COVID-19. NEW YORK, NY, USA

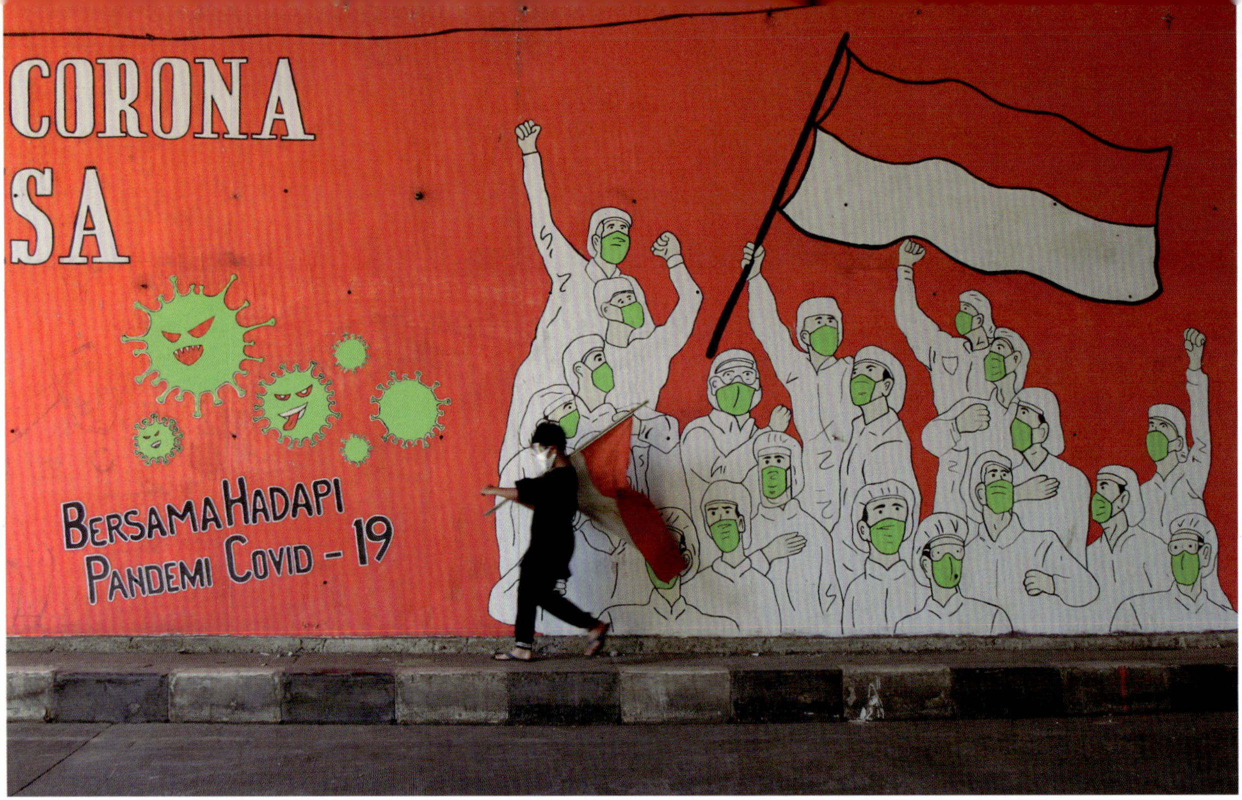

KUNCORO WIDYO RUMPOKO, *Facing the COVID-19 Pandemic Together* |

A boy wearing a mask and face shield runs with a red and white flag in front of the murals raising awareness of the pandemic in the area under the Jakarta Outer Ring Road Toll Road. EAST JAKARTA, INDONESIA

08 23

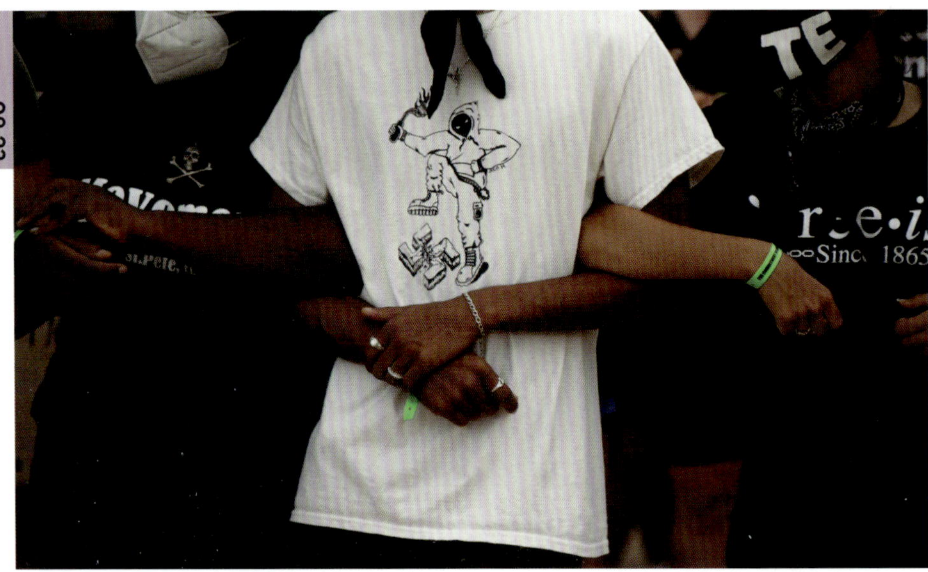

JARRETT ROBERTSON, *We Protect Us* |

A group of frontliners at a Black Lives Matter protest link arms before police rush them. WASHINGTON, DC, USA

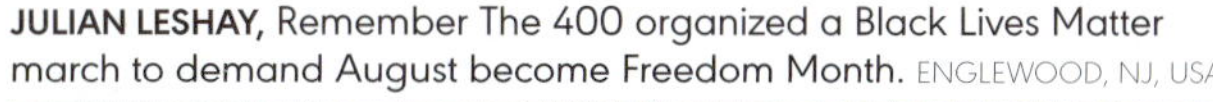

JULIAN LESHAY, Remember The 400 organized a Black Lives Matter march to demand August become Freedom Month. ENGLEWOOD, NJ, USA

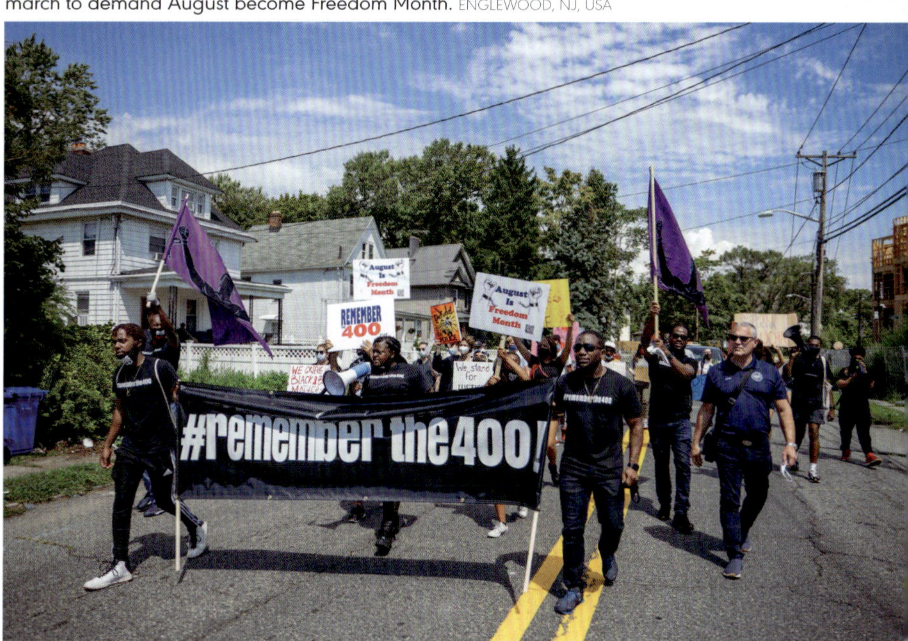

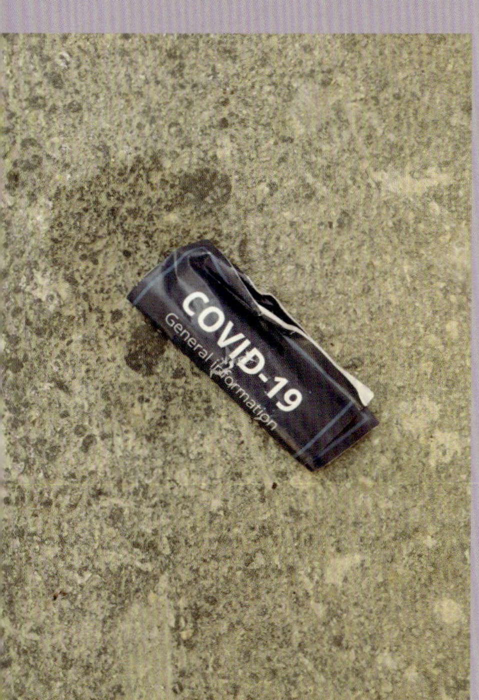

GIOLA CASSAR, *Trashing COVID-19* | The discarded leaflet in the middle of the road reminded me of the excess waste that has been created due to the coronavirus. According to an article published by the United Nations on the on July 27th, around 75% of the coronavirus plastic alone would likely end up in our landfills and seas. However, one doesn't need to go as far to see the waste here in Malta. Masks and other waste products can be found in the middle of the street and sometimes even in trees. This image in particular, is a glimpse into the waste being created on the daily basis around the world. QRENDI, MALTA

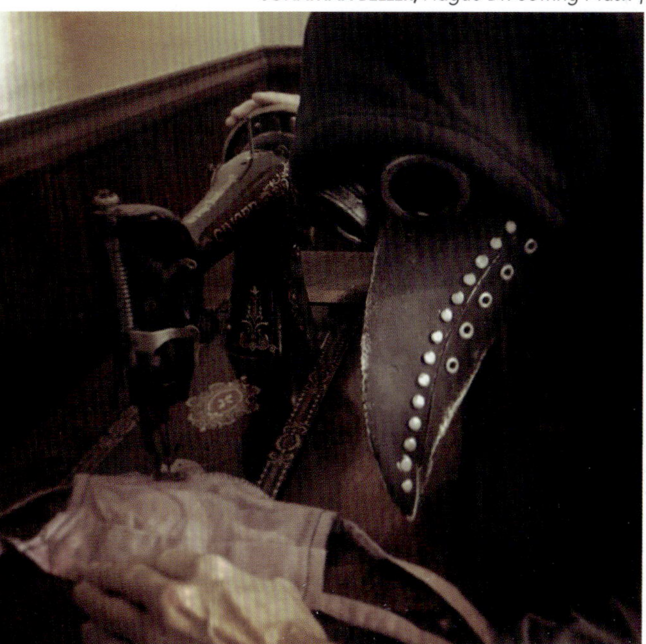

JONATHAN BELLER, *Plague Dr. Sewing Mask* | I got this mask at the beginning of the shutdown and it has helped with depression by allowing creativity during these strange, dark, and crazy times. PROVIDENCE, RI, USA

DESTINY MATA, *March Against Billionaire Landlords* |

Demanding rent cancelation and a stop to the upcoming wave of evictions that was ignited by the pandemic.

NEW YORK PUBLIC LIBRARY, STEPHEN A. SCHWARZMAN BUILDING, NEW YORK, NY, USA

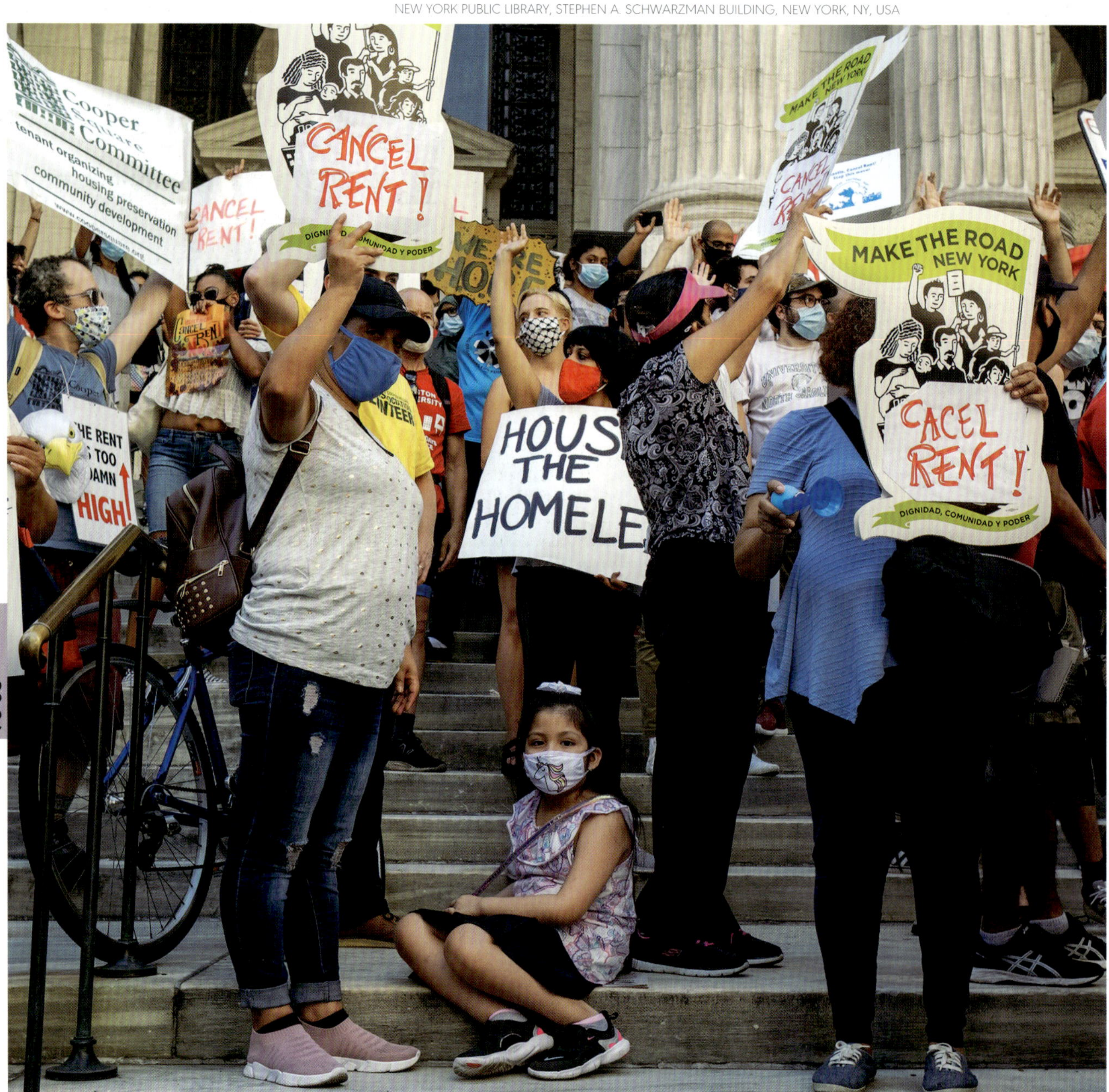

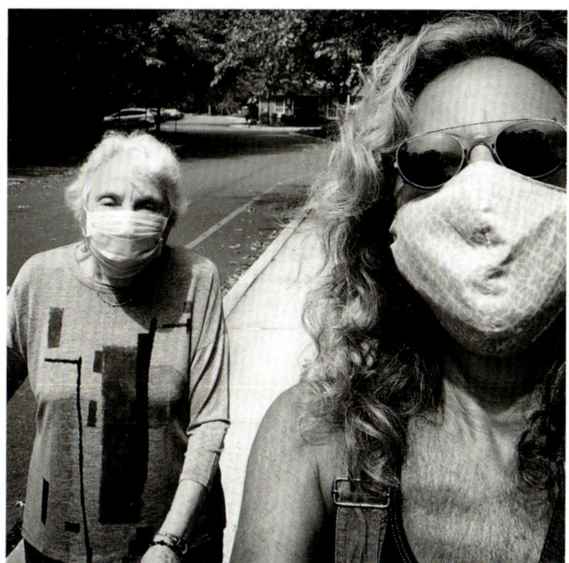

KAREN MARSHALL, *Masked Up Outside Visit With My Mom* | All things considered, we are all doing alright. Just can't wait for the independent living facility where she lives to finally let family visit inside! TEANECK, NJ , USA

CHRISTINA SANTUCCI, *Night Walk in Astoria, Queens* | Each sundown brings a reprieve from the summer heat and a sense of calm amid the chaos. NY, USA

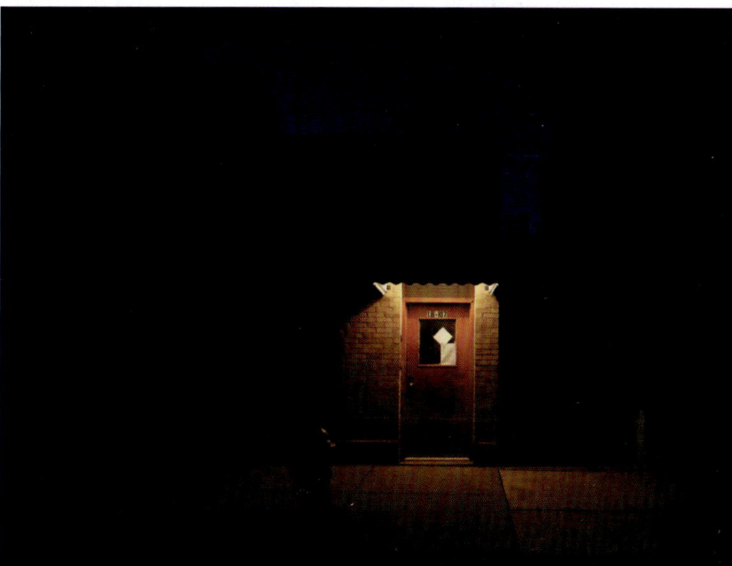

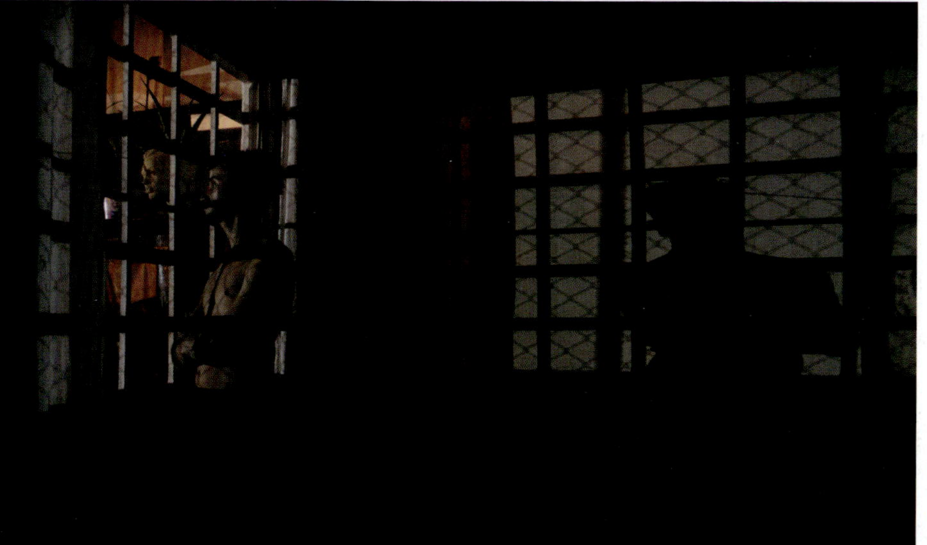

WALTER HURTADO, *Quarantined with Lights and Shadows* | My boyfriend during lockdown. We spent five months together at my house until he could return to Brazil. Taken by the window where the lights from the park shine through. Part of a series called "Quarantine Lights." ARRAIJÁN, PANAMA

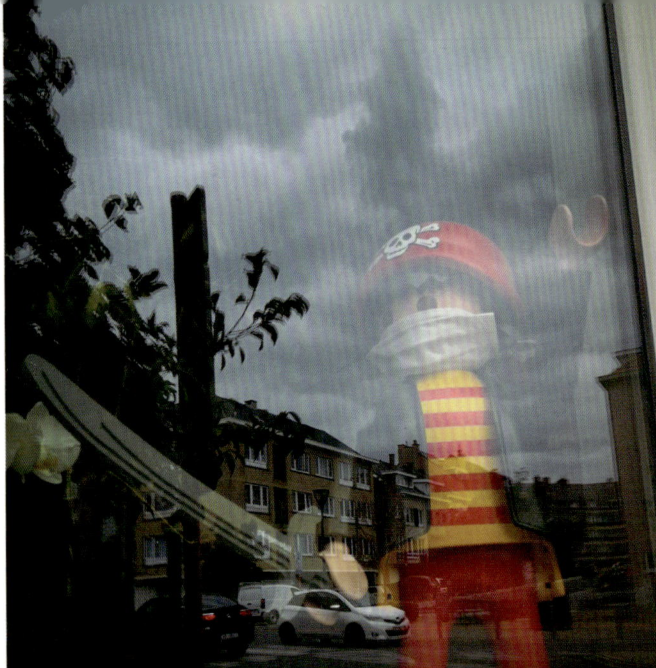

NATHALIE LUGANO, Big Playmobil figure fighting against COVID-19. BRUSSELS, BELGIUM

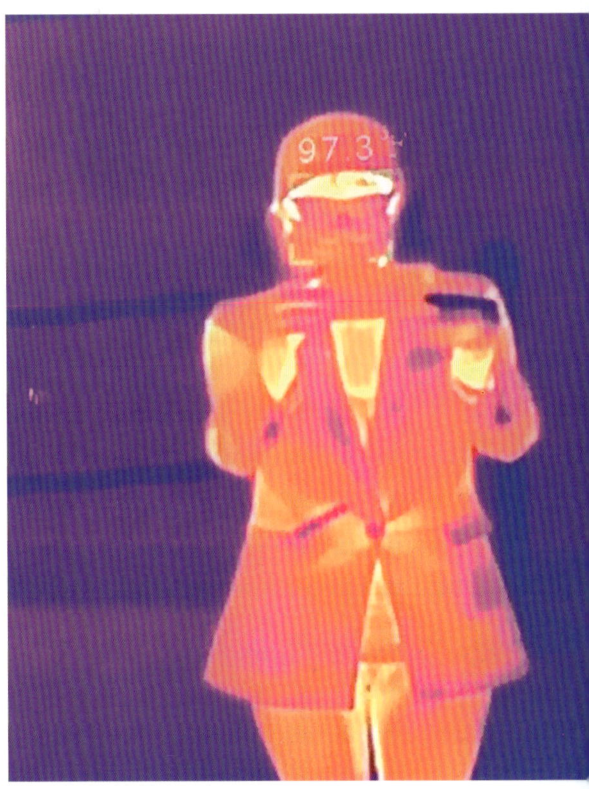

LINDA TROELLER, *97.3F |* Every visitor entering the Hard Rock Casino is automatically temperature screened by an infrared camera. ATLANTIC CITY, NJ, USA

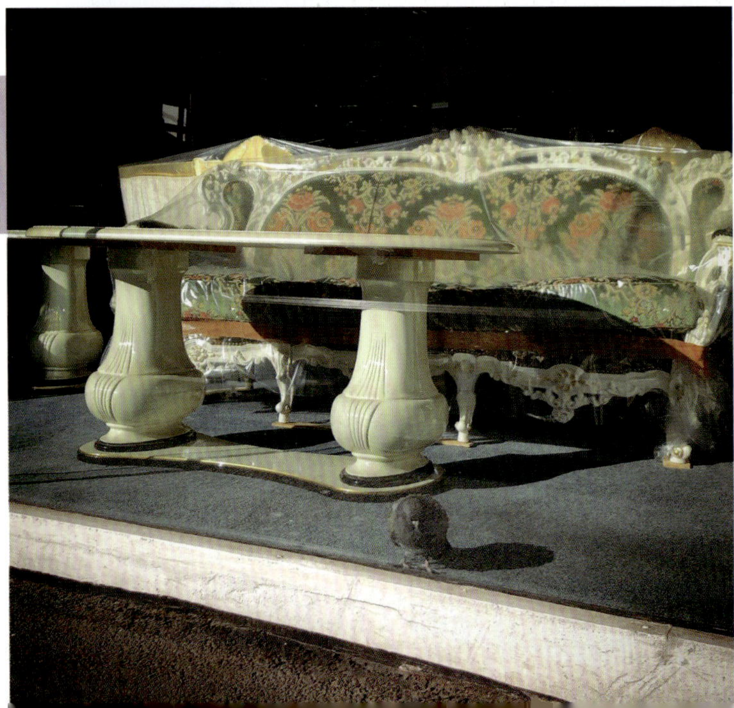

PATRICK POUND, Bird in a store window. MELBOURNE, AUSTRALIA

MOLLY FERRILL,
Covi the rescued white-tailed deer fawn stays inside his rescuer Esmeralda's family house at night to keep safe from passing cars and the neighborhood dogs.
CAMPECHE, MEXICO

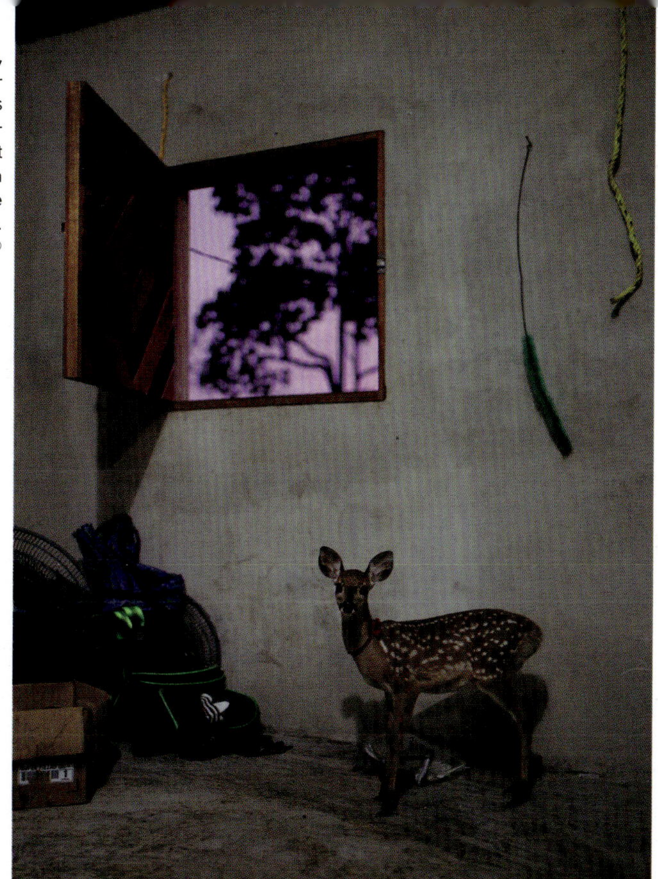

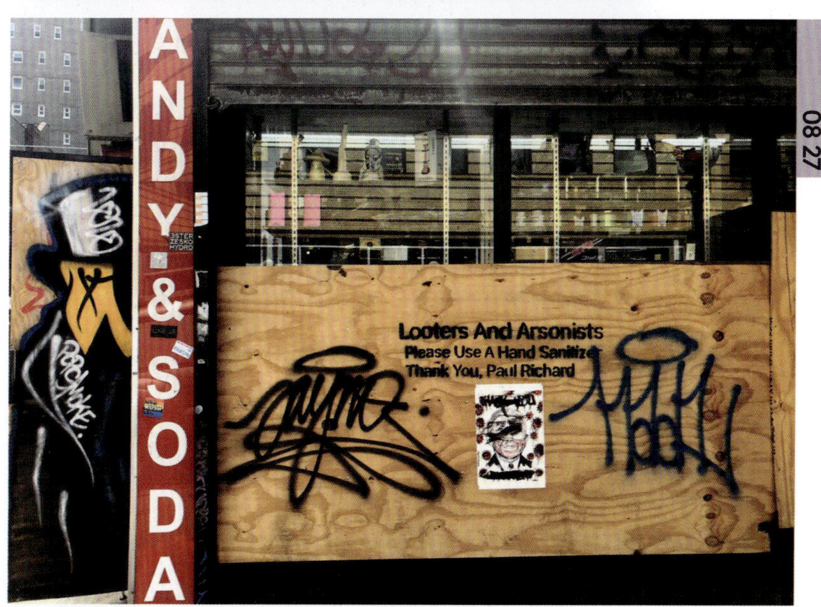

SYNDI PILAR,
Street art on the Village Cigars boarded storefront.
NEW YORK, NY, USA

DAVID ZUNG, Inside the Lincoln Memorial, Reverend Al Sharpton prepares to address the crowd at the 57th Anniversary of Martin Luther King's March on Washington. WASHINGTON, DC, USA

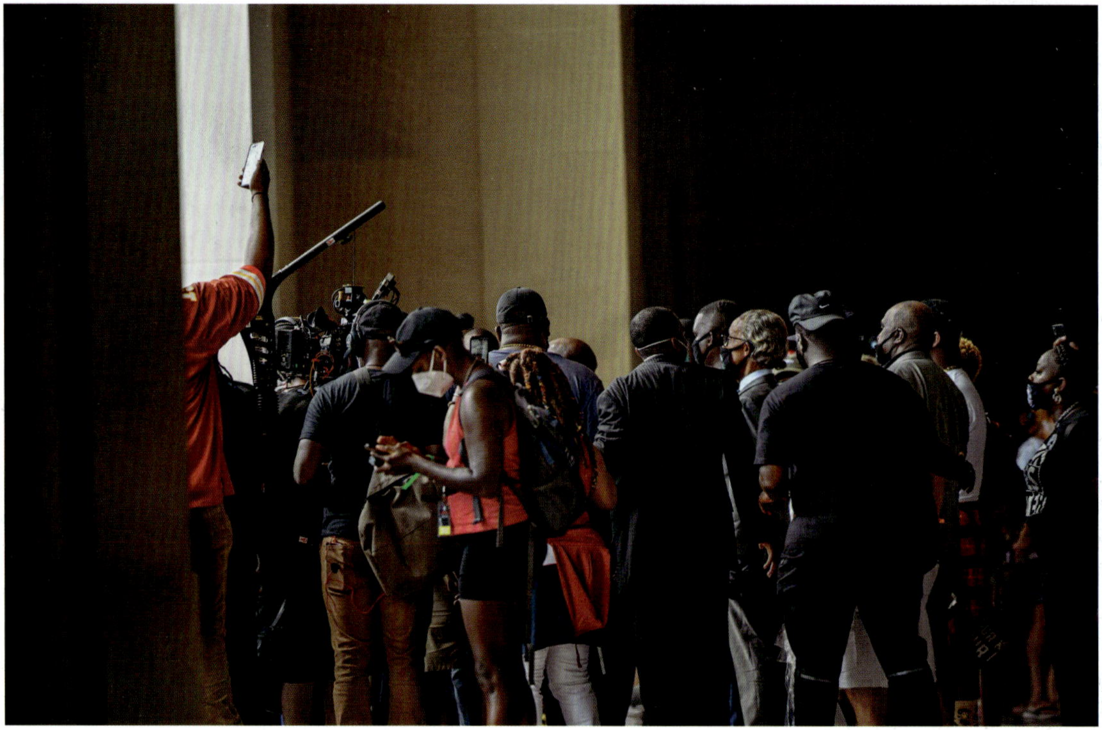

TAKEO KUSHI, *Monuments* |

57th Anniversary of Martin Luther King's March on Washington.
WASHINGTON, DC, USA

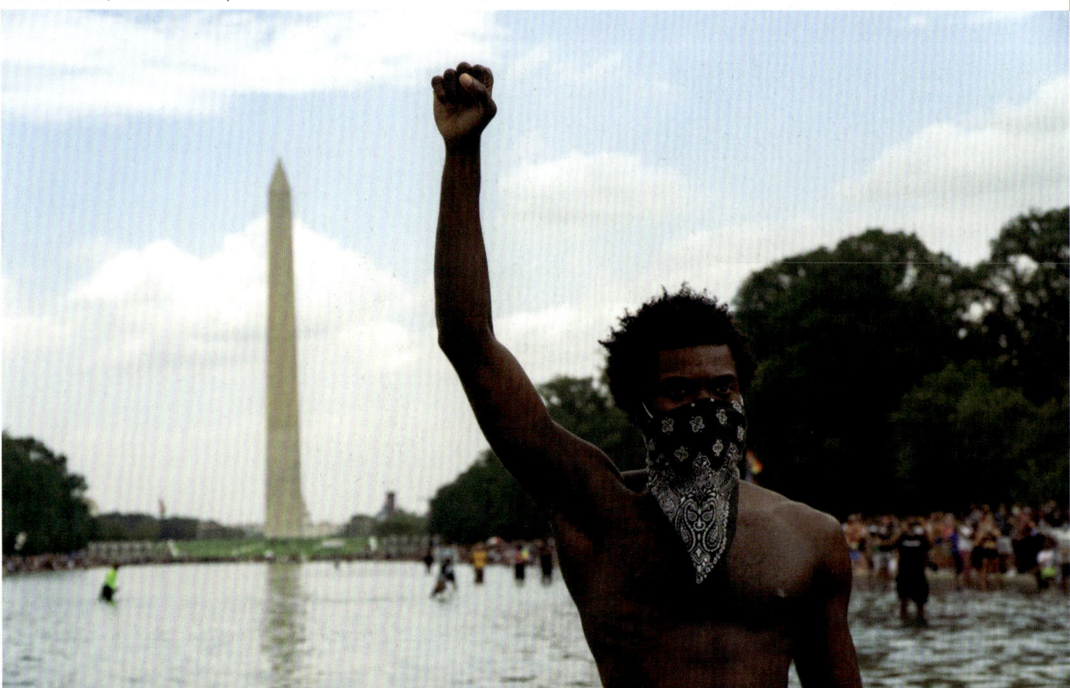

RYAN EDUARD BENAID, Erwin, 28, has been working as an exhumer in a public cemetery in Antipolo City for eight years. PHILIPPINES

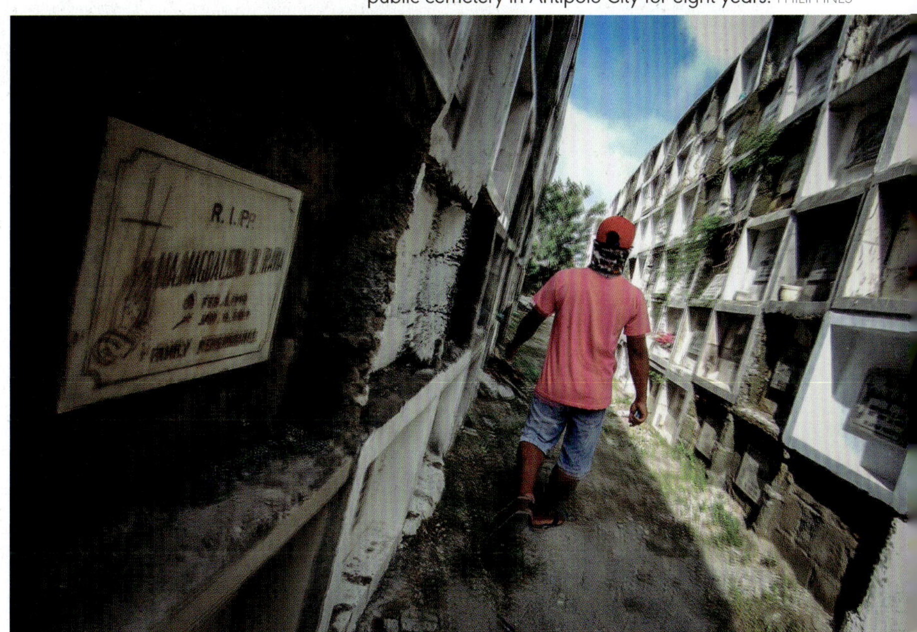

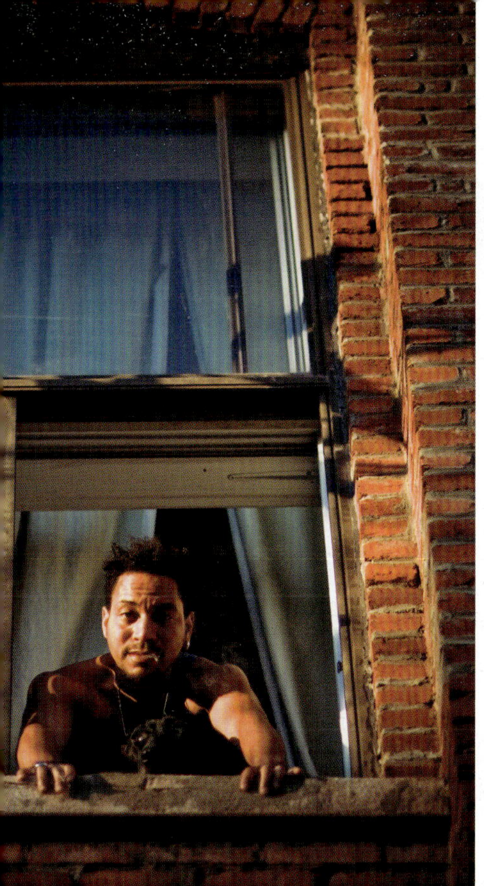

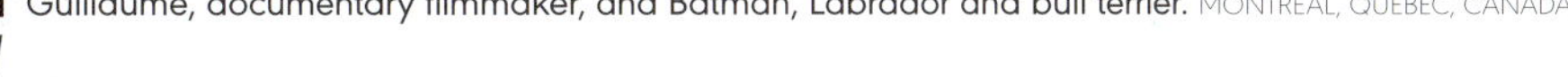

CARLOS VIANI, *Guillaume & Batman* | Guillaume, documentary filmmaker, and Batman, Labrador and bull terrier. MONTREAL, QUEBEC, CANADA

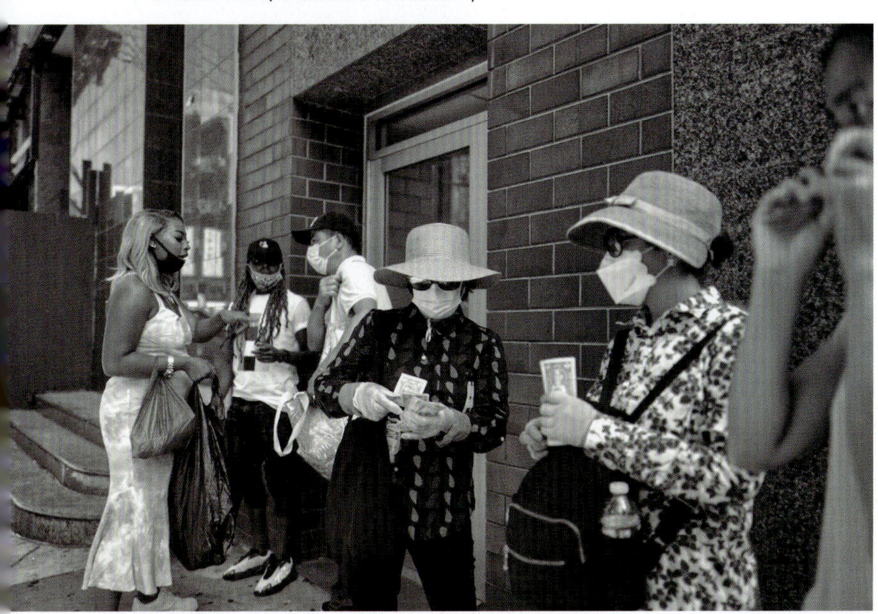

WILLIAM YAN, The Exchange. CHINATOWN, NEW YORK, NY, USA

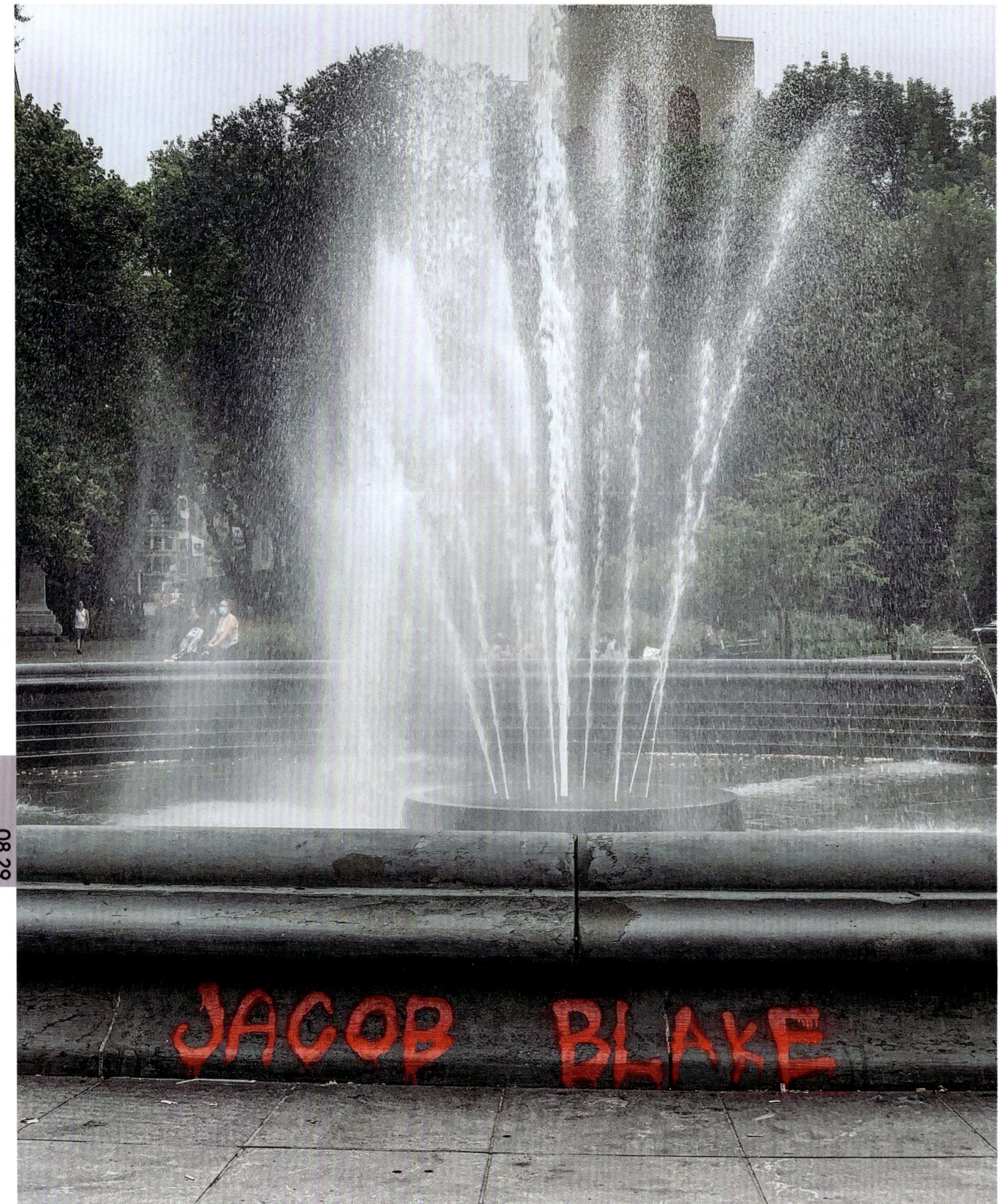

MARJORIE ZIEN, Say His Name. WASHINGTON SQUARE PARK FOUNTAIN, NEW YORK, NY, USA

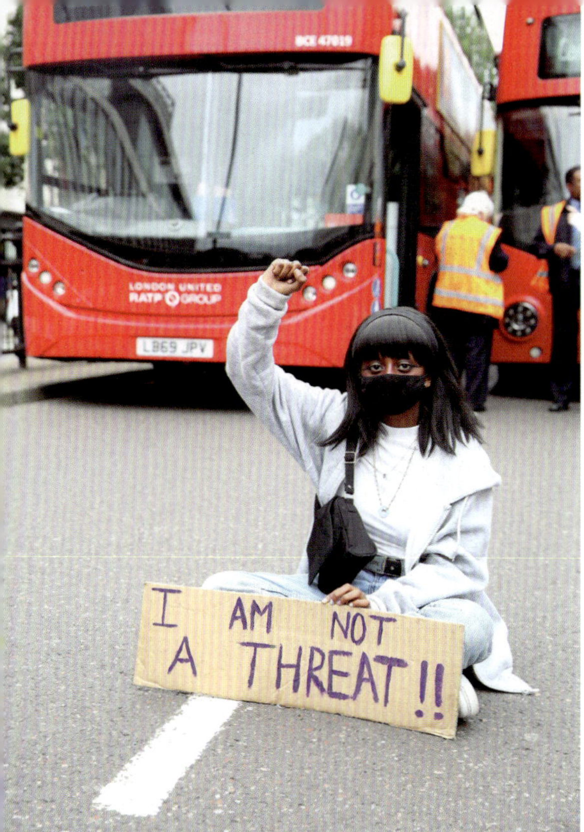

MARCO V. PEREIRA, *Not a Threat!!* |

Portrait of Chiara at the start of the Million People March, one of the many Black Lives Matter protests I documented in London. NOTTING HILL GATE, UNITED KINGDOM

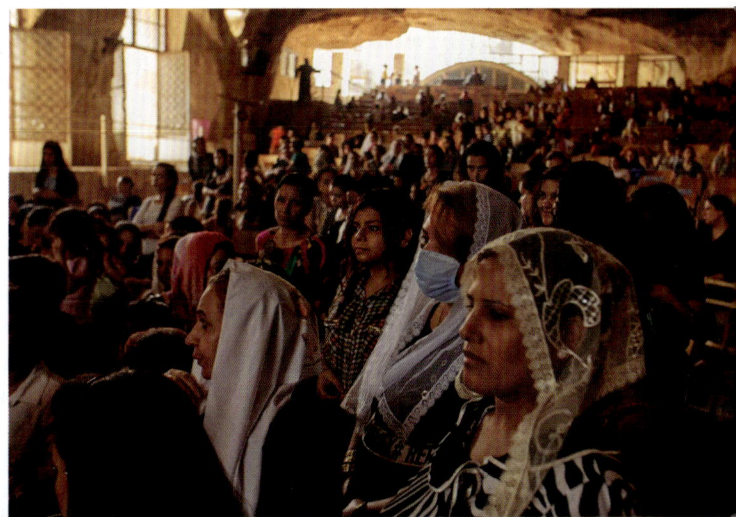

HAMADA ELRASAM,

Most of the Coptic worshipers who attended the Sunday mass in Garbage City after reopening did not wear masks or consider social distancing. CAIRO, EGYPT

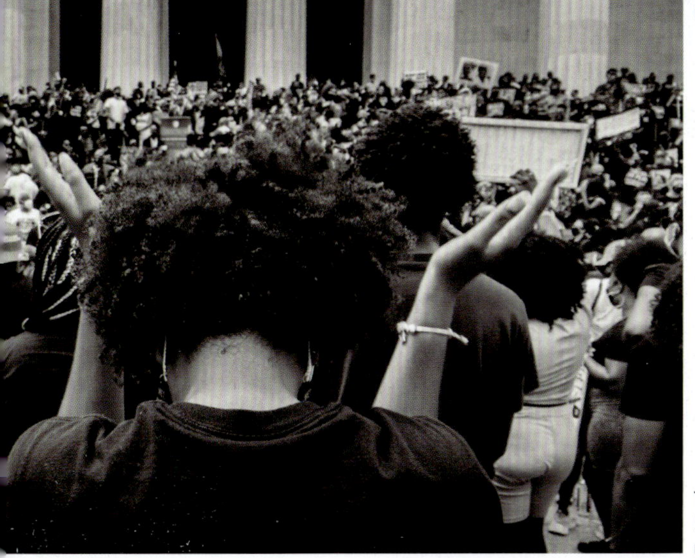

KEVIN MCKEON, *United in Hope* |

Taken at the National Action Network's Commitment March in Washington. The march was put on to demand justice and political change. WASHINGTON, DC, USA

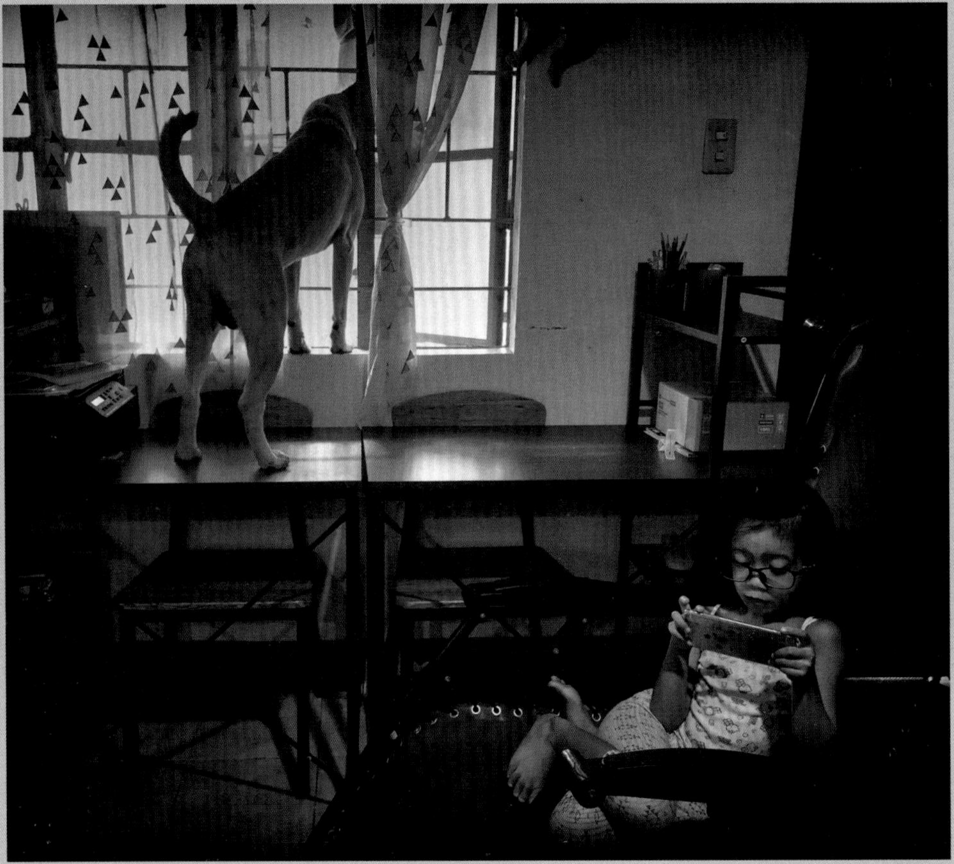

EDWIN TUYAY, Our dog Jiro peeks out of the window as Pearl Jam, my granddaughter, plays with her mobile phone in our living room. The government relaxed the lockdown rules, so people can go to work and earn a living, but the elderly and minors are still not allowed to leave their homes.
PHILIPPINES

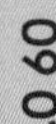

09·20

SEPTEMBER

3_Tracing Apps May Stem CORONAVIRUS Spread Even When Only a Few Use Them: Study *(Reuters)*

24_ More Iowans Now Disapprove than Approve of Gov. Kim Reynolds' Handling of Coronavirus *(Des Moines Register)*

28_ Le virus a fait un million de morts dans le monde *(France Info)*

KERRY PAYNE STAILEY, Optimism eludes me today. Tomorrow, I can try again. PEMAQUID POINT, ME, USA

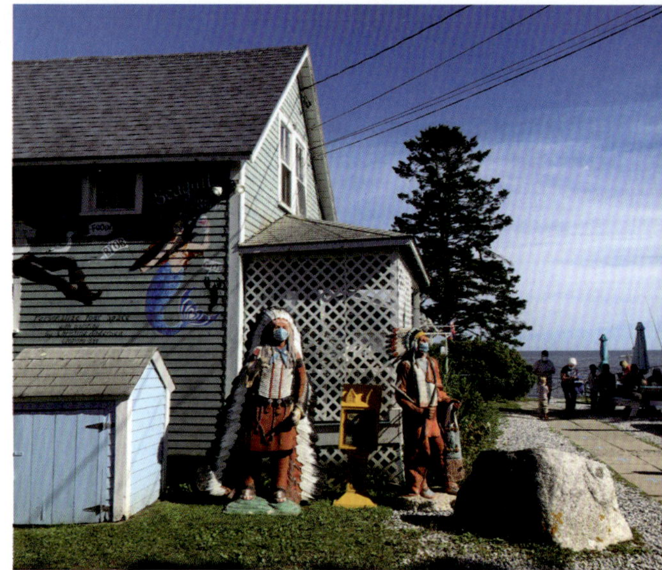

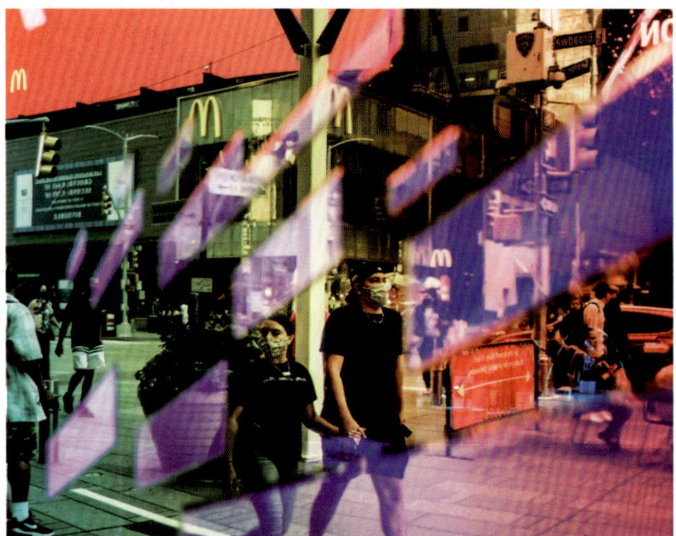

MATTHEW THORNTON, *Shards* | Times Square as it really began to come back to life but with an underlying feeling that things weren't quite right. NEW YORK, NY, USA

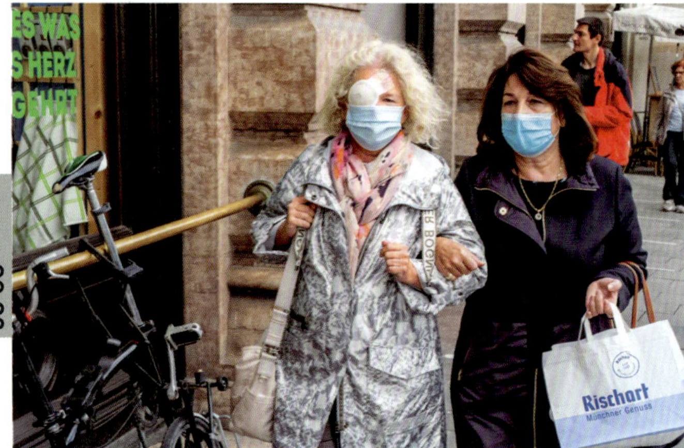

WOLLE TIPPELT, *Double Trouble* | Monocular vision in times of pandemic. Against all odds these two ladies make the best of the day. MUNICH, GERMANY

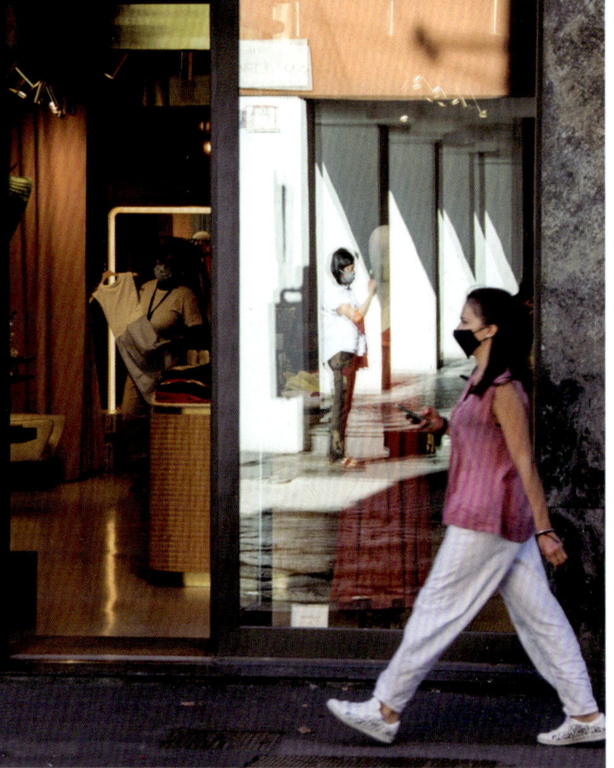

GIANCARLA PANCERA, An ordinary day in unordinary times. MILAN, ITALY

JANET STERNBURG, *Stay Present* | Downtown Los Angeles, Little Tokyo, where I live. CA, USA

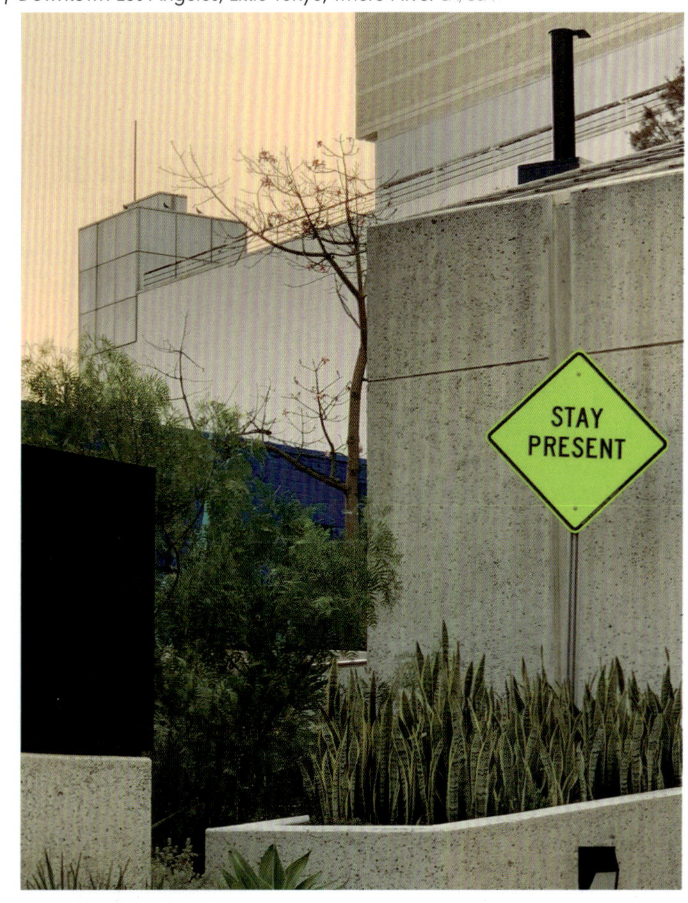

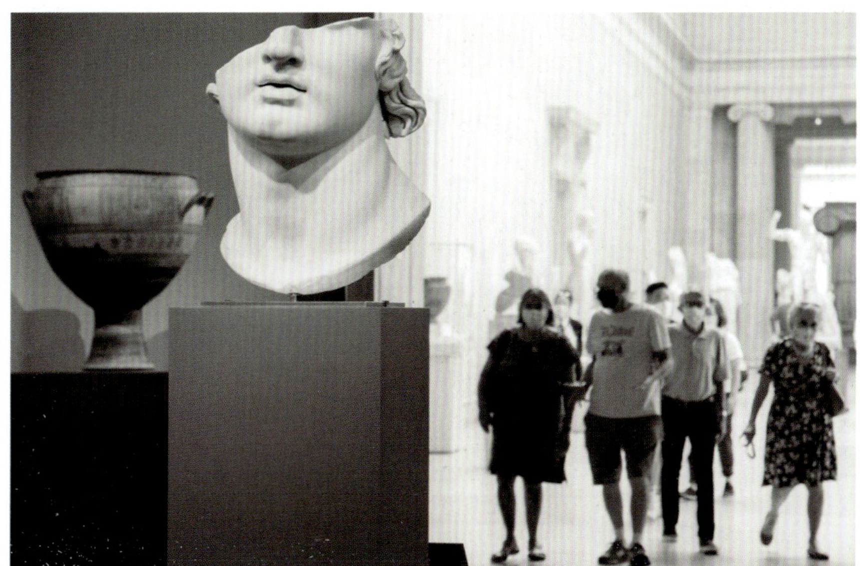

CAROL DRONSFIELD, *Wear a Mask, Art Exempt* | Roaming through the Metropolitan Museum of Art the week it re-opened, all visitors wear wearing masks. The museum guides enforced the rule. Viewing the art brought peace to my heart. NEW YORK, NY, USA

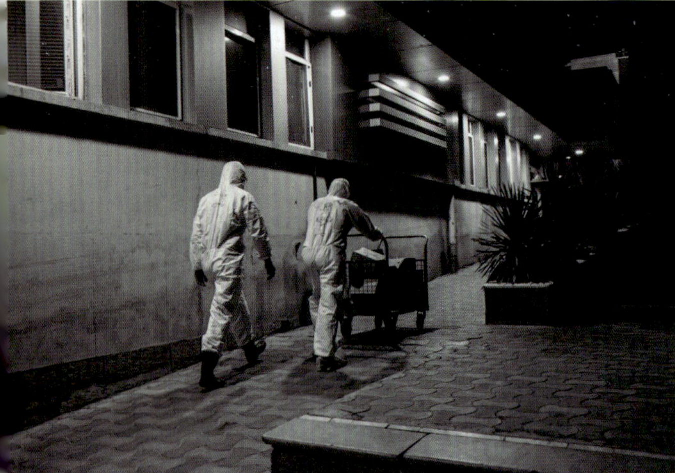

SHERVIN SHIRKOOBI, Two volunteers in isolated clothes carry juice for the medical staff in Amir Alam Hospital. With the outbreak of the coronavirus in Iran, volunteers were hired to help the medical staff in different wards. TEHRAN, IRAN

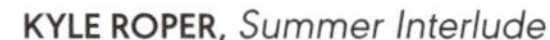

KYLE ROPER, *Summer Interlude* | Double exposure taken with my homemade 8x10 large-format film camera built into the tiny window of my front door. Part of my series "Door Frames." LOS ANGELES, CA, LA

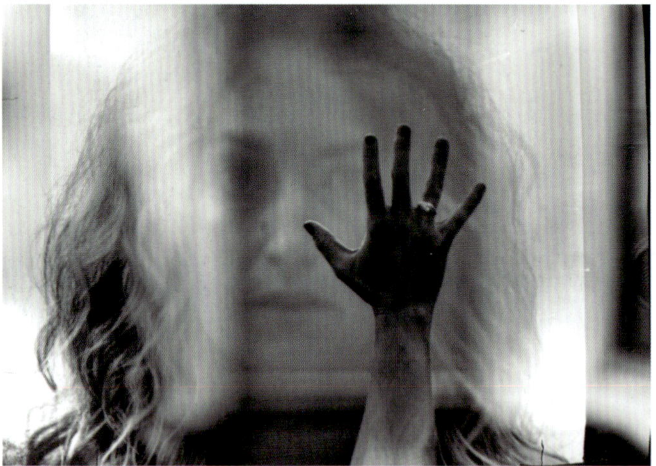

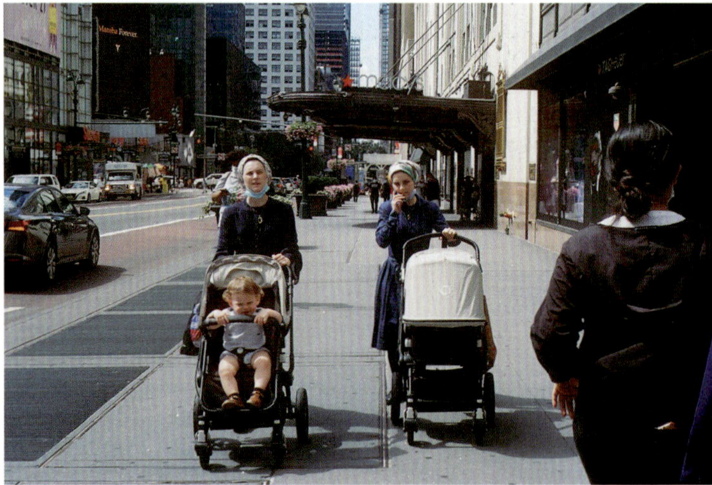

DIANA CUAUTLE, *Sorry Kid, No Chicken Dance* | Two mothers stroll with a rather upset child on a sunny day. NEW YORK, NY, USA

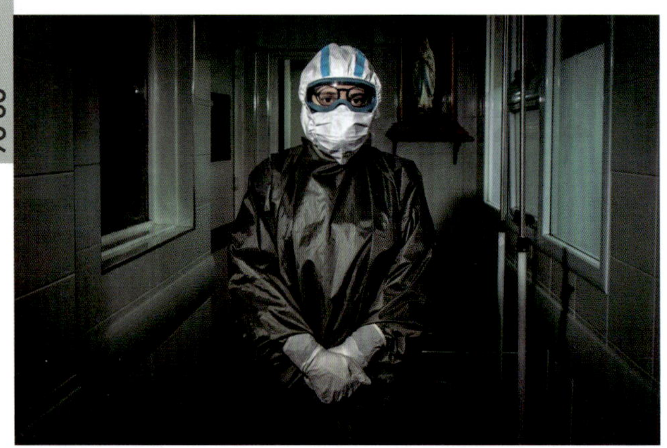

NESTOR GARCÍA, *COVID-19 Portraits* | Essential health workers. Julieta García Accinelli, emergentologist doctor. AVELLANEDA CITY, BUENOS AIRES, ARGENTINA

ALINA BIELOHOLOVA, Awakening. LVIV RAILWAY STATION, UKRAINE

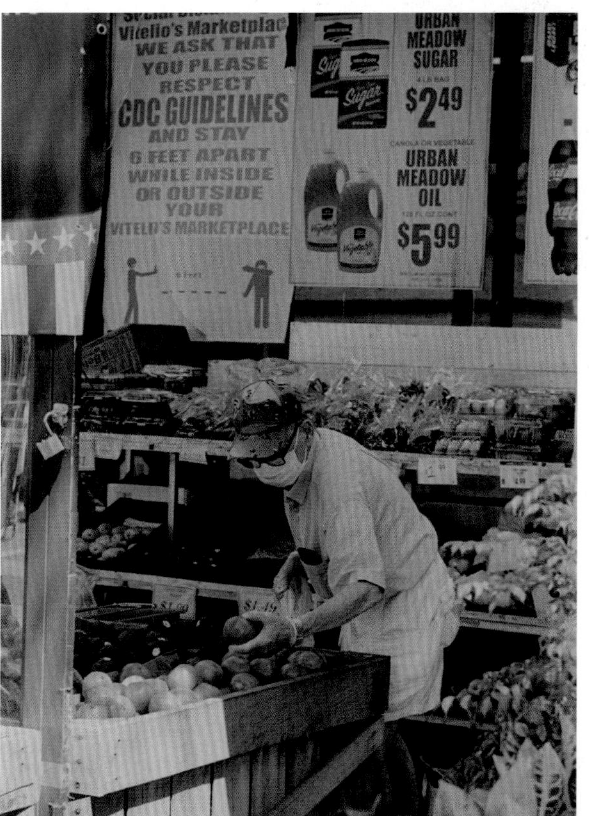

ELI DIKER, Man selecting tomatoes. QUEENS, NY, UISA

JON FEINSTEIN, Smoke-Covered Sunset. SEATTLE, WA, USA

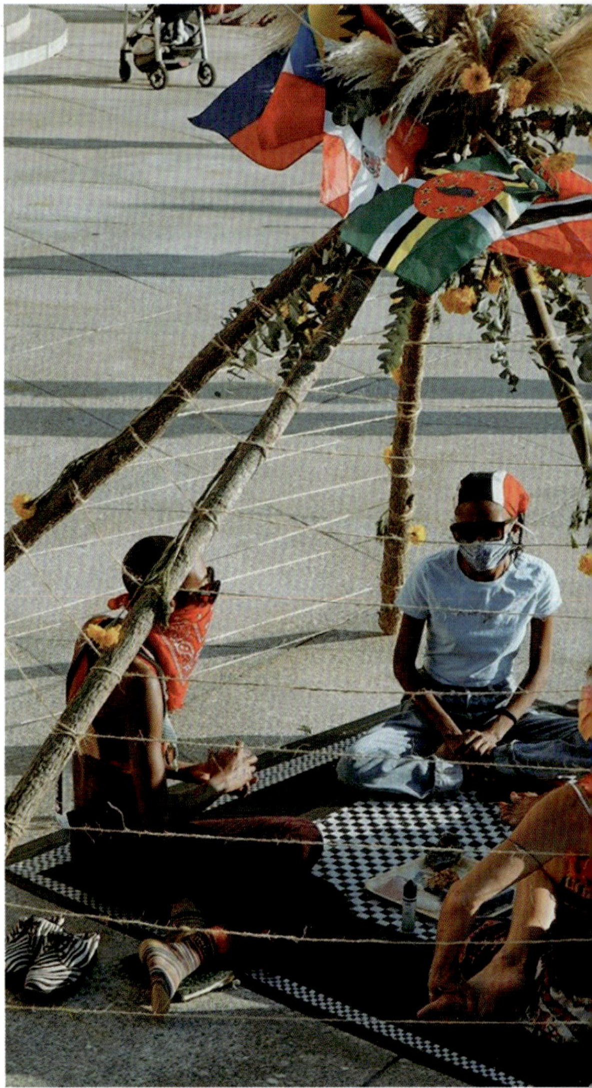

KRIS JULIEN, *Community* | Due to COVID-19, the highly anticipated Caribbean Day Parade was canceled. However the community came together to celebrate the brilliance and beauty of Caribbean culture, also highlighting the need for our voices to be heard while facing systemic racism. GRAND ARMY PLAZA, BROOKLYN, NY, USA

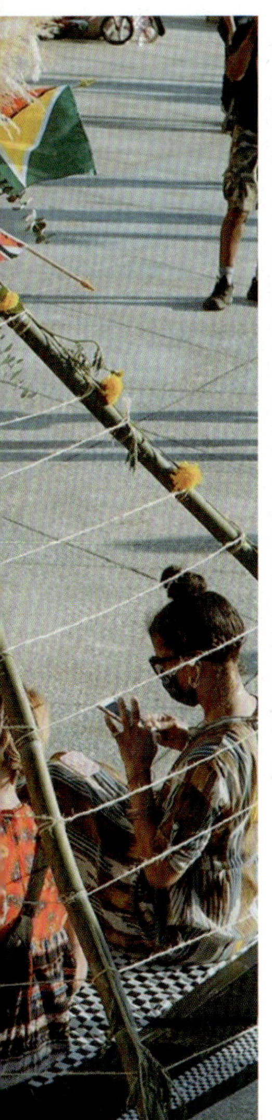

CARLOS BARRADAS, Burning bridges. LISBON, PORTUGAL

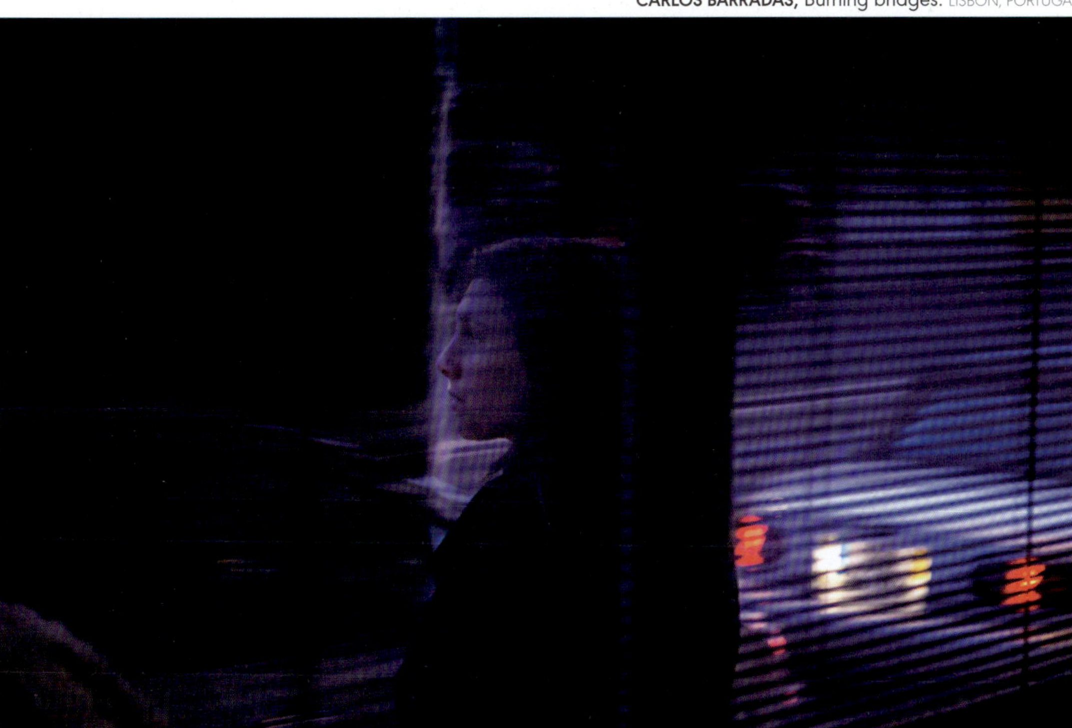

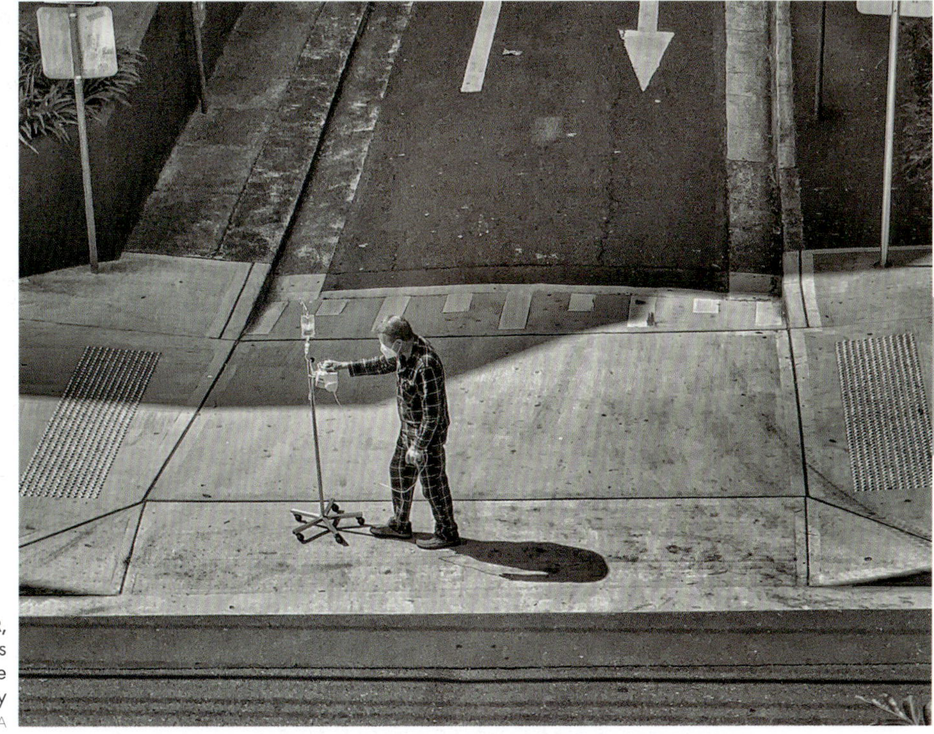

SARAH BARKER,
The most enchanting folx are always on the opposite side of the street. The choreography of everyday life from my balcony view. SYDNEY, AUSTRALIA

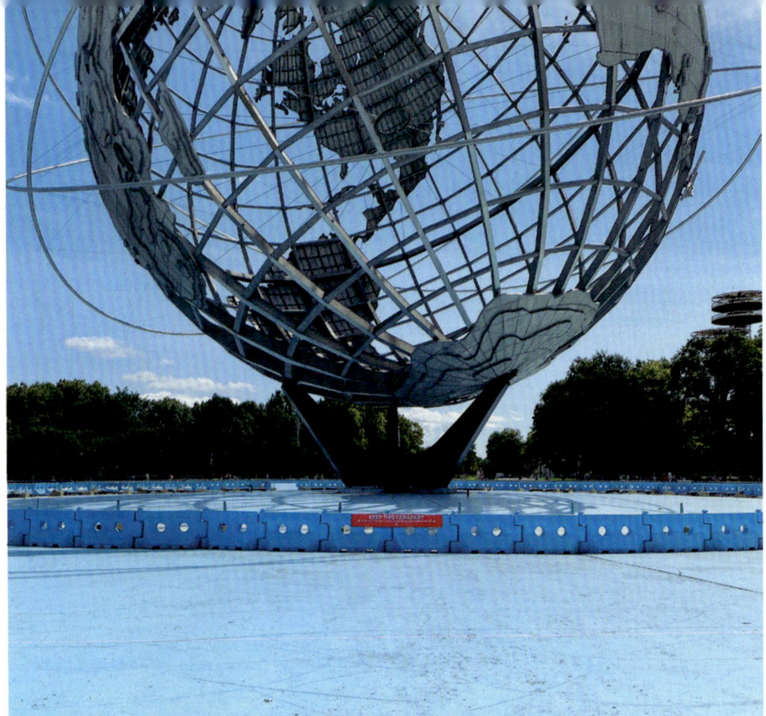

SARA MOSS, The Unisphere, Flushing Meadows Corona Park. QUEENS, NY, USA

ADYSABEL UZCATEGUI SAAVEDRA, This photograph was taken at a protest against the lack of public health protocols in Peru, where the economic situation has been prioritized. LIMA, PERU

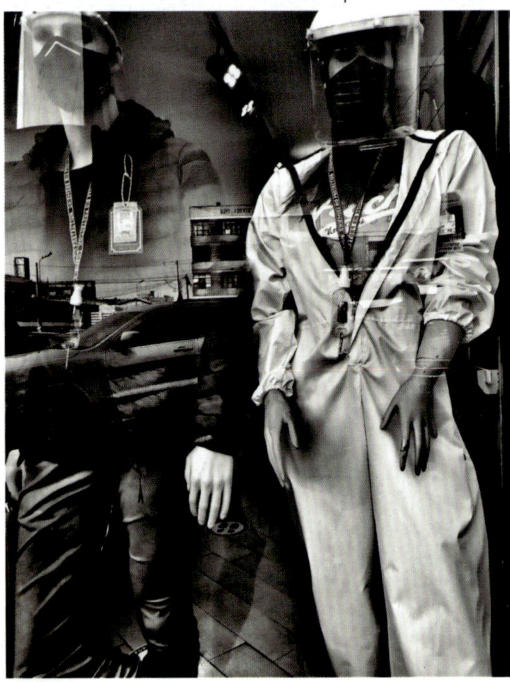

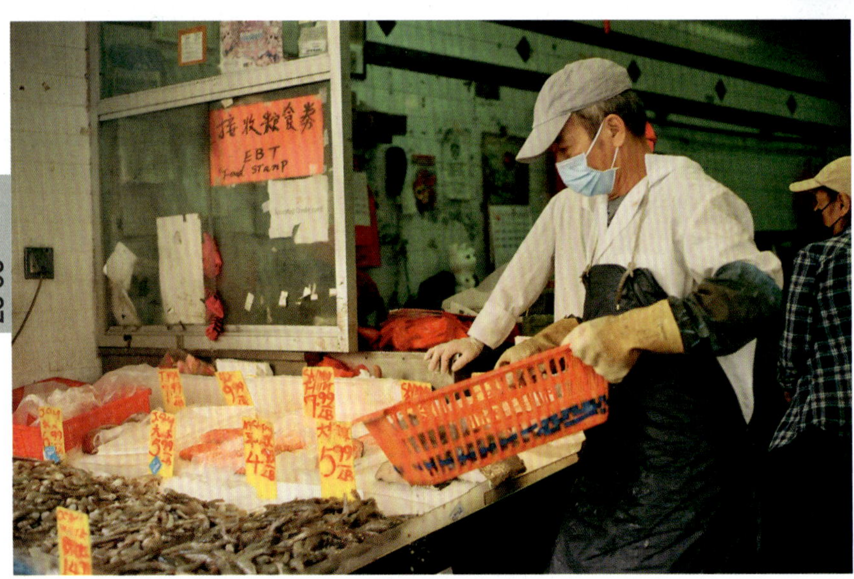

BEATRIZ BENARES, *Employees Must Wear Masks* | It is ironic that many non-Asians decided to avoid areas heavily populated with Asians when these communities were the first to take precautions during this pandemic. NEW YORK, NY, USA

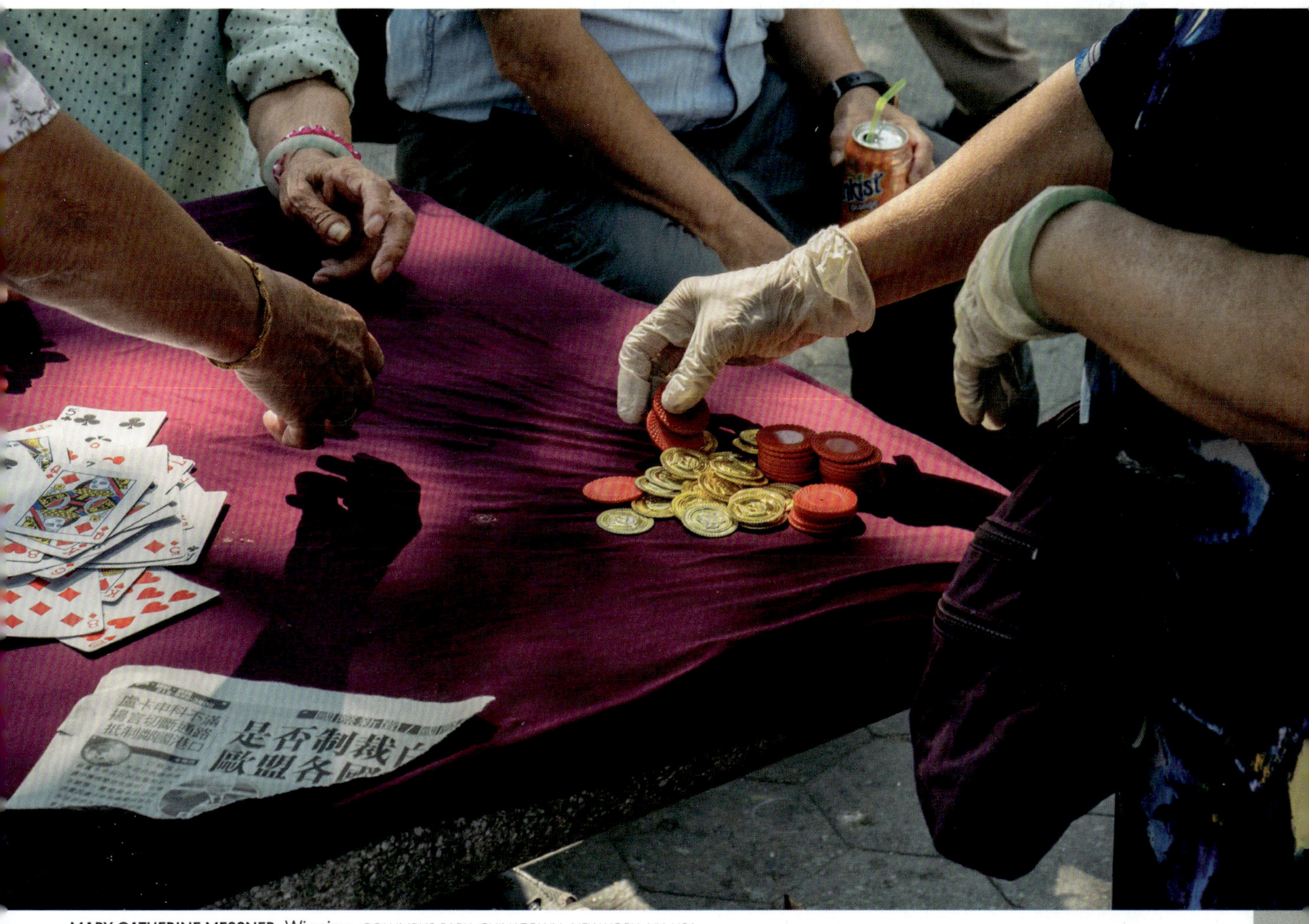

MARY CATHERINE MESSNER, Winning. COLUMBUS PARK, CHINATOWN, NEW YORK, NY, USA

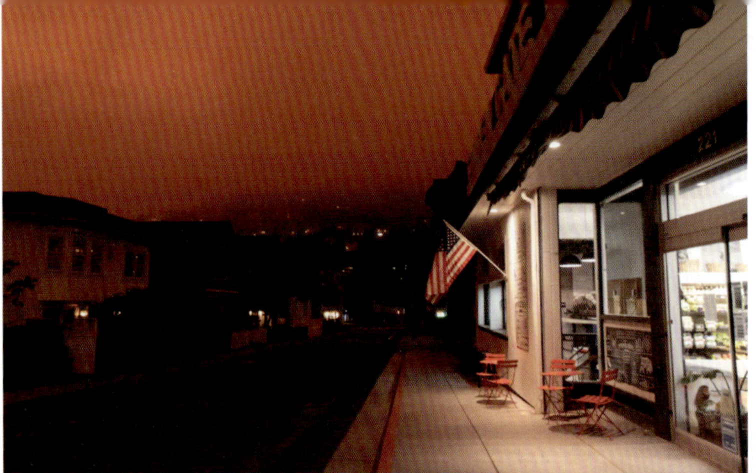

SUZ LIPMAN, Golden Gate Market, 8:15 AM Smoke from multiple wildfires burning in the western United States had become so widespread that it temporarily blocked the sun. SAUSALITO, CA, USA

WILLIE ABLAO, *California Burning* | The Mission District, 1:30PM. SAN FRANCISCO, CA, USA

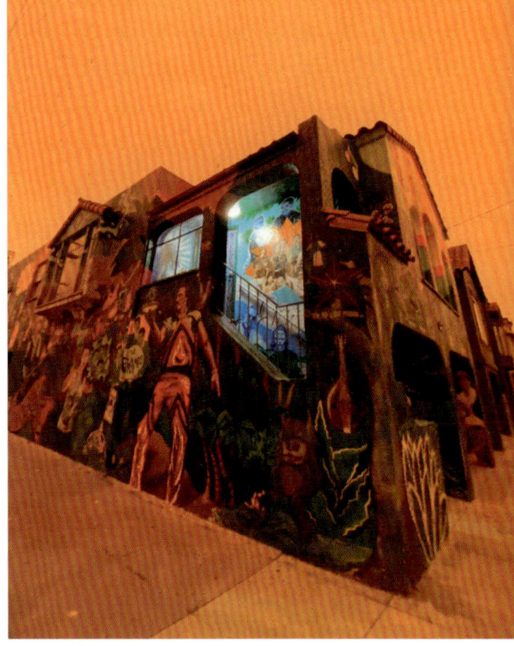

BECKY LOGAN, *Firelight, California* | This image was captured at my house on a day unlike any other I have ever experienced, and I hope that I never experience again, two weeks after a lightning storm started countless fires across our state of California. We had prepared to evacuate our home and had sadly become very used to the orange and pink hues of light since the fires had started. Yet that day was totally different. When we woke, even after the sun rose, it was strangely dark. It was almost like the light that occurs during a total solar eclipse. The whole sky had this orange hue to it, and the air quality was horrible. As the day progressed, it got darker and darker outside. So much so that crickets started chirping in the afternoon. The little light that did enter the house was this very dark orange color. It was like something out of a sci-fi movie, and it was totally apocalyptic. I had thought countless times that 2020 couldn't become any more unsettling, but unfortunately it had. SAN FRANCISCO, CA, USA

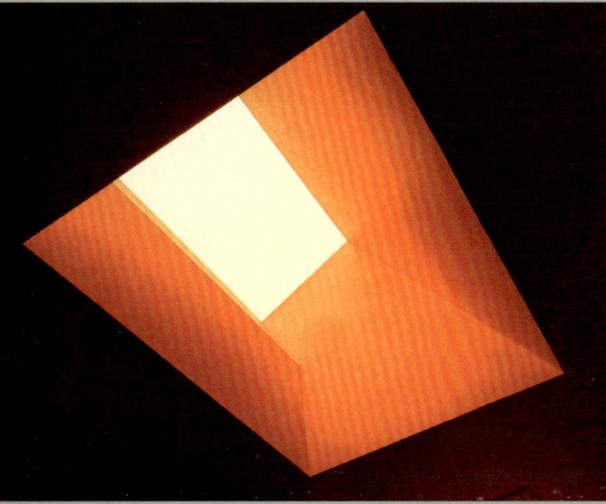

JEFFREY BRAVERMAN, *David and Goliath* | I captured this image mid-day as fires rage across the West Coast. The "David" is a reminder that we can overcome impossible situations in oppressive times. TREASURE ISLAND, CA, USA

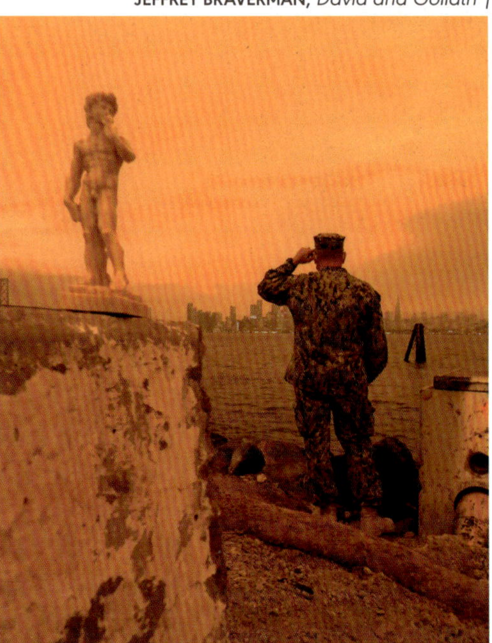

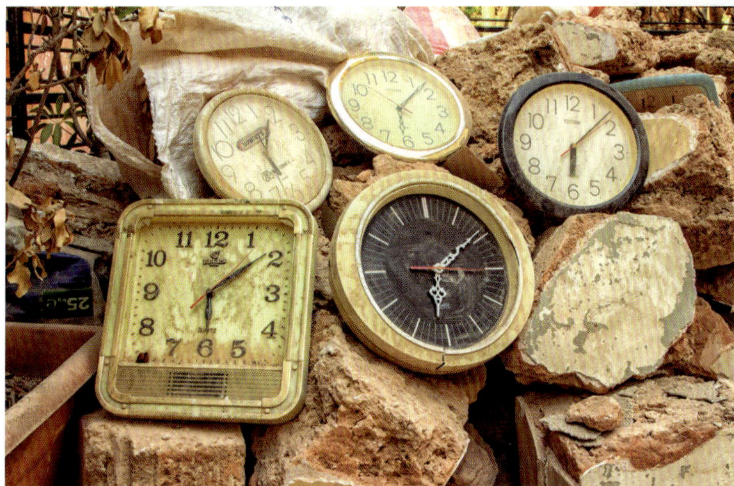

GEORGI BITAR, *Over Here, It's still 6:08 PM* | The image portrays all the clocks that stopped working at 6:08 PM in Beirut on August 4th due to the explosion. LEBANON

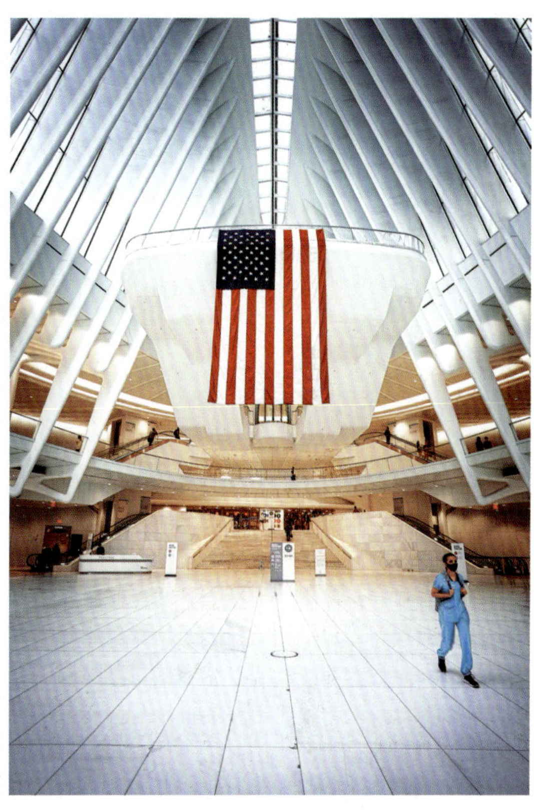

JOSHUA ABRAHAM, Commemorating September 11th in the age of the pandemic. NEW YORK, NY, USA

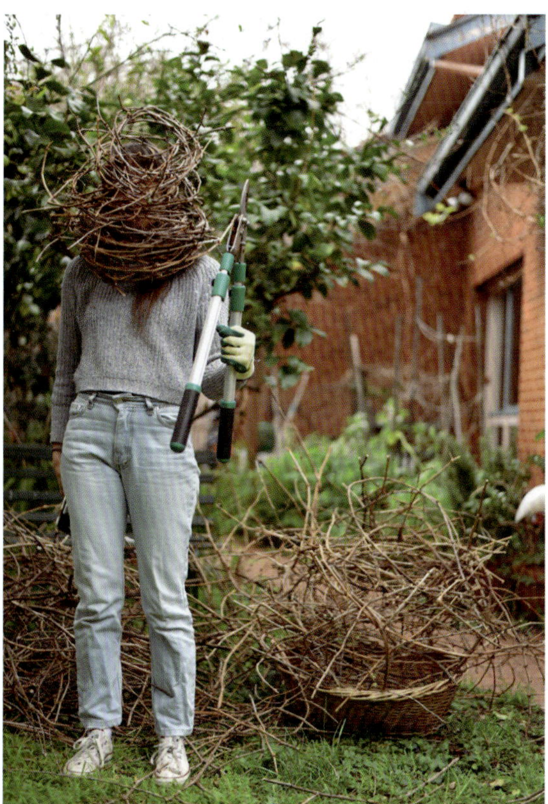

ZOE ARNOTT, *Pruned* | Taken in lockdown. We can only leave to exercise—I busy myself in the garden cutting back the old, making way for the new. MELBOURNE, AUSTRALIA

THIAGO PAIVA, The New Normal in São Paulo City. BRAZIL

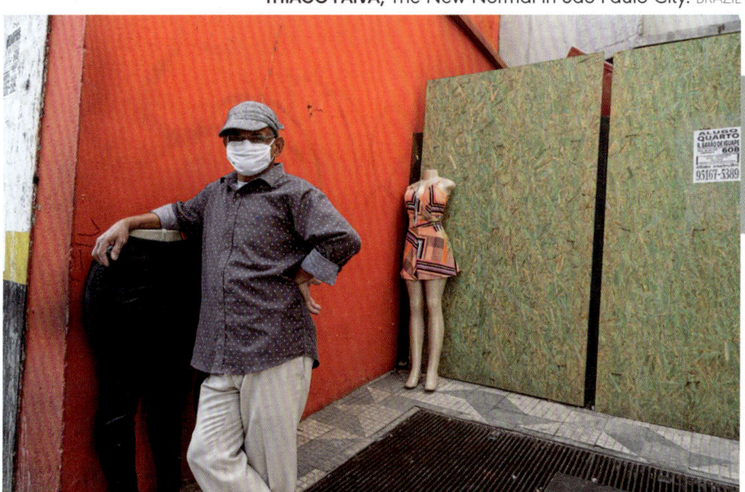

ELA SKOWRONEK, *Marigold and Daisy Steam Stack*

| Fifth Avenue and 52nd Street. Flower Flash in remembrance of 9/11 by Lewis Miller. In his words: "Honoring this day and every day because New Yorkers have been through a lot and we always get up." NEW YORK, NY, USA

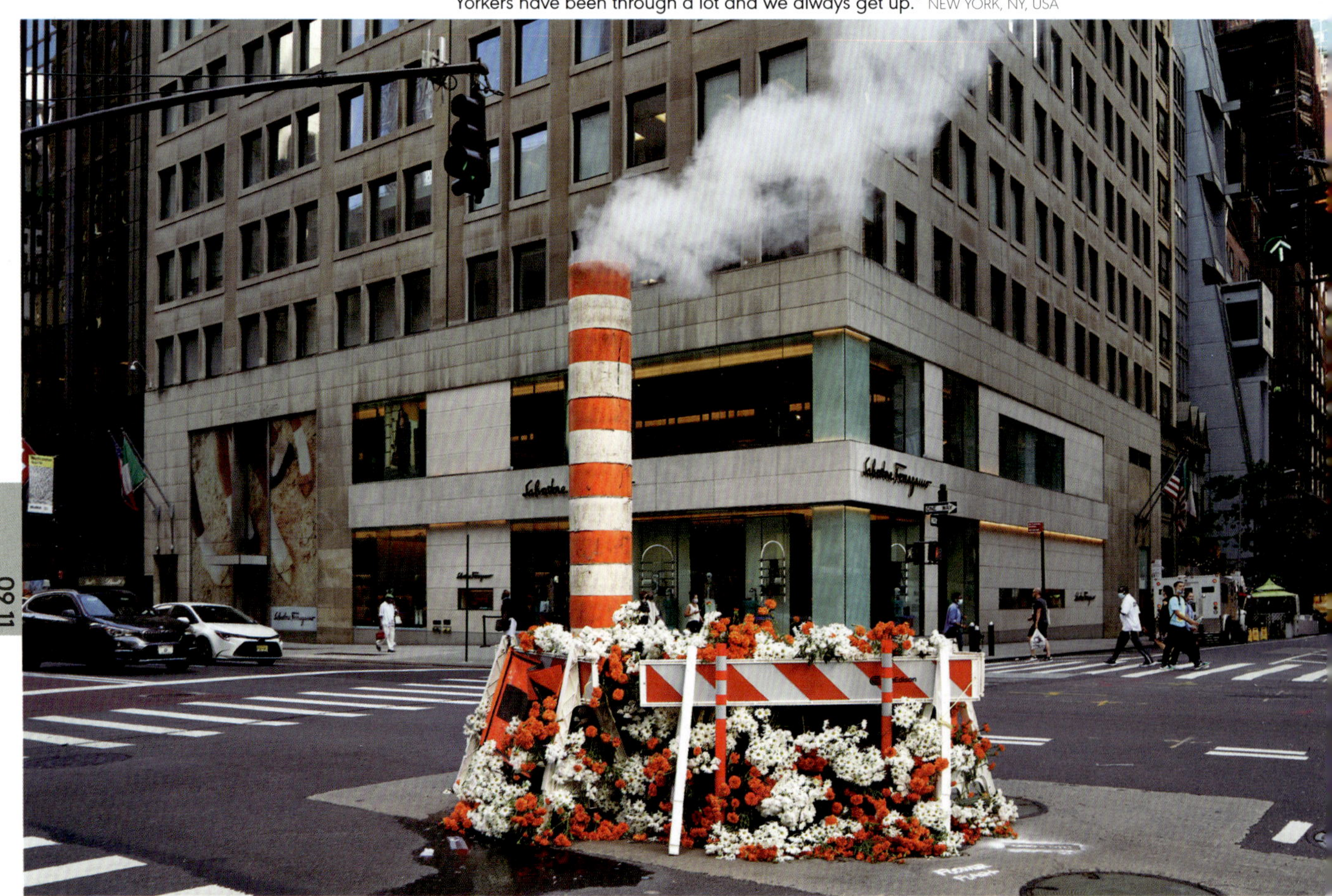

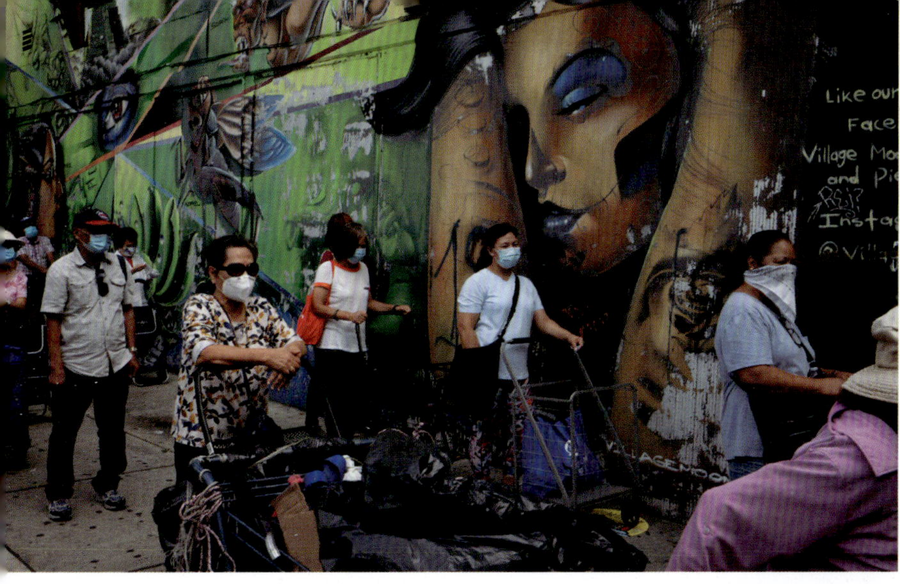

STEPHEN FERRY, People wait for food donations from the Love Wins food pantry, which distributes fresh food to 600 people per week. Love Wins is an LGBTQ-led organization, mostly by residents of Jackson Heights. This neighborhood was one of the worst hit by the pandemic, and the economic fall out is extreme. QUEENS, NY, USA

NATALIA PEDRAZA BRAVO, Going back to school in the "new normal." CHÍA, COLOMBIA

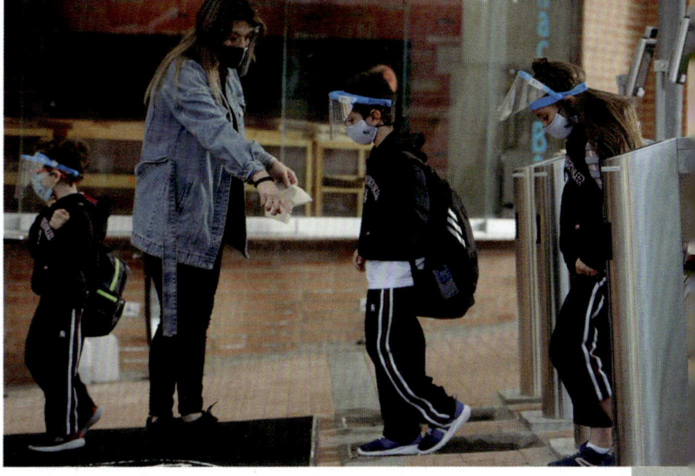

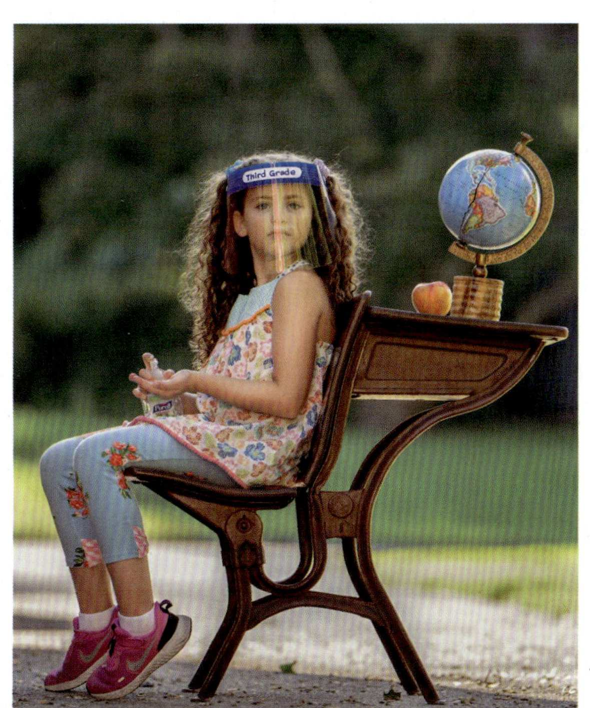

JENNIFER VERDE KING, *Back to school* | First day of third grade. WESTCHESTER, NY, USA

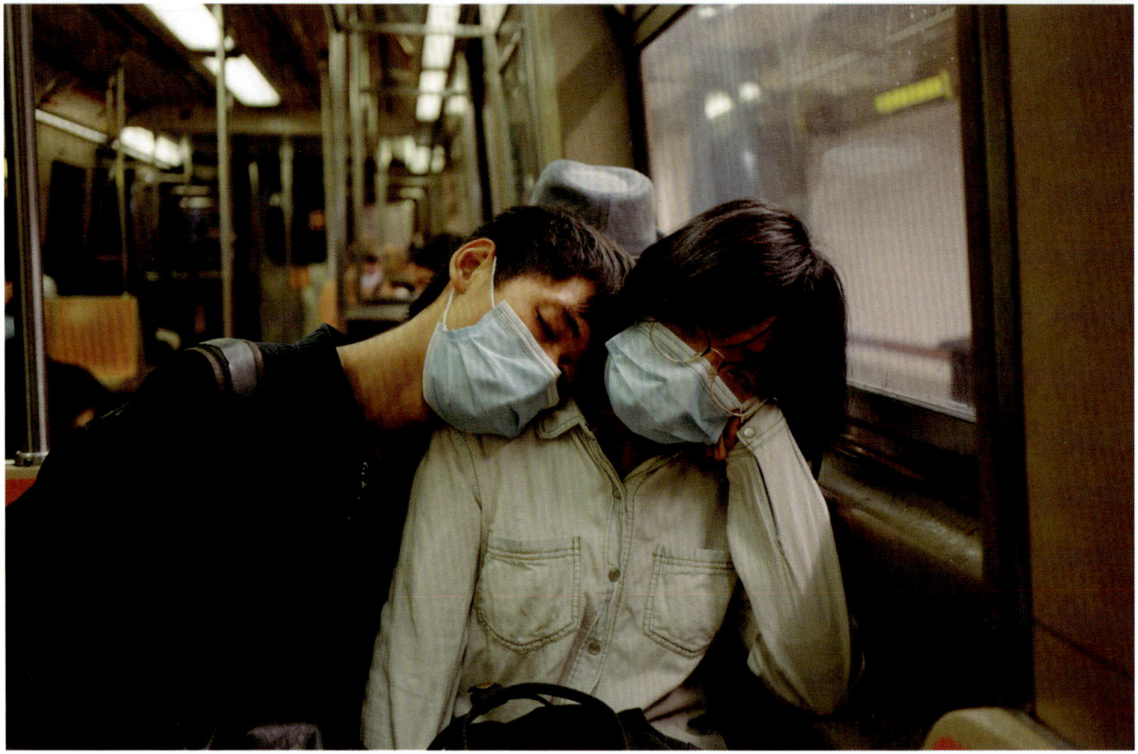

SCOTT ROSSI, Untitled. NEW YORK, NY, USA

JACOB SPETZLER, Trump 2020 signs line the main road in Golden. CO, USA

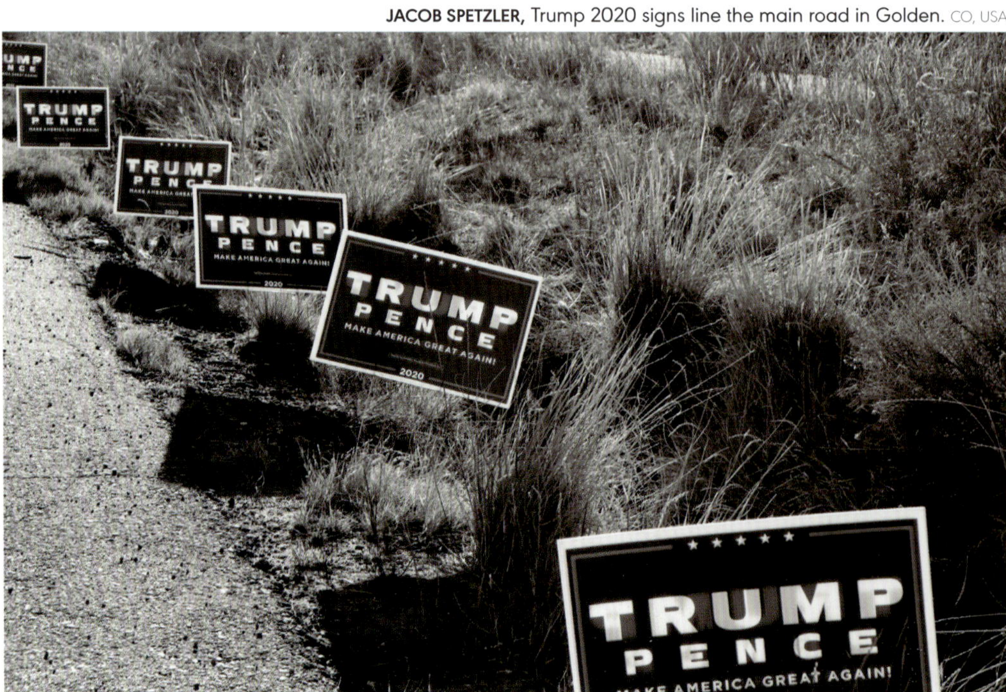

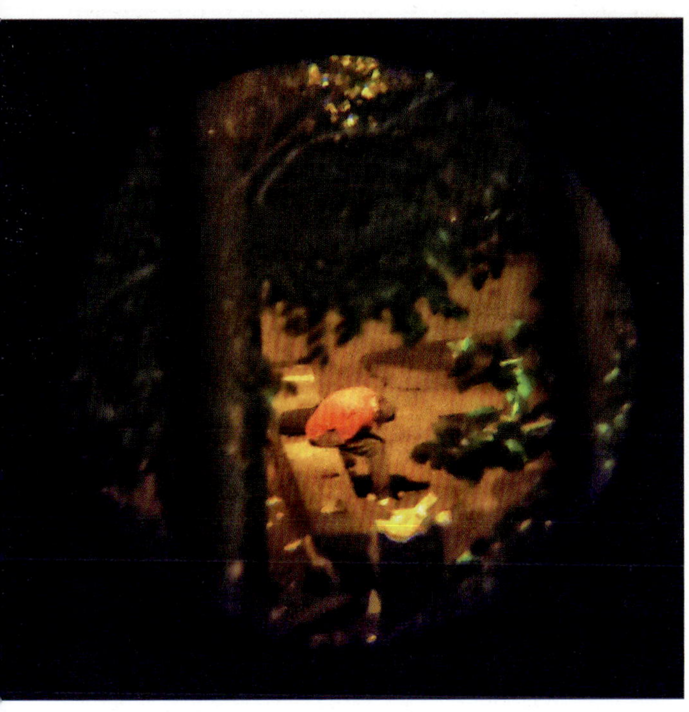

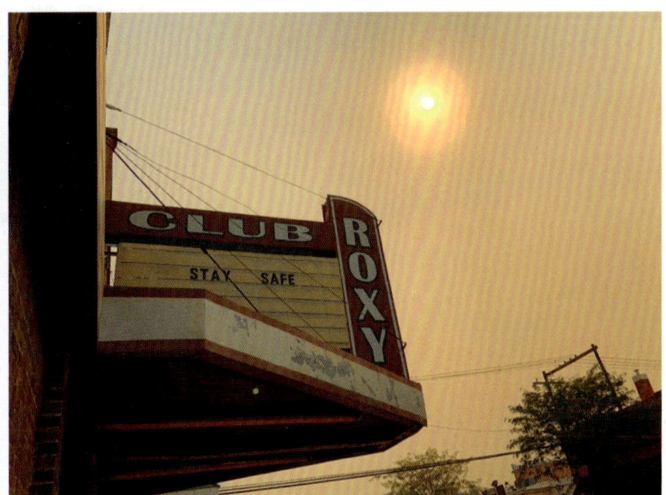

ABBY LINNE, Smoke from wildfires masks the sun over the Roxy marquee. The air quality index reached 157 this afternoon. HAMILTON, MT, USA

ALEXANDER HAHN, Night Shift. SARA D. ROOSEVELT PARK, NEW YORK, NY, USA

PETER HILDEN,

The new normal in restaurants. Restaurant owners try to prevent another closure by instituting social distancing measures. HAMBURG, GERMANY

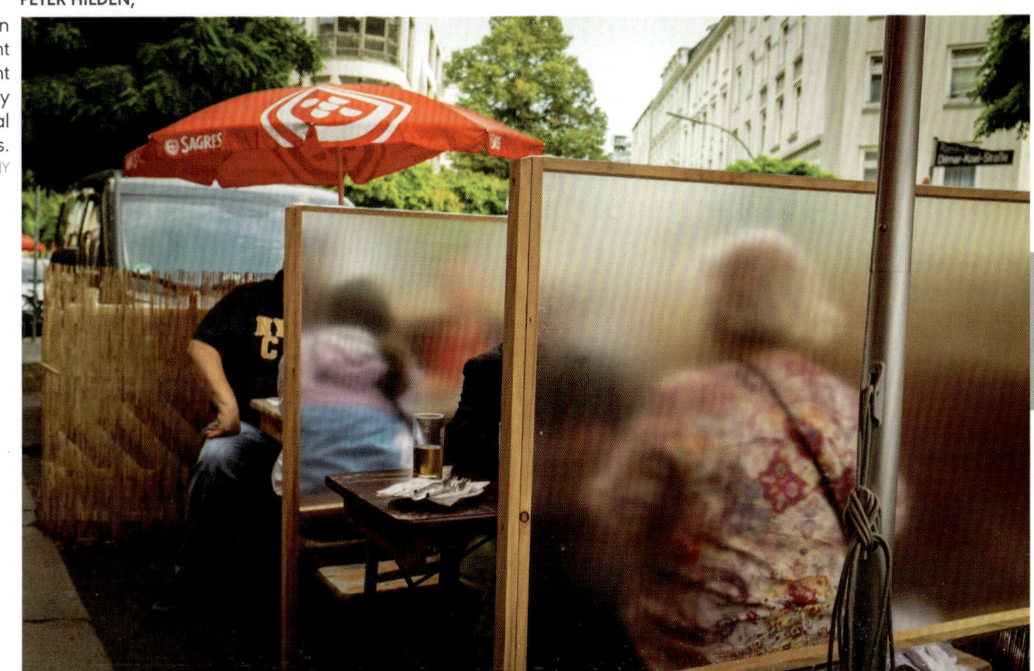

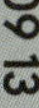

09 13

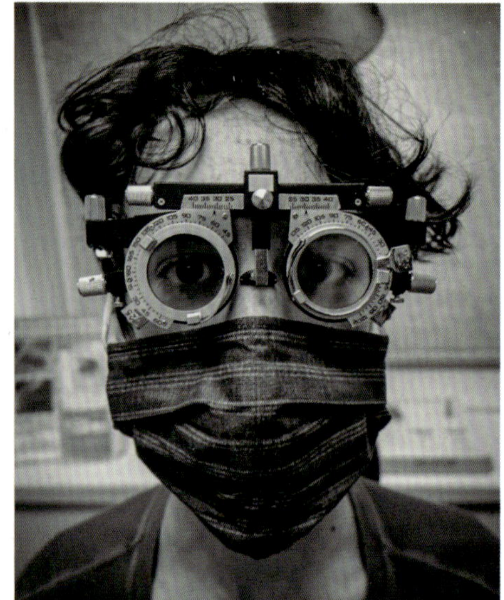

MICHAEL SILVERWISE, Time for Clarity. NEW YORK, NY, USA

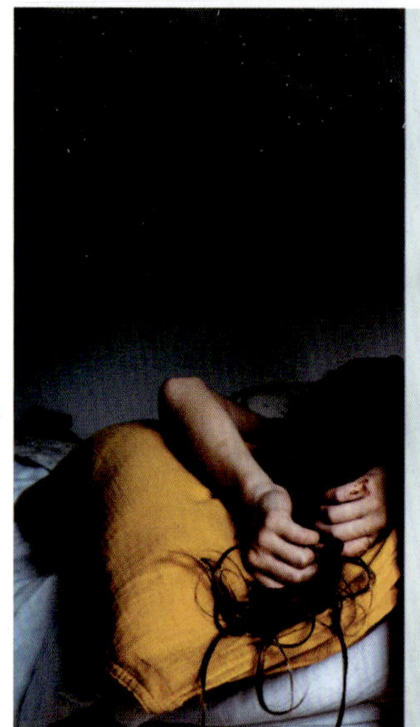

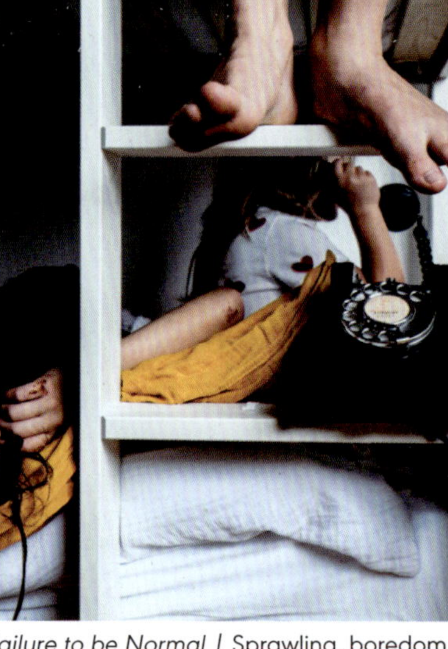

KAREN BRUNEL LAFARGUE, *Failure to be Normal* | Sprawling, boredom, and imaginary conversations on day three of family quarantine. BIARRITZ, FRANCE

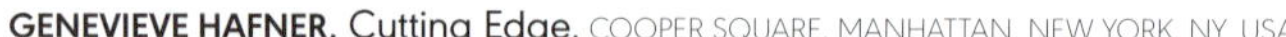

GENEVIEVE HAFNER, Cutting Edge. COOPER SQUARE, MANHATTAN, NEW YORK, NY, USA

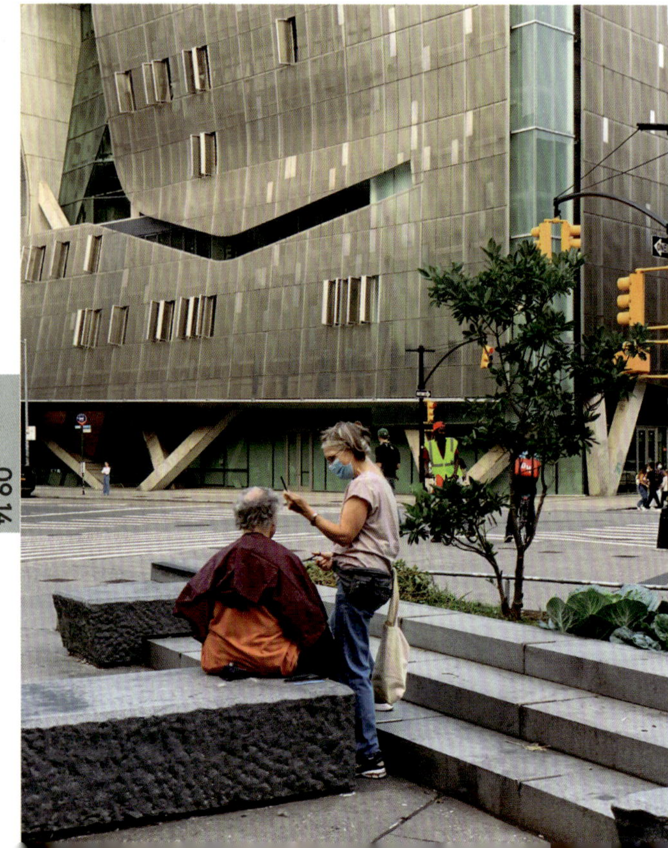

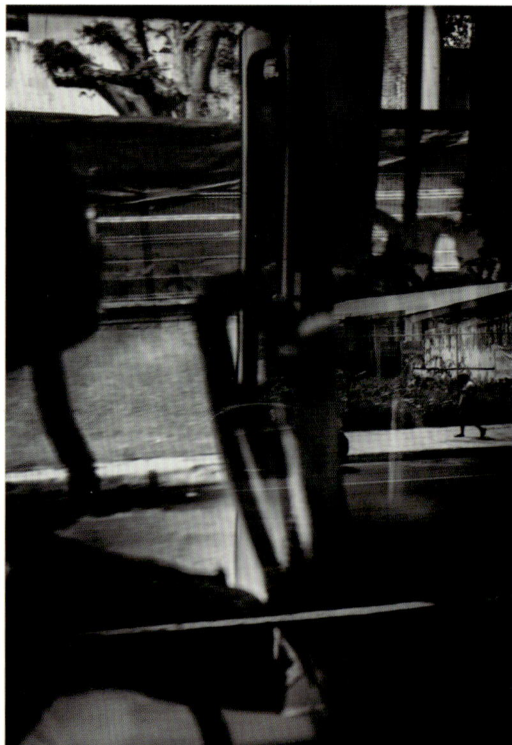

JOSÉ ANTONIO GARCIA, *Beauty of Imperfection* | Reflections on a bus. MAZATLAN, SINALOA, MEXICO

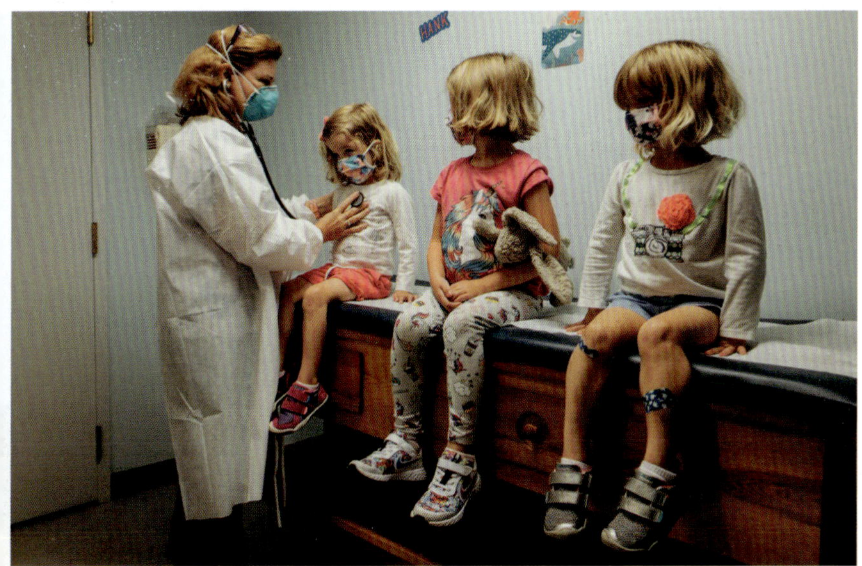

LAURA BETH DAVIDSON, COVID Tests for All. LYNCHBURG, VA, USA

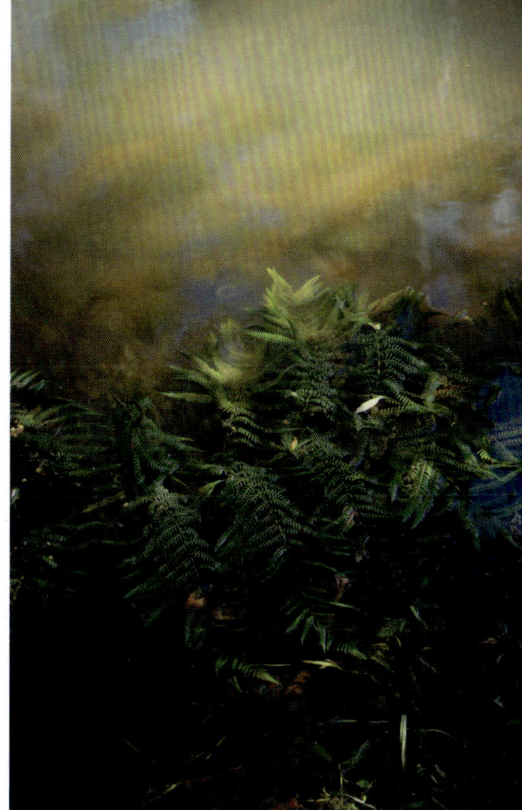

LOU WHELAN, *Birrarung (Ever Flowing) in isolation* | After months of Melbourne's COVID-19 lockdown, the Birrarung river in the small mountain town where I live became a place of peace and reflection. This watery, liminal image evokes a deeper contradiction, elusiveness and ephemerality, of different states of being. AUSTRALIA

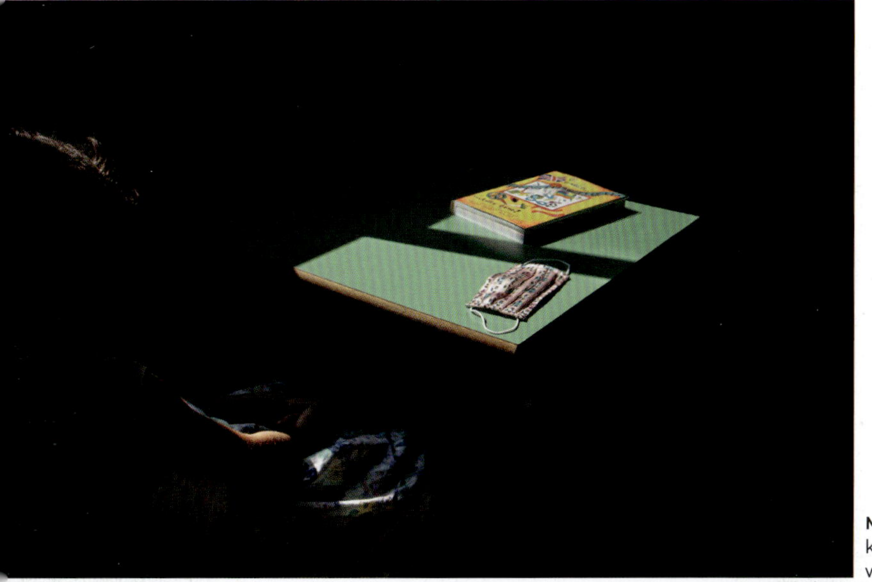

MARZIO TONIOLO, In Santo Stefano Lodigiano, two kilometers from the first red zone in Italy and Europe, we return to school after eight months. ITALY

DOGAN GULCAN, Wall of Faith. PORT JERVIS, NY, USA

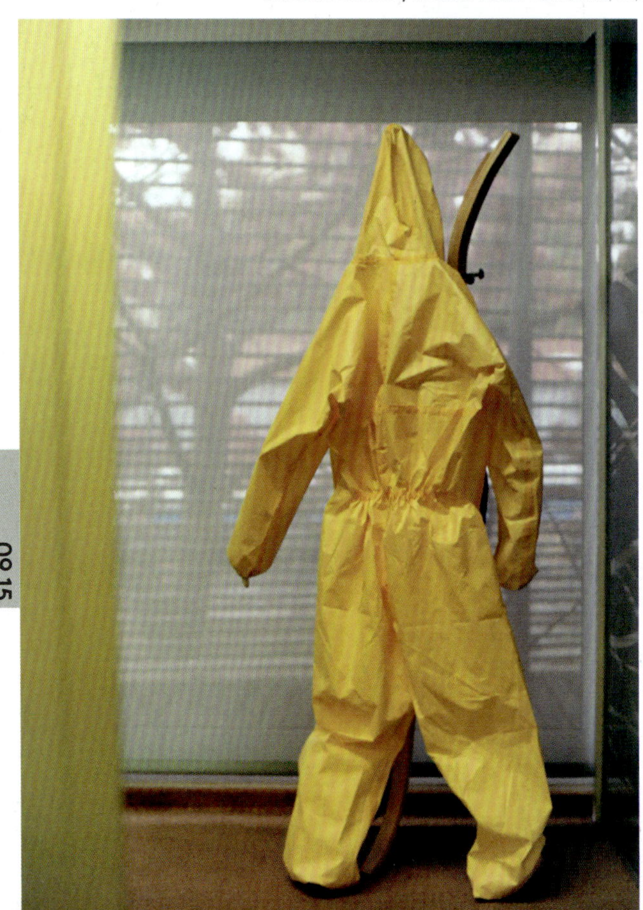

MELISA OECHSLE, *New Friend |*

I took this picture at work in an orthopedic office.
BUENOS AIRES, ARGENTINA

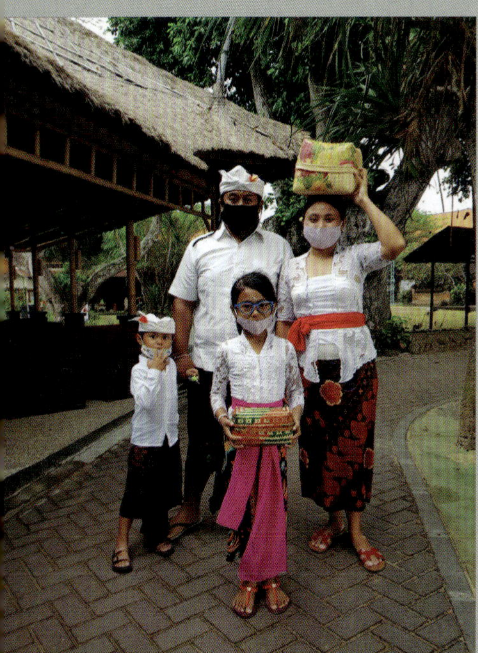

AMIT JANCO, This was the first day of Galungan. A festival celebrated by the millions of Hindus spread across the island. The key significance of Galungan is the triumph of good over evil. It's also the beginning of a ten-day period, during which time the ancestors of Balinese families are set to come down from the heavens to live among their descendants. During this festive time, families visit temples, all of them outdoor and open to the skies, where they gather together with their communities to pray, to receive blessings from a Balinese priest, and to leave offerings for the gods and spirits. This family, dressed in their finest traditional clothes and masks were on their way to a temple, just a stone's throw away from the beach. Despite the massive toll that the pandemic has taken on the inhabitants of this iconic tropical island, with the tourist industry now all but decimated, the Balinese somehow continue to show up with their smiles, the bursts of color, their faith, and more than anything, their resilience.
SANUR, BALI, INDONESIA

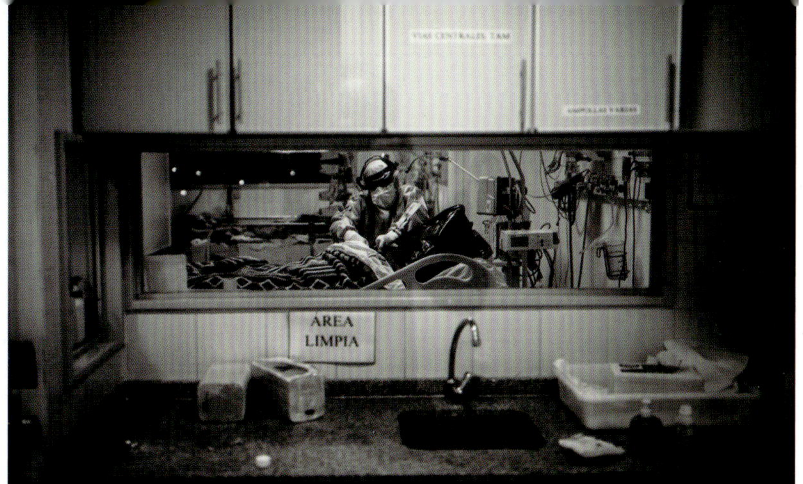

ANIBAL GRECO, A nurse covers the body of a deceased person in the intensive care room for COVID-19 patients at the Posadas hospital in Buenos Aires.
ARGENTINA

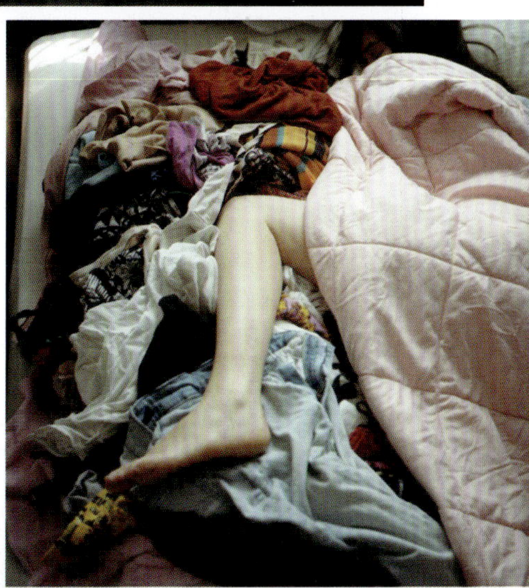

PAOLA MARTÍNEZ FITERRE, *Untitled* | From the series "A Negotiation with Sanity."
QUEENS, NY, USAY

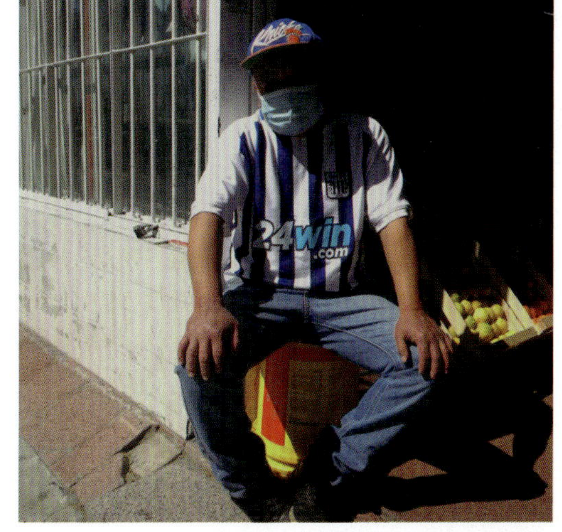

PAOLA NATALIA OLARI UGROTTE, Raul waits for clients at the door of the supermarket where he is the greengrocer. Day 178 of compulsory isolation in the city of Buenos Aires.
ARGENTINA

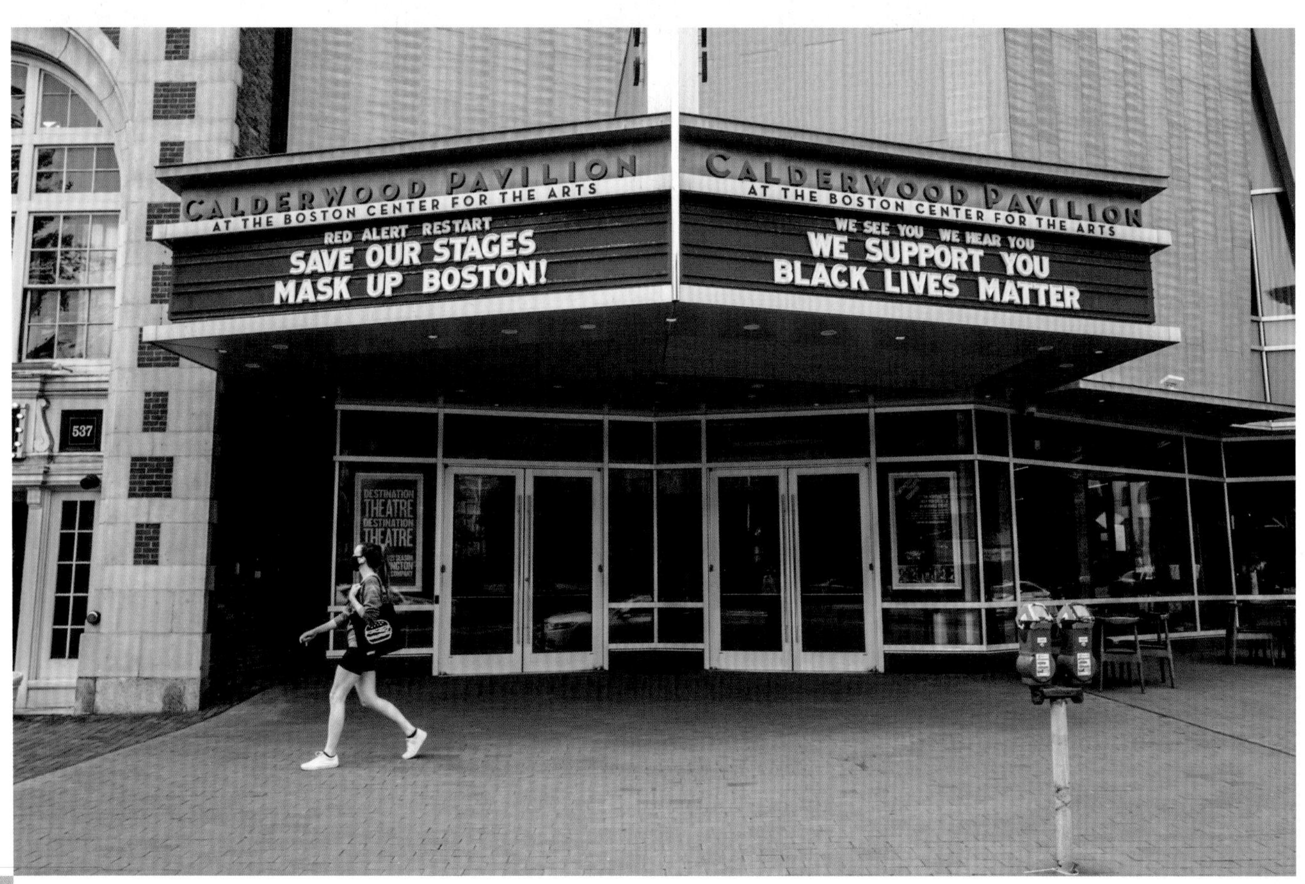

SUSAN BAGGETT, Messages. BOSTON, MA, USA

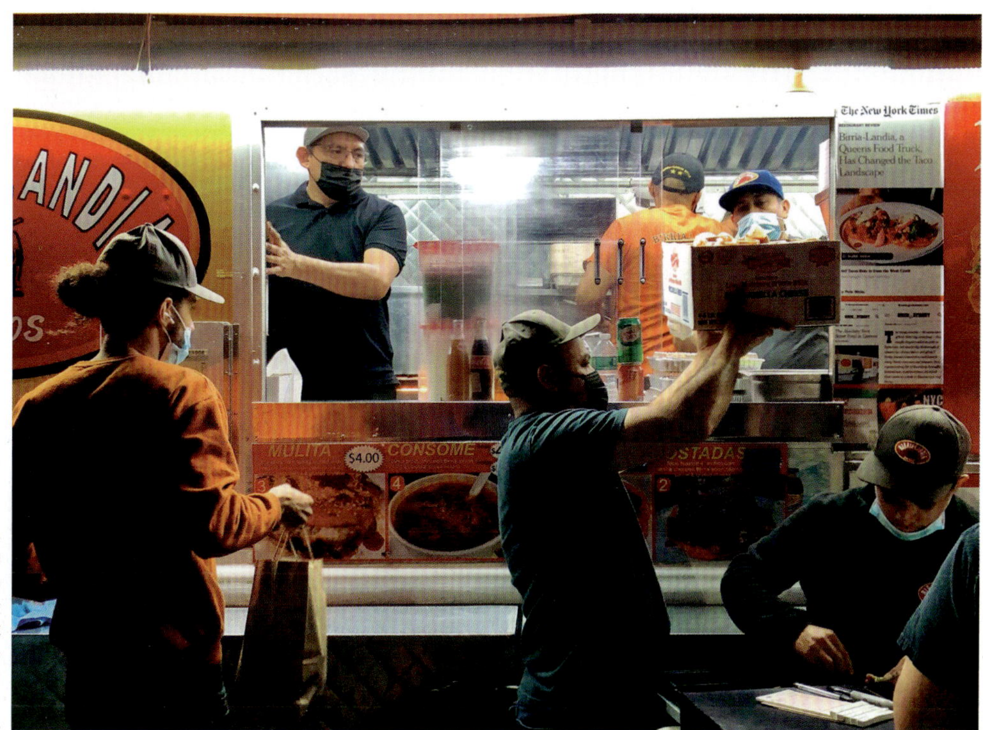

HAZEL HANKIN,
The popular Birria-Landia food truck in Jackson Heights is a well-choreographed operation that has been serving the neighborhood well during the COVID-19 pandemic.
QUEENS, NY, USA

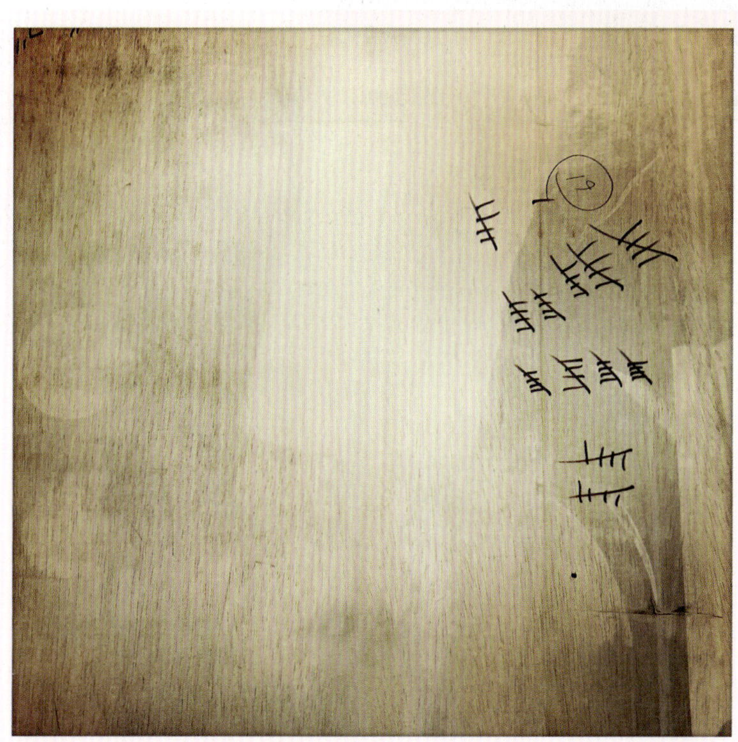

ANTHONY AUSTIN, Discarded Sheet of Plywood, Biding and Mending. LUDLOW STREET, LOWER EAST SIDE, NEW YORK, NY, USA

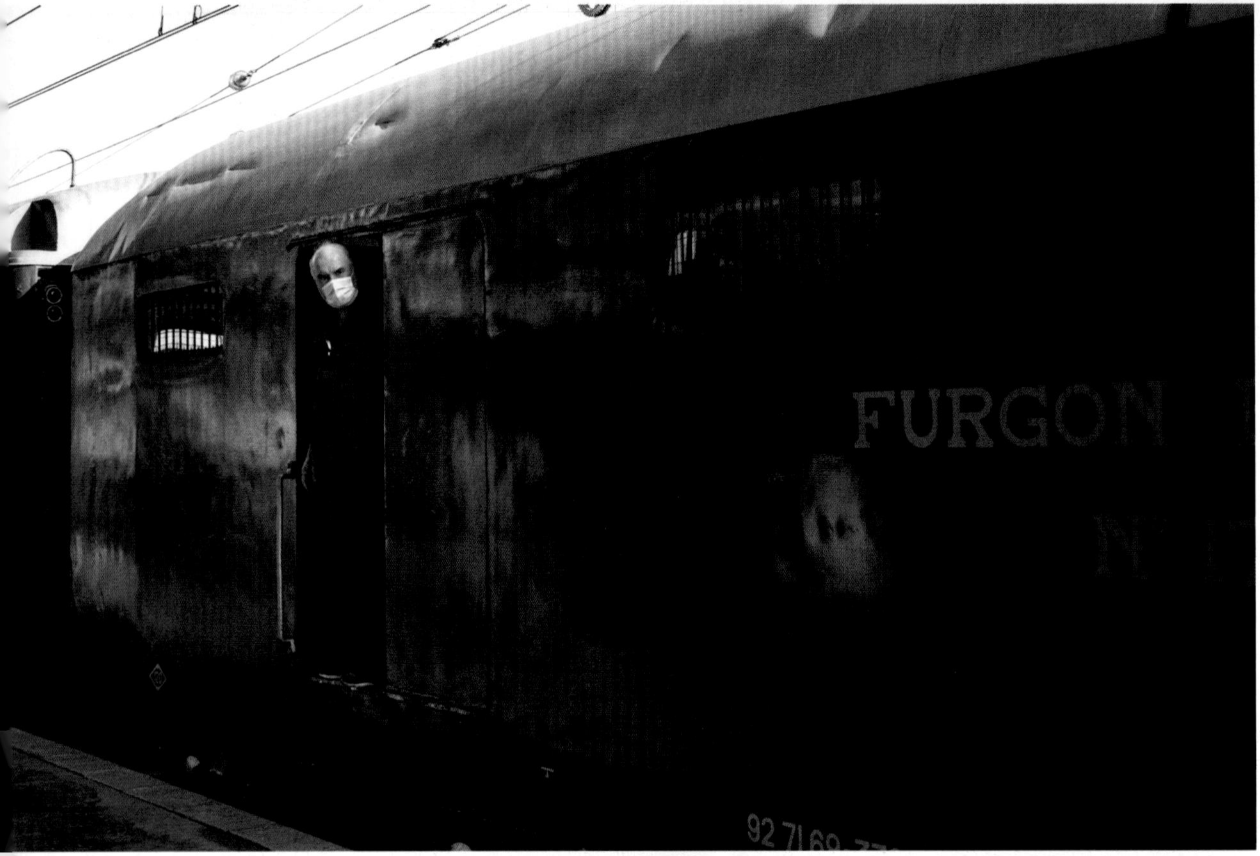

MARCELO AURELIO, *Train of the Lakes* | Lleida Train Station, Catalonia. Locomotive engineer of a classic train, with the mandatory use of a mask. SPAIN

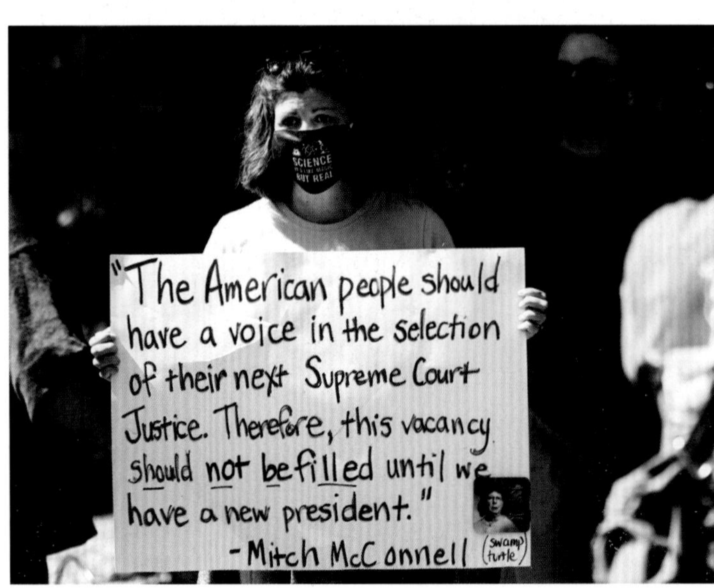

GARY BARRAGAN, *Voicing Hypocrisy* | In front of Mitch McConnell's condo. LOUISVILLE, KY, USA

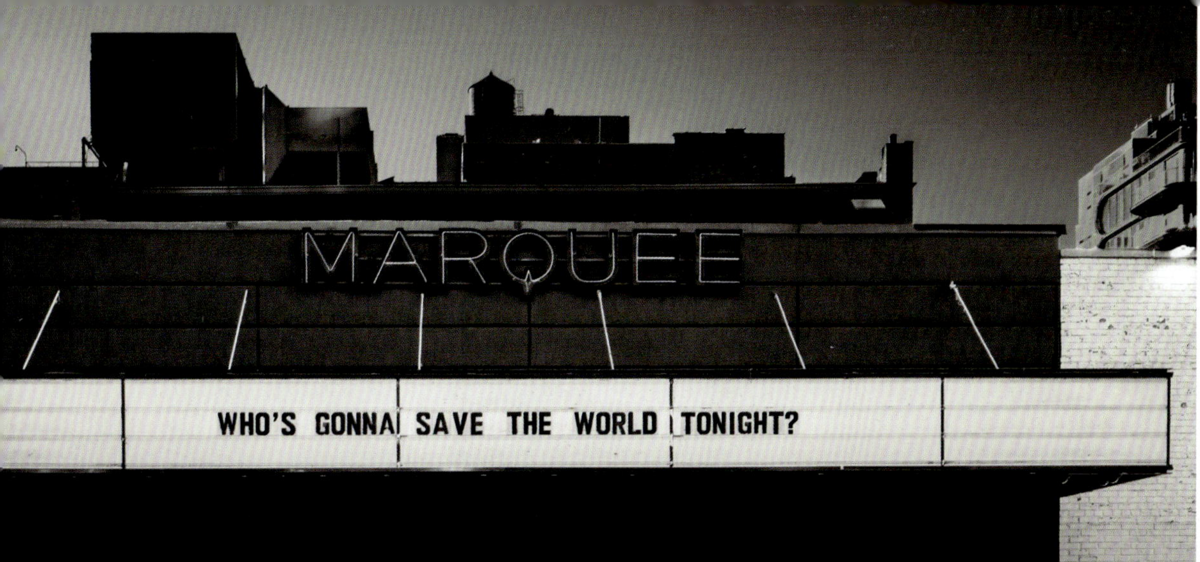

JOSEPH CELA, Who's gonna save the world tonight?
NEW YORK, NY, USA

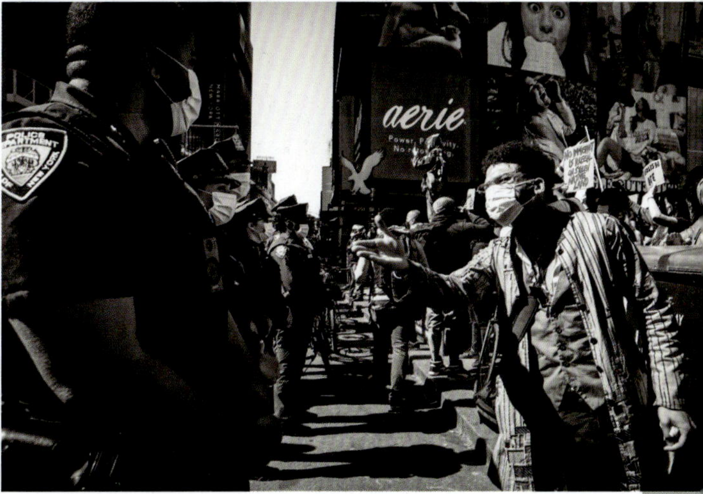

CAROLINE MARDOK, Protest against conditions of detention and sterilization of women by ICE. Protesters are stopped from marching by the police. Eighty-nine people were arrested by the NYPD. NEW YORK, NY, USA

09 19

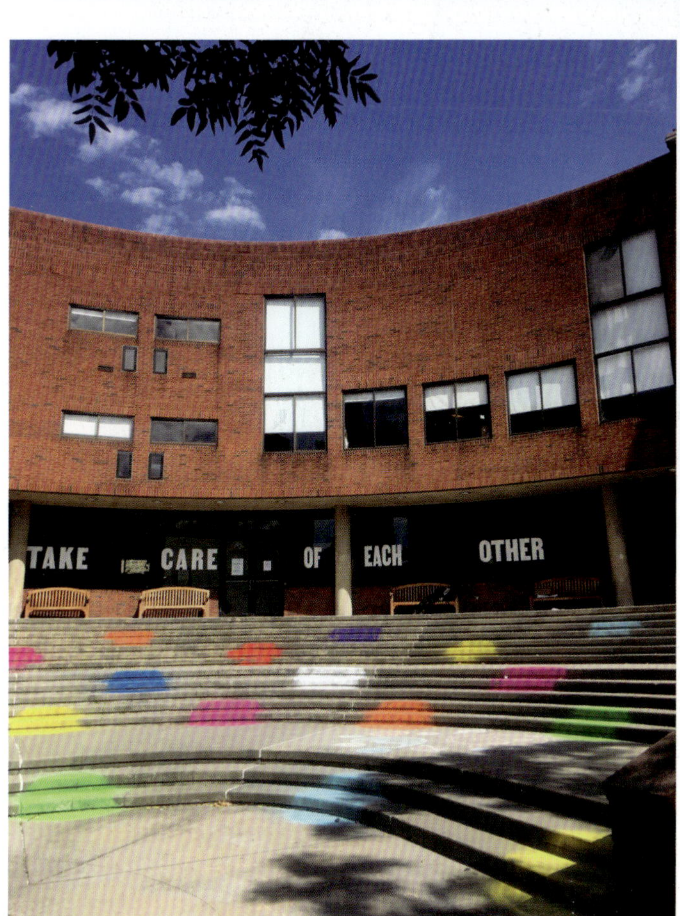

ILANA NOVICK, Take care of each other.
ABRONS ARTS CENTER, LOWER EAST SIDE, NEW YORK, NY, USA

JACQUELINE SILBERBUSH, My Best Friend's COVID Wedding. NEW YORK, NY, USA

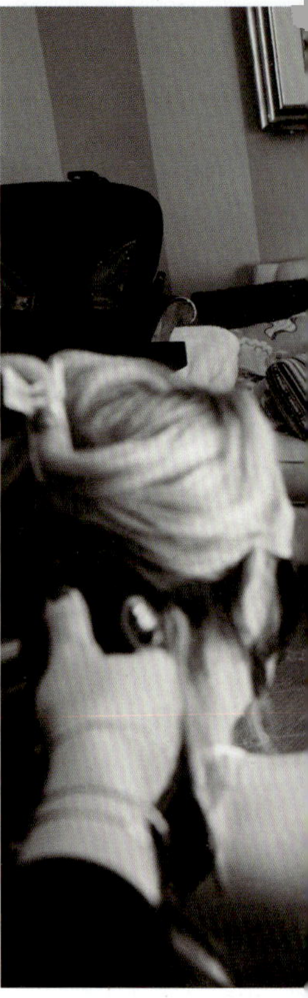

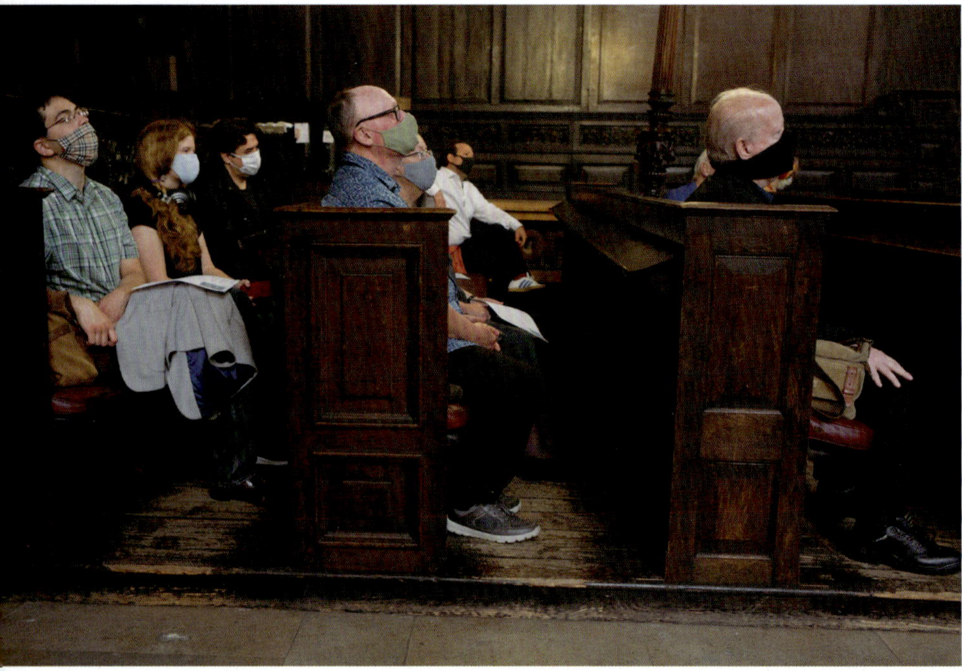

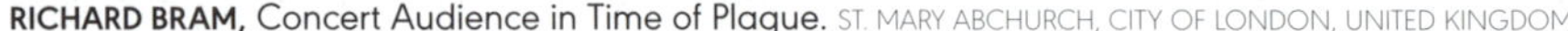

RICHARD BRAM, Concert Audience in Time of Plague. ST. MARY ABCHURCH, CITY OF LONDON, UNITED KINGDOM

NADIA GOMES, Katz's Delicatessen has persisted as a New York City mainstay since 1888. Famous pastrami, salami, and corned beef continue to feed the Lower East Side and its tourists, pandemic or not. NEW YORK, NY, USA

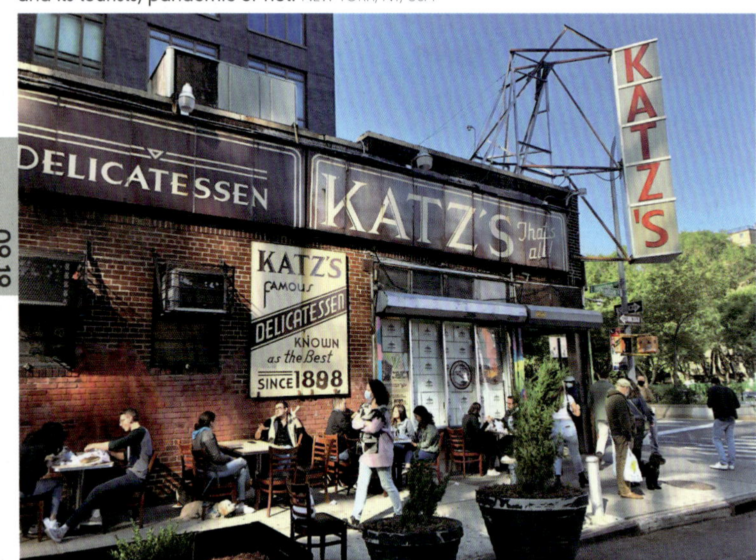

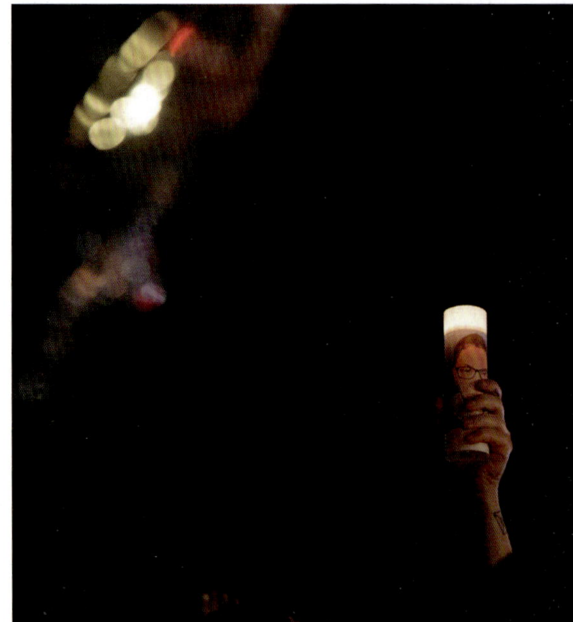

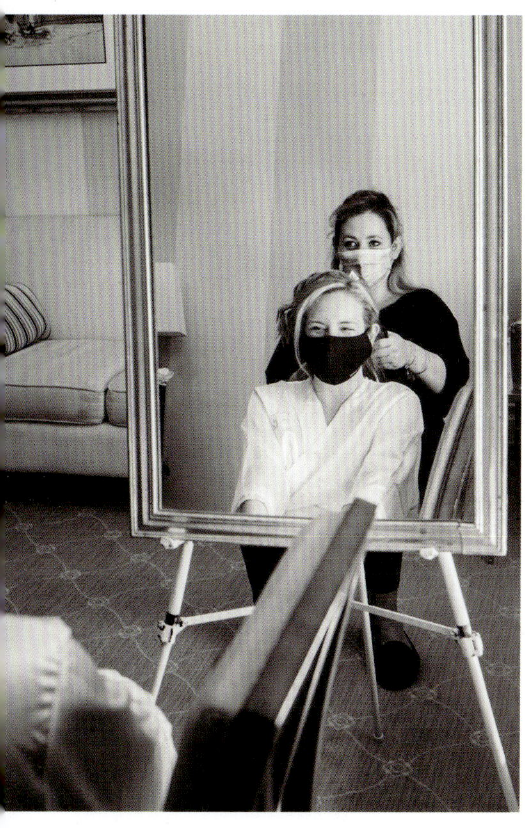

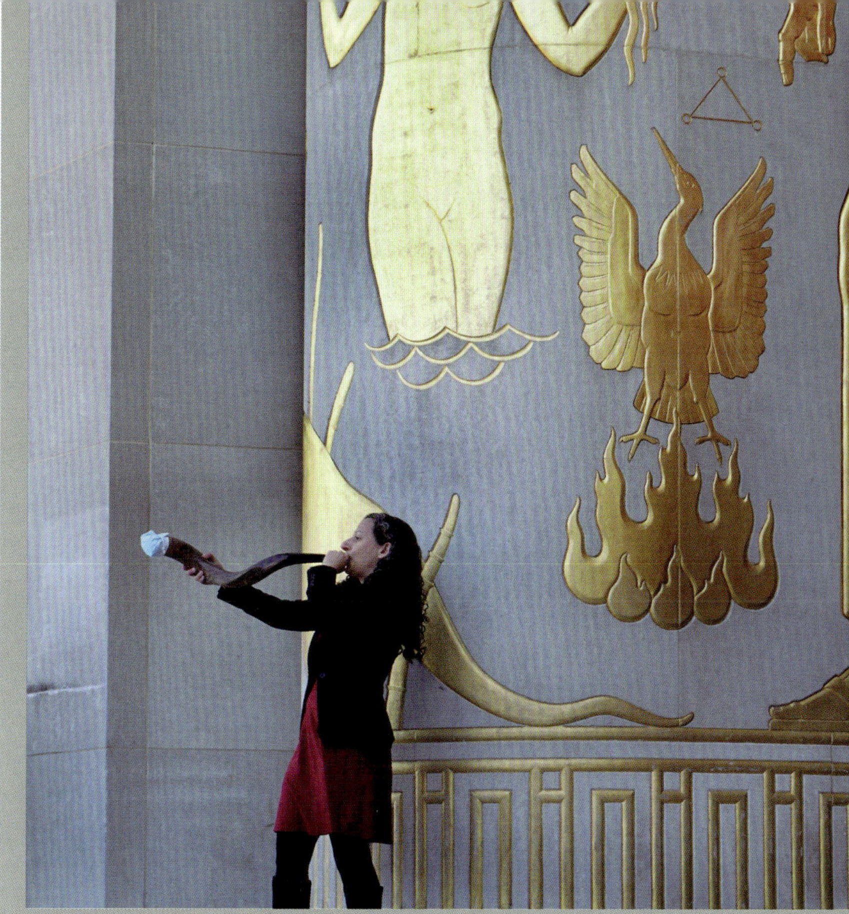

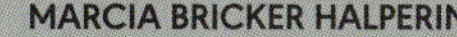

MARCIA BRICKER HALPERIN,

Rosh Hashanah—the Jewish New Year. Temple services were online, but at synagogues across New York City they planned for ritual shofar blowing at outdoor locations. In this photograph the rabbai is blowing the ram's horn on the steps of the Brooklyn Public Library. We had gathered some 20 feet back, and the rabbi put a mask on the shofar as well, because some health specialists claimed that aerosols from instruments, like a trumpet, could travel long distances. Hearing the moving sound of the shofar that day, blown while the rabbi stood before a gilded bas-relief symbol of the Phoenix rising, which flanked the library doors, was a moment when I deeply felt hope and renewal, sorely needed to face the challenging year ahead. BROOKLYN, NY, USA

RACHEL COBB,
A vigil honoring Justice Ruth Bader Ginsberg took place in front of the New York County Supreme Court. Justice Ginsberg died the previous day, just weeks before the presidential election. NEW YORK, NY, USA

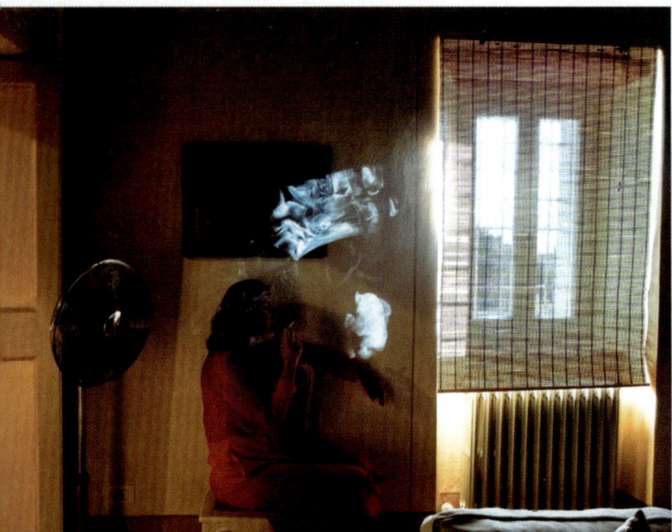

VANESSA PALLOTTA, From "Chromosome XX," a female portrait series documenting women during the COVID-19 pandemic. CAMPELLO SUL CLITUNNO, UMBRIA, ITALY

CAMILLE GARZON, The strength of the Black woman. NEW YORK, NY, USA

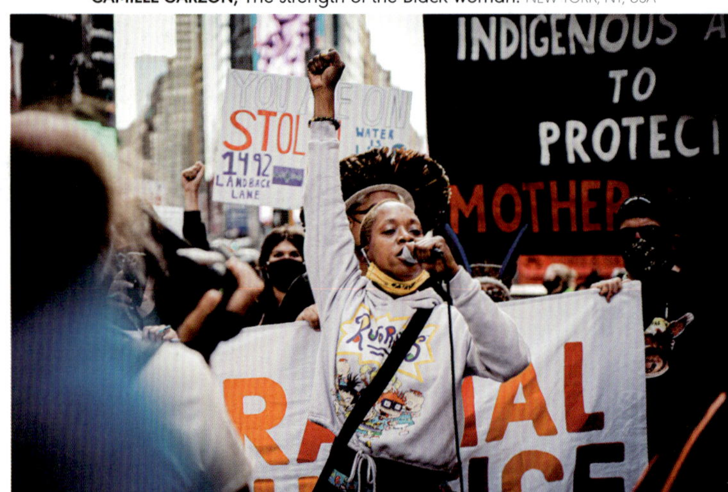

STEPHEN MURPHY, Biking north on a Saturday to join the Green Bay Trail. A schoolyard cut-through had been transformed into a magical tent city of alfresco learning. KENILWORTH, IL, USAY

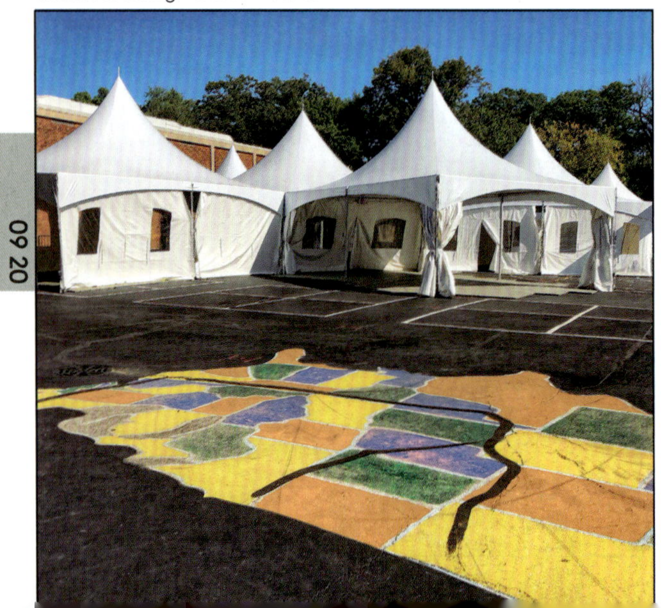

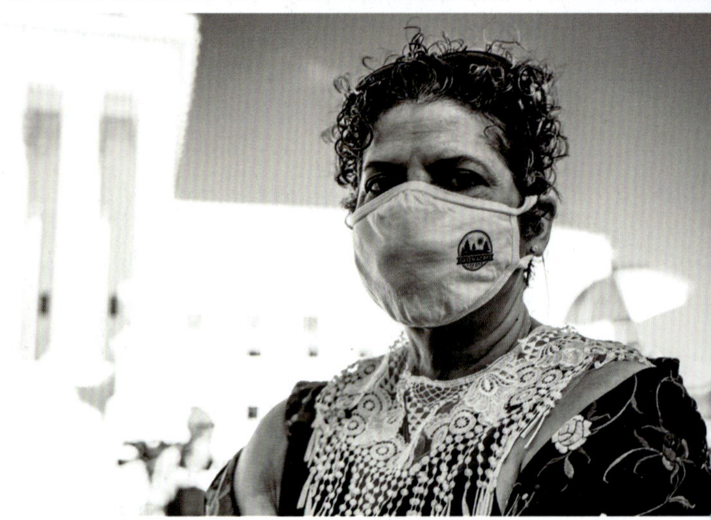

ROBIN FADER, *Mourning Justice Ruth Bader Ginsburg* | As thousands gathered at the Supreme Court leaving tributes in art, chalk and flowers, a woman and her collar become a powerful symbol of respect. WASHINGTON, DC, USA

PATRICIO MURPHY, Cardiologist Juliana Albert speaks during a health workers' press conference demanding supplies and human resources to combat the COVID-19 outbreak. FIRMAT, SANTA FE, ARGENTINA

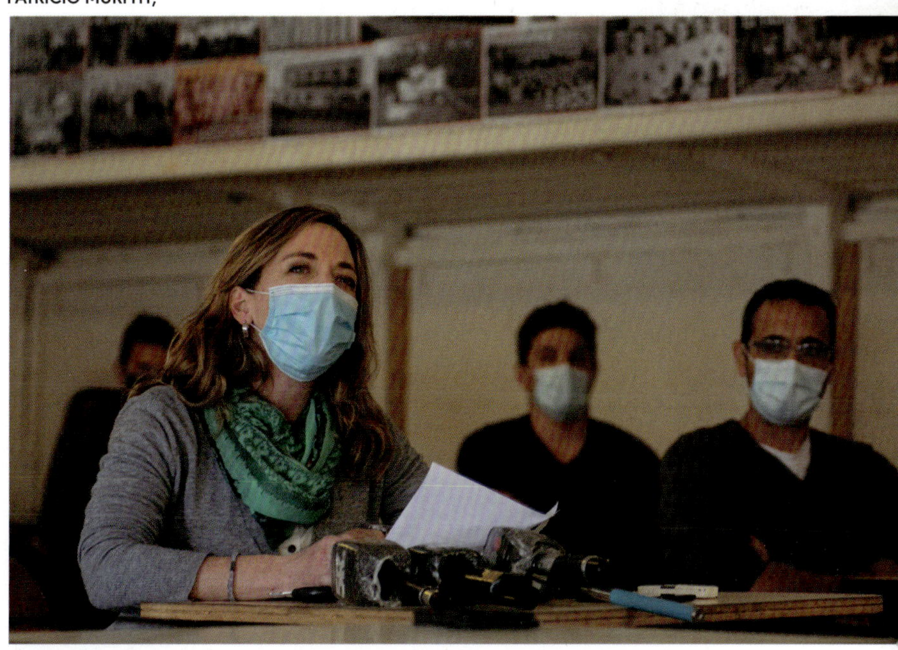

SANTIAGO RAMÍREZ BAQUERO, A group of women protest with dance and cacerolazo in the center of Bogotá against the abuse of the police who murdered a law student eleven days ago. COLOMBIA

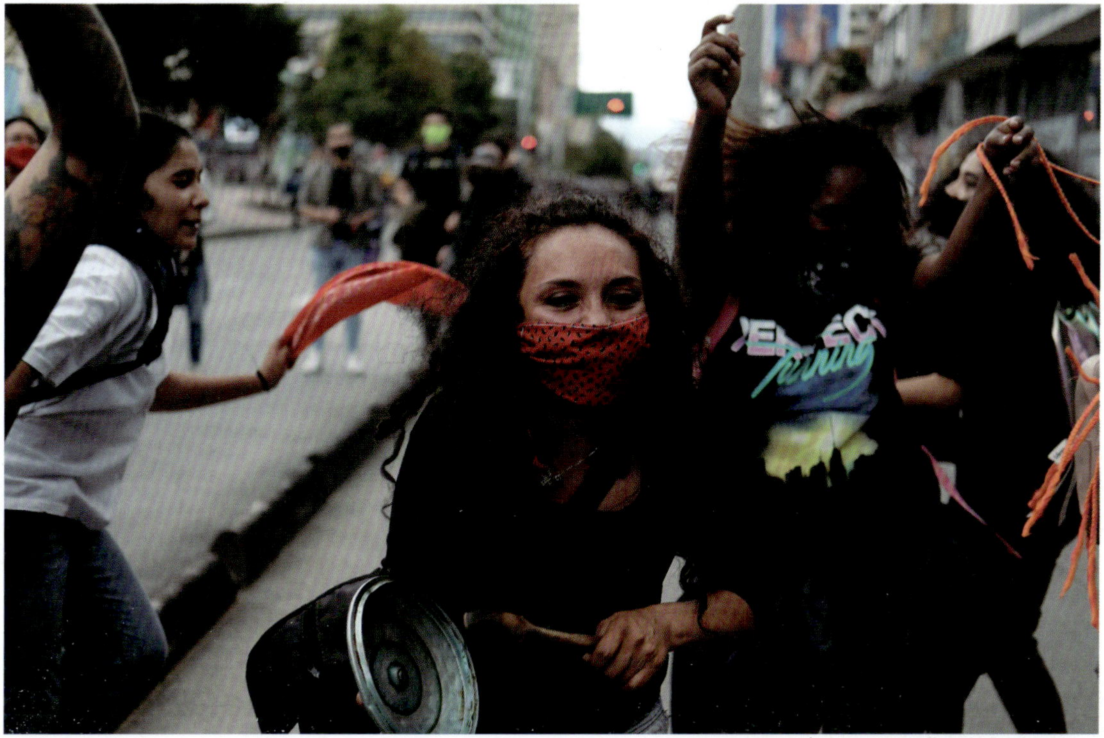

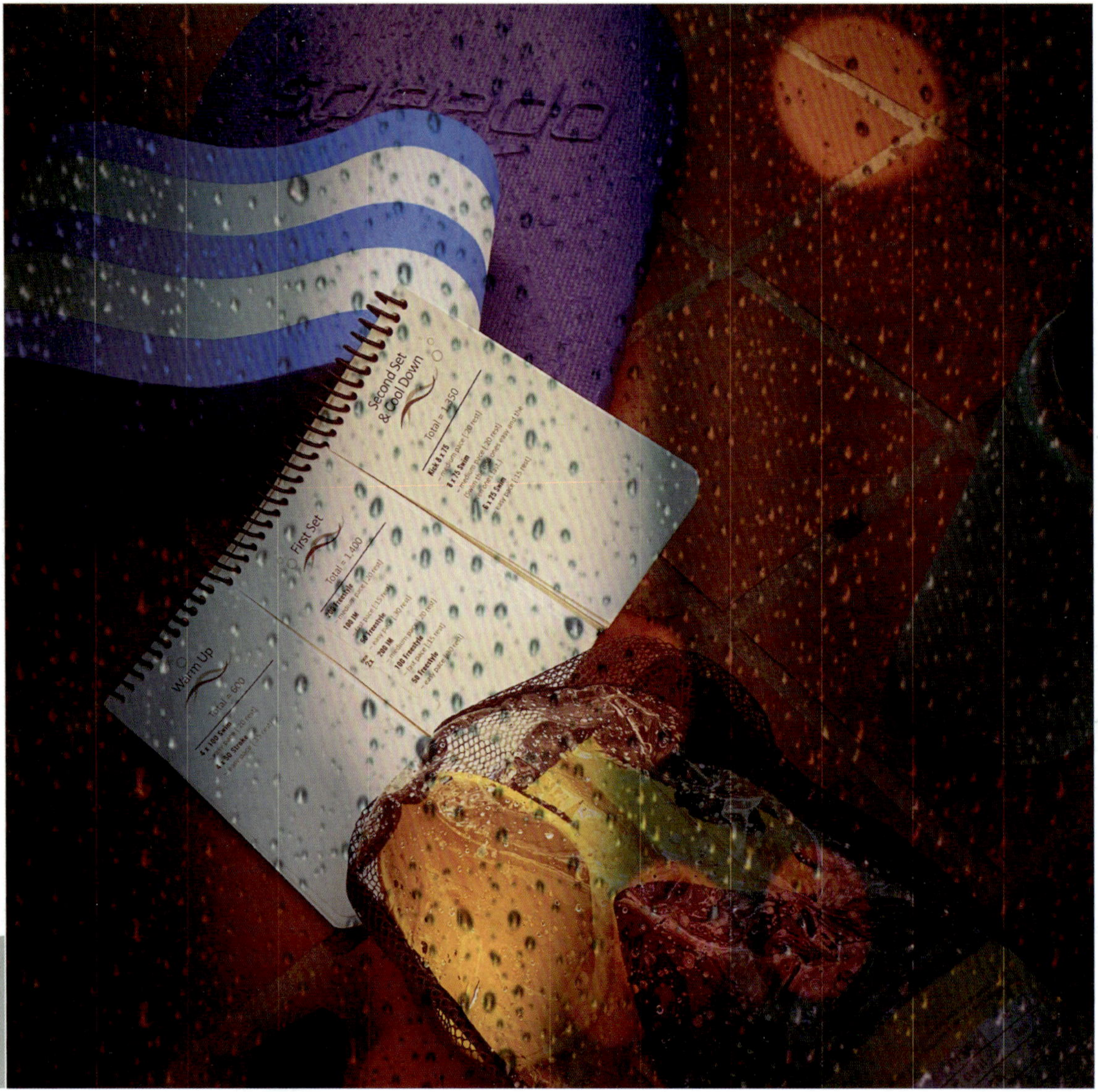

MEGANNE HUETT, *Togetherness.*
VIRGINIA BEACH,
VA, USA

SHEDRICK PELT, This was the scene outside of the Department of Justice the evening of the Breonna Taylor verdict. WASHINGTON, DC, USA

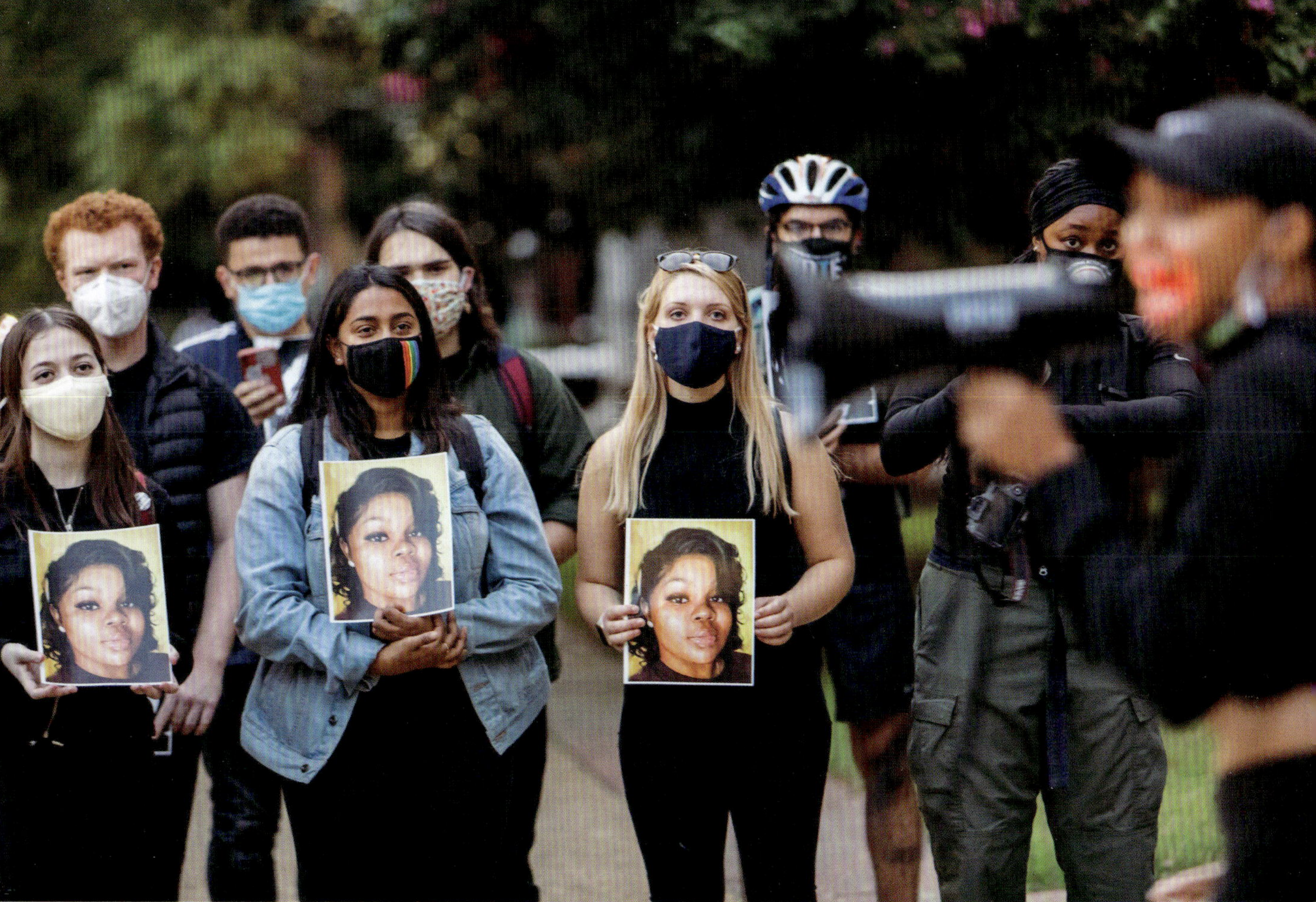

ANN DZAGANIA, Traveling without a face mask on public transport is prohibited. A boy who forgot a face mask covers his face with his shirt. TBILISI, GEORGIA

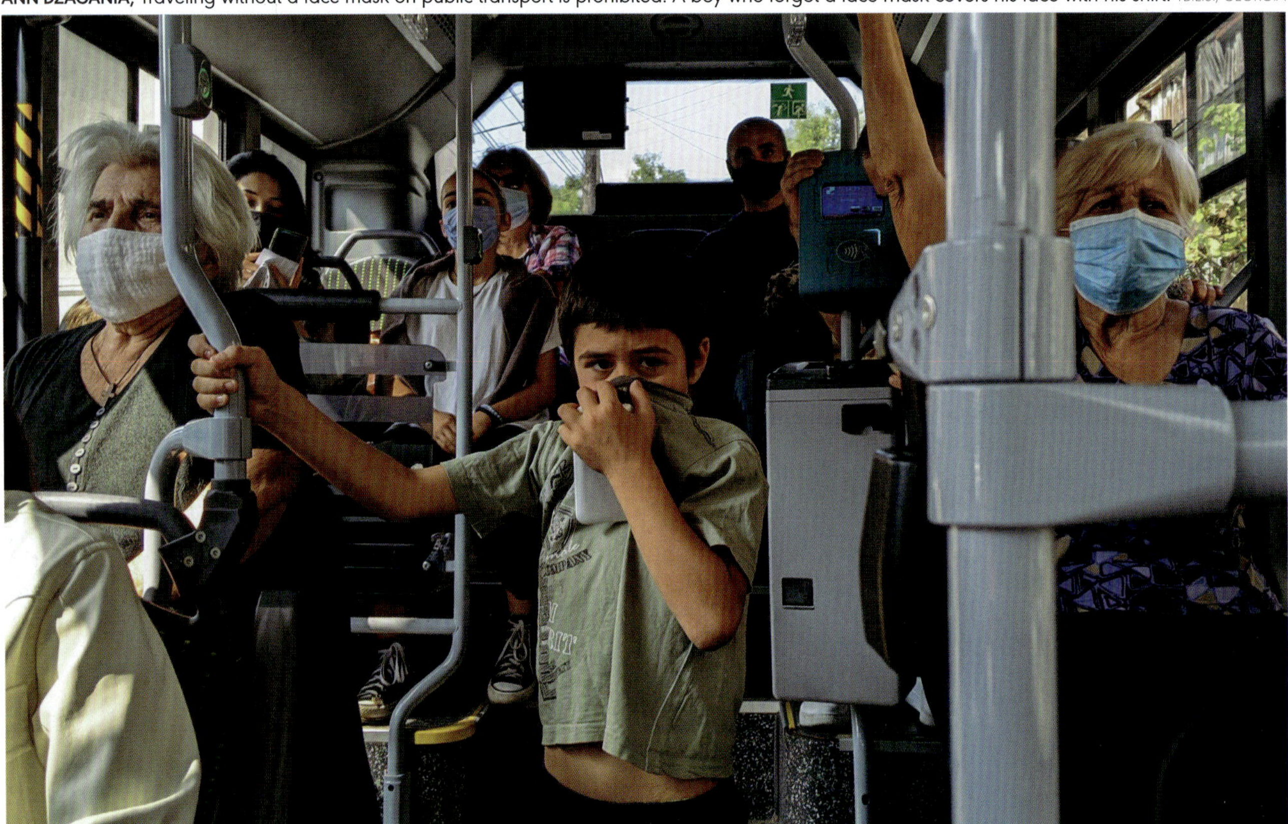

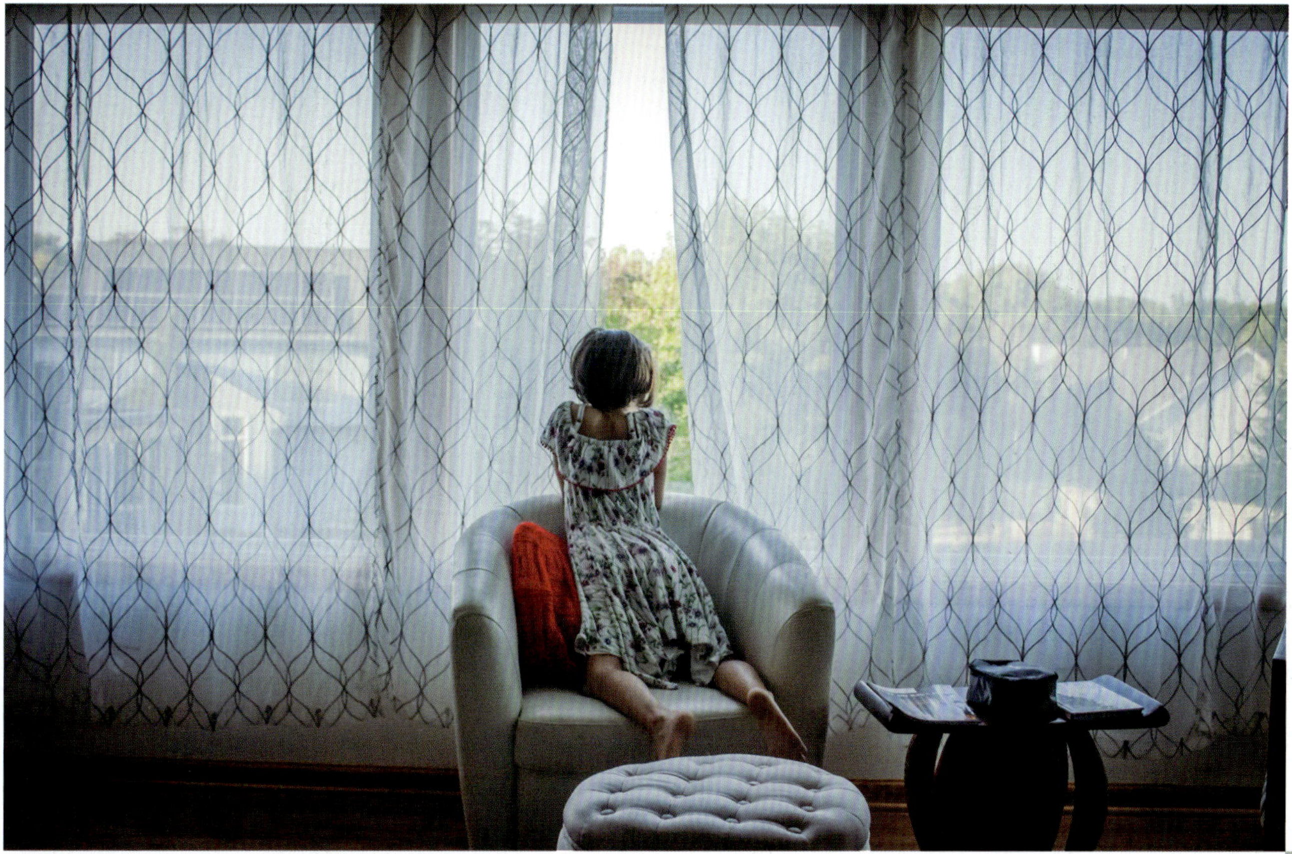

VINEETA SHARMA,

Waiting for Nothing. LENEXA, KS, USA

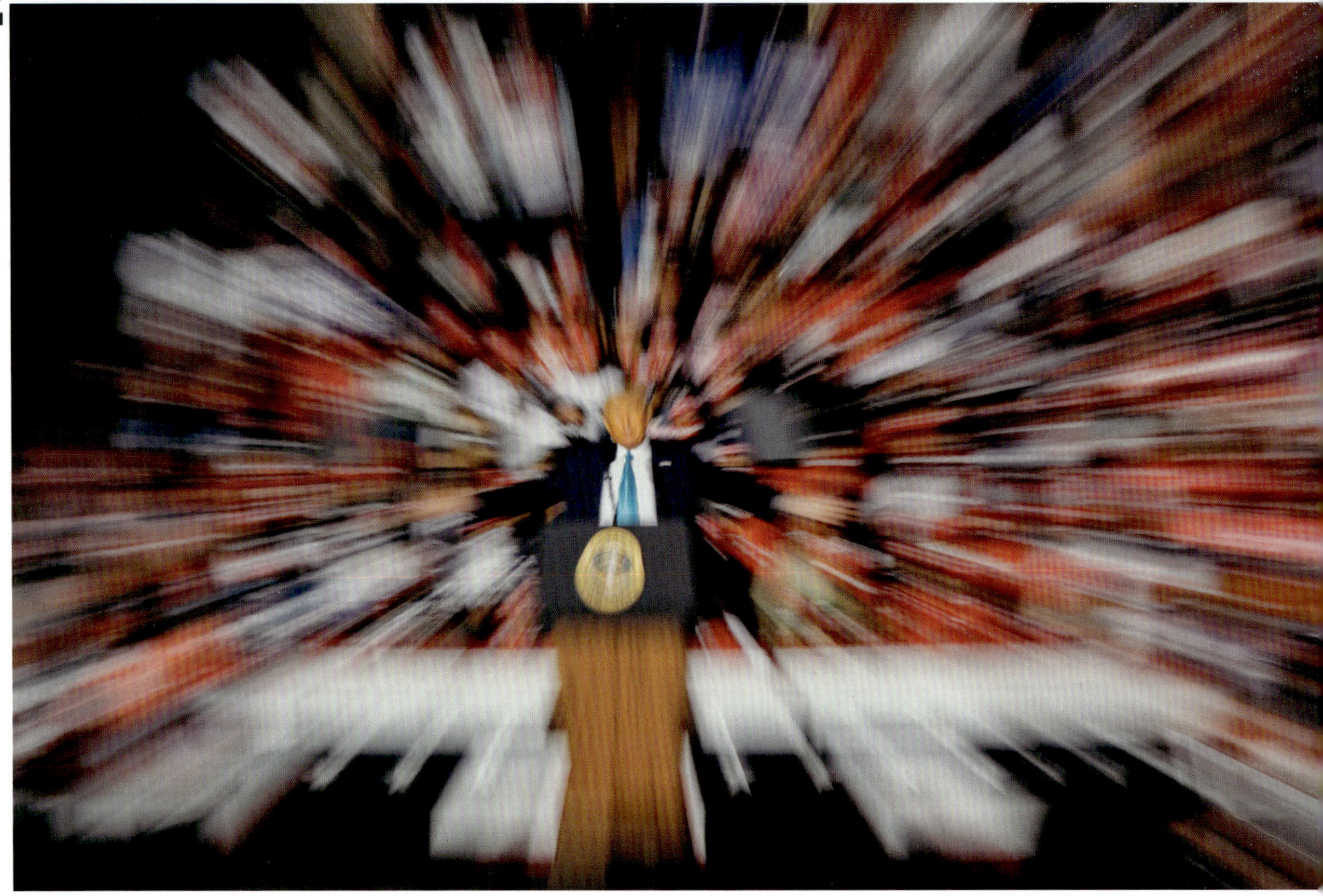

SEAN DISERIO,

After departing a White House ceremony, later deemed a "superspreader event," by Anthony Fauci, Trump headed to a rally in Pennsylvania. Five days later he disclosed that he contracted COVID-19.
MIDDLETOWN, PA, USA

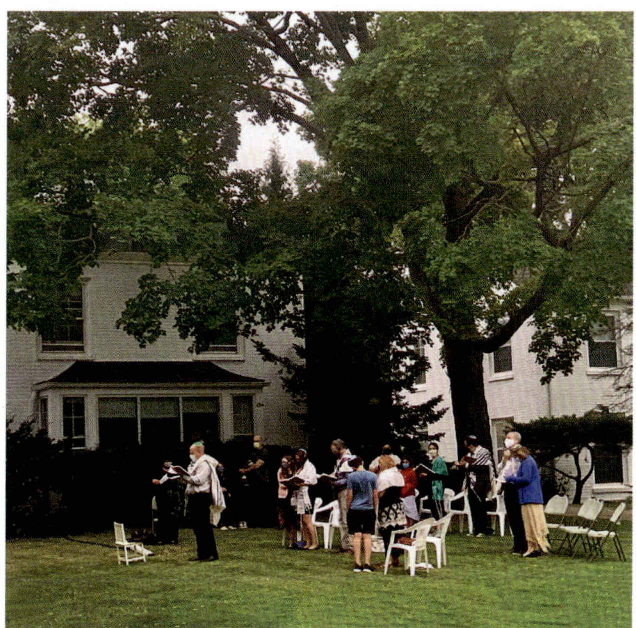

YVETTE MELTZER, *Kol Nidre (All Vows)* | Jewish religious service of chanted prayers being held outdoors, socially distanced, in the front yard of a private home. EVANSTON, IL, USA

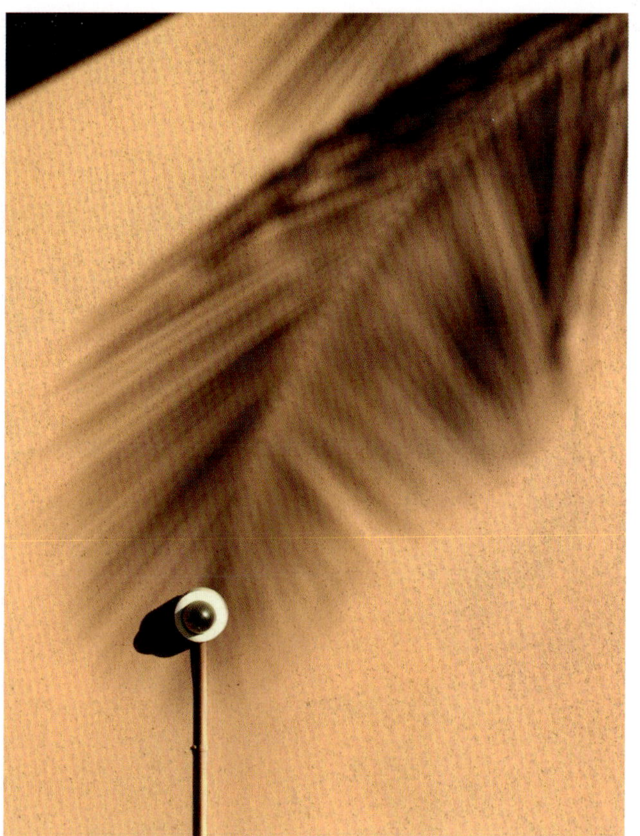

RONALD VER, Tropical Surveillance. HONOLULU, HI, USA

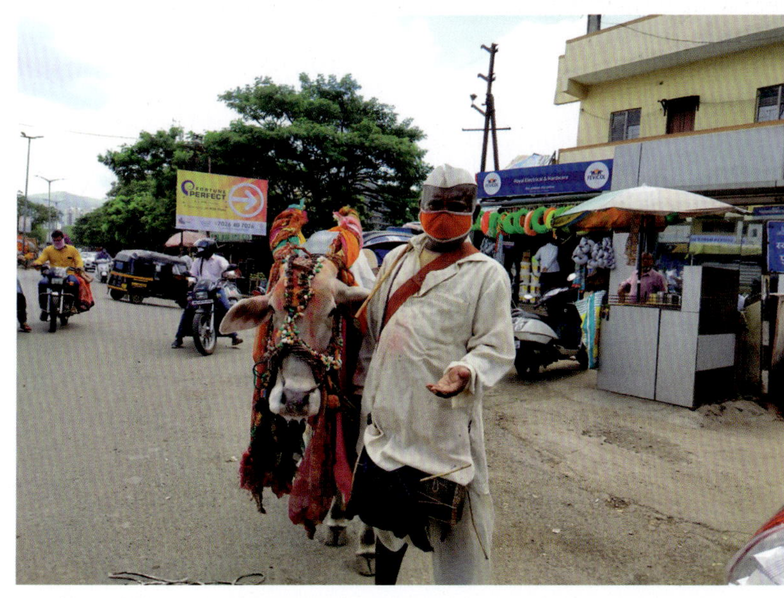

MANAV MENON, Holy Cow. PUNE, MAHARASHTRA, INDIA

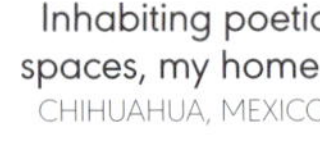

Inhabiting poetic spaces, my home.
CHIHUAHUA, MEXICO

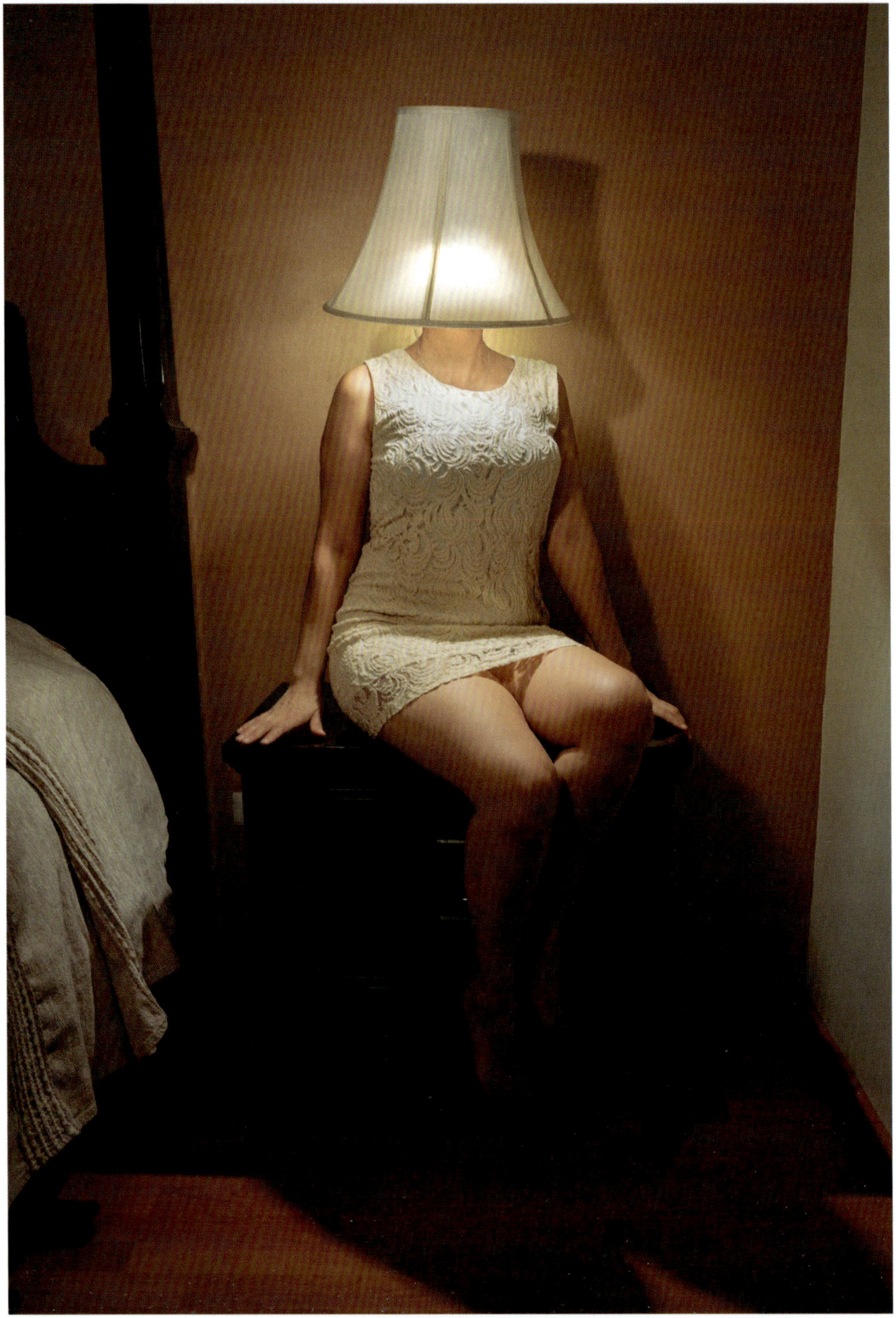

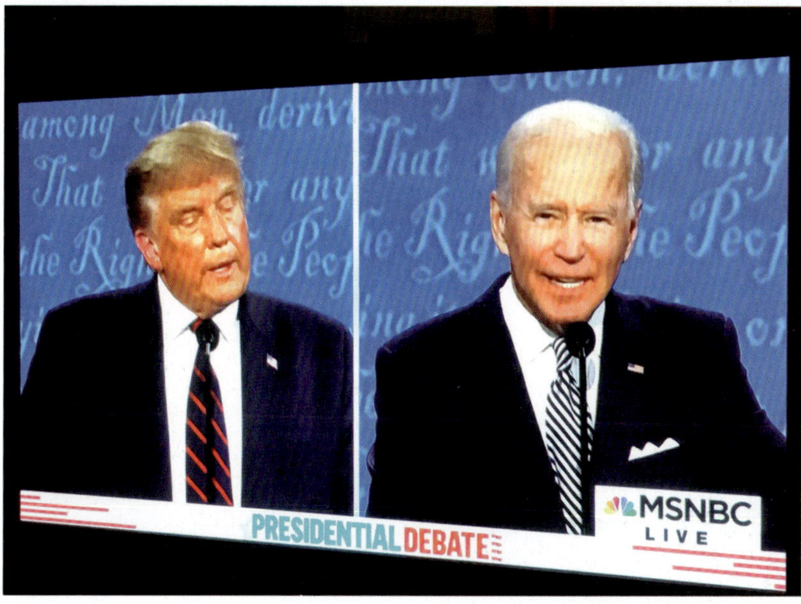

DONNA ROCCO, *First Presidential Debate, Cleveland, Ohio* | Joe Biden to Donald Trump, "Will you just shush for a second?"
NY, USA

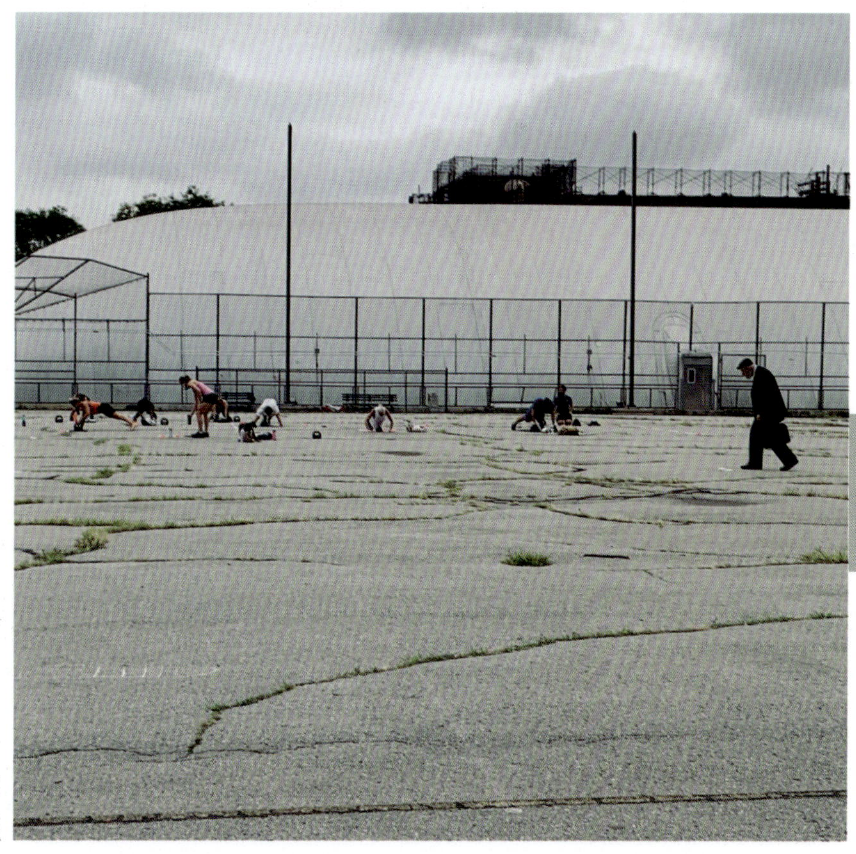

LEANDRO ARTIGALA, *Normality-Normalidad* |
Our new urban scenes, our new daily lives.
WILLIAMSBURG, BROOKLYN, NY, USA

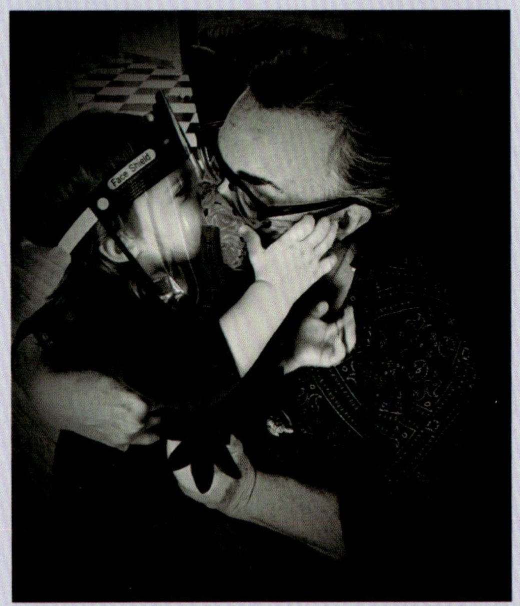

DAVIDA MERLIS GRABER, Reunion. ATLANTA, GA, USA

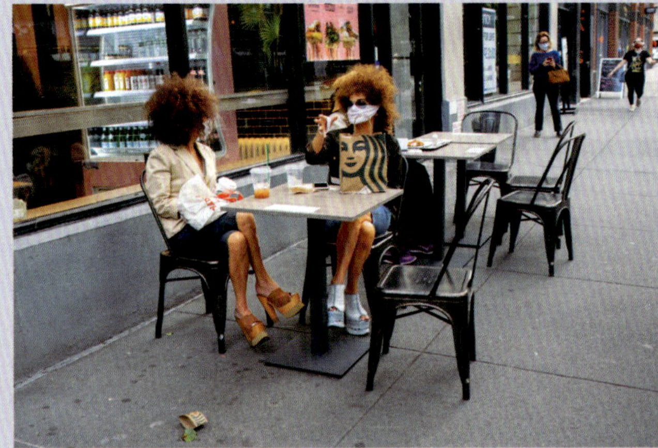

MELANIE EINZIG, Women having coffee on Broadway. NEW YORK, NY, USA

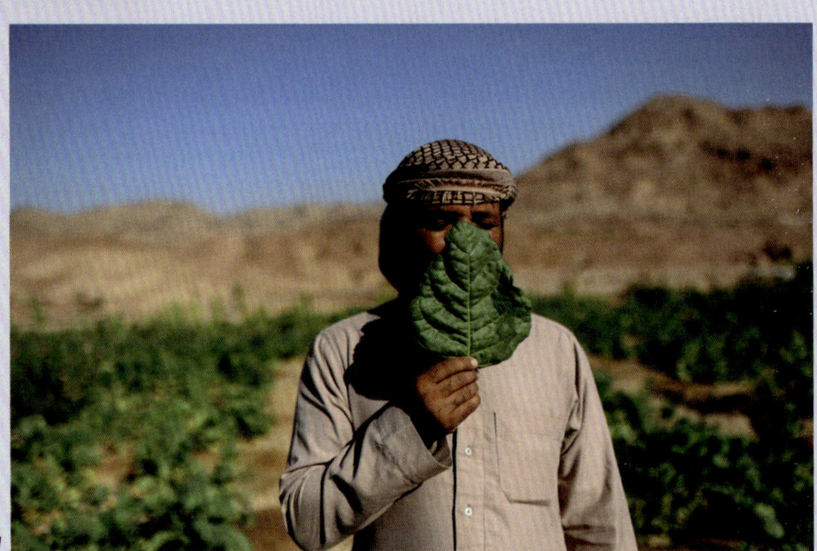

REHAB ELDALIL, *Keepers Of The Land* | Soliman in his garden in the Gharba valley. A major flood occurred after years of drought, providing an agricultural opportunity for the Bedouin community amid COVID-19. SOUTH SINAI, EGYPT

10·20

OCTOBER

10_ Johnson&Johnson Pauses Coronavirus Vaccine Trials Due to Sick Subjects *(Wall Street Journal)*

17_ As the Coronavirus Surges, a New Culprit Emerges: Pandemic Fatigue *(The New York Times)*

26_ LA County Hits New Milestones in Cases, Deaths... *(LA Times)*

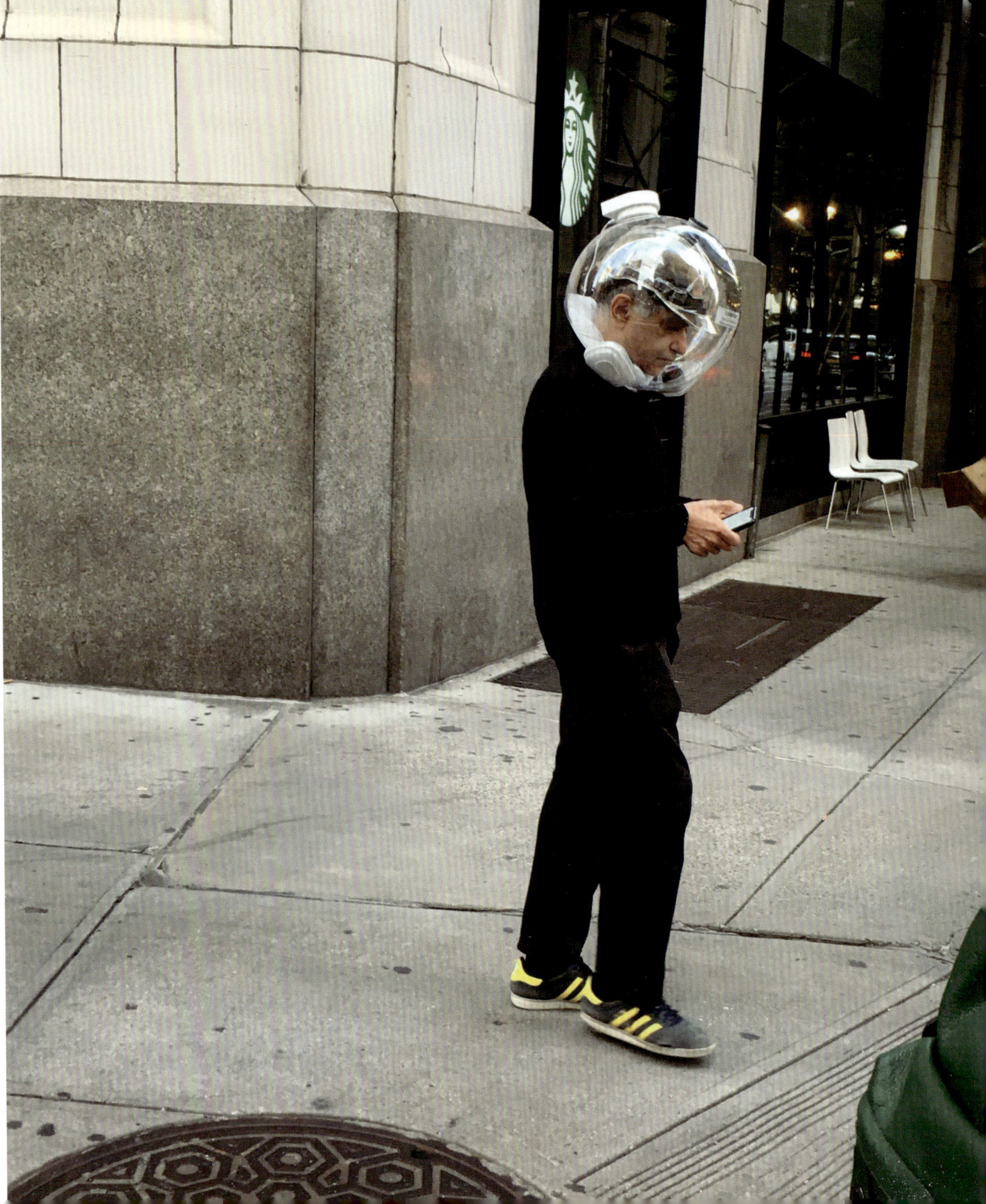

ESTHER LEVINE,
New Reality.
NEW YORK, NY, USA

LAURA MINSK,

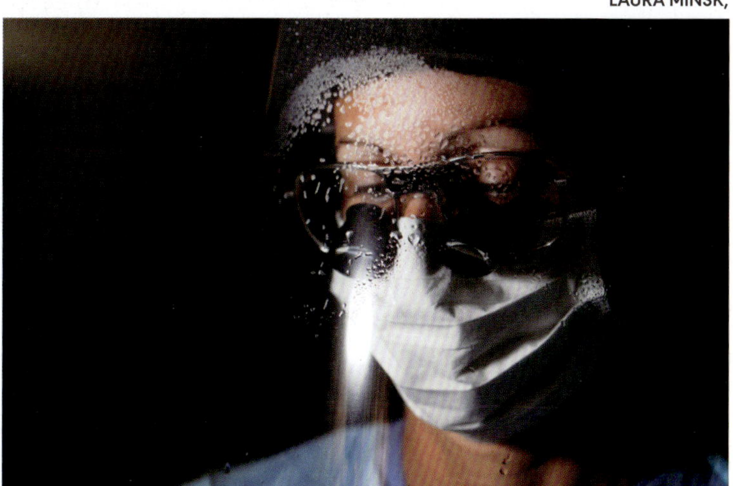

Due to the inherent proximity to patients and the production of aerosols during treatment, dentists face one of the greatest risks of infection of COVID-19. SWARTHMORE, PA, USA

ELI HAIES-GRUNWALD, Teach Peace. GREENWICH VILLAGE, NEW YORK, NY, USA

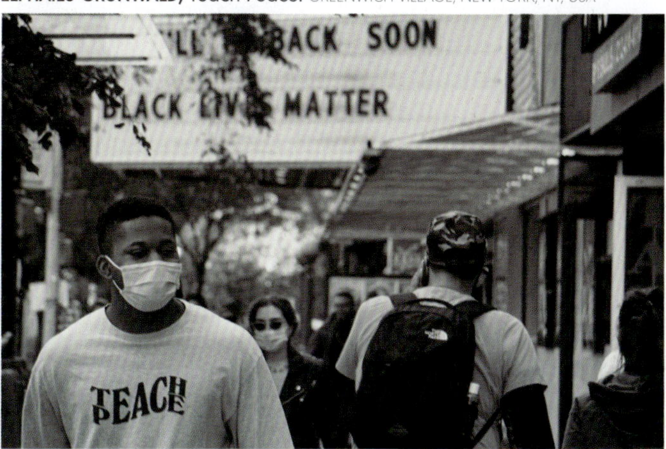

WOLF WEINTRAUB, Prospect Heights, Brooklyn. NEW YORK, NY, USA

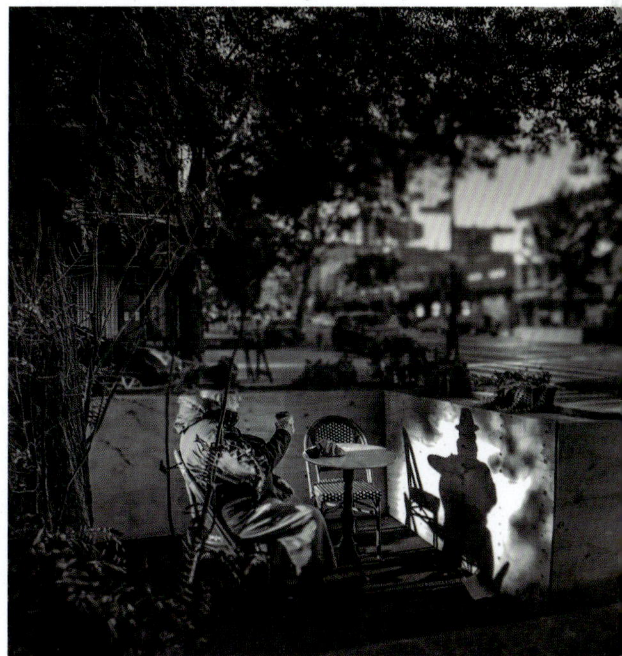

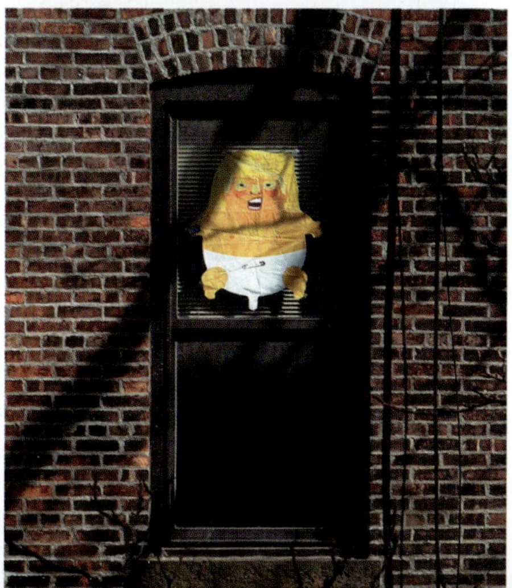

HARRISON WEINSTEIN, Untitled 45. NEW YORK, NY, USA

LISA WINNER, *Under the Sea* |

My son walking through the underground tunnels of the Aquarium by the Bay two weeks after re-opening.

SAN FRANCISCO, CA, USA

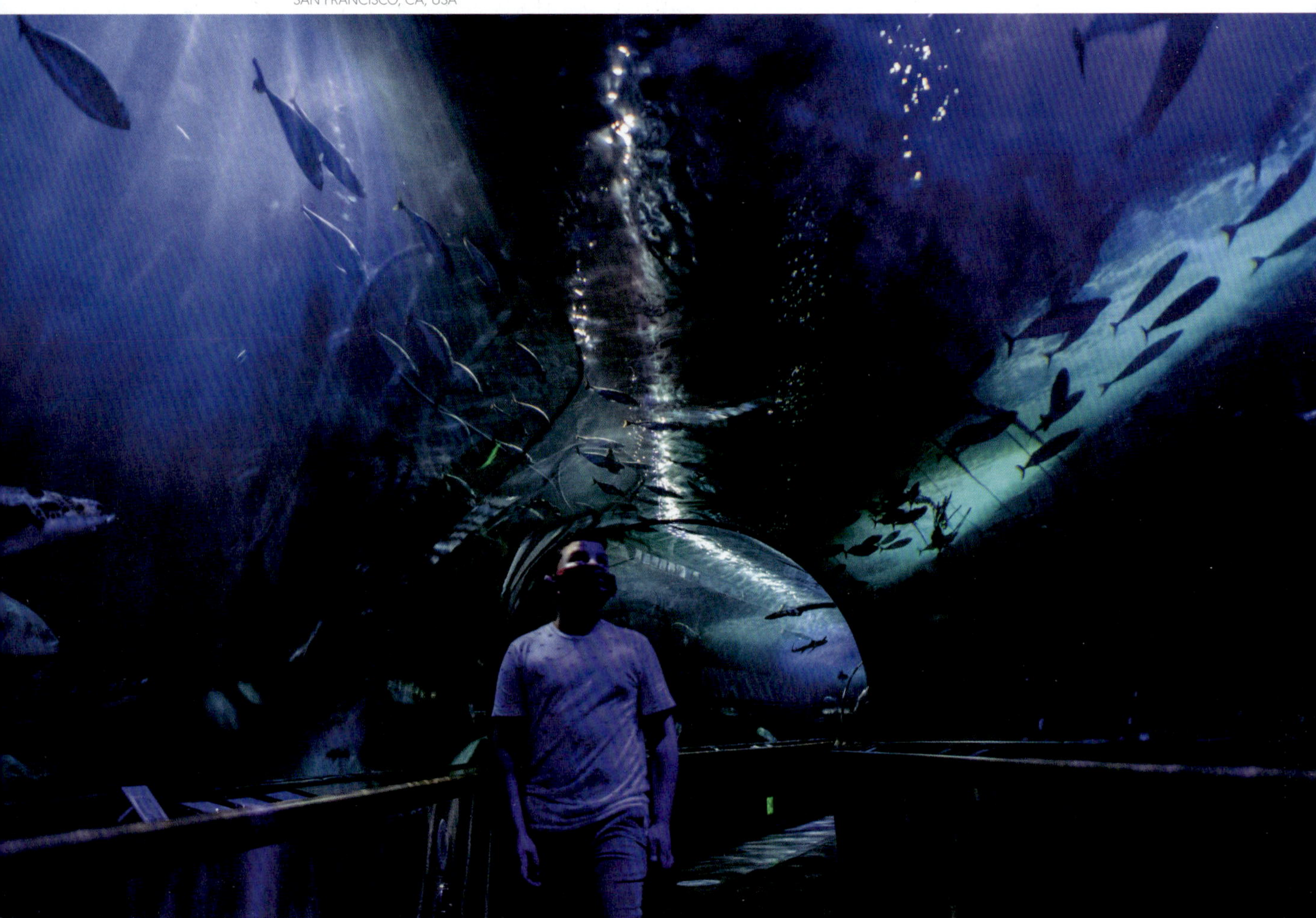

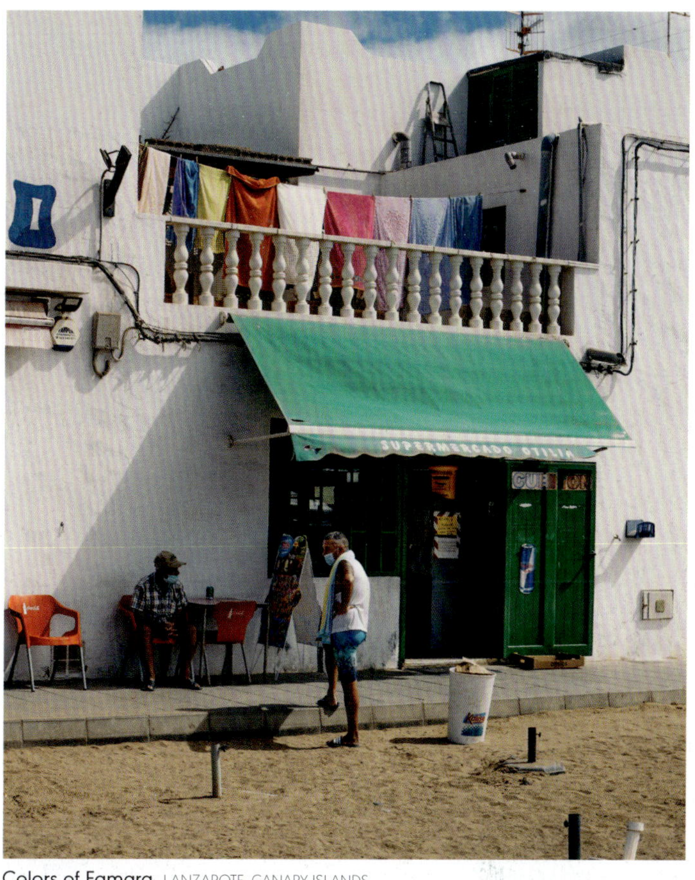

SEAN LEVETT, Colors of Famara. LANZAROTE, CANARY ISLANDS

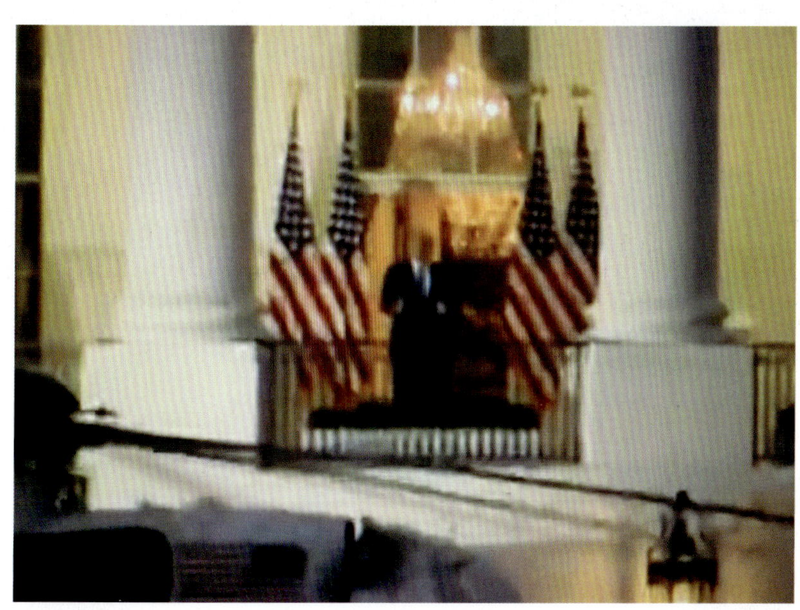

RIK MORAN, 25th Amendment now. NEW YORK, NY, USA

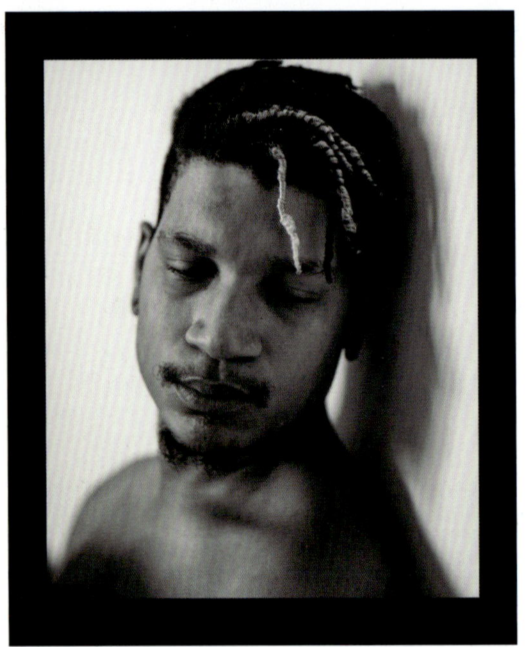

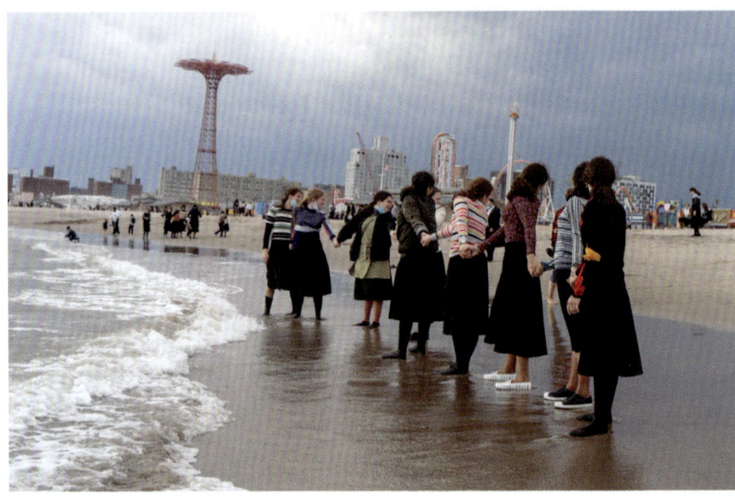

HINDY LEITNER, *Hand in Hand* | This too shall pass. CONEY ISLAND, BROOKLYN, NY, USA

RICHARD BURROWES, A Morning Reflection. WOODSIDE, QUEENS, NY, USA

SOMSAMAY HOMPHOTHICHAK, *Autumn in the City* | Life during the pandemic. MADISON, WI, USA

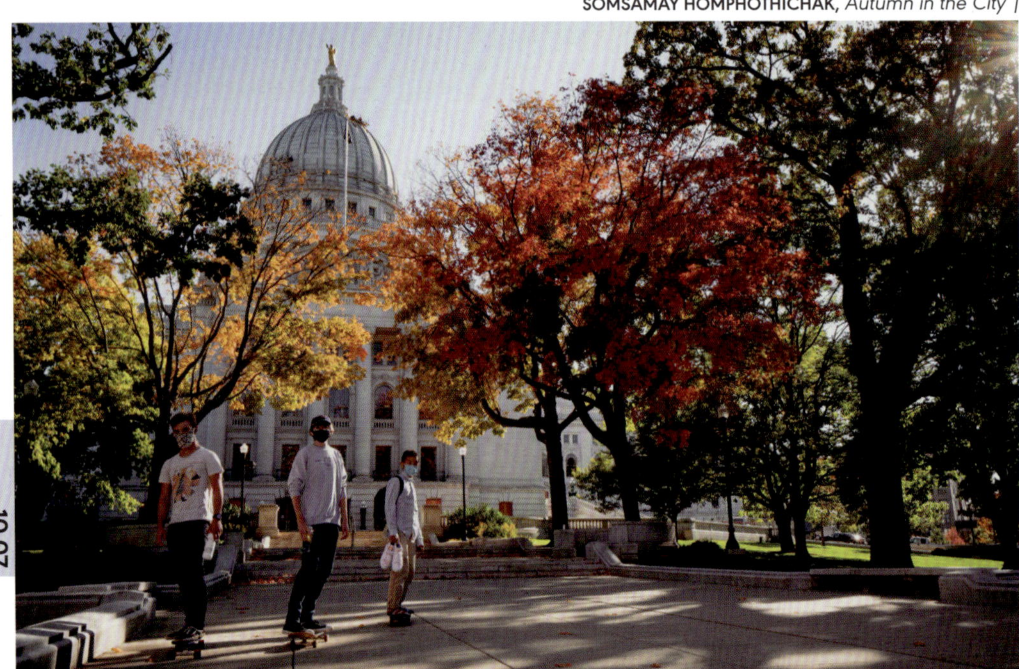

YU-CHEN CHIU, America Seen. CHESTER, VT, USA

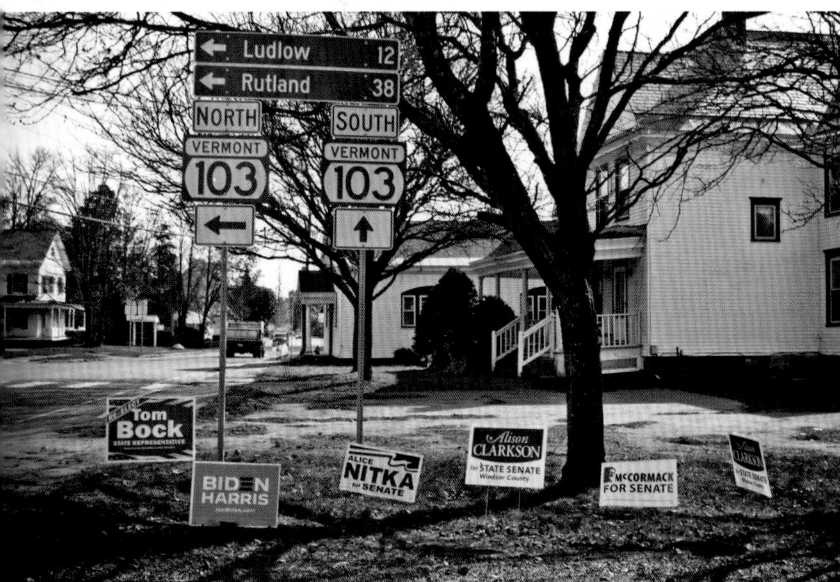

CATIJA REHKAMP, At 8:46 PM the crowd released black balloons into the night sky to celebrate what would have been George Floyd's 47th birthday. BROOKLYN, NY, USA

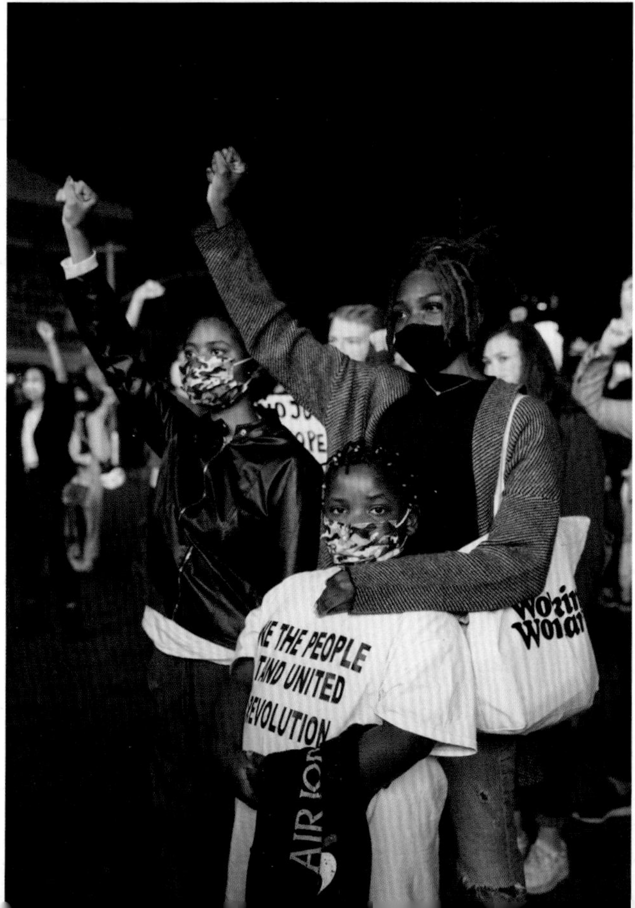

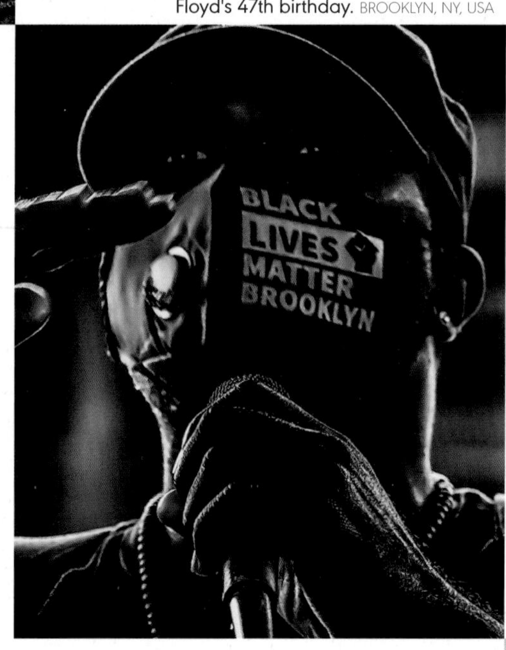

CHAE KIHN, A candlelit vigil was held at the Barclays Center for what would have been George Floyd's 47th Birthday. BROOKLYN, NY, USA

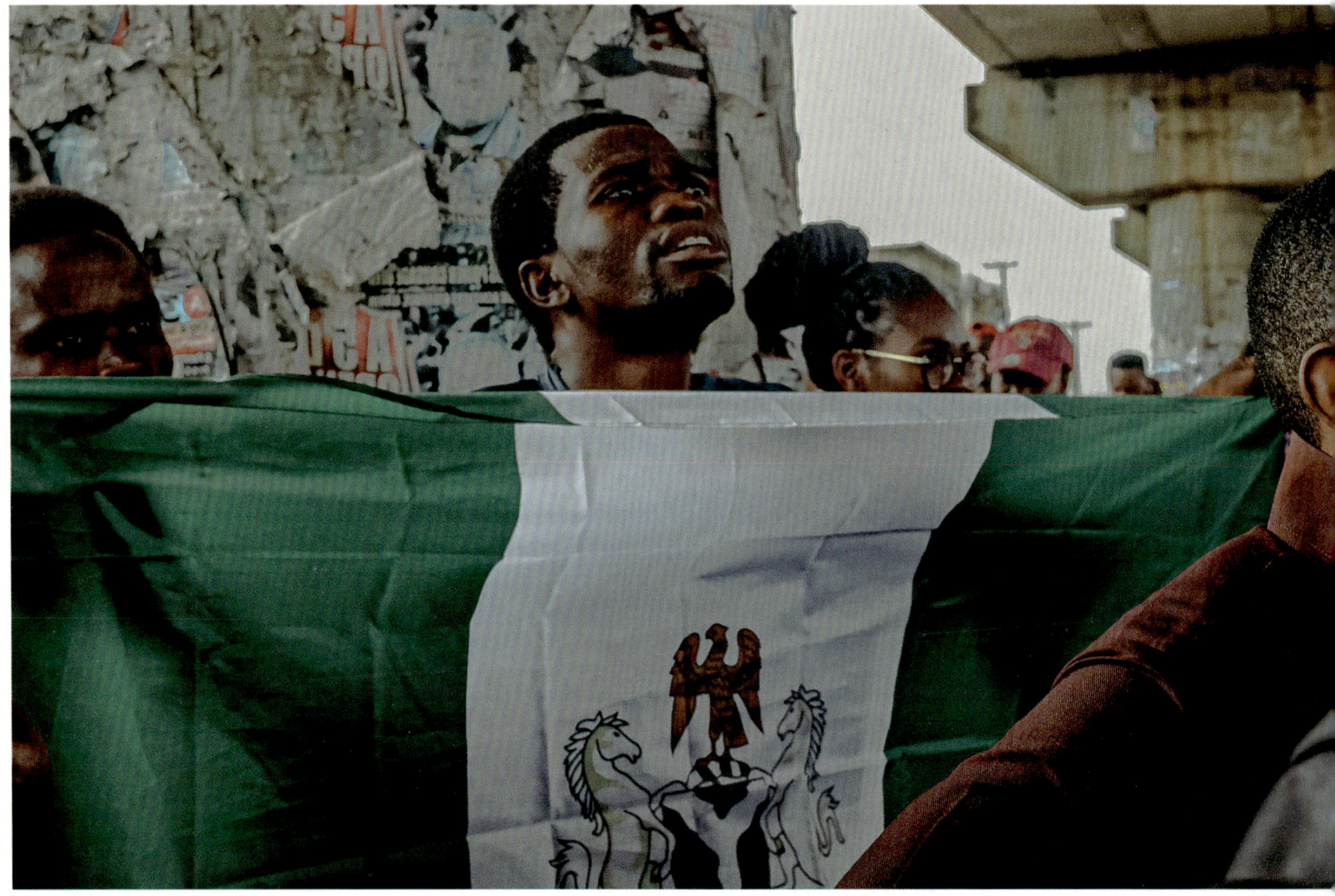

FRANCIS OGUNYEMI, A young man holds the Nigerian flag with the coat of arms during the #EndSARS protests in Kwara State. NIGERIA

GUSTAVO CANDELAS, Counter-protestors clash with police at the Super Happy Fun America Trump Rally in Copley Square. BOSTON, MA, USA

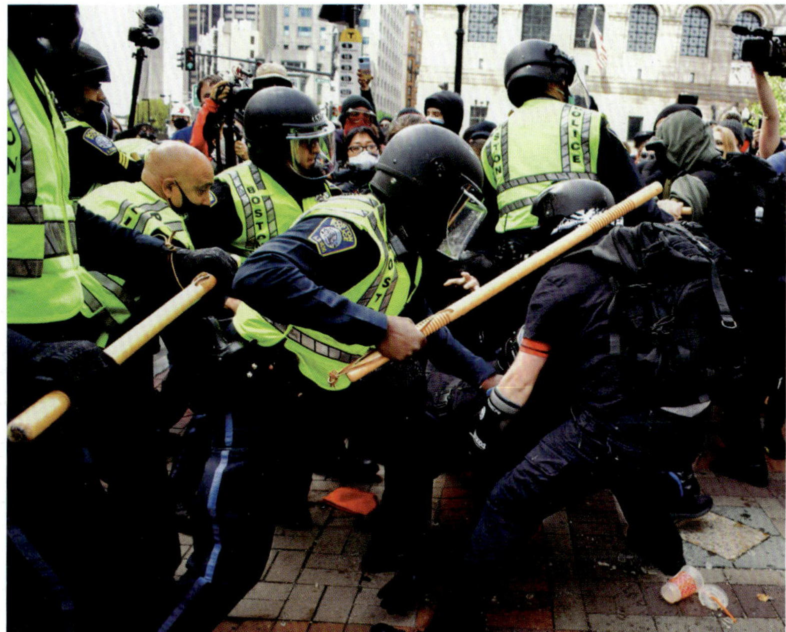

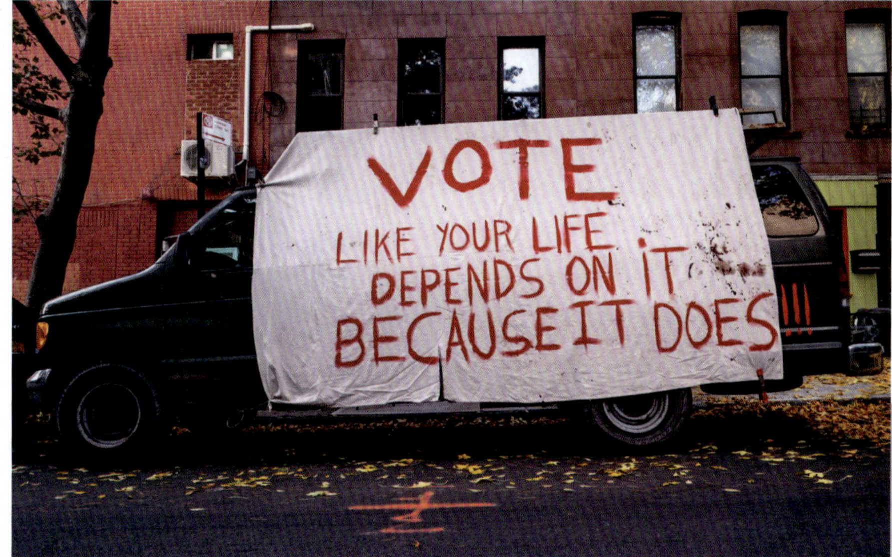

MICHAEL MOONEY, *Vote Like your Life Depends on It Because It Does* | Please vote. BROOKLYN, NY, USA

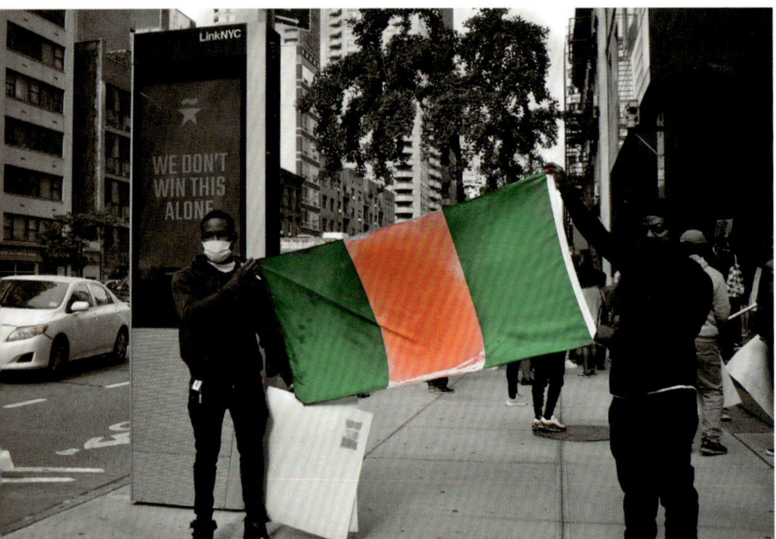

ARMANI ORTIZ, *March For Nigerian Lives | #EndSARS.* NEW YORK, NY, USA

KATIE GODOWSKI,
Riot police at a MAGA rally in lower Manhattan. NEW YORK, NY, USA

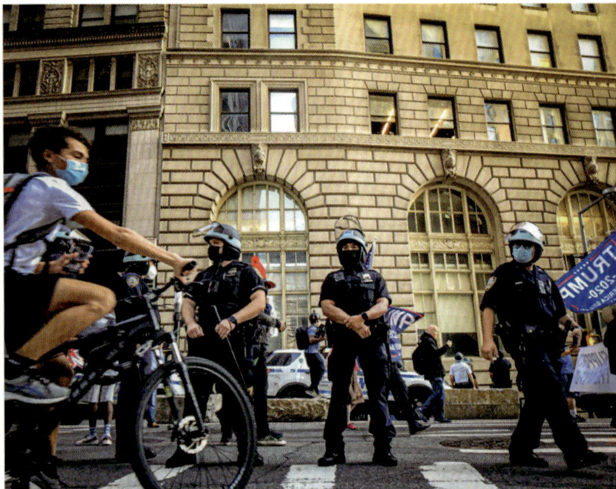

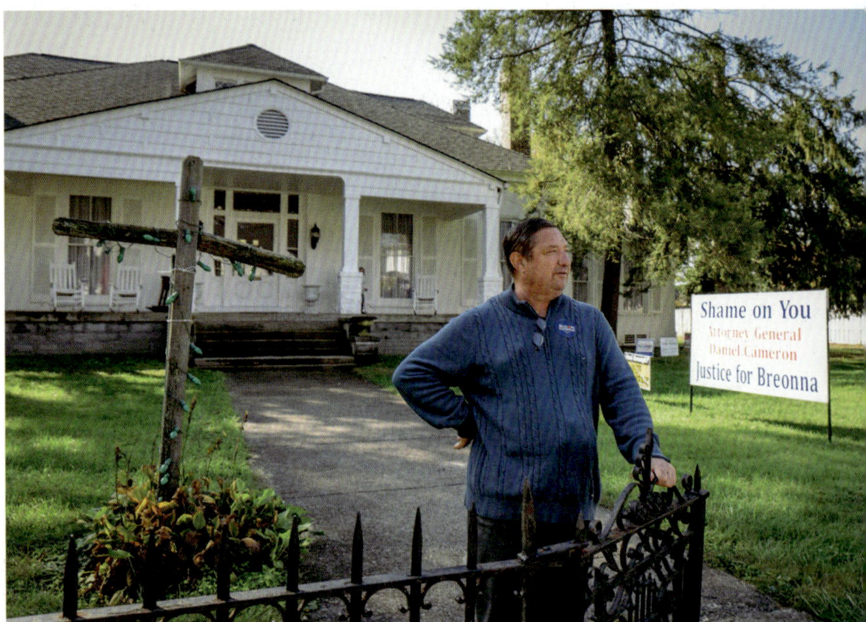

LISA STOCKTON HOWELL, *Justice for Breonna |* The homeowner paid to have this sign made and placed in his yard on the main road through town. GEORGETOWN, KY, USA

BISMA SEPTALISMA, Members of Indonesian trade unions protest against the government's labor reforms in a jobs creation bill. JAKARTA, INDONESIA

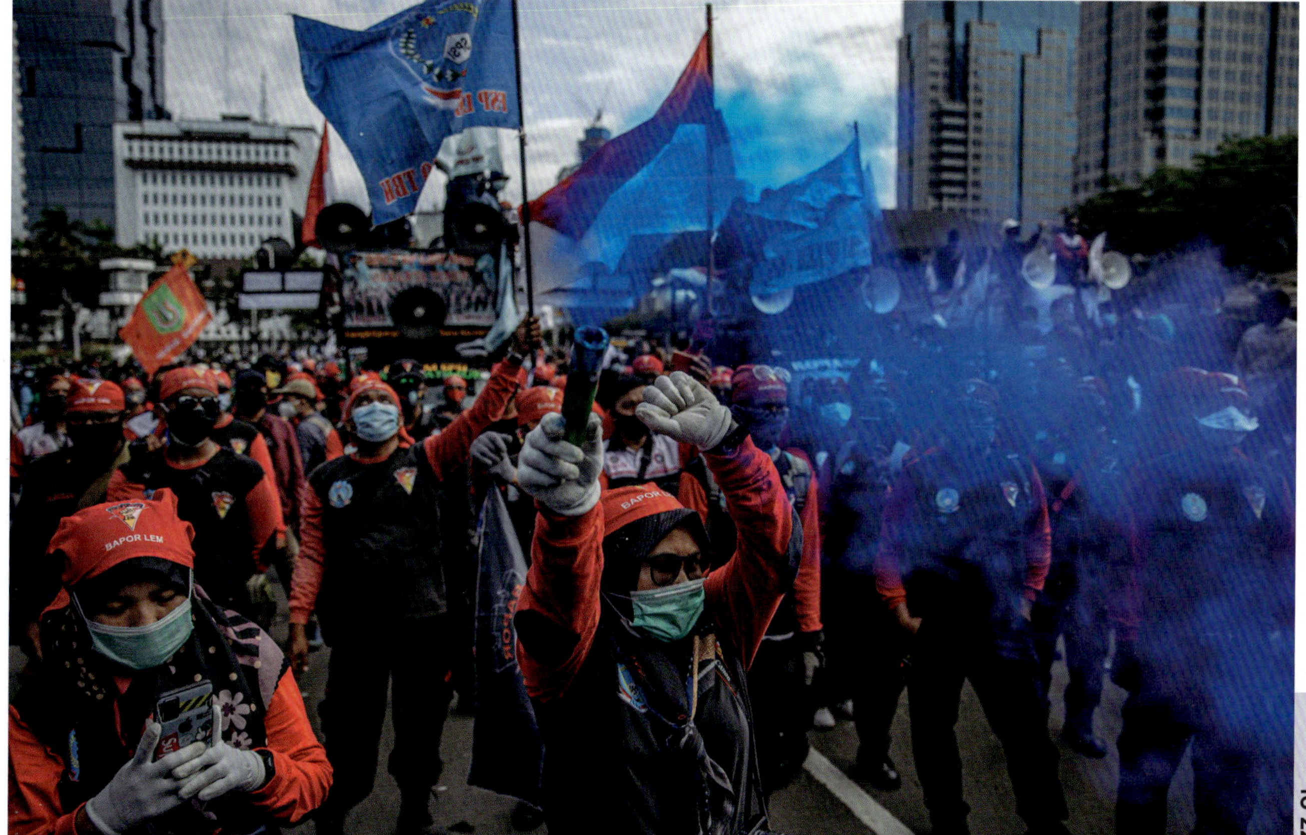

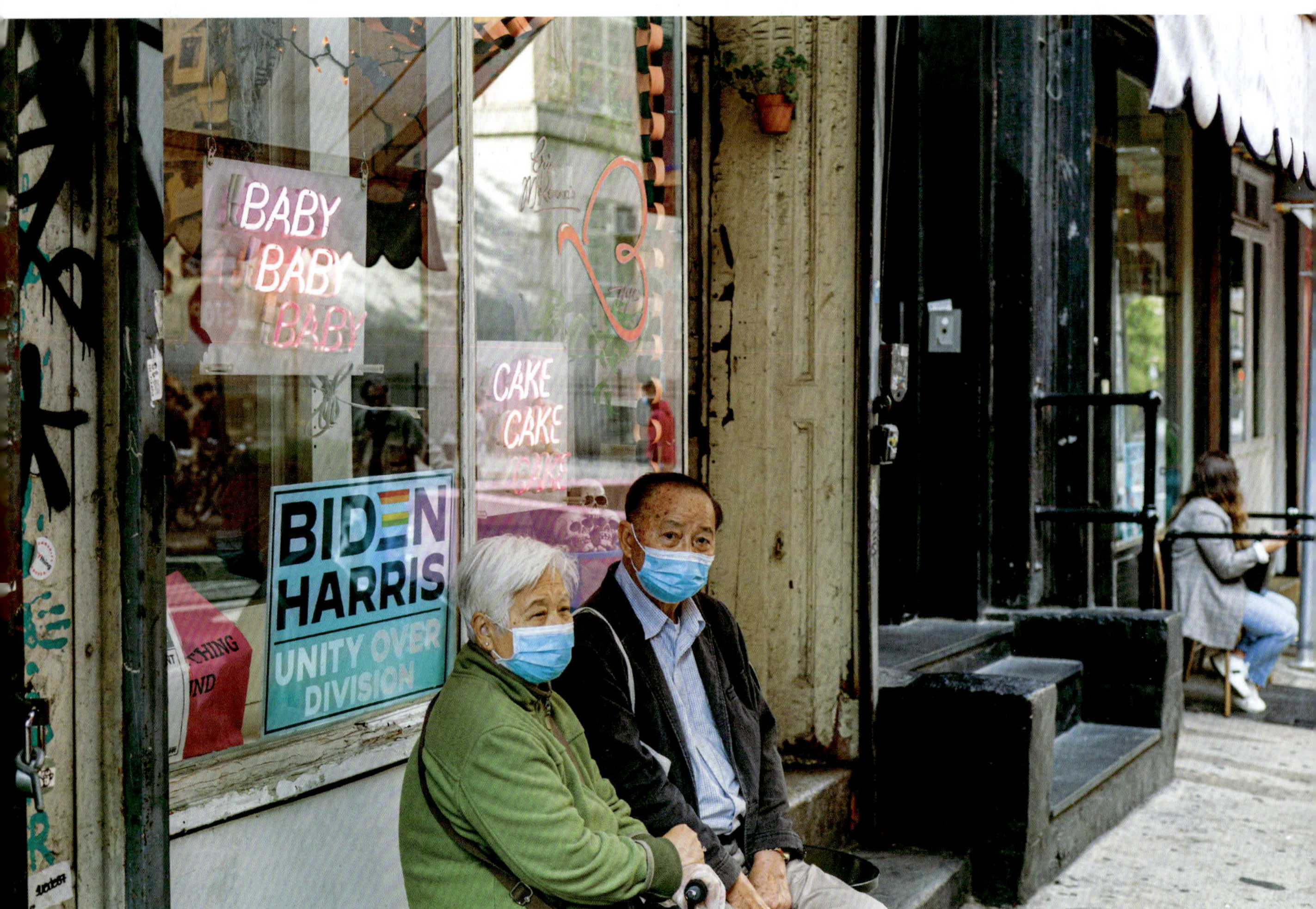

DEEN VAN MEER, A couple resting on a bench in front of a store window on Broome Street with a Biden-Harris sign stating "Unity Over Division."
NEW YORK, NY, USA

10 23

ABIGAIL MONTES, *Marching Cobras of NY* | Celebrating its 35th anniversary, the South Bronx Halloween Parade, though scaled down, provided a moment of normalcy in these uncertain times. NY, USA

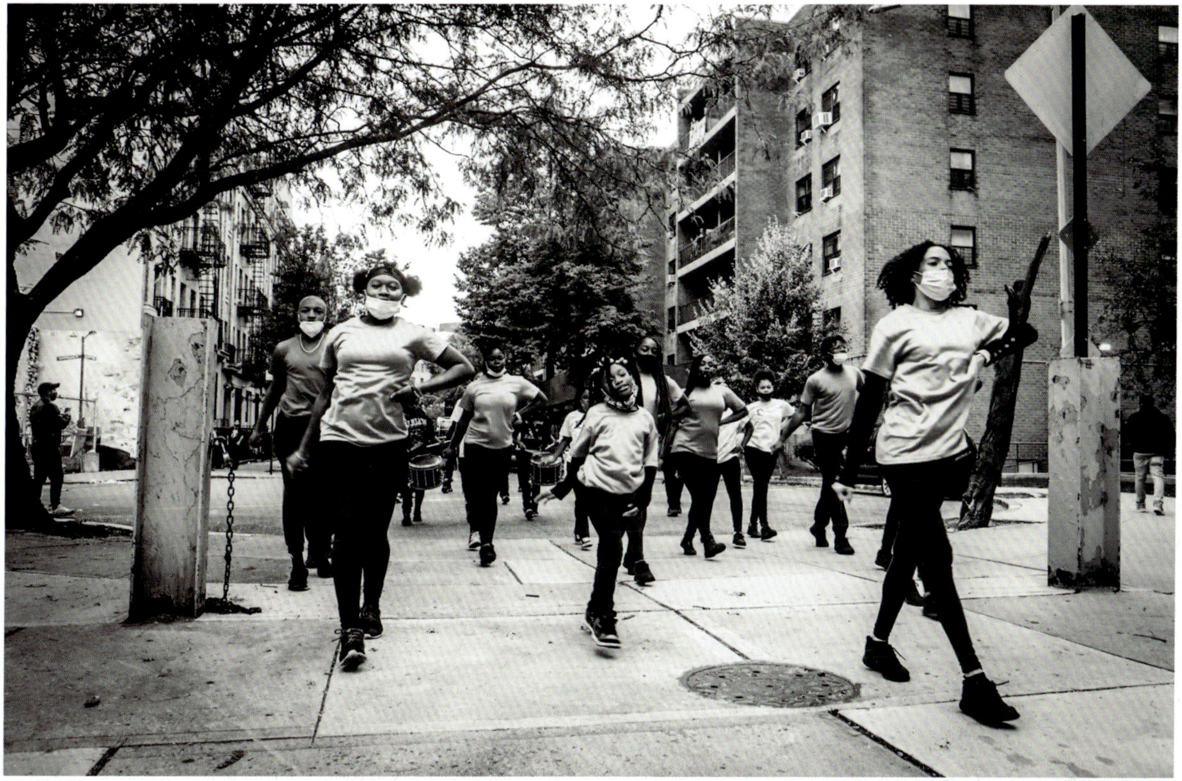

MONIKA PAREKH,

An early voter reminds us that politics were never meant to be world-class entertainment.
NEW YORK, NY, USA

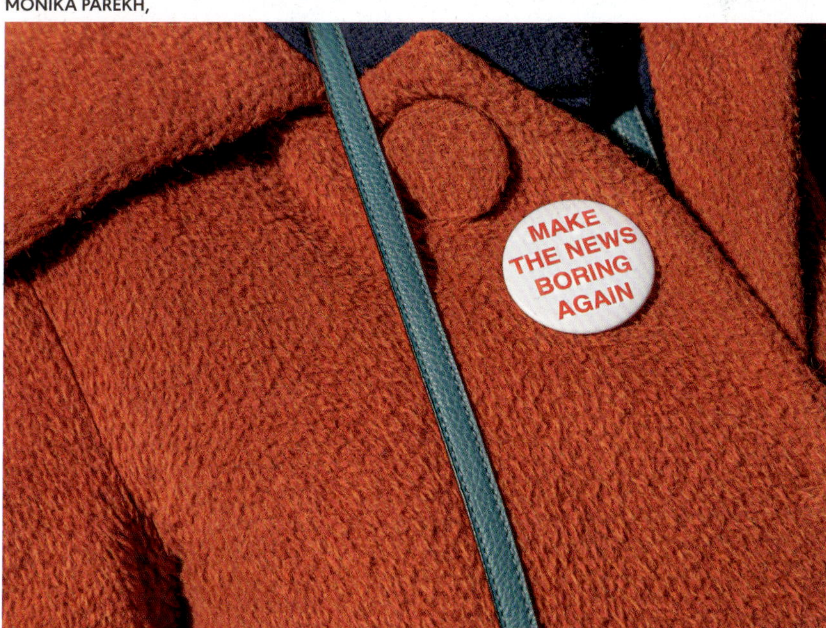

MACKENNA LEWIS, Early voters are out in force—with walkers, wheelchairs, canes, books, knitting, dogs, friends, family, and of course, masks. Love to see it! BROOKLYN, NY, USA

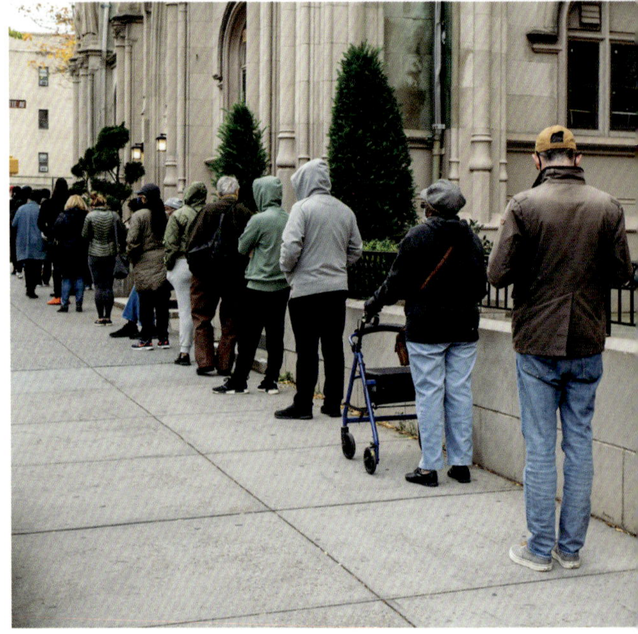

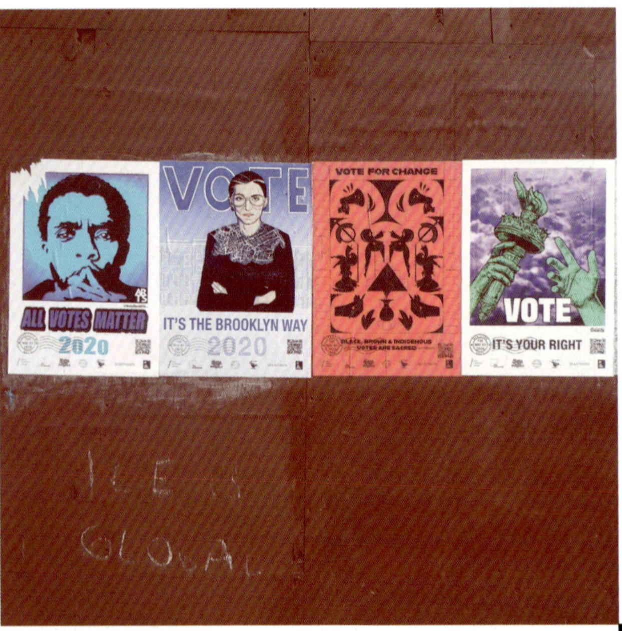

CHRISTINE DOYLE, Voting is the only real power we have.
UPPER WEST SIDE, NEW YORK, NY, USA

ADAM KLUGA, Protest march against the decision of the Constitutional Court, which ruled that abortion in the event of severe fetal impairment is unconstitutional.
TYCHY CITY, POLAND

10 25

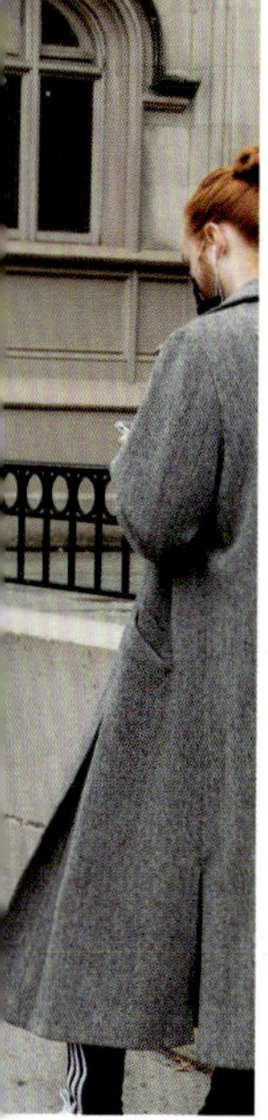

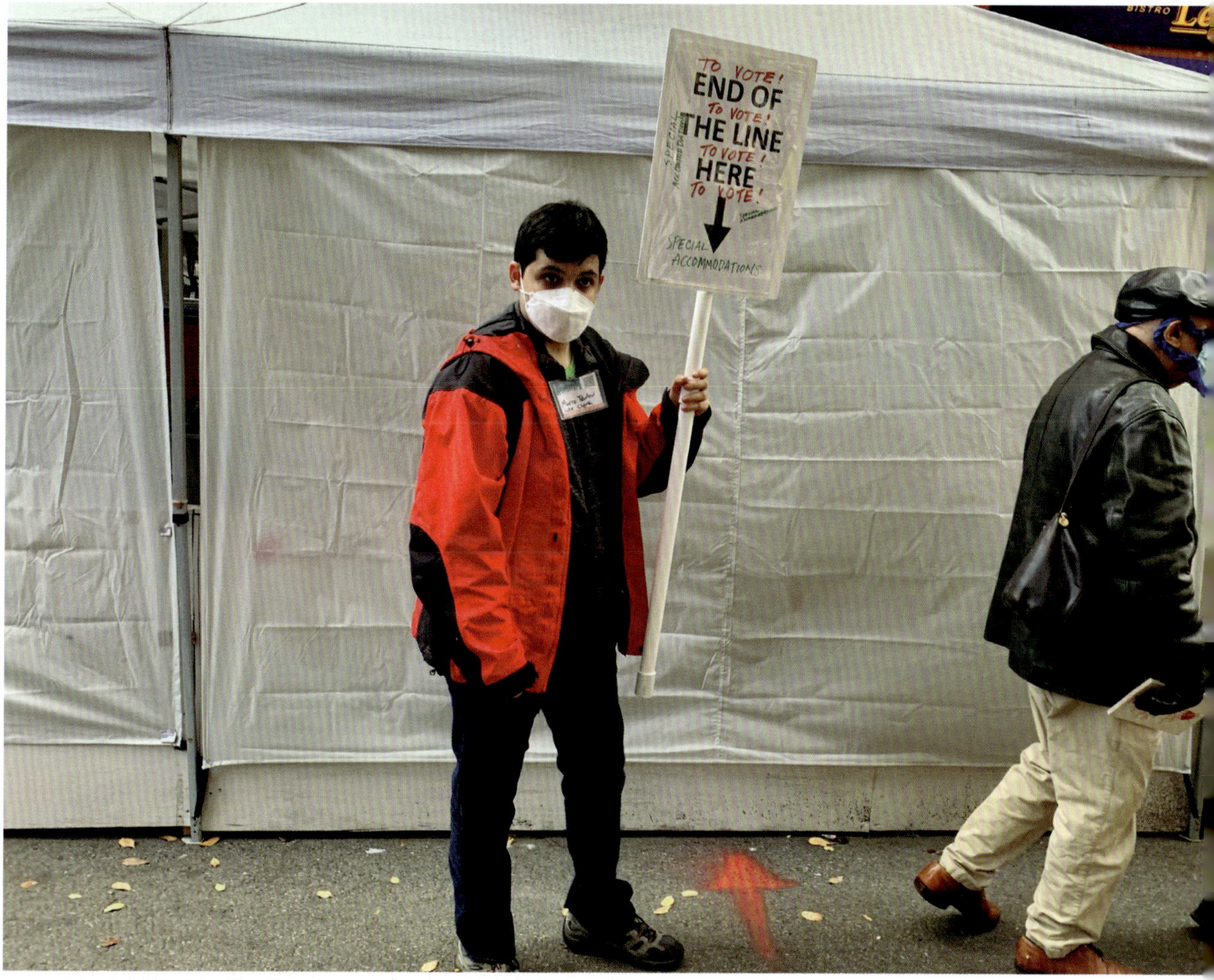

MADELINE ELLIS, *End of the Line Here* |
Taken during early voting when the lines were very long on East 75th Street. NEW YORK, NY, USA

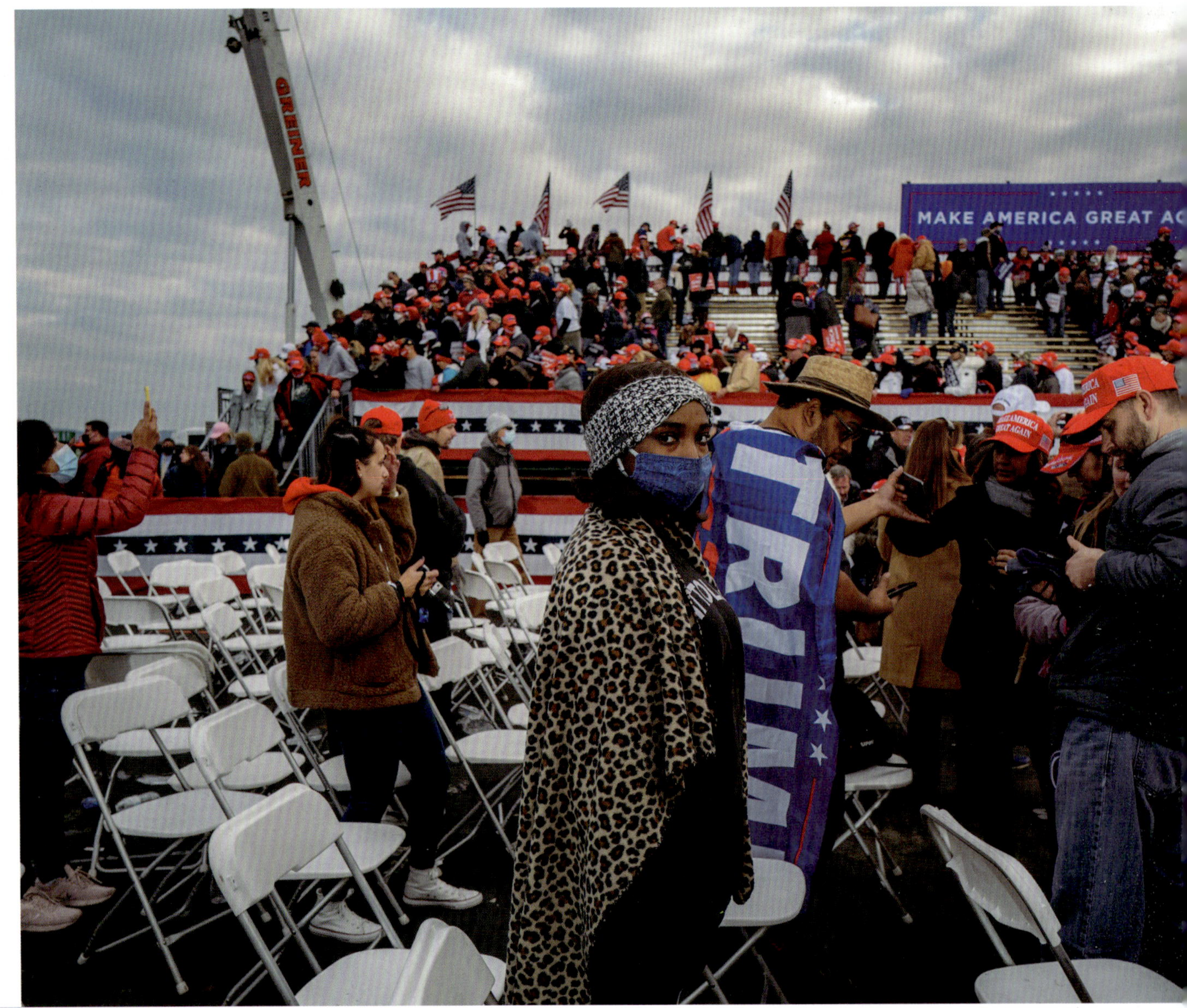

JANICK GILPIN, Young Black Woman at Donald Trump MAGA Rally. READING, PA, USA

10 31

SALVATORE LAFERLITA, Thank You Boulder. CO, USA

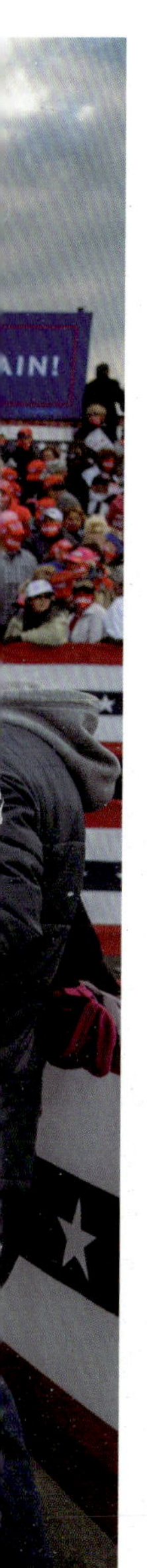

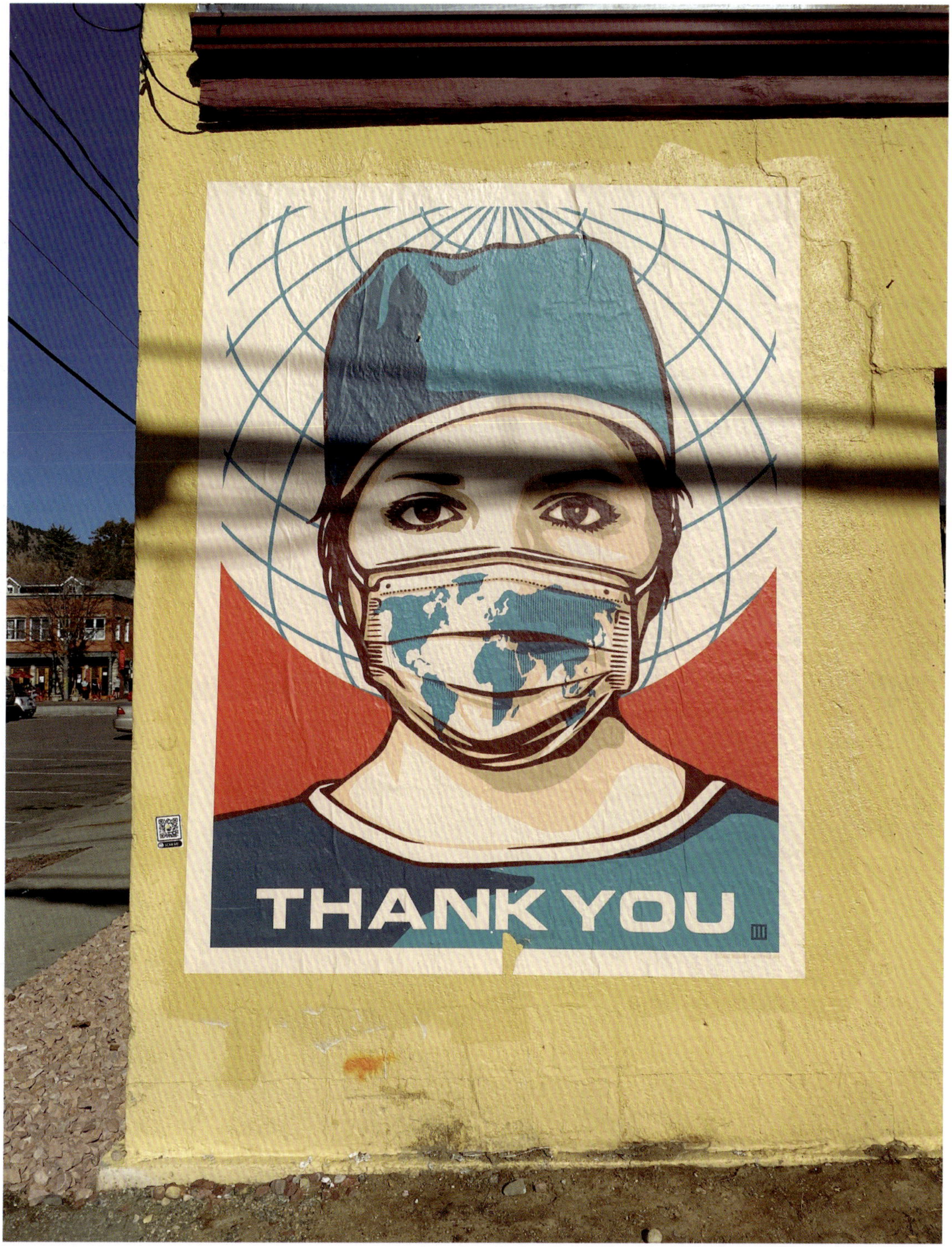

In case of violence, businesses boarded up their windows in anticipation of Election Day. SOHO, NEW YORK, NY, USA

KEN PAPROCKI,

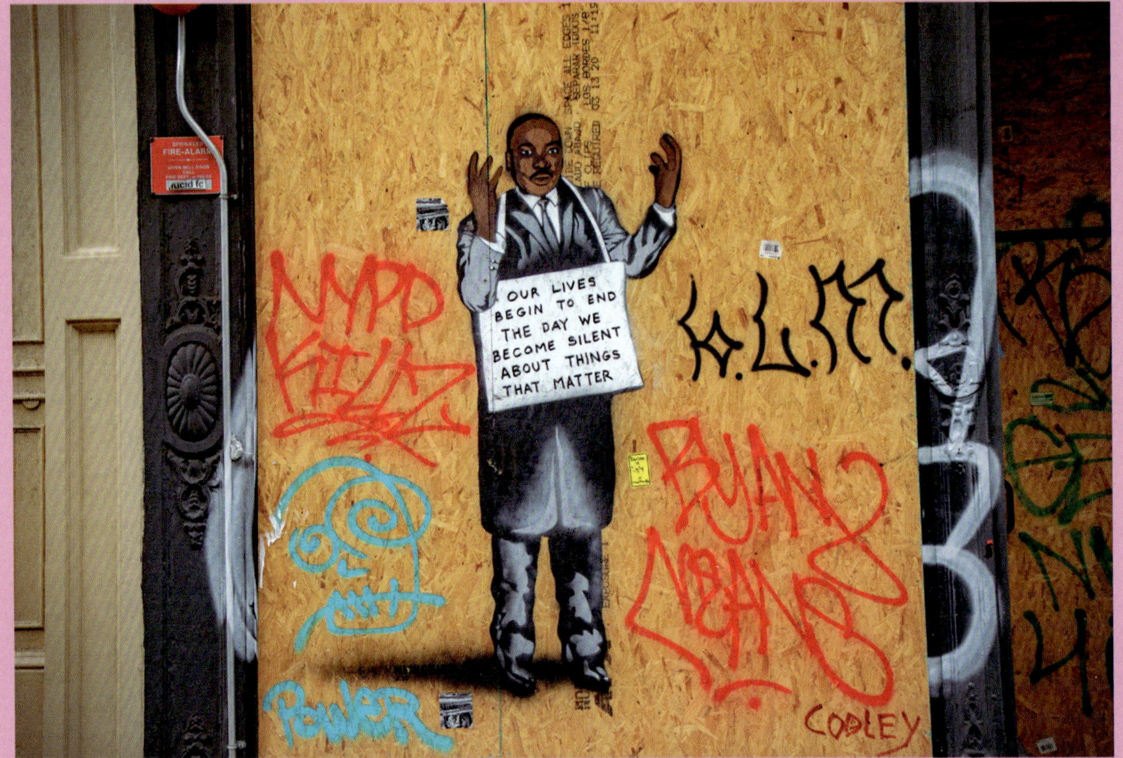

11·20

NOVEMBER

13_US Shatters Case Record Again: More than 10.7 million cases and 243,000 Fatalities Reported *(Washington Post)*

16_Pfizer to Start Pilot Delivery Program for its CORONAVIRUS Vaccine in Four US States *(Reuters)*

20_On Track to be Minnesota's Deadliest Month for CORONAVIRUS *(Star Tribune)*

ANA GUTIERREZ COVARRUBIAS,

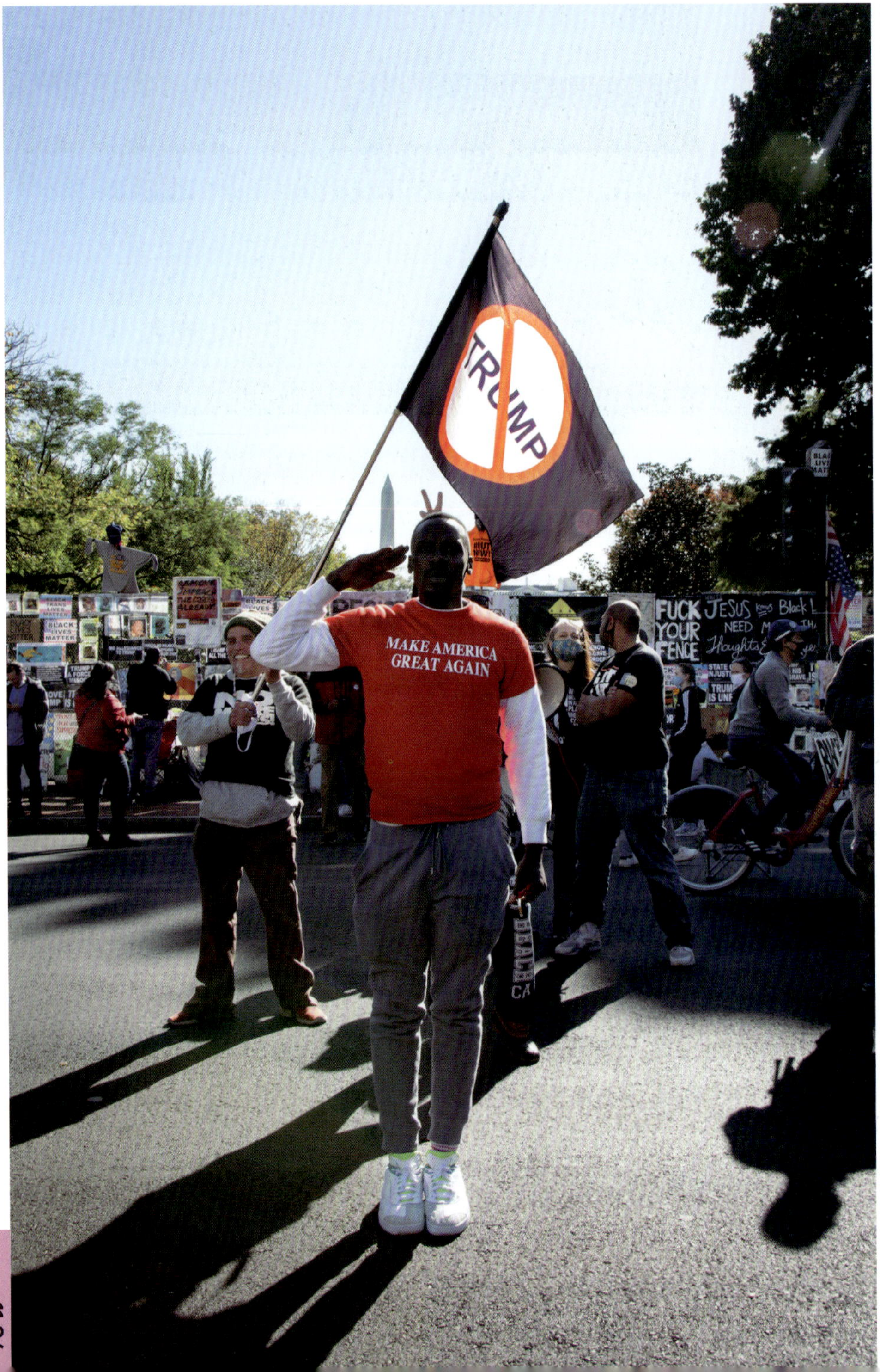

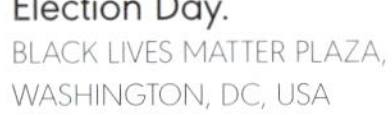

Election Day.
BLACK LIVES MATTER PLAZA,
WASHINGTON, DC, USA

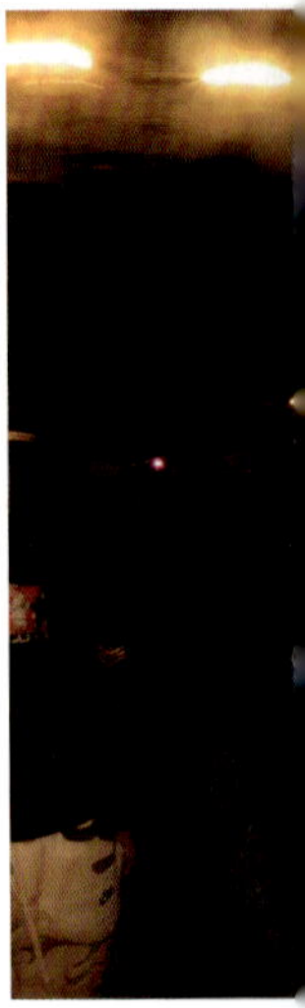

SARA MESSINGER, People dance in the street outside of Washington Square Park in celebration of Biden's projected victory. NEW YORK, NY, USA

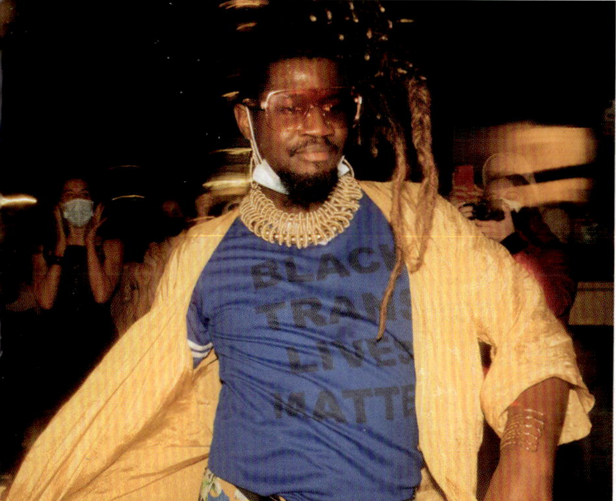

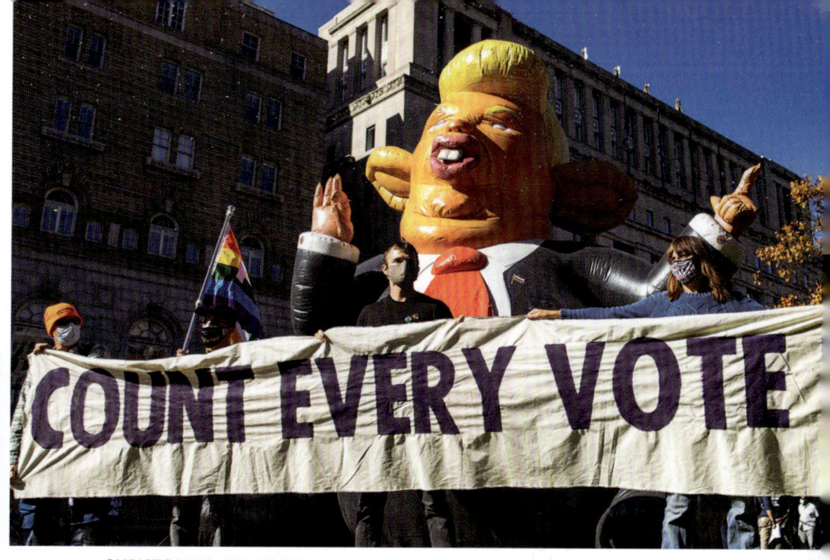

CHRISTOPHER CAMERON, This photo was taken the day before Biden was announced as the winner of the election. WASHINGTON, DC, USA

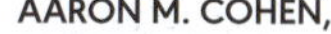

AARON M. COHEN, A young boy is interviewed by the media during a "Count Every Vote" rally and block party outside of the Pennsylvania Convention Center. PHILADELPHIA, PA, USA

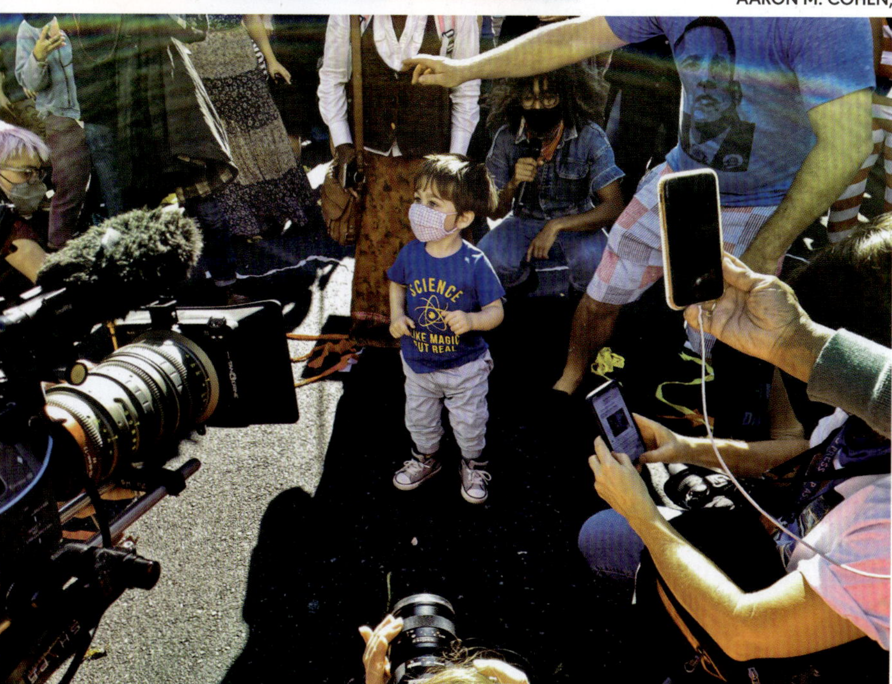

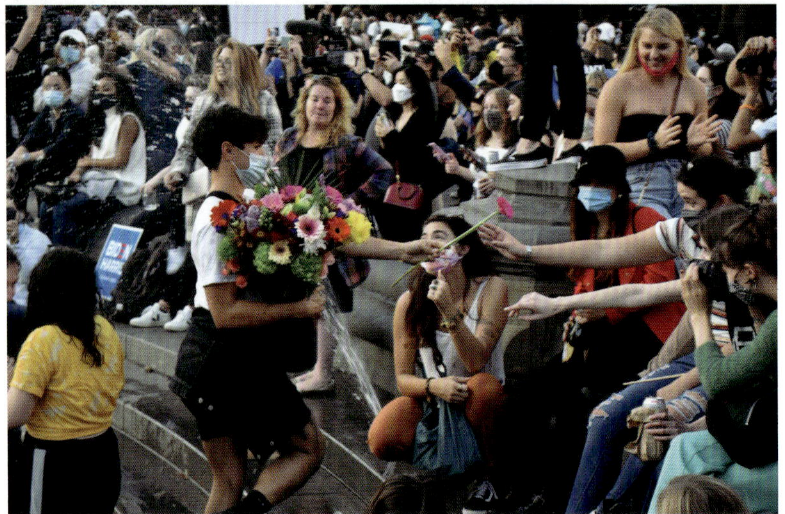

JON FRIER, People celebrating the victory of Biden and Harris in Washington Square Park.
NEW YORK, NY, USA

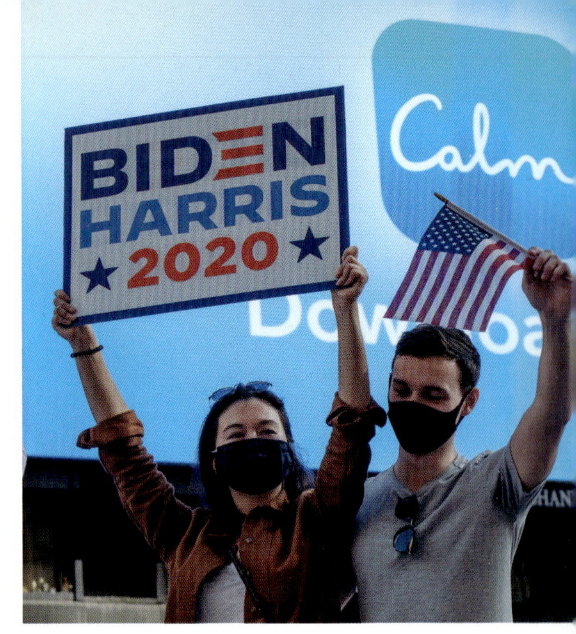

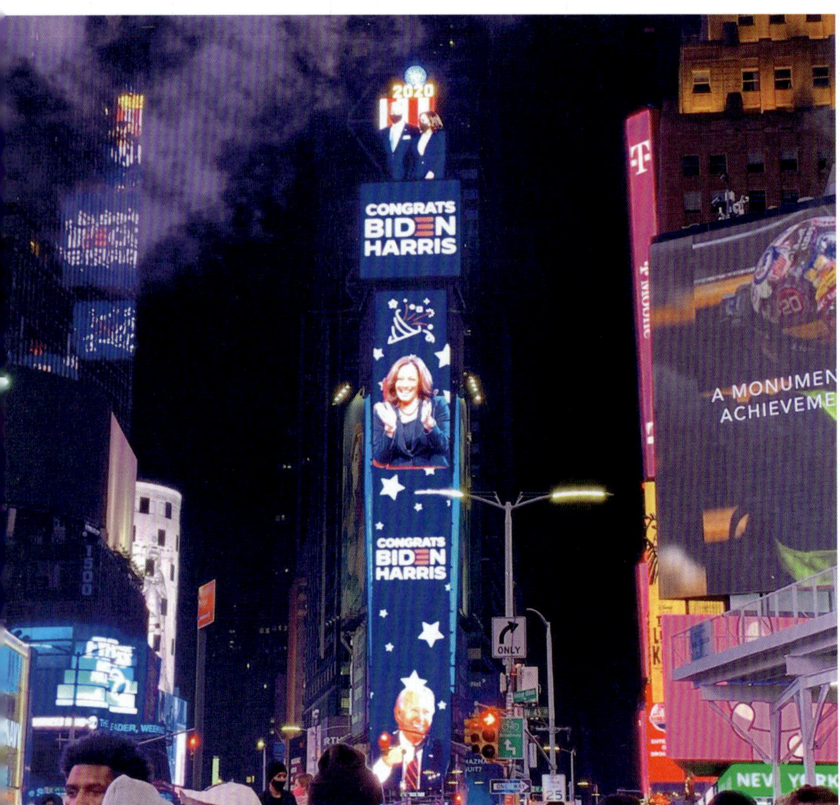

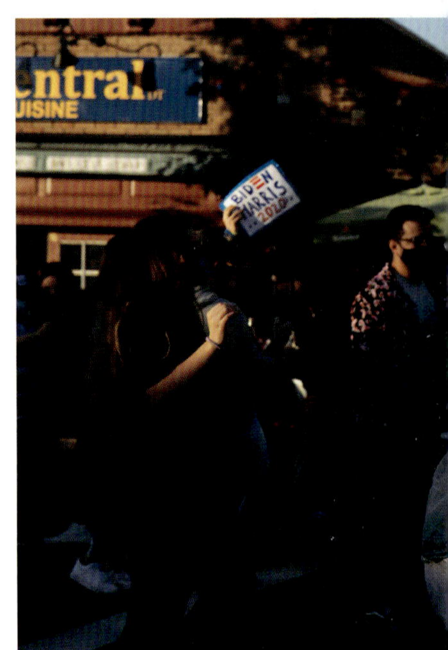

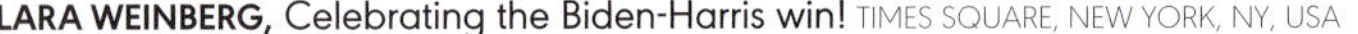
LARA WEINBERG, Celebrating the Biden-Harris win! TIMES SQUARE, NEW YORK, NY, USA

DAMON WEBSTER, Election Day was over, but Biden was not declared the winner until the following Saturday. The streets flooded with revelers and an attitude of positivity not seen for years. TIMES SQUARE, NEW YORK, NY, USA

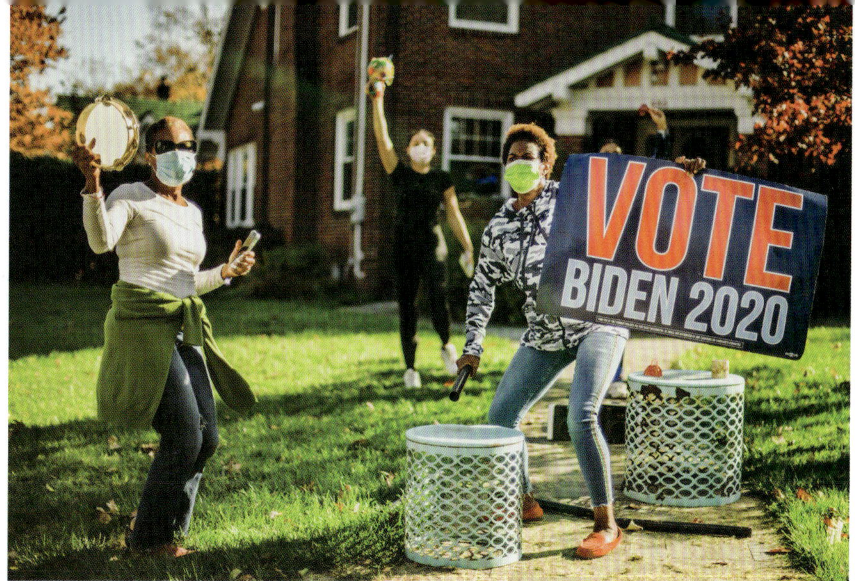

SOPHIE WHITE, *Do You Hear the People Sing?* | Joe Biden is elected president. MAPLEWOOD, NJ, USA

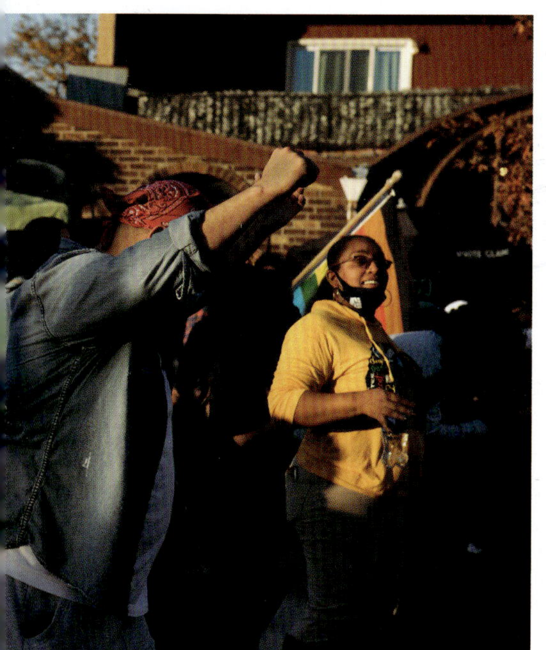

KERRIE SANSKY, *2020 Presidential Election Called for Biden and Harris* | Main Street celebrates. NYACK, NY, USA

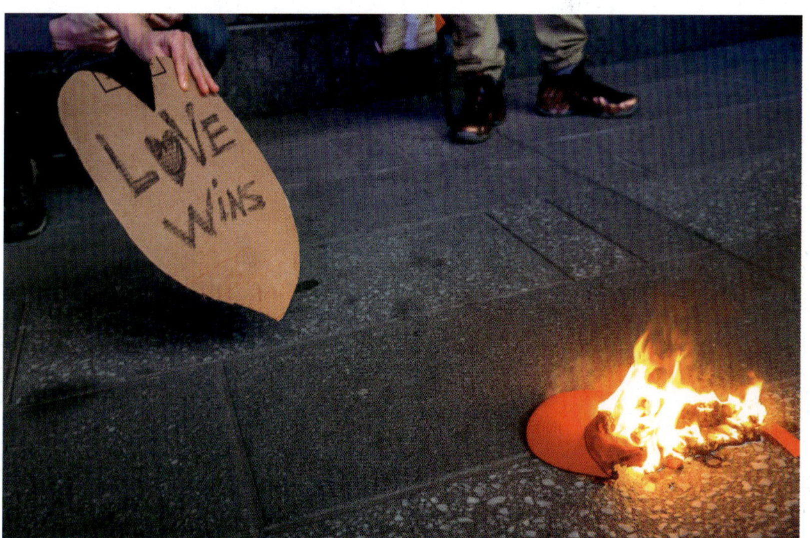

WIAFE MENSAH-BONSU, *Love Wins!* | The world erupted in joy as the US presidential election winner was announced. A red hat burned while a jubilant celebrator waved a "Love Wins" sign. TIMES SQUARE, NEW YORK, NY, USA

EVAN CHRISTENSON, A woman dances amidst the celebrations of Joe Biden's victory. BLACK LIVES MATTER PLAZA, WASHINGTON, DC, USA

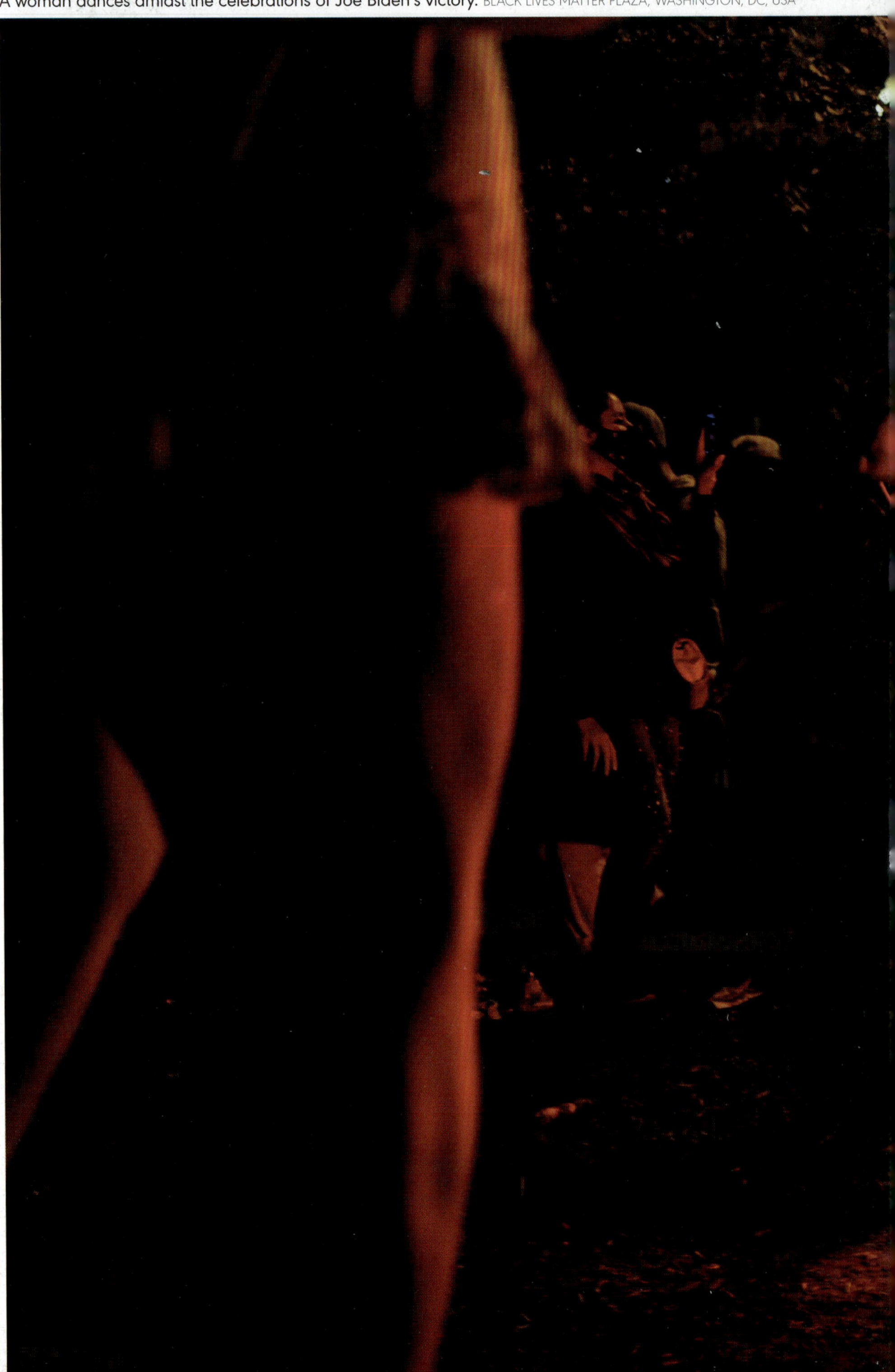

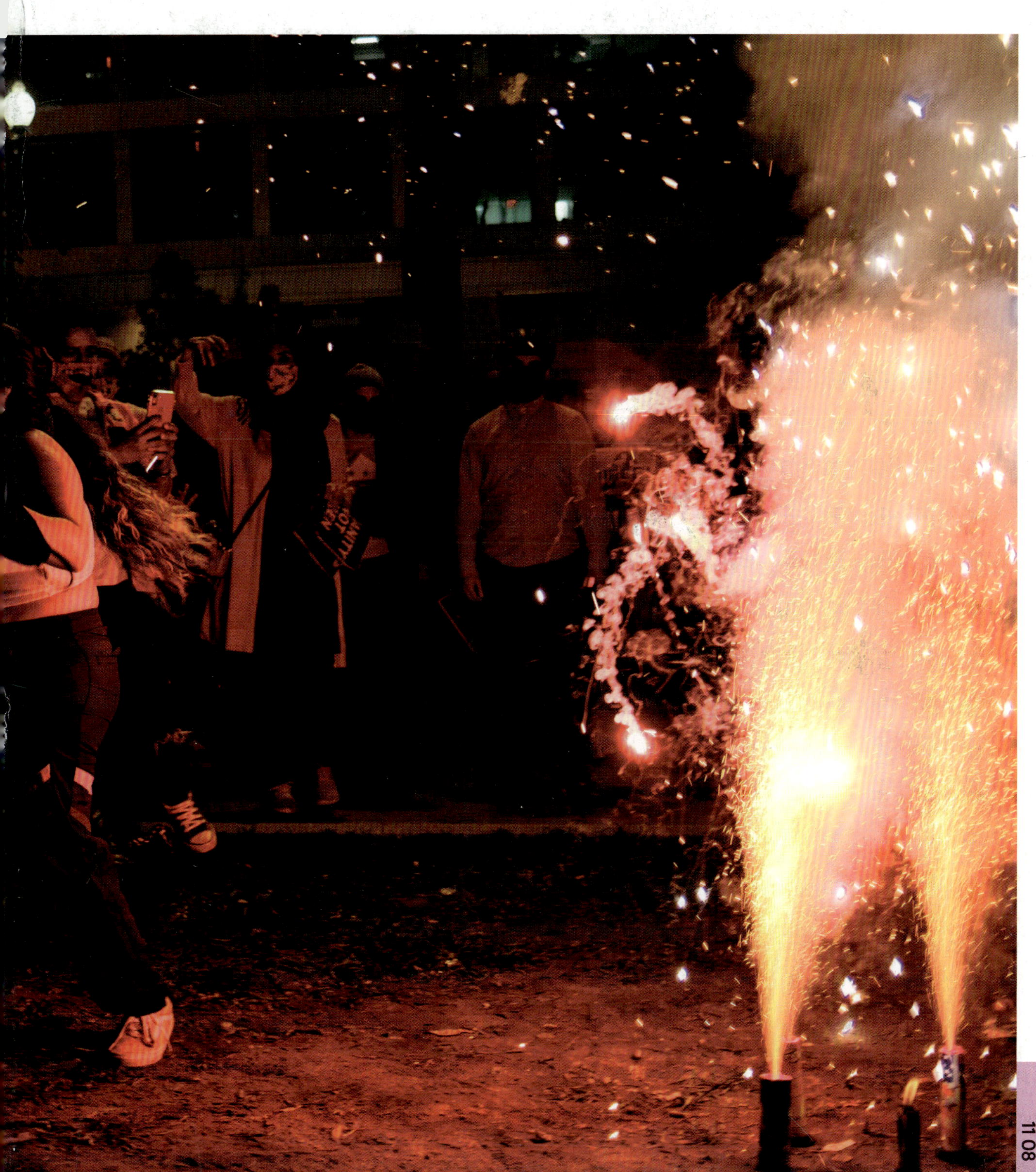

ACKNOWLEDGEMENTS

First and foremost, we are indebted to the entire team at the International Center of Photography for their support, time, and enthusiasm for this project, but we are especially grateful to Colby Anderson, Megan Cross, Carly Goldman, Jacque Donaldson, Anne Massoni, Lauren McCay, Stephanie Routier, Susie Sofranko, Erica Somerwitz, and Sarah Stuby who poured through thousands of images to help select. There is no doubt the exhibition and book are stronger for their contributions.

Additionally, the project could not have happened without the generosity of the ICP Exhibitions Committee: Luana Alesio, Debby Brown, Michael Clinton, Marnie Gelfman, Almudena Legorreta, Elizabeth Richebourg Rea, Helena Sokoloff, and Heather Vrattos. Special thanks to Debby Brown for taking the time to help select images for the show as well, and to Michael Clinton for his continued role in this initiative, from the formulation of the open call to the production of this book.

At ICP, Jacque Donaldson put together an impressive slate of public programs, which were instrumental in giving the exhibition a global reach. Jacque also compiled the audio guide, working with our partners at Gesso, especially Michael Reynolds and Henna Wang, who hosted the guide and answered our many questions. Gigi Loizzo, Lauren McCay, Colby Anderson, and Steve Carter helped expand the reach of the show through their marketing prowess. Lauren provided thoughtful and thorough feedback on all of our exhibition texts, and spent countless hours building out the web presence of *#ICPConcerned*. Florence Grant carefully edited all texts for our reopening exhibitions. Gigi, Jim O'Shea and their visitor experience team dealt with COVID-19 challenges gracefully upon reopening, their hard work ensured we could welcome visitors safely. Dillon Goldschalg, Dean Ebben and Anthony Austin prepared our space and installed a beautiful show amid many obstacles. We're grateful for their good cheer and perseverance. Laura Strom Wondergem designed our website and in-gallery graphics, both are better for her contributions. Deepest thanks to Mark Sweeney who decided to accept our wild challenge and print the exhibition's 800+ images himself in the galleries. His care and patience with them all brought the show together.

Finally, thank you to all of the imagemakers who took time to submit their work through the #ICPConcerned hashtag. We hope this collective experiment provided solace during an overwhelming time.

-David Campany, Managing Director of Programs & Sara Ickow, Manager, Exhibitions and Collections

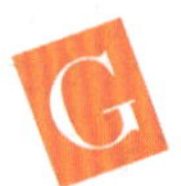

www.geditions.com
media@geditions.com

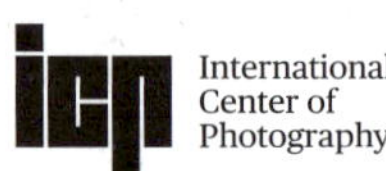

FACEBOOK: International Center of Photography
INSTAGRAM: @icp
TWITTER: @ICPhotog

First Edition, 2021

Library of Congress Cataloging-in-Publication data is available from the publisher.

Hardcover Edition ISBN: 978-1-943876-22-8

Design: Janine Seelen

Printed and bound in China

10 9 8 7 6 5 4 3 2 1

TEAM

Images for this exhibition were chosen by Colby Anderson, Debby Brown, David Campany, Megan Cross, Carly Goldman, Jacque Donaldson, Sara Ickow, Anne Massoni, Lauren McCay, Stephanie Routier, Susie Sofranko, Erica Somerwitz, and Sarah Stuby.

#ICPConcerned: Global Images for Global Crisis was coordinated by David Campany, managing director of programs, and Sara Ickow, manager, exhibitions and collections.

PRODUCTION: Gigi Loizzo, Lauren McCay, Colby Anderson, Jacque Donaldson, Dillon Goldschlag, Mark Sweeney

WEBSITE AND DESIGN: Laura Strom Wondergem

AUDIO GUIDE

Hear directly from a selection of contributing photographers to learn more about the stories behind their images in the *#ICPConcerned: Global Images for Global Crisis* audio guide. Scan the QR code to listen. Transcripts and translations are available in up to 10 languages. Special thanks to Gesso, ICP's audio guide host.

SUPPORT

#ICPConcerned: Global Images for Global Crisis has been made possible by generous support of the ICP Exhibitions Committee: Luana Alesio, Debby Brown, Michael Clinton, Marnie Gelfman, Almudena Legorreta, Elizabeth Richebourg Rea, Helena Sokoloff, and Heather Vrattos.
Exhibitions at ICP are supported, in part, by public funds from the New York City Department of Cultural Affairs in partnership with the City Council and the New York State Council on the Arts with the support of Governor Andrew M. Cuomo and the New York State Legislature. Additional exhibition support is provided by the Joseph and Joan Cullman Foundation for the Arts, Inc.

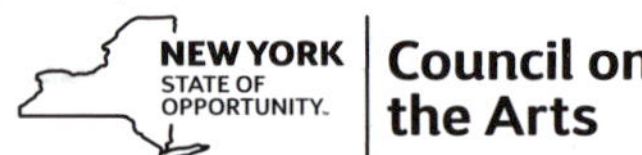

All captions and texts were written by the photographers. They have been edited for spelling and clarity only, all words belong to the individual photographers.

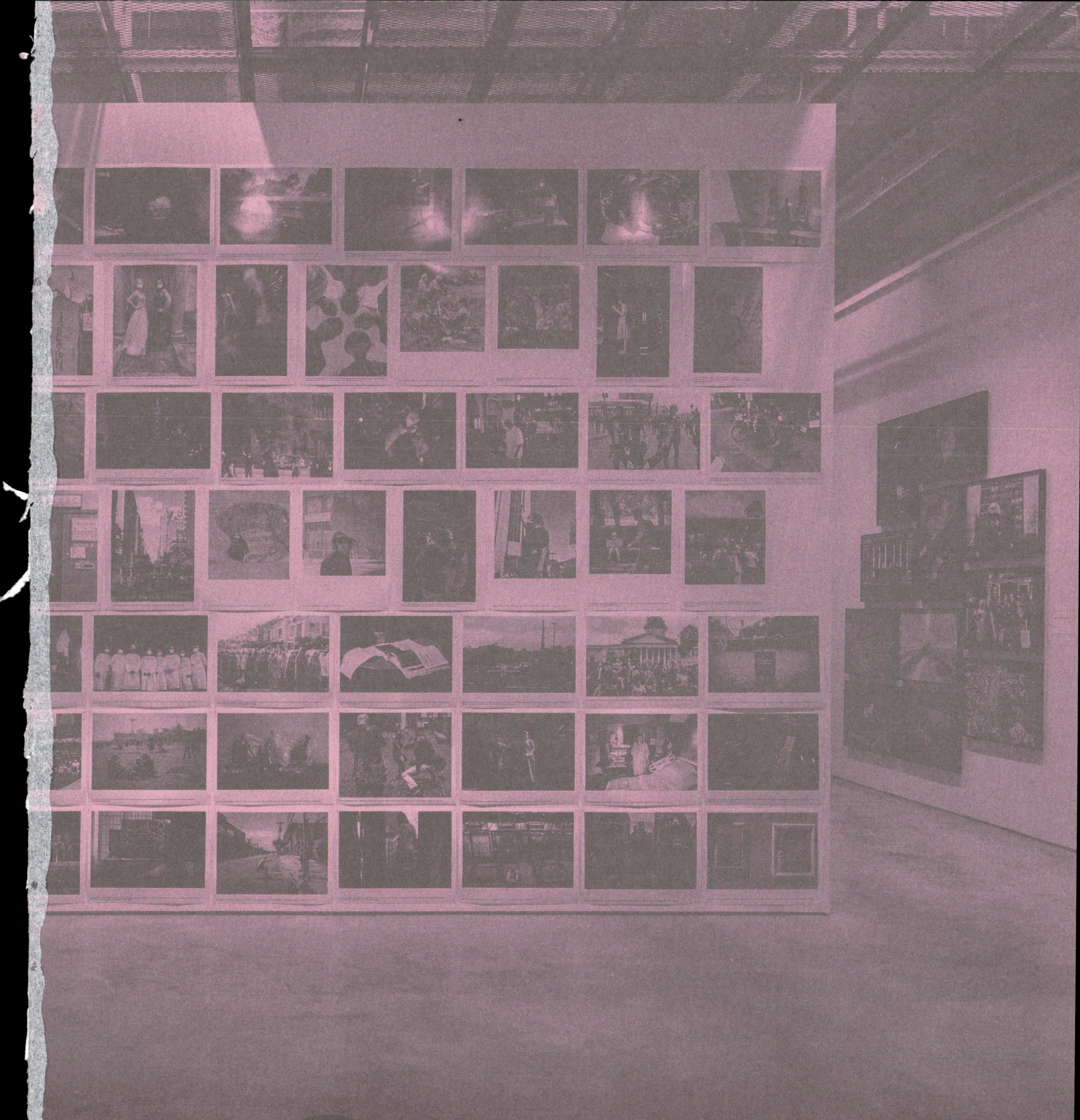
6 FT

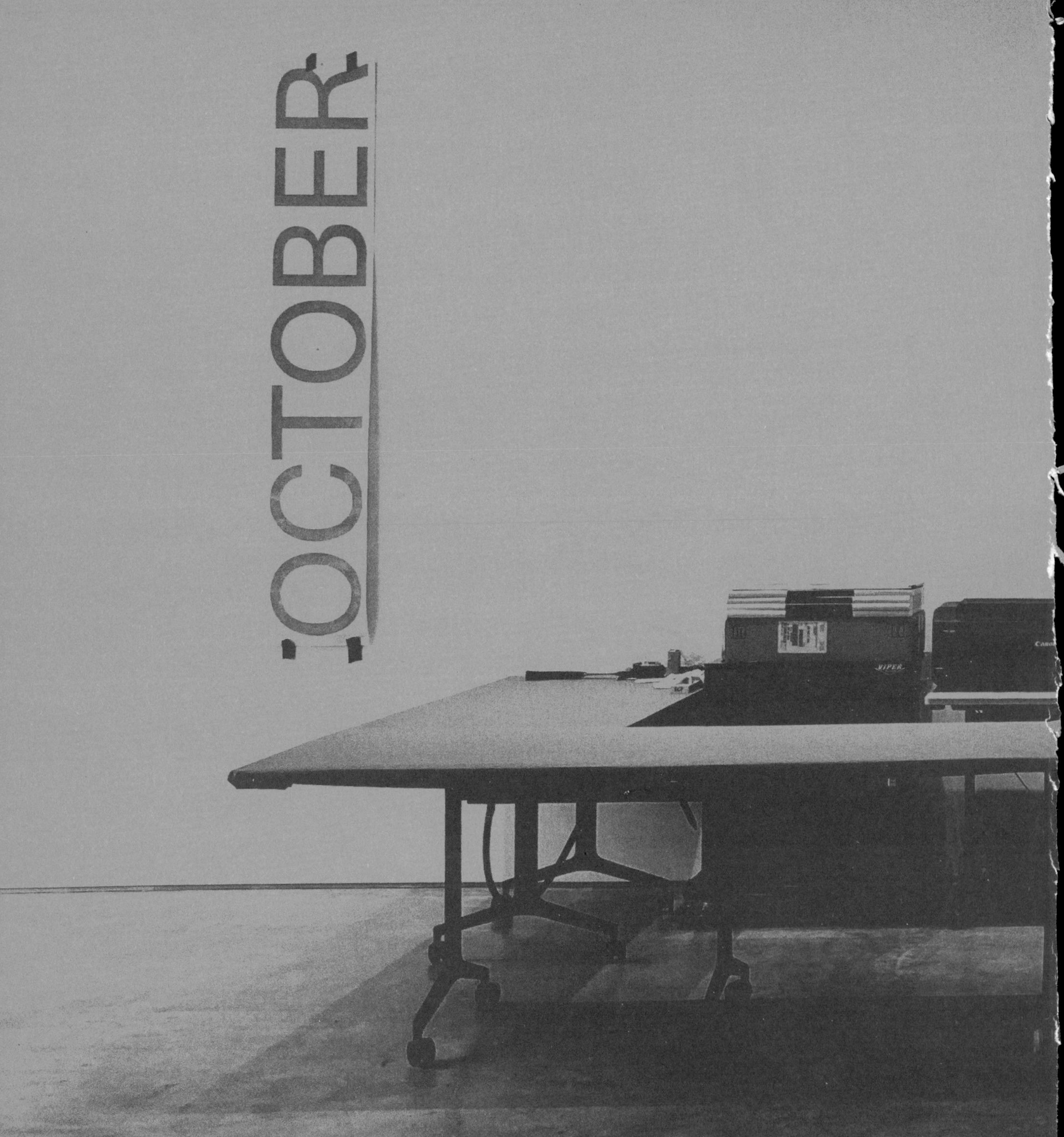
OCTOBER
VIPER